Lecture Notes in Computer Science 1055

Edited by G. Goos, J. Hartmanis and J. van Leeuwen

Advisory Board: W. Brauer D. Gries J. Stoer

Springer
Berlin
Heidelberg
New York
Barcelona
Budapest
Hong Kong
London
Milan
Paris
Santa Clara
Singapore
Tokyo

Tiziana Margaria   Bernhard Steffen (Eds.)

Tools and Algorithms for the Construction and Analysis of Systems

Second International Workshop, TACAS '96
Passau, Germany, March 27-29, 1996
Proceedings

 Springer

Series Editors

Gerhard Goos, Karlsruhe University, Germany

Juris Hartmanis, Cornell University, NY, USA

Jan van Leeuwen, Utrecht University, The Netherlands

Volume Editors

Tiziana Margaria
Bernhard Steffen
Lehrstuhl fur Programmiersysteme
Fakultät für Mathematik und Informatik, Universität Passau
Postfach 2540, D-94030 Passau, Germany

Cataloging-in-Publication data applied for

Die Deutsche Bibliothek - CIP-Einheitsaufnahme

**Tools and algorithms for the construction and analysis of
systems** : second international workshop ; proceedings /
TACAS '96, Passau, Germany, March 27 - 29, 1996. Tiziana
Margaria ; Bernhard Steffen (ed.). - Berlin ; Heidelberg ; New
York ; Barcelona ; Budapest ; Hong Kong ; London ; Milan ;
Paris ; Santa Clara ; Singapore ; Tokyo : Springer, 1996
  (Lecture notes in computer science ; Vol. 1055)
  ISBN 3-540-61042-1
NE: Margaria, Tiziana [Hrsg.]; TACAS <2, 1996, Passau>; GT

CR Subject Classification (1991): F.3, D.2.4, D.2.2, C.2.4

ISBN 3-540-61042-1 Springer-Verlag Berlin Heidelberg New York

© Springer-Verlag Berlin Heidelberg 1996
Printed in Germany

Typesetting: Camera-ready by author
SPIN 10512782   06/3142 – 5 4 3 2 1 0   Printed on acid-free paper

Foreword

This volume contains the proceedings of the Second International Workshop on *Tools and Algorithms for the Construction and Analysis of Systems*, TACAS'96, which took place at the University of Passau (Germany), 27-29 March, 1996. The first workshop of this series took place last year in Aarhus (Denmark) as a satellite of TAPSOFT'95.

TACAS' aim is to bring together researchers and practitioners interested in the development and application of tools and algorithms for specification, verification, analysis, and construction of distributed systems. The overall goal of the workshop is to compare the various methods and the degree to which they are supported by interacting or fully automatic tools. This comprises, in particular, case studies revealing the application profiles of the considered methods.

TACAS'96 comprised four parts:

- **Invited Lectures** by

    - Leslie Lamport, DEC Research Center, Palo Alto, CA - USA
    - Dexter Kozen, Cornell Univ., Ithaca, NY - USA
    - Gerard Holzmann, AT&T Bell Laboratories, Murray Hill, NJ - USA

- **Regular Sessions** featuring 19 papers selected out of 47 submissions, ranging from foundational contributions to explicit tool descriptions.

- **Tool Presentations** demonstrating 11 selected tools in 4 plenary sessions. There were also usual tool demonstrations accompanying the workshop.

- **A Panel** on *Technology Transfer: Trial or Trade*, moderated by Ed Brinksma, University of Twente, NL, with the panelists:

    - Manfred Broy, Techn. Univ. Munich - D,
    - Loe Feijs, Philips, Eindhoven - NL
    - Leslie Lamport, DEC Research Center, Palo Alto, CA - USA
    - Manfred Reitenspieß, Siemens Nixdorf Inform. AG, Munich - D

Grown out of a satellite meeting to TAPSOFT last year, TACAS'96 featured a satellite workshop itself: the *International Workshop on Advanced Intelligent Networks (AIN'96)*, which took place in Passau on March 25-26.

TACAS'96 was hosted and supported by the University of Passau. It was sponsored by Siemens Nixdorf Informationssysteme AG, Bayerisches Staatsministerium für Unterricht, Kultus, Wissenschaft und Kunst, and Deutsche Forschungsgemeinschaft (DFG). The series will be continued next year at the University of Twente in Enschede (NL).

Finally, we would like to thank the program committee and all the referees who assisted in the paper selection, Hildegard Buchhart who helped with the organization and fund raising, Michael von der Beeck, Andreas Holzmann, and Ulrike Lechner who assisted us in the preparation of this volume, and Andreas Claßen, Klaus Schießl, and Volker Braun who took care of the hardware requirements.

March 1996

Tiziana Margaria
Bernhard Steffen

Program Committee

David Basin (D)
Ed Brinksma (NL)
Rance Cleaveland (USA)
Susanne Graf (F)
Kim G. Larsen (DK)
Eric Madelaine (F)
Alan Mycroft (GB)
Scott Smolka (USA)
Bernhard Steffen (D, chair)
Wolfgang Thomas (D)
Frits Vaandrager (NL)

Referees

Roberto Amadio
Karen Bernstein
Dominique Borrione
Amar Bouali
Fredric Boussinot
Costas Courcoubetis
Robert de Simone
Joelle Despeyroux
Jean-Claude Fernandez
Wan Fokkink
Martin Fraenzle
Ranan Fraer
Hubert Garavel
David Griffioen
Kees van Kemenade
Nils Klarlund
Yassine Lakhneche

Helmut Lescow
Xinxin Liu
Florence Maraninchi
Sean Matthews
Olaf Müller
Andreas Podelski
Y.S. Ramakrishna
Annie Ressouche
Judi Romijn
Philip Schnoebelen
Michael Siegel
Friedemann Simon
Oleg Sokolsky
Jan Springintveld
Andrew Uselton
Luca Vigano
Sue-Hwey Wu

Contents

Contents

Invited Lectures

Regular Sessions

Tool Presentations

Early Fault Detection Tools

Gerard J. Holzmann*

ABSTRACT

The traditional software development cycle relies mostly on informal methods to capture design errors in its initial phases, and on more rigorous testing methods during the later phases. It is well understood, though, that those bugs that slip through the early design phases tend to cause the most damage to a design. The anomaly of traditional design is therefore that it excels at catching bugs at the worst possible point in a design cycle: at the end.

In this paper we consider what it would take to develop a suite of tools that has the opposite characteristic: excelling at catching bugs at the start, rather than the end of the design cycle. Such *early fault detection* tools differ from standard formal verification techniques in the sense that they must be able to deal with incomplete, informal design specifications, with possibly ill-defined requirements. They do not aim to replace either testing or formal verification techniques, but to complement their strengths.

1 Introduction

The goal of this paper is to consider the possibility of developing a suite of tools that can help to improve the reliability of a software design process, specifically for distributed systems, from the very early beginnings of that process. Traditional testing techniques come too late to be of much help in this phase. Formal verification techniques, on the other hand, have the disadvantage that they require a fairly solid insight into the design itself, before they can prove to be of value. Users of formal verification tools typically have trouble with two things: (1) to produce a completely defined model of the design, when only partial information or insights are available, and (2) to formalize an adequate set of correctness requirements.

Before formal verification and traditional testing techniques become applicable, there is currently a void of tools. Our aim is to consider if this void could be filled. We propose the term *early fault detection* for a tool or technique that can successfully be applied in the earliest phases of a still incomplete and imprecise design, and that can provide the user with some guidance about potential hazards in the design process as it develops.

*AT&T Bell Laboratories, 600 Mountain Avenue, Murray Hill, NJ 07974, U.S.A.
http://netlib.att.com/netlib/att/cs/home/holzmann.html

2 A Paper Problem

To illustrate the main concepts, we will use a simple, made-up, example of a problem to model the interactions in a pseudo-distributed system. We call this *The Paper Problem*. Consider the interactions between authors, editors, and referees in handling papers that are submitted for publication. The authors, editors and referees together form a peer group, where each person from the group could at various times fulfill any one of the three functions mentioned (authoring, editing, refereeing). There is frequently also consultation within the peer group about problems of current interest. The interactions between author, editor, and referees can therefore be complex. We will treat the modeling problem here as if it were a true industrial design problem, where we have to discover the intricacies of the situation through a systematic process of refinement. For inspiration, we will consider how design problems of this type, though at a much larger scale, may be handled by an industrial design team.

2.1 Structural View

The first thing that must happen is to decide what the main structural components of the new system should be. To make this possible, a very general set of requirements for the new system, as it would operate under ideal circumstances, is drafted. For our paper problem, one such requirement may look as illustrated in Figure 1.

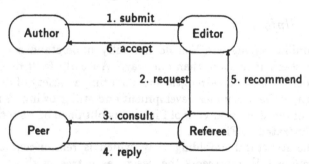

FIGURE 1. Structural View of *The Paper Problem*

Figure 1 represents the main functional entities from our system: the author, the editor, a single referee, and a representative of a peer. One set of possible interactions of these entities is shown. For the time being we will ignore that the functions can actually overlap, as a referee can take on the functions of an author or a peer, etc.

The labels of the arrows between the structural components suggest a time ordering of typical events in this system. In this case, the referee consults with a peer before returning a recommendation to the editor, and, this being an idealized scenario, the editor informs the author that the paper was accepted.

Many things can throw this simple scenario off course. The referee can refuse to handle the paper, or can fail to respond. The author could withdraw the paper, revise it, or become impatient and send additional enquiries to the editor. More to the point, in the case of blind refereeing, the referee might accidentally attempt to consult with the author as a peer, without mentioning the actual reason for doing so. This act could close a dependency cycle in the graph, for instance when the author decides to delay the peer-response to the referee until the final status of the paper is decided by the editor.

The main purpose of the first design phase, however, is to identify the main building blocks for the system, and for now, we merely need to establish that this goal has probably been reached. In practice, requirements engineers may come up with dozens of sketches of the general flavor of Figure 1, showing different scenarios that illustrate the main lines of the intended operation of a new system. The word *sketch* is to be taken literally: these figures often exist only as pencil sketches on paper, or as rough outlines on a white board. They ultimately can reach the status of a figure for reference in a general document for the design rationale, but rarely do they become an integral part of the design process as such.

Our purpose here is to emphasize the very early stages of a design. Our intent is therefore to look very carefully at even the earliest design sketches, to see if they could be amenable to direct tool based support.

2.2 Unfolding

A familiar saying is: "You do not fully understand something until you understand it in more than one way." An early fault detection tool, then, can derive one of its strengths from offering a variety of different views of a design, while it is under development and still growing. A natural alternate view of the structural view of Figure 1 is obtained by its temporal unfolding, as illustrated in Figure 2.

The structural unfolding view, which is reminiscent of the CRC card technique [11], represents the design as a tree, with each path from the root of the tree to a leaf represents a possible scenario. The structural elements are replicated at each node in the tree where they contribute to one of the processing steps. In Figure 2 we have added the possibility of a rejection, as the final outcome of the paper submission process. Where Figure 2 differs from the structural unfolding of Figure 1 is indicated in bold. The purely structural view is superior when architectural questions about the system have to be settled. The view obtained by the structural unfolding is better when good insight needs to be obtained about the interdependencies between different, possibly overlapping, scenarios. Since time sequence information is carried in the labels, one way to preserve the infor-

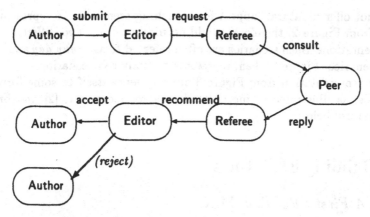

FIGURE 2. Structural Unfolding of an Extension of Figure 1

mation about branching from Figure 2 also in the view of Figure 1 would be to replace the label *6. accept* with *6.1. accept* and to add an arrow from editor to author with label *6.2. reject*. The two views now represent the same design decisions, while emphasizing entirely different aspects of the system.

2.3 Temporal View

Yet another view of the design can be obtained by switching from the representation to a purely temporal view, using basic message sequence charts (MSCs) [12], as illustrated in Figure 3.

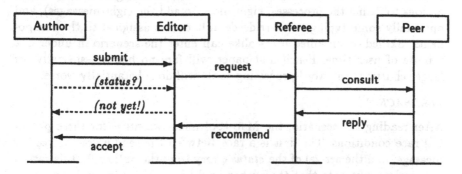

FIGURE 3. Temporal View of an(other) Extension of Figure 1

We have again extended the view from Figure 1 slightly to illustrate the differences in strength of the various views. In this case, we have added (with dashed lines) the possibility of the author interrogating the editor about the status of the paper. The disadvantage of the MSC view is that it does not offer a natural support for branching scenarios. To represent the view from Figure 2, therefore, would normally call for two different MSC representations. Such scenarios are often referred to as *sunny day* and *rainy day* scenarios. Figure 3, then, represents a sunny day scenario.

The representation from Figure 3 directly lends itself to some forms of analysis, as illustrated in more detail in a related paper, [2] and briefly summarized below.

3 Building EFD Tools

3.1 A First EFD Tool: MSC

The three views we have illustrated so far all represent basically the same information about a design, though in different forms, emphasizing different aspects. A single design tool could easily offer all three views, allowing the user to switch between them at will, and revise or add to the growing design from whichever view is most convenient. This (so far) hypothetical tool is the first example of an early fault detection, or *EFD*, tool. Work is currently underway to extend our MSC tool[2] into this type of tool.

At the time of writing, the MSC tool can represent only the temporal view, as in Figure 3. For designers, the MSC tool, when used in this mode, competes with, and is compared with, pencil on paper sketching, despite the additional advantages that the tool may offer for analysis and easy of maintenance. Even on this minimal score, the tool is easily found to be of great value to a designer pressed for time: it takes just twelve mouse actions for the user to define the complete scenario shown in Figure 3 (four mouse actions to define the processes, eight more to add the eight messages), and optionally some typing to override default names assigned to the components. Skilled or unskilled users alike can enter the scenario in under one minute of user time. Pencil and paper will fare no better, especially for larger charts; many word-processing tools will do substantially worse.

FEEDBACK

After reading the scenario, the MSC tool issues warnings for three potential race conditions. The first is a race between the sending of the *request* message, and the arrival of the *status* query from the author. In this case it is harmless, but note that the author could also decide to send a message to *withdraw* or to *revise* his contribution. The editor may have to take different actions, depending on the outcome of the race. There is also a race between the arrival of the *status* query from the author and the arrival of the *recommend* message from the referee, and, finally, a race between the arrival of *recommend* and the sending of *not yet*, at the editor process. Presumably, also a different response from the editor would be called for, depending on the outcome of that race.

If we merge the peer process and the author process into one, to emphasize that the author may be the peer chosen for consultation by the referee, in blind refereeing, the diagram from Figure 4 results.

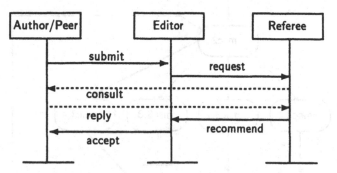

FIGURE 4. Variation on the Scenario in Figure 3

If, further, we would want to define a behavior for the author where the response to the referee's consultation is delayed until after the reception of an *accept* or *reject* message from the editor, we immediately find that this variation cannot be specified without at least one of the message arrows flowing upward in the diagram – against the direction of time. This scenario would create a causal wait cycle that, if it can be specified at all (the Msc tool forbids the creation of message arrows that tilt upwards), can easily be detected and reported as a potential error.

DESIGN PROCESS

Once the design grows, it can be expected that the architectural view, illustrated in Figure 1 will stabilize first. The main structural components of the system are identified and can be refined. Some components may be decomposed, and further detailed, leading to related changes in the structural unfoldings and in the temporal view of the MSCs. It can also be expected that, as the design matures, the temporal view will grow both in importance and in complexity. Large libraries of related scenarios are likely to be built, and keeping track of the inter-dependencies between them becomes an overriding concern.

The inter-dependencies between (perhaps only fragments of) scenarios can be shown graphically in a natural way. Figure 5 shows such a graph, which is based on similar graph from a real design.

The view is similar to the unfolded structural view from Figure 2, but there are important differences. First, the nodes in the graph from Figure 2 represented structural elements, e.g. designated logical or physical processes in the distributed system to be. In Figure 5 the nodes represent scenarios: interaction sequences in which *all* structural components of the system can in principle participate. The first node in Figure 5, labeled *msc1*, for

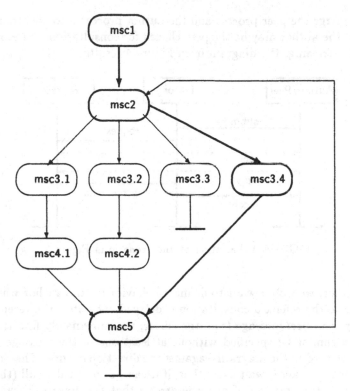

FIGURE 5. Interdependencies of Scenario Fragments

instance, can represent the first series of steps in a call setup procedure for a telephone call. A subsequent processing step, *msc2*, representing say call routing, could have four different outcomes. The call might have to be rejected (*msc3.3*), or it could proceed in various ways, depending on the specific call features that have been invoked.

As indicated, the meta view need not be, and in general will not be, acyclic.

Also indicated in Figure 5, with bold lines, is a possible *traversal* of the graph, from the root to one of the two possible termination points. The graph traversal identifies one possible complete MSC scenario that can be constructed from the fragments *msc1* ⋯ *msc5*.

3.2 A Second EFD Tool: POGA

The graph shown in Figure 5 has a well defined meaning and structure. There is a host of algorithms that can be applied to a directed graph to provide feedback to the user about its properties. Many graphical tools already exist, or are in preparation, for working with generic graphs of this type, e.g., [3]. As part of the investigation of early fault detection tools, we have built a similar tool, which ties in directly with several others, as will be discussed below.

The tool, called POGA (Pictures of Graph Algorithms), consists of a generic graphical interface, written in about 1200 lines of Tcl/Tk [8], a background processor called EULER, written in about 850 lines of ANSI C, and links to a number of existing tools, such as DOT for doing graph layout [4], and MSC [2], which has its own background processors for finding race conditions and causal conflicts in sample scenarios.

The background tool EULER provides access to a collection of generic graph algorithms, such as the computation of shortest paths, strongly connected components, or the roots and leaves of a graph. The EULER tool can also drive a visualization of generic search algorithms, such as depth-first and breadth-first searches starting at a user-selected initial node in the graph. As the name suggests, it is likely to be extended further with algorithms for computing covering paths, e.g. Euler tours, to facilitate the construction of test suites.

The view presented by POGA matches what is shown in Figure 5. The user can interactively select a path through the graph, to indicate scenarios that require inspection. The user iteratively selects nodes from the graph along the desired path. Whenever two nodes are not directly adjacent, the background process, which encapsulates knowledge of graph algorithms, will compute the shortest path between them. The path itself is highlighted on the screen, in much the same fashion as shown in Figure 5 (on color-displays, the path is colored red).

POGA derives much of its utility from the links with other tools that it exploits, such as DOT for graph layout and EULER for generic graph algorithms.

We will consider three other important links in the next section.

3.3 Tool Integration

LINKING POGA WITH MSC

At the request of the user, a path through a graph that is selected in POGA can be expanded into a message sequence scenario, using the reference links stored with the nodes. POGA can then call MSC as an independent background process to allow the user to inspect the specific scenario in more detail. POGA allows the user to provide scenario information in two ways:

- In the *nodes*, as symbolic references to files that contain scenario fragments in ITU standard form, or

- On the *edges*, in a comment field that contains an event description, such as an input or an output action, again in ITU standard form.

At the request of the user, the tool can build a scenario from the fragments that are specified through the nodes and edges along the selected path, and start up the MSC tool in the background for independent processing of the scenario thus created.

The MSC tool can be used to modify the scenario, to repair faults, and update the scenario files, without disturbing or modifying the view of the interdependencies offered by POGA.

The view offered by POGA can readily be extended to support also hierarchical views of a still larger structured collection of scenarios. Each node can then represent either a scenario fragment, or a subgraph. By double clicking a node, the user brings up either MSC for a closer view of the scenario fragment stored at the node, or a second copy of POGA for those nodes that point to subgraphs of scenarios. Scenarios can be nested arbitrarily deeply in this fashion, and the design space can be navigated with relative ease.

LINKING WITH SPIN

Early fault detection tools, by their very nature, do not allow for a very thorough verification of a design. Once the early design phases have been completed, and both the basic structure and the correctness requirements for the design have been settled, it becomes possible to build precise *verification models*. Critical design requirements can then be proven rigorously with specialized tools, such as the model checker SPIN [6]. It is of course attractive if the early fault detection tools can somehow be integrated with the formal verification methods.

To explore this integration, we have built an experimental interface between POGA and the verifiers that are generated by SPIN. With this interface, POGA can be used to visualize the reachable state space of small verification problems, and can offer visual feedback on the precise effect of various types of search algorithms, for instance, SPIN's partial order reduction techniques [7].

Information on actions, input, and output events can be made available on the edges of the graph, by postprocessing the information generated by SPIN with the help of a small AWK filter [1].

The example shown in Figure 6, is part of the reachable state space for a SPIN verification model of our *Paper Problem*, for simplicity restricted to the *sunny day* scenario in which the author will not query the status of the submitted paper, and the referee will not consult with a peer before returning a recommendation to the editor. The state numbers assigned by SPIN indicate the depth-first search order, in which the state space is explored.

Provided with this graph, POGA again offers the user the choice of selecting an arbitrary path, which can then be converted into a message sequence chart in ITU standard form [12], and handed off to MSC as before.

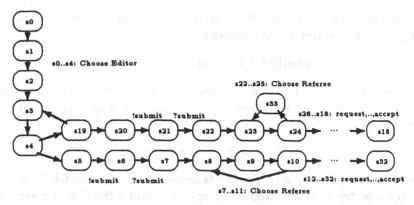

FIGURE 6. POGA View of a State Space Generated by SPIN (partial)

The reachability graph can also be inspected for the presence of strongly connected components, and the like.

The verification model that generated the graph from Figure 6 is 45 lines of PROMELA [6]. A slightly more sophisticated version, of 59 lines, allows for random peer consultation by referees, and allows the author to defer responding to peer consultations until after receiving final word on the status of a paper. We can now attempt to prove the benign liveness property, expressed in the syntax of Linear Temporal Logic [9], that each paper submitted is eventually either accepted or rejected:

$$\Box \ (submitted \rightarrow \Diamond \ (accepted \lor rejected)).$$

In SPIN we can attempt to verify this desirable property by claiming that its negation (a decidedly undesirable property) cannot occur. This negated property is formalized as the language accepted by a two-state Büchi automaton shown in Figure 7.

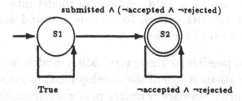

FIGURE 7. SPIN's never claim for Verifying the Paper Problem

A Büchi automaton is an automaton over infinite words, known as a never claim in PROMELA parlance. (The automaton is generated automatically by SPIN from the LTL formula, using the algorithm described in [5].) The initial state of the automaton is S1. The transitions of the automaton are labeled with the state properties that must be true for the transition to be enabled. The automaton, then, can remain in state S1 for an arbitrary length of time. Whenever the property

$$(submitted \land (\lnot\ accepted \land \lnot\ rejected)$$

becomes true, the automaton can non-deterministically choose to switch to the accepting state S2, where it can remain infinitely long only if the property

$$(\lnot\ accepted \land \lnot\ rejected)$$

remains true infinitely long. For the extended verification model, SPIN will report a match of this undesirable property within a fraction of a second, and thus prove that the original liveness requirement can be violated.

Despite the ease with which the potential flaw in the interactions of authors, editors, and referees can be found with a formal verification model, the visual formalism of the message sequence charts can be considered superior in this case. In the MSC tool, it is simply impossible to specify a scenario that could include a causal wait cycle, and hence the system designer may be alerted at an early stage to the possible side-effects of some design decisions. More subtle correctness properties, however, can easily escape attention, and will require more general error checking capabilities.

LINKING WITH CASE TOOLS

The tools described so far can, in principle, span the early phases of the design process. There already exist several competitive design tools that target the later phases of design, for instance, CASE tools such as OB-JECTIME [10]. Just like it is desirable to establish links between formal verification tools and the early fault detection tools MSC and POGA, it can be beneficial to establish a smooth connection with existing CASE tools.

Links can be established in several ways.

- We can convert a SPIN verification model into, for instance, an initial OBJECTIME model, to provide a sound starting point for the development of the final code.

- It is also possible to derive verification models from OBJECTIME models, at various stages of the development, to make sure that essential design properties are correctly preserved throughout the design.

- It can also be attractive to use a library of scenarios (in ITU standard form) and synthesize state machine models, one for each process in the system, that captures all the behavior specified. The synthesis procedure would then have to rely on a judicious use of state names (part of the ITU recommendation) to indicate common points of reference in the various scenarios. Note that each separate scenario defines a path through the state machine of each process that is part of the system. The state machines generated in this way can be used either as an initial verification model, to be fed into SPIN, or as an initial OBJECTIME model, to serve as the starting point of the further development.

- Simulation trails produced by OBJECTIME can be converted into ITU standard format, and provided to the MSC tool for analysis. If race conditions are detected, variations of the scenario can be fed back into OBJECTIME to make sure that the original model is not sensitive to the ordering of events that could be involved in the race.

We are actively exploring all the above options.

4 Conclusions

The initial interest in the early fault detection tools described in this paper has surprised even their authors. We can speculate that the tools derive their appeal not only because of the new checking capabilities they offer, but also because they provide a means to edit and maintain important design documents online, as formal objects. The availability of the new tools makes it unnecessary to maintain offline representations of scenarios, and their dependencies, in a fragile word-processing tool format. Conformance to the ITU standards is an attractive bonus, though not considered essential by many of the tool users.

At the time of writing, the MSC tool is in active use, and the POGA tool is in a prototyping stage. At least one CASE tool provider is in the process of extending their tool so that a direct connection can be made with these early fault detection tools.

Clearly, though, both MSC and POGA are only initial attempts to develop early fault detection tools. There can be a suite of similar tools, each offering different views of (aspects of) the design process. Perhaps the best result we can hope for would be that an improved understanding of the paradigm of early fault detection will help us to render the tools discussed in this paper obsolete.

Acknowledgements: I am grateful to Rajeev Alur, Doron Peled, Brian Kernighan, and Mihalis Yannakakis for many helpful discussions on the topic of this paper. The development of the early fault detection tools is a collaborative effort, to which all the above have made critical contributions.

5 REFERENCES

[1] A.V. Aho, B.W. Kernighan, P.J. Weinberger. *The AWK Programming Language.* Addison-Wesley, 1988.

[2] R. Alur, G.J. Holzmann, D. Peled. An Analyzer for Message Sequence Charts. *This conference.* 1996.

[3] J. Berry, N. Dean, P. Fasel, M. Goldberg, E. Johnson, J. MacCuish, G. Shannon, S. Sklena. *Link: A Combinatorics and Graph theory workbench for applications and research.* DIMACS, Technical Report 95–15, June 1995.

[4] E.R. Gasner, E. Koutsofios, S.C. North, K-P. Vo. A Technique for drawing directed graphs. *IEEE Trans. on Software Eng.* Vol 19, No. 3, May 1993, pp. 214–230.

[5] R. Gerth, D. Peled, M.Y. Vardi, P. Wolper. Simple On-the-fly Automatic Verification of Linear Temporal Logic, *PSTV95, Protocol Specification Testing and Verification.* Warsaw, Poland. Chapman & Hall, Germany, 1995, 173–184.

[6] G.J. Holzmann. *Design and Validation of Computer Protocols.* Prentice Hall, Software Series, 1991.

[7] G.J. Holzmann, D. Peled. An Improvement in Formal Verification. *Proc. 7th Int. Conf. on Formal Description Techniques.* Berne, Switzerland, 1994, 177–194.

[8] J. Ousterhout. *Tcl and the Tk Toolkit.* Addison-Wesley, 1994.

[9] A. Pnueli, The temporal logic of programs, *Proc. of the 18th IEEE Symp. on Foundation of Computer Science.* 1977, 46–57.

[10] B. Selic, G. Gullekson, P.T. Ward. *Real-time object-oriented modeling.* Wiley, New York, 1994.

[11] N.M. Wilkinson. *Using CRC cards: an informal approach to object-oriented development.* SIGS Books, New York, Advances in Object Technology, 1995.

[12] ITU-T (previously CCITT). *Criteria for the use and applicability of formal description techniques. Recommendation Z.120, Message Sequence Chart (MSC).* March 1993, 35 pgs.

Kleene Algebra with Tests and Commutativity Conditions

Dexter Kozen*

ABSTRACT We give an equational proof, using Kleene algebra with tests and commutativity conditions, of the following classical result: every while program can be simulated by a while program with at most one while loop. The proof illustrates the use of Kleene algebra with extra conditions in program equivalence proofs. We also show, using a construction of Cohen, that the universal Horn theory of *-continuous Kleene algebras is not finitely axiomatizable.

1 Introduction

Kleene algebras are algebraic structures with operators $+$, $\cdot$, $*$, 0, and 1 satisfying certain axioms. They arise in various guises in many contexts: relational algebra [28, 34], semantics and logics of programs [19, 29], automata and formal language theory [25, 26], and the design and analysis of algorithms [1, 17, 21]. Many authors have contributed to the development of Kleene algebra [2, 3, 4, 5, 6, 9, 12, 18, 19, 20, 22, 24, 26, 30, 31, 32, 33].

In semantics and logics of programs, Kleene algebra forms an essential component of Propositional Dynamic Logic (PDL) [13], in which it is mixed with Boolean algebra and modal logic to give a theoretically appealing and practical system for reasoning about computation at the propositional level.

Syntactically, PDL is a two-sorted logic consisting of *programs* and *propositions*, defined by mutual induction. A test φ? can be formed from any proposition φ; intuitively, φ? acts as a guard that succeeds with no side effects in states satisfying φ and fails or aborts in states not satisfying φ. Semantically, programs are modeled as binary relations on a set of states, and φ? is interpreted as the subset of the identity relation consisting of all pairs (s, s) such that φ is true in state s.

From a practical point of view, many simple program manipulations, such as loop unwinding and basic safety analysis, do not require the full power of PDL, but can be carried out in a purely equational subsystem using the axioms of Kleene algebra. However, tests are an essential ingredi-

---

*Computer Science Department, Cornell University, Ithaca, New York 14853-7501, USA. kozen@cs.cornell.edu ent, since they are needed to model conventional programming constructs such as conditionals and **while** loops. We define in §2 a variant of Kleene algebra, called *Kleene algebra with tests*, for reasoning equationally with these constructs.

Cohen has studied Kleene algebra in the presence of extra Boolean and commutativity conditions. He has given several practical examples of the use of Kleene algebra in program verification, such as lazy caching [10] and concurrency control [11]. He has also shown that Kleene algebra with extra conditions of the form $p = 0$ remains decidable [9], but that *-continuous Kleene algebra in the presence of extra commutativity conditions of the form $pq = qp$, even for atomic p and q, is undecidable [8].

In this paper we give two results, one of a more practical nature and the other theoretical. In §3, we give a complete equational proof of a classical folk theorem [14, 27] which states that every **while** program can be simulated by another **while** program with at most one **while** loop, provided extra Boolean variables are allowed. The approach we take is that of Mirkowska [27], who gives a set of local transformations that allow every **while** program to be transformed systematically to one with at most one **while** loop. For each such transformation, we give a purely equational proof of correctness. This result illustrates the use of Kleene algebra with tests and commutativity conditions in program equivalence proofs.

In §4, we observe that Cohen's construction establishing the undecidability of *-continuous Kleene algebra with added commutativity conditions actually shows that the universal Horn theory of the *-continuous Kleene algebras is not recursively enumerable, therefore not finitely axiomatizable. This resolves an open question of [22].

2 Kleene Algebra

A *Kleene algebra* [22] is an algebraic structure

$$(K, +, \cdot, {}^*, 0, 1)$$

satisfying (1)–(15) below. As usual, we omit the $\cdot$ from expressions, writing pq for $p \cdot q$. The order of precedence of the operators is ${}^* > \cdot > +$; thus $p + qr^*$ should be parsed as $p + (q(r^*))$. The unary operator ${}^+$ is defined by $q^+ = qq^*$.

$$p + (q + r) = (p + q) + r \tag{1}$$

$$p + q = q + p \tag{2}$$

$$p + 0 = p \tag{3}$$

$$p + p = p \tag{4}$$

$$p(qr) = (pq)r \tag{5}$$

$$
\begin{align}
1p &= p \tag{6}\\
p1 &= p \tag{7}\\
p(q + r) &= pq + pr \tag{8}\\
(p + q)r &= pr + qr \tag{9}\\
0p &= 0 \tag{10}\\
p0 &= 0 \tag{11}\\
1 + pp^* &= p^* \tag{12}\\
1 + p^*p &= p^* \tag{13}\\
q + pr \le r &\;\rightarrow\; p^*q \le r \tag{14}\\
q + rp \le r &\;\rightarrow\; qp^* \le r \tag{15}
\end{align}
$$

where $\le$ refers to the natural partial order on K:

$$
p \le q \;\leftrightarrow\; p + q = q .
$$

Instead of (14) and (15), we might take the equivalent axioms

$$
\begin{align}
pr \le r &\;\rightarrow\; p^*r \le r \tag{16}\\
rp \le r &\;\rightarrow\; rp^* \le r . \tag{17}
\end{align}
$$

Axioms (12)–(17) say essentially that * behaves like the Kleene star operator of formal language theory or the reflexive transitive closure operator of relational algebra. See [23] for an introduction.

A Kleene algebra is said to be *-*continuous* if it satisfies the infinitary condition

$$
pq^*r = \sup_{n \ge 0} pq^n r \tag{18}
$$

where

$$
\begin{align}
q^0 &= 1\\
q^{n+1} &= qq^n
\end{align}
$$

and the supremum is with respect to the natural order $\le$. We can think of (18) as a conjunction of the infinitely many axioms $pq^n r \le pq^*r$, $n \ge 0$, and the infinitary Horn formula

$$
\bigwedge_{n \ge 0} pq^n r \le s \;\rightarrow\; pq^*r \le s .
$$

In the presence of the other axioms, the *-continuity condition (18) implies (14)–(17), and is strictly stronger in the sense that there exist Kleene algebras that are not *-continuous [20].

All true identities between regular expressions, interpreted as regular sets of strings, are derivable from the axioms of Kleene algebra [22]. In the author's experience, two of the most useful such identities are

$$p^*(qp^*)^* = (p+q)^* \tag{19}$$
$$p(qp)^* = (pq)^*p \,. \tag{20}$$

For example, to derive the more complicated identity $(p^*q)^* = 1+(p+q)^*q$, we could reason equationally as follows:

$$
\begin{aligned}
(p^*q)^* &= 1+p^*q(p^*q)^* &&\text{by (12)} \\
&= 1+p^*(qp^*)^*q &&\text{by (20)} \\
&= 1+(p+q)^*q &&\text{by (19).}
\end{aligned}
$$

2.1 Kleene Algebra with Tests

To accommodate tests, we introduce the following variant of Kleene algebra. A *Kleene algebra with tests* is a two-sorted algebra

$$(K,\ B,\ +,\ \cdot,\ ^*,\ 0,\ 1,\ ^-)$$

where $B \subseteq K$ and $^-$ is a unary operator defined only on B, such that

$$(K,\ +,\ \cdot,\ ^*,\ 0,\ 1)$$

is a Kleene algebra and

$$(B,\ +,\ \cdot,\ ^-,\ 0,\ 1)$$

is a Boolean algebra. The elements of B are called *tests*. We reserve the letters p, q, r, s, t, u, v for arbitrary elements of K and a, b, c, d, e for tests. In PDL, a test would be written $b?$, but since we are using different symbols for tests we can omit the ?.

The sequential composition operator $\cdot$ acts as conjunction when applied to tests, and the choice operator $+$ acts as disjunction. Intuitively, a test bc succeeds iff both b and c succeed, and $b+c$ succeeds iff either b or c succeeds.

It follows immediately from the definition that $b \leq 1$ for all $b \in B$. It is tempting to define tests in an arbitrary Kleene algebra to be the set $\{b \in K \mid b \leq 1\}$. This is the approach taken by Cohen [9]. This makes sense in algebras of binary relations [28, 34], but in general the set $\{b \in K \mid b \leq 1\}$ may not extend to a Boolean algebra. For example, in the (min,+) Kleene algebra of the theory of algorithms (see [21]), $b \leq 1$ for all b, but the idempotence law $bb = b$ fails. Thus care must be taken with this approach.

We deliberately forgo this approach in favor of the explicit Boolean subalgebra in order to avoid these difficulties. Even over algebras of binary relations, we would like to admit models with programs whose input/output relations are subsets of the identity (*i.e.*, have no side effects) but whose complements are nevertheless uncomputable. We intend tests b to be viewed as simple predicates that are easily recognizable as such, and that are immediately decidable in a given state (and whose complements are therefore also immediately decidable).

2.2 While Programs

For the results of §3, we work with a PASCAL-like programming language with sequential composition $p;q$, a conditional test **if** b **then** p **else** q, and a looping construct **while** b **do** p. Programs built inductively from atomic programs and tests using these constructs are called *while programs*. We take the sequential composition operator to be of lower precedence than the conditional test or **while** loop, parenthesizing with **begin...end** where necessary; thus

$$\textbf{while } b \textbf{ do } p \,;\, q$$

should be parsed as

$$\textbf{begin while } b \textbf{ do } p \textbf{ end}\,;\, q$$

and not

$$\textbf{while } b \textbf{ do begin } p \,;\, q \textbf{ end}$$

We occasionally omit the **else** clause of a conditional test. This can be considered an abbreviation for a conditional test with the dummy **else** clause 1 (true).

These constructs are modeled in Kleene algebra with tests as follows:

$$
\begin{aligned}
p\,;q &= pq \\
\textbf{if } b \textbf{ then } p \textbf{ else } q &= bp + \bar{b}q \\
\textbf{if } b \textbf{ then } p &= bp + \bar{b} \\
\textbf{while } b \textbf{ do } p &= (bp)^*\bar{b} \,.
\end{aligned}
$$

See [23] for further discussion.

2.3 Commutativity Conditions

We will also be reasoning in the presence of *commutativity conditions* of the form $bp = pb$, where p is an arbitrary element of the Kleene algebra and b is a test. The practical significance of these conditions will become apparent in §3. Intuitively, the execution of program p does not affect the value of b. It stands to reason that if p does not affect b, then neither should it affect $\bar{b}$. This is indeed the case:

Lemma 1 *In any Kleene algebra with tests, the following are equivalent:*

(i) $pb = bp$

(ii) $p\bar{b} = \bar{b}p$

(iii) $bp\bar{b} + \bar{b}pb = 0$.

Proof. By symmetry, it suffices to show the equivalence of (i) and (iii). Assuming (i),

$$bp\bar{b} + \bar{b}pb \;=\; pb\bar{b} + \bar{b}bp \;=\; p0 + 0p \;=\; 0 \,.$$

Conversely, assuming (iii), we have $bp\bar{b} = \bar{b}pb = 0$, thus

$$
\begin{aligned}
pb &= (b + \bar{b})pb = bpb + \bar{b}pb = bpb + 0 = bpb \\
bp &= bp(b + \bar{b}) = bpb + bp\bar{b} = bpb + 0 = bpb \,.
\end{aligned}
$$

$\square$

Of course, any pair of tests commute, *i.e.*, $bc = cb$; this is an axiom of Boolean algebra.

We conclude this section with a pair of useful results that are fairly evident from an intuitive point of view, but nevertheless require formal justification.

Lemma 2 *In any Kleene algebra with tests, if $bq = qb$, then*

$$bq^* \;=\; (bq)^* b \;=\; q^* b \;=\; b(qb)^* \,.$$

Remark Note that it is *not* the case that $bq^* = (bq)^*$: when $b = 0$, the left hand side is 0 and the right hand side is 1.

Proof. We prove the three inequalities

$$bq^* \;\le\; (bq)^* b \;\le\; q^* b \;\le\; bq^* \,;$$

the equivalence of $b(qb)^*$ with these expressions follows from (20). For the first inequality, it suffices by axiom (15) to show that $b + (bq)^* bq \le (bq)^* b$. By Boolean algebra and the commutativity assumption, we have $bq = bbq = bqb$, therefore

$$b + (bq)^* bq \;=\; b + (bq)^* bqb \;=\; (1 + (bq)^* bq)b \;=\; (bq)^* b \,.$$

The second inequality follows from $b \le 1$ and the monotonicity of the Kleene algebra operators.

For the last inequality, it suffices by (14) to show $b + qbq^* \le bq^*$:

$$b + qbq^* \;=\; b + bqq^* \;=\; b(1 + qq^*) \;=\; bq^* \,.$$

Note that in this last argument, we did not use the fact that b was a test.

$\square$

Theorem 3 *In any Kleene algebra, if p is generated by a set of elements all of which commute with q, then p commutes with q.*

Proof. Let p be an expression in the language of Kleene algebra, and assume that all atomic subexpressions of p commute with q. The proof is by induction on the structure of p. The basis and all inductive cases except for programs of the form r^* are straightforward. For the inductive case $p = r^*$, we have by the induction hypothesis that $qr = rq$, and we need to argue that $qr^* = r^*q$. The inequality in one direction is given by the argument in the last paragraph in the proof of Lemma 2, which uses (14), and in the other direction by a symmetric argument using (15). □

3 A Folk Theorem

In this section we give an equational proof, using Kleene algebra with tests and commutativity conditions, of a classical result: *every* **while** *program can be simulated by a* **while** *program with at most one* **while** *loop, provided extra Boolean variables are allowed.* This theorem is the subject of a treatise on folk theorems by Harel [14], who notes that it is commonly but erroneously attributed to Böhm and Jacopini [7], and argues with some justification that it was known to Kleene. The version as stated here is originally due to Mirkowska [27], who gives a set of local transformations that allow every **while** program to be transformed systematically to one with at most one **while** loop. We consider a similar set of local transformations and give a purely equational proof of correctness for each. This result illustrates the use of Kleene algebra with tests and commutativity conditions in program equivalence proofs.

It seems to be a commonly held belief that this result has no purely schematic (*i.e.*, propositional, uninterpreted) proof [14]. The proofs of [15, 27], as reported in [14], use extra variables to remember certain values at certain points in the program, either program counter values or the values of tests. Since having to remember these values seems unavoidable, one might infer that the only recourse is to introduce extra variables, along with an explicit assignment mechanism for assigning values to them. Thus, as the argument goes, proofs of this theorem cannot be purely propositional.

We do not agree completely with this conclusion. The only purpose of these extra variables is to *preserve values across computations*. In our treatment, we only need to preserve the values of certain tests b over certain computations p. We can handle this equationally by introducing a new test c, which we can assume is set to the value of b in some precomputation, and postulating a commutativity condition of the form $cp = pc$, which says intuitively that the value of c is not affected by the execution of p. No explicit assignment mechanism is necessary; we just assume that c already has the correct value.

3.1 An Example

To illustrate this technique, consider the simple program

$$\textbf{if } b \textbf{ then begin } p\,;q \textbf{ end} \tag{21}$$
$$\textbf{else begin } p\,;r \textbf{ end}$$

If the value of b were preserved by p, then we could rewrite this program more simply as

$$p\,; \textbf{ if } b \textbf{ then } q \textbf{ else } r \tag{22}$$

Formally, the assumption that the value of b is preserved by p takes the form of the commutativity condition $bp = pb$. By Lemma 1, we also have $\bar{b}p = p\bar{b}$. Expressed in the language of Kleene algebra, the equivalence of (21) and (22) becomes the equation

$$bpq + \bar{b}pr \;=\; p(bq + \bar{b}r)\,.$$

This identity can be established by simple equational reasoning:

$$
\begin{aligned}
p(bq + \bar{b}r) \;&=\; pbq + p\bar{b}r \quad \text{by (8)}\\
&=\; bpq + \bar{b}pr \quad \text{by the commutativity assumptions.}
\end{aligned}
$$

But what if b is not preserved by p? This situation seems to call for a Boolean variable to remember the value of b across p, and an assignment mechanism to set the value of the variable. However, we do not need to take such a drastic step. We can stay within the realm of uninterpreted equational logic by introducing a new atomic test c and commutativity condition $pc = cp$, intuitively modeling the idea that c tests a variable that is not modified by p. We make the program (22) test c instead of b. We then preface both programs with the guard $bc + \bar{b}\bar{c}$ (in the language of **while** programs, **if** b **then** c **else** $\bar{c}$) which asserts that initially b and c have the same value. Intuitively, *we are assuming that c has already been set to the value of b in some (omitted) precomputation.* We can even include an atomic program s and pretend that s performs this precomputation if we like, although this is not really necessary: if the two programs are already equivalent without the s in front, then they are certainly equivalent with it.

We can now give a purely equational proof of the equivalence of the two programs

$$bc + \bar{b}\bar{c}\,;$$
$$\textbf{if } b \textbf{ then begin } p\,;q \textbf{ end} \tag{23}$$
$$\textbf{else begin } p\,;r \textbf{ end}$$

and

$$bc + \bar{b}\bar{c}\,;$$
$$p\,; \textbf{if } c \textbf{ then } q \textbf{ else } r \tag{24}$$

using the axioms of Kleene algebra with tests and the commutativity conditions $pc = cp$ and $p\bar{c} = \bar{c}p$. Expressed in the language of Kleene algebra, the equivalence of (23) and (24) becomes

$$(bc + \bar{b}\bar{c})(bpq + \bar{b}pr) \;=\; (bc + \bar{b}\bar{c})p(cq + \bar{c}r) \;. \tag{25}$$

Using the distributive laws (8) and (9) and the laws of Boolean algebra, we can simplify the left hand side of (25) as follows:

$$
\begin{aligned}
(bc + \bar{b}\bar{c})(bpq + \bar{b}pr) &= bcbpq + \bar{b}\bar{c}bpq + bc\bar{b}pr + \bar{b}\bar{c}\bar{b}pr \\
&= bcpq + \bar{b}\bar{c}pr \;.
\end{aligned}
$$

The right hand side of (25) simplifies in a similar fashion to the same expression:

$$
\begin{aligned}
(bc + \bar{b}\bar{c})p(cq + \bar{c}r) &= bcpcq + \bar{b}\bar{c}pcq + bcp\bar{c}r + \bar{b}\bar{c}p\bar{c}r \\
&= bccpq + \bar{b}\bar{c}cpq + bc\bar{c}pr + \bar{b}\bar{c}\bar{c}pr \\
&= bcpq + \bar{b}\bar{c}pr \;.
\end{aligned}
$$

Here the commutativity assumptions are used in the second step.

We can even do away with the guard $bc + \bar{b}\bar{c}$ in this argument by the following consideration. If we assume that c is assigned the value of b in the precomputation in both programs, then we might as well test c instead of b in (23) as well as (24). But then we don't need the guard at all, since the two programs are already equivalent without it by the original two-line proof given at the beginning of this section with b replaced by c.

3.2 Normal Form

A program is in *normal form* if it is of the form

$$p \,;\, \textbf{while } b \textbf{ do } q \tag{26}$$

where p and q are **while**-free. The subprogram p is called the *precomputation* of the normal form.

We show that every program can be transformed to a program in normal form. This is done inductively on the structure of the program. Each programming construct accounts for one case in the inductive proof, and we consider each case separately. For each case, we give a transformation that moves an inner **while** loop to the outside and an equational proof of its correctness.

3.3 Conditional

We first show how to move two programs in normal form in the **then** and **else** clauses of a conditional, respectively, outside the conditional. Consider the program

$$\textbf{if } b \textbf{ then begin } p_1 \textbf{ ; while } c_1 \textbf{ do } q_1 \textbf{ end}$$
$$\textbf{else begin } p_2 \textbf{ ; while } c_2 \textbf{ do } q_2 \textbf{ end} \tag{27}$$

We can assume without loss of generality that b commutes with p_1, p_2, q_1, and q_2. If not, we could introduce a new test whose value would be set to the value of b in the precomputation, then use it in place of b in the conditional test, as described in §3.1.

Under these assumptions, we show that (27) is equivalent to

$$\textbf{if } b \textbf{ then } p_1 \textbf{ else } p_2 \textbf{ ;}$$
$$\textbf{while } bc_1 + \bar{b}c_2 \textbf{ do} \tag{28}$$
$$\textbf{if } b \textbf{ then } q_1 \textbf{ else } q_2$$

Note that if the two programs in the **then** and **else** clauses of (27) are in normal form, then (28) is in normal form.

Written in the language of Kleene algebra, (27) becomes

$$bp_1(c_1q_1)^*\bar{c}_1 + \bar{b}p_2(c_2q_2)^*\bar{c}_2 \tag{29}$$

and (28) becomes

$$(bp_1 + \bar{b}p_2)((bc_1 + \bar{b}c_2)(bq_1 + \bar{b}q_2))^*\overline{bc_1 + \bar{b}c_2} \ . \tag{30}$$

The subexpression $\overline{bc_1 + \bar{b}c_2}$ of (30) is equivalent by propositional reasoning to $b\bar{c}_1 + \bar{b}\bar{c}_2$. Here we have used the familiar propositional equivalence

$$bc_1 + \bar{b}c_2 \;\; = \;\; (\bar{b} + c_1)(b + c_2)$$

and a De Morgan law. The starred expression in (30) can be simplified using distributivity and Boolean algebra:

$$(bc_1 + \bar{b}c_2)(bq_1 + \bar{b}q_2) \;\; = \;\; bc_1bq_1 + bc_1\bar{b}q_2 + \bar{b}c_2bq_1 + \bar{b}c_2\bar{b}q_2$$
$$= \;\; bc_1q_1 + \bar{b}c_2q_2 \ .$$

Substituting these simplified expressions in the original expression (30), we obtain

$$(bp_1 + \bar{b}p_2)(bc_1q_1 + \bar{b}c_2q_2)^*(b\bar{c}_1 + \bar{b}\bar{c}_2) \ . \tag{31}$$

Using distributivity, this can be broken up into the sum of four terms:

$$bp_1(bc_1q_1 + \bar{b}c_2q_2)^*b\bar{c}_1 \tag{32}$$
$$+ \;\; bp_1(bc_1q_1 + \bar{b}c_2q_2)^*\bar{b}\bar{c}_2 \tag{33}$$
$$+ \;\; \bar{b}p_2(bc_1q_1 + \bar{b}c_2q_2)^*b\bar{c}_1 \tag{34}$$
$$+ \;\; \bar{b}p_2(bc_1q_1 + \bar{b}c_2q_2)^*\bar{b}\bar{c}_2 \ . \tag{35}$$

Under the commutativity assumptions, Lemma 2 implies that (33) and (34) reduce to 0; and for the remaining two terms (32) and (35),

$$
\begin{aligned}
bp_1(bc_1q_1 + \bar{b}c_2q_2)^*b\bar{c}_1 &= bp_1(bbc_1q_1 + b\bar{b}c_2q_2)^*\bar{c}_1 \\
&= bp_1(c_1q_1)^*\bar{c}_1 \\
\bar{b}p_2(bc_1q_1 + \bar{b}c_2q_2)^*\bar{b}\bar{c}_2 &= \bar{b}p_2(\bar{b}bc_1q_1 + \bar{b}\bar{b}c_2q_2)^*\bar{c}_2 \\
&= \bar{b}p_2(c_2q_2)^*\bar{c}_2 \, .
\end{aligned}
$$

The sum of these two terms is (29).

3.4 Nested Loops

We next consider the case that is perhaps the most interesting: denesting two nested **while** loops. This construction is particularly remarkable in that no commutativity conditions (thus no extra variables) are needed; compare the corresponding transformations of [15, 27], as reported in [14], which do use extra variables.

We show that the program

$$
\begin{aligned}
&\textbf{while } b \textbf{ do begin} \\
&\qquad p\,; \\
&\qquad \textbf{while } c \textbf{ do } q \\
&\textbf{end}
\end{aligned}
\tag{36}
$$

is equivalent to the program

$$
\begin{aligned}
&\textbf{if } b \textbf{ then begin} \\
&\qquad p\,; \\
&\qquad \textbf{while } b + c \textbf{ do} \\
&\qquad\qquad \textbf{if } c \textbf{ then } q \textbf{ else } p \\
&\textbf{end}
\end{aligned}
\tag{37}
$$

This construction transforms a pair of nested **while** loops to a single **while** loop inside a conditional test. No commutativity conditions are assumed in the proof.

After this transformation, the **while** loop can be taken outside the conditional using the transformation of §3.3 (this part does require a commutativity condition). A dummy normal form such as 1; **while** 0 **do** 1 can be supplied for the missing **else** clause. Note that if the program inside the **begin...end** block of (36) is in normal form, then the resulting program will be in normal form.

Not surprisingly, the key property used in the proof is the denesting property (19), which equates a regular expression of *-depth two with another of *-depth one.

Translating to the language of Kleene algebra, (36) becomes

$$
(bp(cq)^*\bar{c})^*\bar{b}
\tag{38}
$$

and (37) becomes

$$bp((b+c)(cq+\bar{c}p))^*\overline{b+c}+\bar{b} \ . \tag{39}$$

The $\bar{b}$ in (39) is for the nonexistent **else** clause of the outermost conditional of (37). Unwinding the outer loop in (38) using (12) and distributing $\bar{b}$ over the resulting sum, we obtain

$$\bar{b}+bp(cq)^*\bar{c}(bp(cq)^*\bar{c})^*\bar{b} \ .$$

Removing $\bar{b}$ and bp from this expression and (39), it suffices to show

$$(cq)^*\bar{c}(bp(cq)^*\bar{c})^*\bar{b} \quad = \quad ((b+c)(cq+\bar{c}p))^*\overline{b+c} \ .$$

Using (20) on the left hand side and propositional reasoning on the right, this simplifies to

$$(cq)^*(\bar{c}bp(cq)^*)^*\bar{c}\bar{b} \quad = \quad ((b+c)(cq+\bar{c}p))^*\bar{c}\bar{b} \ .$$

Removing the $\bar{c}\bar{b}$ on both sides, this further simplifies to

$$(cq)^*(\bar{c}bp(cq)^*)^* \quad = \quad ((b+c)(cq+\bar{c}p))^* \ . \tag{40}$$

Now here is the key step at which the loop is denested. Applying (19) to the left hand side of (40), we obtain

$$(cq+\bar{c}bp)^* \quad = \quad ((b+c)(cq+\bar{c}p))^* \ ,$$

so it suffices to show the equivalence of the subexpressions

$$cq+\bar{c}bp \quad = \quad (b+c)(cq+\bar{c}p) \ .$$

The right hand side is easily transformed to the left using the basic laws of Kleene and Boolean algebra:

$$\begin{aligned}
(b+c)(cq+\bar{c}p) \quad &= \quad bcq+b\bar{c}p+ccq+c\bar{c}p \\
&= \quad bcq+cq+\bar{c}bp \\
&= \quad (b+1)cq+\bar{c}bp \\
&= \quad cq+\bar{c}bp \ .
\end{aligned}$$

3.5 Eliminating Postcomputations

We wish to show that a program occurring after a **while** loop can be absorbed into the **while** loop. Consider a program of the form

$$\textbf{while } b \textbf{ do } p\,;q \tag{41}$$

By introducing a new test if necessary, we can assume without loss of generality that b commutes with q. (Intuitively, the value of the new test will have to be set implicitly both in the precomputation and at the end of p. Formally, we would establish the equivalence of the two programs

$$(bc + \bar{b}\bar{c}) \text{; while } b \text{ do begin } p \text{; } (bc + \bar{b}\bar{c}) \text{ end}$$

$$(bc + \bar{b}\bar{c}) \text{; while } c \text{ do begin } p \text{; } (bc + \bar{b}\bar{c}) \text{ end}$$

We leave this as an exercise.) Under this assumption, we show that the program (41) is equivalent to the program

> **if** $\bar{b}$ **then** q
>   **else while** b **do begin**
> p;   (42)
>   **if** $\bar{b}$ **then** q
>   **end**

Note that if p and q are **while**-free, then (42) consists of a program in normal form inside a conditional, which can be transformed to normal form using the construction of §3.3.

Written in the language of Kleene algebra, (41) becomes

$$(bp)^* \bar{b}q \qquad\qquad\qquad (43)$$

and (42) becomes

$$\bar{b}q + b(bp(\bar{b}q + b))^* \bar{b} . \qquad\qquad (44)$$

Unwinding one iteration of (43) using (12) and distributing $\bar{b}q$ over the resulting sum, we obtain

$$\bar{b}q + bp(bp)^* \bar{b}q .$$

By distributivity, (44) is equivalent to

$$\bar{b}q + b(bp\bar{b}q + bpb)^* \bar{b} .$$

Eliminating the term $\bar{b}q$ from both sides, it suffices to prove

$$bp(bp)^* \bar{b}q = b(bp\bar{b}q + bpb)^* \bar{b} . \qquad (45)$$

At this point we seem to have reached an impasse, since b does not necessarily commute with p, so Lemma 2 does not apply. The trick here is to use the denesting rule (19) in the wrong direction. Starting with the right hand side,

$$b(bp\bar{b}q + bpb)^* \bar{b}$$
$$= b(bpb)^*(bp\bar{b}q(bpb)^*)^* \bar{b} \qquad\qquad \text{by (19)}$$

$$
\begin{aligned}
&= && (bbp)^*b(bp\overline{b}q(1 + bpb(bpb)^*))^*\overline{b} && \text{by (20) and (12)} \\
&= && (bp)^*b(bp\overline{b}q + bp\overline{b}qbpb(bpb)^*)^*\overline{b} && \\
&= && (bp)^*b(bp\overline{b}q)^*\overline{b} && \text{since } \overline{b}qb = \overline{b}bq = 0 \\
&= && (bp)^*b(1 + bp\overline{b}q(1 + bp\overline{b}q(bp\overline{b}q)^*))\overline{b} && \text{by (12)} \\
&= && (bp)^*(b\overline{b} + bp\overline{b}q\overline{b} + bp\overline{b}qbp\overline{b}q(bp\overline{b}q)^*\overline{b}) && \\
&= && (bp)^*bp\overline{b}q\overline{b} && \text{since } b\overline{b} = \overline{b}qb = 0 \\
&= && bp(bp)^*\overline{b}q && \text{by (20).}
\end{aligned}
$$

3.6 Composition

The composition of two programs in normal form

$$
\begin{aligned}
&p_1\,; \\
&\textbf{while } b_1 \textbf{ do } q_1\,; \\
&p_2\,; \\
&\textbf{while } b_2 \textbf{ do } q_2
\end{aligned}
\tag{46}
$$

can be transformed to a single program in normal form. We have actually already done all the work needed to handle this case. First, we use the result of §3.5 to absorb the **while**-free program p_2 into the first **while** loop. We can also ignore p_1, since it can be absorbed into the precomputation of the resulting normal form when we are done. It therefore suffices to show how to transform a program

$$
\begin{aligned}
&\textbf{while } b \textbf{ do } p\,; \\
&\textbf{while } c \textbf{ do } q
\end{aligned}
\tag{47}
$$

to normal form, where p and q are **while**-free.

As argued previously, we can assume without loss of generality that the test b commutes with the program q by introducing a new test if necessary and assuming that its value is set in the precomputation and at the end of p. Since b also commutes with c by Boolean algebra, by Theorem 3 we have that b commutes with the entire second **while** loop. This allows us to use the transformation of §3.5, absorbing the second **while** loop into the first. The resulting program looks like

$$
\begin{aligned}
&\textbf{if } \overline{b} \textbf{ then while } c \textbf{ do } q \\
&\quad\textbf{else } \textbf{ while } b \textbf{ do begin} \\
&\qquad\qquad p\,; \\
&\qquad\qquad \textbf{if } \overline{b} \textbf{ then while } c \textbf{ do } q \\
&\quad\textbf{end}
\end{aligned}
\tag{48}
$$

At this point we can apply the transformation of §3.3 to the subprogram

$$
\textbf{if } \overline{b} \textbf{ then while } c \textbf{ do } q
$$

using a dummy normal form for the omitted **else** clause, giving two nested loops in the **else** clause of (48); then the transformation of §3.4 to the **else** clause of (48); finally, the transformation of §3.3 to the entire resulting program, yielding a program in normal form.

The transformations of §§3.3–3.6 give a systematic method for moving **while** loops outside of any other programming construct. By applying these transformations inductively from the innermost loops outward, we can transform any program into a program in normal form.

None of these arguments needed explicit Boolean variables or any assignment mechanism. Where did they go? Of course they would be there in a real implementation, but they do not play a role in the proofs because they are hidden in "without loss of generality..." assumptions. The point is that it is not significant exactly how a Boolean value is preserved across a computation, but rather that it *can be* preserved; and for the purposes of formal verification, this fact is completely captured by a commutativity assumption. Thus we are justified in our claim that we have given a purely equational proof of this result.

4 Undecidability

Cohen [8] has shown that *-continuous Kleene algebra with extra commutativity conditions of the form $pq = qp$ is undecidable. We reproduce his construction below.

Theorem 4 (Cohen) *It is undecidable whether a given identity holds in all* *-continuous Kleene algebras satisfying a given finite set of identities of the form $pq = qp$.*

Proof. We encode Post's Correspondence Problem (PCP) (see [16]). Let I be an instance of PCP consisting of k pairs of strings $x_i, y_i \in \{p, q\}^+$, $1 \le i \le k$, where p and q are atomic symbols. For $\alpha \in \{1, \ldots, k\}^*$, define x_α inductively by

$$x_\epsilon = \epsilon$$
$$x_{\alpha i} = x_\alpha x_i \,,$$

and define y_α similarly. A *solution* to the instance I of PCP is a string $\alpha \in \{1, \ldots, k\}^+$ such that $x_\alpha = y_\alpha$.

Let $\{p', q'\}$ be a disjoint copy of $\{p, q\}$, and let $z' \in \{p', q'\}^*$ denote the image of the string $z \in \{p, q\}^*$ under the homomorphism $p \mapsto p'$, $q \mapsto q'$. Consider the commutativity conditions

$$uv' = v'u, \quad u, v \in \{p, q\} \,. \tag{49}$$

Let s and t be the expressions

$$s = (x_1 y_1' + x_2 y_2' + \cdots + x_k y_k')^+$$
$$t = (pp' + qq')^* ((p+q)^+ + (p'+q')^+ + (pq'+qp')(p+q+p'+q')^*) \, .$$

Intuitively, modulo the commutativity conditions (49), the regular expression s represents the set of all $x_\alpha y_\alpha$, and the regular expression t denotes the set of all non-solutions to I.

We claim that the inequality $s \leq t$ is a logical consequence of the identities (49) and the axioms of *-continuous Kleene algebra if and only if the instance I of PCP has no solution. In other words, the universal Horn formula

$$pp' = p'p \ \wedge \ pq' = q'p \ \wedge \ qp' = p'q \ \wedge \ qq' = q'q \ \rightarrow \ s \leq t$$

holds in all *-continuous Kleene algebras iff I has no solution.

Suppose I has no solution. For $\alpha \in \{1, \ldots, k\}^+$, let $\alpha = \alpha_1 \alpha_2 \cdots \alpha_n$ where $n \geq 1$ and each $\alpha_i \in \{1, \ldots, k\}$, $1 \leq i \leq n$. Let z be the longest common prefix of x_α and y_α. By the commutativity conditions, $x_\alpha y_\alpha$ is equivalent to a string of the form $zz'pq'w$ or $zz'qp'w$ for w an arbitrary string, or $zz'w$ for w a nonnull string of all primed or all unprimed symbols. There are no other possibilities, since α is not a solution to I. By the commutativity conditions and Kleene algebra, all such strings can be shown to be less than or equal to t. By [21, pp. 221, 246], s is the supremum of all these elements, therefore $s \leq t$.

Conversely, if I has a solution $\alpha = \alpha_1 \alpha_2 \cdots \alpha_n \in \{1, \ldots, k\}^n$, $n \geq 1$, say $x_\alpha = y_\alpha = z$, we claim that $s \leq t$ is not a logical consequence of (49) and the axioms of *-continuous Kleene algebra. It suffices to construct a *-continuous Kleene algebra satisfying (49) in which $s \not\leq t$. Consider the Kleene algebra of binary relations on the set of strings $\{p, q\}^* \cup \{p', q'\}^*$, where the operators have their standard relation-theoretic interpretations. We interpret the symbols p, q, p', q' as follows:

$$u = \{(x, xu) \mid x \in \{p,q\}^*\} \cup \{(u'x', x') \mid x \in \{p,q\}^*\}, \quad u \in \{p, q\}$$
$$u' = \{(x', x'u') \mid x \in \{p,q\}^*\} \cup \{(ux, x) \mid x \in \{p,q\}^*\}, \quad u \in \{p, q\} \, .$$

Let $e = \{(\epsilon, \epsilon)\}$. It is straightforward to verify that the equations (49) hold in this model, and that $epp' = eqq' = e$. It follows that $e(pp' + qq')^* = e$ and $ezz'e = e$. Since $zz' = x_\alpha y_\alpha \leq s$, we have $e \leq ese$, therefore $ese \neq 0$.

Now it also follows that $epq' = eqp' = 0$ and $e(p+q)^+ e = e(p'+q')^+ e = 0$, therefore

$$\begin{aligned} ete &= e((p+q)^+ + (p'+q')^+ + (pq'+qp')(p+q+p'+q')^*)e \\ &= e(p+q)^+ e + e(p'+q')^+ e + e(pq'+qp')(p+q+p'+q')^* e \\ &= 0 \, . \end{aligned}$$

Since $ese \neq 0$ and $ete = 0$, we cannot have $s \leq t$. $\qquad\square$

Let $H(KA)$ (respectively, $H(KA^*)$) denote the universal Horn theory of the Kleene algebras (respectively, the *-continuous Kleene algebras). Cohen's proof establishes more than just the undecidability of $H(KA^*)$: it actually shows that $H(KA^*)$ is not recursively enumerable, therefore not finitely axiomatizable. This is because his proof gives a many-one reduction of PCP to the complement of $H(KA^*)$; *i.e.*, the given instance of PCP is satisfiable iff the resulting Horn formula is *not* valid. Since PCP is r.e.-complete, its complement is not r.e., therefore neither is $H(KA^*)$. This answers an open question of [22], which asked whether the axioms of Kleene algebra were complete for $H(KA^*)$; in other words, do $H(KA)$ and $H(KA^*)$ coincide? The answer is no: the former is recursively enumerable (it is a universal Horn theory), whereas the latter is not.

5 Related Results and Open Problems

Using [21, pp. 221, 246], it can be shown that the equational theory of *-continuous Kleene algebras with tests is complete for relational models, and also admits a free language-theoretic model consisting of sets of "guarded strings". Using this result and a technique based on [22], it can be shown that the equational theories of Kleene algebras with tests and *-continuous Kleene algebras with tests coincide. This result is the analog of [22] for the case of Kleene algebras with tests.

Although Theorem 4 shows that *-continuous Kleene algebra with general commutativity conditions is undecidable, the only commutativity conditions needed in the proof of §3 are of the form $bq = qb$, where b is a test. Lemma 1 shows that these conditions are equivalent to conditions of the form $p = 0$. Cohen [9] shows that Kleene algebra with conditions $p = 0$ reduces efficiently to Kleene algebra without conditions. A construction similar to Cohen's can be used to show that Kleene algebra with tests and conditions $p = 0$ reduces efficiently to Kleene algebra with tests alone, and similarly for *-continuous Kleene algebra with tests.

The following interesting questions present themselves:

1. The equational theory of Kleene algebras with tests can be shown decidable by a simple reduction to PDL. What is its complexity? It is at most deterministic exponential time (since PDL is) and at least *PSPACE*-hard (since the equational theory of Kleene algebras is). We conjecture that it is *PSPACE*-complete.

2. What is the complexity of $H(KA^*)$? It is not r.e., but how high does it go?

3. By the results of §4, there must exist a universal Horn sentence that is true in all *-continuous Kleene algebras but violated in some Kleene algebra. Is there a natural example of such a sentence?

Acknowledgements

Ernie Cohen, David Gries, David Harel, Vaughan Pratt, and Fred B. Schneider provided valuable comments. I am indebted to Ernie Cohen for his kind permission to include his previously unpublished Theorem 4.

6 REFERENCES

[1] Alfred V. Aho, John E. Hopcroft, and Jeffrey D. Ullman. *The Design and Analysis of Computer Algorithms*. Addison-Wesley, 1975.

[2] S. Anderaa. On the algebra of regular expressions. *Appl. Math.*, pages 1–18, January 1965.

[3] K. V. Archangelsky. A new finite complete solvable quasiequational calculus for algebra of regular languages. Manuscript, Kiev State University, 1992.

[4] Roland Carl Backhouse. *Closure Algorithms and the Star-Height Problem of Regular Languages*. PhD thesis, Imperial College, 1975.

[5] Stephen L. Bloom and Zoltán Ésik. Equational axioms for regular sets. Technical Report 9101, Stevens Institute of Technology, May 1991.

[6] Maurice Boffa. Une remarque sur les systèmes complets d'identités rationnelles. *Informatique théoretique et Applications/Theoretical Informatics and Applications*, 24(4):419–423, 1990.

[7] C. Böhm and G. Jacopini. Flow diagrams, Turing machines, and languages with only two formation rules. *Comm. Assoc. Comput. Mach.*, 9(5):366–371, May 1966.

[8] Ernie Cohen, February 1994. Personal communication.

[9] Ernie Cohen. Hypotheses in Kleene algebra.
`ftp://ftp.bellcore.com/pub/ernie/research/homepage.html`,
April 1994.

[10] Ernie Cohen. Lazy caching.
`ftp://ftp.bellcore.com/pub/ernie/research/homepage.html`,
1994.

[11] Ernie Cohen. Using Kleene algebra to reason about concurrency control.
`ftp://ftp.bellcore.com/pub/ernie/research/homepage.html`,
1994.

[12] John Horton Conway. *Regular Algebra and Finite Machines*. Chapman and Hall, 1971.

[13] Michael J. Fischer and Richard E. Ladner. Propositional dynamic logic of regular programs. *J. Comput. Syst. Sci.*, 18(2):194–211, 1979.

[14] David Harel. On folk theorems. *Comm. Assoc. Comput. Mach.*, 23(7):379–389, July 1980.

[15] K. Hirose and M. Oya. General theory of flowcharts. *Comment. Math. Univ. St. Pauli*, 21(2):55–71, 1972.

[16] John E. Hopcroft and Jeffrey D. Ullman. *Introduction to Automata Theory, Languages, and Computation.* Addison-Wesley, 1979.

[17] Kazuo Iwano and Kenneth Steiglitz. A semiring on convex polygons and zero-sum cycle problems. *SIAM J. Comput.*, 19(5):883–901, 1990.

[18] Stephen C. Kleene. Representation of events in nerve nets and finite automata. In Shannon and McCarthy, editors, *Automata Studies*, pages 3–41. Princeton University Press, 1956.

[19] Dexter Kozen. On induction vs. *-continuity. In Kozen, editor, *Proc. Workshop on Logic of Programs*, volume 131 of *Lect. Notes in Comput. Sci.*, pages 167–176. Springer, 1981.

[20] Dexter Kozen. On Kleene algebras and closed semirings. In Rovan, editor, *Proc. Math. Found. Comput. Sci.*, volume 452 of *Lect. Notes in Comput. Sci.*, pages 26–47. Springer, 1990.

[21] Dexter Kozen. *The Design and Analysis of Algorithms.* Springer, 1991.

[22] Dexter Kozen. A completeness theorem for Kleene algebras and the algebra of regular events. *Infor. and Comput.*, 110(2):366–390, May 1994.

[23] Dexter Kozen and Jerzy Tiuryn. Logics of programs. In van Leeuwen, editor, *Handbook of Theoretical Computer Science*, volume B, pages 789–840. North Holland, 1990.

[24] Daniel Krob. A complete system of *B*-rational identities. *Theoretical Computer Science*, 89(2):207–343, October 1991.

[25] Werner Kuich. The Kleene and Parikh theorem in complete semirings. In Ottmann, editor, *Proc. 14th Colloq. Automata, Languages, and Programming*, volume 267 of *Lect. Notes in Comput. Sci.*, pages 212–225. EATCS, Springer, 1987.

[26] Werner Kuich and Arto Salomaa. *Semirings, Automata, and Languages.* Springer, 1986.

[27] G. Mirkowska. *Algorithmic Logic and its Applications*. PhD thesis, University of Warsaw, 1972. In Polish.

[28] K. C. Ng. *Relation Algebras with Transitive Closure*. PhD thesis, University of California, Berkeley, 1984.

[29] Vaughan Pratt. Dynamic algebras as a well-behaved fragment of relation algebras. In D. Pigozzi, editor, *Proc. Conf. Algebra and Computer Science*, volume 425 of *Lect. Notes in Comput. Sci.*, pages 77–110. Springer, June 1988.

[30] Vaughan Pratt. Action logic and pure induction. In J. van Eijck, editor, *Proc. Logics in AI: European Workshop JELIA '90*, volume 478 of *Lect. Notes in Comput. Sci.*, pages 97–120. Springer, September 1990.

[31] V. N. Redko. On defining relations for the algebra of regular events. *Ukrain. Mat. Z.*, 16:120–126, 1964. In Russian.

[32] Jacques Sakarovitch. Kleene's Theorem revisited: a formal path from Kleene to Chomsky. In A. Kelemenova and J. Keleman, editors, *Trends, Techniques, and Problems in Theoretical Computer Science*, volume 281 of *Lect. Notes in Computer Science*, pages 39–50. Springer, 1987.

[33] Arto Salomaa. Two complete axiom systems for the algebra of regular events. *J. Assoc. Comput. Mach.*, 13(1):158–169, January 1966.

[34] A. Tarski. On the calculus of relations. *J. Symb. Logic*, 6(3):65–106, 1941.

Managing Proofs

Leslie Lamport*

ABSTRACT A well-designed proof is a hierarchically structured collection of assumptions and statements. To check the proof with almost any current theorem prover, one must first eliminate the structure and encode the assumptions and statements in the idiosynchratic logic of the prover. One must then check and debug the proof with the particular set of algorithms the prover happens to implement, using an interface that provides an extremely myopic view of the proof. Some people believe that this process can be made wonderful by providing a screen interface that displays typeset formulas and replaces some typing with mouse clicks. In this talk, I propose a more drastic change.

*DEC Research Center, Palo Alto CA (USA), lamport@pa.dec.com

An Analyzer for Message Sequence Charts

Rajeev Alur*
Gerard J. Holzmann*
Doron Peled*

ABSTRACT Message sequence charts (MSCs) are used in the design phase of a distributed system to record intended system behaviors. They serve as informal documentation of design requirements that are referred to throughout the design process and even in the final system integration and acceptance testing. We show that message sequence charts are open to a variety of semantic interpretations. The meaning of an MSC can depend on, for instance, whether one allows or denies the possibility of message loss or message overtaking, and on the particulars of the message queuing policy to be adopted.
We describe an analysis tool that can perform automatic checks on message sequence charts and can alert the user to the existence of subtle design errors, for any predefined or user-specified semantic interpretation of the chart. The tool can also be used to specify time constraints on message delays, and can then return useful additional timing information, such as the minimum and the maximum possible delays between pairs of events.

1 Introduction

Message sequence charts (MSCs)—also known as time sequence diagrams, message flow diagrams, or object interaction diagrams—are a popular visual formalism for documenting design requirements for concurrent systems. MSCs are often used in the first attempts to formalize design requirements for a new system and the protocols it supports. MSCs represent typical execution scenarios, providing examples of either normal or exceptional executions of the proposed system.

Like any other aspect of the design process, MSCs are amenable to errors, the most common of which are *race conditions*. A race condition exists when two events appear in one (visual) order in the MSC, but can be shown to occur in the opposite order during an actual system execution. These conflicts can result from incorrect or incomplete assumptions about chains

---

*AT&T Bell Laboratories, 600 Mountain Avenue, Murray Hill, NJ 07974.
Email: {alur,gerard,doron}@research.att.com

of dependencies in the design, or from conflicting semantic assumptions about the underlying communication system. The ambiguities may lead to unspecified reception errors, deadlocks, loss of messages, and other types of incorrect behavior in the final system. Some semantic interpretations of the MSC may permit the occurrence of race conditions, while others may circumvent them. The specific version of the semantics used is influenced by the underlying communication architecture that will be chosen for the final design. The semantics are different, for instance, when processes have a single input queue or multiple queues, and it can depend on whether or not the messages are stored in FIFO order.

We describe some generic algorithms for analyzing message sequence charts, and a tool that implements them. The tool allows the user to construct and edit message sequence charts interactively, in graphical form, and to store these charts in either Z.120 textual form [5], or in graphical form as PostScript files. The tool provides the user with a menu of possible semantic interpretations of a given MSC, and can detect conflicts such as causality cycles and race conditions.

When the user specifies additional information, the tool can also perform timing analysis. The additional information consists of user-defined bounds on message delays, and bounds on delays between successive send operations. The analyzer can check whether the timing constraints are consistent, and can derive additional information such as the minimum and the maximum expiration times for timers.

The analyzer can serve as a convenient means to integrate formal verification techniques into the design process, in a way that is almost invisible to the users. The MSC analyzer, for instance, can be extended to produce formal models in the input language of standard model checkers, such as SPIN [4], to permit more detailed analyses of a design.

There have been several attempts to define an appropriate formal semantics for MSCs, e.g., [6], [7]. These approaches provide semantics definitions that correspond to, what we will define to be, the *visual order* of events. Our approach allows the user to formalize more specifically the assumptions that the user can make about the underlying (or target) architecture of the system, and compare the resulting semantics against the visual order.

2 Message Sequence Charts and their Semantics

A sample MSC is shown in Figure 1. For illustrative purposes, it reflects only a small number of the possible features. For a more complete description of MSCs, refer to the ITU recommendation Z.120 [5]. The tool we will describe supports all the features of basic message sequence charts. As yet, it does not include additional features such as creation or destruction of processes, co-regions (to be discussed below), and sub-MSCs.

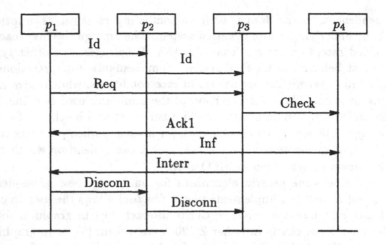

FIGURE 1. A message sequence chart

Vertical lines in the chart correspond to asynchronous processes or autonomous agents. Messages exchanged between these processes are represented by arrows. The tail of each arrow corresponds to the event of sending a message, while the head corresponds to its receipt. Arrows can be drawn either horizontally or sloping downwards, but not upwards.

2.1 Formalization

To formalize MSCs and allow their analysis, consider the MSC of Figure 2. It contains 3 processes, numbered from left to right p_1, p_2, p_3. For each process p in the system there is a vertical line which defines a local visual order, denoted $<_p$, on all the events belonging to p. Each event is either a send or a receive event, and belongs to one specific process. The events of sending and receiving messages are labeled by s_1, s_2, s_3, r_1, r_2, and r_3. For each send event, there exists a matching receive event, and vice versa. This means that, in the charts that we will use here, there are no anonymous *environment* processes. If an environment process is used, it is represented by a vertical line in the MSC. As we will see in the sequel, the actual order of occurrence of any two events in the MSC may or may not correspond to the visual order in the chart, depending on the semantic interpretation that is used.

A message sequence chart M defines a labeled directed acyclic graph with the following components:

- *Processes:* A finite set P of processes.

- *Events:* A finite set S of send events and a finite set R of receive events such that $S \cap R$ is empty. The set $S \cup R$ is denoted by E.

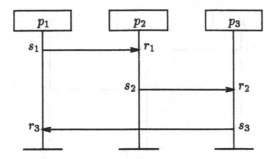

FIGURE 2. A simple MSC

- *Process Labels:* A labeling function $L : E \mapsto P$ that maps each event e to a process $L(e) \in P$. The set of events belonging to a process p is denoted by E_p.

- *Send-receive Edges:* A *compatibility* bijection $c : S \mapsto R$ such that each send event s is mapped to a unique receive event $c(s)$ and each receive event r is mapped to a unique send event $c^{-1}(r)$.

- *Visual Order:* For every process p there is a local total order $<_p$ over the events E_p which corresponds to the order in which the events are displayed. The relation

$$< \triangleq (\cup_p <_p) \cup \{(s, c(s)) \mid s \in S\}$$

  contains the local total orders and all the edges, and is called the *visual order*.

The visual order defines an acyclic graph over the events since send-receive edges cannot go upwards in the chart. The visual order does not necessarily reflect the semantics of the MSC. Although some event e may appear before an event f in the visual order, this may be only due to the two dimensionality of the diagram; it may be that e and f can in practice occur in either order. An automated scenario analyzer can, then, warn the designer that events may occur in an order that differs from the visual one.

2.2 Ambiguities

To illustrate the potential ambiguities of MSC specifications, two questions need to be addressed in assigning semantics to MSCs:

1. Which causal precedences are enforced by the underlying architecture?

2. Which causal precedences are likely to be inferred by the user?

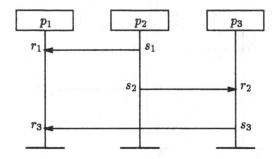

FIGURE 3. Another simple MSC

Any discrepancy between the answers to the above two questions could lead to design errors and requires the user's attention.

Consider Figures 2 and 3. In Figure 2, it is reasonable to infer that receive event r_3 occurs after send event s_1. The intuition is that p_2's send event s_2 is delayed until the arrival of r_1, and p_3's send event s_3 is delayed until the arrival of r_2. Since a message cannot be received before it is sent, we have

$$s_1 \ll r_1 \ll s_2 \ll r_2 \ll s_3 \ll r_3$$

where the symbol $\ll$ represents causal precedence.

However, it is not clear if the receive event r_1 precedes the receive event r_3 in Figure 3. It is possible that the message sent from p_2 to p_1 takes longer than the total time it takes for the messages from p_2 to p_3 and then from p_3 to p_1. Although the user may be persuaded to assume, based on the visual order, that r_3 must always follow r_1, this is not necessarily the case. An implementation of the protocol that is based on this assumption may encounter unspecified reception errors, it may deadlock, or, if it cannot distinguish between the two messages and merely assumes that one will always precede the other, it may end up deriving information from the wrong message.

The ITU Z.120 recommendation contains a mechanism for defining that the order of occurrence of events is either unknown or immaterial, using *co-regions*. For the user, however, it can be hard to assess correctly where precisely co-regions are required, where they are redundant, or even invalid. The analysis tool can identify the regions accurately in all cases.

The semantics of the enforced order can also depend on the underlying architecture of the system. Consider, for instance, two subsequent messages, sent one after the other from one process to the other. The arrival of the messages in the same order in which they were sent is guaranteed only if the architecture guarantees a FIFO queuing discipline. When this is not guaranteed, an alternative semantics in which messages can overtake each other is called for.

2.3 Interpreted MSCs

As discussed above, the correct semantic interpretation may depend on many things that cannot be standardized, such as the particulars of the underlying architecture or the communication medium and queueing disciplines that are used. We therefore adopt a user-definable semantics, and predefine only a small number of reasonable semantic interpretations.

There are three types of causal precedences that we will distinguish in this paper:

The *visual* order $<$. As explained in Section 2.1, the visual order corresponds to the scenario as drawn.

The *enforced* order $\ll$. This order contains all the event pairs that the underlying architecture can guarantee to occur only in the order specified. For example, if a send event s follows a receive event r in the enforced order, then the implementation can force the process to wait for the receive event r before allowing the send event s to take place. The message sent may, for instance, need to carry information that is acquired from the received message r.

The *inferred* order $\sqsubset$. Events that are ordered according to the inferred order are likely to be assumed by the user to occur in that order. A tool can check that the inferred order is valid by computing the transitive closure of the enforced order.

The enforced and the inferred orders can both be defined as subsets of the visual order, i.e., $(\ll \cup \sqsubset) \subseteq <$. Different semantic interpretations correspond to different rules for extracting the enforced and inferred order from the visual order. For example, a pair $(s, c(s))$ of a send and a corresponding receive event is always in the enforced order. On the other hand, a pair (r_1, r_2) of receive events in the visual order may appear in either the enforced order or in the inferred order, but it need not appear in either.

Formally, an *interpreted message sequence chart* M consists of the following components:

- An MSC $\langle P, S, R, L, c, \{<_p \,|p \in P\}\rangle$,

- For every process p, a binary relation $\ll_p$ over E_p: $e \ll_p f$ means that event e *is known* to precede event f. It is required that $\ll_p$ is a subset of the visual order $<_p$. The enforced order $\ll$ is

$$(\cup_p \ll_p) \cup \{(s, c(s))|s \in S\}.$$

- For every process p, a binary relation $\sqsubset_p$ over E_p: $e \sqsubset_p f$ means that event e *is assumed* to precede event f. It is required that $\sqsubset_p$ is a subset of the visual order $<_p$. The inferred order $\sqsubset$ is $\cup_p \sqsubset_p$.

Since the enforced order $\ll$ corresponds to the causality in the system, one can compute the order $\ll^*$ among the set of events, i.e., its transitive closure. It can then be checked whether $\sqsubseteq$ is a subset of $\ll^*$. If this is not the case, there is a conflict between the enforced and the inferred orders, and the user is likely to make an invalid inference about the behavior of the system. For example, the race conflict in Figure 3 corresponds to the interpretation that $\ll$ is $\{(s_1, r_1), (r_1, s_2), (s_2, r_2), (r_2, s_3), (s_3, r_3)\}$, while (s_1, r_3) is in $\sqsubseteq$.

Observe that since the visual order is acyclic, so is the relation $\ll^*$ due to the requirement that each $\ll_p$ is a subset of $<_p$. Also note that the two orders $\ll$ and $\sqsubseteq$ cannot conflict since both are consistent with the visual order.

There is more than one reasonable semantic interpretation of an MSC. We consider four sample choices, each tied to a different choice for the underlying architecture. Consider two events of the same process p. Each event is either a send or a receive event, with a matching receive or send event in some other process. Figure 4 illustrates the corresponding five cases that are relevant to our default set of interpretations.

Four default choices for the relations $\ll$ and $\sqsubseteq$ are indicated, as enumerated below. Cases A, B, and C, share the same interpretations in all four defaults. Cases A and C formalize the notion that a send event is a controlled event, that is only issued when the preceding events in the visual order have occurred. The order is therefore enforced in both cases, under all semantic interpretations. In case B, the inference is made that the receive event r can happen only after the send event s to account for the case where s is meant to provoke the reception r. Cases D and E distinguish between the the case when the two matching send events for two receive events that arrive to the same process p belong to the same process q or to two different processes q and r, and are interpreted differently in different defaults:

1. *Single FIFO-queue per process:* Each process p has a single FIFO queue to store all the messages received by p. Messages received by p from the same source arrive in the order in which they are sent (case E), but messages received by p from different sources (case D) need not arrive in the order sent. The inferred order of receive events corresponds to the visual order. In this semantics, if a process is waiting to receive a message r_1, and if r_2 arrives before r_1, then r_2 may be lost, or a deadlock may occur.

2. *One FIFO queue per source:* Each process p has one FIFO queue for every process q to store all the messages received by p from q. Since messages received from different sources are stored in different buffers, no order is inferred for the two receives in case D. This is because with multiple queues, a process has direct access to the first message arriving from each process, and the relative order of two

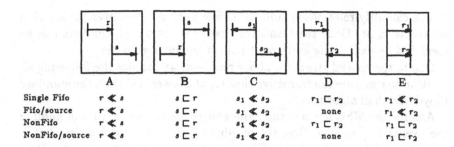

	A	B	C	D	E
Single Fifo	$r \ll s$	$s \sqsubset r$	$s_1 \ll s_2$	$r_1 \sqsubset r_2$	$r_1 \ll r_2$
Fifo/source	$r \ll s$	$s \sqsubset r$	$s_1 \ll s_2$	none	$r_1 \ll r_2$
NonFifo	$r \ll s$	$s \sqsubset r$	$s_1 \ll s_2$	$r_1 \sqsubset r_2$	$r_1 \sqsubset r_2$
NonFifo/source	$r \ll s$	$s \sqsubset r$	$s_1 \ll s_2$	none	$r_1 \sqsubset r_2$

FIGURE 4. Defaults for interpreted MSCs

messages arriving from difference processes is unimportant. If the wrong message arrives first, the receiving process would still be able to wait for the arrival of the other message, and after processing the second one, the first one would still be in its own message input queue.

3. *Single Non-FIFO queue per process:* The order in which messages are received is not necessarily the same as the order in which the messages are sent. Thus, for case E, no order between r_1 and r_2 is known. The inferred order between receive events corresponds to the visual order.

4. *One Non-FIFO per source:* Each process p has one FIFO queue for every process q to store all the messages received by p from q. Due to non-FIFO nature, for case E, the order among receives is only inferred, and not necessarily enforced. Due to multiple queues, for case D no order is inferred for receives from different sources.

Alternative interpretations may be provided for different choices of the underlying queuing model. The user can also be given an explicit override capability, to make different semantic choices for specific, user-selected, event pairs.

3 The Analysis of MSCs

Consider an interpreted MSC with visual order $<$, enforced order $\ll$, and inferred order $\sqsubset$. To find inconsistencies the transitive closure $\ll^*$ of the enforced order is computed and compared against the inferred order.

> *Race Condition:* Events e and f from the same process p are said to be in a race if $(e \sqsubset f)$ but (not $e \ll^* f$).

The MSC analysis problem is to compute all the races of a given interpreted MSC.

The causality relations $\ll$ and $\ll^*$ define partial orders over the set E of all events in M. Once the transitive closure is computed, conflicts can be identified by examining each event pair in the inferred order.

Due to the special structure of our problem, we can use the following algorithm to compute the transitive closure, at a lower cost than the standard Floyd-Warshall algorithm.

Assume the MSC has n events. Since there are no cycles, we can number the events $1 \ldots n$, such that the numbering defines a total order that is consistent with visual order $<$. The numbering can be done in time $\mathcal{O}(n)$, using a standard topological sort algorithm (see e.g., [10]). A boolean two-dimensional matrix C is used to store the pairs in $\ll^*$. All entries of C are initially false.

Algorithm 1:
for $e := 1$ **to** n **do**
  for $f := e - 1$ **downto** 1 **do**
    if *not* $C[f][e]$ **and** $f \ll e$ **then**
      $C[f][e] := true$;
      for $g := 1$ **to** $f - 1$ **do**
        if $C[g][f]$ **then** $C[g][e] := true$

In this algorithm, the value of each of the n^2 entries in C can change from false to true at most once. Call event f an *immediate predecessor* of event e if $f \ll e$ and there is no event g such that $f \ll g \ll e$. Observe that the innermost loop of the algorithm is executed for a pair (e, f) only if the event f is an immediate predecessor of the event e.

Theorem 3.1 *Given an interpreted MSC with n events. If relation $\ll$ contains ℓ pairs (f, e) such that event f is an immediate predecessor of event e, then the computational complexity of Algorithm 1 is $n^2 + \ell n$.*

For the default choices of Figure 4, ℓ is bounded by $2n$, which means that for these choices the computational complexity of Algorithm 1 is $O(n^2)$.

4 MSCs with Timing Constraints

In this section, we describe an extension of MSCs to specify timing constraints on a message flow. As an example, consider the MSC in Figure 5. The label $[1, 2]$ on the edge from s_1 to r_1 specifies the lower and upper bounds on the delay of message delivery. The label $[5, 6]$ on the vertical line from r_1 to s_2 specifies bounds on the delay between r_1 to s_2, and models an assumption about the speed of process p_2. The event *set_timer* corresponds to setting a timer which expires after 4 time units. The timing information, in this case, is consistent with the visual order of the two receive events *expire* and r_2. In fact, we can deduce that the timer will

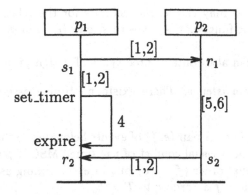

FIGURE 5. An MSC with timing constraints

always expire before the receive event r_2. Thus, the timing information can be used to deduce additional causal information, or to rule out possible race conflicts. It can also be used to compute maximum and minimum delays between pairs of events. For instance, the separation between the events *expire* and r_2 is at least 1 and at most 5.

Let R^+ be the set of nonnegative real numbers, and let us consider intervals of R^+ with integer endpoints. Intervals may be open, closed or half-closed, and may extend to infinity on the right. Examples of intervals are $(0, \infty)$, $[2, 5]$, $(3, 7]$, where the round brace indicates an open interval, and the square brace a closed one. The set of intervals is denoted by I.

A *timed MSC M* consists of

- An interpreted MSC with enforced order $\ll$ and inferred order $\sqsubseteq$.

- A timing function $T_\ll : \ll \mapsto I$ that maps each pair (e, f) in the enforced order $\ll$ to an interval $T_\ll(e, f)$. This function models the known timing relationships: the event f is known to occur within the interval $T_\ll(e, f)$ after the event e.

- A timing function $T_\sqsubseteq : \sqsubseteq \mapsto I$ that maps each pair (e, f) in the inferred order $\sqsubseteq$ to an interval $T_\sqsubseteq(e, f)$. This function models the timing constraints that the user wants to check for consistency.

A *timing assignment* for a timed MSC M is a function $T : E \mapsto R^+$ that assigns, to each event e, a time-stamp $T(e)$ such that for every pair (e, f) in the enforced relation $\ll$ the time difference $T(f) - T(e)$ belongs to the interval $T_\ll(e, f)$. Thus, a timing assignment gives the possible times at which events may occur. A sample timing assignment for the MSC of Figure 5 is

$$T(s_1) = 0, \qquad T(set\_timer) = 1.5, \quad T(r_1) = 2$$
$$T(expire) = 5.5, \quad T(s_2) = 7, \qquad\qquad T(r_2) = 8.$$

As before, the user may choose the defaults for the relations $\ll$ and $\sqsubset$. The default timing function $T_{\ll}$ maps each pair (e, f) in $\ll$ to the interval $(0, \infty)$.

Timed MSCs can also contain three types of design problems:

1. *Timing Inconsistency:* There exists no timing assignment for the MSC.

2. *Visual Conflicts:* A pair (e, f) of events belonging to the same process p is said to be a visual conflict of the timed MSC if f appears before e in the visual order ($f <_p e$) but in every timing assignment T, e happens before f according to T.

3. *Timing Conflicts:* A pair (e, f) of events is said to be a timing conflict of the timed MSC if e is assumed to occur before f ($e \sqsubset f$), but there is a timing assignment T such that the time difference $T(f) - T(e)$ does not belong to the interval $T_{\sqsubset}(e, f)$.

Timing inconsistency corresponds to an unsatisfiable set of timing constraints. The visual conflict corresponds to the case when the timing constraints imply that the event e always precedes f, in an order opposite to their visual order. Timing conflict corresponds to the case that the inferred bounds are not necessarily satisfied by the timing assignments. The MSC of Figure 5 has no conflicts. Observe that timing imposes additional ordering, and hence, it may be the case that the underlying interpreted MSC has races, but the timed MSC has no conflicts.

The analysis problem for timed MSCs is defined as follows. The input to the timed MSC analysis problem consists of a timed MSC M. If M has timing inconsistency then the output reports inconsistent specification. If M is consistent then the answer to the MSC analysis problem is the set of all visual and timing conflicts.

The timing constraints imposed by the timing function $T_{\ll}$ are linear constraints, where each constraint puts a bound on the difference of two variables. Solving such constraints can be reduced to computing negative-cost cycles and shortest distances in weighted digraphs [9].

The analysis can include both strict and nonstrict inequalities. In order to deal with different types of bounds uniformly, the cost domain D can be defined to be $Z \times \{0, 1\}$, where Z is the set of all integers (such analysis is typical of algorithms for timing verification, see, for instance, [1, 2]). The costs of the edges of the graph is from the domain D. To compute shortest paths, we need to add costs and compare costs. The ordering $\prec$ over D is the lexicographic ordering: $\langle a, b \rangle \prec \langle a', b' \rangle$ iff (1) $a < a'$, or (2) $a = a'$ and $b < b'$. The addition is defined by $\langle a, b \rangle + \langle a', b' \rangle = \langle a + a', b + b' \rangle$ (note that $+$ over the boolean component is disjunction). A strict inequality $x - y < a$ is now written as $x - y \leq \langle a, 1 \rangle$ and a nonstrict inequality $x - y \leq a$ is now written as $x - y \leq \langle a, 0 \rangle$

Given a timed MSC M, define a weighted digraph G_M as follows. The set of vertices of G_M is the set E of events. The cost of the edge from an event e to an event f gives an upper bound on the difference $T(e) - T(f)$ for a timing assignment for M. Consider a pair (e, f) in the enforced order. If $T_{\ll}(e, f) = [a, b]$, the graph G_M has an edge from e to f with cost $\langle -a, 0 \rangle$, and from f to e with cost $\langle b, 0 \rangle$. If $T_{\ll}(e, f) = (a, b]$, the graph G_M has an edge from e to f with cost $\langle -a, 1 \rangle$, and from f to e with cost $\langle b, 0 \rangle$. If $T_{\ll}(e, f) = [a, \infty)$ then the graph G_M has an edge from e to f with cost $\langle -a, 0 \rangle$, and there no edge from f to e. The cases $[a, b)$, (a, b), and (a, ∞) are handled similarly.

Lemma 4.1 *The timed MSC M is timing inconsistent iff the graph G_M has a negative cost cycle.*

Suppose M is timing consistent. Let d_{ef} be the length of the shortest path from e to f in the graph G_M (let d_{ef} be ∞ if no such path exists). The paths in G_M, then, represent all the timing assignments for M:

Lemma 4.2 *Let M be a consistent timed MSC. A function $T : E \mapsto R^+$ is a timing assignment for M iff $T(e) - T(f) \prec d_{ef}$ for all events e, f.*

Consequently, a pair (e, f) of events belonging to a process p with $e <_p f$ is a visual conflict iff there is a path from f to e with negative cost (i.e. $d_{fe} < 0$). Let (e, f) be a pair of events in $\sqsubset$. The pair (e, f) is a timing conflict iff the interval $T_{\sqsubset}(e, f)$ is included in the interval $[-d_{ef}, d_{fe}]$. It is clear that the timed MSC analysis problem can be solved by computing the shortest paths in G_M. To compute shortest paths, we use the classical dynamic programming algorithm [3, 11]. This immediately leads to the following theorem:

Theorem 4.3 *Given a timed MSC M with n events the timed MSC analysis problem is solvable in time $O(n^3)$.*

5 An MSC Analysis Tool

In this section, we briefly describe the features of the message sequence chart analyzer that we have implemented to illustrate these ideas. The graphical interface to the MSC analyzer was written in Tcl/Tk [8]. The analyzer itself was written in ANSI standard C.

The most important features of the tool can be summarized as follows.

- The tool allows the user to construct, edit, and analyze MSCs interactively. The charts may be stored in the ITU standard form (Z.120), in textual form as conventional annotated scenarios, or in graphical form, as PostScript files. Annotations to the MSC can be entered in *comment* boxes that become part of the scenario as displayed.

- For the online analysis of interpreted MSCs, the tool supports the four pre-defined semantics choices listed in Figure 4 through menu choices. Other user-defined semantics can easily be incorporated.

- The analysis for race conditions is invoked by clicking on a button labeled 'Check..'. A menu is then created listing all conflicts that can occur for the chosen semantic interpretation of the chart. By selecting a conflict from a menu-list, the corresponding event pair is highlighted in the chart. The user can also set preferences so that only certain types of conflicts (eg. between two receives, or between a send and a receive) are entered into the conflict menus.

- The user can also select an event e, with a mouse click, and ask the tool to identify all related (or optionally all unrelated) events. Related are all those events that necessarily precede or follow e in the partial order $\ll^*$. The two types of events (i.e., following or preceding the selected event) are marked in different colors.

- For timing analysis, the user can annotate the chart with intervals, both on message transmissions and on local process states (see Figure 5). Timing conflicts, for the chosen semantic interpretation, are requested as before, with a mouse click.

- The user can also select an event e, again with a mouse click, and ask the tool to identify for every related event f the interval in which f may happen relative to e. This capability can be used, for instance, to identify the required upper and lower bounds for timer expirations.

The runtime requirements to perform an exhaustive analysis of a scenario are negligible for even large MSCs (in the order of 10^3 events, spanning ten to twenty pages when printed). The analysis tool therefore runs comfortably on even small laptop computers. The tool has been applied successfully to detect race conditions in several routine industrial MSC applications.

The tool can be used to analyze cyclic scenarios by unfolding the MSCs a finite number of times before the analysis begins. If there is a simple cycle, i.e., the complete scenario can repeat, then it is sufficient to analyze only two subsequent copies of the MSC. Thus, in this case there is no need for special machinery: the user can check for race conditions by importing the same MSC twice, one after the other. This will create two subsequent copies, with events of the second copy in process p ordered to appear later than events of the first copy in p in the new local order $<_p$.

6 Conclusions

We have shown that message sequence charts are sensitive to various semantic interpretations. Under different semantics, different race conditions may occur.

We have proposed and implemented a tool which can be used to analyze message sequence charts to locate and visualize design errors as early as possible in a design cycle. The tool conforms to ITU recommendation Z.120. We have noted that extensions of the tool, to gently integrate formal verification techniques further into the design process, are possible. It is our intention to use the formal representation of MSCs described here as a vehicle for exploring such extensions.

Acknowledgements: We thank Chuck Kalmanek, Bob Kurshan, and Mihalis Yannakakis for many fruitful discussions. We are also grateful to Brian Kernighan, who developed a port of the MSC analyzer for Windows PCs.

7 REFERENCES

[1] R. Alur, A. Itai, R.P. Kurshan, M. Yannakakis. Timing verification by successive approximation. *Information and Computation* **118(1)**, pp. 142–157, 1995.

[2] D.L. Dill. Timing assumptions and verification of finite-state concurrent systems. In *Automatic Verification Methods for Finite State Systems*, LNCS 407, pp. 197–212, 1989.

[3] R.W. Floyd. Algorithm 97 (Shortest Path). *Communications of the ACM* **5** (1962), pp. 365.

[4] G.J. Holzmann. *Design and Validation of Computer Protocols*, Prentice Hall Software Series, 1991.

[5] ITU-T Recommendation Z.120, Message Sequence Chart (MSC), March 1993. (Includes [7] as Annex B.)

[6] P.B. Ladkin, S. Leue. What do message sequence charts mean. In *Formal Description Techniques*, VI 1994 (FORTE'94), Elsevier, pp. 301–315.

[7] S. Mauw, M.A. Reniers. An algebraic semantics of basic message sequence charts. *The Computer Journal*, **37(4)** (1994).

[8] J. Ousterhout. *Tcl and the Tk toolkit*, Addison-Wesley, 1994.

[9] C.H. Papadimitriou, K. Steiglitz. *Combinatorial Optimization–Algorithms and Complexity*, Prentice-Hall, 1982.

[10] T.H. Cormen, C.E. Leiserson, R.L. Rivest. *Introduction to Algorithms*, MIT press, 1990.

[11] S. Warshall. A theorem on boolean matrices. *Journal of the ACM*, **9** (1962), pp. 11-12.

Relation-Algebraic Analysis of Petri Nets with RELVIEW

Rudolf Berghammer *
Burghard von Karger *
Christiane Ulke *

ABSTRACT We present a method for specifying and implementing algorithms for the analysis of Petri nets. It is formally grounded in relational algebra. Specifications are written in ordinary predicate logic and then transformed systematically into relational programs which can be executed directly in RELVIEW, a graphical computer system for calculating with relations. Our method yields programs that are correct by construction. Its simplicity and efficiency is illustrated in many examples.

1 Introduction

Petri nets [9, 10] are widely used for designing and modeling concurrent and interacting processes. The success of Petri nets derives from their intuitive graphical representation which has great appeal even for people who are not familiar with the underlying theory. Furthermore, they have a well-defined semantics which unambiguously defines the behaviour of a net and allows formal analysis. And, finally, since they may contain cycles, a large class of processes can be represented by finite nets of manageable sizes.

In recent years, Tarski's relational algebra [13] has been used successfully for formal problem specification, prototyping, and algorithm development. Relations are well suited for reasoning about discrete structures in general and graphs in particular [12, 2, 3]. Since the static part of a Petri net is a directed graph, relational algebra is very promising for computer-aided investigations of their structure. Many interesting properties of Petri nets can be expressed in relational algebra. This is easiest for static properties such as causality and free choice but possible also for dynamic qualities like reachability and liveness.

The design of a relational algorithm starts from a logical problem specification that describes the desired result of a computation. With the aid of simple but rigorous transformation rules the specification is translated

*Institut für Informatik und Praktische Mathematik, Christian-Albrechts-Universität Kiel, Preusserstraße 1–9, D–24105 Kiel, Germany

stepwise into a relational term. The goal of this transformation is the elimination of all quantifiers. In case of success, the resulting relational expression can be executed directly and efficiently in RELVIEW [4]. In this way, a program is built up very quickly and its correctness is guaranteed by a completely formal development.

Since RELVIEW can manipulate relations very efficiently, the performance of our programs is often good enough. However, in some cases optimizations are possible. Then again the formal framework of relational algebra can be very helpful because we can use its highly developed apparatus for transforming a given relational expression into a more efficient one.

The relational approach to specification, prototyping and design applies, at least in principle, to all discrete structures that can be represented naturally by binary relations. For the purpose of presentation we restrict ourselves here to a certain class of Petri nets, known as condition/event nets. A quite different set of graph-theoretic algorithms has been handled in the same style in [2, 3].

2 Relation-Algebraic Preliminaries

A *typed relation* $R : X \leftrightarrow Y$ consists of a domain X, a range Y and a set $R \subseteq X \times Y$. The set of all (typed) relations with domain X and range Y is denoted by $[X \leftrightarrow Y]$. When the type is clear, we abbreviate $R : X \leftrightarrow Y$ to R.

If X and Y are finite and of cardinality m and n, respectively, then we may consider R as a Boolean matrix with m rows and n columns. Since this matrix interpretation is well suited for a graphical representation, we use Boolean matrix notation and write R_{xy} instead of $(x, y) \in R$.

We assume the reader to be familiar with the basic operations on relations, viz. R^{T} (transposition), $\overline{R}$ (negation), $R \cup S$ (join), $R \cap S$ (meet), and $R; S$ (composition). The empty relation is denoted by O, the universal relation by L, and the identity relation by I. The latter relation is the relation-level description of the meta-level symbol "$=$". For relation inclusion we write $R \subseteq S$. In a component-free manner, now we introduce some further relational notions which are needed in this article. Further details can be found in the textbook [12].

2.1 Closures

A relation $R : X \leftrightarrow X$ is reflexive if $\mathsf{I} \subseteq R$ and transitive if $R; R \subseteq R$. The least transitive relation containing R is called the transitive closure of R and denoted by $R^+ = \bigcup_{i \geq 1} R^i$, while the least reflexive and transitive relation containing R is called the reflexive-transitive closure of R and denoted by

$R^* = \bigcup_{i \geq 0} R^i$. Obviously, we have the equations $R^+ = R; R^* = R^*; R$ and $R^* = I \cup R^+$.

2.2 Mappings

Let $R : X \leftrightarrow Y$ be a relation. Then R is said to be functional if $R^\mathsf{T}; R \subseteq I$, and total if $R; L = L$. As usual, a functional and total relation is called a mapping. A relation R is injective if R^T is functional and surjective if R^T is total.

2.3 Description of Sets

Relational algebra offers two different ways of describing the subsets of a given set.

The first representation uses vectors, i.e., relations $v : X \leftrightarrow Y$ with $v = v; L$. This condition means: Whatever set Z and universal relation $L : Y \leftrightarrow Z$ we choose, an element x from X is either in relation $v; L$ to none of the elements of Z or to all elements of Z. As for a vector $v : X \leftrightarrow Y$ the set Y is irrelevant, we consider in the following only vectors $v : X \leftrightarrow 1$ with a specific singleton set 1 as range and omit the second subscript. Such a vector can be considered as a Boolean matrix with exactly one column, i.e., as a Boolean column vector, and describes the subset $\{x \in X : v_x\}$ of X.

A vector $v : X \leftrightarrow 1$ is said to be a point if it is injective and surjective. These properties mean that it describes a singleton set. In the matrix model, hence a point is a Boolean column vector in which exactly one component is true.

Instead of vectors, we can use injective mappings for representing subsets. Given an injective mapping $\imath : Y \leftrightarrow X$, we call Y a subset of X given by $\imath$. If Y is a subset of X given by $\imath$, then the vector $\imath^\mathsf{T}; L : X \leftrightarrow 1$, where $L : Y \leftrightarrow 1$, describes Y in the above sense. Clearly, the transition in the other direction, i.e., the construction of an injective mapping $\imath(v) : Y \leftrightarrow X$ from a given vector $v : X \leftrightarrow 1$ describing Y, is also possible. In combination with the set-theoretic membership relation

$$\varepsilon : X \leftrightarrow 2^X \qquad \varepsilon_{xs} :\Longleftrightarrow x \in s, \tag{1}$$

the relation-level equivalent of the meta-level symbol "$\in$", injective mappings can be used to enumerate sets of sets. More specifically, if the vector $v : 2^X \leftrightarrow 1$ describes a subset S of the powerset 2^X, then it is straightforward to compute an injection $\imath(v) : S \leftrightarrow 2^X$, from which we obtain the elements of S as the columns of the relation $\varepsilon; \imath(v)^\mathsf{T} : X \leftrightarrow S$. If X is finite, this leads to an economic representation of S by a Boolean matrix with $|X|$ rows and $|S|$ columns.

2.4 Residuals and Symmetric Quotients

Residuals are the greatest solutions of certain inclusions. The left residual of S over R (in symbols S / R) is the greatest relation X such that $X; R \subseteq S$ and the right residual of S over R (in symbols $R \setminus S$) is the greatest relation X such that $R; X \subseteq S$. We will also need relations which are left and right residuals simultaneously, viz. symmetric quotients. The symmetric quotient $\text{syq}(R, S)$ of two relations R and S is defined as the greatest relation X such that $R; X \subseteq S$ and $X; S^{\mathsf{T}} \subseteq R^{\mathsf{T}}$. In terms of the basic operations we have

$$S / R = \overline{\overline{S}; R^{\mathsf{T}}} \qquad R \setminus S = \overline{R^{\mathsf{T}}; \overline{S}} \qquad \text{syq}(R, S) = (R \setminus S) \cap (R^{\mathsf{T}} / S^{\mathsf{T}}).$$

The left residual is only defined if both relations have the same range and the right residual and the symmetric quotient are only defined if both relations have the same domain. Translating the first two equations into component-wise predicate logic notation yields

$$(S / R)_{yx} \Longleftrightarrow \forall z \; R_{xz} \to S_{yz} \qquad (R \setminus S)_{xy} \Longleftrightarrow \forall z \; R_{zx} \to S_{zy}. \qquad (2)$$

In particular, for $S : Y \leftrightarrow Z$ and $R : Z \leftrightarrow X$ we obtain the two correspondences

$$(S / \mathsf{L})_y \Longleftrightarrow \forall z \; S_{yz} \qquad (\overline{R} \setminus \mathsf{O})_x \Longleftrightarrow \forall z \; R_{zx} \qquad (3)$$

for single first-order universal quantification using a relation $\mathsf{L} : 1 \leftrightarrow Z$ and a vector $\mathsf{O} : Z \leftrightarrow 1$. And, finally, in component-wise notation the symmetric quotient satisfies the equivalence

$$\text{syq}(R, S)_{xy} \Longleftrightarrow \forall z \; R_{zx} \leftrightarrow S_{zy}. \qquad (4)$$

Let us consider (4) for the special case where R is a membership relation $\varepsilon : X \leftrightarrow 2^X$ and S is a vector $v : X \leftrightarrow 1$. Then the type of $\text{syq}(\varepsilon, v)$ is $[2^X \leftrightarrow 1]$ and for each set Y from 2^X we have $\text{syq}(\varepsilon, v)_Y$ if and only if $\forall z \; z \in Y \leftrightarrow v_z$. As a consequence, $\text{syq}(\varepsilon, v) : 2^X \leftrightarrow 1$ is exactly the point in the powerset corresponding to the vector v.

3 Nets and their Relational Representation

In this section we recall the basics of condition/event nets and explain their representation in the RELVIEW tool.

3.1 Nets

A *(condition/event) net* $\mathcal{N}$ is a bipartite directed graph, which we represent as a a a quadruple $\mathcal{N} = (C, E, R, S)$ with relations $R : C \leftrightarrow E$ and $S : E \leftrightarrow C$. The elements of C and E are called *conditions* and *events*, respectively, and we require that $C \cap E = \emptyset$. In the graphical representation, conditions (also known as *places*) are drawn as circles whereas events appear as squares. A *marking* is simply a subset M of C. A marked net $(\mathcal{N}, M)$ is visualized by decorating each condition $c \in M$ with a bullet, called a *token*. For example,

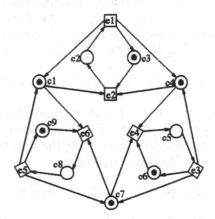

depicts a marked net with nine conditions $C = \{c_1, \ldots, c_9\}$, six events $E = \{e_1, \ldots, e_6\}$ and marking $M = \{c_1, c_3, c_4, c_6, c_7, c_9\}$. The relation R (resp. S) is coded by the set of arrows leading into (resp. out of) squares.

A net is a statical structure whereas markings are subject to change. The dynamic evolution of a marked net is described by a simple token game which specifies the effect of events on the current marking. An event e is currently *enabled* if all its predecessors but none of its successors carry a mark. In this case the *execution* (or *firing*) of e results in a new marking N which is obtained from the previous marking M by removing all predecessors of e and then adding all successors of e, i.e., by $N = (M \setminus \mathsf{pred}(e)) \cup \mathsf{succ}(e)$. In this way, by

$$M \xrightarrow{e} N \quad :\Longleftrightarrow \quad \text{e is enabled by M and its execution transforms M into N}$$

every (unmarked) net induces a labeled transition relation on markings.

The above net is a somewhat simplified description of E.W. Dijkstra's dining philosophers [5]. Three philosophers are sitting round a table with a large bowl of tangled spaghetti in the middle. A hungry philosopher needs two forks to eat but there are only three forks on the entire table, one between each pair of neighbours. Each philosopher is thinking most of the time but can decide to start eating at any time provided both his forks are free. After eating his fill, he is supposed to return the forks to their places and go back into thinking mode. The initial marking indicates that all philosophers are busy thinking (c_3, c_6, and c_9) and all three forks are available (c_1, c_4, and c_7). The eating states c_2, c_5, and c_8 are unmarked.

The transitions e_2, e_4, and e_6 from thinking to eating are enabled (although the philosophers may only eat one at a time) whereas the transitions from eating to thinking are disabled.

3.2 The RELVIEW System

RELVIEW [4] is a relation-based computer system for visualization, analysis and manipulation of discrete structures. Written in the C programming language, it runs under X windows and makes full use of the graphical user interface. Currently RELVIEW is used in about 30 installations all over the world.

All data are represented as binary relations, which RELVIEW visualizes in different ways. RELVIEW offers several different algorithm for pretty-printing a relation as a directed graph, including an algorithm for drawing bipartite graphs such as Petri nets. Alternatively, a relation may be displayed as a Boolean matrix which is very useful for visual editing and also for discovering various structural properties that are not evident from a graphical presentation.

For example, in RELVIEW the marked dining philosophers net is represented by the following relations (matrices) R and S and the (column) vector *init*:

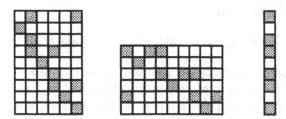

RELVIEW can manage as many relations simultaneously as memory allows and the user may manipulate and analyse them by combining them with the operators of relational algebra. The elementary operations can be accessed through simple mouse-click and combined into *relational programs* which can then be stored and applied to many sets of input data. Because RELVIEW often is used on large input data, we have incorporated some very efficient routines for computing relational products, residuals and transitive closures.

Relational programs are extremely compact: Every program considered in this paper easily fits on a single line. To the uninitiated they seem arcane. However, that does not mean relational programming is difficult. On the contrary, each program is constructed from its obvious logical specification in a short series of refinement steps each of which is formally based on one of a very small set of transformation rules. As a result, every relational program we present in this paper is *correct by construction*.

4 Reachability and Liveness

Given a net and two markings M and N, we say that N is reachable from M iff there is a sequence of transitions $M \xrightarrow{e_1} \ldots \xrightarrow{e_n} N$ that transforms M into N. Many safety properties of nets depend on the (un-)reachability of certain markings. Unlike the properties we considered in the previous section, reachability is a dynamic quality in the sense that its definition involves a potentially large number of transition steps. As a consequence, the costs of computing reachability are inherently exponential. Nevertheless the relational program for testing reachability which we derive in Sec. 4.1 is very useful for experimenting with small to medium-sized nets. It can be used as a building block for analysing more specific properties such as liveness which we investigate in Sec. 4.2.

4.1 Reachability

Reachability is defined in terms of sequences of transitions. Therefore, in the first step of our development we consider a single transition from a marking M to a marking N which is caused by the execution of an event e. We have to transscribe the definition of the transition relation of a net into a logical predicate. The first condition in that definition requires that M enables e which yields

$$(\forall c \ R_{ce} \rightarrow c \in M) \wedge (\forall c \ S_{ec} \rightarrow c \notin M).$$

Now we represent events by points from $[E \leftrightarrow 1]$. Then $R; e : C \leftrightarrow 1$ is the vector of the set of predecessors and $S^\mathsf{T}; e : C \leftrightarrow 1$ the vector of set of the successors of the point $e : E \leftrightarrow 1$. Furthermore, a condition c is a predecessor of e if and only if $(R; e)_c$ and a successor of e if and only if $(S^\mathsf{T}; e)_c$. Hence, the above formula becomes

$$(\forall c \ (R; e)_c \rightarrow c \in M) \wedge (\forall c \ (S^\mathsf{T}; e)_c \rightarrow c \notin M).$$

Using the correspondences between certain kinds of logical and relation-algebraic constructions, our next aim is to replace the set-theoretic and logical symbols of this formula with relational operations and "outermost" subscripts M, N following the general method outlined in the introduction. The desired form is derived by

$$(\forall c \ (R; e)_c \rightarrow c \in M) \wedge (\forall c \ (S^\mathsf{T}; e)_c \rightarrow c \notin M)$$

$$\Longleftrightarrow (\forall c \ (R; e)_c \rightarrow \varepsilon_{cM}) \wedge (\forall c \ (S^\mathsf{T}; e)_c \rightarrow \bar{\varepsilon}_{cM}) \qquad (1), \ \varepsilon : C \leftrightarrow 2^C$$

$$\Longleftrightarrow (\forall c \ (R; e; \mathsf{L})_{cN} \rightarrow \varepsilon_{cM}) \wedge (\forall c \ (S^\mathsf{T}; e; \mathsf{L})_{cN} \rightarrow \bar{\varepsilon}_{cM}) \ \mathsf{L} : 1 \leftrightarrow 2^C$$

$$\Longleftrightarrow (R; e; \mathsf{L} \setminus \varepsilon)_{NM} \wedge (S^\mathsf{T}; e; \mathsf{L} \setminus \bar{\varepsilon})_{NM} \qquad (2)$$

$$\Longleftrightarrow ((R; e; \mathsf{L} \setminus \varepsilon)^\mathsf{T} \cap (S^\mathsf{T}; e; \mathsf{L} \setminus \bar{\varepsilon})^\mathsf{T})_{MN},$$

where composition binds more than the residuals. If e is executed, the new marking N results from the old marking M by replacing the predecessors of e with its successors. On account of our point representation $e : E \leftrightarrow 1$ of events and since thus $\overline{R;e} : C \leftrightarrow 1$ is the complement of set of the predecessors of e, this is specified by the formula

$$\forall c \; (c \in M \wedge \overline{R;e_c}) \vee (S^{\mathsf{T}};e)_c \leftrightarrow c \in N.$$

Again, we are able to replace all the set-theoretic and predicate logic symbols with relational operations and subscripts M and N; a possible derivation is

$$\forall c \; (c \in M \wedge \overline{R;e_c}) \vee (S^{\mathsf{T}};e)_c \leftrightarrow c \in N$$

$$\Longleftrightarrow \forall c \; (\varepsilon_{cM} \wedge \overline{R;e_c}) \vee (S^{\mathsf{T}};e)_c \leftrightarrow \varepsilon_{cN} \qquad (1), \varepsilon : C \leftrightarrow 2^C$$

$$\Longleftrightarrow \forall c \; (\varepsilon_{cM} \wedge (\overline{R;e};\mathsf{L})_{cM}) \vee (S^{\mathsf{T}};e;\mathsf{L})_{cM} \leftrightarrow \varepsilon_{cN} \quad \mathsf{L} : 1 \leftrightarrow 2^C$$

$$\Longleftrightarrow \forall c \; ((\varepsilon \cap \overline{R;e};\mathsf{L}) \cup S^{\mathsf{T}};e;\mathsf{L})_{cM} \leftrightarrow \varepsilon_{cN}$$

$$\Longleftrightarrow \mathsf{syq}((\varepsilon \cap \overline{R;e};\mathsf{L}) \cup S^{\mathsf{T}};e;\mathsf{L},\varepsilon)_{MN} \qquad (4).$$

Now we can remove the subscripts M and N in the results of the last two derivations. Putting together the remainig relation-algebraic expressions, we arrive at the component-free specification

$$\begin{aligned} trans(R,S,e) := \quad & (R;e;\mathsf{L} \setminus \varepsilon)^{\mathsf{T}} \\ \cap \; & (S^{\mathsf{T}};e;\mathsf{L} \setminus \overline{\varepsilon})^{\mathsf{T}} \\ \cap \; & \mathsf{syq}((\varepsilon \cap \overline{R;e};\mathsf{L}) \cup S^{\mathsf{T}};e;\mathsf{L},\varepsilon) \end{aligned}$$

of a relation $trans(R,S,e) : 2^C \leftrightarrow 2^C$ that describes all possible single transitions between markings of $\mathcal{N}$ which are caused by an execution of the event (point) $e : E \leftrightarrow 1$.

Having derived a relational specification of the transition relation, we have solved the most difficult part of the reachability problem. By definition, the reachability relation on markings we have searched for is precisely the reflexive-transitive closure of the union of all transition relations. Hence, we define a relation

$$reach(R,S) := (\; \bigcup_{e \in \mathsf{P}(E)} trans(R,S,e))^*$$

the type of which is also $[2^C \leftrightarrow 2^C]$, where $\mathsf{P}(E)$ denotes the set of all points from $[E \leftrightarrow 1]$.

Also testing whether one marking can be reached from another is now trivial. If they are given as vectors $m : C \leftrightarrow 1$ and $n : C \leftrightarrow 1$, we then produce the corresponding points $\mathsf{syq}(\varepsilon,m) : 2^C \leftrightarrow 1$ and $\mathsf{syq}(\varepsilon,n) : 2^C \leftrightarrow 1$ in the powerset as described in Sec. 2.4 and have that n is reachable from a marking vector m if and only if $\mathsf{syq}(\varepsilon,m);\mathsf{syq}(\varepsilon,n)^{\mathsf{T}} \subseteq reach(R,S)$.

To obtain the set of all markings reachable from $m : C \leftrightarrow 1$, we start by computing the vector $Reach(R, S, m) : 2^C \leftrightarrow 1$ of the relation-theoretic successors (wrt. the reachability relation) of the point corresponding to m using

$$Reach(R, S, m) := reach(R, S)^\mathsf{T}; \mathsf{syq}(\varepsilon, m) .$$

Then, we represent the elements contained in the subset of 2^C described by the vector $Reach(R, S, m)$ as the columns of a Boolean matrix as described in Sec. 2.3.

We have formulated the above specifications in the RELVIEW system and applied to the relational representation of the philosophers net given in Sec. 3.2. The left-hand of the following two RELVIEW pictures shows the column-wise representation of the four markings reachable from the initial one; on the right-hand we have the "transition matrix" describing the possible transitions between these markings. This latter matrix is obtained as value of the relational expression $\imath(r); (\bigcup_e trans(R, S, e)); \imath(r)^\mathsf{T}$, where e ranges over the points $\mathsf{P}(E)$ and $r := Reach(R, S, init)$.

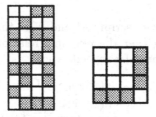

The last column of the first matrix describes the initial marking *init* (all philosophers are thinking). Three different markings are reachable (exactly one philosopher eats) and each of them corresponds to one of the first three columns. The 4×4 transition matrix shows that each of the three eating states can evolve into the thinking state and vice versa, but that no other transitions are possible. Thus, every sequence of markings/events of the token game of the philosophers net which starts with the initial marking corresponds to a run of a philosopher's dinner and vice versa.

4.2 Liveness

In the literature one finds several notions of liveness. Five different formal definitions of a marking to be live are given, investigated, and compared in [8]. All of them can easily be specified in our relational framework. In the following, we concentrate on the version which is preferred by [8]: Given a net $\mathcal{N} = (C, E, R, S)$, an event e is said to be *dead* under a marking M if there is no reachable marking N which enables e, and a marking M is called *live* if for all markings N reachable from M and all events e we have that e is not dead under N.

We start our development of an executable relational specification of liveness by reconsidering the predicate logic formula

$$(\forall c\; R_{ce} \to c \in M) \land (\forall c\; S_{ec} \to c \notin M)$$

which specifies that the marking M enables the event e. In contrast with Sec. 4.1, however, we do not represent events by points in the relational sense. This allows the following derivation which replaces the set-theoretic and predicate logic symbols with relational operations and the subscripts M and e:

$$
\begin{aligned}
&(\forall c\; R_{ce} \to c \in M) \land (\forall c\; S_{ec} \to c \notin M) \\
\Longleftarrow\; &(\forall c\; R_{ec}^{\mathsf{T}} \to \varepsilon_{Mc}^{\mathsf{T}}) \land (\forall c\; S_{ec} \to \overline{\varepsilon^{\mathsf{T}}}_{Mc}) \qquad (1),\; \varepsilon : C \leftrightarrow 2^C \\
\Longleftarrow\; &(\varepsilon^{\mathsf{T}} / R^{\mathsf{T}})_{Me} \land (\overline{\varepsilon^{\mathsf{T}}} / S)_{Me} \qquad (2) \\
\Longleftarrow\; &((\varepsilon^{\mathsf{T}} / R^{\mathsf{T}}) \cap (\overline{\varepsilon^{\mathsf{T}}} / S))_{Me}\,.
\end{aligned}
$$

Now the subscripts M and e can be removed, yielding

$$enable(R,S) := (\varepsilon^{\mathsf{T}} / R^{\mathsf{T}}) \cap (\overline{\varepsilon^{\mathsf{T}}} / S)$$

as a component-free specification of the enabling relation of type $[2^C \leftrightarrow E]$. In the Boolean matrix model this means that the entry in the M-row and e-column of $enable(R,S)$ is true if and only if e is enabled by M.

Combining the above relation $enable(R,S)$ with the reachability relation $reach(R,S)$ derived in Sec. 4.1, we have that e is dead under M if and only if

$$\neg\exists N\; reach(R,S)_{MN} \land enable(R,S)_{Ne}\,.$$

So the set of all such pairs M, e, the "is-dead-under" relation, is given by

$$dead(R,S) := \overline{reach(R,S); enable(R,S)}$$

which is a relational specification of type $[2^C \leftrightarrow E]$.

To specify liveness in predicate logic, finally, we use the reachability relation $reach(R,S)$ again, but now in combination with $dead(R,S)$. We get that a marking M is live if and only if the formula

$$\forall N\; \forall e\; reach(R,S)_{MN} \to \neg dead(R,S)_{Ne}$$

holds. In this case, the replacement of the set-theoretic and predicate logic symbols with relational operations and the subscript M proceeds as follows:

$$
\begin{aligned}
&\forall N\; \forall e\; reach(R,S)_{MN} \to \neg dead(R,S)_{Ne} \\
\Longleftrightarrow\; &\forall N\; reach(R,S)_{MN} \to \neg\exists e\; dead(R,S)_{Ne} \\
\Longleftrightarrow\; &\neg\exists N\; reach(R,S)_{MN} \land \exists e\; dead(R,S)_{Ne} \\
\Longleftrightarrow\; &\neg\exists N\; reach(R,S)_{MN} \land (dead(R,S); \mathsf{L})_N \qquad \mathsf{L} : E \leftrightarrow 1 \\
\Longleftrightarrow\; &\overline{reach(R,S); dead(R,S); \mathsf{L}}_M\,.
\end{aligned}
$$

Finally, a removal of the subscript M yields

$$live(R, S) := \overline{reach(R, S); dead(R, S); \mathsf{L}}$$

as the desired vector of type $[2^C \leftrightarrow 1]$ which describes all markings of $\mathcal{N}$ which are live. Considered as Boolean column vector this means that for a subset M of 2^C the M-component of $live(R, S)$ is true if and only if M is a live marking.

The following picture shows the column-wise representation of the eight live markings of the philosophers net as computed by RELVIEW:

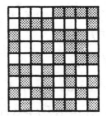

From the columns 1, 2, 5, and 6 of this matrix we see that every marking reachable from *init* is live. This means that the marked philosophers net is live, a result which can also be verified with RELVIEW using the test *Reach*$(R, S, init) \subseteq live(R, S)$. There are four more live markings, but none of them corresponds to a "real" state in a philosopher's dinner. For example, the marking depicted in the third column describes the impossible situation where each philosopher is eating

5 Protoptyping Some Further Dynamic Properties

Now we consider further examples for prototyping relational specifications of dynamic net properties. First, we consider concurrency and conflicts. Then we are then concerned with deadlocks and traps. Finally, we treat the notion of contact-freeness.

5.1 Concurrency and Conflicts

When we use nets to model concurrent and interacting processes, we cannot state whether and when an event will happen, but can only specify conditions that enable it. In this connection, however, it is very interesting to know which events can take place concurrently at a given state. This leads to the following notion. Two events e and f are *concurrently enabled* by a marking M if both of them are enabled by M in the sense of Sec. 3.1 and they have neither a predecessor nor a successor in common.

Assume $\mathcal{N} = (C, E, R, S)$ is a net. Expressed as logical formulae, the first part of the definition of the two events e and f being concurrently enabled by the marking M reads as

$$(\forall c\ R_{ce} \rightarrow c \in M) \wedge (\forall c\ S_{ec} \rightarrow c \notin M)$$
$$\wedge\ (\forall c\ R_{cf} \rightarrow c \in M) \wedge (\forall c\ S_{fc} \rightarrow c \notin M)$$

and the second part as

$$\neg(\exists c\ R_{ce} \wedge R_{cf}) \wedge \neg(\exists c\ S_{ec} \wedge S_{fc})\,.$$

Compared with Sec. 4.1 and Sec. 4.2, in the sequel we choose a third variant for a transformation of the formulae describing that a marking enables an event. Assume the marking to be represented by a vector $m : C \leftrightarrow 1$. Then $c \in M$ resp. $c \notin M$ will be replaced by m_c resp. $\overline{m}_c$ and we get for the first part the derivation

$$(\forall c\ R_{ce} \rightarrow m_c) \wedge (\forall c\ S_{ec} \rightarrow \overline{m}_c)$$
$$\wedge\ (\forall c\ R_{cf} \rightarrow m_c) \wedge (\forall c\ S_{fc} \rightarrow \overline{m}_c)$$
$$\Longleftrightarrow (R \setminus m)_e \wedge (S^\mathsf{T} \setminus \overline{m})_e \wedge (R \setminus m)_f \wedge (S^\mathsf{T} \setminus \overline{m})_f \qquad (2)$$
$$\Longleftrightarrow ((R \setminus m) \cap (S^\mathsf{T} \setminus \overline{m}))_e \wedge ((R \setminus m) \cap (S^\mathsf{T} \setminus \overline{m}))_f$$
$$\Longleftrightarrow (((R \setminus m) \cap (S^\mathsf{T} \setminus \overline{m}))\,; ((R \setminus m) \cap (S^\mathsf{T} \setminus \overline{m}))^\mathsf{T})_{ef}\,.$$

A transformation of the second part is even simpler. We obtain

$$\neg(\exists c\ R_{ce} \wedge R_{cf}) \wedge \neg(\exists c\ S_{ec} \wedge S_{fc})$$
$$\Longleftrightarrow \overline{R^\mathsf{T}; R}_{ef} \wedge \overline{S; S^\mathsf{T}}_{ef}$$
$$\Longleftrightarrow \overline{R^\mathsf{T}; R \cup S; S^\mathsf{T}}_{ef}\,.$$

Combining the results of these two derivations and dropping the subscripts e and f, we arrive at the relational specification

$$concur(R, S, m) := aux(R, S, m)\,; aux(R, S, m)^\mathsf{T} \cap \overline{R^\mathsf{T}; R \cup S; S^\mathsf{T}}$$

of type $[E \leftrightarrow E]$, where the auxiliary function aux is defined by

$$aux(R, S, m) := (R \setminus m) \cap (S^\mathsf{T} \setminus \overline{m})\,.$$

It computes for the net $\mathcal{N}$ and a given marking vector $m : C \leftrightarrow 1$ all pairs of events which are concurrently enabled by m. If we evaluate $concur(R, S, m)$ using Boolean matrices and vectors and their standard procedures for implementing relational algebra, then the run time is determined by the times needed for the compositions $R^\mathsf{T}; R$ and $S; S^\mathsf{T}$.

The dual notion to concurrency is that of a conflict. Given a marking M, two events e and f are in *conflict* under M if they are both enabled by M in the sense of Sec. 3.1, have a common predecessor or a common successor, and are different. In a predicate logic form we have, hence, the conjunction of the above formula describing that e and f are enabled by the marking M with

$$(\exists c\ R_{ce} \wedge R_{cf}) \vee (\exists c\ S_{ec} \wedge S_{fc}),$$

saying that $\mathsf{pred}(e) \cap \mathsf{pred}(f) \neq \emptyset$ or $\mathsf{succ}(e) \cap \mathsf{succ}(f) \neq \emptyset$, and the inequality $e \neq f$. For a net $\mathcal{N} = (C, E, R, S)$ and a vector $m : C \leftrightarrow 1$ representing the marking, this immediately leads (using the function aux again) to

$$conf(R, S, m) := aux(R, S, m); aux(R, S, m)^{\mathsf{T}} \cap (R^{\mathsf{T}}; R \cup S; S^{\mathsf{T}}) \cap \overline{\mathsf{I}}$$

as a relational specification of type $[E \leftrightarrow E]$ for computing all pairs of events which are in conflict under m. It has the same time complexity as $concur(R, S, m)$.

Let us apply the results to our running example. Since two or more philosophers cannot eat at the same time, one would expect that no two events are concurrently enabled by a marking reachable from $init$. The RELVIEW system confirms this conjecture. For every column m_i of the column-wise representation of $Reach(R, S, init)$ given in Sec. 4.1, the evaluation of the relational specification $concur(R, S, m_i)$ yields the empty Boolean 6×6 matrix. On the other hand, conflicts do exist. For the columns m_1, m_2, m_3 the conflict matrix is empty, but for the last column – the initial marking vector – RELVIEW yields the following Boolean 6×6 matrix:

Hence, in the initial state we have conflicts between each pair of events representing transitions from eating to thinking. This result agrees with the transition matrix shown in Sec. 4.1.

5.2 Deadlocks and Traps

Let $\mathcal{N} = (C, E, R, S)$ be a net. A set D of conditions is called a *deadlock* if each of its predecessors is also a successor. The dual notion is that of a *trap*: A subset T of C is said to be a *trap* if its successor set is a subset of its predecessor set. Both deadlocks and traps are useful for reasoning about liveness properties; details about the deadlock approach to the liveness problem can be found in [7].

If we represent sets of conditions by vectors of type $[C \leftrightarrow 1]$, then $S; v$ describes the set of predecessors and $R^{\mathsf{T}}; v$ the set of successors of $v : C \leftrightarrow 1$.

Hence, it is very easy to test a single set to be a deadlock or a trap. We have that $d : C \leftrightarrow 1$ is a deadlock if and only if $S; d \subseteq R^\mathsf{T}; d$ and, by exchanging the rôle of the relations S and R^T, also that $t : C \leftrightarrow 1$ is a trap if and only if $R^\mathsf{T}; t \subseteq S; t$. These inclusions can be tested efficiently if we implement R, S by Boolean matrices and d, t by Boolean vectors and use again the standard procedures for the relational operations.

In the following we concentrate on algorithms describing all deadlocks and traps. For a net without restrictions, the number of deadlocks and traps can grow exponentially with its size. As in the case of the algorithms of Sec. 4, therefore, our approach will lead to a complexity which is exponential in time and space.

Expressed in predicate logic we have that a set D of conditions is a deadlock if and only if the formula

$$\forall e\, (\exists c\, c \in D \wedge S_{ec}) \to (\exists c\, c \in D \wedge R_{ce})$$

is valid and that a set T of conditions is a trap if and only if

$$\forall e\, (\exists c\, c \in T \wedge R_{ce}) \to (\exists c\, c \in T \wedge S_{ec})$$

holds. The first formula can be transformed as follows, in doing so replacing the set-theoretic and logical symbols with relational operations and the subscript D:

$$\forall e\, (\exists c\, c \in D \wedge S_{ec}) \to (\exists c\, c \in D \wedge R_{ce})$$

$$\Longleftrightarrow \forall e\, (\varepsilon^\mathsf{T}; S^\mathsf{T})_{De} \to (\varepsilon^\mathsf{T}; R)_{De} \qquad\qquad (1),\ \varepsilon : C \leftrightarrow 2^C$$

$$\Longleftrightarrow \forall e\, (\overline{\varepsilon^\mathsf{T}; S^\mathsf{T}} \cup \varepsilon^\mathsf{T}; R)_{De}$$

$$\Longleftrightarrow ((\overline{\overline{S;\varepsilon}^\mathsf{T}} \cup \varepsilon^\mathsf{T}; R)\,/\,\mathsf{L})_D \qquad\qquad (3),\ \mathsf{L} : 1 \leftrightarrow E.$$

Therefore, changing to a component-free relation-algebraic notation, we get

$$deadlock(R, S) := (\overline{\overline{S;\varepsilon}^\mathsf{T}} \cup \varepsilon^\mathsf{T}; R)\,/\,\mathsf{L}$$

as specification of the vector of type $[2^C \leftrightarrow 1]$ describing all deadlocks of the net $\mathcal{N}$. In the same way one obtains from the above predicate logic description of traps by exchanging the rôle of the relations R and S^T that

$$trap(R, S) := (\overline{\overline{\varepsilon^\mathsf{T}; R}} \cup (S;\varepsilon)^\mathsf{T})\,/\,\mathsf{L}$$

is the vector of type $[2^C \leftrightarrow 1]$ describing all traps of $\mathcal{N}$.

Using RELVIEW to compute the set of all deadlocks of the philosophers net (which coincides with the set of all traps due to the net's symmetric form), we obtain the following column-wise representation:

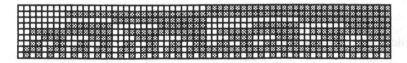

Since none of these 64 deadlocks can be reached from *init*, so the (marked) philosophers net is deadlock-free. To verify this by hand is troublesome; a mechanical verification with RELVIEW is easy. We only need to evaluate the expressions $Reach(R, S, init) \cap deadlock(R, S)$ and test the result for emptiness.

5.3 Contact-Freeness

Suppose we have a net and a present marking M. A necessary condition for an event to be executed is that no condition of its successor set is contained in M. If an execution of an event is prevented since the successors are marked, then one speaks of a contact situation. Contact situations are undesirable. A marking M is said to be *contact-free* if it is true for every event e that $\mathsf{pred}(e) \subseteq M$ implies $\mathsf{succ}(e) \subseteq C \setminus M$ and $\mathsf{succ}(e) \subseteq M$ implies $\mathsf{pred}(e) \subseteq C \setminus M$.

Assume an event e and a marking M. Then we have that $\mathsf{pred}(e) \subseteq M$ implies $\mathsf{succ}(e) \subseteq C \setminus M$ if and only if

$$(\forall c\, R_{ce} \to c \in M) \to (\forall c\, S_{ec} \to c \notin M)$$

holds, and that $\mathsf{succ}(e) \subseteq M$ implies $\mathsf{pred}(e) \subseteq C \setminus M$ if and only if

$$(\forall c\, S_{ec} \to c \in M) \to (\forall c\, R_{ce} \to c \notin M)$$

is valid. In the first case, the replacement of the logical and set-theoretic symbols with relational operations and the subscripts e and M proceeds as follows:

$$
\begin{aligned}
&(\forall c\, R_{ce} \to c \in M) \to (\forall c\, S_{ec} \to c \notin M) \\
\iff{}& (\forall c\, R_{ce} \to \varepsilon_{cM}) \to (\forall c\, S^{\mathsf{T}}_{ce} \to \overline{\varepsilon}_{cM}) && (1),\ \varepsilon : C \leftrightarrow 2^C \\
\iff{}& (R \setminus \varepsilon)_{eM} \to (S^{\mathsf{T}} \setminus \overline{\varepsilon})_{eM} && (2) \\
\iff{}& (\overline{R \setminus \varepsilon} \cup (S^{\mathsf{T}} \setminus \overline{\varepsilon}))_{eM}\,.
\end{aligned}
$$

By exchanging the rôle of the two relations R and S^{T} in this derivation, the second predicate logic formula for contact-freeness is transformed into

$$(\overline{S^{\mathsf{T}} \setminus \varepsilon} \cup (R \setminus \overline{\varepsilon}))_{eM}\,.$$

Now we combine these expressions and obtain

$$
\begin{aligned}
&\forall e\, (\overline{R \setminus \varepsilon} \cup (S^{\mathsf{T}} \setminus \overline{\varepsilon}))_{eM} \wedge (\overline{S^{\mathsf{T}} \setminus \varepsilon} \cup (R \setminus \overline{\varepsilon}))_{eM} \\
\iff{}& \forall e\, ((\overline{R \setminus \varepsilon} \cup (S^{\mathsf{T}} \setminus \overline{\varepsilon})) \cap (\overline{S^{\mathsf{T}} \setminus \varepsilon} \cup (R \setminus \overline{\varepsilon})))_{eM} \\
\iff{}& ((\overline{R \setminus \varepsilon} \cup (S^{\mathsf{T}} \setminus \overline{\varepsilon})) \cap (\overline{S^{\mathsf{T}} \setminus \varepsilon} \cup (R \setminus \overline{\varepsilon})) \setminus \mathsf{O})_e && (3),\ \mathsf{O} : E \leftrightarrow 1
\end{aligned}
$$

which in turn yields the vector

$$contactfree(R, S) := \overline{(\overline{R \setminus \varepsilon} \cup (S^{\mathsf{T}} \setminus \overline{\varepsilon})) \cap (\overline{S^{\mathsf{T}} \setminus \varepsilon} \cup (R \setminus \overline{\varepsilon}))} \setminus \mathsf{O}$$

of type $[2^C \leftrightarrow 1]$ as component-free relational specification of the set of all contact-free markings of $\mathcal{N} = (C, E, R, S)$. As with deadlocks and traps, the complexity of this algorithm is exponential in time and space. Evaluating this term for the philosophers net reveals that there are exactly 95 contact-free markings. Their column-wise representation is:

Moreover, RELVIEW can check that $Reach(R, S, init) \subseteq contactfree(R, S)$ holds, thereby proving that no contact situation can be reached from the initial marking of the philosophers net. A marked net with this property is said to be *contact-free*.

6 Testing Structural Properties of Nets

Structural (or static) properties of a net can be decided from its definition as a bipartite graph without considering the token game. Their main purpose is to characterize subclasses of nets with nice characteristics. As an example, for the special subclass of nets called "synchronisation graphs" the reachability problem is polynomial in the size of the net [6]. By means of some examples, in this section we demonstrate how structural properties of nets can be decided using a relational approach.

6.1 Free Choice Nets

In general nets there may occur the situation that a marking can only enable an event if two further concurrently enabled events are executed in a specific order. To exclude such a confused situation, i.e., to allow that the choice of the event to execute is taken locally, the specific class of free choice nets has been introduced in [7]. Formally, a net $\mathcal{N} = (C, E, R, S)$ is called a *free choice net* if for all conditions c and events e from R_{ce} it follows that $succ(c) = \{e\}$ or $pred(e) = \{c\}$. This means that an event with a forward-branching predecessor may not be backwards-branching.

For a relation-algebraic specification of a net to be free choice we follow the pattern of Sec. 5.3. Hence, we start the formula

$$\forall e \, \forall c \; R_{ce} \rightarrow (\forall f \; R_{cf} \rightarrow e = f) \vee (\forall d \; R_{de} \rightarrow d = c)$$

expressing that $\mathcal{N}$ is a free choice net and remove then the universal quantification over e and c. A transformation of the resulting formula (now with free ocurrences of e and c) into a form with only relational operations and

the subscripts e, c is obtained by

$$R_{ce} \to (\forall f \; R_{cf} \to e = f) \vee (\forall d \; R_{de} \to d = c)$$
$$\iff \overline{R^\mathsf{T}}_{ec} \vee (\forall f \; R_{cf} \to I_{ef}) \vee (\forall d \; R_{de} \to I_{dc})$$
$$\iff \overline{R^\mathsf{T}}_{ec} \vee (I / R)_{ec} \vee (R \setminus I)_{ec} \qquad (2)$$
$$\iff (\overline{R^\mathsf{T}} \cup (I / R) \cup (R \setminus I))_{ec} .$$

Note that we have used two identity relations during this development, viz. $I : E \leftrightarrow E$ in the left residual I / R and $I : C \leftrightarrow C$ in the right residual $R \setminus I$. As an immediate consequence from the above derivation we obtain

$$\mathcal{N} \text{ is a free choice net}$$
$$\iff \forall e \; \forall c \; (\overline{R^\mathsf{T}} \cup (I / R) \cup (R \setminus I))_{ec}$$
$$\iff \overline{R^\mathsf{T}} \cup (I / R) \cup (R \setminus I) = \mathsf{L} \qquad \mathsf{L} : E \leftrightarrow C .$$

In the standard Boolean matrix model for relational algebra, the latter equality can be tested in a time complexity which is determined by the costs for computing the residuals.

The philosophers net is not a free choice net. Using RELVIEW, this can easily be verified and the system then yields:

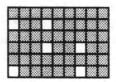

This Boolean 6×9 matrix relates the events and conditions which fulfil the free choice property. A comparison of this matrix with the 6×9 universal matrix shows that this property is violated by exactly 6 pairs, viz. by (e_2, c_1), (e_2, c_4), (e_4, c_4), (e_4, c_7), (e_6, c_1), and (e_6, c_7).

6.2 Synchronisation Graphs and State Machines

We say that a net is a *synchronisation graph* (or *S-graph*) if every condition has at most one predecessor and at most one successor. Such nets model the branching (or splitting) of a process into concurrent threads and the synchronisation of these threads. Due to the absence of branching conditions for synchronisation graphs the reachability problem can be solved in polynomial time. The same holds in nets without branching events, i.e., in the case that every event has at most one predecessor and at most one successor. Such a net is said to be a *state machine* (or *T-graph*).

On account of our special representation of a net as a relational structure $\mathcal{N} = (C, E, R, S)$ we have that $\mathcal{N}$ is a synchronisation graph if and only if

S is injective and R is functional and that $\mathcal{N}$ is a state machine if and only if R is injective and S is functional. Efficient tests for Boolean matrices to be functional resp. injective inspect row by row resp. column by column, i.e., need only two nested loops.

Using the method outlined in the introduction, we are also able to develop relational specifications of the vectors of non-branching conditions resp. non-branching events such that the resulting algorithms are polynomial. In the case of a condition c, first we consider the property that it has at most one predecessor. The derivation of a relational specification from its predicate logic description proceeds as follows:

$$\forall e\, \forall f\, S_{ec} \wedge S_{fc} \to e = f$$
$$\Longleftrightarrow \forall e\, S_{ec} \to \forall f\, S_{fc} \to \mathrm{I}_{fe} \qquad \mathrm{I} : E \leftrightarrow E$$
$$\Longleftrightarrow \forall e\, S_{ec} \to (S \setminus \mathrm{I})_{ce} \qquad\qquad (2)$$
$$\Longleftrightarrow \forall e\, (\overline{S^{\mathsf{T}}} \cup (S \setminus \mathrm{I}))_{ce}$$
$$\Longleftrightarrow ((\overline{S^{\mathsf{T}}} \cup (S \setminus \mathrm{I})) / \mathsf{L})_c \qquad (3),\ \mathsf{L} : 1 \leftrightarrow E\,.$$

Next, we deal with the property that c has at most one successor. Its logical formalization is

$$\forall e\, \forall f\, R_{ce} \wedge R_{cf} \to e = f$$

and a replacement of S by R^{T} in the above derivation transforms it into

$$((\overline{R} \cup (R^{\mathsf{T}} \setminus \mathrm{I})) / \mathsf{L})_c\,.$$

It remains to put the two relational forms together and to remove the subscript c. In doing so, we arrive at

$$s\text{-}graph(R, S) := ((\overline{S^{\mathsf{T}}} \cup (S \setminus \mathrm{I})) / \mathsf{L}) \cap ((\overline{R} \cup (R^{\mathsf{T}} \setminus \mathrm{I})) / \mathsf{L})$$

as the vector $s\text{-}graph(R, S) : C \leftrightarrow 1$ of non-branching conditions. Hence, the net $\mathcal{N}$ is a synchronisation graph if and only if $s\text{-}graph(R, S)$ equals the universal vector $\mathsf{L} : C \leftrightarrow 1$.

If we change the rôle of the relations R and S in the development of $s\text{-}graph(R, S)$, then the result is the component-free specification

$$t\text{-}graph(R, S) := ((\overline{R^{\mathsf{T}}} \cup (R \setminus \mathrm{I})) / \mathsf{L}) \cap ((\overline{S} \cup (S^{\mathsf{T}} \setminus \mathrm{I})) / \mathsf{L})$$

of a vector of type $[E \leftrightarrow 1]$ for enumerating the non-branching events. In this specification we use an identity relation $\mathrm{I} : C \leftrightarrow C$ and an universal relation $\mathsf{L} : 1 \leftrightarrow C$.

For small examples these properties can easily be read off the matrix representation. For example, the philosophers net is neither a synchronisation graph nor a state machine, because R and S have both rows and columns with more than one entry.

6.3 Causal Nets

As a last structural property we consider causal nets introduced in [11]. A net is a *causal net* if it is a synchronisation graph and the set of its arcs, called its "flow relation", is cycle-free. The latter property implies that each event can occur only once. If we define a partial order on events by $e \leq f$ if and only if f can be executed only after e, then a causal net can be seen as the net-theoretic way to represent this partial order.

In Sec. 6.2 we have shown how to decide the property to be a synchronisation graph using relational algebra. Therefore, it remains to develop a similar test for cycle-freeness. To this end, let us represent the net $\mathcal{N} = (C, E, R, S)$ as an "ordinary" directed graph $\mathcal{N} = (V, F)$, where $V := C \cup E$ and the flow relation $F : V \leftrightarrow V$ has the special form[1]

$$F = \begin{pmatrix} O & R \\ S & O \end{pmatrix}.$$

The relation F is acyclic if and only if its transitive closure is contained in $\overline{I} : V \leftrightarrow V$. A simple induction on the powers F^i of F shows the equation

$$F^+ = \begin{pmatrix} (R;S)^+ & (R;S)^+;R \\ (S;R)^+;S & (S;R)^+ \end{pmatrix}.$$

Thus, F is cyclefree if and only if $(R;S)^+ \subseteq \overline{I}$ and $(S;R)^+ \subseteq \overline{I}$. In the Boolean matrix model, the costs for these tests are the same as for computing the transitive closures, for instance we obtain cubic time complexity if S. Warshall's well-known algorithm is used.

7 Conclusion

We have captured many properties of condition/event nets in single-line relational programs which can be immediately executed in the RELVIEW system. This experience has taught us to use the RELVIEW system as a "programmable pocket calculator" for Petri nets. It cannot, of course, compete in machine efficiency with special purpose tools (although the complexities are usually the same). For structural properties such as causality and free choice the RELVIEW algorithms are easily sufficient whereas dynamic properties like reachability and liveness can only be tested for small to medium-sized nets. For example, the reachability relation for the philosophers net can be computed on a SUN workstation for up to five philosophers.

---

[1] We can also express F relation-algebraically in terms of R and S. But to achieve this, we need a relational specification of disjoint union which is beyond the aim of this article.

The real attraction of RELVIEW lies in its flexibility: New properties of nets (and new types of nets!), are introduced all the time and RELVIEW is an ideal tool for toying with new concepts while avoiding unnecessary overhead. We have used the system on many more examples, including a fair version of the philosophers net.

Even in those cases where the obvious transcription of a logical specification yields a relational algorithm of unacceptable complexity all hope is not lost. Relational algebra is a powerful transformation tool and it is often possible to derive an efficient algorithm from a prototype. A number of examples of this technique can be found in [2, 3].

We have performed the translation from logical specifications to relational programs manually, but our experience suggests that certain patterns occur very frequently, so that mechanical aid could be helpful. Of course, the transformation technique presented in this article is not sufficient for translating arbitrary first-order formulae to relational expressions and in some cases where a translation exists, a certain amount of creativity is required. Theoretically, completeness can be achieved by including the direct product of relations and adding appropriate rules. However, the use of products may lead to inefficient and obscure relational programs and is therefore best avoided.

For ease of presentation we have considered only condition/event nets in this paper, but other types of Petri nets can be explored in a similar way. In this context it is important to know that the natural numbers can be axiomatized very naturally within relational algebra [1], so that places with multiple tokens can be modelled.

8 REFERENCES

[1] Berghammer R., Zierer H.: Relational algebraic semantics of deterministic and nondeterministic programs. Theoret. Comput. Sci. 43, 123-147 (1986)

[2] Berghammer R., Gritzner T., Schmidt G.: Prototyping relational specifications using higher-order objects. In: Heering, J., Meinke, K., Möller, B., Nipkow, T. (eds.): Proc. Int. Workshop on Higher Order Algebra, Logic and Term Rewriting (HOA 93), Amsterdam, The Netherlands, Sept. 1993, LNCS 816, Springer, 56-75 (1994)

[3] Berghammer R., von Karger B.: Algorithms from relational specification. In: Brink C., Schmidt G., Albrecht R. (eds.): Relational methods in Computer Science, Supplement volume of Computing (to appear 1996)

[4] Berghammer R., Schmidt G.: RELVIEW – A computer system for the manipulation of relations. In: Nivat M., Rattray C., Rus T., Scollo G.

(eds.): Proc. 3rd Conf. on Algebraic Methodology and Software Technology (AMAST 93), University of Twente, The Netherlands, June 1993, Workshops in Computing, Springer, 405-406 (1993)

[5] Dijkstra E.W.: Hierarchical ordering of sequential processes. Acta Informatica 1, 115-138 (1971)

[6] Genrich H.J., Lautenbach K.: Synchronisationsgraphen. Acta Informatica 2, 143-161 (1973)

[7] Hack M.: Analysis of production schemata by Petri nets. TR-94, MIT-MAC (1972)

[8] Lautenbach K.: Liveness in Petri nets. Bericht 02.1/75-7-29, Gesellschaft für Mathematik und Datenverarbeitung, St. Augustin (1975)

[9] Reisig W.: Petri nets – An introduction. EATCS Monographs on Theoret. Comput. Sci., Springer (1985)

[10] Olderog E.-R.: Nets, terms and formulas. Cambridge Tracts in Theoret. Comput. Sci., Cambridge University Press (1991)

[11] Petri C.A.: Non-sequential processes. Bericht GMD-ISF-77-5, Gesellschaft für Mathematik und Datenverarbeitung, St. Augustin (1977)

[12] Schmidt G., Ströhlein T.: Relations and graphs. Discrete Mathematics for Computer Scientists, EATCS Monographs on Theoret. Comput. Sci., Springer (1993)

[13] Tarski A.: On the calculus of relations. J. Symbolic Logic 6, 73-89 (1941)

Efficient Search as a Means of Executing Specifications

Craig A. Damon*
Daniel Jackson

ABSTRACT The utility of directly executing formal specifications is briefly touched upon and the concept of exhaustive search as a means of execution is introduced. A mechanism for improving the efficiency of such searches is presented in some detail. Finally, the results of an implementation of the mechanism are presented.

KEYWORDS model generation, constraint satisfaction, exhaustive testing, formal specifications, executable specifications.

1 Introduction

One common prescription for curing the ills of software development involves the development of a formal specification in a language such as Z [Spi89]. However, beyond the clarity brought about by the very act of writing a formal specification, it is unclear what additional benefits the development of a specification actually brings.

One possible benefit arises if one is able to execute the specification. Such an execution can be used to validate and help debug a specification. Unfortunately, it is not obvious how to directly execute a Z specification. One approach [Val91] involves restricting Z to a constructive (and therefore executable) subset.

Hayes and Jones [HJ89] argue that forcing any form of determinism into the specification is a disservice, in that it may lead to restrictions in the programs that meet the specification. They provide numerous examples where this type of constructive style leads to over-specification.

Fuchs [Fu92], in response, argues that any finite specification can be executed,

* Authors' address: School of Computer Science, Carnegie Mellon University, 5000 Forbes Avenue, Pittsburgh, PA 15213. WWW: http://www.cs.cmu.edu/~{cdamon,dnj}. Email:{craig.arthur.damon, daniel.jackson}@cs.cmu.edu. Fax: (412) 268-5576.

This research was sponsored in part by a Research Initiation Award from the National Science Foundation (NSF), under grant CCR-9308726, by a grant from the TRW Corporation, and by the Wright Laboratory, Aeronautical Systems Center, Air Force Materiel Command, USAF, and the Advanced Research Projects Agency (ARPA), under grant F33615-93-1-1330.

albeit inefficiently, by performing a search over the possible results. Ignoring quantification for the moment, it is straightforward and efficient to test whether a particular case is a legal execution of a specification of some operation. Thus if a system could enumerate all possible cases, checking each case against the specification, it could find all possible executions. Such a search can be easily extended to support both universal and existential quantification.

We have built just such a system, called Nitpick[1] [JD96]. The goal of Nitpick is to allow interactive exploration of formal specifications by generating instances of states satisfying invariants, executions of operations and counterexamples of claims about a specification. As all of these scenarios amount to finding models of a formula, this paper will focus only the ability to discover valid executions.

To force a finite search space, we require the user to artificially restrict the scope of the search by limiting the number of elements of each type under consideration. Because of this limitation, Nitpick is not a verifier, since it can never search what is in general an infinite state space. Rather it is more like a debugger or tester, allowing the user to improve the specification, without ever certifying perfection.

Even for a small specification and small scope, the search can easily require checking 10^{20} total possible cases and we have seen examples (still simple) where the total space has approached 10^{40} total possible cases. The naive approach to fully searching these entire case spaces is clearly untenable.

Our approach in Nitpick is to employ a collection of sound case space reduction techniques. We currently have implemented three such techniques: derived variable detection [JD95], isomorph elimination [JJD96] and enumeration tree pruning. With derived variable detection, we detect relationships that must hold within the specification and can be determined constructively. This allows us to remove certain variables from the enumeration space, constructing their values from the other variables which are enumerated. Isomorph elimination removes cases which are only relabelings of each other. The remainder of this paper focuses on the concept, implementation and effectiveness of enumeration tree pruning, including its interaction with isomorph elimination.

2 Overview

Nitpick evaluates specifications and claims written in a simplified form of the Z specification language called NP, that retains the essential non-constructive nature of Z [Ja96]. In particular, formulas are built from simple relation and set operators, composed with **and, or, not,** $\Rightarrow$ (logical implication) and $\Leftrightarrow$ (logical equivalence). Formulas themselves are grouped into schemas, which are named collec-

---

[1] The Nitpick specification analyzer is freely available (in binary form for the Macintosh) from the authors or from http://www.cs.cmu.edu/~nitpick.

tions of formulas with associated variable declarations. Schemas are used to describe legal states of data structures as well as appropriate transitions of those data structures. Claims about the states are written in essentially the same formula language, allowing the user to make assertions about the specification.

Although the Nitpick tool is built around the Z specification language, this reduction technique is not limited just to Z specifications. Rather, it could be applied more broadly to find satisfying assignments for the variables in many logical expressions. All we rely on is the standard logical connectives and the ability to efficiently evaluate the terms for a given assignment.

An assignment is a mapping from each free variable found in the specification to a value. Typically, in the execution of an operation, some of these variables represent the state prior to execution while others represent the final state after the execution of the operation. An assignment which satisfies all of the restrictions of the specification is called a satisfying assignment. We use the term case to describe a single assignment, satisfying or not. When looking for sample executions, a satisfying assignment is an interesting case.

To find these assignments, Nitpick identifies the free variables involved in the specification, enumerates all of the possible values for each of those variables (based on the scope restrictions provided by the user), and constructs an enumeration tree, with each level corresponding to a single free variable. The specification is then evaluated against each leaf and the satisfying assignments are reported back to the user.

As a simple example, consider the formula

$$a = \{ \} \text{ or } a = b \text{ or } b = c$$

with a, b and c each declared elsewhere to be sets of type T. For this example there are three free variables, a, b and c. Assuming that T is defined to consist only of the values t_1 and t_2, a possible enumeration tree can be seen in Figure 1.

Given this simple formula and this enumeration tree, the enumeration tree can be pruned in an obvious way. If the first portion of the formula ($a = \{\}$) is tested first for each value of a, it is clear that when a is empty the value of the entire formula is true and does not depend on which values of b or c are chosen. Because of this, the entire leftmost sub-tree below a can be pruned. Similarly, if a is equal to b, the value of the formula is independent of the value chosen for c and the appropriate sub-trees of b can be pruned. The reduced tree is shown in Figure 2.

Note that this reduction does not occur statically, that is merely by examining the specification. On the contrary, at each node of the enumeration tree, starting from the root, the specification is partially evaluated given the variables bound thus far. If this partial assignment gives a definite value to the formula as a whole, the tree traversal can be safely terminated and the tree can be pruned at that node. Otherwise, each child of that node must be evaluated for possible pruning.

73

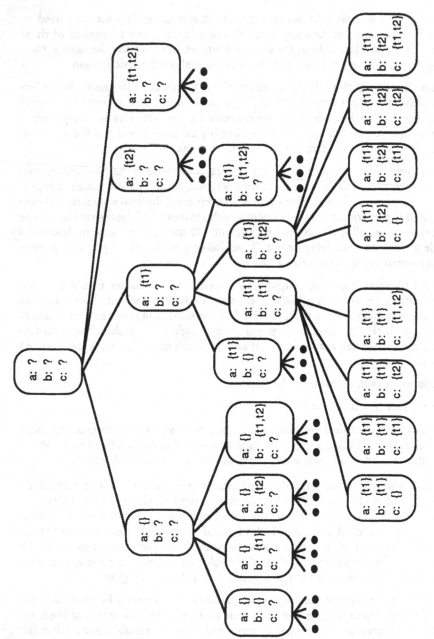

Figure 1: Full Enumeration Tree

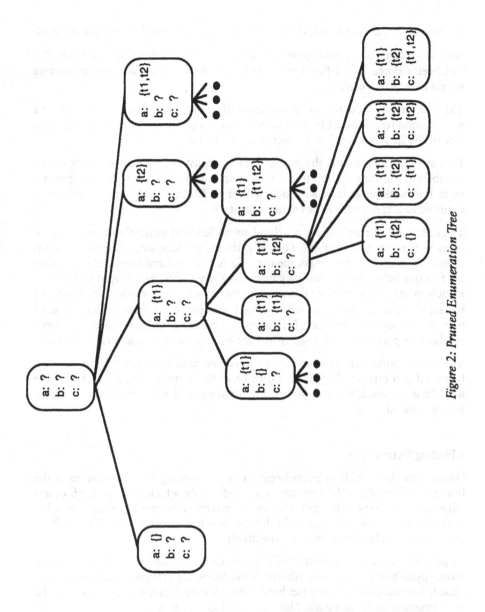

Figure 2: Pruned Enumeration Tree

Because of this, the pruning is done on the fly while the search is being performed.

Something could easily have gone wrong with this short circuiting of the tree. If c had been defined as the first level of the tree, only a small amount of pruning would have been possible.

The goal of this reduction is to automatically remove as many leaves from the enumeration tree as possible. This should occur regardless of the order and structure of the specification that the user provides to Nitpick.

To maximize the pruning, the implementation must the optimal ordering of the variables in the enumeration tree. This is non-trivial to compute, so we approximate this, seeking at least a "good" ordering. This is in addition to the work required to actually prune the enumeration tree.

To understand this analysis, it is helpful to understand more about how Nitpick actually executes specifications. Logically, there are three steps Nitpick performs to evaluate a specification. First, the formula is analyzed and compiled into a simple function which takes a full assignment of the variables as its input and returns a boolean indicating whether this assignment satisfies the specification. Next, the full set of potential values for each variable is computed[2] and these values are used to define the enumeration tree. Finally all combinations of these values are tested by checking partial and full assignments for each node in the enumeration tree.

The enumeration tree, of course, need never be held in memory in its entirety. Using a depth first search, only an indicator of the current value for each variable need be maintained. Because of this, the memory utilization of a Nitpick execution is minimal.

3 Finding Determinants

Discovering the variable ordering begins with discovering the determinants of the formula. Informally, a determinant is a sub-formula which can, by itself, determine the value of the entire formula. Some determinants only determine the value of the formula if they are true and others only when they are false. We call these true and false value determinants respectively.

To give a more formal definition of determinants, it is necessary to give a more formal definition of a formula. Although the following grammar is obviously simplified, it is sufficient for purposes here, since this reduction is independent of the term structure of the language. This simplified grammar is

Formula = Formula **and** Formula I Formula **or** Formula I

not Formula I **predicate**$(x_1, \ldots, x_n)$

[2] To further reduce our memory requirements, we do not fully enumerate the set of values for most variables. Instead we initially compute the number of possible values and provide simple calculations which can compute each value quickly from a simple ordinal.

where predicate represents a function which takes n variables as its arguments and returns a boolean.

The sets of true and false value determinants for a formula F can then be defined as the smallest sets of sub-formulas of F satisfying:

> F∈ trueDeterms **and** F ∈ falseDeterms
>
> **if** f ∈ trueDeterms **and** f = g **or** h
>> **then** g∈ trueDeterms **and** h ∈ trueDeterms
>
> **if** f ∈ falseDeterms **and** f = g **and** h
>> **then** g∈ falseDeterms **and** h ∈ falseDeterms
>
> **if** f ∈ trueDeterms **and** f = **not** g
>> **then** g∈ falseDeterms
>
> **if** f ∈ falseDeterms **and** f = **not** g
>> **then** g∈ trueDeterms

This formalism can easily be extended to include the entire NP language (as well as many others). The logical implication operator ($\Rightarrow$) can be converted into **not** and **or** in the standard manner, f $\Rightarrow$ g = **not** f **or** g. All of the standard relational and set tests can be modelled as predicates, with specialized predicates to handle more complicated expressions.

For our example above, a = {} **or** (a = b **or** b = c), the sets of determinants are

$$trueDeterms = \left\{\, a = \{\}, a = b, \ b = c \,\right\}$$
$$falseDeterms = \left\{\, a = \{\} \textbf{ or } (a = b \textbf{ or } b = c) \,\right\}$$

Note that it is possible for a formula to be both a true value and a false value determinant. Although not true in the example above, it is even possible for a formula to be a member of both miminal determinant sets. When this occurs, all other portions of the formula are extraneous since they do not effect the ultimate evaluation of the formula. As will be seen later, however, these other determinants may be useful to reduce the number of cases needed to be considered.

4 Variable and Formula Ordering

To find a good ordering of the variables, two special functions are used: one to estimate the chance of a sub-formula being known to be true given values for a subset of the variables and a similar one to estimate the chance of it being known to be false. These functions, called *known value estimators*, estimate what percentage of all assignments will make a given formula true or false, given knowledge of only a subset of variables.

```
selectedVariables := empty
variableOrdering := empty
remainingVariables = all free variables
while not remainingVariables = {}
    bestChance := 0
    foreach variable v in remainingVariables
        chance := 0
        testSet := selectedVariables ∪ {v}
        foreach true determinant d
            chance := 1.0 - ((1.0  - chance) *
                    (1.0 - trueValueEstimator(d,testSet)))
        end foreach
        foreach false determinant d
            chance := 1.0 - ((1.0  - chance) *
                    (1.0 - falseValueEstimator(d,testSet)))
        end foreach
        if chance > bestChance
            bestVariable := v
            bestChance := chance
        end if
    end foreach
    if  bestChance = 0
            /* no best selected yet, so choose an element */
        bestVariable := choose (remainingVariables)
    end if
    remainingVariables := remainingVariables \ {bestVariable}
    selectedVariables := selectedVariables ∪ {bestVariable}
    variableOrdering := append(variableOrdering,bestVariable)
end while
```

Figure 3. Simple Variable Ordering Algorithm

For example, the true known value estimator may estimate that the formula $a = \{\}$ will be true 12.5% of the time if the set of known variables contains a. If the set of known variables was $\{b, c\}$ however, it would estimate a 0% chance of knowing that the formula was true.

With these two functions, Nitpick performs a simple search to discover a good ordering of the variables. The algorithm for this search is given in Figure 3. The search is begun by using these functions to check each of the determinants against each single variable. The single variable with the aggregate best chance to induce tree pruning is thus identified. This process is then repeated, checking each remaining variable, in combination with the variables already selected, for their chance of pruning each determinant.

If at any point, no single variable provides any additional opportunities for pruning the enumeration tree, the full algorithm also checks all pairs of variables. If any pair gives opportunities for pruning while neither individual variable offers any, either variable can be chosen without preference. For performance reasons, we do not currently consider triples or larger groups of variables.

If no best variable is found, we apply some heuristics to determine the best candidate, implemented by our *choose* function from Figure 3. Our best heuristic to date is to take the variable with the smallest set of possible values, as this will create the cheapest tree if pruning does occur. Finally, we just arbitrarily choose one.

Currently, we use a very rough approximation for the known value estimators. The first check, of course, verifies that enough variables are defined to have any knowledge of the value of the formula. Where sufficient variables are defined, we use some very rough hardwired approximations, such as estimating boolean equality as 1/2 true and 1/2 false, while set equality is estimated at 1/8 true and 7/8 false[3].

Coming back to our original example, $a = \{\}$ or $a = b$ or $b = c$, the ordering process can be easily demonstrated. During the first iteration, it is determined that a has a 1/8 chance of being true for the determinant $a = \{\}$, while no other single variable could give a value to any other determinant. Therefore, a will be the first variable enumerated. During the second iteration, it is seen that the pair of variables $\{a, b\}$ has an approximate 1/8 chance of making $a = b$ true (in addition to the $a = \{\}$ chance), whereas the pair $\{a, c\}$ could not determine any new determinants. The variable ordering is now determined to be $<a, b, ?>$. Since there is only a single variable remaining, no additional iterations are required and the final ordering is $<a, b, c>$, which is in fact the optimal variable ordering for this simple example.

Given a variable ordering, the appropriate ordering of determinants can now be defined. To test a single case, the determinants will be checked in this order, halting when the value of the formula is first known (i.e. when a determinant has been evaluated to its determining value).To maximize pruning, we need to evaluate those determinants which are well defined higher in the enumeration tree before those that are only well defined lower in the tree.

To implement this ordering, each determinant, whether true or false value, is tagged with the level of the lowest variable in the enumeration tree which is required by the determinant. They are then sorted, highest level first, based on these tags so that they may be evaluated in that order.

---

3 The values for structured types, such as sets and relations, are based on an assumed cardinality of three, which is the default for the scope settings. It remains to be seen whether refining these values by using the actual scope restrictions will improve the orderings.

```
foreach variable v
    resetValue (v)

variableLevel := 1
done := false
repeat
    while variableLevel <= numVariables
        /* Check Determinants */
        foreach determinant d where tag (d) = variableLevel
            if eval (d,case) = determingValue (d)
                goto valueDetermined
        /* Nothing determined yet */
        variableLevel := variableLevel + 1
        continue while loop


    valueDetermined:
        displayCase (case,formula)
        repeat
            v := variables[variableLevel]
            if moreValues (v)
                nextValue (v)
                exit repeat
            else
                resetValue (v)
                variableLevel := variableLevel - 1
        until variableLevel = 0
        if variableLevel = 0
            done := true
    end while

    /* Got to a leaf - Start back up */
    variableLevel := variableLevel + 1
    repeat
        v := variables[variableLevel]
        if moreValues (v)
            nextValue (v)
            exit repeat
        else
            resetValue (v)
            variableLevel := variableLevel - 1
    until variableLevel = 0
    if variableLevel = 0
        done := true
until done
```

Figure 4. *Partial Depth Pruning Search Algorithm*

```
foreach variable v
    resetValue (v)

variableLevel := numVariables
done := false
repeat
    /* Check Determinants */
    foreach determinant d in order
            if eval (determinant,case) = determiningValue (d)
                    variableLevel := tag (d)
                    exit foreach

    displayCase (case,formula)

    /* Find next unpruned case */
    repeat
        v := variables[variableLevel]
        if moreValues (v)
                nextValue (v)
                exit repeat
        else
                resetValue (v)
                variableLevel := variableLevel - 1
    until variableLevel = 0
    if variableLevel = 0
            done := true
until done
```

Figure 5. Full Depth Pruning Search Algorithm

5 Pruning The Tree

To prune the tree, we want to find the highest nodes in the enumeration tree for which the value of the formula is known. This can be easily determined using a pre-order walk of the tree. At each node of the enumeration tree, a subset of the determinants is evaluated. Only the determinants that have been associated with this level of the tree need to be evaluated, i.e. those determinants which use the variable corresponding to this level, but do not reference any lower variables. Having already sorted the determinants, this set is trivially recognized.

If any of these determinants do in fact determine the value of the formula, the enumeration tree can be pruned here, ignoring all descendent nodes. If the formula is not resolved at this node, each descendant node in turn must be similarly checked.

As noted earlier, the full enumeration tree is never, of course, maintained in memory. Instead, only a means for determining the next value for each variable is necessary. Pruning the tree at a given level simply involves choosing the next value for the variable at the appropriate level, and resetting (starting back at the first value) the variable at each subsequent level in the "tree". The algorithm for searching the tree is given in Figure 4.

Partly for implementation reasons, Nitpick actually does a full enumeration down to a leaf before evaluatuing any of the determinants. This approach has the side effect of always providing a full assignment of variables, even if their values are not significant to the example discovered.

To make the evaluation of a single case as efficient as possible, Nitpick compiles the formula (currently into a simple interpretable stream). The code is generated in the order that was determined above. The state of each logical connective is modelled by position in the code, with a single branch in the code mapping to each logical connective (and, or, etc.). To determine where pruning can occur, the generated code actually tracks which variables have been used.

This variable tracking is done by tagging each branch in the generated code with the level of the lowest variable used in determining this branch. The modified algorithm for doing full depth searches with pruning is given in Figure 5.

6 Measured Reductions

This approach to reduce the state explosion has been implemented as a part of Nitpick. Nitpick consists of about 40,000 lines of C code and runs on Macintosh computers. Although we have not found instances where it is advantageous to turn off any of the space reductions techniques, we do allow them to be disabled for research purposes.

To illustrate the effectiveness of this approach, we measured the search space with and without the tree pruning reduction for three different small to moderate example specifications, each run with a smaller and larger scope setting. The Style example is a simple abstraction of a word processing paragraph style mechanism; the Phone example is a toy specification modelling call forwarding in a phone system; and the Desktop example models the move operation for the Macintosh desktop in the face of aliases. These examples range in size from fifty to a hundred lines of NP specification. For all of these runs, the total memory utilized by Nitpick was less than a megabyte all of which was allocated statically at compile time.

The results of these measurements are shown in Table 1. In this table, the *# Vars* column gives the number of free variables enumerated in the example. *Space Size* gives the total state size that would have to be searched without pruning. *Search Size* gives the number of states that remained after pruning. *Time* give the time in seconds (s), minutes (m) or hours (h) that the pruned search required when run on a Power Macintosh 7500. *Improv* is the (linear) improvement factor gained from the pruning. *Log Ratio* is the ratio of the logs of the *Search Size* and *Space Size*

Example	Scope	# Vars	Space Size	Search Size	Time	Improv	Log Ratio
Style	Small	8	9.8E8	4.6 E3	0.9 s	105	0.41
Style	Large	8	1.7E14	6.5 E6	12m	107	0.46
Phone	Small	3	2.9E5	5.2 E4	31s	6	0.87
Phone	Large	3	6.5E8	5.1E7	4h	10	0.94
Desktop	Small	6	7.9E6	1.1E3	1.7s	104	0.49
Desktop	Large	6	1.2E13	5.3E6	36m	106	0.51

Table 1. Results Of Pruning For Various Examples.

columns. All of these examples make use of derived variable detection, but do not utilize isomorph elimination. Since both the *Space Size* and *Search Size* columns include the derived variable detection reduction, the *Improv* and *Log Ratio* columns reflect only the gain from the tree pruning.

As the table shows, the gains from this tree pruning can be huge, with a 10^7 linear reduction in the large style example. The most interesting column, however, is the rightmost one, *Log Ratio*. This indicates the exponential reduction gained by the pruning.

One goal with Nitpick is to develop a number of reductions which each approach a log ratio of 0.5. As can be seen from the table, the pruning for all but the Phone example is near or beyond this goal. Such factors can drastically slow the exponential growth of state spaces. Although the growth of course remains exponential, reducing the exponent by a relatively constant small fraction flattens and shifts the growth curve to the right, yielding manageable search sizes for small to moderate specifications. Derived variable detection also typically gives a ratio around 0.5 (although this varies substantially depending on the style and structure of the specification). Like pruning, isomorph elimination, will meet this goal on many specifications, while occasionally dropping to the 0.9 range.

In general, and as could be expected, the gains from pruning seem to be most significant with more variables and smaller individual scopes. The positive correlation with the number of variables bodes well for the ability to scale into larger and more complex specifications, since larger specifications will typically have a greater number of variables.

This also blends nicely with the isomorph elimination work, which yields the largest reductions with fewer variables and larger scopes. Because of this combination, the product of the log ratios of these two mechanisms is nearly always better than 0.5, even if one or the other is significantly over that target.

7 Future Work

Based on earlier, more approximate orderings, it is clear to us that the gain is heavily dependent on choosing a good ordering. As was noted earlier, our current estimation functions for truth and false values are quite rough. Over time we may need to investigate more exacting measures, although these are likely to be more computationally expensive than the current tests.

Another future research area is the possibility of adding additional determinants which can be computed more cheaply, in terms of the number of variables used, than the existing ones. For example, consider the following formula, where a and b are sets of type T and e is an element of T:

$$a \setminus \{e\} = b$$

(The \ operator is set difference.) The smaller formula

$$e \notin b$$

can be derived from this formula. This additional formula can be conjoined to the first without changing its meaning, thus is seemingly redundant. This change does however allow enumeration tree pruning to occur before evaluating a (when e is in b).

One final possibility is to record some information about the nature of the pruning at the point that it is discovered and then use this information to quickly find the next appropriate value. For example, consider a formula where the sub-formula $a \in b$ is a determinant and the enumeration tree has a above b. If $a \in b$ caused tree pruning with a having the value t_2 and b having the value $\{\}$, the tree walker could go directly to the value $\{t_2\}$ for b, skipping over $\{t_1\}$. If such value selections were sufficiently cheap, this significantly improve the search time.

8 Related Work

The first author's background with traditional compiler optimization [ASU86] was the basis for this work. However, there are fundamental differences between the expression re-ordering done by compilers and this work. Most notable among these is the goal itself. Compilers sort the executable trying to minimize the number of instructions required to compute an expression. Thus they sort the cheapest determinants to the front. And few programming languages give the compiler writer the freedom to re-order evaluation on the scale required here.

Related approaches have also been tried in search problems over the last two decades in the AI field [KK88], particularly game playing and optimization problems. These approaches tend to be much less rewarding in game playing since the problems tend to be much less absolute. In particular, no single sub-expression can generally definitively determine the outcome of the entire search. Rather a numeric weighting is typically established for each case investigated and the weightings compared. So related pruning strategies can only remove cases which are clearly inferior to ones already established, thus markedly reducing the effectiveness of the pruning. In addition, searches for winning strategies in game playing, by their very nature, cannot re-order the evaluation tree, further limiting the effectiveness of this approach.

Recently, work has been done on variable ordering heuristics for speeding searches for solving constraint satisfaction problems[SF91]. While many of these heuristics are tailored to help with specific constraints, generally job shop scheduling, there are some general approaches which Nitpick may be able to exploit. Most interesting is the use of dynamic reordering of the search tree during the search. This is computationally very expensive and would only be useful if a significant further reduction in the search space was gained.

Slaney's FINDER program [Sla94] uses similar techniques for different goals. Its purpose is to find models of formulas in first-order logic with uninterpreted function symbols. Unlike Nitpick, FINDER constructs functions point-wise, and can thus exploit more fine-grained backtracking. By considering entire relation values, Nitpick, on the other hand, can combine backtracking search with isomorph elimination. FINDER depends on the user to provide variable orderings, and thus, although it may outperform this pruning algorithm when used by a skilled practioner, is less automatic.

9 Conclusion

The common belief has been that an "executable" specification language was necessary in order to be able to directly execute formal specifications. However, as Fuchs [Fu92] pointed out, most specifications, even non-constructive and non-deterministic ones, can be used as the test for an exhaustive search. This can then be viewed as a very inefficient form of executing the specification.

We have shown one mechanism which can be used to significantly reduce the search space required to execute a specification. While this mechanism alone does not allow efficient execution of specifications through searching, in combination with other such mechanisms it does allow a large body of specifications to be executed reasonably efficiently. This mechanism is particularly valuable here, since it becomes more effective as the specification becomes more complex (and would thus be thought to be more expensive to analyze).

With such executions, a more exploratory and interactive environment can be provided to the specification writer. Nitpick is a first step towards such an environment, allowing less sophisticated users a means to become more comfortable with formal specifications.

Further research is still needed to find more of these reductions, which in turn will enlarge the potential range of specifications which can be executed. As the suite of reductions becomes more powerful, the dream of executing arbitrary specifications may perhaps be realized without sacrificing the enormous advantages of non-constructive specifications.

Appendix: Interaction with Isomorph Elimination

There is an interaction between enumeration tree pruning and the isomorph elimination technique [JJD96] also employed by Nitpick. When using isomorph elimination, only isomorphically distinct values are used in the enumeration tree, with each value being "unlabeled". In the earlier enumeration example, four distinct values were enumerated for the sets a and b: {}, {t_1}, {t_2}, {t_1,t_2}. The middle two values are isomorphic, so the isomorphic enumeration yields only three values: {}, {•}, and {•,*}, where • and * are canonical values to be bound to specific values in the labeling.

Before labeling, it is undetermined whether • or * maps to t_1 (or to t_2) in any given variable. The appropriate detection and generation of these labelings is beyond the scope of this paper. The reader here only needs to understand that the final labelings will generate a complete set of isomorphically distinct cases utilizing actual values.

At each leaf of the original enumeration tree, the complete necessary set of labelings of these canonical values is evaluated. These additional values can be thought of as a new tree rooted at each leaf of the enumeration tree, where each level of this new tree corresponds to a variable which must be labeled. The labeling tree labels each relevant value used in each variable, so that an actual value can be tested for each variable.

In this context, there are really two opportunities for pruning, one for each kind of tree. The pruning of the labeling trees looks much like the original pruning of the enumeration tree. It can be pruned if the value of the formula at some leaf of the labeling tree is independent of the lowest levels of the labeling tree. To ensure that the most effective chance of pruning can be obtained, the labeling trees always utilize the same variable ordering discovered earlier for use by the enumeration tree.

The enumeration tree can only be pruned if the value of the entire formula is known without considering any of the pruned variables for all leaves of the associated labeling trees. In other words, the enumeration tree can only be pruned back to the lowest pruning performed across all of the paths of the associated labeling tree. Note that it does not have to be the same determinant causing each pruning of the labeling tree, just that each pruning of the labeling tree must occur at the same (or higher) level as the pruning of the enumeration tree. As can be expected, this greatly reduces the effectiveness of pruning of the enumeration tree, although most of the loss is recovered by the pruning of the labeling tree.

References

[ASU86]   A. Aho, R. Sethi and J. Ulman, *Compilers Principles, Techniques and Tools*, Addison Wesley 1986.

[Fu92]   N. E. Fuchs. Specifications are (preferably) executable. *Software Engineering Journal*, 1992, 7, (5), pp 323-334.

[HJ89]   I. J. Hayes and C. B. Jones, Specifications are not (necessarily) executable, *Software Engineering Journal*, 1989, 4, (6), pp 330-338.

[JD95]   D. Jackson and C. A. Damon. *Semi-Executable Specifications*, Technical Report CMU-CS-95-216, School of Computer Science, Carnegie Mellon University, Pittsburgh, PA, 1995.

[Ja96]   D. Jackson, Nitpick: A Checkable Specification Language, Workshop of Formal Methods in Software Practice (FMSP '96), San Diego, 1996.

[JD96]   D. Jackson and C. A. Damon. Elements of Style: Analyzing a Software Design Feature with a Counterexample Detector. *Proc. ISSTA 96*, San Diego, CA, 1996.

[JJD96]   D. Jackson, S. Jha and C. Damon. Faster Checking of Software Specifications by Eliminating Isomorphs. *Proc. Principles of Programming* St. Petersburg, Florida, USA, 1996.

[KK88]   L. Kanal and V. Kumar, Ed. Search in Artificial Intelligence, Springer-Verlag, New York, 1988.

[SF91]   N. M. Sadeh and M. S. Fox. *Variable and Value ordering Heuristics for Hard Constraint Satisfaction Problems: An Application to Job Shop Scheduling*, Technical Report CMU-RI-TR-91-23, Robotics Institute, Carnegie Mellon University, Pittsburgh, PA, 1991.

[Sla94]   J. K. Slaney. Finder: Finite Domain Enumerator, System Description. *Proc. 12th International Conference on Automated Deduction*, Lecture Notes in Artificial Intelligence series, Springer Verlag, Berlin, 1994, pp. 798-801.

[Spi89]   J. M. Spivey , *The Z Notation: A Reference Manual*, Prentice-Hall International, 1989.

[Val91]   S. H. Valentine. Z--, an executable subset of Z. In J. E. Nicholls (ed.), *Z User Workshop*, York, 1991. Springer-Verlag Workshops in Computing 1992.

An Improvement of McMillan's Unfolding Algorithm

Javier Esparza*
Stefan Römer*
Walter Vogler†

ABSTRACT McMillan has recently proposed a new technique to avoid the state explosion problem in the verification of systems modelled with finite-state Petri nets. The technique requires to construct a finite initial part of the unfolding of the net. McMillan's algorithm for this task may yield initial parts that are larger than necessary (exponentially larger in the worst case). We present a refinement of the algorithm which overcomes this problem.

1 Introduction

In a seminal paper [10], McMillan has proposed a new technique to avoid the state explosion problem in the verification of systems modelled with finite-state Petri nets. The technique is based on the concept of net unfolding, a well known partial order semantics of Petri nets introduced in [12], and later described in more detail in [4] under the name of *branching processes*. The unfolding of a net is another net, usually infinite but with a simpler structure. McMillan proposes an algorithm for the construction of a *finite* initial part of the unfolding which contains full information about the reachable states. We call an initial part satisfying this property (in fact slightly stronger one) a *finite complete prefix*. He then shows how to use these prefixes for deadlock detection.

The unfolding technique has been later applied to other verification problems. In [7, 8, 11] it is used to check relevant properties of speed independent circuits. In [5], an unfolding-based model checking algorithm for a simple branching time logic is proposed.

Although McMillan's algorithm is simple and elegant, it sometimes gen-

---

*Institut für Informatik, Technische Universität München.
E–mail: {esparza|roemer}@informatik.tu-muenchen.de.
Partially supported by the Teilprojekt A3 SAM of the Sonderforschungsbereich 342 "Werkzeuge und Methoden für die Nutzung paralleler Rechnerarchitekturen".
†Institut für Mathematik, Universität Augsburg.
E–mail: Walter.Vogler@informatik.uni-augsburg.de.

erates prefixes much larger than necessary. In some cases a minimal complete prefix has $O(n)$ in the size of the Petri net, while the algorithm generates a prefix of size $O(2^n)$. In this paper we provide an algorithm which generates a minimal complete prefix (in a certain sense to be defined). The prefix is always smaller than or as large as the prefix generated with the old algorithm.

The paper is organised as follows. Section 2 contains basic definitions about Petri nets and branching processes. In Section 3 we show that McMillan's algorithm is just an element of a whole family of algorithms for the construction of finite complete prefixes. In Section 4 we select an element of this family, and show that it generates minimal prefixes in a certain sense. Finally, in Section 5 we present experimental results.

2 Basic Definitions

2.1 Petri Nets

A triple (S, T, F) is a *net* if $S \cap T = \emptyset$ and $F \subseteq (S \times T) \cup (T \times S)$. The elements of S are called *places*, and the elements of T *transitions*. Places and transitions are generically called *nodes*. We identify F with its characteristic function on the set $(S \times T) \cup (T \times S)$. The *preset* of a node x, denoted by ${}^\bullet x$, is the set $\{y \in S \cup T \mid F(y, x) = 1\}$. The *postset* of x, denoted by $x^\bullet$, is the set $\{y \in S \cup T \mid F(x, y) = 1\}$.

A *marking* of a net (S, T, F) is a mapping $S \to I\!N$. We identify a marking M with the multiset containing $M(s)$ copies of s for every $s \in S$. A 4-tuple $\Sigma = (S, T, F, M_0)$ is a *net system* if (S, T, F) is a net and M_0 is a marking of (S, T, F) (called the *initial marking* of Σ). A marking M *enables* a transition t if $\forall s \in S \colon F(s, t) \leq M(s)$. If t is enabled at M, then it can *occur*, and its occurrence leads to a new marking M' (denoted $M \xrightarrow{t} M'$), defined by $M'(s) = M(s) - F(s, t) + F(t, s)$ for every place s. A sequence of transitions $\sigma = t_1 t_2 \ldots t_n$ is an *occurrence sequence* if there exist markings M_1, M_2, ..., M_n such that

$$M_0 \xrightarrow{t_1} M_1 \xrightarrow{t_2} \ldots M_{n-1} \xrightarrow{t_n} M_n$$

M_n is the marking reached by the occurrence of σ, also denoted by $M_0 \xrightarrow{\sigma} M_n$. M is a *reachable marking* if there exists an occurrence sequence σ such that $M_0 \xrightarrow{\sigma} M$.

The *reachability graph* of a net system Σ is a labelled graph having the set of reachable markings of Σ as nodes and the relations $\xrightarrow{t}$ between markings as edges.

A marking M of a net is *n-safe* if $M(s) \leq n$ for every place s. We identify 1-safe markings with the set of places s such that $M(s) = 1$. A net system Σ is n-safe if all its reachable markings are n-safe.

In this paper we consider only net systems satisfying the following two additional properties:

- The number of places and transitions is finite.

- Every transition of T has a nonempty preset *and* a nonempty postset.

2.2 Occurrence Nets

Let (S, T, F) be a net and let x_1, $x_2 \in S \cup T$. The nodes x_1 and x_2 are in *conflict*, denoted by $x_1 \# x_2$, if there exist distinct transitions $t_1, t_2 \in T$ such that ${}^\bullet t_1 \cap {}^\bullet t_2 \neq \emptyset$, and (t_1, x_1), (t_2, x_2) belong to the reflexive and transitive closure of F. In other words, x_1 and x_2 are in conflict if there exist two paths leading to x_1 and x_2 which start at the same place and immediately diverge (although later on they can converge again). For $x \in S \cup T$, x is in *self-conflict* if $x \# x$.

An *occurrence net* is a net $N = (B, E, F)$ such that:

- for every $b \in B$, $|{}^\bullet b| \leq 1$,

- F is acyclic, i.e. the (irreflexive) transitive closure of F is a partial order,

- N is finitely preceded, i.e., for every $x \in B \cup E$, the set of elements $y \in B \cup E$ such that (y, x) belongs to the transitive closure of F is finite, and

- no event $e \in E$ is in self-conflict.

The elements of B and E are called *conditions* and *events*, respectively. $Min(N)$ denotes the set of minimal elements of $B \cup E$ with respect to the transitive closure of F.

The (irreflexive) transitive closure of F is called the *causal relation*, and denoted by $<$. The symbol $\leq$ denotes the reflexive and transitive closure of F. Given two nodes $x, y \in B \cup E$, we say $x \ co \ y$ if neither $x < y$ nor $y < x$ nor $x \# y$.

2.3 Branching Processes

Branching processes are "unfoldings" of net systems containing information about both concurrency and conflicts. They were introduced by Engelfriet in [4]. We quickly review the main definitions and results of [4].

Let $N_1 = (S_1, T_1, F_1)$ and $N_2 = (S_2, T_2, F_2)$ be two nets. A *homomorphism* from N_1 to N_2[1] is a mapping $h: S_1 \cup T_1 \to S_2 \cup T_2$ such that:

---

[1]In [4], homomorphisms are defined between net systems, instead of between nets, but this is only a small technical difference without any severe consequence.

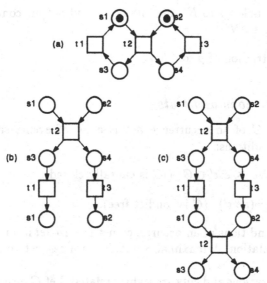

FIGURE 1. A net system and two of its branching processes

- $h(S_1) \subseteq S_2$ and $h(T_1) \subseteq T_2$, and

- for every $t \in T_1$, the restriction of h to ${}^\bullet t$ is a bijection between ${}^\bullet t$ (in N_1) and ${}^\bullet h(t)$ (in N_2), and similarly for $t^\bullet$ and $h(t)^\bullet$.

In other words, a homomorphism is a mapping that preserves the nature of nodes and the environment of transitions.

A *branching process* of a net system $\Sigma = (N, M_0)$ is a pair $\beta = (N', p)$ where $N' = (B, E, F)$ is an occurrence net, and p is a homomorphism from N' to N such that

(i) The restriction of p to $Min(N')$ is a bijection between $Min(N')$ and M_0,

(ii) for every $e_1, e_2 \in E$, if ${}^\bullet e_1 = {}^\bullet e_2$ and $p(e_1) = p(e_2)$ then $e_1 = e_2$.

Figure 1 shows a 1-safe net system (part (a)), and two of its branching processes (parts (b) and (c)).

Two branching processes $\beta_1 = (N_1, p_1)$ and $\beta_2 = (N_2, p_2)$ of a net system are *isomorphic* if there is a bijective homomorphism h from N_1 to N_2 such that $p_2 \circ h = p_1$. Intuitively, two isomorphic branching processes differ only in the names of conditions and events.

It is shown in [4] that a net system has a unique maximal branching process up to isomorphism. We call it the *unfolding* of the system. The unfolding of the 1-safe system of Figure 1 is infinite.

Let $\beta' = (N', p')$ and $\beta = (N, p)$ be two branching processes of a net system. β' is a *prefix* of β if N' is a subnet of N satisfying

- if a condition belongs to N', then its input event in N also belongs to N', and

- if an event belongs to N', then its input and output conditions in N also belong to N'.

and p' is the restriction of p to N'.

2.4 Configurations and Cuts

A *configuration* C of an occurrence net is a set of events satisfying the following two conditions:

- $e \in C \Rightarrow \forall e' \leq e : e' \in C$ (C is causally closed).

- $\forall e, e' \in C : \neg(e \# e')$ (C is conflict-free).

A set B' of conditions of an occurrence net is a *co-set* if its elements are pairwise in *co* relation. A maximal co-set B' with respect to set inclusion is called a *cut*.

Finite configurations and cuts are tightly related. Let C be a finite configuration of a branching process $\beta = (N, p)$. Then the co-set $Cut(C)$, defined below, is a cut:

$$Cut(C) = (Min(N) \cup C^{\bullet}) \setminus {}^{\bullet}C.$$

In particular, given a finite configuration C the set of places $p(Cut(C))$ is a reachable marking, which we denote by $Mark(C)$.

A marking M of a system Σ is *represented* in a branching process β of Σ if β contains a finite configuration C such that $Mark(C) = M$. It is easy to prove using results of [1, 4] that every marking represented in a branching process is reachable, and that every reachable marking is represented in the unfolding of the net system.

For 1–safe systems, we have the following result, which will be later used in Section 4:

Proposition 2.1

Let x_1 and x_2 be two nodes of a branching process of a 1-safe net system. If x_1 co x_2, then $p(x_1) \neq p(x_2)$. ∎ 2.1

Given a cut c of a branching process $\beta = (N, p)$, we define $\Uparrow c$ as the pair (N', p'), where N' is the unique subnet of N whose set of nodes is $\{x \mid (\exists y \in c : x \geq y) \land \forall y \in c : \neg(x \# y)\}$ and p' is the restriction of p to the nodes of N'. Further, we define $p(c)$ as the multiset containing an instance of the place $p(b)$ for every $b \in c$. The following result will also be used later:

Proposition 2.2

If β is a branching process of (N, M_0) and c is a cut of β, then $\Uparrow c$ is a branching process of $(N, p(c))$. ∎ 2.2

3 An Algorithm for the Construction of a Complete Finite Prefix

3.1 Constructing the Unfolding

We give an algorithm for the construction of the unfolding of a net system. First of all, let us describe a suitable data structure for the representation of branching processes.

We implement a branching process of a net system Σ as a list $n_1, \ldots, n_k$ of nodes. A node is either a condition or an event. A condition is a pair (s, e), where s is a place of Σ and e the input event. An event is a pair (t, B), where t is a transition of Σ, and B is the set of input conditions. Notice that the flow relation and the labelling function of a branching process are already encoded in its list of nodes. How to express the notions of causal relation, configuration or cut in terms of this data structure is left to the reader.

The algorithm for the construction of the unfolding starts with the branching process having the conditions corresponding to the initial marking of Σ and no events. Events are added one at a time together with their output conditions.

We need the notion of "events that can be added to a given branching process".

Definition 3.1

> Let $\beta = n_1, \ldots, n_k$ be a branching process of a net system Σ. The *possible extensions* of β are the pairs (t, B), where B is a co-set of conditions of β and t is a transition of Σ such that
>
> * $p(B) = {}^\bullet t$, and
> * β contains no event e satisfying $p(e) = t$ and ${}^\bullet e = B$
>
> $PE(\beta)$ denotes the set of possible extensions of β.   ∎ 3.1

Procedure 3.2 *The unfolding algorithm*

> **input**: A net system $\Sigma = (N, M_0)$, where $M_0 = \{s_1, \ldots, s_n\}$.
> **output**: The unfolding Unf of Σ.
> **begin**
> $Unf := (s_1, \emptyset), \ldots, (s_n, \emptyset)$;
> $pe := PE(Unf)$;
> **while** $pe \neq \emptyset$ **do**
>   append to Unf an event $e = (t, B)$ of pe and a
>   condition (s, e) for every output place s of t;
> $pe := PE(Unf)$
> **endwhile**
> **end**
>
> ∎ 3.2

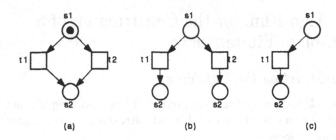

FIGURE 2. A 1-safe net system, its unfolding, and a prefix

The procedure does not necessarily terminate. In fact, it terminates if and only if the input system Σ does not have any infinite occurrence sequence. It will eventually produce any reachable marking only under the fairness assumption that every event added to pe is eventually chosen to extend Unf (the correctness proof follows easily from the definitions and from the results of [4]).

Constructing a Finite Complete Prefix

We say that a branching process β of a net system Σ is *complete* if for every reachable marking M there exists a configuration C in β such that:

- $Mark(C) = M$ (i.e., M is represented in β), and

- for every transition t enabled by M there exists a configuration $C \cup \{e\}$ such that $e \notin C$ and e is labelled by t.

The unfolding of a net system is always complete. A complete prefix contains as much information as the unfolding, in the sense that we can construct the unfolding from it as the least fixpoint of a suitable operation. This property does not hold if we only require every reachable marking to be represented. For instance, the net system of Figure 2(a) has Figure 2(b) as unfolding. Figure 2(c) shows a prefix of the unfolding in which every reachable marking is represented. The prefix has lost the information indicating that t_2 can occur from the initial marking. Observe that the prefix is not complete.

Since an n-safe net system has only finitely many reachable markings, its unfolding contains at least one complete finite prefix. We transform the algorithm above into a new one whose output is such a prefix.

We need some preliminary notations and definitions:

Given a configuration C, we denote by $C \oplus E$ the fact that $C \cup E$ is a configuration such that $C \cap E = \emptyset$. We say that $C \oplus E$ is an *extension* of C, and that E is a *suffix* to C. Obviously, if $C \subset C'$ then there is a suffix E of C such that $C \oplus E = C'$.

Let C_1 and C_2 be two finite configurations such that $Mark(C_1) = Mark(C_2)$. It follows easily from the definitions that $\Uparrow Cut(C_i)$ is isomorphic to the unfolding of $\Sigma' = (N, Mark(C_i))$, $i = 1, 2$; hence, $\Uparrow Cut(C_1)$ and $\Uparrow Cut(C_2)$ are isomorphic. Moreover, there is an isomorphism $I_{C_1}^{C_2}$ from $\Uparrow Cut(C_1)$ to $\Uparrow Cut(C_2)$. This isomorphism induces a mapping from the finite extensions of C_1 onto the extensions of C_2: it maps $C_1 \oplus E$ onto $C_2 \oplus I_{C_1}^{C_2}(E)$.

We can now introduce the three basic notions of the algorithm:

Definition 3.3

A partial order $\prec$ on the finite configurations of a branching process is an *adequate order* if:

- $\prec$ is well-founded,
- $\prec$ refines $\subset$, i.e. $C_1 \subset C_2$ implies $C_1 \prec C_2$, and
- $\prec$ is preserved by finite extensions, meaning that if $C_1 \prec C_2$ and $Mark(C_1) = Mark(C_2)$, then $C_1 \oplus E \prec C_2 \oplus I_{C_1}^{C_2}(E)$.

$\blacksquare$ 3.3

Definition 3.4 *Local configuration*

The local configuration $[e]$ of an event of a branching process is the set of events e' such that $e' \leq e$.[2] $\blacksquare$ 3.4

Definition 3.5 *Cut-off event*

Let β be a branching process and let $\prec$ be an adequate partial order on the configurations of β. An event e is a *cut-off event* (with respect to $\prec$) if β contains a local configuration $[e']$ such that

(a) $Mark([e]) = Mark([e'])$, and

(b) $[e'] \prec [e]$.

$\blacksquare$ 3.5

The new algorithm has as parameter an adequate order $\prec$, i.e. every different adequate order leads to a different algorithm.

Algorithm 3.6 *The complete finite prefix algorithm*

input: An n-safe net system $\Sigma = (N, M_0)$, where $M_0 = \{s_1, \ldots, s_k\}$.
output: A complete finite prefix Fin of Unf.
begin
$Fin := (s_1, \emptyset), \ldots, (s_k, \emptyset);$
$pe := PE(Fin);$
$cut\text{-}off := \emptyset;$

---

[2]It is immediate to prove that $[e]$ is a configuration.

> **while** $pe \neq \emptyset$ **do**
>> choose an event $e = (t, B)$ in pe such that $[e]$ is minimal
>>> with respect to $\prec$;
>> **if** $[e] \cap$ *cut-off* $= \emptyset$ **then**
>>> append to *Fin* the event e and a condition
>>> (s, e) for every output place s of t;
>>> $pe := PE(Fin)$;
>>> **if** e is a cut-off event of *Fin* **then**
>>>> *cut-off* $:=$ *cut-off* $\cup \{e\}$
>>> **endif**
>> **else** $pe := pe \setminus \{e\}$
>> **endif**
> **endwhile**
> **end**

■ 3.6

McMillan's algorithm in [10] corresponds to the order

$$C_1 \prec_m C_2 :\Leftrightarrow |C_1| < |C_2|.$$

It is easy to see that $\prec_m$ is adequate.

The reason of condition (a) in the definition of cut-off event is intuitively clear in the light of this algorithm. Since $Mark([e']) = Mark([e])$, the continuations of Unf from $Cut([e])$ and $Cut([e'])$ are isomorphic. Then, loosely speaking, all the reachable markings that we find in the continuation of Unf from $Cut([e])$ are already present in the continuation from $Cut([e'])$, and so there is no need to have the former in *Fin*. The rôle of condition (b) is more technical. In fact, when McMillan's algorithm is applied to "ordinary" small examples, condition (b) seems to be superfluous, and the following strategy seems to work: if an event e is added and *Fin* already contains a local configuration $[e']$ such that $Mark([e]) = Mark([e'])$, then mark e as cut-off event. The following example (also independently found by K. McMillan) shows that this strategy is incorrect. Consider the 1-safe net system of Figure 3.

The marking $\{s_{12}\}$ is reachable. Without condition (b) we can generate the prefix of Figure 4.

The names of the events are numbers which indicate the order in which they are added to the prefix. The events 8 and 10 are cut-off events, because their corresponding markings $\{s_7, s_9, s_{10}\}$ and $\{s_6, s_8, s_{11}\}$ are also the markings corresponding to the events 7 and 9, respectively. This prefix is not complete, because $\{s_{12}\}$ is not represented in it.

Observe that *Fin* contains all the events of the set *cut-off*. We could modify the algorithm to remove all these events, and the prefix so obtained would still enjoy the property that every reachable marking is represented in it. However, the prefix would not be necessarily complete. Consider for

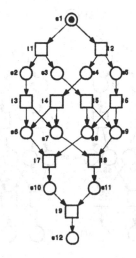

FIGURE 3. A 1–safe net system

example the net system of Figure 2(a). Algorithm 3.6 generates the branching process of Figure 2(b), and one of the two events of the process (the maximal one with respect to ≺) is a cut-off event. If this event is removed, we obtain an incomplete prefix.

We now prove the correctness of Algorithm 3.6.

Proposition 3.7

Fin is finite.

Proof: Given an event e of *Fin*, define the *depth* of e as the length of a longest chain of events

$e_1 < e_2 < \ldots < e$; the depth of e is denoted by $d(e)$. We prove the following results:

(1) For every event e of *Fin*, $d(e) \leq n+1$, where n is the number of reachable markings of Σ.

Since cuts correspond to reachable markings, every chain of events $e_1 < e_2 < \ldots < e_n < e_{n+1}$ of *Unf* contains two events e_i, e_j, $i < j$, such that $Mark([e_i]) = Mark([e_j])$. Since $[e_i] \subset [e_j]$ and ≺ refines ⊂, we have $[e_i] \prec [e_j]$, and therefore $[e_j]$ is a cut-off event of *Unf*. Should the finite prefix algorithm generate e_j, then it has generated e_i before and e_j is recognized as a cut-off event of *Fin*, too.

(2) For every event e of *Fin*, the sets $^\bullet e$ and $e^\bullet$ are finite.

By the definition of homomorphism, there is a bijection between $p(e)^\bullet$ and $p(e^\bullet)$, where p denotes the homomorphism of *Fin*, and similarly for $^\bullet p(e)$ and $p(^\bullet e)$. The result follows from the finiteness of N.

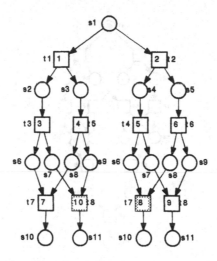

FIGURE 4. A prefix of the net system of Figure 3

(3) For every $k \geq 0$, *Fin* contains only finitely many events e such that $d(e) \leq k$.

By complete induction on k. The base case, $k = 0$, is trivial. Let E_k be the set of events of depth at most k. We prove that if E_k is finite then E_{k+1} is finite. Define $E_k^\bullet = \{b | e \in E_k, b \in e^\bullet\}$. By (2) and the induction hypothesis, $E_k^\bullet$ is finite. Since ${}^\bullet E_{k+1} \subseteq E_k^\bullet \cup Min(Fin)$, we get by property (ii) in the definition of a branching process that E_{k+1} is finite.

It follows from (1) and (3) that *Fin* only contains finitely many events. By (2) it contains only finitely many conditions. ■ 3.7

Proposition 3.8

Fin is complete.

Proof: We first prove that every reachable marking of Σ is represented in *Fin*.

Let M be an arbitrary reachable marking of Σ. There exists a configuration C of *Unf* such that $Mark(C) = M$. If C is not a configuration of *Fin*, then it contains some cut-off event e, and so $C = [e] \oplus E$ for some set of events E. By the definition of a cut-off event, there exists a local configuration $[e']$ such that $[e'] \prec [e]$ and $Mark([e']) = Mark([e])$.

Consider the configuration $C' = [e'] \oplus I_{[e]}^{[e']}(E)$. Since $\prec$ is preserved by finite extensions, we have $C' \prec C$. Morever, $Mark(C') = M$. If C' is not a configuration of *Fin*, then we can iterate the procedure and find a configuration C'' such that $C'' \prec C'$ and $Mark(C'') = M$. The procedure cannot be iterated infinitely often because $\prec$ is well-founded. Therefore, it terminates in a configuration of Fin.

Now we show that Fin is complete. We have to prove that for every reachable marking M there exists a configuration C in β such that:

- $Mark(C) = M$, and
- for every transition t enabled by M there exists a configuration $C \cup \{e\}$ such that $e \notin C$ and e is labelled by t.

Let M be an arbitrary reachable marking of Σ. Since M is represented in Fin, the set of configurations C of Fin satisfying $Mark(C)$ $= M$ is nonempty. By well-foundedness, this set has at least a minimal element C_m with respect to $\prec$. If C_m would contain some cut-off event, then we would find as above another configuration C' satisfying $C' \prec C_m$ and $Mark(C') = M$, which contradicts the minimality of C_m. So C_m contains no cut-off event.

Let t be an arbitrary transition enabled by M. Then there exists a configuration $C_m \cup \{e\}$ of Unf such that $e \notin C_m$ and e is labelled by t. Assume that $C_m \cup \{e\}$ is not a configuration of Fin. Since Fin contains all the events of the set *cut-off* in Algorithm 3.6, it also contains a cut-off event $e' < e$. This implies $e' \in C_m$, which contradicts that C_m contains no cut-off event. So $C_m \cup \{e\}$ is a configuration of Fin. ∎ 3.8

4 An Adequate Order for the 1–Safe Case

As we mentioned in the introduction, McMillan's algorithm may be inefficient in some cases. An extreme example, due to Kishinevsky and Taubin, is the family of systems on the left of Figure 5.

While a minimal complete prefix has size $O(n)$ in the size of the system (see the dotted line in Figure 5), the branching process generated by McMillan's algorithm has size $O(2^n)$. The reason is that, for every marking M, all the local configurations $[e]$ satisfying $Mark([e]) = M$ have the same size, and therefore there exist no cut-off events with respect to McMillan's order $\prec_m$.

Our parametric presentation of Algorithm 3.6 suggests how to improve this: it suffices to find a new adequate order $\prec_r$ that refines McMillan's order $\prec_m$. Such an order induces a weaker notion of cut-off event; more precisely, every cut-off event with respect to $\prec_m$ is also a cut-off event with respect to $\prec_r$, but maybe not the other way round. Therefore, the instance of Algorithm 3.6 which uses the new order generates at least as many cut-off events as McMillan's instance, and maybe more. In the latter case, Algorithm 3.6 generates a smaller prefix.

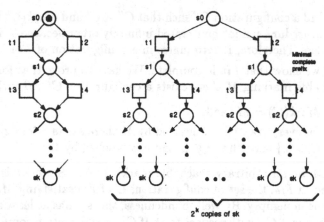

2^k copies of sk

FIGURE 5. A Petri net and its unfolding

The order $\prec_r$ is particularly good if in addition it is *total*. In this case, whenever an event e is generated after some other event e' such that $Mark([e]) = Mark([e'])$, we have $[e'] \prec_r [e]$ (because events are generated in accordance with the total order $\prec_r$), and so e is marked as a cut-off event. So we have the following two properties:

- the guard "e is a cut-off event of *Fin*" in the inner **if** instruction of Algorithm 3.6 can be replaced by "*Fin* contains a local configuration $[e']$ such that $Mark([e]) = Mark([e'])$", and

- the number of events of the complete prefix which are not cut-off events cannot exceed the number of reachable markings.

In the sequel, let $\Sigma = (N, M_0)$ be a fixed net system, and let $\ll$ be an arbitrary total order on the transitions of Σ. We extend $\ll$ to a partial order on sets of events of a branching process as follows: for a set E of events, let $\varphi(E)$ be that sequence of transitions which is ordered according to $\ll$ and contains each transition t as often as there are events in E with label t. Now we say that $E_1 \ll E_2$ if $\varphi(E_1)$ is shorter than $\varphi(E_2)$, or if they have the same length but $\varphi(E_1)$ is lexicographically smaller than $\varphi(E_2)$. Note that E_1 and E_2 are incomparable with respect to $\ll$ iff $\varphi(E_1) = \varphi(E_2)$. In particular, if E_1 and E_2 are incomparable with respect to $\ll$, then $|E_1| = |E_2|$.

We now define $\prec_r$ more generally on suffixes of configurations of a branching process (recall that a set of events E is a suffix of a configuration if there exists a configuration C such that $C \oplus E$).

Definition 4.1 *Total order* $\prec_r$

Let E_1 and E_2 be two suffixes of configurations of a branching process β and let $Min(E_1)$ and $Min(E_2)$ denote the sets of minimal elements of E_1 and E_2 with respect to the causal relation. We say $E_1 \prec_r E_2$ if:

- $E_1 \ll E_2$, or
- $\varphi(E_1) = \varphi(E_2)$ and
    - $Min(E_1) \ll Min(E_2)$, or
    - $\varphi(Min(E_1)) = \varphi(Min(E_2))$ and $E_1 \setminus Min(E_1) \prec_r E_2 \setminus Min(E_2)$.

$\blacksquare$ 4.1

Notice that this definition would not be correct for configurations only, because $E \setminus Min(E)$ need not be a configuration even if E is one.

The second condition of this definition could be expressed as: the Foata-Normal-Form of E_1 is smaller than that of E_2 with respect to $\ll$, cf. e.g. [3].

Theorem 4.2

Let β be a branching process of a 1-safe net system. $\prec_r$ is an adequate total order on the configurations of β.

Proof: a) $\prec_r$ is a partial order.

It is easy to see by induction on $|E|$ that $\prec_r$ is irreflexive. Now assume $E_1 \prec_r E_2 \prec_r E_3$. Clearly, $E_1 \prec_r E_3$ unless $\varphi(E_1) = \varphi(E_2) = \varphi(E_3)$, which in particular implies $|E_1| = |E_2| = |E_3|$. For such triples with these equalities we apply induction on the size: if $Min(E_1) \ll Min(E_2)$ or $Min(E_2) \ll Min(E_3)$, we conclude $E_1 \prec_r E_3$, and otherwise we apply induction to $E_i \setminus Min(E_i)$, $i = 1, 2, 3$, which are also suffixes of configurations.

b) $\prec_r$ is total on configurations.

Assume that C_1 and C_2 are two incomparable configurations, i.e. $|C_1| = |C_2|$, $\varphi(C_1) = \varphi(C_2)$, and $\varphi(Min(C_1)) = \varphi(Min(C_2))$. We prove $C_1 = C_2$ by induction on $|C_1| = |C_2|$.

The base case gives $C_1 = C_2 = \emptyset$, so assume $|C_1| = |C_2| > 0$.

We first prove $Min(C_1) = Min(C_2)$. Assume without loss of generality that $e_1 \in Min(C_1) \setminus Min(C_2)$. Since $\varphi(Min(C_1)) = \varphi(Min(C_2))$, $Min(C_2)$ contains an event e_2 such that $p(e_1) = p(e_2)$. Since ${}^\bullet Min(C_1)$ and ${}^\bullet Min(C_2)$ are subsets of $Min(N)$, and all the conditions of $Min(N)$ carry different labels by Proposition 2.1, we have ${}^\bullet e_1 = {}^\bullet e_2$. This contradicts condition (ii) of the definition of branching process.

Since $Min(C_1) = Min(C_2)$, both $C_1 \setminus Min(C_1)$ and $C_2 \setminus Min(C_2)$ are configurations of the branching process $\Uparrow Cut(Min(C_1))$ of $(N, Mark(Min(C_1)))$ (Proposition 2.2); by induction we conclude $C_1 = C_2$.

c) $\prec_r$ is well-founded.

In a sequence $C_1 \succ_r C_2 \succ_r \ldots$ the size of the C_i cannot decrease infinitely often; also, for configurations of the same size,

C_i cannot decrease infinitely often with respect to $\ll$, since the sequences $\varphi(C_i)$ are drawn from a finite set; an analogous statement holds for $Min(C_i)$. Hence, we assume that all $|C_i|$, all $\varphi(C_i)$ and all $\varphi(Min(C_i))$ are equal and apply induction on the common size. For $|C_i| = 0$, an infinite decreasing sequence is impossible. Otherwise, we conclude as in case b) that we would have $C_1 \setminus Min(C_1) \succ_r C_2 \setminus Min(C_2) \succ_r \ldots$ in $\Uparrow Cut(Min(C_1))$, which is impossible by induction.

d) $\prec_r$ refines $\sqsubseteq$.

Obvious.

e) $\prec_r$ is preserved by finite extensions.

This is the most intricate part of the proof, and here all the complications in Definition 4.1 come into play. Take $C_1 \prec_r C_2$ with $Mark(C_1) = Mark(C_2)$. We have to show that $C_1 \oplus E \prec_r C_2 \oplus I_{C_1}^{C_2}(E)$, and we can assume that $E = \{e\}$ and apply induction afterwards. The case $C_1 \ll C_2$ is easy, hence assume $\varphi(C_1) = \varphi(C_2)$, and in particular $|C_1| = |C_2|$. We show first that e is minimal in $C_1' = C_1 \cup \{e\}$ if and only if $I_{C_1}^{C_2}(e)$ is minimal in $C_2' = C_2 \cup \{I_{C_1}^{C_2}(e)\}$. So let e be minimal in C_1', i.e. the transition $p(e)$ is enabled under the initial marking. Let $s \in {}^\bullet p(e)$; then no condition in ${}^\bullet C_1 \cup C_1^\bullet$ is labelled s, since these conditions would be in co relation with the s-labelled condition in ${}^\bullet e$, contradicting Proposition 2.1. Thus, C_1 contains no event e' with $s \in {}^\bullet p(e')$, and the same holds for C_2 since $\varphi(C_1) = \varphi(C_2)$. Therefore, the conditions in $Cut(C_2)$ with label in ${}^\bullet p(e)$ are minimal conditions of β, and $I_{C_1}^{C_2}(e) = e$ is minimal in C_2'. The reverse implication holds analogously, since about C_1 and C_2 we have only used the hypothesis $\varphi(C_1) = \varphi(C_2)$.

With this knowledge about the positions of e in C_1' and $I_{C_1}^{C_2}(e)$ in C_2', we proceed as follows. If $Min(C_1) \ll Min(C_2)$, then we now see that $Min(C_1') \ll Min(C_2')$, so we are done. If $\varphi(Min(C_1)) = \varphi(Min(C_2))$ and $e \in Min(C_1')$, then

$$C_1' \setminus Min(C_1') = C_1 \setminus Min(C_1) \prec_r C_2 \setminus Min(C_2) = C_2' \setminus Min(C_2')$$

hence $C_1' \prec_r C_2'$. Finally, if $\varphi(Min(C_1)) = \varphi(Min(C_2))$ and $e \notin Min(C_1')$, we again argue that $Min(C_1) = Min(C_2)$ and that, hence, $C_1 \setminus Min(C_1)$ and $C_2 \setminus Min(C_2)$ are configurations of the branching process $\Uparrow Cut(Min(C_1))$ of $(N, Mark(Min(C_1)))$; with an inductive argument we get $C_1' \setminus Min(C_1') \prec_r C_2' \setminus Min(C_2')$ and are also done in this case. ∎ 4.2

We close this section with a remark on the minimality of the prefixes generated by the new algorithm, i.e. by Algorithm 3.6 with $\prec_r$ as adequate order. Figure 1(b) and (c) are a minimal complete prefix and the prefix generated by the new algorithm for the 1-safe system of Figure 1(a), respectively. It follows that the new algorithm does not always compute a minimal complete prefix.

However, the prefixes computed by the algorithm are minimal in another sense. The algorithm stores only the reachable markings corresponding to local configurations, which for the purpose of this discussion we call *local markings*. This is the feature which makes the algorithm interesting for concurrent systems: the local markings can be a very small subset of the reachable markings, and therefore the storage of the unfolding may require much less memory than the storage of the state space. In order to find out that the prefix of Figure 1(b) is complete, we also need to know that the initial marking $\{s_1, s_2\}$ appears again in the prefix as a non-local marking. If we only store information about local markings, then the prefix of Figure 1(c) is minimal, as well as all the prefixes generated by the new algorithm. The reason is the observation made above: all the local configurations of *Fin* which are not induced by cut-off events correspond to different markings; therefore, in a prefix smaller than *Fin* we lose information about the reachability of some marking.

5 Implementation Issues and Experimental Results

The implementation of the Algorithm 3.6 has been carried out in the context of the model checker described in [5], which allows to efficiently verify formulae expressed in a simple branching time temporal logic.

For the storage of Petri nets and branching processes we have developed an efficient, universal data structure that allows fast access to single nodes [14]. This data structure is based on the underlying incidence matrix of the net. Places, transitions and arcs are represented by nodes of doubly linked lists to support fast insertion and deletion of single nodes.

The computation of new elements for the set PE involves the combinatorial problem of finding sets of conditions B such that $p(B) = {}^\bullet t$ for some transition t. We have implemented several improvements in this combinatorial determination, which have significant influence on the performance of the algorithm. The interested reader is referred to [6].

Algorithm 3.6 is very simple, and can be easily proved correct, but is not efficient. In particular, it computes the set PE of possible extensions each time a new event is added to *Fin*, which is clearly redundant. Similarly to McMillan's original algorithm [10], in the implementation we use a queue to store the set PE of possible extensions. The new events of *Fin* are extracted from the head of this list, and, when an event is added, the new possible extensions it generates are appended to its tail.

The simplest way to organize the list would be to sort its events according to the total order $\prec_r$. However, this is again inefficient, because it involves

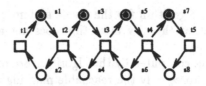

FIGURE 6. n–buffer for $n = 4$.

n	Original net			Unfolding			time [s]	
	$|S|$	$|T|$	$|[M_0\rangle|$	$|B|$	$|E|$	$cutoffs$	McMillan	New algorithm
20	40	21	2^{20}	421	211	1	0.22	0.20
40	80	41	2^{40}	1641	821	1	2.40	2.50
60	120	61	2^{60}	3661	1831	1	17.45	18.08
80	160	81	2^{80}	6481	3241	1	66.70	67.85
100	200	101	2^{100}	10101	5051	1	191.58	197.34
120	240	121	2^{120}	14521	7261	1	444.60	437.30
140	280	141	2^{140}	19741	9871	1	871.93	869.50
160	320	161	2^{160}	25761	12881	1	1569.90	1563.74
180	360	181	2^{180}	32581	16291	1	2592.93	2597.86

TABLE 1. Results of the n buffer example[3].

performing unneccessary comparisons. The solution is to sort the events according to the size of their local configuration, as in [10], and compare events with respect to $\prec_r$ only when it is really needed.

With this implementation, the new algorithm only computes more than McMillan's when two events e and e' satisfy $Mark([e]) = Mark([e'])$ and $|[e]| = |[e']|$. But this is precisely the case in which the algorithm behaves better, because it always identifies either e or e' as a cut-off event. In other words: when the complete prefix computed by McMillan's algorithm is minimal, our algorithm computes the same result with no time overhead.

The running time of the new algorithm is $O((\frac{|B|}{\xi})^\xi)$, where B is the set of conditions of the unfolding, and ξ denotes the maximal size of the presets of the transitions in the original net (notice that this is not a measure in the size of the input). The dominating factor in the time complexity is the computation of the possible extensions. The space required is linear in the size of the unfolding because we store a fixed amount of information per event.

Finally, we present some experimental results on three scalable examples. We compare McMillan's algorithm and the new algorithm, both implemented using the universal data structure and the improvements in the combinatorial determination mentioned above.

The first example is a model of a concurrent n–buffer (see Figure 5). The net has $2n$ places and $n + 1$ transitions, where n is the buffer's capacity. While the number of reachable markings is 2^n, Fin has size $O(n^2)$ and contains one single cut–off event (see Table 1). In this example, the complete prefix computed by McMillan's algorithm is minimal. The new algorithm computes the same prefix without time overhead, as expected.

Our second example, Figure 5, is a model of a slotted ring protocol taken from [13]. Here the size of the prefix produced by the new algorithm grows

---

[3] All the times have been measured on a SPARCstation 20 with 48 MB main memory.

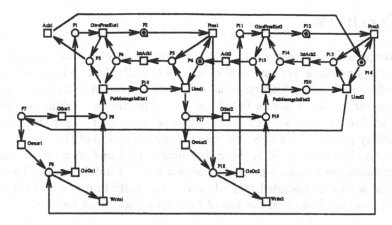

FIGURE 7. Slotted ring protocol for $n = 2$.

n	Original net			McMillan's algorithm				New algorithm			
	$|S|$	$|T|$	$|[M_0>|$	$|B|$	$|E|$	c	time [s]	$|B|$	$|E|$	c	time [s]
1	10	10	$1.2 \cdot 10^1$	18	12	3	0.00	18	12	3	0.00
2	20	20	$2.1 \cdot 10^2$	100	68	12	0.00	90	62	14	0.00
3	30	30	$4.0 \cdot 10^3$	414	288	60	0.13	267	186	42	0.05
4	40	40	$8.2 \cdot 10^4$	1812	1248	296	1.72	740	528	128	0.38
5	50	50	$1.7 \cdot 10^6$	8925	6240	1630	45.31	1805	1280	300	1.58
6	60	60	$3.7 \cdot 10^7$	45846	31104	8508	1829.48	4470	3216	792	11.08
7	70	70	$8.0 \cdot 10^8$				—[4]	10143	7224	1708	79.08
8	80	80	$1.7 \cdot 10^{10}$				—[4]	23880	17216	4256	563.69
9	90	90	$3.8 \cdot 10^{11}$				—[4]	52209	37224	8820	2850.89
10	100	100	$8.1 \cdot 10^{12}$				—[4]	119450	86160	21320	15547.67

TABLE 2. Results of the slotted ring protocol example; $c = |cutoffs|$.

more slowly than in the case of McMillan's algorithm. For $n = 6$ the output is already one order of magnitude smaller. The slow growth in size can cause an even more dramatic reduction in the running time.

n	Original net			McMillan's algorithm				New algorithm			
	$|S|$	$|T|$	$|[M_0>|$	$|B|$	$|E|$	c	time [s]	$|B|$	$|E|$	c	time [s]
3	23	17	43	94	44	8	0.02	52	23	4	0.00
6	47	35	639	734	361	64	0.48	112	50	7	0.02
9	71	53	7423	5686	2834	512	22.90	172	77	10	0.05
12	95	71	74264	45134	22555	4096	1471.16	232	104	13	0.13

TABLE 3. Results of Milner's cyclic scheduler; $c = |cutoffs|$.

In Table 3, we give the times for an example taken from [2] that models Milner's cyclic scheduler for n tasks. While the size of the unfolding produced by the McMillan's algorithm grows exponentially with the number of tasks, we get linear size using our new one.

---

[4] These times could not be calculated; for $n = 7$ we interrupted the computation after more than 12 hours.

6 Conclusions

We have presented an algorithm for the computation of a complete finite prefix of an unfolding. We have used a refinement of McMillan's basic notion of cut-off event. The prefixes constructed by the algorithm contain at most n non-cut-off events, where n is the number of reachable markings of the net. Therefore, we can guarantee that the prefix is never larger than the reachability graph, which does not hold for the algorithm of [10].

Recently, Kondratyev et al. have independently found another partial order between events which permits to obtain reduced unfoldings [9]. Their technique works for bounded nets. However, the partial order is not total, and so the upper bound on the size of the unfolding cannot be derived.

Acknowledgements

We thank Michael Kishinevsky, Alexander Taubin and Alex Yakovlev for drawing our attention to this problem, Burkhard Graves for detecting some mistakes, and an anonymous referee for helpful comments.

7 REFERENCES

[1] E. Best and C. Fernández: Nonsequential Processes – A Petri Net View. EATCS Monographs on Theoretical Computer Science 13 (1988).

[2] James C. Corbett: Evaluating Deadlock Detection Methods. University of Hawaii at Manoa (1994).

[3] V. Diekert: Combinatorics on Traces. LNCS 454 (1990).

[4] J. Engelfriet: Branching processes of Petri nets. Acta Informatica 28, pp. 575–591 (1991).

[5] J. Esparza: Model Checking Using Net Unfoldings. Science of Computer Programming 23, pp. 151–195 (1994).

[6] J. Esparza, S. Römer and W. Vogler: An improvement of McMillan's unfolding algorithm. Informatik Bericht, TU München, in preparation.

[7] M. Kishinevsky, A. Kondratyev, A. Taubin, and V. Varshavsky: Concurrent Hardware: The Theory and Practice of Self-Timed Design, Wiley (1993).

[8] A. Kondratyev and A. Taubin: Verification of speed-independent circuits by STG unfoldings. Proceedings of the Symposium on Advanced Research in Asynchronous Circuits and Systems, Utah (1994).

[9] A. Kondratyev, A. Taubin, M. Kishinevsky and S. Ten: Analysis of Petri Nets by Ordering Relations. Technical Report TR:95-2-002, University of Aizu (1995).

[10] K.L. McMillan: A Technique of a State Space Search Based on Unfolding. Formal Methods in System Design 6(1), pp. 45–65 (1995)

[11] K.L. McMillan: Trace theoretic verification of asynchronous circuits using unfoldings. Proceedings of the 7th Workshop on Computer Aided Verification, Liege (1995).

[12] M. Nielsen, G. Plotkin and G. Winskel: Petri Nets, Event Structures and Domains. Theoretical Computer Science 13(1), pp. 85–108 (1980).

[13] E. Pastor, O. Roig, J. Cortadella and R.M. Badia: Petri Net Analysis Using Boolean Manipulation. Proc. Application and Theory of Petri Nets '94, LNCS 815, pp. 416–435 (1994).

[14] S. Römer: Implementation of a Compositional Partial Order Semantics of Petri Boxes. Diploma Thesis (in German). Universität Hildesheim (1993).

Efficient Local Model-Checking for Fragments of the Modal μ-Calculus

Girish Bhat* Rance Cleaveland*

ABSTRACT This paper develops efficient local model-checking algorithms for expressive fragments of the modal μ-calculus. The time complexity of our procedures matches that of the best existing global algorithms; however, in contrast to those routines, ours explore a system's state space in a need-driven fashion and do not require its *a priori* construction. Consequently, our algorithms should perform better in practice. Our approach relies on a novel reformulation of the model-checking problem for the modal mu-calculus in terms of checking whether certain linear-time temporal formulas are satisfied by generalized Kripke structures that we call *and-or* Kripke structures.

1 Introduction

Over the last decade *model checking* has emerged as a useful technique for automatically verifying concurrent systems. [1, 4, 8, 15, 19]. In this approach, one attempts to determine whether or not a system satisfies a formula that typically comes from a temporal logic. A variety of different temporal logics have been proposed for this purpose [4, 10, 18]; one particularly expressive one is the modal μ-calculus [13], which is capable of encoding numerous existing temporal logics [12].

When systems are finite-state, mu-calculus model checking becomes decidable; for such systems, a variety of model-checking algorithms have been developed. Two major approaches may be identified. *Global* routines [6, 12, 14] require the *a priori* construction of the entire state space of the system being analyzed; a subsequent pass over the state space then determines the truth or falsity of the formula. Such algorithms typically exhibit good worst-case behavior; however, in practice, the overhead of computing the whole state space is often unnecessary, as the truth or falsity of the property can be deduced from an investigation of a small part

---

*Research supported by NSF/DARPA grant CCR-9014775, NSF grant CCR-9120995, ONR Young Investigator Award N00014-92-J-1582, NSF Young Investigator Award CCR-9257963, NSF grant CCR-9402807, and AFOSR grant F49620-95-1-0508.

of it. *Local*, or *on-the-fly*, algorithms [1, 5, 16, 20] attempt to remedy this shortcoming by exploring the state space in *demand-driven* fashion. The procedures that have been proposed for the full mu-calculus, however, have uniformly had very poor worst-case behavior in comparison to the global approaches. An efficient algorithm for the alternation-free fragment has been given in [1], but this fragment is incapable of expressing certain fairness constraints that are often needed in practice.

In this paper we present efficient local model-checking algorithms for fragments of the mu-calculus introduced by Emerson et al. in [11]. One of these fragments contains more expressive power than CTL* [10] and hence is capable of encoding properties involving subtle fairness constraints. Our algorithms also have worst-case behavior that matches that of the best existing global model-checking algorithms for these logics [11]. However, since our routines explore state spaces in a need-driven fashion, we expect them to perform much better in practice than the global approaches.

The remainder of this paper is organized as follows. The next section presents the syntax and semantics of μ-calculus and defines the fragments L_1 and L_2 that we consider. In Section 3 we define a variant of traditional Kripke structures that we call *and-or Kripke structures* and give the semantics of a linear-time temporal logic with respect to them. The section following then shows how the model-checking problem for the modal mu-calculus may be reduced to one of model-checking and-or Kripke structures against temporal formulas of a restricted form. Section 5 presents our algorithms; in particular, we explain how the restricted form of L_1 and L_2 may be exploited to give very efficient on-the-fly procedures, and we briefly discuss some implementation issues. The last section contains our conclusions and directions for future research.

2 The Modal μ-calculus

This section presents the syntax and semantics of the modal μ-calculus and defines the sublogics L_1 and L_2. Throughout this section we fix a set $(A, B \in)\mathcal{A}$ of *atomic propositions*.

2.1 Syntax

The syntax of μ-calculus formulas is parameterized with respect to a set $(X, Y \in)\mathcal{V}$ of propositional variables and a set $(a, b \in)Act$ of actions. Formulas are given by the following grammar.

$$\phi \quad ::= \quad A \mid X \mid \neg\phi \mid \phi \vee \phi \mid \phi \wedge \phi \mid [a]S \mid \langle a \rangle S \mid \mu X.\phi \mid \nu X.\phi$$

Formulas must also obey the following syntactic restriction: in $\mu X.\phi$ or $\nu X.\phi$, all free occurrences of X in ϕ must fall within the scope of an even number of negations. We use ϕ, ψ, γ to range over formulas. We refer to $[a]$ and $\langle a \rangle$ operators as *modalities* and to μ and ν as the least and greatest fixpoint operators, respectively, and we call a formula of the form A or $\neg A$ a *literal* and use $(L \in) \mathcal{L}$ to stand for the set of all literals. If a formula has form $\mu X.\phi$ then we sometimes call it a μ-formula, while if it has form $\nu X.\phi$ we refer to it as a ν-formula. In what follows we also assume the usual definitions for (proper, maximal) subformula, for free and bound variable, and for closed formulas, and we write $\phi[\gamma/X]$ to represent the capture-free simultaneous substitution of γ for all free occurrences of X in ϕ. We also introduce the following syntactic normal forms.

Definition 2.1 *Let ϕ be a closed μ-calculus formula.*

1. *ϕ is in positive normal form (PNF) if the only negated subformulas it has are literals.*

2. *ϕ is L_2 normal form (LNF) if every variable is bound at most once and the only negated subformulas it has are closed.*

It is trivial to show that for any closed formula there are semantically equivalent PNF and LNF formulas.

Alternation Levels and the Fischer-Ladner Closure.

We now introduce the notions of *alternation level* and *Fischer-Ladner closure* for LNF formulas. The former notion is defined for the fixpoint subformulas of a given formula; intuitively, it records the number of "alternations" in interdependent fixpoint constructors encountered in the path in the parse tree from the root of the formula to the root of the subformula. To define it precisely, we introduce the following. For formulas ϕ_1 and ϕ_2 let $\phi_1 \preceq \phi_2$ iff ϕ_1 is a subformula of ϕ_2. We also write $\phi_1 \prec_M \phi_2$ iff ϕ_1 is a *maximal* proper subformula of ϕ_2. We use σ to range over $\{\mu, \nu\}$ and $\bar{\sigma}$ to represent the dual of σ.

Definition 2.2 *Let ϕ be a mu-calculus formula in L_2 normal form, with $\psi \equiv \sigma X.\psi' \preceq \phi$. Then $al_\phi(\psi)$ is defined as follows.*

- *If ψ is closed then $al_\phi(\psi) = 1$.*

- *If ψ is not closed then let $\gamma \equiv \sigma'Y.\gamma' \preceq \phi$ be such that $\psi \prec_M \gamma$. If $\sigma' = \bar{\sigma}$ and there exists a $\xi \equiv \sigma''.\xi'$ with $\sigma'' = \bar{\sigma}$, $\gamma \preceq \xi$ and Z appearing free in γ', then $al_\phi(\psi) = 1 + al_\phi(\gamma)$. Otherwise $al_\phi(\psi) = al_\phi(\gamma)$.*

The notion of alternation level can be used to define the more usual one of alternation depth as follows.

Definition 2.3 *Let ϕ be a formula. Then the alternation depth, $ad(\phi)$, of ϕ is given as follows. If ϕ contains fixpoint subformulas $\psi_1, \ldots, \psi_n (n \geq 1)$ then $ad(\phi) = max\{al_\phi(\psi_1), \ldots, al_\phi(\psi_n)\}$. If ϕ contains no fixpoint subformulas, then $ad(\phi) = 0$.*

We refer to a formula ϕ as *alternation-free* when $ad(\phi) \leq 1$. It should be noted that our definition is a slight variant of the usual one given in [12] that corrects a minor anomaly in the treatment of open formulas. The above definition of alternation depth always returns a value less than or equal to the one produced by [12].

We now present the Fisher-Ladner closure [13] for a μ-calculus formula and extend the notion of alternation level to the elements of the closure.

Definition 2.4 *Let ϕ be an μ-calculus formula. Then the Fisher-Ladner closure of ϕ, denoted by $Cl(\phi)$, is the smallest set for which the following hold.*

- *$\phi \in Cl(\phi)$.*

- *If $\neg\psi \in Cl(\phi)$ then $\psi \in Cl(\phi)$.*

- *If $\psi_1 \vee \psi_2 \in Cl(\phi)$ or $\psi_1 \wedge \psi_2 \in Cl(\phi)$ then $\psi_1, \psi_2 \in Cl(\phi)$.*

- *If $[a]\psi \in Cl(\phi)$ or $\langle a \rangle \psi \in Cl(\phi)$ then $\psi \in Cl(\phi)$.*

- *If $\sigma X.\psi \in Cl(\phi)$ then $\psi[\sigma X.\psi/X] \in Cl(\phi)$.*

The next lemma establishes that there is a one-to-one correspondence between the subformulas of a LNF formula ϕ and $Cl(\phi)$.

Lemma 2.5 *Let ϕ be in LNF, with $\psi \preceq \phi$ and $\gamma \in Cl(\phi)$. There there is a unique $\psi' \in Cl(\phi)$ and substitution ρ such that $\psi' \equiv \psi[\rho]$, and there is a unique $\gamma' \preceq \phi$ and subsitution ρ' such that $\gamma \equiv \gamma'[\rho']$.*

Proof. Follows by induction on the definitions of $\preceq$ and Cl and the fact that variables are bound at most once in LNF formulas.
If $\gamma \in Cl(\phi)$ then we use $s(\phi)$ to denote the subformula of ϕ whose existence is guaranteed by the lemma. We may now define $al_\phi(\gamma)$ as follows.

Definition 2.6 *Let ϕ be in LNF, and let $\gamma \in Cl(\phi)$. Then $al_\phi(\gamma) = al_\phi(s(\gamma))$.*

2.2 Semantics

Labeled transitions systems are used to interpret μ-calculus formulas.

Definition 2.7 *A labeled transition system is a quadruple $\langle S, Act, \rightarrow, I \rangle$, where*

$$[A]_Te = \mathcal{V}(A)$$
$$[X]_Te = e(X)$$
$$[\neg\phi]_Te = S - [\phi]_Te$$
$$[\phi_1 \vee \phi_2]_Te = [\phi_1]_Te \cup [\phi_2]_Te$$
$$[\phi_1 \wedge \phi_2]_Te = [\phi_1]_Te \cap [\phi_2]_Te$$
$$[\langle a\rangle\phi]_Te = \{s \mid \exists s'. s \xrightarrow{a} s' \wedge s' \in [\phi]_Te\}$$
$$[[a]\phi]_Te = \{s \mid \forall s'. s \xrightarrow{a} s' \Rightarrow s' \in [\phi]_Te\}$$
$$[\mu X.\phi]_Te = \bigcup\{S \subseteq \mathcal{S} \mid S \subseteq [\phi]_Te[X \to S]\}$$
$$[\nu X.\phi]_Te = \bigcap\{S \subseteq \mathcal{S} \mid [\phi]_Te[X \mapsto S] \subseteq S\}$$

FIGURE 1. Semantics of formulas for $T = \langle S, Act, \to, I\rangle$.

- S *is a set of states;*

- *Act is a set of actions;*

- $\to \subseteq S \times Act \times S$ *is the transition relation; and*

- $I \in A \to 2^S$ *is the interpretation.*

If $T = \langle S, Act, \to, I\rangle$ is a labeled transition system and $s \in S$, then we refer to the pair $\langle T, s\rangle$ as a labeled transition structure; in this case, we call s the start state.

Intuitively, a labeled transition system encodes the operational behavior of a system, with S containing the possible system states, Act the actions the system may engage in, $\to$ the transitions between states that occurs as a result of execution of actions, and I indicating which states a given atomic proposition is true in. A labeled transition system additionally contains a designated start state. Following traditional usage we write $s \xrightarrow{a} s'$ in lieu of $\langle s, a, s'\rangle \in \to$ and call s' an a-*derivative* of s. When $|S| < \infty$ and $|Act| < \infty$ we call labeled transition system $\langle S, Act, \to, I\rangle$ *finite-state*.

The semantics of μ-calculus formulas shown in Figure 2.2 is given with respect to a labeled transition system $T = \langle S, Act, \to, I\rangle$ and an environment $e : \mathcal{V} \to 2^S$. The environment $e[X \mapsto S]$ is the environment obtained from e by updating X to S. Intuitively, the semantics maps a formula to a set of states for which the formula holds. Accordingly, the meaning of an atomic proposition is given by I, and the meaning of a propositional variable is the set of states bound to it by the environment e. The boolean constructs are interpreted in the usual fashion. The meaning of $[a]\phi$ contains the set of states all of whose the a-derivatives satisfy ϕ. Similarly, $\langle a\rangle\phi$ represents the set of states for which there is some a-derivative satisfying ϕ.

The semantics of $\mu X.\phi$ and $\nu X.\phi$ are taken to be the least and greatest fixpoints of the function $\phi_e(S) = [\![\phi]\!]_{\mathcal{T}} e[X \mapsto S]$ repectively. The existence of these fixpoints is guaranteed by the monotonicity of ϕ_e over the lattice of sets of states and the Tarski Fixpoint Theorem [17].

We now define what it means for a labeled transition structure to satisfy a formula.

Definition 2.8 *Let $\langle \mathcal{T}, s \rangle$ be a labeled transition structure and e an environment. Then $s \models^e_{\mathcal{T}} \phi$ iff $s \in [\![\phi]\!]_{\mathcal{T}} e$.*

If ϕ is closed then the environment e does not influence $[\![\phi]\!]_{\mathcal{T}} e$. In this case we write $s \models_{\mathcal{T}} \phi$ when $s \models^e_{\mathcal{T}} \phi$ holds for some (hence any) e.

2.3 The L_1 and L_2 Sublogics

We now present the syntax of two fragments of μ-calculus. The first, L_1, is the set of formulas formed by the following rules.

1. All atomic propositions and variables are elements of L_1.

2. If ϕ_1, ϕ_2 are in L_1 then

   (a) $\phi_1 \vee \phi_2$, $\langle a \rangle \phi_1$, $\mu X.\phi$ and $\nu X.\phi$ are in L_1.

   (b) $\neg \phi$ is in L_1 provided that ϕ is atomic.

   (c) $\phi_1 \wedge \phi_2$ is in L_1 provided ϕ_1 is a literal.

   (d) $[a]\phi_1$ is in L_1 provided ϕ_1 is a literal.

It should be noted that this definitions differs slightly from the one given in [11]; the difference, however, is insignificant for the purposes of this paper.

To obtain L_2 we modify rules 2(b), 2(c) and 2(d) by replacing "atomic" and "literal" with "closed formula". Note that L_1 is a sublogic of L_2. It is also straightforward to establish that for any formula in L_2, there is an equivalent LNF formula that is also in L_2 (hence the motivation for LNF). The same does not hold for PNF; in general, L_2 formulas do not have PNF equivalents that are also in L_2.

The expressiveness of L_2 has been studied by Emerson et al. [11]; in particular they have shown that it has the same expressive power as Wolper's ECTL* [18] and hence is strictly more expressive than CTL* [10].

3 And-Or Kripke Structures and Temporal Logic

In this paper we wish to present algorithms for solving the model-checking problem for closed formulas in L_1 and L_2 interpreted over finite-state labeled transition structures. This problem may be phrased as follows.

> Given L_1/L_2 formula ϕ and labeled transition structure $\langle T, s \rangle$, does $s \models_T \phi$?

Our approach uses this general strategy.

1. From $\langle T, s \rangle$ and ϕ, generate an intermediate structure representing the possible "attempted proofs" that $s \models_T \phi$.

2. Check whether one of the attempted proofs is valid.

It turns out that the construction of the intermediate structure can be combined with the check for validity, thereby yielding an on-the-fly algorithm.

In this section, we introduce the intermediate structures used in our methodology. They resemble the traditional Kripke structures used in defining the semantics of temporal logics; the main difference is that the underlying graph structure is an *and-or* graph. Hence we call these structures *and-or Kripke structures*. We also show how a linear-time temporal logic may be interpreted over these structures; we use this logic to define the "validity check" referred to above.

3.1 And-Or Kripke Structures

And-or Kripke structures may be defined formally as follows.

Definition 3.1 *An and-or Kripke structure is a tuple* $\langle Q, A, R, L, P, q_0 \rangle$ *where*

- Q *is a set of* states;

- A *is a set of* atomic propositions;

- $R \subseteq Q \times Q$ *is the* transition relation, *which is total: for every* $q \in Q$ *there must exist a* $q' \in Q$ *with* $\langle q, q' \rangle \in R$;

- $L : Q \to 2^A$ *is the* propositional labeling;

- $P : Q \to \{\vee, \wedge\}$ *is the* and-or labeling; *and*

- $q_0 \in Q$ *is the start state.*

If $P(s) = \vee$ then we sometimes refer to s as a $\vee$-state, and similarly for $\wedge$. And-or Kripke structures differ from traditional Kripke structures in the inclusion of the and-or labeling P. In a traditional Kripke structure, an execution, or *run*, of the system is typically defined as a maximal sequence of states $q_0 q_1 \ldots$ where $\langle q_i, q_{i+1} \rangle \in R$. In an and-or Kripke structure, a run will instead be a *tree* of states, with $\wedge$-states having multiple successors, in general. This intuition is captured by the following definition.

Definition 3.2 *Let* $\mathcal{K} \equiv \langle Q, A, R, L, P, q_0 \rangle$ *be an and-or Kripke structure. Then a* run *of* $\mathcal{K}$ *is a maximal (hence infinite) tree with nodes labeled by elements of* Q *that satisfies the following properties.*

- *The root of the tree is labeled by q_0.*

- *Let σ be a node labeled by q.*

  - *If $P(q) = \wedge$ and $\{q' \mid \langle q, q' \rangle \in R\} = \{q_1, \ldots q_m\}$ then σ has exactly m successors $\sigma_1, \ldots, \sigma_m$, with σ_i labeled by q_i.*

  - *If $P(q) = \vee$ then σ has exactly one successor, σ', and σ' is labeled by some q' such that $\langle q, q' \rangle \in R$.*

We use $R(\mathcal{K})$ to represent the set of all runs of $\mathcal{K}$.

Note that if an and-or Kripke structure contains only $\vee$-states, then its runs are sequences; in this case, the notion of run coincides exactly with the one found for traditional Kripke structures.

We also use the following notions in the rest of the paper.

Definition 3.3 *Let $\mathcal{K} \equiv \langle Q, A, R, L, P, q_0 \rangle$ be an and-or Kripke structure.*

- *A path through $\mathcal{K}$ is a maximal sequence $q_0' q_1' \ldots$ such that $\langle q_i', q_{i+1}' \rangle \in R$.*

- *Let $r \in R(\mathcal{K})$. Then $\pi(r)$, the paths through r, contains all sequences of the form $q_0' q_1' \ldots$, where q_0' labels the root of r and q_{i+1}' labels a successor σ_{i+1} of σ in r if q_i' labels node σ_i in r.*

And-or Kripke structures may also be viewed as variations on amorphous alternating tree automata [2], the main difference being that tree automata have an explicit acceptance condition used for defining runs and have propositional labelings on their transitions rather than states.

3.2 A Linear Temporal Logic

We now introduce a simple linear-time temporal logic and show how formulas may be interpreted with respect to and-or Kripke structures. The semantics of the logic, which we call LTL, is given as follows, where $(A \in)A$ is assumed to be a set of atomic propositions.

$$\phi ::= A \mid \phi \wedge \phi \mid \phi \vee \phi \mid F\phi \mid G\phi$$

The boolean operations are interpreted in the usual manner, while F and G represent the standard "eventually" and "henceforth" operators.

Traditionally, LTL formulas are interpreted with respect to paths in Kripke structures. We recall the definition here.

Definition 3.4 *Let $\mathcal{K} \equiv \langle Q, A, R, L, P, q_0 \rangle$ be an and-or Kripke structure, let $x \equiv q_0' q_1' \ldots$ be a path in $\mathcal{K}$, and let ϕ be an LTL formula. Then $x \models_{\mathcal{K}} \phi$ is defined inductively as follows.*

- $x \models_\mathcal{K} A$ *iff* $A \in L(q_0')$.

- $x \models_\mathcal{K} \phi_1 \wedge \phi_2$ *iff* $x \models_\mathcal{K} \phi_1$ *and* $x \models_\mathcal{K} \phi_2$.

- $x \models_\mathcal{K} \phi_1 \vee \phi_2$ *iff* $x \models_\mathcal{K} \phi_1$ *or* $x \models_\mathcal{K} \phi_2$.

- $x \models_\mathcal{K} F\phi$ *iff there is a suffix* $x^i = q_i' q_{i+1}' \ldots$ *of* x *such that* $x^i \models_\mathcal{K} \phi$.

- $x \models_\mathcal{K} G\phi$ *iff for every suffix* $x^i = q_i' q_{i+1}' \ldots$ *of* x, $x^i \models_\mathcal{K} \phi$.

We may now extend the notion of $\models_\mathcal{K}$ to *runs* of $\mathcal{K}$ as follows.

Definition 3.5 *Let* $\mathcal{K}$ *be an and-or Kripke structure with* $r \in R(\mathcal{K})$, *and let* ϕ *be an LTL formula. Then* $r \models_\mathcal{K} \phi$ *iff for every* $x \in \pi(r), x \models_\mathcal{K} \phi$.

Finally, we may identify two different ways in which an and-or Kripke structure satisfies an LTL formula.

Definition 3.6 *Let* $\mathcal{K}$ *be an and-or Kripke structure, and let* ϕ *be an LTL formula. Then:*

- $\mathcal{K} \models_\exists \phi$ *iff there is an* $r \in R(\mathcal{K})$ *such that* $r \models_\mathcal{K} \phi$.

- $\mathcal{K} \models_\forall \phi$ *iff for every* $r \in R(\mathcal{K})$, $r \models_\mathcal{K} \phi$.

4 μ-Calculus Model Checking via And-Or Kripke Structures

We now show how model-checking for the general μ-calculus can be reduced to the model-checking problem for LTL interpreted over and-or Kripke structures. The reduction proceeds as follows.

1. We give a set of "proof rules" for establishing that a labeled transition structure satisfies a μ-calculus formula in PNF.

2. We then show how one may use the rules to generate an and-or Kripke structure from a labeled transition structure and μ-calculus formula.

3. Finally, we describe how to build a formula in LTL that is satisfied by the and-or Kripke structure if and only if the labeled transition structure satisfies the original μ-calculus formula.

The proof rules for inferring if a labeled transition structure satisfies a PNF formula are given in Figure 5. They work on *assertions* of form $s \vdash_\mathcal{T} \phi$; intuitively, $s \vdash_\mathcal{T} \phi$ represents the statement that transition structure $\langle \mathcal{T}, s \rangle$ satistifies ϕ. In what follows we use $(\sigma, \sigma' \in) \Sigma$ to refer to the set of all assertions. The proof rules are also goal-directed, meaning that given an assertion to be proved, an application of a proof rule yields subassertions to be proved. The following lemma establishes the soundness of the rules.

$$\vee \; \frac{s \vdash_T L}{true} \quad (s \models_T L)$$

$$\wedge \; \frac{s \vdash_T \phi_1 \wedge \phi_2}{s \vdash_T \phi_1 \quad s \vdash_T \phi_2} \qquad \vee \; \frac{s \vdash_T \phi_1 \vee \phi_2}{s \vdash_T \phi_1 \quad s \vdash_T \phi_2}$$

$$\wedge \; \frac{s \vdash_T [a]\phi}{s_1 \vdash_T \phi, .., s_m \vdash_T \phi} \quad \{s_1, \ldots, s_m\} = \{s' | s \xrightarrow{a} s'\}$$

$$\vee \; \frac{s \vdash_T \langle a\rangle\phi}{s_1 \vdash_T \phi, .., s_m \vdash_T \phi} \quad \{s_1, \ldots, s_m\} = \{s' | s \xrightarrow{a} s'\}$$

$$\vee \; \frac{s \vdash_T \mu X.\phi}{s \vdash_T \phi[\mu X.\phi/X]} \qquad \vee \; \frac{s \vdash_T \nu X.\phi}{s \vdash_T \phi[\nu X.\phi/X]}$$

FIGURE 2. Proof rules for the μ-calculus, where $T = \langle S, Act, \rightarrow, I\rangle$.

Lemma 4.1 *Let $\sigma \equiv s \vdash_T \phi$ be an assertion.*

1. *If the subgoals resulting from applying a rule to σ have the form $s_1 \vdash_T \phi_1, \ldots, s_m \vdash_T \phi_m$, then $s \models_T \phi$ iff $s_i \models_T \phi_i$ for each i.*

2. *If the subgoal resulting from applying a rule to σ is true then $s \models_T \phi$.*

3. *If no rule can be applied to σ then $s \not\models_T \phi$.*

Proof. Follows from the semantics of μ-calculus formulas.
We now introduce the notion of *proof structure*.

Definition 4.2 *Let $V \subseteq \Sigma \cup \{true\}$, $E \subseteq V \times V$ and $\sigma \in \Sigma$. Then $\langle V, E\rangle$ is a proof structure for σ if $\sigma \in V$ and V and E are maximal sets satisfying the following for every $\sigma' \in V$: σ' is reachable from σ using edges in E, and the set $\{\sigma'' | \langle \sigma', \sigma''\rangle \in E\}$ is the result of applying a rule from Figure 5 to σ'.*

Note that a proof structure for a given σ is unique, since at most one rule is applicable to any assertion. Intuitively, a proof structure for σ in intended to encode all possible ways of "proving" that σ holds. A "candidate proof" may be obtained from a proof structure by removing all but one outgoing edge from all assertions to which a rule labeled by $\vee$ has been applied. It is also the case that proof structures may contain cycles, owing to the presence of the fixpoint operators in the logic; this fact complicates a determination of when a proof structure for σ contains a "valid proof" of σ. In traditional proof theory, circular reasoning is always deemed incorrect; in such a setting, a proof for σ that contains a cycle could not be used as evidence of the truth of σ. However, in the μ-calculus, while one may not use such "circular reasoning" to establish that $s \vdash_T \mu X.\phi$ holds, one may use it in order to prove $s \vdash_T \nu X.\phi$. Consequently, in order to determine if a proof structure contains a valid proof, one should permit cycles in which the "top-level" formula in a ν-formula. More specifically, a cycle is allowed in a proof if the formulas with the lowest alternation level on the cycle are ν-formulas. Our approach to checking this condition is as follows.

1. Represent the proof structure for an assertion σ as an and-or Kripke structure whose runs are attempted proofs of σ; and

2. devise an LTL formula that holds of runs whose paths satisfy the "good cycles" condition.

In order to determine if a proof structure contains a proof for σ, one would then check whether the resultant and-or Kripke structure satisfies the LTL formula.

To convert a proof structure $\langle V, E \rangle$ for assertion $\sigma \equiv s \vdash_T \phi$ into an and-or Kripke structure, we must specify the set of states Q, the set of atomic propositions A, the transition relation R, the propositional labeling L, the and-or labeling P, and the start state q_0. Most of these are straightforward.

- For the state set, take $Q = V$.

- For the transition relation R it is tempting to take E. However, R is required to be total, while E may not be (there may be "leaves" in the proof structure). To handle this, we extend E to a total relation by adding self loops to every leaf. Formally,

$$R = E \cup \{ \langle \sigma', \sigma' \rangle \mid \forall \sigma'' \in V. \langle \sigma', \sigma'' \rangle \notin R \}$$

- As remarked above, for any given assertion at most one rule is applicable. So we define $P(\sigma)$ to be the label of the rule in Figure 5 applicable to σ, if such a rule exists; if no such rule exists, we take $P(\sigma)$ to be $\vee$.

- For the start state, we take $q_0 = \sigma$.

In order to complete our definition, we need to specify A and L. Our intention is to use the atomic propositions in order to record the alternation level of fixpoint formulas contained in assertions; accordingly, we the atomic propositions to be of form ν_i and $\mu_{>i}$, where $i \leq ad(\phi)$ (recall that ϕ is the formula in the "root assertion" in the proof structure). Formally, if ϕ is the μ-calculus formula being checked then the set of atomic propositions $A = \{true\} \cup \{ \nu_i \mid i \leq ad(\phi) \} \cup \{ \mu_{>i} \mid i \leq ad(\phi) \}$. The function L can now be defined as follows, where $\sigma' \equiv s' \vdash_M \phi'$. $\nu_i \in L(\sigma')$ iff ϕ' is a ν-formula and $al_\phi(\phi') = i$. $\mu_{>i} \in L(\sigma')$ iff either ϕ' is a non-μ-formula or ϕ' is a μ-formula and $al_\phi(\phi') > i$. If σ' is of form $true$, then $L(\sigma) = \{true\}$.

$$\vee \, \frac{s \vdash_T \phi_1 \wedge \phi_2}{s \vdash_T \phi_2} \; (s \models_T \phi_1)$$

$$\vee \, \frac{s \vdash_T [a]\phi}{true} \; (\forall s'' \in \{ s' \mid s \xrightarrow{a} s' \}.s'' \models_T \phi)$$

FIGURE 3. Modified proof rules for L_1.

The following theorem states that the μ-calculus model-checking problem may be reduced to checking specific LTL formulas on and-or Kripke structures.

Theorem 4.3 *Let $\mathcal{K}_\sigma$ be the and-or Kripke structure corresponding to $\sigma \equiv s \vdash_T \phi$. Then $s \models_M \phi$ iff $\mathcal{K}_\sigma \models_\exists F(true) \vee \bigvee_{i=1}^{ad(\phi)} (GF\nu_i \wedge FG\mu_{>i})$.*

The proof of this theorem appears in an appendix, but the intuition is as follows. Suppose that $\mathcal{K}_\sigma$, where $\sigma \equiv s \vdash_T \phi$, contains a run r satisfying $GF\nu_i \wedge FG\mu_{>i}$ for some $i \leq ad(\phi)$. Suppose further that the run contains a cycle. It then follows that the run contains a path that traverses this cycle an infinite number of times. In order for this path to satisfy this formula, it must follow that some ν-formula of level i appears infinitely often while μ-formulas of level $\leq i$ can only appear finitely often. This implies that the cyclic reasoning implicit in the cycle is being used in support a ν-formula and hence that the cycle is allowable. Similarly, if all cycles in a run satisfy the "good cycle" condition then given LTL formula must hold the infinite paths in the run.

5 Model Checking for L_1 and L_2

The previous characterization of μ-calculus model checking in terms of and-or Kripke structures does not by itself suggest efficient algorithms for determining whether states satisfy formulas in the full calculus. However, when the formulas are in L_1 or L_2, it turns out that the and-or Kripke structures have a special structure that permits them to be manipulated efficiently. In the remainder of this section we use these facts to develop local model-checking algorithms for these logics.

5.1 Efficient L_1 Model Checking

Recall that the syntactic restrictions on the L_1 sublogic stipulate that in formulas of the form $\phi_1 \wedge \phi_2$ and $[a]\phi$, ϕ_1 and ϕ must be literals. These facts imply that proof structures involving formulas of these types have a restricted form. In particular, in a structure built for assertion $s \vdash_T \phi_1 \wedge \phi_2$, the left child of the root ($s \vdash_T \phi_1$, where ϕ_1 is atomic) is either a leaf if

$s \not\models_T \phi_1$ or has the leaf *true* as its only child otherwise. A similar property holds for all children of $s \vdash_T [a]\phi$ when ϕ is atomic; by only looking at the a-derivatives of s and no other states, one may determine if a successful proof structure may be constructed for this assertion.

Using these observations, we may alter the proof rules for the full μ-calculus to obtain the ones given in Figure 3. What is noteworthy about these is the absence of rules labeled by $\wedge$; instead, side conditions are used to handle the left conjuncts in conjunctions and formulas using the $[a]$ modality.

From the definition of the procedure for constructing and-or Kripke structures from models and μ-calculus formulas, it immediately follows that if ϕ is in L_1 then the and-or Kripke structure for assertion $s \vdash_T \phi$ contains no $\wedge$-states. This implies that all the runs of this structure degenerate to sequences of states, as branching in a run arises only from $\wedge$-states. Therefore, checking if there exists a run which satisfies an LTL formula is equivalent to checking if there exists a path satisfying the formula. As we observed before, this is the LTL model-checking problem for traditional Kripke structures, for which an efficient on-the-fly algorithm has been developed [3]. As the proof rules permit us to construct the Kripke structure on-the-fly, we therefore obtain an on-the-fly model-checking routine for L_1.

Time Complexity

In order to quantify the time complexity of this algorithm we first characterize the size of the proof structure yielded by applying the rules in Figure 3. First, note that in any assertion $s' \vdash_T \phi'$ found in a proof structure for $s \vdash_T \phi$, $\phi' \in Cl(\phi)$. This leads the following result.

Theorem 5.1 *Let $\langle T, s \rangle$ be a labeled transition structure, let ϕ a L_1 formula, and let $\langle V, E \rangle$ be a proof structure for $s \vdash_T \phi$. Then $|V| + |E| \leq |\phi| * |T|$.*

Also observe that the formula we give in Theorem 4.3 is $O(ad(\phi))$ in size. Consequently, as the LTL model-checking algorithm in [3] has complexity $2^{O(|\psi|)} * |\mathcal{K}|$ for a Kripke structure $\mathcal{K}$ and LTL formula ψ, one would expect the complexity of our algorithm for L_1 formula ϕ and labeled transition structure $\langle T, s \rangle$ to be $2^{O(|ad(|\phi|)|)} * |\phi| * |T|$. However, recall that formula under consideration has the form $Ftrue \vee \bigvee_{i=1}^{ad(\phi)}(GF\nu_i \wedge FG\mu_{>i})$, where *true* and the ν_i and $\mu_{>i}$ are atomic propositions. It can be shown that for formulas in this form the algorithm in [3] takes time in $O(ad(\phi)*c)$ where c is constant. Intuitively, this is due to the observation that to check whether a there is a path in a Kripke structure satisfying $(\bigvee_{i=1}^{n}(GFp \wedge FGq))$, it suffices to check each disjunct in isolation. As a result our model-checking algorithm for the logic L_1 has time complexity $O(ad(\phi) * |\phi| * |T|)$.

$$\vee \; \frac{s \vdash_\mathcal{T} \neg\phi}{true} \; (s \not\models_\mathcal{T} \phi)$$

FIGURE 4. Additional rule for L_2.

5.2 Efficient L_2 Model Checking

The model checker for L_2 uses the same essential observations as the one given above for L_1. Indeed, the same proof rules are used (with one rule, given in Figure 4, to handle negation). However, the side conditions in the rules for propositions of the form $\neg\phi$, $\phi_1 \wedge \phi_2$ and $[a]\phi$ are nontrivial to handle because ϕ_1 and ϕ are no longer assumed to be atomic; in L_2 they are only required to be closed. We may nevertheless exploit the following observations. Suppose we wish to build a proof structure for an assertion σ using the proof rules for the full μ-calculus, and suppose further $s' \vdash_\mathcal{T} \phi_1 \wedge \phi_2$ is an assertion in the proof structure and that ϕ_1 is closed. It then follows that the substructure computed for $s' \vdash_\mathcal{T} \phi_1$ will have no edges leading to any other part of the proof structure; in other words, $s' \vdash_\mathcal{T} \phi_1$ may be checked independently. Our L_2 model checker thus handles the side conditions for the negation rule and for the former $\wedge$-rules by invoking itself recursively on them. The resulting algorithm may be shown also to have time complexity $O(ad(\phi) * |\phi| * |\mathcal{T}|)$ using a simple induction on the structure of formulas.

5.3 Implementation Concerns

We have implemented our algorithm in the NCSU Concurrency Workbench, which is a re-implementation of the tool for analyzing concurrent systems described in [7], and have experimented with the implementation using several small and medium-sized (up to 5,000 states) examples, including a train signalling scheme. In its current prototype form, and running on a Sun SparcStation 20 with 512 MB of memory, the implementation seems to be capable of processing roughly 1,000 states per minute.

However, a number of tricks can be used to improve the performance of the algorithm. Firstly, we are explicitly calling an implementation of the LTL model checker of [3] in our μ-calculus model checker. However, since the LTL formulas we use have an extremely restricted form, *partially evaluating* the LTL model checker with respect to these formulas would yield a substantial time and space savings. Secondly, the LTL formulas being checked can be "optimized" to yield formulas for which the (partially evaluated) model checker exhibits better behavior. For example, the LTL formula $FGp \wedge GFq$, where p and q are atomic, is logically equivalent to $FG(p \wedge Fq)$; the latter, however, is much more efficient to process in the scheme of [3] than the former.

6 Conclusion

In this paper we have presented efficient on-the-fly model-checking algorithms for fragments of the modal μ-calculus. In contrast with existing algorithms for these logics [11] our routines construct the system state space in a demand-driven manner; the fragments are also capable of expressing fairness constraints that are beyond the expressive power of fragments of the μ-calculus for which efficient on-the-fly algorithms have been developed [1]. Our approach relies on a reduction of the model-checking problem for the full μ-calculus to the model checking problem for LTL interpreted over novel structures that we call and-or Kripke structures. We have also implemented our algorithms in the Concurrency Workbench [7], a tool for analyzing concurrent systems.

7 REFERENCES

[1] H.R. Andersen. Model checking and boolean graphs. In *Proceedings of the European Symposium on Programming*, volume 582 of *Lecture Notes in Computer Science*, pages 1–19, Rennes, France, March 1992. Springer-Verlag.

[2] O. Bernholtz, M.Y. Vardi, and P. Wolper. An automata-theoretic approach to branching-time model checking. In Dill [9], pages 142–155.

[3] G. Bhat, R. Cleaveland, and O. Grumberg. Efficient on-the-fly model checking for CTL*. In *Tenth Annual Symposium on Logic in Computer Science (LICS '95)*, pages 388–397, San Diego, July 1995. IEEE Computer Society Press.

[4] E.M. Clarke, E.A. Emerson, and A.P. Sistla. Automatic verification of finite-state concurrent systems using temporal logic specifications. *ACM Transactions on Programming Languages and Systems*, 8(2):244–263, April 1986.

[5] R. Cleaveland. Tableau-based model checking in the propositional mu-calculus. *Acta Informatica*, 27(8):725–747, September 1990.

[6] R. Cleaveland, M. Klein, and B. Steffen. Faster model checking for the modal mu-calculus. In G.v. Bochmann and D.K. Probst, editors, *Computer Aided Verification (CAV '92)*, volume 663 of *Lecture Notes in Computer Science*, pages 410–422, Montréal, June/July 1992. Springer-Verlag.

[7] R. Cleaveland, J. Parrow, and B. Steffen. The Concurrency Workbench: A semantics-based tool for the verification of finite-state systems. *ACM Transactions on Programming Languages and Systems*, 15(1):36–72, January 1993.

[8] R. Cleaveland and B. Steffen. A linear-time model-checking algorithm for the alternation-free modal mu-calculus. *Formal Methods in System Design*, 2:121–147, 1993.

[9] D.L. Dill, editor. *Computer Aided Verification (CAV '94)*, volume 818 of *Lecture Notes in Computer Science*, Stanford, California, June 1994. Springer-Verlag.

[10] E.A. Emerson and J.Y. Halpern. 'Sometime' and 'not never' revisited: On branching versus linear time temporal logic. *Journal of the Association for Computing Machinery*, 33(1):151–178, 1986.

[11] E.A. Emerson, C. Jutla, and A.P. Sistla. On model-checking for fragments of μ-calculus. In C. Courcoubetis, editor, *Computer Aided Verification (CAV '93)*, volume 697 of *Lecture Notes in Computer Science*, pages 385–396, Elounda, Greece, June/July 1993. Springer-Verlag.

[12] E.A. Emerson and C.-L. Lei. Efficient model checking in fragments of the propositional mu-calculus. In *Symposium on Logic in Computer Science (LICS '86)*, pages 267–278, Cambridge, Massachusetts, June 1986. IEEE Computer Society Press.

[13] D. Kozen. Results on the propositional μ-calculus. *Theoretical Computer Science*, 27:333–354, 1983.

[14] D.E. Long, A. Browne, E.M. Clarke, S. Jha, and W.R. Marrero. An improved algorithm for the evaluation of fixpoint expressions. In Dill [9], pages 338–350.

[15] O. Sokolsky and S. Smolka. Incremental model-checking in the modal mu-calculus. In Dill [9], pages 352–363.

[16] C. Stirling and D. Walker. Local model checking in the modal mu-calculus. In *TAPSOFT*, volume 352 of *Lecture Notes in Computer Science*, pages 369–383, Barcelona, March 1989. Springer-Verlag.

[17] A. Tarski. A lattice-theoretical fixpoint theorem and its applications. *Pacific Journal of Mathematics*, 25(2):285–309, 1955.

[18] M. Vardi and P. Wolper. Yet another process logic. In E.M. Clarke and D. Kozen, editors, *Workshop on Logics of Programs*, volume 164 of *Lecture Notes in Computer Science*, pages 501–512, Pittsburgh, June 1983. SV.

[19] M. Vardi and P. Wolper. An automata-theoretic approach to automatic program verification. In *Symposium on Logic in Computer Science (LICS '86)*, pages 332–344, Cambridge, Massachusetts, June 1986. IEEE Computer Society Press.

[20] G. Winskel. A note on model checking the modal ν-calculus. In G. Ausiello, M. Dezani-Ciancaglini, and S. Ronchi Della Rocca, editors, *Automata, Languages and Programming (ICALP '89)*, volume 372 of *Lecture Notes in Computer Science*, pages 761–772, Stresa, Italy, July 1989. Springer-Verlag.

8 Appendix : Proof of Theorem 4.3

We use the result in [5] to prove our theorem. First, we say that an and-or Kripke structure is *successful* if satisfies the temporal formula in Theorem 4.3. Our goal is to show that an assertion $s \models_M \phi$ is true iff the corresponding and-or Kripke structure is successful. In [5], necessary and sufficient condition for the truth of $s \vdash_T \phi$ is given. Therefore, our goal now can be reduced to showing that the and-or Kripke Structure corresponding an assertion $\sigma \equiv s \vdash_T \phi$ is successful iff σ satisfies this condition.

We first give a brief description of the technique in [5]. The model checking technique in [5] is also a goal oriented approach based on the use of *proof rules*. But the assertions they use are of a slightly different form. Their assertions are of form $H : s \vdash_T \phi$ where H is referred to as the hypothesis set whose elements are of form $s' \vdash_T \phi'$. Intuitively, the hypothesis set records information about the assertions seen on the path from the root. The proof rules in [5] with some minor modifications is shown in Fig 5.

A leaf σ is successful iff

- σ is of form *true*.

- σ is of form $H : s \vdash_T [a]\phi$ and s does not have any a transitions.

- σ is of form $H : s \vdash_T \nu X.\phi'$

A tableau for an assertion is *successful* iff all the leaves in the tableau are successful.

Theorem 8.1 *For an assertion $\sigma \equiv \{\} : s \vdash_T \phi$, $s \models_T \phi$ iff σ has a successful tableau.*

Before we present our proof, we introduce what we refer to as *proof trees*. We use these structures as means to connect the notions of and-or Kripke structures and tableaus.

Let $\mathcal{K} \equiv \langle \mathcal{Q}, \mathcal{A}, R, L, P, q_0 \rangle$ be the and-or Kripke structure corresponding to the assertion $s \vdash_T \phi$. Let $\alpha \in \{\mu, \nu\}$. Also let $\bar{\alpha} = \mu$ iff $\alpha = \nu$ and vice versa.

Definition 8.2 *A proof tree for an assertion σ is a finite tree satisfying the following.*

1. *Every node in the tree is labelled with an element of Q.*

2. *The root of the tree is labelled with σ.*

3. *Let n be a node labeled by σ.*

   - *If $P(\sigma) = \wedge$ and $\{\sigma' \mid \langle \sigma, \sigma' \rangle \in R\} = \{\sigma_1, \ldots \sigma_m\}$ then n has exactly m successors $n_1, \ldots, n_m$, with n_i labeled by σ_i.*

   - *If $P(\sigma) = \vee$ then n has exactly one successor, n', and n' is labeled by some σ' such that $\langle \sigma, \sigma' \rangle \in R$.*

4. *Every leaf σ in the tree is of the form*

   - *true or*
   - *$s \vdash_T L$ where $s \not\models_T L$ or*
   - *$s \vdash_T \alpha X.\phi$ and there exists an internal no de σ' such that $\sigma' = \sigma, \sigma'$ is an ancestor of σ and for every assertion σ'' of form $s' \vdash_T \bar\alpha Y.\phi'$ on the path from σ' to σ, $al(\bar\alpha Y.\phi') > al(\alpha X.\phi)$.*

A leaf n labelled with σ is successful iff $\sigma \equiv s \vdash_T \nu X.\phi'$ or $\sigma \equiv true$. A proof tree is successful iff all the leaves in the tree are successful.

Our proof now follows from the following two theorems.

Theorem 8.3 *An assertion $\sigma \equiv s \vdash_T \phi$ has a successful proof tree iff the and-or Kripke structure corresponding to the assertion is successful.*

Proof. '$\Rightarrow$' Assume σ has a successful proof tree. Now if we unwind the proof tree into an infinite tree, we get a run of the and-or Kripke structure corresponding to σ. From the definition of a successful proof tree, it is clear that this run satisfies the temporal formula in Theorem 4.3.

'$\Leftarrow$' Assume that the and-or Kripke structure corresponding to σ is successful. Then there exists a run of the Kripke structure that satisfies the LTL formula in Theorem 4.3. We now show how a successful proof tree can be constructed from this run. Since the run satisfies the LTL formula in Theorem 4.3, we know that on every path starting from the root in the run either (i) eventually there is a node labelled with *true* or (ii) an assertion $\sigma' \equiv s' \vdash_T \nu X.\phi$ occurs infinitely often and no assertion of form $s'' \vdash_T \mu Y.\phi''$, such that $al(\mu Y.\phi'') \leq al(\nu X.\phi')$, occurs infinitely often on the path. In the first case, we terminate the path when we hit node labelled with *true*. In the second case we know there exists an node n_1 on the path labelled with σ' and there exists an ancestor n_2 of n_1 such that for every node labelled with $s'' \vdash_T \mu Y.\phi''$ on the path from n_1 to n_2, $al(\mu Y.\phi'') > al(\nu X.\phi')$. We terminate the path at such a node. It clear that all the leaves the leaves the resulting tree are successful. It remains to be shown that the tree resulting from this construction is finite. Assume that the constructed proof tree is not finite. By König's Lemma, there exists an infinite path in the tree. This is contradiction since this path is successful and would be terminated by our construction.

Theorem 8.4 *An assertion σ has a successful proof tree iff it has a successful tableau.*

Proof. '$\Leftarrow$' Assume σ has a successful tableau. Replace every assertion $H : s \vdash_T \phi$ by the assertion $s \vdash_T \phi$. Our claim is that the resulting tree is a successful proof tree. It clear that this tree satisfies all requirements except 4. So we need to prove that every leaf n in the constructed tree satisfies the requirements for the leaves in a proof tree. If the leaf is labelled with *true* it obviously does. If the leaf is labelled with $s \vdash_T \nu X.\phi$ then we know that this corresponds to a tableau leaf labelled with $H : s \vdash_T \nu X.\phi$ where $\nu X.\phi \in H$. Now, from the tableau construction it follows that the leaf has an ancestor labelled with $H' : s \vdash_T \nu X.\phi$ and for every node on the path from this ancestor to the leaf there exists no assertion of form $H'' : s' \vdash_T \mu Y.\phi'$ such that $al(\mu Y.\phi') \leq \nu X.\phi$. It follows from the above observation that the leaf n in the constructed proof tree satisfies the necessary requirement.

'$\Rightarrow$' In this case we consider the *smallest* successful proof tree and map it to a successful tableau. Basically, an assertion $\sigma' \equiv s \vdash_T \phi$ in the proof tree is replaced by the assertion $H : s \vdash_T \phi$ in the tableau where $H = \{\sigma'' \mid \sigma'' \equiv \alpha X.\phi'$ is an ancestor of σ, and for every assertion of form $\bar{\alpha} Y.\phi''$, $al(\bar{\alpha} Y.\phi'') > al(\alpha X.\phi')\}$. To show that the resulting structure is indeed a successful tableau, we need to show that (i) tableau rules can be applied at each internal node n, and the successors of n correspond to assertions obtained as a result of an application of a rule in Figure 5. (ii) the leaves are indeed leaves and are successful (Recall that a successful leaf in a tableau is labelled with true or of labelled with $H : s \vdash_T \nu X.\phi$ where $s \vdash_T \nu X.\phi \in H$).

The latter case is straightforward. The first case requires an analysis of the structure of the formula appearing in the the assertion labelling node n. Most of the cases are straightforward. The interesting cases are when the assertion has form $H : s \vdash_T \nu X.\phi$ or $H : s \vdash_T \mu X.\phi$. For the first case, assume no tableau rule can be applied at node n. This implies that $s \vdash_T \nu X.\phi \in H$. From our construction it follows that node n' which is the pre-image of n in the original proof tree has an ancestor n'' labelled with $s \vdash_T \nu X.\phi$ and on the path from n' to n'' there is no μ-formula with lower alternation level. Therefore, n' can be a leaf in the proof tree. This would mean there exists a smaller successful proof tree which contradicts our assumption the original proof tree was the smallest successful proof tree.

For the second case, again assume that no tableau rule can be applied at node n. This implies that $s \vdash_T \mu X.\phi \in H$. From our construction it follows that node n' which is the pre-image of n in the original proof tree has an ancestor n'' labelled with $s \vdash_T \mu X.\phi$. Let the subtrees at nodes n'

$$R1 \frac{H : s \vdash_T L}{true} \quad (s \models_T L)$$

$$R2 \frac{H : s \vdash_T \phi_1 \wedge \phi_2}{H : s \vdash_T \phi_1 \quad H : s \vdash_T \phi_2} \qquad R3 \frac{H : s \vdash_T \phi_1 \vee \phi_2}{H : s \vdash_T \phi_1}$$

$$R4 \frac{H : s \vdash_T \phi_1 \vee \phi_2}{H : s \vdash_T \phi_2}$$

$$R5 \frac{H : s \vdash_T [a]\phi}{H : s_1 \vdash_T \phi, .., H : s_m \vdash_T \phi} \quad \{s_1, \ldots, s_m\} = \{s' | s \xrightarrow{a} s'\}$$

$$R6 \frac{H : s \vdash_T \langle a \rangle \phi}{H : s_1 \vdash_T \phi} \quad (s \xrightarrow{a} s_1)$$

$$R7 \frac{H : s \vdash_T \alpha X.\phi}{H' : s \vdash_T \phi[\mu X.\phi/X]} \quad (s \vdash_T \alpha X.\phi \notin H)$$

where $\alpha \in \{\mu, \nu\}$, $\bar{\alpha} = \mu(\nu)$ if $\alpha = \mu(\nu)$
and $H' = H - \{s' \vdash_T \bar{\alpha} X'.\phi' | al(\bar{\alpha} X'.\phi') > al(\alpha X.\phi)\}$

FIGURE 5. Proof rules for the μ-calculus, where $T = \langle S, Act, \rightarrow, I \rangle$.

and n'' be T'_n and T''_n respectively. Now, in the original proof tree, if we replace the subtree T''_n at node n' by the T'_n, the resulting tree is a smaller successful proof tree. This again is a contradiction as we assumed that the original proof tree was the smallest successful proof tree.

Test Generation with Inputs, Outputs, and Quiescence

Jan Tretmans*

ABSTRACT This paper studies testing based on labelled transition systems, using the assumption that implementations communicate with their environment via inputs and outputs. Such implementations are formalized by restricting the class of transition systems to those systems that can always accept input actions, as in input/output automata. Implementation relations, formalizing the notion of conformance of these implementations with respect to labelled transition system specifications, are defined analogous to the theory of testing equivalence and preorder. A test generation algorithm is given, which is proved to produce a sound and exhaustive test suite from a specification, i.e., a test suite that fully characterizes the set of correct implementations.

1   Introduction

Testing is an operational way to check the correctness of a system implementation by means of experimenting with it. Tests are applied to the implementation under test, and based on observations made during the execution of the tests a verdict about the correct functioning of the implementation is given. The correctness criterion that is to be tested is given in the system specification, preferably in some formal language. The specification is the basis for the derivation of test cases, when possible automatically, using a test generation algorithm.

Testing and verification are complementary techniques for analysis and checking of correctness of systems. While verification aims at proving properties about systems by formal manipulation on a mathematical model of the system, testing is performed by exercising the real, executing implementation (or an executable simulation model). Verification can give certainty about satisfaction of a required property, but this certainty only applies to the model of the system: any verification is only as good as the validity of the system model. Testing, being based on observing only a small subset of all possible instances of system behaviour, can never be complete: testing can only show the presence of errors, not their absence. But since testing can be applied to the real implementation, it is useful in those cases when a

*University of Twente, PO Box 217, NL-7500 AE Enschede, *tretmans@cs.utwente.nl*

valid and reliable model of the system is difficult to build due to complexity, when the complete system is a combination of formal parts and parts which cannot be formally modelled (e.g., physical devices), when the model is proprietary (e.g., third party testing), or when the validity of a constructed model is to be checked with respect to the physical implementation.

Many different aspects of a system can be tested: does the system do what it should do, i.e., does its behaviour comply with its functional specification (conformance testing), how fast can the system perform its tasks (performance testing), how does the system react if its environment does not behave as expected (robustness testing), and how long can we rely on the correct functioning of the system (reliability testing). This paper focuses on conformance testing based on formal specifications, in particular it aims at giving an algorithm for the generation of conformance test cases from transition system-based specifications.

The ingredients for defining such an algorithm comprise, apart from a formal specification, a class of implementations. An implementation under test, however, is a physical, real object, that is in principle not amenable to formal reasoning. It is treated as a black box, exhibiting behaviour, and interacting with its environment. We can only deal with implementations in a formal way, if we make the assumption that any real implementation has a formal model, with which we could reason formally. This formal model is only assumed to exist, but it is not known a priori. This assumption is referred to as the test hypothesis [1, 10, 15]. Thus the test hypothesis allows to reason about implementations as if they were formal objects, and to express the correctness of implementations with respect to specifications by a formal relation between such models of implementations and specifications. This relation is called the implementation relation [3, 10]. Conformance testing now consists of performing experiments to decide how the unknown model of the implementation relates to the specification. The experiments are specified in test cases. Given a specification, a test generation algorithm must produce a set of such test cases (a test suite), which must be sound, i.e., which give a negative verdict only if the implementation is not correct, and which, if the implementation is not correct, have a high probability to give a negative verdict.

One of the formalisms studied in the realm of conformance testing is that of labelled transition systems. A labelled transition system is a structure consisting of states with transitions, labelled with actions, between them. The formalism of labelled transition systems can be used for modelling the behaviour of processes, such as specifications, implementations, and tests, and it serves as a semantic model for various, well-known formal languages, e.g., ACP, CCS, and CSP. Also (most parts of) the semantics of standardized languages like LOTOS [9], SDL [4], and Estelle [8] can be expressed in labelled transition systems.

Traditionally, for labelled transition systems the term testing theory does not refer to conformance testing. Instead of starting with a specification to find a test suite to characterize the class of its conforming implementations, these testing theories aim at defining implementation relations, given a class of tests: a transition systems p is equivalent to a system q if any test case leads to the same observations with p as with q (or more generally, p relates to q if for all possible tests, the observations made of p are related in some sense to the observations made of q). Different relations are defined by variations of the class of tests, the way they are executed, and the required relation between observations, see e.g., [5, 7]. Conformance testing for labelled transition systems has been studied especially in the context of testing communication protocols with the language LOTOS, e.g., [2, 11, 15, 19]. This paper uses both kinds of testing theories: first an implementation relation is defined by using a class of tests, and, once defined, test generation from specifications for this particular relation is investigated.

Almost all of the testing theory mentioned above is based on synchronous, symmetric communication between different processes: communication between two processes occurs if both processes offer to interact on a particular action, and if the interaction takes place it occurs synchronously in both participating processes. Both processes can propose and block the occurrence of an interaction; there is no distinction between input and output actions. For testing, a particular case where such communication occurs, is the modelling of the interaction between a tester and an implementation under test during the execution of a test. We will refer to above theories as testing with symmetric interactions.

This paper approaches communication in a different manner by distinguishing explicitly between the inputs and the outputs of a system. Such a distinction is made, for example, in Input/Output Automata [12], Input-Output State Machines [13], and Queue Contexts [17]. Outputs are actions that are initiated by, and under control of the system, while input actions are initiated by, and under control of the system's environment. A system can never refuse to perform its input actions, while its output actions cannot be blocked by the environment. Communication takes place between inputs of the system and outputs of the environment, or the other way around. It implies that an interaction is not symmetric anymore with respect to the communicating processes. Many real-life implementations allow such a classification of their actions, communicating with their environment via inputs and outputs, so it can be argued that such models have a closer link to reality. On the other hand, the input-output paradigm lacks some of the possibilities for abstraction, which can be a disadvantage when designing and specifying systems at a high level of abstraction. In an attempt to use the best of both worlds, this paper assumes that implementations communicate via inputs and outputs (as part of the test hypothesis), whereas specifications, although interpreting the same actions as inputs, respectively outputs, are allowed to refuse their inputs, which implies that technically specifications are just normal transition systems.

The aim of this paper is to study conformance testing and test generation algorithms for implementations that communicate via inputs and outputs, based on specifications that are labelled transition systems. The implementations are modelled by input-output transition systems, a special kind of labelled transition systems, where inputs are always enabled. These are introduced in section 2. Input-output transition systems differ only marginally from the input/output automata of [12]. Section 3 recalls some of the testing theory for symmetric interactions, in particular the definition of some often used implementation relations. Implementation relations with inputs and outputs are discussed in section 4. The first relation is defined following a testing scenario à la [5]. It is analogous to the scenario used in [14] to obtain a testing characterization of the relation quiescent trace preorder on input/output automata [18], and analogous results are obtained. However, it is shown that this relation does not make full use of the freedom to have specifications which are not input-enabled. A class of weaker implementation relations is defined, of which quiescent trace preorder is a special case. These relations allow to use the abstractness made possible by non-input-enabled specifications. A fully abstract model with respect to these relations is presented. Section 5 formalizes conformance testing by introducing test cases, test suites, and how to run, execute, and pass a test case. Finally, a test generation algorithm that produces provably correct test cases for any of the implementation relations of section 4 is developed in section 6. Some concluding remarks are given in section 7; for complete proofs we refer to [16].

2 Models

The formalism of labelled transition systems is used for describing the behaviour of processes, such as specifications, implementations, and tests.

Definition 2.1
A *labelled transition system* is a 4-tuple $\langle S, L, T, s_0 \rangle$, consisting of a countable, non-empty set S of states, a countable set L of labels, a transition relation $T \subseteq S \times (L \cup \{\tau\}) \times S$, and an initial state $s_0 \in S$. □

The labels in L represent the observable interactions of a system; the special label $\tau \notin L$ represents an unobservable, internal action. We denote the class of all labelled transition systems over L by $\mathcal{LTS}(L)$. For technical reasons we restrict $\mathcal{LTS}(L)$ to labelled transition systems that are strongly converging, i.e., ones that do not have infinite compositions of transitions with internal actions.

A *trace* is a finite sequence of observable actions. The set of all traces over L is denoted by L^*, with ϵ denoting the empty sequence. If $\sigma_1, \sigma_2 \in L^*$, then $\sigma_1 \cdot \sigma_2$ is the concatenation of σ_1 and σ_2.

Let $p = \langle S, L, T, s_0 \rangle$ be a labelled transition system with $s, s' \in S$, $\mu_{(i)} \in L \cup \{\tau\}$, $a_{(i)} \in L$, and $\sigma \in L^*$, then the following standard notations are used. Note that we identify the process p with its initial state s_0.

$$s \xrightarrow{\mu} s' \quad =_{def} \quad (s, \mu, s') \in T$$

$$s \xrightarrow{\mu_1 \cdots \mu_n} s' \quad =_{def} \quad \exists s_0, \ldots, s_n : s = s_0 \xrightarrow{\mu_1} s_1 \xrightarrow{\mu_2} \ldots \xrightarrow{\mu_n} s_n = s'$$

$$s \xrightarrow{\mu_1 \cdots \mu_n} \quad =_{def} \quad \exists s' : s \xrightarrow{\mu_1 \cdots \mu_n} s'$$

$$s \overset{\epsilon}{\Longrightarrow} s' \quad =_{def} \quad s = s' \text{ or } s \xrightarrow{\tau \cdots \tau} s'$$

$$s \overset{a}{\Longrightarrow} s' \quad =_{def} \quad \exists s_1, s_2 : s \overset{\epsilon}{\Longrightarrow} s_1 \xrightarrow{a} s_2 \overset{\epsilon}{\Longrightarrow} s'$$

$$s \xrightarrow{a_1 \cdots a_n} s' \quad =_{def} \quad \exists s_0 \ldots s_n : s = s_0 \overset{a_1}{\Longrightarrow} s_1 \overset{a_2}{\Longrightarrow} \ldots \overset{a_n}{\Longrightarrow} s_n = s'$$

$$s \overset{\sigma}{\Longrightarrow} \quad =_{def} \quad \exists s' : s \overset{\sigma}{\Longrightarrow} s'$$

$$s \overset{\sigma}{\nRightarrow} \quad =_{def} \quad \text{not } \exists s' : s \overset{\sigma}{\Longrightarrow} s'$$

$$traces(p) \quad =_{def} \quad \{ \sigma \in L^* \mid p \overset{\sigma}{\Longrightarrow} \}$$

$$init(p) \quad =_{def} \quad \{ a \in L \mid p \overset{a}{\Longrightarrow} \}$$

A process p has *finite behaviour* if there is a natural number n, such that all traces in $traces(p)$ have length smaller than n; p is *deterministic* if for all $\sigma \in L^*$, there is at most one p' such that $p \overset{\sigma}{\Longrightarrow} p'$. If $\sigma \in traces(p)$, then this p' is denoted by p **after** σ.

We represent a labelled transition system in the standard way, either by a tree or a graph, or by a process-algebraic behaviour expression, with a syntax inspired by LOTOS [9]:

$$B =_{def} \textbf{stop} \mid a ; B \mid i ; B \mid B \square B \mid B \| B \mid \Sigma \mathcal{B}$$

Here $a \in L$, and $\mathcal{B}$ is a countable set of behaviour expressions. The operational semantics are given in the standard way by the following axioms and inference rules:

$$\vdash \quad a; B \xrightarrow{a} B$$

$$\vdash \quad i; B \xrightarrow{\tau} B$$

$$B_1 \xrightarrow{\mu} B_1', \ \mu \in L \cup \{\tau\} \quad \vdash \quad B_1 \square B_2 \xrightarrow{\mu} B_1'$$

$$B_2 \xrightarrow{\mu} B_2', \ \mu \in L \cup \{\tau\} \quad \vdash \quad B_1 \square B_2 \xrightarrow{\mu} B_2'$$

$$B_1 \xrightarrow{\tau} B_1' \quad \vdash \quad B_1 \| B_2 \xrightarrow{\tau} B_1' \| B_2$$

$$B_2 \xrightarrow{\tau} B_2' \quad \vdash \quad B_1 \| B_2 \xrightarrow{\tau} B_1 \| B_2'$$

$$B_1 \xrightarrow{a} B_1', \ B_2 \xrightarrow{a} B_2', \ a \in L \quad \vdash \quad B_1 \| B_2 \xrightarrow{a} B_1' \| B_2'$$

$$B \xrightarrow{\mu} B', \ B \in \mathcal{B}, \ \mu \in L \cup \{\tau\} \quad \vdash \quad \Sigma \mathcal{B} \xrightarrow{\mu} B'$$

Communication between processes modelled as labelled transition systems is based on symmetric interaction, as expressed by the composition operator $\|$. An interaction can occur if both the process and its environment are able to perform that interaction, implying that both processes can also block the occurrence of an interaction. If both processes offer more than one interaction then it is assumed that by some mysterious negotiation mechanism they will agree on a common interaction. There is no notion of input or output, nor of initiative or direction. All actions are treated in the same way for both communicating partners.

Many real systems, however, communicate in a different manner. They do make a distinction between inputs and outputs, and one can clearly distinguish whether the initiative for a particular interaction is with the system or with its environment. There is a direction in the flow of information from the initiating communicating process to the other. The initiating process determines which interaction will take place. Even if the other one decides not to accept the interaction, this is usually implemented by first accepting it, and then initiating a new interaction in the opposite direction explicitly signalling the non-acceptance. One could say that the mysterious negotiation mechanism is made explicit by exchanging two messages: one to propose an interaction and a next one to inform the initiating process about the (non-)acceptance of the proposed interaction.

We use *input-output transition systems*, analogous to input/output automata [12], to model systems for which the set of actions can be partitioned into *output actions*, for which the initiative to perform them is with the system, and *input actions*, for which the initiative is with the environment. If an input action is initiated by the environment, the system is always prepared to participate in such an interaction: all the inputs of a system are always enabled; they can never be refused. Naturally an input action of the system can only interact with an output of the environment, and vice versa, implying that output actions can never be blocked by the environment. Although the initiative for any interaction is in exactly one of the communicating processes, the communication is still synchronous: if an interaction occurs it occurs at exactly the same time in both processes. The communication, however, is not symmetric: the communicating processes have different roles in an interaction.

Definition 2.2
An *input-output transition system* p is a labelled transition system in which the set of actions L is partitioned into input actions L_I and output actions L_U ($L_I \cup L_U = L$, $L_I \cap L_U = \emptyset$), and for which all inputs are always enabled in any state:

$$\text{whenever} \quad p \stackrel{\sigma}{\Longrightarrow} p' \quad \text{then} \quad \forall a \in L_I : p' \stackrel{a}{\Longrightarrow}$$

The class of input-output transition systems with input actions in L_I and output actions in L_U is denoted by $\mathcal{IOTS}(L_I, L_U) \subseteq \mathcal{LTS}(L_I \cup L_U)$. $\quad\Box$

Example 2.3
Figure 1 gives some input-output transition systems with $L_I = \{but_{in}\}$ and $L_U = \{liq_{out}, choc_{out}\}$. In q_1 we can push the *button*, which is an input for the candy machine, and then the machine outputs *liquorice*. After the *button* has been pushed once, and also after having obtained *liquorice*, any more pushing of the *button* does not make anything happen: the machine makes a self-loop. In the sequel we use the convention that a self-loop of a state that is not explicitly labelled, is labelled with all inputs that cannot occur in that state (and also not via τ-transitions, cf. definition 2.2). $\quad\Box$

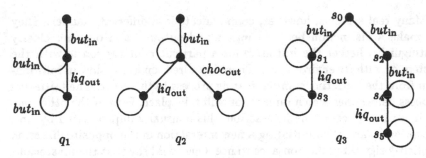

FIGURE 1. Input-output transition systems

When studying input-output transition systems the notational convention will be that $a, b, c \ldots$ denote input actions, and $z, y, x, \ldots$ denote output actions. Since input-output transition systems are labelled transition systems all definitions for labelled transition systems apply. In particular, the synchronous parallel communication can be expressed by $\|$, but now care should be taken that the outputs of one process interact with the inputs of the other.

Note that input-output transition systems differ marginally from input/output automata [12]: instead of requiring *strong input enabling* as in [12] ($\forall a \in L_I : p' \xrightarrow{a}$), input-output transition systems allow input enabling via internal transitions (*weak input enabling, $\forall a \in L_I : p' \xRightarrow{a}$*).

3   Testing with Symmetric Interactions

Before going to the test hypothesis that all implementations can be modelled by input-output transition systems in sections 4, 5, and 6, this section will briefly review the conformance testing theory that is based on the weaker hypothesis that implementations can be modelled as labelled transition systems. In this case correctness of an implementation with respect to a specification is expressed by an implementation relation on $\mathcal{LTS}(L)$. Many different relations have been studied, e.g., bisimulation equivalence, failure equivalence and preorder, testing equivalence and preorder, and many others [7]. A straightforward example is *trace preorder* $\leq_{tr}$, which requires inclusion of trace sets. The intuition behind this relation is that an implementation $i \in \mathcal{LTS}(L)$ may show only behaviour, in terms of traces of observable actions, which is specified in the specification $s \in \mathcal{LTS}(L)$.

Definition 3.1
Let $i, s \in \mathcal{LTS}(L)$, then $i \leq_{tr} s$ $=_{def}$ $traces(i) \subseteq traces(s)$ $\qquad\qquad$ □

Another, more sophisticated relation is *testing preorder* $\leq_{te}$. In addition to requiring that the traces observed with the implementation are contained in those observed with the specification, testing preorder requires that any possible observer, or tester, encountering a deadlock with the implementation will experience the same deadlock when interacting with the specification. We formalize it using a testing scenario that is slightly different from the one in [5].

Definition 3.2
Let $p, i, s \in \mathcal{LTS}(L)$, $\sigma \in L^*$, and $A \subseteq L$, then

1. p **after** σ **ref** A $=_{def}$ $\exists p' : p \overset{\sigma}{\Longrightarrow} p'$ and $\forall a \in A : p' \overset{a}{\nRightarrow}$
2. p **after** σ **deadlocks** $=_{def}$ p **after** σ **ref** L
3. The sets of *observations*, obs and obs' respectively, that an observer $u \in \mathcal{LTS}(L)$ can make of process $p \in \mathcal{LTS}(L)$ are given by the deadlocks, respectively the traces of their synchronization $u \,\|\, p$:

$$obs(u, p) \quad =_{def} \quad \{\, \sigma \in L^* \mid (u \,\|\, p) \text{ after } \sigma \text{ deadlocks} \,\}$$
$$obs'(u, p) \quad =_{def} \quad \{\, \sigma \in L^* \mid u \,\|\, p \overset{\sigma}{\Longrightarrow} \,\}$$

4. $i \leq_{te} s$ $=_{def}$ $\forall u \in \mathcal{LTS}(L) : \quad obs(u, i) \subseteq obs(u, s)$
   and $\quad obs'(u, i) \subseteq obs'(u, s)$ $\qquad$ □

The definition of $\leq_{te}$ in definition 3.2 is extensional, i.e., in terms of how the environment (i.c. the observers u) perceives a system. It can be rewritten into an intensional characterization, i.e., a characterization in terms of properties of the transition systems themselves. This characterization, given in terms of failure pairs is known to coincide with failure preorder on our class of strongly converging transition systems [5].

Proposition 3.3
$i \leq_{te} s$ iff $\forall \sigma \in L^*, A \subseteq L : i$ **after** σ **ref** A implies s **after** σ **ref** A $\qquad$ □

An implementation relation that is strongly related to $\leq_{te}$ is the relation **conf** [2]. It is a modification of $\leq_{te}$ by restricting all observations to only those traces that are contained in the specification s. This restriction makes testing a lot easier: only traces of the specification have to be considered, not the huge complement of this set, i.e., the traces not explicitly specified. Saying it in other words, **conf** requires that an implementation does what it should do, not that it does not do what it is not allowed to do. It is for the relation **conf** that several test generation algorithms have been developed and implemented, that generate provably correct test cases, e.g., [2, 15, 19].

Definition 3.4
i **conf** s $=_{def}$ $\forall u \in \mathcal{LTS}(L) : \quad (obs(u, i) \cap traces(s)) \subseteq obs(u, s)$
   and $\quad (obs'(u, i) \cap traces(s)) \subseteq obs'(u, s)$ $\qquad$ □

Proposition 3.5
i **conf** s iff
$\quad \forall \sigma \in traces(s), A \subseteq L : i$ **after** σ **ref** A implies s **after** σ **ref** A $\qquad$ □

4 Relations with Inputs and Outputs

We now make the test assumption that implementations can be modelled by input-output transition systems: we consider implementation relations $\subseteq \mathcal{IOTS}(L_I, L_U) \times \mathcal{LTS}(L_I \cup L_U)$.

The implementation relations $\leq_{te}$ and **conf** were defined by relating the observations, made of the implementation by a symmetrically interacting observer $u \in \mathcal{LTS}(L)$, to the observations made of the specification (definitions 3.2 and 3.4). An analogous testing scenario can be defined for input-output transition systems, using the fact that communication takes place along the lines explained in section 2: the input actions of the observer synchronize with the output actions of the implementation, and vice versa, so an input-output implementation in $\mathcal{IOTS}(L_I, L_U)$ communicates with an 'output-input' observer in $\mathcal{IOTS}(L_U, L_I)$. In this way the *input-output testing relation* $\leq_{iot}$ is defined between $i \in \mathcal{IOTS}(L_I, L_U)$ and $s \in \mathcal{LTS}(L_I \cup L_U)$ by requiring that any possible observation made of i by any 'output-input' transition system is a possible observation of s by the same observer (cf. definition 3.2).

Definition 4.1
For $i \in \mathcal{IOTS}(L_I, L_U)$ and $s \in \mathcal{LTS}(L_I \cup L_U)$:

$$i \leq_{iot} s \quad =_{def} \quad \forall u \in \mathcal{IOTS}(L_U, L_I): \quad obs(u, i) \subseteq obs(u, s)$$
$$\text{and} \quad obs'(u, i) \subseteq obs'(u, s) \qquad \square$$

Note that, despite what was said above about the communication between the implementation and the observer, the observations made of s are based on the communication between an input-output transition system and a standard labelled transition system, since s need not be an input-output system. Technically there is no problem in making such observations: the definitions of obs, obs', $\|$, and . **after** . **deadlocks** apply to labelled transition systems, not only to input-output transition systems. Below we will elaborate on this possibility to have $s \in \mathcal{LTS}$.

In [14] the testing scenario of testing preorder [5] was applied to define a relation on input/output automata, completely analogous to definition 4.1. It was shown to yield the implementation relation *quiescent trace preorder* introduced in [18]. Although we are more liberal with respect to the specification, $s \in \mathcal{LTS}(L_I \cup L_U)$, exactly the same intensional characterization is obtained: $\leq_{iot}$ is fully characterized by trace inclusion and inclusion of (weakly) quiescent traces. A weakly quiescent trace (output-suspension trace in [16]) is a trace after which no more outputs are possible. Note again the marginal difference with the original definition of quiescence on input/output automata [18]: there quiescence requires the absence of outputs and internal actions. We will refer to the latter as strong quiescence. It is easy to see that on our class of strongly converging transition systems both definitions coincide, but for diverging processes strong quiescence has some counter-intuitive properties. For example, let d be a divergent loop, $d := \tau; d$, then the trace a is not a strongly quiescent trace of $a; d$, which results in some counter-intuitive implementations following strongly quiescent trace preorder (cf. [14]).

Definition 4.2
Let $p \in \mathcal{LTS}(L)$. A trace $\sigma \in L^*$ is *weakly quiescent*, if p after σ ref L_U. The set of weakly quiescent traces of p is denoted by $\delta\text{-}traces(p)$. $\square$

Proposition 4.3
$i \leq_{iot} s$ iff $traces(i) \subseteq traces(s)$ and $\delta\text{-}traces(i) \subseteq \delta\text{-}traces(s)$ $\square$

Comparing the intensional characterization of $\leq_{iot}$ in proposition 4.3 with the one for $\leq_{te}$ (proposition 3.3), we see that the restriction to input-output systems simplifies the corresponding intensional characterization. Instead of sets of pairs consisting of a trace and a set of actions (failure pairs), it suffices to look at just two sets of traces. This relatively simple characterization suggests to transform a labelled transition system into another one representing exactly these two sets of traces, so that the relation can be characterized by trace preorder $\leq_{tr}$ (definition 3.1) on the results of this transformation. Such a transformation on a labelled transition system p can be defined, and the result is called the $\delta\text{-}trace$ *automaton* Δ_p. To obtain Δ_p a special transition is attached to each state where quiescence is possible. Then the resulting transition system is determinized. The special transition indicating output quiescence has label δ, and goes to a state **stop**, from where no other transitions can be made. The label δ indicates the absence of output actions in a state, i.e., it makes the absence of output actions to an explicit observable action.

Definition 4.4
Let $p = \langle S, L_I \cup L_U, T, s_0 \rangle \in \mathcal{LTS}(L_I \cup L_U)$, then the $\delta\text{-}trace$ *automaton* of p, Δ_p, is the transition system $\langle S_\delta, L_\delta, T_\delta, q_0 \rangle \in \mathcal{LTS}(L_I \cup L_U \cup \{\delta\})$, where

- $S_\delta =_{def} \mathcal{P}(S) \cup \{\textbf{stop}\}$, with **stop** a unique state;
  ($\mathcal{P}(S)$ is the powerset of S)
- $L_\delta =_{def} L_I \cup L_U \cup \{\delta\}$, with $\delta \notin L_I \cup L_U$;
- $T_\delta =_{def} \{ q \xrightarrow{a} q' \mid a \in L_I \cup L_U, q, q' \in S_\delta,$
  $q' = \{ s' \in S \mid \exists s \in q : s \xRightarrow{a} s' \} \neq \emptyset \}$
  $\cup \{ q \xrightarrow{\delta} \textbf{stop} \mid \exists s \in q, \forall x \in L_U : s \xRightarrow{x}\not\!\!\rightarrow \}$
- $q_0 =_{def} \{ s' \in S \mid s_0 \xRightarrow{\epsilon} s' \}$ $\square$

Proposition 4.5
1. $traces(p) = traces(\Delta_p) \cap L^*$
2. $\delta\text{-}traces(p) = \{ \sigma \in L^* \mid \sigma \cdot \delta \in traces(\Delta_p) \}$
3. Δ_p is deterministic.
4. $\forall \sigma \in traces(\Delta_p) \cap L^*, \exists x \in L_U \cup \{\delta\} : (\Delta_p \text{ after } \sigma) \xrightarrow{x}$ $\square$

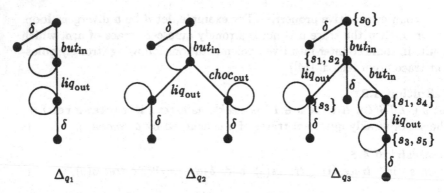

FIGURE 2. δ-trace automata for figure 1

Example 4.6

Figure 2 gives the δ-trace automata for q_1, q_2, and q_3 of figure 1. For Δ_{q_3} the states, subsets of states of q_3, have been added. Note that the nondeterminism of q_3 is removed, and that state $\{s_1, s_2\}$ has a δ-transition, since there is a state in $\{s_1, s_2\}$, i.c. s_2, that refuses all outputs. □

An immediate corollary of propositions 4.3 and 4.5 is that the input-output testing relation is completely characterized by trace preorder $\leq_{tr}$ on the corresponding δ-trace automata: they serve as a fully abstract model modulo $\leq_{iot}$. The δ-trace automaton of a specification is sufficient and necessary to define the class of $\leq_{iot}$-conforming implementations, and it will be the basis for the discussion of testing in section 6.

Theorem 4.7

$i \leq_{iot} s$ iff $\Delta_i \leq_{tr} \Delta_s$ □

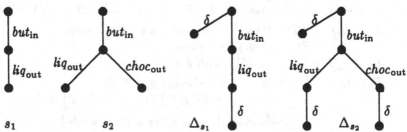

FIGURE 3. Two specifications and their δ-trace automata

Example 4.8

From Δ_{q_1}, Δ_{q_2}, and Δ_{q_3} (figures 1 and 2), using theorem 4.7, it follows that $q_1 \leq_{iot} q_2$: an implementation capable of only producing *liquorice* conforms to a specification that prescribes to produce either *liquorice* or *chocolate*. Although q_2 looks deterministic, it in fact specifies that after *button* there is a nondeterministic choice between supplying *liquorice* or *chocolate*. It also implies that for this kind of testing q_2 is equivalent to but_{in}; liq_{out}; **stop** $\Box$ but_{in}; $choc_{out}$; **stop** (omitting the input self-loops), an equivalence which does not hold for $\leq_{te}$ in the symmetric case. If we want to specify a machine that produces both *liquorice* and *chocolate*, then two buttons are needed to select the respective candies:

$$liq\text{-}button; liq_{out}; \textbf{stop} \ \Box \ choc\text{-}button; choc_{out}; \textbf{stop}$$

On the other hand, $q_2 \not\leq_{iot} q_1, q_3$: if the specification prescribes to produce only *liquorice*, then an implementation should not have the possibility to produce *chocolate*. We have $q_1 \leq_{iot} q_3$, but $q_3 \not\leq_{iot} q_1, q_2$, since q_3 may refuse to produce anything after the *button* has been pushed once, while both q_1 and q_2 will always output something. Formally: $but_{in} \cdot \delta \in traces(\Delta_{q_3})$, while $but_{in} \cdot \delta \notin traces(\Delta_{q_1}), traces(\Delta_{q_2})$.

Figure 3 presents two non-input-output transition system specifications with their δ-trace automata, but none of q_1, q_2, q_3 correctly implements s_1 or s_2; the problem occurs with non-specified input traces of the specification: $but_{in} \cdot but_{in} \in traces(\Delta_{q_1}), traces(\Delta_{q_2}), traces(\Delta_{q_3})$, while $but_{in} \cdot but_{in} \notin traces(\Delta_{s_1}), traces(\Delta_{s_2})$. $\Box$

For the relation $\leq_{iot}$ it is allowed that the specification is not an input-output transition system: a specification may have states that can refuse input actions. Such a specification is interpreted as a not-completely specified input-output transition system, i.e., a transition system where a distinction is made between inputs and outputs, but where some inputs are not specified in some states. The intention of such specifications often is that the specifyer does not care about the responses of an implementation on such non-specified inputs. If a candy machine is specified to deliver liquorice after pushing a button as in s_1 in figure 3, then it is intentionally left open what an implementation may do after pushing the button twice: perhaps ignoring it, supplying one of the candies, or responding with an error message. Intuitively, q_1 would conform to s_1, however, $q_1 \not\leq_{iot} s_1$, as was shown in example 4.8. The implementation freedom, intended with non-specified inputs, cannot be expressed with the relation $\leq_{iot}$. From theorem 4.7 the reason can be deduced: since the implementation can always perform input actions, all inputs must always be enabled in any state of the specification in order to satisfy trace inclusion, so the specification must be an input-output transition system, too, otherwise no implementation can exist.

For input/output automata a solution to this problem is given in [6], using the so-called demonic semantics for process expressions. In this semantics a transition to a demonic process Ω is added for each non-specified input. Since Ω exhibits any behaviour, the behaviour of the implementation is not prescribed after such a non-specified input. We choose another solution to allow for non-input-output transition system specifications to express implementation freedom for non-enabled inputs: we introduce a weaker implementation relation. To define this relation, *i/o-conformance* **ioconf**, we first give an alternative characterization of $\leq_{iot}$ (proposition 4.10) to see where the problem occurs, and how it might be solved. For this characterization the output actions $out(\Delta)$ of a δ-trace automaton are defined, where δ occurs as a special output action as explained above.

Definition 4.9
For Δ be a δ-trace automaton, $out(\Delta) =_{def} init(\Delta) \cap (L_U \cup \{\delta\})$ □

The set $out(\Delta)$ will be used particularly in expressions of the form $out(\Delta \text{ after } \sigma)$ to denote the set of outputs (possibly including δ) of the state reached after σ. If $\sigma \notin traces(\Delta)$, then we define $out(\Delta \text{ after } \sigma) = \emptyset$.

Proposition 4.10
$i \leq_{iot} s$ iff $\forall \sigma \in L^* : out(\Delta_i \text{ after } \sigma) \subseteq out(\Delta_s \text{ after } \sigma)$ □

In proposition 4.10 we see that $\leq_{iot}$ requires that the outputs of the implementation are included in the outputs of the specification after any trace: traces of the specification, and traces that are not in the specification. A weaker implementation relation is obtained if this requirement is relaxed to inclusion for those traces that are explicitly specified in the specification (cf. the relation between $\leq_{te}$ and **conf**, definitions 3.2 and 3.4, and propositions 3.3 and 3.5).

Definition 4.11
$i \text{ ioconf } s =_{def} \forall \sigma \in traces(\Delta_s) \cap L^* : out(\Delta_i \text{ after } \sigma) \subseteq out(\Delta_s \text{ after } \sigma)$□

Example 4.12
Consider again figures 1, 2, and 3. Indeed we have $q_1 \text{ ioconf } s_1$. On the other hand, $q_2 \text{ ioc}\!\!\not\phi\text{nf } s_1$, since q_2 can produce more than *liquorice* after the *button* has been pushed: $out(\Delta_{q_2} \text{ after } but_{in}) = \{liq, choc\} \not\subseteq \{liq\} = out(\Delta_{s_1} \text{ after } but_{in})$. Moreover, $q_1, q_2 \text{ ioconf } s_2$, but $q_3 \text{ ioc}\!\!\not\phi\text{nf } s_1, s_2$, since $\delta \in out(\Delta_{q_3} \text{ after } but_{in})$, while $\delta \notin out(\Delta_{s_1} \text{ after } but_{in}), out(\Delta_{s_2} \text{ after } but_{in})$.
□

The form of the characterizations of $\leq_{iot}$ in proposition 4.10 and of **ioconf** in definition 4.11 suggests to generalize them into a class of relations **ioconf**$_{\mathcal{F}}$ for any set of traces $\mathcal{F}$. Implementation relations of the form **ioconf**$_{\mathcal{F}}$ will be the basis for test generation in section 6.

Definition 4.13
Let $\mathcal{F} \subseteq L^*$, $i \in \mathcal{IOTS}(L_I, L_U)$, $s \in \mathcal{LTS}(L_I \cup L_U)$, then

$i \text{ ioconf}_{\mathcal{F}} s =_{def} \forall \sigma \in \mathcal{F} : out(\Delta_i \text{ after } \sigma) \subseteq out(\Delta_s \text{ after } \sigma)$ □

5 Testing Input-Output Transition Systems

Now that we have formal specifications, expressed as labelled transition systems, implementations, modelled by input-output transition systems, and a formal definition of conformance, expressed by one of the implementation relations $\mathbf{ioconf}_{\mathcal{F}}$, the next point of discussion is how tests look like, and how tests are executed.

A test case is a specification of the behaviour of a tester in an experiment to be carried out with an implementation under test. Such behaviour, like other behaviours, can be described by a labelled transition system. But to guarantee that the experiment lasts for a finite time, a test case should have finite behaviour. Moreover, a tester executing a test case would like to have control over the testing process as much as possible, so a test case should be specified in such a way that unnecessary nondeterminism is avoided. First of all, this implies that the test case itself must be deterministic. But also we will not allow test cases with a choice between an input action and an output action, nor a choice between multiple input actions (input and output with respect to the implementation). Both introduce unnecessary nondeterminism in the test run: if a test case can offer multiple input actions, or a choice between input and output, then the continuation of the test run is unnecessarily nondeterministic, since any input-output implementation can always accept any input action. This implies that in any state of a test case either one particular input is offered to the implementation, or all possible outputs are accepted. Finally, to be able to decide about the success of a test, a verdict (**pass** or **fail**) is attached to each state of the test. Altogether, we come to the following definition of a test case.

Definition 5.1

1. A *test case* t is a 6-tuple $\langle S, L_U, L_I, T, \nu, s_0 \rangle$, such that:

   o $\langle S, L_U \cup L_I, T, s_0 \rangle$ is a deterministic labelled transition system with finite behaviour;

   o for any state t' of the test case, either $init(t') = \{a\}$ for some $a \in L_I$, or $init(t') = L_U$, or $init(t') = \emptyset$;

   o $\nu : S \to \{\mathbf{fail}, \mathbf{pass}\}$ is a *verdict function*.

   The class of test cases over L_U and L_I is denoted as $\mathcal{IOTS}_t(L_U, L_I)$.

2. A *test suite* T is a set of test cases: $T \subseteq \mathcal{IOTS}_t(L_U, L_I)$. $\square$

Note that L_I and L_U refer the inputs and outputs from the point of view of the implementation under test, so L_I denotes the outputs, and L_U denotes the inputs of the test case. The definitions of $\mathcal{LTS}(L)$ are extended to $\mathcal{IOTS}_t(L_U, L_I)$ by defining them over the underlying transition system.

A test run of an implementation with a test case is modelled by the synchronous parallel execution of the test case with the implementation under test, which continues until no more interactions are possible, i.e., until a deadlock occurs (definition 3.2). This deadlock may occur when the (finite) test case reaches a final state, or when the combination reaches a state where the test case expects an output from the implementation which is not produced. An implementation passes a test run if and only if the verdict of the test case in the state where the deadlock is reached is **pass**. Since an implementation can behave nondeterministically different test runs of the same test case with the same implementation may lead to different final states, and hence to different verdicts. An implementation passes a test case if and only if all possible test runs lead to the verdict **pass**. This means that each test case must be executed several times in order to give a final verdict, theoretically even infinitely many times.

Definition 5.2

1. A *test run* of a test case $t \in \mathcal{IOTS}_t(L_U, L_I)$ with an implementation $i \in \mathcal{IOTS}(L_I, L_U)$ is a trace of the synchronous parallel composition of t and i, $t \| i$, leading to deadlock.

2. An implementation i *passes* a test case t, if all the test runs of t and i lead to a **pass**-state of t:

$$i \text{ passes } t \quad =_{def} \quad \forall \sigma \in L^* : \quad (t \| i) \text{ after } \sigma \text{ deadlocks}$$
$$\text{implies} \quad \nu(t \text{ after } \sigma) = \text{pass}$$

3. An implementation i *passes* a test suite T, if it passes all test cases in T: i **passes** $T =_{def} \forall t \in T : i$ **passes** t. If i does not pass the test suite, it fails: i **fails** $T =_{def} \exists t \in T : i$ **passes** t. $\quad\square$

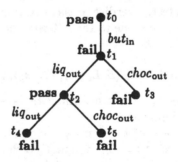

FIGURE 4. A test case

Example 5.3

For q_2 (figure 1) there are two test runs with t in figure 4:

$$t \| q_2 \xrightarrow{but_{in} \cdot liq_{out}} t_2 \| q_2' \quad \text{and} \quad \forall a \in L : t_2 \| q_2' \xrightarrow{a} \!\!\!\!\!/$$

$$t \| q_2 \xrightarrow{but_{in} \cdot choc_{out}} t_3 \| q_2'' \quad \text{and} \quad \forall a \in L : t_3 \| q_2'' \xrightarrow{a} \!\!\!\!\!/$$

where q_2' and q_2'' are the final states of q_2 after the $liq_{out}-$ and $choc_{out}-$ actions, respectively. Although $\nu(t_2) = \text{pass}$, we have that q_2 fails t, since $\nu(t_3) = \text{fail}$. Similarly, q_1 passes t and q_3 fails t. $\quad\square$

6 Test Generation for Inputs and Outputs

Now all ingredients are there to present an algorithm $gen_{\mathbf{ioconf}_{\mathcal{F}}}$ to generate test suites from labelled transition system specifications for any of the implementation relations $\mathbf{ioconf}_{\mathcal{F}}$. A generated test suite $gen_{\mathbf{ioconf}_{\mathcal{F}}}(s)$ must test implementations for conformance with respect to s and $\mathbf{ioconf}_{\mathcal{F}}$. Ideally, an implementation should pass the test suite if and only if it is conforming. In this case the test suite is called *complete* [10]. Unfortunately, in almost all practical cases such a test suite would be infinitely large, hence for practical testing we have to restrict to test suites that can only detect non-conformance, but that cannot assure conformance. Such test suites are called *sound*. Test suites that can only assure conformance, but not non-conformance are called *exhaustive*.

Definition 6.1
Let s be a specification, and T a test suite, then for an implementation relation $\mathbf{ioconf}_{\mathcal{F}}$:

T is complete	$=_{def}$	$\forall i:$	$i\ \mathbf{ioconf}_{\mathcal{F}}\ s$	iff	i **passes** T
T is sound	$=_{def}$	$\forall i:$	$i\ \mathbf{ioconf}_{\mathcal{F}}\ s$	implies	i **passes** T
T is exhaustive	$=_{def}$	$\forall i:$	$i\ \mathbf{ioconf}_{\mathcal{F}}\ s$	if	i **passes** T $\square$

We aim at producing sound test suites. To get some idea how such test cases will look like we consider the definition of **ioconf**. In definition 4.11 we see that to test for **ioconf** we have to check for each $\sigma \in traces(\Delta_s) \cap L^*$ whether $out(\Delta_i\ \mathbf{after}\ \sigma) \subseteq out(\Delta_s\ \mathbf{after}\ \sigma)$. Basically, this can be done by having a test case t that executes σ:

$$t\,\|\,i \stackrel{\sigma}{\Longrightarrow} t'\,\|\,i'$$

and then checks $out(\Delta_i\ \mathbf{after}\ \sigma)$ by having transitions to pass-states for all allowed outputs (those in $out(\Delta_s\ \mathbf{after}\ \sigma)$), and transitions to fail-states for all erroneous outputs (those not in $out(\Delta_s\ \mathbf{after}\ \sigma)$). Special care should be taken for the special output δ: δ actually models the absence of any output, so no transition will be made at all if i' 'outputs' δ; the test run will deadlock in $t'\,\|\,i'$. This can be checked by having the verdict **pass** in the state t' if δ is allowed ($\delta \in out(\Delta_s\ \mathbf{after}\ \sigma)$), and by having the verdict **fail** in t', if the specification does not allow to have quiescence at that point. All this is reflected in the following recursive algorithm. The algorithm is nondeterministic in the sense that in each recursive step it can be continued in many different ways: termination of the test case in choice 1, any input action satisfying the requirement of choice 2, or checking the allowed outputs in choice 3. Each continuation will result in another sound test case (theorem 6.4.1), and all possible test cases together form an exhaustive (and thus complete) test suite (theorem 6.4.2), so there are no errors in implementations that are principally undetectable with test suites generated with the algorithm. However, if the behaviour of the specification is infinite, the algorithm allows to construct infinitely many different test cases, which can be arbitrarily long, but which all have finite behaviour. To define the algorithm one additional definition is needed.

Definition 6.2
Let $\mathcal{F} \subseteq L^*$ and $a \in L$, then $\mathcal{F}$ **after** a $=_{def}$ $\{\sigma \in L^* \mid a \cdot \sigma \in \mathcal{F}\}$. $\quad\square$

Algorithm 6.3
Let Δ be the δ-trace automaton of a specification, and let $\mathcal{F} \subseteq L^*$, then a test case $t \in \mathcal{IOTS}_t(L_U, L_I)$ is obtained by a finite number of recursive applications of one of the following three nondeterministic choices:

1. (∗ terminate the test case ∗)

   $t \quad := \quad$ **stop** ;

   $\nu(t) \quad := \quad$ **pass** ;

2. (∗ give a next input to the implementation ∗)

   $t \quad := \quad a \; ; \; t'$;

   $\nu(t) \quad := \quad$ **pass** ;

   where $a \in L_I$, such that $\mathcal{F}$ **after** $a \neq \emptyset$, and t' is obtained by recursively applying the algorithm for $\mathcal{F}$ **after** a and Δ', with $\Delta \xrightarrow{a} \Delta'$.

3. (∗ check the next output of the implementation ∗)

   $t \quad := \quad \Sigma \{ x \; ; \; \textbf{stop} \mid x \in L_U, \; x \notin out(\Delta) \}$

   $\qquad\qquad \square \; \Sigma \{ x \; ; \; t_x \mid x \in L_U, \; x \in out(\Delta) \}$;

   $\nu(t) \quad := \quad$ if $(\delta \in out(\Delta)$ or $\epsilon \notin \mathcal{F})$ then **pass** else **fail** ;

   where $\nu(\textbf{stop}) :=$ if $\epsilon \in \mathcal{F}$ then **fail** else **pass** for all x in the first operand, and t_x is obtained by recursively applying the algorithm for $\mathcal{F}$ **after** x and Δ', with $\Delta \xrightarrow{x} \Delta'$.

   $\quad\square$

Theorem 6.4

1. A test case obtained with algorithm 6.3 from Δ_s and $\mathcal{F}$ is sound for s with respect to **ioconf**$_{\mathcal{F}}$.

2. The set containing all possible test cases that can be obtained with algorithm 6.3 is exhaustive.

   $\quad\square$

Example 6.5
We generate a test case for s_1 from Δ_{s_1} for the implementation relation **ioconf** $=$ **ioconf**$_{traces(s)}$ (figure 3). We start with giving an input:
$but_{in} \in init(\Delta_{s_1}) \cap L_I$, so $t := but_{in}; t'$ and $\nu(t) = $ **pass**.
In the next step we generate the test case t' from $\Delta' = liq_{out}; \delta; $ **stop**, where we check the outputs:
$t' := \Sigma\{x; \textbf{stop} \mid x \in L_U, x \notin \{liq_{out}\}\} \; \square \; \Sigma\{x; t_x \mid x \in L_U, x \in \{liq_{out}\}\}$
$= choc_{out}; \textbf{stop} \; \square \; liq_{out}; t_{liq_{out}}$.
Since $\delta \notin out(\Delta')$, we have $\nu(t') = $ **fail**. Moreover, $\nu(\textbf{stop}) = $ **fail**.
Now generating $t_{liq_{out}}$ from $\Delta'' = \delta; $ **stop** we again check the outputs:
$t_{liq_{out}} := \Sigma\{x; \textbf{stop} \mid x \in L_U, x \notin \{\delta\}\} \; \square \; \Sigma\{x; t_x \mid x \in L_U, x \in \{\delta\}\}$

$= choc_{out}; \textbf{stop} \; \square \; liq_{out}; \textbf{stop},$

with for both branches $\nu(\textbf{stop}) = \textbf{fail}$, and $\nu(t_{liq_{out}}) = \textbf{pass}$.

Combining $t_{liq_{out}}$ and t' into t we obtain the test case t of figure 4 as a sound test case for s_1, which is consistent with the results found in examples 4.12 and 5.3: q_1 **ioconf** s_1, q_2 **iocǿnf** s_1, and q_3 **iocǿnf** s_1, and indeed q_1 **passes** t, q_2 **fails** t, and q_3 **fails** t. □

7   Concluding Remarks

This paper presented a theory for conformance testing of implementations that communicate via inputs and outputs. The main ingredients of this theory are the implementation relations $\leq_{iot}$, **ioconf**, and **ioconf**$_{\mathcal{F}}$, and a sound and exhaustive test generation algorithm. The resulting theory and algorithm are somewhat simpler than the corresponding theory and algorithms for testing with symmetric interactions (e.g., compare proposition 4.3 with 3.3, and compare algorithm 6.3 with the **conf**-based test generation algorithm in [15]). The theory and the algorithm can form the basis for the development of test generation tools. They can be applied to those domains where implementations can be assumed to communicate via inputs and outputs, which is the case for many realistic systems, and where specifications can be expressed in labelled transition systems, which also holds for many specification formalisms.

It was indicated that input-output transition systems only marginally differ from input/output automata [12], having weaker requirements on input-enabling and on quiescence. We think that in a few cases these weaker requirements are easier and more intuitive. This was indicated for quiescence with the example in section 4, just above definition 4.2, but it was also indicated that for strongly-converging systems the two coincide. For a precise comparison a more elaborate investigation of divergence in input-output transition systems is necessary. The weaker requirement on input enabling allows some systems that are $\mathcal{IOTS}$ but not IOA. For example, when the communication between an IOA system and a bounded input buffer is hidden, then the whole system is not IOA anymore: when the buffer is full, no input actions are possible anymore without first performing an internal event. Such a system is $\mathcal{IOTS}$.

The model of input-output transition systems is also very much related to the model of input-output state machines [13]. The idea for the δ-trace automaton is inspired by the way the absence of output is treated in [13], but there are subtle differences in the way the δ-transitions are added.

The implementation relations and algorithm in this paper generalize those for queue systems [17]. Queue systems are transition systems in a queue context, i.e., to which two unbounded queues are attached to model asynchronous communication, one queue for inputs, and one queue for outputs.

An unbounded queue clearly has the property that input can never be refused, while the output queue makes that from the system's point of view output actions can never be refused by the environment.

Another open issue is the atomicity of actions. Although we allow specifications to be labelled transition systems, the actions are classified as inputs and outputs, and they have a one-to-one correspondence to those of the implementation. An interesting area for further investigation occurs if implementation relations are combined with action refinement, so that one abstract symmetric interaction of the specification is implemented using multiple inputs and outputs, e.g., implementing an abstract interaction by means of a hand-shake protocol. Tests could be derived from the specification using symmetric algorithms (section 3) and then refined, or the specification could be refined after which the input-output based algorithm is used. The precise relation between testing, inputs and outputs, and action refinement needs further investigation.

A second open problem is the well-known test selection problem (test-suite size reduction [10]). Algorithm 6.3 can generate infinitely many sound test cases, but which ones shall be really executed? Solutions can be sought by defining coverage measures, fault models, stronger test hypotheses, etc. [1, 10, 13, 15]. Another aspect is the incorporation of data in the test generation procedure. The state explosion caused by the data in specifications needs to be handled in a symbolic way, otherwise automation of the test generation algorithm in test tools will probably not be feasible. A last, more practical problem is the implementation of the observation of quiescence. In practical test execution tools, timers will have to be used, for which the time-out values need to be chosen carefully, in order not to observe quiescence where there is none.

8 REFERENCES

[1] G. Bernot. Testing against formal specifications: A theoretical view. In S. Abramsky and T. S. E. Maibaum, eds., *TAPSOFT'91*, 99–119. LNCS 494, Springer-Verlag, 1991.

[2] E. Brinksma. A theory for the derivation of tests. In S. Aggarwal and K. Sabnani, eds., *Prot. Spec., Test., and Ver. VIII*, 63–74. North-Holland, 1988.

[3] E. Brinksma, R. Alderden, R. Langerak, J. van de Lagemaat, and J. Tretmans. A formal approach to conformance testing. In J. de Meer, et al., eds., *Protocol Test Systems II*, 349–363. North-Holland, 1990.

[4] ITU-T. SDL. Recommendation Z.100, 1992.

[5] R. De Nicola. Extensional equivalences for transition systems. *Acta Informatica*, 24:211–237, 1987.

[6] R. De Nicola and R. Segala. A process algebraic view of input/output automata. *TCS*, 138:391–423, 1995.

[7] R.J. van Glabbeek. The linear time – branching time spectrum. In J.C.M. Baeten and J.W. Klop, eds., *CONCUR'90*, LNCS 458, 278–297. Springer-Verlag, 1990.

[8] ISO. Estelle – International Standard IS-9074, 1989.

[9] ISO. LOTOS – International Standard IS-8807, 1989.

[10] ISO/IEC JTC1/SC21 WG7, ITU-T SG 10/Q.8. *Formal Methods in Conformance Testing, working draft.* September 1995.

[11] G. Leduc. A framework based on implementation relations for implementing LOTOS specifications. *Computer Networks and ISDN Systems*, 25(1):23–41, 1992.

[12] N.A. Lynch and M.R. Tuttle. An introduction to input/output automata. *CWI Quarterly*, 2(3):219–246, 1989.

[13] M. Phalippou. *Relations d'Implantation et Hypothèses de Test sur des Automates à Entrées et Sorties.* PhD thesis, L'Université de Bordeaux I (F), 1994.

[14] R. Segala. Quiescence, fairness, testing, and the notion of implementation. In E. Best, ed., *CONCUR'93*, 324–338. LNCS 715, Springer-Verlag, 1993.

[15] J. Tretmans. *A Formal Approach to Conformance Testing.* PhD thesis, University of Twente (NL), 1992.

[16] J. Tretmans. Testing labelled transition systems with inputs and outputs. Memorandum INF-95-26, University of Twente (NL), 1995.

[17] J. Tretmans and L. Verhaard. A queue model relating synchronous and asynchronous communication. In R.J. Linn and M.Ü. Uyar, eds., *Prot. Spec., Test., and Ver. XII*, 131–145. North-Holland, 1992.

[18] F. Vaandrager. On the relationship between process algebra and input/output automata. In *Logic in Computer Science*, 387–398. Sixth Annual IEEE Symposium, 1991.

[19] C. D. Wezeman. The CO-OP method for compositional derivation of conformance testers. In E. Brinksma, et al., eds., *Prot. Spec., Test., and Ver. IX*, 145–158. North-Holland, 1990.

Breaking and Fixing the Needham-Schroeder Public-Key Protocol Using FDR

Gavin Lowe*

ABSTRACT In this paper we analyse the well known Needham-Schroeder Public-Key Protocol using FDR, a refinement checker for CSP. We use FDR to discover an attack upon the protocol, which allows an intruder to impersonate another agent. We adapt the protocol, and then use FDR to show that the new protocol is secure, at least for a small system. Finally we prove a result which tells us that if this small system is secure, then so is a system of arbitrary size.

1 Introduction

In a distributed computer system, it is necessary to have some mechanism whereby a pair of agents can be assured of each other's identity—they should become sure that they really are talking to each other, rather than to an intruder impersonating the other agent. This is the role of an *authentication protocol*.

In this paper we use the Failures Divergences Refinement Checker (FDR) [11, 5], a model checker for CSP, to analyse the Needham-Schroeder Public-Key Authentication Protocol [8]. FDR takes as input two CSP processes, a specification and an implementation, and tests whether the implementation refines the specification [6]. It has been used to analyse many sorts of systems, including communications protocols [10], distributed databases [12], and puzzles; we show here how it may be used to analyse security protocols.

We model the agents taking part in the protocol as CSP processes. We also model the most general intruder who can interact with the protocol: the intruder can observe and intercept messages, and so learn information— such as the values of nonces—and then use this information to introduce fake messages into the system. We use FDR to test whether the protocol correctly achieves authentication, and discover an attack upon the protocol,

---

*Oxford University Computing Laboratory, Wolfson Building, Parks Road, Oxford, OX1 3QD, United Kingdom. e-mail gavin.lowe@comlab.ox.ac.uk.

which allows the intruder to imitate an agent A in a run of the protocol with another agent B. This attack was previously reported in [7].

We then adapt the protocol, and use FDR to show that the new protocol is secure, at least for a small system with a single initiator and a single responder. We then prove that this implies that a system of arbitrary size is secure: we prove that if there were an attack on any system running the protocol, no matter how large, then there would be an attack on this small system. This proof is by hand, rather than being fully automatic; however, we believe that this proof is considerably simpler than a direct proof of the security of an arbitrarily-sized system.

We believe that security protocols provide an excellent subject for analysis using process algebra tools. It is obviously important to get these protocols right, particularly given the increasing commercial and financial use of the internet. However, many protocols have appeared in the literature only to be later broken. Often the attacks are somewhat subtle and hard to spot—the protocol discussed in this paper appeared 17 years before it was eventually broken. Further, existing formalisms for analysing protocols have not proved very effective—an incorrect proof of the protocol of this paper has appeared in [2].

The main contributions of this paper are two-fold: (1) a study of how errors may be found in security protocols using a tool such as FDR; and (2) a study of how a protocol, running on a system of arbitrary size, may be verified by considering just a single, small system.

2 The Needham-Schroeder Public-Key Protocol

The Needham-Schroeder Public-Key Protocol [8] aims to establish mutual authentication between an *initiator* A and a *responder* B. The protocol uses *public key cryptography* [4, 9]. Each agent A possesses a *public key*, denoted K_a, which any other agent can obtain from a key server. It also possesses a *secret key*, K_a^{-1}, which is the inverse of K_a. We will write $\{m\}_k$ for message m encrypted with key k. Any agent can encrypt a message m using A's public key to produce $\{m\}_{K_a}$; only A can decrypt this message, so this ensures secrecy.

The protocol also uses *nonces*: random numbers generated with the purpose of being used in a *single* run of the protocol. We denote nonces by N_a and N_b: the subscripts are intended to denote that the nonces were generated by A and B, respectively.

The complete Needham-Schroeder Public-Key Protocol involves seven steps. However, in this paper we consider a reduced version with only three steps. In the steps we omit, the two agents request and receive each other's public keys from a key server: omitting these steps is equivalent to assuming that each agent initially has the other's public key. There is a well known attack upon the full protocol [3], which allows an intruder to replay old, compromised public keys, because the key delivery messages contain no proof of freshness; however, this attack is easily prevented. The attack we consider in this paper is newer, and more subtle.

The reduced protocol can be described as:

Message 1. $A \rightarrow B$: $A.B.\{N_a.A\}_{PK(B)}$
Message 2. $B \rightarrow A$: $B.A.\{N_a.N_b\}_{PK(A)}$
Message 3. $A \rightarrow B$: $A.B.\{N_b\}_{PK(B)}$.

Here A is an initiator who seeks to establish a session with responder B. A selects a nonce N_a, and sends it along with its identity to B (message 1), encrypted using B's public key. When B receives this message, it decrypts the message to obtain the nonce N_a. It then returns the nonce N_a, along with a new nonce N_b, to A, encrypted with A's key (message 2). When A receives this message it would seem that he should be assured that he is talking to B, since only B should be able to decrypt message 1 to obtain N_a. A then returns the nonce N_b to B, encrypted with B's key. It would seem that B should be assured that he is talking to A, since only A should be able to decrypt message 2 to obtain N_b.

3 Using FDR to find an attack on the Needham-Schroeder Public-Key Protocol

In this section we model the protocol using CSP. We assume that the reader is familiar with CSP, as described in [6]. We model the protocol by defining CSP processes corresponding to each of the two agents. We also give a CSP description of the most general intruder who can interact with the protocol. We then use the FDR refinement checker to test whether the intruder can successfully attack the protocol.

We assume the existence of the sets *Initiator* of initiators, *Responder* of responders, *Key* of public keys, and *Nonce* of nonces. We will represent a protocol message of the form:

Message 1. $A \rightarrow B$: $A.B.\{N_a.A\}_{K_b}$

by the CSP event $comm.Msg1.A.B.Encrypt.K_b.N_a.A$, etc. We are modelling a protocol message with an encrypted component of the form $\{m\}_k$ by a CSP event containing fields of the form $Encrypt.k.m$. We define the sets of communications events corresponding to the three steps in the protocol:

$MSG1 \triangleq \{Msg1.a.b.Encrypt.k.n_a.a' \mid$
$a \in Initiator, a' \in Initiator, b \in Responder,$
$k \in Key, n_a \in Nonce\},$

$$MSG2 \;\hat{=}\; \{Msg2.b.a.Encrypt.k.n_a.n_b \mid$$
$$a \in Initiator, b \in Responder,$$
$$k \in Key, n_a \in Nonce, n_b \in Nonce\},$$

$$MSG3 \;\hat{=}\; \{Msg3.a.b.Encrypt.k.n_b \mid$$
$$a \in Initiator, b \in Responder, k \in Key, n_b \in Nonce\},$$

$$MSG \;\hat{=}\; MSG1 \cup MSG2 \cup MSG3.$$

Standard communications in the system will be modelled by the channel *comm*. We also want to model the fact that the intruder can fake or intercept messages, and so we introduce extra channels *fake* and *intercept*. We declare these channels:

$$\textbf{channel } comm, fake, intercept : MSG.$$

We will ensure that the receiver of a faked message is not aware that it is a fake, and that the sender of an intercepted message is not aware that it is intercepted.

We introduce two extra channels, defining the external interface of the protocol. We represent a request from a user for initiator a to connect with responder b by the event $user.a.b$; we represent the resulting session by the event $session.a.b$. We also add channels to represent the state of the agents: these will be useful in the subsequent analysis of the system. We represent the initiator a thinking it is taking part in a run of the protocol with b by the event $I\_running.a.b$, and represent the responder b thinking it is taking part in a run of the protocol with a by the event $R\_running.a.b$; we represent the initiator committing to the session by the event $I\_commit.a.b$, and represent the responder committing to the session by $R\_commit.a.b$. We declare these channels by:

$$\textbf{channel } user, session, I\_running, R\_running, I\_commit, R\_commit :$$
$$Initiator.Responder.$$

We will represent a responder with identity a, who has a single nonce n_a, by the CSP process $INITIATOR(a, n_a)$. If we want to consider a responder with more than one nonce, then we can compose several such processes, either sequentially or interleaved. Ignoring, for the moment, the possibility of intruder action, the process can be defined by:

$$INITIATOR(a, n_a) \;\hat{=}\;$$
$$user.a?b \rightarrow I\_running.a.b \rightarrow$$
$$comm!Msg1.a.b.Encrypt.key(b).n_a.a \rightarrow$$
$$comm.Msg2.b.a.Encrypt.key(a)?n'_a.n_b \rightarrow$$
$$\textbf{if} \quad n_a = n'_a$$
$$\textbf{then} \quad comm!Msg3.a.b.Encrypt.key(b).n_b \rightarrow$$
$$\qquad\quad I\_commit.a.b \rightarrow session.a.b \rightarrow Skip$$
$$\textbf{else} \quad Stop.$$

The initiator receives a request from the user to connect with responder b, and so starts what he believes is a run of the protocol with b. He sends a message 1, containing the nonce n_a, encrypted with b's public key. He receives a message 2 back, and checks the value of the first nonce. He then sends back the corresponding message 3, commits to the session, and carries out the session.

We now introduce the possibility of enemy action by applying a renaming to the above process. Our renaming should ensure that message 1s and message 3s sent by the initiator can be intercepted, and message 2s can be faked. We define an initiator with identity A and nonce N_a by:[1]

$$INITIATOR1 \cong$$
$$INITIATOR(A, N_a)$$
$$[[comm.Msg1 \leftarrow comm.Msg1, comm.Msg1 \leftarrow intercept.Msg1,$$
$$comm.Msg2 \leftarrow comm.Msg2, comm.Msg2 \leftarrow fake.Msg2,$$
$$comm.Msg3 \leftarrow comm.Msg3, comm.Msg3 \leftarrow intercept.Msg3]].$$

We can define a CSP process representing the responder, similarly.

3.1 The intruder

We want to model the intruder as a process that can perform any attack that we would expect a real-world intruder to be able to perform. Thus the intruder should be able to:

- Overhear and/or intercept any messages being passed in the system;

- Decrypt messages that are encrypted with his own public key, so as to learn new nonces;

- Introduce new messages into the system, using nonces he knows;

- Replay any message he has seen (possibly changing plain-text parts), even if he does not understand the contents of the encrypted part.

We assume that the intruder is a user of the computer network, and so can take part in normal runs of the protocol, and other agents may initiate runs of the protocol with him. We will define the most general (i.e. the most non-deterministic) intruder who can act as above. We consider an intruder with identity I, with public key K_i, who initially knows a nonce N_i. All of our refinement tests are in the traces model, so—for reasons of efficiency—we define the intruder using external choices, where nondeterministic choices might seem more natural.

---

[1]This is the process that can perform either a $comm.Msg1$ or $intercept.Msg1$ event whenever $INITIATOR(A, N_a)$ can perform a corresponding $comm.Msg1$, etc.

At any instant, the state of the intruder can be parameterized by the knowledge it has acquired. More precisely, our model of the intruder will be parameterized by the sets $m1s$, $m2s$ and $m3s$ of message 1s, message 2s and message 3s that it has been unable to decrypt, and the set ns of nonces that it knows.

The intruder can observe messages being passed in the system, possibly intercepting them. If the messages are encrypted with its own key K_i, then it can learn new nonces; otherwise it remembers the encrypted component. It can introduce fake messages into the system using nonces that it knows, or by replaying encrypted components that it has been unable to decrypt. This is captured by the following (rather long, but reasonably uniform) CSP definition[2].

$I(m1s, m2s, m3s, ns) \mathrel{\widehat{=}}$
$\quad comm.Msg1?a.b.Encrypt.k.n.a' \rightarrow$
$\qquad$ if $k = K_i$ then $I(m1s, m2s, m3s, ns \cup \{n\})$
$\qquad$ else $I(m1s \cup \{Encrypt.k.n.a'\}, m2s, m3s, ns)$
$\quad \Box\ intercept.Msg1?a.b.Encrypt.k.n.a' \rightarrow$
$\qquad$ if $k = K_i$ then $I(m1s, m2s, m3s, ns \cup \{n\})$
$\qquad$ else $I(m1s \cup \{Encrypt.k.n.a'\}, m2s, m3s, ns)$
$\quad \Box\ comm.Msg2?b.a.Encrypt.k.n.n' \rightarrow$
$\qquad$ if $k = K_i$ then $I(m1s, m2s, m3s, ns \cup \{n, n'\})$
$\qquad$ else $I(m1s, m2s \cup \{Encrypt.k.n.n'\}, m3s, ns)$
$\quad \Box\ intercept.Msg2?b.a.Encrypt.k.n.n' \rightarrow$
$\qquad$ if $k = K_i$ then $I(m1s, m2s, m3s, ns \cup \{n, n'\})$
$\qquad$ else $I(m1s, m2s \cup \{Encrypt.k.n.n'\}, m3s, ns)$
$\quad \Box\ comm.Msg3?a.b.Encrypt.k.n \rightarrow$
$\qquad$ if $k = K_i$ then $I(m1s, m2s, m3s, ns \cup \{n\})$
$\qquad$ else $I(m1s, m2s, m3s \cup \{Encrypt.k.n\}, ns)$
$\quad \Box\ intercept.Msg3?a.b.Encrypt.k.n \rightarrow$
$\qquad$ if $k = K_i$ then $I(m1s, m2s, m3s, ns \cup \{n\})$
$\qquad$ else $I(m1s, m2s, m3s \cup \{Encrypt.k.n\}, ns)$
$\quad \Box\ fake.Msg1?a.b?m:m1s \rightarrow I(m1s, m2s, m3s, ns)$
$\quad \Box\ fake.Msg2?a.b?m:m2s \rightarrow I(m1s, m2s, m3s, ns)$
$\quad \Box\ fake.Msg3?a.b?m:m3s \rightarrow I(m1s, m2s, m3s, ns)$
$\quad \Box\ fake.Msg1?a.b!Encrypt?k?n:ns?a' \rightarrow I(m1s, m2s, m3s, ns)$
$\quad \Box\ fake.Msg2?b.a!Encrypt?k?n:ns?n':ns \rightarrow I(m1s, m2s, m3s, ns)$
$\quad \Box\ fake.Msg3?a.b!Encrypt?k?n:ns \rightarrow I(m1s, m2s, m3s, ns)$.

We consider an intruder who initially knows the nonce N_i:

$$INTRUDER \mathrel{\widehat{=}} I(\{\}, \{\}, \{\}, \{N_i\}).$$

---

[2]In practice, it is more efficient to define the intruder slightly differently, as the interleaving of four components.

3.2 Analyzing the system

We may now define a system with an intruder:[3]

$AGENTS \; \hat{=}$
$\quad INITIATOR1 \, |[\, \{comm, session.A.B\} \,]| \, RESPONDER1,$
$SYSTEM \; \hat{=} \; AGENTS \, |[\, \{fake, comm, intercept\} \,]| \, INTRUDER.$

We can use FDR to test whether the protocol correctly authenticates the two agents. FDR takes as two inputs, a specification and an implementation, and test whether the implementation refines the specification. In this paper we are working in the traces model of CSP [6], so checking for refinement amounts to testing whether each trace of the implementation is also a trace of the specification.

To test whether the protocol correctly authenticates the responder, we need to find a specification that allows only those traces where the initiator A commits to a session with B only if B has indeed taken part in the protocol run. The initiator committing to a session is represented by an $I\_commit.A.B$ event; the responder taking part in a run of the protocol with A is represented by $R\_running.A.B$. Thus the authenticity of the responder can be tested using the specification AR:

$$AR_0 \; \hat{=} \; R\_running.A.B \rightarrow I\_commit.A.B \rightarrow AR_0,$$
$$A_1 \; \hat{=} \; \{R\_running.A.B, I\_commit.A.B\},$$
$$AR \; \hat{=} \; AR_0 \, ||| \, RUN(\Sigma \setminus A_1).$$

AR_0 expresses that an $I\_commit.A.B$ event should only occur after an $R\_running.A.B$ event; interleaving this specification with $RUN(\Sigma \setminus A_1)$ (where Σ is the set of all events) allows all other events to occur in an arbitrary order.

FDR can be used to verify that $SYSTEM$ refines AR, and so the protocol does indeed correctly authenticate the responder[4].

We now consider authentication of the initiator. The protocol should ensure that the responder B commits to a session with initiator A only if A took part in the protocol run. Formally, an $R\_commit.A.B$ event should occur only if there has been a corresponding $I\_running.A.B$ event. This requirement is captured by the specification AI:

$$AI_0 \; \hat{=} \; I\_running.A.B \rightarrow R\_commit.A.B \rightarrow AI_0,$$
$$A_2 \; \hat{=} \; \{I\_running.A.B, R\_commit.A.B\},$$
$$AI \; \hat{=} \; AI_0 \, ||| \, RUN(\Sigma \setminus A_2).$$

---

[3]Our notation differs a little from [6]: we write $P \, |[\, A \,]| \, Q$ for the parallel composition of P and Q, synchronizing on the set of events A; we write $\{c_1, \ldots, c_n\}$ for the set of all communications over channels $c_1, \ldots, c_n$.

[4]The FDR input files used for this case study can be obtained from URL http://www.comlab.ox.ac.uk/oucl/users/gavin.lowe/Security/NSPKP/index.html.

FDR can be used to discover that $SYSTEM$ does *not* refine AI. It finds that after the trace:

$$\langle user.A.I\,,\ I\_running.A.I\,,$$
$$intercept.Msg1.A.I.Encrypt.K_i.N_a.A\,,$$
$$fake.Msg1.A.B.Encrypt.K_b.N_a.A\,,$$
$$intercept.Msg2.B.A.Encrypt.K_a.N_a.N_b\,,$$
$$fake.Msg2.I.A.Encrypt.K_a.N_a.N_b\,,$$
$$intercept.Msg3.A.I.Encrypt.K_i.N_b\,,$$
$$fake.Msg3.A.B.Encrypt.K_b.N_b\rangle$$

the system can perform $R\_commit.A.B$. Thus the responder B commits to a session with A even though A is not trying to establish a session with B (there has been no corresponding $I\_running.A.B$ event).

We can rewrite this attack as follows. The attack consists of the interleaving of two runs, which we write as α and β. (We use the term *run* for a particular instance of the protocol; we use the term *attack*, for any sequence of events leading to a breach of security.) In run α, A tries to establish a session with I, while in run β, the intruder impersonates A to establish a false session with B. We write, for example, $\beta.2$ to represent message 2 of run β; we write $I(A)$ to represent the intruder imitating A.

Message $\alpha.1$.	$A \rightarrow I$	:	$A.I.\{N_a.A\}_{PK(I)}$
Message $\beta.1$.	$I(A) \rightarrow B$	:	$A.B.\{N_a.A\}_{PK(B)}$
Message $\beta.2$.	$B \rightarrow I(A)$	:	$B.A.\{N_a.N_b\}_{PK(A)}$
Message $\alpha.2$.	$I \rightarrow A$	:	$I.A.\{N_a.N_b\}_{PK(A)}$
Message $\alpha.3$.	$A \rightarrow I$	:	$A.I.\{N_b\}_{PK(I)}$
Message $\beta.3$.	$I(A) \rightarrow B$	:	$A.B.\{N_b\}_{PK(B)}.$

In message $\alpha.1$, A tries to establish a session with I, sending the none N_a encrypted with I's key. In message $\beta.1$, the intruder imitates A to start a run of the protocol with B, sending the same nonce N_a. B responds by choosing a new nonce N_b, and returning it in message $\beta.2$. The intruder cannot decrypt this message to obtain N_b, but instead uses A as an oracle, by replaying this message in message $\alpha.2$; note that this message is of the form expected by A in run α. A decrypts the message to obtain N_b, and returns this to I in message $\alpha.3$. I can then decrypt this message to obtain N_b, which he returns to B in message $\beta.3$, thus completing run β of the protocol. Hence B believes that he has correctly carried out a run of the protocol with A.

4 A corrected protocol

It is easy to adapt the protocol to prevent the attack found above; we simply include the identity of the responder within the encrypted part of message 2:

$$\text{Message 1.} \quad A \to B \; : \; A.B.\{N_a.A\}_{PK(B)}$$
$$\text{Message 2.} \quad B \to A \; : \; B.A.\{N_a.N_b.B\}_{PK(A)}$$
$$\text{Message 3.} \quad A \to B \; : \; A.B.\{N_b\}_{PK(B)} \, .$$

This prevents the above attack, because message $\beta.2$ would become:

$$\text{Message } \beta.2. \quad B \to I(A) \; : \; B.A.\{N_a.N_b.B\}_{PK(A)} \, ,$$

and the intruder can not successfully replay this in message $\alpha.2$, because A is expecting a message containing I's identity.

We may adapt our CSP representation of the protocol and the intruder. FDR then fails to find any attacks on the protocol in the case where the initiator A and responder B each have a *single* nonce, and so can take part in a *single* run of the protocol. We conclude that the protocol is safe, at least for this small system.

The question remains, though: is a more general system safe from attack? If the agents had more nonces, could the intruder obtain enough knowledge from several runs to be able to attack the protocol? How about if there were more than just the two honest agents involved? Or how about if the same agent could act both as initiator and responder?

These kind of questions arise in many model checking problems, and are not unique to the area of security protocols. We may typically use a tool to verify a small system of fixed size; but this does not necessarily tell us that larger systems are also correct. One solution is to prove—by some method—that if a system of arbitrary size were incorrect, then this would imply that the small system were also incorrect. Following this idea, in Section 6 we prove that if there were an attack on a more general system running the Needham-Schroeder protocol, then there would be an attack on the small system we considered above. But first, we define some notation, and prove a useful result concerning the way in which an intruder responds to a nonce challenge. We adopt a very general setting, so that our results may be applicable to a wide class of protocols.

5 A logic for analyzing protocols

5.1 Messages

We begin by defining the data type of messages. A message may be an atom, the concatenation of two simpler messages, or a message encrypted with a key. We may define the set Msg of messages by the following BNF expression:

$$a \; \in \; Atom \; ::= \; C \mid N \mid k \mid \ldots,$$
$$m \; \in \; Msg \; ::= \; a \mid m.m \mid \{m\}_k,$$

where C ranges over the set *Agent* of agent names, k over the set *Key* of keys, and N over the set *Nonce* of nonces. We take the concatenation operator "." to be associative. For each key k, we assume the existence of an inverse k^{-1}, such that a message encrypted with k can be decrypted with k^{-1}: in symmetric crypto-systems, each key is its own inverse; in public key systems, the public and secret keys are inverses.

We may also define what it means for a message to *contain* another:

$$a \text{ contains } m \ \hat{=} \ a = m,$$
$$m_1.m_2 \text{ contains } m \ \hat{=} \ m_1.m_2 = m \lor m_1 \text{ contains } m \lor m_2 \text{ contains } m,$$
$$\{m_1\}_k \text{ contains } m \ \hat{=} \ \{m_1\}_k = m \lor m_1 \text{ contains } m.$$

We may use this to define the submessages of a particular message:

$$\text{sub-msgs}(m) \ \hat{=} \ \{m' \in Msg \mid m \text{ contains } m'\}.$$

We will want to be able to discuss which messages an intruder can produce given the messages that he has seen so far. We write $B \vdash m$ to represent that the intruder may derive message m from the finite set of messages B. The following definition is adapted from [13].

$$m \in B \ \Rightarrow \ B \vdash m, \tag{1}$$
$$B \vdash m \land B \vdash m' \ \Rightarrow \ B \vdash m.m', \tag{2}$$
$$B \vdash m.m' \ \Rightarrow \ B \vdash m \land B \vdash m', \tag{3}$$
$$B \vdash m \land B \vdash k \ \Rightarrow \ B \vdash \{m\}_k, \tag{4}$$
$$B \vdash \{m\}_k \land B \vdash k^{-1} \ \Rightarrow \ B \vdash m. \tag{5}$$

If the intruder has already seen message m (i.e. $m \in B$) then he can produce that message (rule 1). If he can produce both halves of a concatenated message, then he can produce the entier message (rule 2), and vice versa (rule 3). If he can produce a message m and a key k, then he can encrypt m with k (rule 4). If we can produce an encrypted message and the corresponding decrypting key, then he can decrypt the message (rule 5). We also write $B \nvdash m$ for $\neg (B \vdash m)$.

We state a few lemmas about the $\vdash$ relation that will prove useful. These may be proved by rule induction.

Lemma 1: If m may be derived from some set of information B, then it may be derived from any larger set of information:

$$B \vdash m \land B \subseteq B' \ \Rightarrow \ B' \vdash m.$$

Lemma 2: Derived messages may be used in subsequent derivations:

$$B \vdash m' \land B \cup \{m'\} \vdash m \ \Rightarrow \ B \vdash m.$$

Lemma 3: If m may be derived from B, but some sub-message X may not:

$$B \vdash m \ \wedge \ m \text{ contains } X \ \wedge \ B \nvdash X,$$

then there is some encrypted sub-message Y of m, which contains X, may be derived from B, is contained in some element of B, but which cannot be decrypted:

$$\exists Y \in \text{sub-msgs}(m) \bullet Y \text{ contains } X \wedge B \vdash Y \wedge \exists b \in B \bullet b \text{ contains } Y$$
$$\wedge \exists Z \in Msg \,;\, k \in Key \bullet Y = \{Z\}_k \wedge B \nvdash k^{-1}.$$

Lemma 4: Suppose $A \cup B \vdash x$, x contains a, and $a \in Atom$. Then either some element of B contains a key, some sub-message of x containing a may be derived from A, or a is contained in some element of B:

$$\exists k \in Key \bullet \exists b \in B \bullet b \text{ contains } k \wedge A \nvdash k \wedge A \cup B \vdash k$$
$$\vee \ \exists z \in \text{sub-msgs}(x) \bullet z \text{ contains } a \wedge A \vdash z$$
$$\vee \ \exists b \in B \bullet b \text{ contains } a \wedge A \nvdash a.$$

5.2 Traces

We let $RunId$ be the space of *run identifiers*, ranged over by α, β, etc. We define a *message number* to be a (run identifier, natural number) pair.

$$MsgNo \ \widehat{=} \ RunId \times \mathbf{N}.$$

We write $\alpha.i$ for message i of run α.

As above, we will write $I(A)$ to represent the intruder imitating agent A. We define the set $Agent^+$ to contain all agent identifiers, and all such $I(A)$:

$$Agent^+ \ \widehat{=} \ Agent \cup \{I(A) \mid A \in Agent \setminus \{I\}\}.$$

We also define the set of agent identifiers representing the intruder:

$$IntId \ \widehat{=} \ \{I\} \cup \{I(A) \mid A \in Agent \setminus \{I\}\}.$$

We define a *communication* to be a quadruple where the fields are: (1) the message number, (2) the sender of the communication, where $I(A)$ represents the intruder imitating A, (3) the receiver, where $I(A)$ represents the intruder intercepting a message meant for A, and (4) the actual message that is sent:

$$Communication \ \widehat{=} \ MsgNo \times Agent^+ \times Agent^+ \times Msg.$$

When convenient, we will represent the communication $(\alpha.i, A, B, m)$ by the more conventional, and visually more pleasing:

$$\text{Message } \alpha.i. \quad A \to B \,:\, m.$$

We define a *run* to be a sequence s of such communications where all the communications have the same run identifier:

$$\exists \alpha \cdot \forall (\beta.i, C, D, m) \text{ in } s \cdot \beta = \alpha,$$

and the honest agents follow the protocol.

We define a *trace* to be a sequence of communications, formed from the interleaving of several runs with distinct run identifiers. We let tr, tr' range over traces.

We may abstract the data included in the communications of a particular run:

$$\mathsf{data}(tr) \;\hat{=}\; \{m \mid \exists \alpha, i, A, B \cdot (\alpha.i, A, B, m) \text{ in } tr\}.$$

We make the assumption that when an honest agent introduces a new nonce into a run of the protocol, the nonce really is freshly chosen; this means that the agent will introduce different nonces into different runs, that no other honest agent will introduce the same nonce, and that the intruder does not initially know the value of the nonce. We term this assumption the *nonce assumption*.

5.3 Intruders

We assume that the intruder has some initial knowledge, which may be represented by a set of atoms IK_0. This will normally include the identities of all agents in the system, all the public keys, and I's own secret key. We may define the intruder's knowledge after a particular trace:

$$\mathsf{knowledge\text{-}after}\, tr \;\hat{=}\; \{m \mid IK_0 \cup \mathsf{data}(tr) \vdash m\}.$$

The intruder knows the message m after trace tr if m may be derived from the data in tr and I's initial knowledge.

We define a trace to be *valid* if the intruder only produces messages that are derivable from the knowledge that it has acquired:

$\mathsf{valid}(tr) \;\hat{=}$
$\qquad \forall tr' \in Trace \,;\, \alpha.i \in Msg\_No \,;\, m \in Msg \,;\, I' \in IntId \,;\, C \in Agent \cdot$
$\qquad tr' ^\frown \langle (\alpha.i, I', C, m) \rangle \leq tr \Rightarrow m \in \mathsf{knowledge\text{-}after}\, tr'.$

If the intruder sends a message m after observing tr', then m is in the intruder's knowledge at that point.

We write I learns X from $\alpha.i$ if the intruder learns the piece of information X from message number $\alpha.i$:

$\qquad (I \text{ learns } X \text{ from } \alpha.i)(tr) \;\hat{=}$
$\qquad\qquad \exists m \in Msg \,;\, A, B \in Agent \,;\, tr' \in Trace \cdot$
$\qquad\qquad\quad tr' ^\frown \langle (\alpha.i, A, B, m) \rangle \leq tr$
$\qquad\qquad\quad \wedge\, X \notin \mathsf{knowledge\text{-}after}\, tr'$
$\qquad\qquad\quad \wedge\, X \in \mathsf{knowledge\text{-}after}(tr' ^\frown \langle (\alpha.i, A, B, m) \rangle).$

We drop the argument *tr* when it is obvious from context.

We write I says X in $\alpha.i$ if the intruder sends the communication $\alpha.i$, which contains X as a sub-message:

$$(I \text{ says } X \text{ in } \alpha.i)(tr) \;\hat{=}\; \exists m \in Msg; I' \in IntId; A \in Agent \bullet$$
$$(\alpha.i, I', A, m) \text{ in } tr \wedge m \text{ contains } X.$$

5.4 Nonce challenges

We now prove a result concerning the way in which an intruder meets a nonce challenge. We make some additional assumptions about the protocol in question:

- The encrypted parts of differently numbered messages in the protocol are textually distinct: if M_i is a valid message i, and M_j is a valid message j, and M_i contains $\{M\}_k$ and M_j contains $\{M\}_k$ then $i = j$. Thus it is always possible to tell which message an encrypted part comes from; this means, for example, that the intruder cannot replay some encrypted text taken from a message 1, and have it interpreted as a message 2.

- All runs of the protocol have essentially the same form.

- The intruder does not learn any additional keys during a trace: if $k \in$ knowledge-after tr then $k \in IK_0$.

Note that the Needham-Schroeder Public Key Protocol satisfies these assumptions: that the intruder does not learn any additional keys during a trace follows from the fact that that secret keys are never passed during the protocol (this can be proved formally using Lemma 4).

Theorem 5: Consider a valid trace tr that includes a nonce challenge, met by the intruder:

$$\text{Message } \alpha.i. \qquad A \to I(B) \;:\; M_1(N)$$
$$\text{Message } \alpha.j. \qquad I(B) \to A \quad\; :\; M_2(N),$$

where $M_1(N)$ and $M_2(N)$ contain the nonce N:

$$M_1(N) \text{ contains } N \;\wedge\; M_2(N) \text{ contains } N,$$

and the nonce is first introduced in message $\alpha.i$, and first returned in $\alpha.j$. Suppose further that

$$\forall z \in \text{sub-msgs}(M_2(N)) \bullet$$
$$z \text{ contains } N \Rightarrow IK_0 \cup \{z\} \vdash N \vee IK_0 \cup \{z\} \vdash M_2(N). \tag{6}$$

Then one of the following holds:

1. The intruder can produce either N or $M_2(N)$ immediately from message $\alpha.i$:

$$I \text{ learns } N \text{ from } \alpha.i \ \lor \ I \text{ learns } M_2(N) \text{ from } \alpha.i.$$

2. The intruder replays some encrypted sub-message Y of $\alpha.i$ in message i of some other run β:

$$\exists Y \cdot M_1(N) \text{ contains } Y \land Y \text{ contains } N \land I \text{ says } Y \text{ in } \beta.i$$
$$\land \exists Z \in Msg \, ; k \in Key \cdot Y = \{Z\}_k \land k^{-1} \notin IK_0,$$

and learns either N or $M_2(N)$ from a later message of β:

$$\exists k > i \cdot I \text{ learns } N \text{ from } \beta.k \ \lor \ I \text{ learns } M_2(N) \text{ from } \beta.k.$$

Proof: Assume the conditions of the theorem. By the nonce assumption, the intruder does not know the value of N or $M_2(N)$ before message $\alpha.i$. Clearly, the intruder must, at some point, learn $M_2(N)$ in order to produce message $\alpha.j$. Suppose the intruder first learns either N or $M_2(N)$ from message $\beta.k$ with contents M_3:

$$\text{Message } \beta.k. \quad C \to D \ : \ M_3.$$

Formally:

$$tr' ^\frown \langle (\beta.k, C, D, M_3) \rangle \leq tr$$
$$\land \ N, M_2(N) \notin \text{knowledge-after } tr'$$
$$\land \ (N \in \text{knowledge-after}(tr' ^\frown \langle (\beta.k, C, D, M_3) \rangle))$$
$$\lor \ M_2(N) \in \text{knowledge-after}(tr' ^\frown \langle (\beta.k, C, D, M_3) \rangle)).$$

If $\alpha.i = \beta.k$ then we have case 1. Otherwise, $\beta.k$ occurs after $\alpha.i$, but before $\alpha.j$.

We now show that M_3 contains N. If the intruder learns N from message $\beta.k$, i.e. $IK_0 \cup \text{data} \, tr' \cup \{M_3\} \vdash N$, then the result follows from Lemma 4 and the assumption that the intruder's key knowledge is constant. If the intruder learns $M_2(N)$ from message $\beta.k$, i.e. $IK_0 \cup \text{data} \, tr' \cup \{M_3\} \vdash M_2(N)$, then again from Lemma 4 we have:

$$\exists z \in \text{sub-msgs} \, M_2(N) \cdot z \text{ contains } N \land IK_0 \cup \text{data} \, tr' \vdash z$$
$$\lor \ M_3 \text{ contains } N.$$

But the first disjunct and equation 6 would imply that $IK_0 \cup \text{data} \, tr' \vdash N$ or $IK_0 \cup \text{data} \, tr' \vdash M_2(N)$, contradicting the above. Hence M_3 contains N.

By the assumption that $\alpha.j$ is the first message after $\alpha.i$ that contains N, we have $\alpha \neq \beta$. From the nonce assumption, we must have that the nonce N

is introduced into run β by the intruder, say in message $\beta.l$ $(l < k)$, following trace tr'':

$$\exists I' \in IntId \,;\, E \in Agent \cdot tr'' ^\frown \langle (\beta.l, I', E, M_4(N)) \rangle \leq tr'$$
$$\wedge \, M_4(N) \text{ contains } N.$$

That is:

$$\text{Message } \beta.l. \qquad I' \rightarrow E \ : \ M_4(N).$$

By assumption, the trace is valid, so $IK_0 \cup \text{data } tr'' \vdash M_4(N)$. Hence, from Lemma 3 and the fact that the intruder does not know N after tr'', $M_4(N)$ contains some encrypted sub-message Y of some previous message $\gamma.m$ with contents $M_5(N)$:

$$\exists Y \cdot M_4(N) \text{ contains } Y \wedge Y \text{ contains } N \wedge Y \in \text{knowledge-after } tr''$$
$$\wedge \, \exists F, G \in Agent \cdot (\gamma.m, F, G, M_5(N)) \text{ in } tr'' \wedge M_5(N) \text{ contains } Y$$
$$\wedge \, \exists Z \in Msg \,;\, k \in Key \cdot Y = \{Z\}_k \wedge k^{-1} \notin \text{knowledge-after } tr''.$$

That is:

$$\text{Message } \gamma.m. \qquad F \rightarrow G \ : \ M_5(N).$$

By the assumption that encrypted components of differently numbered messages are textually distinct, we must have that $M_4(N)$ and $M_5(N)$ have the same message number, i.e. $l = m$; hence $\beta \neq \gamma$. Either $\alpha = \gamma$ or $\alpha \neq \gamma$; we show that the latter case leads to a contradiction.

So suppose that $\alpha \neq \gamma$. By the nonce assumption, N must have been introduced into run γ by the intruder, say in message $\gamma.n$ $(n < l)$. By the assumption that all runs take the same form, message $\beta.n$ must also contain N. But this contradicts the assumption that N was introduced into β in message $\beta.l$.

Hence we have that $\alpha = \gamma$. Message $\alpha.m$ precedes $\alpha.j$ and contains N, and so must be $\alpha.i$. Collecting all the above information gives us case 2.

□

6 Verifying systems of arbitrary size

In this section we show that if there is an attack upon a system of arbitrary size running the corrected protocol given in Section 4, then there is an attack upon the small system described above, with a single initiator A and a single responder B, each of which has a single nonce, and so can carry out a single run of the protocol. The proofs proceed by considering a run leading to a failure of authentication, and considering how many extra runs are needed for the intruder to learn any additional information it uses.

6.1 Attacks upon the initiator

In this section we show that if the intruder may imitate the responder to attack the initiator in a system of arbitrary size, then there is a similar attack upon the small system described above.

Consider a run, α, where the intruder imitates the responder B to attack the initiator A:

$$
\begin{aligned}
&\text{Message } \alpha.1. \qquad A \to I(B) \;:\; A.B.\{N_a.A\}_{PK(B)} \\
&\text{Message } \alpha.2. \quad I(B) \to A \quad:\; B.A.\{N_a.N_b.B\}_{PK(A)} \\
&\text{Message } \alpha.3. \qquad A \to I(B) \;:\; A.B.\{N_b\}_{PK(B)}.
\end{aligned}
$$

Note that the intruder only needs to send message 2 in this run, so the only additional runs necessary are those that are needed in order to produce $B.A.\{N_a.N_b.B\}_{PK(A)}$.

The intruder cannot decrypt message $\alpha.1$, because he does not know B's secret key. Hence he learns neither N_a nor $B.A.\{N_a.N_b.B\}_{PK(A)}$ from $\alpha.1$:

$$\neg \,(I \text{ learns } N_a \text{ from } \alpha.1) \;\wedge\; \neg \,(I \text{ learns } B.A.\{N_a.N_b.B\}_{PK(A)} \text{ from } \alpha.1),$$

so from Theorem 5, the intruder must replay the encrypted part of message $\alpha.1$ in message 1 of another run, β say, and learn either N_a or $B.A.\{N_a.N_b.B\}_{PK(A)}$ from message $\beta.2$:

$$
\begin{aligned}
&I \text{ says } \{N_a.A\}_{PK(B)} \text{ in } \beta.1 \\
&\wedge\, (I \text{ learns } N_a \text{ from } \beta.2 \;\vee\; I \text{ learns } B.A.\{N_a.N_b.B\}_{PK(A)} \text{ from } \beta.2).
\end{aligned}
$$

Note that the responder in run β must be B, because message $\beta.1$ is encrypted with B's public key. The intruder does not need any additional information in order to carry out this second run, so only the two runs are needed.

Thus if the intruder can imitate the responder B to attack A, then such an attack would have been found by considering the small system above.

6.2 Attacks upon the responder

Consider an attack where the intruder succeeds in imitating the initiator A in a run, α say, of the protocol with responder B:

$$
\begin{aligned}
&\text{Message } \alpha.1. \qquad I(A) \to B \quad:\; A.B.\{N_a.A\}_{PK(B)} \\
&\text{Message } \alpha.2. \qquad B \to I(A) \quad:\; B.A.\{N_a.N_b.B\}_{PK(A)} \\
&\text{Message } \alpha.3. \qquad I(A) \to B \quad:\; A.B.\{N_b\}_{PK(B)}.
\end{aligned}
$$

Note that the intruder only needs to produce Messages 1 and 3 in this run, so the only additional runs necessary are those that are needed in order for the intruder to learn something that it sends in one of these messages.

Firstly consider the nonce handshake using N_b. The intruder cannot decrypt message $\alpha.2$, so he learns neither N_b nor $A.B.\{N_b\}_{PK(B)}$ from $\alpha.2$:

$$\neg \ (I \text{ learns } N_b \text{ from } \alpha.2) \ \wedge \ \neg \ (I \text{ learns } A.B.\{N_b\}_{PK(B)} \text{ from } \alpha.2),$$

so from Theorem 5 the intruder must replay the encrypted part of message $\alpha.2$ in message 2 of some other run, β say, and learn N_b or $A.B.\{N_b\}_{PK(B)}$ from message $\beta.3$:

$$I \text{ says } \{N_a.N_b.B\}_{PK(A)} \text{ in } \beta.2$$
$$\wedge \ (I \text{ learns } N_b \text{ from } \beta.3 \vee I \text{ learns } A.B.\{N_b\}_{PK(B)} \text{ from } \beta.3).$$

Note that the initiator of run β must be A, because message $\beta.2$ is encrypted with A's public key. Further, from the form of message $\beta.2$ we see that A must believe that he is communicating with B. Hence run β is of the form:

$$\begin{array}{lll} \text{Message } \beta.1. & A \to I(B) & : \ A.B.\{N_a.A\}_{PK(B)} \\ \text{Message } \beta.2. & I(B) \to A & : \ B.A.\{N_a.N_b.B\}_{PK(A)} \\ \text{Message } \beta.3. & A \to I(B) & : \ A.B.\{N_b\}_{PK(B)}. \end{array}$$

Now we see that the intruder learns the component $\{N_a.A\}_{PK(B)}$ from message $\beta.1$, and replays this in $\alpha.1$, and so only these two runs are necessary for the intruder to learn all the knowledge it uses in the attack. Thus if the intruder can imitate the initiator A to attack the responder B, then such an attack would have been found by considering the small system above.

In fact, in this case, we have shown that if there were an attack, it would be of the above form; but the above does not lead to any error of authentication; we may deduce that there is no such attack on the system— even without the aid of FDR.

6.3 Summary

Above we showed that in order to discover an attack upon the protocol, it is enough to consider a system with a single initiator and responder, each with a single nonce.

We now prove a similar result concerning the intruder: it is enough to consider an intruder with a single identity, I say, and a single public key, K_i say. Thus, two intruders working together are no more powerful than a single intruder. Further, it is enough to consider an intruder who initially knows a single nonce, N_i say.

We make the assumption that the honest agents act the same way regardless of the actual values of nonces introduced by other agents; we term this *data independence*.

Suppose, then, that there is a successful attack where the intruder uses more than one identity, more than one public key, and/or more than one nonce. Consider the attack where each intruder's identity is renamed to I, each intruder's key is renamed to K_i, and each intruder's nonce is renamed to N_i. Then, by the data independence assumption, each run proceeds as before. Further, at each stage or the new attack, the intruder's knowledge is related to his knowledge at the corresponding stage of the original attack, in the obvious way, i.e. by the above renaming (this can be proved formally from the definition of the $\vdash$ relation). Thus the intruder is able to produce all of his messages in the new attack. Hence the new attack is indeed successful, and is made by an attacker with a single identity, single public key, and single nonce.

Putting together all these results, we deduce that if there is an attack on a system running the protocol, we would have found it by applying FDR to the small system in Section 4. Hence the protocol is secure.

7 Conclusion

In this paper we have used the Failures Divergences Refinement Checker for CSP to analyse the Needham-Schroeder Public-Key Protocol. We have encoded the protocol and an intruder in CSP, and used FDR to discover a security flaw. We have adapted the protocol to remove this flaw, and used FDR to verify that there are no attacks upon a small system running the protocol. We then proved that this was enough to prove that there are no attacks upon a more general system.

We should be clear as to precisely what we have proved. We have proved that the protocol in Section 4 is secure subject to the assumptions we have made about the method of encryption used, encapsulated in the definition of the $\vdash$ relation. We have assumed that the encryption used is reasonable, in that the intruder is unable to guess the values of keys it does not know. Further, we assume that secret keys are indeed kept secret. We have also assumed that the intruder may not alter an encrypted message before replaying it (unless the message is encrypted using the intruder's key). However, if Cipher Block Chaining is used (see e.g. [14]) then (subject to certain assumptions) it is possible to split an encrypted message into encrypted sub-messages; using the notation of this paper:

$$B \vdash \{m_1.m_2\}_k \ \Rightarrow \ B \vdash \{m_1\}_k \wedge B \vdash \{m_2\}_k.$$

Thus, our proof in not valid in this case. See [1] for examples of attacks upon protocols using CBC.

We believe that this method of analyzing security protocols is very practical. Encoding the protocol and the intruder in CSP is normally straightforward. And the tests using FDR are fast, typically taking less than two minutes. The proof that the security of a small system implies the security of an arbitrarily-sized system is by hand, rather than being fully automatic.

However, we believe that this proof is considerably simpler than a direct proof of the security of an arbitrarily-sized system: we effectively prove the general form an attack must take, and use FDR to do the tedious checking of details.

We intend to analyse more protocols using this approach. In particular, we would like to produce more lemmas and theorems that are useful in proving results concerning the size of system it is necessary to consider in order to be sure that there are no attacks upon a protocol; eventually, we hope to identify properties of protocols (concerning, for example, the number of nonce challenges) that are enough to give us such results directly.

8 REFERENCES

[1] Colin Boyd. Hidden assumptions in cryptographic protocols. *Proceedings of the IEE*, 137, Part E(6):433–436, November 1990.

[2] Michael Burrows, Martín Abadi, and Roger Needham. A logic of authentication. *Proceedings of the Royal Society of London A*, 426:233–271, 1989. A preliminary version appeared as Digital Equipment Corporation Systems Research Center report No. 39, 1989.

[3] Dorothy E. Denning and Giovanni Maria Sacco. Timestamps in key distribution protocols. *Communications of the ACM*, 24(8):533–536, 1981.

[4] W. Diffie and M. Hellman. New directions in cryptography. *IEEE Transactions on Information Theory*, 22:644–654, 1976.

[5] Formal Systems (Europe) Ltd. *Failures Divergence Refinement—User Manual and Tutorial*, 1993. Version 1.3.

[6] C. A. R. Hoare. *Communicating Sequential Processes*. Prentice Hall, 1985.

[7] Gavin Lowe. An attack on the Needham-Schroeder public-key authentication protocol. *Information Processing Letters*, 56:131–133, 1995.

[8] Roger Needham and Michael Schroeder. Using encryption for authentication in large networks of computers. *Communications of the ACM*, 21(12):993–999, 1978.

[9] R. L. Rivest, A. Shamir, and L. Adleman. A method for obtaining digital signatures and public-key cryptosystems. *Communications of the ACM*, 21(2):120–126, February 1978.

[10] A. W. Roscoe. Developing and verifying protocols in CSP. In *Proceedings of Mierlo workshop on protocols*. TU Eindhoven, 1993.

[11] A. W. Roscoe. Model-checking CSP. In *A Classical Mind, Essays in Honour of C. A. R. Hoare*. Prentice-Hall, 1994.

[12] A. W. Roscoe and Helen MacCarthy. Verifying a replicated database: A case study in model-checking CSP. Submitted for publication.

[13] Steve Schneider. Security properties and CSP. In preparation, 1995.

[14] Bruce Schneier. *Applied Cryptography*. Wiley, 1994.

Automatic Compositional Verification of Some Security Properties

R. Focardi*
R. Gorrieri*

ABSTRACT [1] The Compositional Security Checker (CSC for short) is a semantic tool for the automatic verification of some compositional information flow properties. The specifications given as inputs to CSC are terms of the Security Process Algebra, a language suited for the specification of systems where actions belong to two different levels of confidentiality. The information flow security properties which can be verified by CSC are some of those classified in [4]. They are derivations of some classic notions, e.g. Non Interference [6]. The tool is based on the same architecture of the Concurrency Workbench [2], from which some modules have been integrally imported. The usefulness of the tool is tested with the significative case-study of an access-monitor.

1   Introduction

Security is a crucial property of system behaviour, requiring a strict control over the information flow among parts of the system. The main problem is to limit, and possibly to avoid, the damages produced by malicious programs, called *Trojan Horses*, which try to broadcast secret information. There are several approaches to solve this problem.

In the *Discretionary Access Control* security (DAC for short), every *subject* decides the access properties of its *objects*. An example of DAC is the file management in Unix where a user can decide the access possibilities of her/his files. So, if a user executes a Trojan Horse program, this can modify the security properties of user's objects.

A solution to this problem is the *Mandatory Access Control* (MAC for short), where access rules are imposed by the system. An example of MAC is *Multilevel Security* [1]: every object is bounded to a security level, and so every subject is; information can flow from a certain object to a certain

*Dipartimento di Scienze dell'Informazione, Università di Bologna, Piazza di Porta San Donato 5, I – 40127 Bologna (Italy). e_mail:{focardi,gorrieri}@cs.unibo.it
[1] Research supported in part by CNR and MURST.

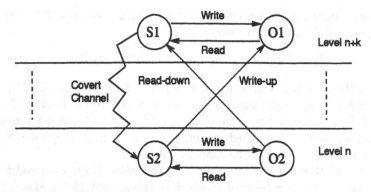

FIGURE 1. Information flows in multilevel security.

subject only if the level of the subject is greater than the level of the object. So a Trojan Horse, which operates at a certain level, has no way to *downgrade* information, and its action is restricted inside such a level. There are two access rules: *No Read Up* (a subject cannot read data from an upper level object) and *No Write Down* (a subject cannot write data to a lower level object).

However, these access rules are not enough. It could be possible to indirectly transmit information using some system *side effect*. For example, if two levels – 'high' and 'low' – share some finite storage resource, it is possible to transmit data from level 'high' to level 'low' by using the 'resource full' error message. For a high level transmitter, it is sufficient to alternatively fill or empty the resource in order to transmit a '1' or a '0' datum. Simultaneously, the low level receiver tries to write on the resource, decoding every error message as a '1' and every successful write as a '0'. It is clear that such indirect ways of transmission, called *covert channels*, do not violate the two multilevel access rules (see Figure 1). Therefore it is necessary to integrate a MAC discipline with a covert channel analysis (see e.g. [10]).

An alternative, more general approach to security requires to control directly the whole flow of information, rather than the accesses of subjects to objects. To make this, it is necessary to choose a formal model of system behaviour and to define the information flow on such a model. By imposing some information flow rule, we can control any kind of transmission, be it direct or indirect.

In the literature, there are many different definitions of this kind based on several system models (see e.g. [6, 11]). In [4] we have rephrased them in the uniform setting of *Security Process Algebra* (SPA, for short), then compared and classified. SPA is an extension of CCS [9] which permits to describe systems where actions belong to two different levels of confidentiality.

For some of the investigated information flow properties, we provided useful algebraic characterizations. They are all of the following form. Let E be an SPA process term, let X be a security property, let $\approx$ be a semantic equivalence among process terms and let $\mathcal{C}_X$ and $\mathcal{D}_X$ be two SPA contexts for property X. Then, we can say:

$$E \text{ is } X\text{-secure if and only if } \mathcal{C}_X[E] \approx \mathcal{D}_X[E].$$

Hence, checking the X-security of E is reduced to the "standard" problem of checking semantic equivalence between two terms having E as a subterm. In recent years a certain number of tools for checking semantic equivalence have been presented; among them, the Concurrency Workbench (CW for short) [2] is one of the most famous.

The aim of this work is to present a tool called Compositional Security Checker which can be used to check automatically (finite state) SPA specifications against some information flow security properties. The tool has the same modular architecture of CW (Version 6.1), from which some modules have been integrally imported and some others only modified.

The tool is equipped with a parser, which transforms an SPA specification into a parse-tree; then, for the parsed specification CSC builds the labelled transition system following the operational rules defined in Plotkin' SOS style. When a user wants to check if an SPA process E is X-secure, CSC first provides operational semantic descriptions to the terms $\mathcal{C}_X[E]$ and $\mathcal{D}_X[E]$ in the form of two lts's; then verifies the semantic equivalence of $\mathcal{C}_X[E]$ and $\mathcal{D}_X[E]$ using their lts representations.

An interesting feature of CSC is the exploitation of the compositionality of some security property. The main problem in the verification of security properties is the exponential state explosion due to parallel composition. As an example consider two agents E_1 and E_2; the number of states of their parallel composition $E_1|E_2$ is equal to the product of the states of E_1 and E_2. Now if we have a compositional security property X, i.e. such that $F_1|F_2$ is X-secure whenever F_1 and F_2 are X-secure, then we can apply the following strategy: check the X-security of E_1 and E_2; if it is satisfied conclude that $E_1|E_2$ is X-secure, otherwise check the X-security of the whole agent $E_1|E_2$. Using this strategy for compositional security properties, CSC is able to avoid, in some cases, the exponential state explosion due to parallel composition operator.

The paper is organized as follows. In Section 2 we present SPA. In Section 3 we recall from [4] some of the security properties which are verified by CSC giving some examples. Section 4.1 reports the input-output behavior of CSC, while in Section 4.2 we describe the architecture of the tool. The implementation of the security predicates is the subject of Section 5. Then, a sample session with the interactive tool is described in Section 6.1 and Section 6.2 is devoted to a case-study (access-monitor). Finally, Section 7 is about the state explosion problem and the compositional algorithm.

2 SPA and Semantic Equivalences

In the following, systems will be specified using the *Security Process Algebra* (SPA for short), a slight extension of Milner's CCS [9]. SPA includes two more operators, namely the hiding operator E/L of CSP [7] and the (new) input restriction operator $E \setminus_I L$, which are useful in characterizing some security properties in an algebraic style. Intuitively $E \setminus_I L$ can execute all the actions process E is able to do, provided that they are not inputs in L. Moreover the set of visible actions is partitioned into high level actions and low level ones in order to specify multilevel systems. [2]

SPA syntax is based on the following elements: a set $I = \{a, b, \ldots\}$ of *input* actions, a set $O = \{\bar{a}, \bar{b}, \ldots\}$ of *output* actions, a set $\mathcal{L} = I \cup O$ of *visible* actions, (ranged over by α) and the usual function $\bar{\cdot} : \mathcal{L} \to \mathcal{L}$ such that $a \in I \implies \bar{a} \in O$ and $\bar{a} \in O \implies \bar{\bar{a}} = a \in I$; two sets Act_H and Act_L of high and low level actions such that $\overline{Act_H} = Act_H$, $\overline{Act_L} = Act_L$, $Act_H \cup Act_L = \mathcal{L}$ and $Act_H \cap Act_L = \emptyset$ where $\bar{L} \stackrel{\text{def}}{=} \{\bar{a} : a \in L\}$; a set $Act = \mathcal{L} \cup \{\tau\}$ of actions (τ is the internal, invisible action), ranged over by μ; a set K of constants, ranged over by Z. The syntax of SPA *agents* is defined as follows:

$$E ::= \underline{0} \mid \mu.E \mid E + E \mid E|E \mid E \setminus L \mid E \setminus_I L \mid E/L \mid E[f] \mid Z$$

where $L \subseteq \mathcal{L}$ and $f : Act \to Act$ is such that $f(\bar{\alpha}) = \overline{f(\alpha)}$, $f(\tau) = \tau$. Moreover, for every constant Z there must be the corresponding definition: $Z \stackrel{\text{def}}{=} E$. The meaning of $\underline{0}$, $\mu.E$, $E + E$, $E|E$, $E \setminus L$, $E[f]$ and $Z \stackrel{\text{def}}{=} E$ is as for CCS [9].

Let $\mathcal{E}$ be the set of *closed* and *guarded* [9] SPA agents, ranged over by E, F. Let $\mathcal{L}(E)$ denote the *sort* of E, i.e., the set of the (possibly executable) actions occurring syntactically in E. The sets of high level agents and low level ones are defined as $\mathcal{E}_H \stackrel{\text{def}}{=} \{E \in \mathcal{E} \mid \mathcal{L}(E) \subseteq Act_H \cup \{\tau\}\}$ and $\mathcal{E}_L \stackrel{\text{def}}{=} \{E \in \mathcal{E} \mid \mathcal{L}(E) \subseteq Act_L \cup \{\tau\}\}$, respectively. The operational semantics of SPA is given (as usual) associating to each agent a particular state of the labelled transition system $(\mathcal{E}, Act, \to)$ where $\to \subseteq \mathcal{E} \times Act \times \mathcal{E}$ and, intuitively, $E \stackrel{\mu}{\to} E'$ means that agent E can execute μ moving to E'.

We recall here the definition of weak bisimulation [9] over SPA agents. In the following the expression $E \stackrel{\alpha}{\Longrightarrow} E'$ is a shorthand for $E(\stackrel{\tau}{\to})^* E_1 \stackrel{\alpha}{\to} E_2(\stackrel{\tau}{\to})^* E'$, where $(\stackrel{\tau}{\to})^*$ denotes a (possibly empty) sequence of τ labelled transitions. Moreover $E \stackrel{\hat{\mu}}{\Longrightarrow} E'$ stands for $E \stackrel{\mu}{\Longrightarrow} E'$ if $\mu \in \mathcal{L}$, and for $E(\stackrel{\tau}{\to})^* E'$ if $\mu = \tau$ (note that $(\stackrel{\tau}{\to})^*$ means "zero or more τ labelled transitions" while $\Longrightarrow$ requires at least one τ labelled transition).

---

[2] Actually, only two-level systems can be specified; note that this is not a real limitation because it is always possible to deal with the multilevel case by grouping – in several ways – the various levels in two clusters.

Definition 2.1 *A relation $R \subseteq \mathcal{E} \times \mathcal{E}$ is a* weak bisimulation *if $(E, F) \in R$ implies, for all $\mu \in Act$,*

- *whenever $E \xrightarrow{\mu} E'$ then there exists $F' \in \mathcal{E}$ such that $F \xRightarrow{\hat{\mu}} F'$ and $(E', F') \in R$;*

- *conversely, whenever $F \xrightarrow{\mu} F'$ then there exists $E' \in \mathcal{E}$ such that $E \xRightarrow{\hat{\mu}} E'$ and $(E', F') \in R$.*

Two SPA agents $E, F \in \mathcal{E}$ are observational equivalent, *notation $E \approx_B F$, if there exists a weak bisimulation containing the pair (E, F). Note that $\approx_B$ is an equivalence relation.* ∎

Now we present a value-passing extension of SPA (VSPA, for short). All the examples contained in this paper will be done using such value passing calculus, because it originates more readable specifications than those written in pure SPA. As in [9], the semantics of the value-passing calculus can be given via translation into the pure calculus [3].

The syntax of VSPA agents is defined as follows:

$$
\begin{aligned}
E \quad ::= \quad & \underline{0} \mid a(x_1, \ldots, x_n).E \mid \bar{a}(e_1, \ldots, e_n).E \mid \tau.E \mid E + E \mid E|E \mid \\
& \mid E \setminus L \mid E \setminus_I L \mid E/L \mid E[f] \mid A(e'_1, \ldots, e'_n) \mid \\
& \mid \text{if } b \text{ then } E \mid \text{if } b \text{ then } E \text{ else } E
\end{aligned}
$$

where the variables $x_1, \ldots, x_n$ and the value expressions $e_1, \ldots, e_n$ and $e'_1, \ldots, e'_n$ must be consistent with the arity of the action a and constant A respectively (the arity specifies the sorts of the parameters) and b is a boolean expression. An example of VSPA agent specification follows.

Example 2.2 Consider the following system specified using VSPA:

$$
\begin{aligned}
Access\_Monitor\_1 \quad &\overset{\text{def}}{=} \quad (Monitor|Object(1,0)|Object(0,0)) \setminus L \\
Monitor \quad &\overset{\text{def}}{=} \quad access\_r(l, x).(\text{if } x \leq l \text{ then } r(x, y).\overline{val}(l, y).Monitor \\
& \qquad \text{else } \overline{val}(l, err).Monitor) + \\
& \qquad + access\_w(l, x).write(l, z).(\text{if } x \geq l \text{ then} \\
& \qquad \overline{w}(x, z).Monitor \text{ else } Monitor) \\
Object(x, y) \quad &\overset{\text{def}}{=} \quad \bar{r}(x, y).Object(x, y) + w(x, z).Object(x, z)
\end{aligned}
$$

where $x, y, z, l \in \{0, 1\}$, $L = \{r, w\}$ and $\forall i \in \{0, 1\}$ we have $r(1, i)$, $w(1, i)$, $access\_r(1, i)$, $val(1, i)$, $val(1, err)$, $access\_w(1, i)$, $write(1, i) \in Act_H$ and all the others actions are low level ones. The process $Access\_Monitor\_1$ (Figure 2) handles read and write requests from high and low level users on two binary variables: a high level and a low level one. It achieves *no read up* and *no write down* access control rules allowing a high level user to read from both objects and write only on the high one; conversely, a low level user is allowed to write on both objects and read only from the low

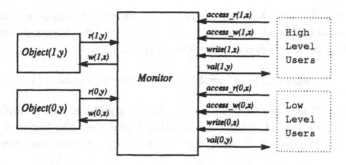

FIGURE 2. The Access Monitor for Example 2.2.

one. Users interact with the monitor through the following access actions: $access\_r(l, x), access\_w(l, x), write(l, z)$ where l is the user level ($l = 0$ low, $l = 1$ high), x is the object ($x = 0$ low, $x = 1$ high) and z is the binary value to be written. As an example, consider $access\_r(0, 1)$ which represents a low level user ($l = 0$) read request from the high level object ($x = 1$), and $access\_w(1, 0)$ followed by $write(1, 0)$ which represents a high level user ($l = 1$) write request of value 0 ($z = 0$) on the low object ($x = 0$). Read results are returned to users through the output actions $val(l, y)$. ∎

3 Some Information Flow Properties

In this section we present some of the security properties (see [3, 4] for more details) which can be verified using CSC.

Bisimulation Non-deterministic Non Interference (*BNNI*, for short) is a generalization of *Non Interference* [6]. Intuitively, the high level does not interfere with the low level if and only if a low level user cannot distinguish between processes E and $E \setminus_I Act_H$. In other words a system is *BNNI* if what a low level user sees of the system cannot be modified by any high level input.

Definition 3.1 $E \in BNNI \Leftrightarrow (E \setminus_I Act_H)/Act_H \approx_B E/Act_H$ ∎

Example 3.2 Consider the following modified monitor [3] which does not control write accesses:

$$Access\_Monitor\_2 \stackrel{def}{=} (Monitor|Object(1, 0)|Object(0, 0)) \setminus L$$

$$Monitor \stackrel{def}{=} access\_r(l, x).(\text{if } x \leq l \text{ then } r(x, y).\overline{val}(l, y).Monitor$$
$$\text{else } \overline{val}(l, err).Monitor) +$$
$$+ access\_w(l, x).write(l, z).\overline{w}(x, z).Monitor$$

---

[3] In the following, if an agent is not specified (e.g. $Object(x, y)$) we mean that it has not been modified with respect to previous examples.

Now it is possible for a high level user to write down (actions *access_w*$(1, 0)$ and *access_w*$(1, 1)$) so the system is not secure. In fact, *Access_Monitor_2* is not *BNNI* as it can execute the following trace:

$$\gamma = access\_w(1, 0).write(1, 1).access\_r(0, 0).\overline{val}(0, 1)$$

In γ we have 2 accesses to the monitor: first a high level user modifies the value of the low object writing-down value 1 and then the low user reads value 1 from the object. If we purge γ of high level actions we obtain the sequence

$$\gamma' = access\_r(0, 0).\overline{val}(0, 1)$$

that, clearly, can not be a trace for *Access_Monitor_2*. In fact, in γ', we have that a low level user reads 1 from the low level object without other interactions between the monitor and the environment (note that the initial values of the objects is 0). Moreover it is not possible to obtain a trace for *Access_Monitor_2* adding to γ' only high level outputs, because all the high level outputs in *Access_Monitor_2* are prefixed by high level inputs. Hence γ' is not a trace for $(Access\_Monitor\_2 \setminus_I Act_H)/Act_H$ too. In other words, it is not possible to find a trace γ'' with the same low level actions of γ and without high level inputs.

Since γ' is a trace for agent *Access_Monitor_2*$/Act_H$ but not for agent $(Access\_Monitor\_2 \setminus_I Act_H)/Act_H$, we conclude that *Access_Monitor_2* is not *BNNI*.

Hence, *BNNI* is able to detect if high level inputs interfere with low level executions, i.e. if a low level user can deduce something about high level inputs by observing only low level actions. ∎

In [4] we proposed a more intuitive notion of information flow security: *Bisimulation Non Deducibility on Compositions* (*BNDC*, for short). A system E is *BNDC* if for every high level process Π a low level user cannot distinguish between processes E and $(E|\Pi) \setminus Act_H$. In other words, a system E is *BNDC* if what a low level user sees of the system is not modified by composing any high level process Π to E.

Definition 3.3 $E \in BNDC \Leftrightarrow \forall \Pi \in \mathcal{E}_H, \; E/Act_H \approx_B (E \mid \Pi) \setminus Act_H$. ∎

A static characterization of *BNDC* − which does not involve composition with every processes Π − is not immediate. As a matter of fact, this problem is still open. In [5] we proposed the *SBSNNI* property which is static, compositional (i.e. if two systems are *SBSNNI* their composition is *SBSNNI*, too) and strictly stronger than *BNDC*. We first define *Bisimulation Strong Non-deterministic Non Interference* (*BSNNI*, for short), a property which differs from *BNNI* only because it restricts system E over all the high level actions rather than only over high level inputs.

Definition 3.4 $E \in BSNNI \Leftrightarrow E/Act_H \approx_B E \setminus Act_H$. ∎

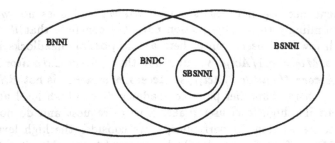

FIGURE 3. The inclusion diagram for bisimulation-based properties

Now we can define *Strong BSNNI* (*SBSNNI*, for short).

Definition 3.5 *A system* $E \in SBSNNI$ *if and only if for all* E' *reachable from* E *we have* $E' \in BSNNI$.　∎

The following holds [5]:

Proposition 3.6 *SBSNNI* $\subset$ *BNDC*　∎

In the automatic verification of security properties it can be very useful to work on a *reduced* system, i.e. a system equivalent to the original one, but with a minimum number of states. The Concurrency Workbench provides a procedure to this aim and we imported it in CSC. This is very useful because we can prove that if a system E is *BNDC*, then any other observational equivalent system F is *BNDC*. This also holds for all the other security properties.

Theorem 3.7 *If* $E \approx_B F$, *then* $E \in X \Leftrightarrow F \in X$, *where* X *can be BNNI, BSNNI, BNDC, SBSNNI*.　∎

Figure 3 summarizes the relations among the security properties defined above.

The following example shows that *BSNNI* and *BNNI* are not able to detect some deadlocks due to high level activities which, on the contrary, are revealed by *BNDC* (this because they do not check the system against all the possible high level interactions, as *BNDC* does).

Example 3.8 Consider the first version of the monitor *Access_Monitor_1*. Using CSC we can verify that such system is *BSNNI* and *BNNI*, but it is not *BNDC*. This happens because a high level user can make a read request without accepting the corresponding output from the monitor (remember that communications in SPA are synchronous). In particular, consider $\Pi = \overline{access\_r}(1,1).\underline{0}$. System $(Access\_Monitor\_1 | \Pi) \setminus Act_H$ will be deadlocked immediately after the execution of the read request by Π, blocking in the following state

$$(\overline{val}(1,0).Monitor \mid Object(0,0) \mid Object(1,0)) \setminus L \mid 0) \setminus Act_H$$

This happens because Π executes a read request and does not wait for the corresponding return value (action val). We conclude that Π can interfere with low level users. Since there are no possible deadlocks in process $Access\_Monitor\_1/Act_H$, we find out that $(Access\_Monitor\_1|\Pi) \setminus Act_H \not\approx_B Access\_Monitor\_1/Act_H$, so $Access\_Monitor\_1$ is not $BNDC$.

Moreover, there is another possible deadlock due to high level activity; this happens if a high level user makes a write request and do not send the value to be written. In particular, if we consider the high level user $\Pi' = \overline{access\_w}(1,0).\underline{0}$, it will deadlock system $(Access\_Monitor\_1|\Pi') \setminus Act_H$ immediately after the execution of the write request by Π', blocking in the following state:

$$(((write(1,0).Monitor + write(1,1).Monitor) \mid Object(0,0) \mid$$
$$\mid Object(1,0)) \setminus L \mid 0) \setminus Act_H$$

This happens because Π' executes a write request and does not send the corresponding value through action $write(1,0)$ or $write(1,1)$. Again, we have that $(Access\_Monitor\_1|\Pi') \setminus Act_H \not\approx_B Access\_Monitor\_1/Act_H$. In order to obtain a $BNDC$ system, we modify the monitor by adding an output buffer for each level (this makes communications asynchronous) and using an atomic action for write request and value sending. The resulting system follows:

$$Access\_Monitor\_3 \stackrel{def}{=} (Monitor|Object(1,0)|Object(0,0)|Buf(1,empty)|$$
$$|Buf(0,empty)) \setminus L$$

$$Monitor \stackrel{def}{=} access\_r(l,x).(\text{if } x \leq l \text{ then } r(x,y).\overline{val}(l,y).Monitor$$
$$\text{else } \overline{val}(l,err).Monitor) +$$
$$+ access\_w(l,x,z).(\text{ f } x \geq l \text{ then } \overline{w}(x,z).Monitor$$
$$\text{else } Monitor)$$

$$Buf(x,j) \stackrel{def}{=} \overline{res}(x,j).Buf(x,empty) + val(x,k).Buf(x,k)$$

where $k \in \{0,1,err\}$ and $j \in \{0,1,err,empty\}$; $L = \{r, w, val\}$. Moreover output actions $res(x,j)$ of buffer substitute output actions $val(x,k)$ in the interactions with users, with $res(1,i) \in Act_H, \forall i \in \{0,1,err,empty\}$.

Using CSC it is possible to automatically verify that $Access\_Monitor\_3$ is $SBSNNI$ and so $BNDC$. ■

4 What is the Compositional Security Checker

4.1 Input-Output

The inputs of CSC are concurrent systems expressed as SPA agents. The outputs are answers to questions like: "does this system satisfy that specific

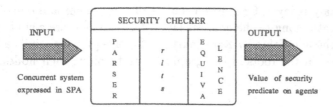

FIGURE 4. Structure of the CSC

security property ?". The structure of CSC is described in Figure 4. In detail, the tool is able:

- to parse SPA agents, saving them in suitable environments as parse trees;

- to give a semantic to these parse trees, building the corresponding rooted labelled transition systems (*rlts* for short);

- to check if an agent satisfies a certain security property; the implemented routine for this purpose verifies the equivalence of two particular agents modeled as rlts. In this way, future changes of the language will not compromise the validity of the core of the tool.

4.2 Architecture

The CSC has the same general architecture of the CW. In its implementation we have decided to exploit the characteristic of versatility and extensibility of CW. In particular CSC maintains the strongly modular characteristic of CW. The modules of the system are partitioned in three main layers: interface layer, semantic layer, analysis layer.

In the interface layer we have the command interpreter. It allows us to define the agents and the set of high level actions; it also allows to invoke the security predicates and the utility functions on the behaviour of an agent. Then we have a parser which recognizes the SPA syntax of agents and stores them as parse trees in appropriate environments. The partition of the set of visible actions in the sets of high and low level actions has been obtained by defining the set of high level actions; by default, all the other possible actions are considered at low level. Then we have defined a transition function that, according to the operational semantic rule of SPA, provides all possible transitions for an agent. This function allows the construction of the transition graph associated to an agent.

In the semantic layer, CSC uses a transformation routine to translate transition graphs into observational graphs [2]. Since it refers to processes modeled as transition graphs, it has been imported from CW in CSC without any modification.

In the analysis layer, CSC uses a routine of equivalence and one of minimization that belong to the analysis layer of CW. These are a slight modification of the algorithm by Kanellakis and Smolka [8] which finds a bisimulation between the roots of two graphs by partitioning their nodes.

5 Security Predicates

Now, we want to explain briefly how the system works in evaluating security predicates *BNNI, BSNNI, SBSNNI*, discussing, at the same time, about their computational complexity. CSC computes the value of these predicates over *finite state agents* (i.e. agents possessing a finite state transition graph), based on the definitions given in Section 2 that we report below in CSC syntax: [4]

$$E \in BNNI \quad \Leftrightarrow \quad E!Act_H \approx_B (E?Act_H)!Act_H$$
$$E \in BSNNI \quad \Leftrightarrow \quad E!Act_H \approx_B E \setminus Act_H$$
$$E \in SBSNNI \quad \Leftrightarrow \quad E' \in BSNNI, \ \forall E' \ reachable \ from \ E$$

As for CW, the inner computation of the CSC follows three main phases.

Phase a) CSC builds the transition graphs of the two agents of which it wants to compute the equivalence. For example in the case of *BNNI*, CSC computes the transition graph for $(E?Act_H)!Act_H$ and $E!Act_H$. In this phase we do not have any particular problem with complexity, except for the intrinsic exponential explosion in the number of nodes of the graphs due to parallel composition.

Phase b) The two transition graphs obtained in Phase a) are transformed into observational graphs using the classic algorithms for the product of two relations and the reflexive transitive closure of a relation. This transformation has a $O(n^3)$ complexity, in which n is the number of nodes in the original graph.

Phase c) The general equivalence algorithm [8] is applied to the graphs obtained in Phase b). Time and space complexities of this algorithm are $O(k*l)$ and $O(k+l)$ respectively, where l is the number of nodes and k is the number of edges in the two graphs. This is not a limiting factor in the computation of the observational equivalence. In particular we have that in most cases 80% of computation time is due to the routine for reflexive transitive closure of Phase b).

---

[4] In the CSC the hiding and input restriction operators are respectively represented by ! and ?, for easy of parsing.

Since *SBSNNI* is verified by testing *BSNNI* over all the n states of the original graph, the resulting complexity will be n times the *BSNNI* complexity.

It is interesting to observe that the exponential explosion of the number of nodes of the transition graphs (Phase a), due to the operator of parallel composition, influences negatively the following phases, but it can not be avoided because of its intrinsic nature. A solution to this problem for the predicate *SBSNNI* could be based on the exploitation of compositional properties proved in [4] and recalled in Section 7.

6 Using CSC

6.1 Sample session

The style used in specifying SPA agents in CSC is the same used for CCS agents in CW. For example the command line [5]

> Command: bi   *A*   *h.'l.'h.A* $+'$ *h.'l.A*

defines the agent $A \overset{\text{def}}{=} h.\bar{l}.\bar{h}.A + \bar{h}.\bar{l}.A$. As in CW the first letter of agents must be a capital letter and output actions have to be prefixed by $'$.

We assumed that the set of visible actions $\mathcal{L}$ is partitioned in two subsets Act_H and Act_L of high and low level actions respectively. With the command

> Command: acth   *h*

we specify that $Act_H = \{h,' h\}$. In this way we obtain that $h,' h$ are considered as high level actions and any other action as low level one.

Now, we can check whether agent *A* is *BNNI* secure:

> Command: bnni   *A*
> true

CSC tells us that *A* is *BNNI* secure. Now we can check if agent *A* is *BSNNI* secure too:

> Command: bsnni   *A*
> false

So *A* is *BNNI* secure but is not *BSNNI* secure. Finally the command **quit** causes an exit to the shell.

---

[5] Here we use the typewriter style for CSC messages (such as the prompt "Command:"); the bold style for CSC commands and the italic style for the remaining text (such as agents, sets) inserted by users.

```
bi Access_Monitor_1
(Monitor | Object_10 | Object_h0)\ L

bi Monitor
access_r_hh.(rh0.'val_h0.Monitor + rh1.'val_h1.Monitor) + \
access_r_lh.'val_l_err.Monitor + \
access_r_hl.(rl0.'val_h0.Monitor + rl1.'val_h1.Monitor) + \
access_r_ll.(rl0.'val_l0.Monitor + rl1.'val_l1.Monitor) + \
access_w_hh.(write_h0.'wh0.Monitor + write_h1.'wh1.Monitor) + \
access_w_lh.(write_l0.'wh0.Monitor + write_l1.'wh1.Monitor) + \
access_w_hl.(write_h0.Monitor + write_h1.Monitor) + \
access_w_ll.(write_l0.'wl0.Monitor + write_l1.'wl1.Monitor)

bi Object_h0
'rh0.Object_h0 + wh0.Object_h0 + wh1.Object_h1

bi Object_h1
'rh1.Object_h1 + wh0.Object_h0 + wh1.Object_h1

bi Object_10
Object_h0[rl0/rh0,rl1/rh1,wl0/wh0,wl1/wh1]

basi L
rh0  rh1  rl0  rl1  wh0  wh1  wl0  wl1

acth
rh0 rh1 wh0 wh1 access_r_hh access_r_hl val_h0 val_h1 val_h_err \
access_w_hh access_w_hl write_h0 write_h1
```

TABLE .1. Translation of Access_Monitor_1 into CSC syntax.

6.2 Checking the Access Monitor

In this Section we use CSC to analyze the systems of Example 3.8. Since CSC works on SPA agents we have to translate all the VSPA specifications into SPA. Consider system *Access_Monitor*_1. Table.1 reports the translation of *Access_Monitor*_1 specification into the CSC syntax. [6] The new command **basi** has been used to bind a set of actions to an identifier. Moreover, the \ character at the end of a line does not represent the restriction operator, but is the special character that permits to break in more lines the description of long agents and long action lists.

We can write to a file the contents of Table.1 and load it, in CSC, with command **if** <*filename*>. Now we can check that *Access_Monitor*_1 satisfies all the security properties except *SBSNNI* using the following command lines:

> Command: **bnni**   *Access_Monitor*_1
> true
> Command: **bsnni**   *Access_Monitor*_1

---

[6] In the translation, we use $\{l, h\}$ in place of $\{0, 1\}$ for the levels of users and objects in order to make the SPA specification more clear. Formally we make the translation considering variables l and x ranging in $\{l, h\}$. As an example $access\_r(1,0)$ becomes access_r_hl

```
true
Command: sbsnni   Access_Monitor_1
false: ('val_h1.Monitor | Object_11 | Object_h1) \ L 7
```

Note that when *SBSNNI* fails for a process E, CSC gives as output an agent
E' which is reachable from E and is not *BSNNI*. In the following we will
show that this can be useful to decide if E is *BNDC*. So we have found that
Access_Monitor_1 $\in$ *BSNNI, BNNI* and *Access_Monitor_1* $\notin$ *SBSNNI*
Since *SBSNNI* $\subset$ *BNDC* $\subset$ *BSNNI, BNNI* (see Proposition 3.6), we cannot conclude whether *Access_Monitor_1* is *BNDC* or not. However using
the output of *SBSNNI* it is easy to find a high level process Π which
can deadlock the monitor. In fact, in the state given as output by *SB-
SNNI*, the monitor is waiting for the high level action 'val_h1; so, if we
find a process Π which leads the system to such a state and does not
execute the val_h1 action, we will have a high level process able to deadlock the monitor. It is sufficient to consider Π = 'access_r_hh.0. System
$(Access\_Monitor\_1|\Pi) \setminus Act_H$ will be deadlocked immediately after the execution of the read request by Π, blocking in the following state

$$(('val\_h0.Monitor \mid Object\_10 \mid Object\_h0) \setminus L \mid 0) \setminus Act_H$$

(this state differs from the one given as output by *SBSNNI* only for the
values stored in objects). We verify that *Access_Monitor_1* is not *BNDC* by
checking that $(Access\_Monitor\_1|\Pi) \setminus Act_H \not\approx_B Access\_Monitor\_1/Act_H$
using the following commands:

```
    Command: bi  Pi  'access_r_hh.0
    Command: eq
    Agent: (Access_Monitor_1 | Pi) \ acth
    Agent: Access_Monitor_1 ! acth
    false
```

As we said in Example 3.8, such a deadlock is caused by synchronous
communications in SPA. Moreover, using the CSC output again, we can
find out that also the high level process Π' = 'access_w_hl.0 can deadlock *Access_Monitor_1*, this because it executes a write request and does
not send the corresponding value. Hence, in Example 3.8 we proposed the
modified system *Access_Monitor_3* with an output buffer for each level
and atomic actions for write request and value sending. We finally check
that this version of the monitor is *SBSNNI*, hence *BNDC* too:

```
    Command: sbsnni   Access_Monitor_3
    true
```

---

[7] We write Object_11 instead of Object_h1[r10/rh0,r11/rh1,w10/wh0,w11/wh1]

agent	B	D	B|D|B	B|D|D|B
state number	3	3	27	81
time spent	<1 sec.	<1 sec.	~11 sec.	~270 sec.

TABLE .2. Number of states and time spent on a SPARC station 5.

7 State Explosion and Compositionality

We now want to plain out how the parallel composition operator can increase exponentially the number of states of the system, and then how it can slow down the execution speed of security predicate verification. Let us define in CSC the two agents B, D and the set Act_H of high level actions:

```
Command: bi    B   y.a.b.B + a.b.B
Command: bi    D   'a.'b.(x.D + D)
Command: acth  x   y
```

Let us check now if B and D are *SBSNNI* secure:

```
Command: sbsnni  B
true
Command: sbsnni  D
true
```

As we will see that *SBSNNI* is preserved by system composition, the two agents $B|D|B$ and $B|D|D|B$ must also be *SBSNNI* secure. Hence the verification of these two agents can be reduced to the verification of their two basic components B and D only. The time spent in verifying *SBSNNI* directly on $B|D|B$ and $B|D|D|B$ is very long. Using the **size** command of CSC, which computes the number of states of an agent, we can fill in Table.2, which points out the exponential increase of the number of states and the consequent increase of the computation time for verification of *SBSNNI*.

Theorem 7.1 [5] *The following hold:*

(i) $E, F \in SBSNNI \implies (E|F) \in SBSNNI$

(ii) $E \in SBSNNI, L \subseteq \mathcal{L} \implies E \setminus L \in SBSNNI$ ∎

In the following $\mathcal{E}_{FS} \subseteq \mathcal{E}$ will denote the set of closed and guarded SPA agents with a finite lts. CSC is able to exploit the compositionality of security properties through the following algorithm:

Definition 7.2 *(Compositional Algorithm) Let $P \subseteq \mathcal{E}$ be a set of SPA agents such that*

- $E, E' \in P \implies E|E' \in P$

- $E \in P, L \subseteq \mathcal{L} \implies E \setminus L \in P$

and A_P be an algorithm which checks if a certain agent $E \in \mathcal{E}_{FS}$ belongs to P; in other words $A_P(E) = \textbf{true}$ if $E \in P$ and $A_P(E) = \textbf{false}$ otherwise. Then we can define a compositional algorithm $A'_P(E)$ in the following way:

1) if E is in the form $E' \setminus L$ (recursively) calculate $A'_P(E')$; if $A'_P(E') = \textbf{true}$ then return $\textbf{true}$ else return the result of $A_P(E)$;

2) if E is in the form $E_1 | E_2$ (recursively) calculate $A'_P(E_1)$ and $A'_P(E_2)$; if $A'_P(E_1) = A'_P(E_2) = \textbf{true}$ then return $\textbf{true}$ else return the result of $A_P(E)$;

3) otherwise return $A_P(E)$. ∎

Note that the algorithm requires that property P is closed with respect to restriction and uses this in step 1. This could seem useless; however, the parallel composition is often in the following form: $(A|B) \setminus L$ (in order to force some synchronization) and so if we want to check P over A and B separately, we must be granted that P is preserved by both parallel and restriction operators. We have the following correctness result for the compositionality algorithm:

Theorem 7.3 Let $F \in \mathcal{E}_{FS}$ be a finite state SPA agent. If, every time the algorithm executes step 1, E' belongs to $\mathcal{E}_{FS}$, then $A'_P(F)$ terminates and $A_P(F) = A'_P(F)$.

PROOF. First, note that in step 1 of A'_P it is $E' \in \mathcal{E}_{FS}$ (by hypothesis) and in step 2 if $E \in \mathcal{E}_{FS}$ then $E_1, E_2 \in \mathcal{E}_{FS}$. As $F \in \mathcal{E}_{FS}$, then we recursively obtain that every E, E' and E_1, E_2 of steps 1, 2 and 3 belong to $\mathcal{E}_{FS}$. So, when the algorithm executes $A_P(E)$ in steps 1,2 or 3, it terminates because $E \in \mathcal{E}_{FS}$.

We still have to prove that, in steps 1 and 2, $A'_P(E')$ and $A'_P(E_1)$, $A'_P(E_2)$ terminate. In particular we must prove that for every $F' \in \mathcal{E}_{FS}$ the evaluation of $A'_P(F')$ never needs to evaluate $A'_P(F')$ itself (going into an infinite loop). This holds because agents in $\mathcal{E}_{FS}$ are guarded; so the evaluation of $A'_P(F')$ could at most need to evaluate $A'_P(\mu.F')$ where μ is the guard for F'. Hence $A'_P(F)$ terminates.

When the algorithm calculates $A_P(E)$ in steps 1, 2 and 3 it is always $E \in \mathcal{E}_{FS}$, so $A_P(E) = \textbf{true}$ if $E \in P$ and $A_P(E) = \textbf{false}$ if $E \notin P$. Hence, by (partial) structural induction and using compositionality properties, we obtain that $A_P(F) = A'_P(F)$. ∎

The theorem above requires that, every time the algorithm executes step 1, E' belongs to $\mathcal{E}_{FS}$; i.e. in $A'_P(E)$, if E is in the form $E' \setminus L$ then E' must be finite state. As an example, consider a finite state system $E \setminus L$ such that $E \notin \mathcal{E}_{FS}$; then $A_P(E \setminus L)$ terminates while $A'_P(E \setminus L)$ possibly do not, because it tries to calculate $A_P(E)$ and E is not finite state.

Note that such a condition trivially holds if we specify systems as composition and restriction of finite state subsystems. In particular we can use

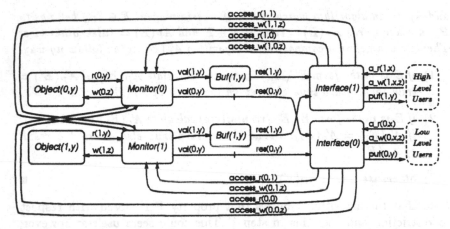

FIGURE 5. The compositional Access_Monitor

the following syntax which defines the so called *nets of automata*:

$$p \quad ::= \quad \underline{0} \mid \mu.p \mid p + p \mid Z$$
$$E \quad ::= \quad p \mid E|E \mid E \setminus L \mid E \setminus_I L \mid E/L \mid E[f]$$

where for every constant Z there must be the corresponding definition $Z \stackrel{\text{def}}{=} p$.

It not necessary to use such a syntax in order to satisfy theorem hypotheses. As an example consider the following agent $B \stackrel{\text{def}}{=} a.\underline{0} + D \setminus \{i\}$ with $D \stackrel{\text{def}}{=} i.(o.\underline{0}|D)$ which is finite state but it is not a net of automata. Since the top operator is a $+$ then $A'_P(B)$ behaves just like $A_P(B)$ and so it terminates (theorem hypotheses trivially hold in this case).

Example 7.4 Consider again *Access_Monitor_3*. The verification of the *SBSNNI* property on such a system requires a lot of time (more than 1 hour on a SUN5 workstation) because of the above mentioned exponential state explosion due to parallel composition. We can try to verify *SBSNNI* using the compositional algorithm. Unfortunately we have that *Monitor* is not *SBSNNI* and so, in this case, the compositional technique cannot help us to reduce the execution time. This happens because the *BNDC*-security of *Access_Monitor_3* depends on both monitor and objects; i.e. process *Monitor* is not able to guarantee multilevel security for every possible object connected to it. As an example, consider the following modified objects:

$$Object(x, y) \quad \stackrel{\text{def}}{=} \quad \overline{r}(x, y).Object(x, 0) + w(x, z).Object(x, z)$$

which reset (to zero) their value every time they are read. Using these objects, we obtain a system which is not *BSNNI* and so is not *BNDC*. In such a system, a high level user can change (to zero) the value of the low level variable by simply reading it. This is generally called "half-bit" covert channel because the high level user can set the low level variable only to one of the two possible values (in this case 0) and so can transmit only a half-bit information to low level. In [3] we show how to construct a 1-bit channel using some half-bit ones.

Finally we present a version of the Access Monitor (Figure 5) which can be verified very efficiently by exploiting the compositionality of $SBSNNI$. Here every object has a "private" monitor which implements the access functions for such (single) object. To make this, we have decomposed process **Monitor** (which is not $BNDC$) into two different processes, one for each object; then we have composed such processes to respective objects together with a high level buffer obtaining the $BNDC$-secure **Modh** and **Modl** agents. In particular, $Monitor(x)$ handles the accesses to object x ($x = 0$ low, $x = 1$ high). We also have an interface which guarantees the exclusive use of the monitor within the same level. Moreover the new interface actions $a\_r(l, x)$, $a\_w(l, x, z)$ and $put(l, y)$ substitute actions $access\_r(l, x)$, $access\_w(l, x, z)$ and $res(l, y)$ in the interaction between the users and the monitor.

$$
\begin{aligned}
Access\_Monitor\_4 &\stackrel{\text{def}}{=} (Modh|Modl|Interf) \setminus L \\
Modh &\stackrel{\text{def}}{=} ((Monitor(1)|Object(1,0)|Buf(1, empty)) \setminus Lh) \\
&\qquad [res(0, y)/val(0, y)] \\
Modl &\stackrel{\text{def}}{=} ((Monitor(0)|Object(0,0)|Buf(1, empty)) \setminus Ll) \\
&\qquad [res(0, y)/val(0, y)] \\
Interf &\stackrel{\text{def}}{=} Interf(0)|Interf(1) \\
Interf(l) &\stackrel{\text{def}}{=} a\_r(l, x).\overline{access\_r}(l, x).res(l, y).\overline{put}(l, y).Interf(l) + \\
&\qquad + a\_w(l, x, z).\overline{access\_w}(l, x, z).Interf(l) \\
Monitor(x) &\stackrel{\text{def}}{=} access\_r(l, x).(\text{ if } x \le l \text{ then } r(x, y).\overline{val}(l, y). \\
&\qquad Monitor(x) \text{ else } \overline{val}(l, err).Monitor(x)) + \\
&\qquad + access\_w(l, x, z).(\text{ if } x \ge l \text{ then } \overline{w}(x, z).Monitor(x) \\
&\qquad \text{ else } Monitor(x)) \\
Object(x, y) &\stackrel{\text{def}}{=} \overline{r}(x, y).Object(x, y) + w(x, z).Object(x, z) \\
Buf(x, j) &\stackrel{\text{def}}{=} \overline{res}(x, j).Buf(x, empty) + val(x, k).Buf(x, k)
\end{aligned}
$$

where $L = \{res, access\_r, access\_w\}$, $Lh = \{r, w, val(1, y)\}$ and $Ll = \{r, w, val(1, y)\}$. Table.3 reports the output of the (successful) verification of $SBSNNI$ on $Access\_Monitor\_4$. This task requires about 1 minute on a SUN5 workstation. We can also check that $Access\_Monitor\_4 \approx_B$ $(Access\_Monitor\_3|Interf) \setminus L$ with $L = \{res, access\_r, access\_w\}$; i.e. this Access Monitor version is equivalent to the $Access\_Monitor\_3$ with the interface. Such equivalence verification requires about 10 minutes. Note that, by Theorem 3.7, we can conclude that also $(Access\_Monitor\_3|Interf) \setminus L$ is $BNDC$, even if a direct (non compositional) check would take about

```
Verifying Modh | Modl | Interf
  Verifying Modh
  Verifying Modl
  Verifying Interf
    Verifying Interf_h
    Verifying Interf_l
true
```

TABLE .3. Verification of *SBSNNI* on *Access_Monitor_4* exploiting compositionality.

20 minutes (about 20 times longer than checking the equivalent process *Access_Monitor_4*). Note that checking $(Access\_Monitor\_3|Interf) \setminus L$ requires less time than checking *Access_Monitor_3* alone. So for this agent the compositional algorithm takes more time with respect to direct checking. This happens because $(Access\_Monitor\_3|Interf) \setminus L$ has less states than *Access_Monitor_3*; in fact, the interface reduces the internal parallelism in system *Access_Monitor_3* (in particular the parallelism given by the action of the buffers). Hence it is useful to adopt the compositional technique when building complex systems as parallel composition of simpler ones, i.e. when the number of states increases (e.g. as in *Access_Monitor_4*).

∎

8 REFERENCES

[1] D. E. Bell and L. J. La Padula. "Secure Computer Systems: Unified Exposition and Multics Interpretation". *ESD-TR-75-306, MITRE MTR-2997*, March 1976.

[2] R. Cleaveland, J. Parrow, and B. Steffen. "The Concurrency Workbench: a Semantics Based Tool for the Verification of Concurrent Systems". *ACM Transactions on Programming Languages and Systems*, Vol. 15 No. 1:36–72, January 1993.

[3] R. Focardi and R. Gorrieri. "The Compositional Security Checker: A Tool for the Automatic Compositional Verification of Security Properties". Forthcoming.

[4] R. Focardi and R. Gorrieri. "A Classification of Security Properties for Process Algebras". *Journal of Computer Security*, 3(1):5–33, 1994/1995.

[5] R. Focardi, R. Gorrieri, and V. Panini. "The Security Checker: a Semantics-based Tool for the Verification of Security Properties". In *Proceedings Eight IEEE Computer Security Foundation Workshop, (CSFW'95) (Li Gong Ed.)*, pages 60–69, Kenmare (Ireland), June 1995. IEEE Press.

[6] J. A. Goguen and J. Meseguer. "Security Policy and Security Models". In *Proceedings of the 1982 Symposium on Security and Privacy*, pages 11–20. IEEE Computer Society Press, April 1982.

[7] C. A. R. Hoare. *Communicating Sequential Processes*. Prentice-Hall, 1985.

[8] P. Kanellakis and S.A. Smolka. "CCS Expression, Finite State Processes, and Three Problems of Equivalence". *Information & Computation 86*, pages 43–68, May 1990.

[9] R. Milner. *Communication and Concurrency*. Prentice-Hall, 1989.

[10] C. R. Tsai, V. D. Gligor, and C. S. Chandersekaran. "On the Identification of Covert Storage Channels in Secure Systems". *IEEE Transactions on Software Engineering*, pages 569–580, June 1990.

[11] J. T. Wittbold and D. M. Johnson. "Information Flow in Nondeterministic Systems". In *Proceedings of the 1990 IEEE Symposium on Research in Security and Privacy*, pages 144–161. IEEE Computer Society Press, 1990.

Permutable Agents in Process Algebras

François Michel[*]
Pierre Azéma[*]
François Vernadat[*]

ABSTRACT
Within the framework of symmetrical systems, an extension of CCS [6], so-called PCCS, is described. PCCS equips CCS with the concept of pool of agents by means of the explicit structure of Pool expressions. The symmetries whithin a Pools of agents may then be used to simplify the validation process of concurrent systems.

An equivalence relation, so-called Permutability, is formally introduced : two PCCS expressions are permutable iff they can be obtained from each other by a permutation of expressions within a pool. Permutability can be decided in a polynomial time w.r.t. the length of expressions. The Permutability notion allows the definition of symbolic Processes, which describe the system behaviour when inside a pool the agent identities are removed . A transitional semantics is defined and behavioral verifications may be conducted over symbolic Processes.

Key words : Process Algebras, Symmetries, Concurrent Systems, Verification

1   Introduction

In concurrent systems, a single behaviour may be shared by several processes, in other words, all this processes are instances of a same process class. Furthermore, this kind of systems often exhibits architectural symmetries, e.g. two processes of the same class may be substituted one for each other without modifying the system behavior.

In order to study these symmetrical systems, some procedures have ever been designed. Their main advantage lies in the simplification of the validation step by elimination of symmetrical cases in behavioral studies. This approach, initiated by [8] with HL-Trees, formally consists of three steps (cf. Figure 1) :

1. Extraction of a group of symmetries from the formal description. Two states are symmetrical iff they satisfy a symmetry relationship. This

---

[*]LAAS/CNRS 7,Avenue du Colonel Roche - 31077 Toulouse Cedex - France

group of symmetries defines the equivalence relation "is symmetrical to" among states.

2. As a consequence, a quotient graph may be considered. This quotient graph may be directly built from the formal description, that is on line. Such a construction algorithm is easily derived from any standard enumeration algorithm, by replacing the syntactical equality among states by the relation "is symmetrical to".

3. The symmetrical properties, i.e. which hold for all the symmetrical states in a class, may be verified over the quotient graph. Study of structural properties (deadlocks, connectivity,....) [3, 5, 9], and temporal logic model checking [2, 1] have been adapted to these quotient graphs.

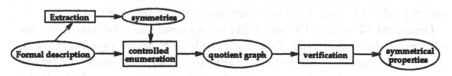

FIGURE 1. The symmetrical approach

The symmetry approach faces two difficulties : the symmetry derivation from the formal description, on one hand, and the computation efficiency for deciding whether two states are symmetrical, on the other hand.

A main contribution of this paper is to propose an efficient application of symmetries to Process Algebras for each step of the former symmetry approach. The motivation is twofold. On one hand, the validation of symmetrical systems described by process algebras will be conducted over reduced graph modulo system symmetries. Consequently, when the reduced graph derivation cost is low, space saving and time speed-up are expected. From a design point of view, on the other hand, the process composition is performed by means of algebraic operators, these operators have to preserve the symmetries of each components. This is the reason why Pool expressions will be introduced.

The purpose is not to promote a new Process Algebra but to present the ingredients which may be added to a Process Algebra, here CCS, in order to use symmetries. These ingredients concern the description formalism and specific types of symmetry :

Description Formalism : The detection of symmetries in the case of usual formalisms is a complex problem, e.g. Symmetries of Petri Nets [9]. Specific formalisms have been designed in order to *explicitly state* symmetries rather than to detect them : the Well-Formed Nets [3, 5], the language $Mur\varphi$ extended by scalarsets [4]. Like in $Mur\varphi$, an already existing formalism, CCS, will be extended by symmetrical structures, Pools of concurrent agents, resulting in PCCS.

The second section briefly introduces the syntax, semantics and behav-

ioral equivalence in CCS, the third section extends these three issues to
PCCS.

Symmetries : [2] has shown that, in the general case, to determine
whether two states are symmetrical is as hard as the graph isomorphism
problem for which no polynomial solution is known. For this reason, PCCS
only implements a particular kind of symmetries : all agents in a pool are
pairwise permutable. In this context, the relation "is symmetrical to" is
called Permutability. Permutability is defined syntactically : two PCCS expressions are permutable iff they can be obtained from each other by an
agent permutation within the Pool expressions. The behavioural interpretation of Permutability is made precise by means of the P-Equivalence,
which is a specific strong equivalence.

The Permutability definition, its interpretation and its computation,
polynomial w.r.t. length of terms, are presented in forth section.

Quotient Graphs : Permutability allows symbolic Processes to be defined as an equivalence class. From each symbolic Process, a symbolic L.T.S.
(the quotient graph in the symmetry approach) can be derived by a transitional semantics. An efficient construction algorithm manages to built the
symbolic L.T.S. for any PCCS expression.

Symmetrical Properties : The behavior verification is conducted on
the symbolic L.T.S.. That is, properties of states, which are symbolic Processes, are derived from the Permutability interpretation by means of the
P-Equivalence.

The symbolic Processes and their properties are developed in the fifth
section.

PCCS seems to offer a good balance between a low (polynomial) computation cost and a high reduction rate. This question is discussed in a
deeper way in the sixth section.

2 CCS Algebra

CCS is a Process Algebra whose basic elements are a set of names $\mathcal{A}$, the
associated co-names $\overline{\mathcal{A}}$ and a set $\mathcal{K}$ of agent constants. $\mathcal{L} = \mathcal{A} \cup \overline{\mathcal{A}}$ denotes
the set of labels and $Act = \mathcal{L} \cup \{\tau\}$ denotes the set of actions. Its syntax is
described in the first part, its transitional semantics in second part. In the
third part, three notions of equivalence among processes are given: strong
equivalence, observation equivalence and observation congruence.

2.1 Syntax of CCS

The agent expressions are : $0 \qquad a.E \qquad E + F \qquad E|F \qquad E \setminus L \qquad E[f]$
where E, F are agent expressions, $a \in \mathcal{L}$, $L \subset \mathcal{L}$ and f is a relabeling
function, that is a function from $\mathcal{L}$ to $\mathcal{L}$ such that $\overline{f(l)} = f(\overline{l})$; f is extended
to Act by $f(\tau) = \tau$.

Every constant A in $\mathcal{K}$ is assumed to have a definition :

$$A \stackrel{def}{=} E \text{ where E is an agent expression.}$$

Remark: the operator $\Sigma_{i \in I} E_i$, where I is any set of indexes, is not included in our version of CCS. Indeed, it will be assumed in the sequel of the article, that *the length of expressions is finite and so is the set of constant names.*

2.2 Transitional semantics of CCS

The semantics of CCS is defined in terms of labelled transition systems (L.T.S.). Their states are agent expressions, and transition labelled by actions are ruled by :

$$\frac{}{a.E \xrightarrow{a} E} \qquad \frac{E_1 \xrightarrow{a} E_1'}{E_1 + E_2 \xrightarrow{a} E_1'} \qquad \frac{E_2 \xrightarrow{a} E_2'}{E_1 + E_2 \xrightarrow{a} E_2'}$$

$$\frac{E_1 \xrightarrow{a} E_1'}{E_1|E_2 \xrightarrow{a} E_1'|E_2} \qquad \frac{E_2 \xrightarrow{a} E_2'}{E_1|E_2 \xrightarrow{a} E_1|E_2'} \qquad \frac{E_1 \xrightarrow{a} E_1' \; E_2 \xrightarrow{\bar{a}} E_2'}{E_1|E_2 \xrightarrow{\tau} E_1'|E_2'}$$

$$\frac{E \xrightarrow{a} E'}{E \setminus L \xrightarrow{a} E' \setminus L}(a, \bar{a}, \notin L) \qquad \frac{E \xrightarrow{a} E'}{E[f] \xrightarrow{f(a)} E[f]} \qquad \frac{E \xrightarrow{a} E'}{A \xrightarrow{a} E'}(A \stackrel{def}{=} E)$$

Consequently, with each agent expression E, a L.T.S. can be associated.

2.3 Behavioral Equivalence of processes

In [7], three kind of equivalences are introduced; from the strongest to the weakest: strong equivalence, observation congruence, and observation equivalence. The first two relations are also congruence for the operators of CCS. They are all defined according to the same idea : *If two processes are equivalent then they can perform the same action and then become equivalent processes.* Only the semantics of "perform an action" changes.

Strong equivalence is defined as the union of all strong bisimulation :

Definition 2.1 (Strong bisimulation, strong equivalence) *a binary relation among agent expressions, B, is a strong bisimulation iff it verifies :*

$$P \; B \; Q \Rightarrow \forall a, \; \forall P', (P \xrightarrow{a} P' \Rightarrow \exists Q', Q \xrightarrow{a} Q' \text{ and } P' \; B \; Q')$$
$$\text{and} \quad \forall Q', (Q \xrightarrow{a} Q' \Rightarrow \exists P', P \xrightarrow{a} P' \text{ and } P' \; B \; Q')$$

the relation $\sim = \cup_{B strong \; bisimulation} B$ *is an equivalence relation called strong equivalence.*

To define observation equivalence, the particular action τ, representing internal computation, is considered.Transition relations $\Rightarrow$ and $\Rightarrow_{ref}$ are defined by abstracting internal computation :

- $\forall$ P,Q agent expressions, $\forall a \in Act$: $P \xrightarrow{a} Q \Leftrightarrow P \xrightarrow{\tau^* a \tau^*} Q$
- $\Rightarrow_{ref} = \Rightarrow \cup \{ (P, \tau, P) / P \text{ agent expression } \}$

The definition of weak bisimulation and observation equivalence is obtained by substituting $\Rightarrow_{ref}$ for $\rightarrow$ in Definition 2.1. Unfortunately, observation equivalence is not a congruence for the operator "+", that is why the stronger observation congruence is introduced :

Definition 2.2 (observation congruence, equality)
P and Q are observation equivalent iff
$$\forall a \in Act, \quad \forall P', \; (P \xrightarrow{a} P' \Rightarrow \exists Q', Q \xRightarrow{a} Q' \text{ and } P' \approx Q')$$
$$\text{and } \forall Q', (Q \xrightarrow{a} Q' \Rightarrow \exists P', P \xRightarrow{a} P' \text{ and } P' \approx Q')$$
Observation congruence is also called equality and denoted by the usual symbol "=".

In the sequel, the symbol $\cong$ denotes $\sim$, $\approx$ or $=$ in properties verified by three equivalences.

3   PCCS presentation

In order to explicitly declare symmetries, new concepts are introduced into CCS, resulting in an extended CCS, so-called Pool CCS (PCCS). PCCS describes in a simple way pools of concurrent processes sharing a class of possible behaviours. For each pool of agents, an unique name `Pool_id` is introduced. | `Pool_id` | is the number of agents in `Pool_id`. | `Pool_id` |. | `Pool_id` | is an integer constant, that is, the number of agents for a given pool is constant. agents in the pool are assumed to be numbered from 1 to | `Pool_id` |.

Moreover, the set of labels is partitioned into :

- the set of common labels $\mathcal{L}_{com}$, which enables communication between distinct pools (with distinct pool identifiers),
  $Act_{com} = \mathcal{L}_{com} \cup \{\tau\}$ is the set of common actions,
- the sets of symbolic labels $\mathcal{L}(\text{Pool\_id})$ attached to each pool `Pool_id`. Label a of $\mathcal{L}(\text{Pool\_id})$ represents label a_i of any agent i of pool `Pool_id`.

Example : The Jobshop example described in [7] is extended. Let us consider that n jobbers share p hammers and q mallets to manufacture objects brought by a different conveyer belt for each jobbers. The whole system, depicted in Figure 2, may be represented by 3 pools `JOBBERS`, `HAMMERS` and `MALLETS` such that $\mid JOBBERS \mid = n$, $\mid HAMMERS \mid = p$ and $\mid MALLETS \mid = q$. As each jobber is working on his own conveyer belt, entering and leaving of objects is expressed by symbolic labels `in`, `out` in `JOBBERS`. The other labels `geth`, `puth`, `getm`, `putm` are common labels. In Figure 2, agents J_i, the ith jobbers, H_k, the kth hammers, and M_l, the lth mallets are represented.

The communications between distinct pools are restricted to labels of $\mathcal{L}_{com}$ in order to not break the pool agent symmetry by composition. For instance, suppose that pool `One_Object` is inserted in the Jobshop system, its symbolic labels are $\{in\}$ (cf. Figure 3). The ith agent in `One_Object`

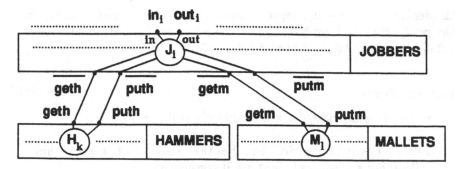

FIGURE 2. Jobshop system

prevents the ith jobber to manufacture more than one object. Now, assume that $|\,One\_Object\,| = 1$, then only the first jobber cannot manufacture two objects, i.e., symmetry among jobbers is broken.

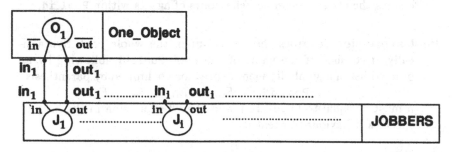

FIGURE 3. Breaking symmetries by communication on symbolic labels

The syntax and the transitional semantics are detailed in the next two parts. The relations between PCCS and behavioral equivalences are explained in the third part. The last part compares the expressive power of CCS and PCCS.

3.1 Syntax of PCCS

The new syntactical elements are :

- pool declaration, to define new pools,
- Pool expression, to define a pool behaviour,

The Pool expression addition to standard CCS expressions results in PCCS expressions.

Declaration of Pools

A pool is declared by : `POOL Pool_id  n { symbolic_labels }`
`POOL` is a key word introducing the declaration. `Pool_id` is the identifier of

the declared pool, n is an integer constant defining the number of agents in the pool, | Pool_id |. symbolic_labels is a sequence of distinct identifiers defining symbolic labels of Pool_id, $\mathcal{L}$(Pool_id).

Pool expressions

There are three imbricated syntactical levels in PCCS :

Symbolic agent expression describes the behaviour of agents within a Pool. For a given pool, Pool_id, it consists of :
- a CCS expression using $\mathcal{L}_{com} \cup \mathcal{L}$(Pool_id) as labels,
- a constant A such that $A \stackrel{def}{=} E$ and E is a symbolic agent expression of Pool, Pool_id.

The set of symbolic agent expressions attached to a pool, Pool_id, defines the class of possible behaviours of agents within Pool_id.

Pool expression describes the behaviour of the whole pool. Syntactically, it consists of the name of the pool, Pool_id, following by an ordered list of n symbolic agent expressions delimited by parenthesis :
$$\text{Pool\_id}(E_1, E_2, \ldots, E_i, \ldots, E_{n-1}, E_n)$$
n must be equal to | Pool_id |, and the ith expression in the list, E_i, specifies behaviour of agent i.

PCCS expression describes a system where several agent pools are working and consists of usual CCS operators and Pool expressions.

In the sequel, $E_i, F_i, \ldots$ will range over the symbolic agent expressions, $P, Q, \ldots$ will range over PCCS expressions, and Pool_id is a pool of n agents.

Remark : as symbolic agent expressions are usual CCS terms, the imbrication of pools is forbidden in PCCS (this choice is explained in part 6).

Example : In the Jobshop system, the three pools are declared by :
POOL JOBBERS n {in,out}   POOL HAMMERS p {}   POOL MALLETS q {}
The behaviour of agents are expressed by the symbolic agent expression :
$$J \stackrel{def}{=} in.(\overline{geth}.\overline{puth}.\overline{out}.J + \overline{getm}.\overline{putm}.\overline{out}.J)$$
$$H \stackrel{def}{=} geth.puth.H \qquad\qquad M \stackrel{def}{=} getm.putm.M$$
Behaviours of pools are expressed by Pool expressions :
$$\overbrace{\text{JOBBERS}(J,\ldots,J)}^{n\ times} \qquad \overbrace{\text{HAMMERS}(H,\ldots,H)}^{p\ times} \qquad \overbrace{\text{MALLETS}(M,\ldots,M)}^{q\ times}$$
The whole system is specified by the PCCS expression :
(JOBBERS$(J,\ldots,J)$ | HAMMERS$(H,\ldots,H)$ | MALLETS$(M,\ldots,M)$) \ L
where L = {geth, getm, putm, puth}

3.2 Transitional semantics of PCCS

The PCCS semantics is defined in terms of labelled transition systems like in CCS. The specification rules of the behaviour of Pool expressions are defined in the first part. The PCCS rules are the standard CCS rules plus specific rules for Pool expressions. Some minor modifications are introduced for restriction and relabeling in the case of symbolic labels.

Transitional semantics of Pool expressions

The transitional semantics of a symbolic agent expression is given by the usual CCS rules. The following extra rules define the semantics of Pool expressions :

$$\text{Com} \frac{E_i \xrightarrow{a} E_i'}{\text{Pool\_id}(...E_{i-1}, E_i, E_{i+1}...) \xrightarrow{a} \text{Pool\_id}(...E_{i-1}, E_i', E_{i+1}...)} (a \in Act_{com})$$

$$\text{Symb} \frac{E_i \xrightarrow{a} E_i'}{\text{Pool\_id}(..., E_i, ...) \xrightarrow{a_i} \text{Pool\_id}(..., E_i', ...)} (a \in \mathcal{L}(\text{Pool\_id}))$$

Com is the production of common action a by agent i.

Symb shows how a symbolic label catches the identity of the issuing agent, i.e. the symbolic agent expression is instantiated.

Intra-pool Communications obey to ($sync$ is a distinguished action in $\mathcal{L}_{com}$) :

$$\text{Rdv}_2 \frac{E_i \xrightarrow{a} E_i' \qquad E_j \xrightarrow{\bar{a}} E_j'}{\text{Pool\_id}(..., E_i, ..., E_j, ...) \xrightarrow{\tau} \text{Pool\_id}(..., E_i', ..., E_j', ...)} \left(\begin{array}{c} a, \bar{a} \in \mathcal{L}_{com} \\ a, \bar{a} \neq sync \end{array} \right)$$

$$\text{Rdv}_{all} \frac{E_i \xrightarrow{\overline{sync}} E_i' \text{ and } \forall j \neq i, E_j \xrightarrow{sync} E_j'}{\text{Pool\_id}(E_1, ..., E_n) \xrightarrow{\tau} \text{Pool\_id}(E_1', ..., E_n')}$$

Rdv$_2$ represents the communication between agents i and j in the pool on a common label. Only agents i and j are moving.

Rdv$_{all}$ is a natural rule of atomic multicast within a pool. This kind of multi-synchronization is not in the spirit of CCS but it is very convenient to build high-level specifications; furthermore, it is restricted within a pool. Nevertheless, this rule is not essential and can be deleted from PCCS without altering the results of the next sections.

Example : in the Jobshop system, a jobber which detects a default on its input object, must stop the production in the Jobshop. Thus, the other jobbers must stop working after having manufactured their current object. The description of the new system is obtained by replacing the symbolic agent expression J by J_{watch} in the previous description :

$$J_{watch} \stackrel{def}{=} in.(sync.0 + \overline{geth}.\overline{puth}.O_{watch} + \overline{getm}.\overline{putm}.O_{watch})$$

$$O_{watch} \stackrel{def}{=} \overline{sync}.0 + \overline{out}.J_{watch}$$

Transitional semantics of PCCS

Pool expressions can be used in usual CCS expressions. Transitional semantics of "+" and "|" and "." remains the same, only restriction and relabeling have a different semantics when they are applied with labels of $\mathcal{L}(\mathtt{Pool\_id})$:

$$\frac{E \xrightarrow{a_i} E'}{E \setminus L \xrightarrow{a_i} E' \setminus L}(a \in \mathcal{L}(\mathtt{Pool\_id}) \; and \; a, \bar{a}, \notin L) \qquad \frac{E \xrightarrow{a_i} E'}{E[f] \xrightarrow{f(a)_i} E'[f]}(a \in \mathcal{L}(\mathtt{Pool\_id}))$$

Moreover, a relabeling function must respect the domains :

$$f(\mathcal{L}(\mathtt{Pool\_id})) \subseteq \mathcal{L}(\mathtt{Pool\_id})$$

Remarks : $\mathcal{L}(\mathtt{Pool\_id}) \cap \mathcal{L}(\mathtt{Pool\_id'}) = \emptyset$ prevents different pools from communicating on symbolic labels. However, two expressions of a single pool may communicate on symbolic labels.

3.3   PCCS behavioral equivalences

The former three equivalence definitions are still valid in the case of PCCS. Moreover, they are congruences for operator $\mathtt{Pool\_id}$:

Property 3.1 (Pool expressions and behavioural equivalences)
$E_i \cong F_i \; \Rightarrow \; \mathtt{Pool\_id}(E_1, \ldots, E_i, \ldots, E_n) \cong \mathtt{Pool\_id}(E_1, \ldots, F_i, \ldots, E_n)$

Proof (sketch of) :
$B = \{(\mathtt{Pool\_id}(E_1, \ldots, E_i, \ldots, E_n), \mathtt{Pool\_id}(E_1, \ldots, F_i, \ldots, E_n)/E_i \cong F_i\}$
is a strong (resp. weak) bisimulation if $\cong$ is $\sim$ (resp. $\cong$ is $\approx$) as a consequence of the transitional semantics of Pool expressions.
($\cong$ is $=$) as a consequence of ($\cong$ is $\approx$). $\square$.

3.4   PCCS power of expression

As any CCS expression is a PCCS expression, PCCS expressive power is greater than CCS. Conversely :

Property 3.2 *If the rule* **Rdv**$_{all}$ *is not used then there exists a set of rewriting rules changing each PCCS expression, in a CCS expression having the same derived L.T.S..*

Sketch of proof : For each $\mathtt{Pool\_id}$, a family $(f_i)_{1 \leq i \leq n}$ of relabeling functions is defined :
$$f_i(a) = \begin{cases} a & if a \in \mathcal{L}_{com} \\ a_i & if a \in \mathcal{L}(\mathtt{Pool\_id}) \end{cases}$$
Then, a CCS expression is obtained from each PCCS expression by the rewriting rules :
$$\mathtt{Pool\_id}(E_1, \ldots, E_n) \to E_1[f_1] \mid \ldots \mid E_i[f_i] \mid \ldots \mid E_n[f_n]$$
Finally, verify that the obtained CCS expression share the same derived L.T.S. than P. $\square$

From this property, one could claim that the concept of pool is useless since it can be replaced by usual CCS expressions. But, in this case, the compositional issue of PCCS is lost : nothing ensure that symmetries in CCS expressions will be preserved by composition (see for instance, the example of One_Object in the jobshop). Hence, symmetries should be recomputed for each CCS expression.

4 PCCS Symmetries

PCCS symmetries are defined for Pool expressions of the same pool. They involve the notion of Permutability. Two expressions are permutable iff it exists an agent permutation within the pool which make them equal. A deductive system, introduced in the next part, makes this definition precise. The behaviour interpretation of permutability is explained in part two. An efficient permutability computation is presented in part three.

4.1 Permutable expressions

Permutability is defined as the union of Φ-equalities. Two expressions are related by a Φ-equality iff they are equal up to permutation Φ of symbolic agents in pool expressions. Φ-equality and Permutability of pool expressions are first defined. The extension to any PCCS expression is then carried out by means of a deductive system. The recursion problem needs a particular treatment. Φ-equality is decidable over PCCS and so is Permutability. Permutability is finally defined, as an equivalence relation.

Permutable Pool expressions

Symmetries are derived from agent permutations :

Definition 4.1 (Permutable Pool expressions)
Let φ be permutation over $\{1,..,n\}$.
Pool_id$(E_1, ..., E_n)$ *and* **Pool_id**$(E'_1, ..., E'_n)$ *are equal up to φ or φ-equal iff $\forall i \in \{1, \ldots, n\}$, E_i and $E'_{\varphi(i)}$ are syntactically equal. Two Pool expressions are permutable iff it exists φ such that they are equal up to φ.*

Remark : a more simple definition of permutable pool expression can be : two pool expressions are permutable iff they are syntactically equal up to associativity and commutativity among processes within a pool. However, the extension of permutability to any PCCS expressions requires to identify the permutation which makes two Pool expressions equal. This is the reason why φ-equality is introduced.

PCCS Φ-equality

The extension to any PCCS expression is performed by first, defining a mapping Φ over Pool identifiers such that :
$\forall\texttt{Pool\_id}$, $\Phi(\texttt{Pool\_id})$ is a permutation over $\{1,\ldots,|\texttt{Pool\_id}|\}$.

Equality up to Φ, or Φ-equality, denoted $\overset{\Phi}{=}$, is then defined by a deductive system. Obviously, the notion of Φ-equality over Pool expressions remains the same that in 4.1 :

$$(A_1)\ \frac{\texttt{Pool\_id}(E_1,\ldots)\ \text{and}\ \texttt{Pool\_id}(E_1',\ldots)\ \text{are}\ \Phi(\texttt{Pool\_id})\text{-equal}}{\texttt{Pool\_id}(E_1,\ldots)\overset{\Phi}{=}\texttt{Pool\_id}(E_1',\ldots)}$$

As our motivation is to preserve symmetries by composition, Φ-equality is naturally extended as a congruence :

$$(A_2)\frac{}{0\overset{\Phi}{=}0}\qquad (R_1)\frac{P\overset{\Phi}{=}Q}{P[f]\overset{\Phi}{=}Q[f]}\qquad (R_2)\frac{P\overset{\Phi}{=}Q}{P\setminus L\overset{\Phi}{=}Q\setminus L}\qquad (R_3)\frac{P\overset{\Phi}{=}Q}{a.P\overset{\Phi}{=}a.Q}$$

$$(R_4)\frac{P_1\overset{\Phi}{=}Q_1\ \text{and}\ P_2\overset{\Phi}{=}Q_2}{(P_1+P_2)\overset{\Phi}{=}(Q_1+Q_2)}\qquad (R_5)\frac{P_1\overset{\Phi}{=}Q_1\ \text{and}\ P_2\overset{\Phi}{=}Q_2}{(P_1\mid P_2)\overset{\Phi}{=}(Q_1\mid Q_2)}$$

In rules R_4, R_5 commutativity of "+" and "|" are not used. Indeed, commutativity would render the computation very complex. For instance, the comparison of $A_1+\cdots+A_n$ and $B_1+\cdots+B_n$, would require the examination of all the possible orderings of $A_1,\ldots,A_n$ and $B_1,\ldots B_n$. $n!$ operations are to be performed, and the computation is no more polynomial with the length of the expressions.

Recursion

Recursion requires a specific treatment. A naive idea would be to write the rule :

$$\frac{E\overset{\Phi}{=}Q}{A\overset{\Phi}{=}Q}(A\overset{def}{=}E)$$

But, the query, $\vdash\ A\overset{\Phi}{=}0+A$ where $A\overset{def}{=}0+A$, will lead to infinite computation.

So, a new construction, which preserves during the computation the substitution induced by $\overset{def}{=}$ is defined : $\Delta\rightsquigarrow P\overset{\Phi}{=}Q$ where Δ is a set of terms $P_i\overset{\Phi}{=}Q_i$. It means that $P\overset{\Phi}{=}Q$ under the assumption that for all i, $P_i\overset{\Phi}{=}Q_i$.
The following axiom is then a direct consequence :

$$(A_3)\ \frac{}{\Delta\cup\{P\overset{\Phi}{=}Q\}\rightsquigarrow P\overset{\Phi}{=}Q}$$

This construction is related to the former ones by the relation :

$$(R_6)\ \frac{P\overset{\Phi}{=}Q}{\Delta\rightsquigarrow P\overset{\Phi}{=}Q}\text{(for any }\Delta\text{ set of }\Phi\text{-equalities)}$$

The recursion rules can finally be completed :

$$(R_7) \frac{\Delta \cup \{A \stackrel{\Phi}{=} Q\} \rightsquigarrow E \stackrel{\Phi}{=} Q}{\Delta \rightsquigarrow A \stackrel{\Phi}{=} Q}(A \stackrel{def}{=} E) \quad (R_8) \frac{\Delta \cup \{Q \stackrel{\Phi}{=} A\} \rightsquigarrow Q \stackrel{\Phi}{=} E}{\Delta \rightsquigarrow Q \stackrel{\Phi}{=} A}(A \stackrel{def}{=} E)$$

Φ-equality Decidability

By taking into account the former set of axioms and inferences rules, $\stackrel{\Phi}{=}$ is decidable :

Property 4.1 *it can be decided by finite applications of* $A_1, \ldots, R_8$ *whether* $\vdash P \stackrel{\Phi}{=} Q$

Sketch of proof: The derivation tree whose root is $\vdash P \stackrel{\Phi}{=} Q$ is shown to be finite :
(a) as the length of expressions is assumed to be finite, the number of sons of each node in the derivation tree is finite. (b) as the number of constant names is assumed to be finite, the number of possible sets Δ is finite, hence the depth of the tree is finite. (a) and (b) $\Rightarrow$ the derivation tree is finite. $\square$

Permutability

P and Q are said to be permutable, denoted by $P \stackrel{P}{=} Q$, iff it exists Φ such that $\vdash P \stackrel{\Phi}{=} Q$.

Property 4.2 *Permutability is an equivalence relation*

Sketch of proof: the set of all mappings Φ is a group from laws :

- $\Phi \circ \Phi'(\texttt{Pool\_id}) = \Phi(Pool_i d) \circ \Phi'(\texttt{Pool\_id})$
- and $\Phi^{-1}(\texttt{Pool\_id}) = (\Phi(\texttt{Pool\_id}))^{-1}$

This group structure implies an equivalence relation, more particularly, neutral element $\Rightarrow$ reflexivity, inverse $\Rightarrow$ symmetry, internal composition law $\Rightarrow$ transitivity. $\square$

4.2 Interpretation of Permutability

Interpretation of Φ-equality

The interpretation of Φ-equality is similar to the other behavioral equivalences : *two processes are equal up to Φ iff if they can perform the same action up to Φ and then become Φ-equal processes* . The meaning of equal actions up to Φ is made precise by :
$$\begin{cases} if \ a \in \mathcal{L}(\texttt{Pool\_id}) \ then \ \Phi(a_i) = a_j \ with \ j = \Phi(\texttt{Pool\_id})(i), \\ if \ a \in \mathcal{L}com \ then \ \Phi(a) = a \end{cases}$$
The bisimulation and equivalence up to Φ may then be defined :

Definition 4.2 *A binary relation B_Φ is a bisimulation up to Φ iff*

$$PB_\Phi Q \Rightarrow \quad \forall a, \quad \forall P', \ (P \xrightarrow{a} P' \Rightarrow \exists Q', \ Q \xrightarrow{\Phi(a)} Q' \text{ and } P'B_\Phi Q')$$
$$\text{and} \quad \forall Q', \ (Q \xrightarrow{\Phi(a)} Q' \Rightarrow \exists P', \ P \xrightarrow{a} P' \text{ and } P'B_\Phi Q')$$

The relation $\overset{\Phi}{\sim} = \cup\, B_\Phi$ is called Φ-equivalence.

The Φ-equality is sound for the Φ-equivalence :

Property 4.3 (Soundness of Φ-equality) $\vdash P \overset{\Phi}{=} Q \Rightarrow P \overset{\Phi}{\sim} Q$

Sketch of proof: $\{(P,Q)/P \overset{\Phi}{=} Q\}$ is a bisimulation up to Φ (use $A_1, \ldots, R_8$).
$\square$

Interpretation of Permutability

Permutability is defined as the union of all Φ-equalities, so permutability interpretation is defined as the union of all Φ-equivalences, or P-Equivalence, denoted $\overset{P}{\sim}$.

The Φ-equalities properties entail the following property:

Property 4.4 (Interpretation of $\overset{P}{=}$) $P \overset{P}{=} Q \Rightarrow P \overset{P}{\sim} Q$

4.3 Efficient Computation of Permutability

Processing Pool expression

Let $\mid X \mid$ be the cardinal of the finite set X. To decide whether two Pool expressions are permutable does not require the exhaustive enumeration of all the $\mid$ Pool_id $\mid$! possible permutations because of the following fundamental property :

Property 4.5 *Let $\{P_1, \ldots, P_m\}$ and $\{Q_1, \ldots, Q_m\}$ partitions of $\{1, ..., n\}$,*
$(\forall 1 \le i \le m :\mid P_i \mid = \mid Q_i \mid) \Leftrightarrow (\exists\, \Phi$ *permutation of* $\{1, ..., n\} : \Phi(P_i) = Q_i)$

In the case of Pool expressions, partitions are induced by the notion of P-state : The P-state of a Pool expression $\texttt{Pool\_id}(E_1, \ldots, E_n)$, denoted $s(\texttt{Pool\_id}(E_1, \ldots, E_n))$ is the set $\{(P_k, E^k)/1 \le k \le m\}$ such that $P_k \subset \{1, ..., n\}$, is the set of agents which share the same symbolic expression E^k. $\{P_k/1 \le k \le m\}$ constitutes a partition of $\{1, ..., n\}$.

$\mid s \mid$ is the set $\{(\mid P_k \mid, E^k)/1 \le k \le m\}$ which gives for each k the number of agents which share E^k.

Example : in a Jobshop system with 3 hammers, it holds that:
$$s(\,HAMMERS(H, puth.H, H)\,) = \{\ (\{1,3\}, H),\ (\{2\}, puth.H)\ \}$$
$$\mid s(\,HAMMERS(H, puth.H, H)\,)\mid = \{\ (2, H),\ (1, puth.H)\ \}$$

If s (resp. s') denotes the P-state of a Pool expression P (resp. P') then from property 4.5 :

Property 4.6 $\mid s \mid = \mid s' \mid \Leftrightarrow P \overset{p}{=} P'$

Example : $HAMMERS(H, puth.H, H) \stackrel{P}{=} HAMMERS(H, H, puth.H)$ since:
$$| \; s(\; HAMMERS(H, puth.H, H) \;) \; | \quad = | \; s(\; HAMMERS(H, H, puth.H) \;) \; |$$
$$= \{(2, H), (1, puth.H)\}$$
Intuitively, in both cases, there are two free hammers.

Extension to PCCS

The extension of P-state to PCCS is similar to the extension of Φ-equality. The whole process is rather technical. Therefore, it is detailed in appendix 1. Basically, it uses the fact that Φ-equality is defined as a congruence and P-state is computed by intersection of partitions.

5 Validation in PCCS

PCCS symmetries may be applied for an efficient reduction of the state space. This reduction is performed by associating symbolic process $\overline{P}$ with each PCCS process P, as defined in the next section. The transitional semantics of symbolic Processes, derived from the PCCS transitional semantics, is then used to build a L.T.S.. The algorithm, described in section 2, takes, as input, a PCCS expression P and constructs the L.T.S. derived from the symbolic Process $\overline{P}$. The symbolic Process properties are presented in section 3.

5.1 Symbolic Processes

A symbolic Process is an equivalence class of PCCS processes with respect to the equivalence relation $\stackrel{P}{=}$. The equivalence class of process P is denoted $\overline{P}$. It represents a process up to a permutation among agents in Pools. This abstraction can be extended to actions by the mapping **abst**:
$$\begin{cases} if \; a \in \mathcal{L}_{com} \; then & abst(a) = a \\ if \; a = b_i \; with \; b \in \mathcal{L}(\text{Pool\_id}) \; then & abst(a) = b \\ for \; all \; co\text{-}action \; \overline{a}, & abst(\overline{a}) = \overline{abst(a)} \end{cases}$$
The transitional semantics of symbolic Processes is defined by the rule:

$$\frac{P \stackrel{a}{\longrightarrow} Q}{\overline{P} \stackrel{abst(a)}{\longrightarrow} \overline{Q}}$$

That is, the identity of agents is abstracted. This rule is not ambiguous since two processes, attached to the same symbolic Process gives the same symbolic transitions by the previous rule. In other words :

Property 5.1 $(\overline{P} = \overline{R} \; and \; P \stackrel{a}{\longrightarrow} Q) \Rightarrow$
$(\exists b, \; \exists T, \; abst(a) = abst(b) \; and \; \overline{Q} = \overline{T} \; and \; R \stackrel{b}{\longrightarrow} T)$

Sketch of proof: from the interpretation of Permutability by P-Equivalence. □

The symbolic L.T.S. of PCCS process P is the L.T.S. which can be derived from $\overline{P}$ using the transitional semantics of symbolic Processes.

5.2 The symbolic L.T.S.

The algorithm, depicted in Table .1, build the symbolic L.T.S. of P. The algorithm consists of a partial exploration of the L.T.S. which can be derived from P. An equivalence class of processes is represented by a class member, the first reached one (line (*) in the algorithm).

In the algorithm, $\rightarrow$ denotes the set of the symbolic L.T.S. transition relation, the reached states are putted in set **Reached**, the states whose transitions are to be fired are stored in stack **To_Explore**.

```
PROCEDURE SYMBOLIC_LTS( P : IN PCCS expression) IS
    Reached := {P}; Push(To_Explore,P) ; →= ∅;
    WHILE To_Explore ≠ empty_stack LOOP
        Pop(To_Explore,Q);
        FOR ALL (Q,a,R) PCCS transitions
            IF ∃ R' ∈ Reached such that R ≟ R'                (*)
                THEN →=→ ∪{(Q,abst(a),R')});
                ELSE Reached := Reached ∪ {R};
                    →:=→ ∪{(Q,abst(a),R)});
            END IF;
        END FOR ALL;
    END WHILE;
END PROCEDURE;
```

TABLE .1. Symbolic L.T.S. derivation algorithm

Property 5.2 (Soundness) *The algorithm of Table .1 builds the symbolic L.T.S. of P*

Sketch of proof: consequence of Property 5.1. □

5.3 Properties of symbolic Processes

The property of symbolic Processes can be deduced from the interpretation of Permutability in terms of P-Equivalence.

The Φ-equivalence notion is similar to the usual behavioral equivalences :

Property 5.3 $Q \overset{\Phi}{\sim} P$ and $Q \cong R$ and $R \overset{\Phi}{\sim} T \Rightarrow P \cong T$

The following property may then be deduced :

Property 5.4 $P \cong Q \Rightarrow \overline{P} \cong \overline{Q}$

This property is interesting in its negative form : $\overline{P} \not\cong \overline{Q} \Rightarrow P \not\cong Q$
That is it can be deduced over symbolic processes that two PCCS expressions are not linked by a behavioral equivalence.

Unfortunately, the converse property is false as shown by Figure 4.

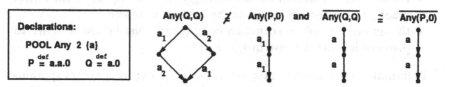

FIGURE 4. Counter example

Some weaker properties can nevertheless be decided :

1. $\mathcal{L}(\texttt{Pool\_id}) = \emptyset \Rightarrow \texttt{Pool\_id}(E_1, \ldots, E_n) \sim \overline{\texttt{Pool\_id}(E_1, \ldots, E_n)}$,
2. P is a deadlock $\Leftrightarrow \overline{P}$ is a deadlock,
3. P is divergent $\Leftrightarrow \overline{P}$ is divergent
   (P is divergent iff it can perform an infinite sequence of τ)

Sketch of proof: (1) consequence of property 5.1, and by noticing that a $= abst(a)$ if a $\in Act_{com}$. (2)+(3) from Property 5.1. $\square$
Property (1) is very interesting since it allows a partial compositional analysis by substituting $\overline{\texttt{Pool\_id}(E_1, \ldots, E_n)}$ for $\texttt{Pool\_id}(E_1, \ldots, E_n)$ in the system description. Moreover, it expresses a simple intuitive idea as shows the following example:

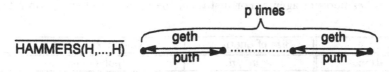

FIGURE 5. Symbolic L.T.S.

Example : in the Jobshop system, the symbolic L.T.S. of pool expression $HAMMERS(H, \ldots, H)$ is described in Figure 5. In CCS, it can be expressed by the agent ham_p such that :

$$\forall 1 \leq j \leq p-1, ham_j \stackrel{def}{=} geth.ham_{j-1} + puth.ham_{j+1}$$
$$ham_0 \stackrel{def}{=} puth.ham_1 \qquad ham_p \stackrel{def}{=} geth.ham_{p-1}$$

The same process can be applied to pool $MALLETS$. And the system described by :

$(JOBBERS(J, \ldots, J) \mid ham_p \mid mallet_q) \setminus \{geth, puth, getm, putm\}$

is strongly equivalent to the initial description of section 3 by Property (1). Hence, a conceptually simple expression can be automatically replaced by an expression easier to analyze.

6 PCCS enhancement

Two criteria are essential for a symmetrical formalism :

- the number of states of the quotient graph with respect to the initial graph. The reduction rate must be as high as possible.
- the quotient graph construction complexity must be low in order to preserve in time the save in space.

To formalize the reduction rate, let us consider a set of n agents (parameter n represents the complexity of the system). Each agent behaviour has m states. The agent composition is assumed to not restrict their reachable states, that is, the number of states of the whole systems is m^n: the number of state grows exponentially with the complexity.

The quotient graph state number of this system is now computed for several groups of agent permutations. This defines the theoretical reduction power of each permutation group.

The procedure complexity for determining whether two states are symmetrical is directly related to the computation complexity.

Table .2 shows the results in the case of four symmetries:

- The group of rotation, the agents are located on a ring,
- The dihedral group, the agents are located on a polygon,
- PCCS, i.e the group of all permutations, the agents are in a set (or a complete net),
- 2D-PCCS, an extension of PCCS where a pool of agents can contain other pools of agents. For instance, the agents are located on a tree.

	Size of quotient	Complexity w.r.t n
Rotations	$\geq m^n/n$	polynomial
Dihedral group	$\geq m^n/2n$	polynomial
PCCS	$C_{n+m-1}^n \leq (n+m)^m$	polynomial
2D-PCCS	$\leq ((n/2)+m)^{2m}$	equivalent to the graph isomorphism problem

TABLE .2. Results for different kinds of symmetries

It seems not interesting to use rotations or dihedral groups in order to fight against combinatorial explosion, because their reduction rate is low.

2D-PCCS could be a good candidate but the complexity of computation constitutes a handicap. Finally, PCCS seems to be a good trade-off. Besides, the list is not exhaustive, and other kind of symmetries may combine good figures.

7 Conclusion

PCCS supplies a suitable formalism for Pools of agents and their symmetries. The agent Pools are described by a new structure: Pool expressions. The symmetries are expressed by means of Permutability concept. As Permutability is an equivalence relation, symbolic Processes can be defined as an equivalence class. A symbolic transitional semantics is brought to symbolic processes. Furthermore, an algorithm is available for computing the symbolic L.T.S. of a PCCS expression. Permutability can be decided in polynomial time, consequently the computation cost of the symbolic L.T.S. is low. The Permutability interpretation in terms of P-Equivalence, makes possible verifications over symbolic L.T.S. : divergence, showing that two processes are not related by behaviour equivalences . . .

Now, we are working on solutions to verify behavioral equivalence on symbolic processes. We think that it can be performed by introducing new synchronization operators $\|$ such that behavioral equivalence between P and Q can be verified upon the symbolic process $\overline{P \parallel Q}$.

8 REFERENCES

[1] A. Sistla E. Emerson. Symmetry and model checking. In *Computer Aided Verification*, pages 463–478. Lecture Notes in Computer Science 697, June-July 1993.

[2] T. Filkorn E.M. Clarke and S. Jha. Exploiting symmetry in temporal logic model checking. In *Computer Aided Verification*, pages 451–462. Lecture Notes in Computer Science 697, June-July 1993.

[3] G. Franceschinis G. Chiola, C. Dutheillet and S. Haddad. On well-formed coloured nets and their symbolic reachability graph. In *High-Level Petri Nets*, pages 373–396. Springer-Verlag, 1991.

[4] C. Ip and D. Dill. Better verification through symmetry. In *Int. Symp. on Computer Hardware Description language and their Application*, 1993.

[5] Claude Dutheillet Lamonthezie. *Symétrie dans les Réseau Colorés*. PhD thesis, Université Paris 6, 1991.

[6] Robin Milner. *A Calculus of Communication Systems*, volume 92. Springer-Verlag, lncs edition, 1980.

[7] Robin Milner. *Communication and Concurrency*. Prentice Hall, 1989.

[8] L.O. Jepsen P. Huber, A.M. Jensen and K. Jensen. Reachability trees for high-level petri nets. In *High-Level Petri Nets*, pages 319–350. Springer-Verlag, 1991.

[9] K. Schmidt. Symmetries of petri nets. Informatik-Berichte 33, Humbolt-Universität zu Berlin, 1994.

1 Efficient Computation of Permutabilty

1.1 P-states of Pool expression sets

The notion of P-state is generalized to sets of Pool expressions by :
Let $(\texttt{Pool\_id}(E_1^i, \ldots, E_n^i))_{1 \leq i \leq l}$ be a family of l Pool expressions of the same Pool, Pool_id.
The P-state of this family is the set: $s = \{ (P_k, V_k) \ / \ 1 \leq k \leq m \}$ where

- $(V_k)_{1 \leq k \leq m}$ is a family of vectors of length l :
  $V_k = (V_k^1, \ldots, V_k^l)$ where V_k^h is a symbolic agent expression.
- j and g in P_k means that, for each $1 \leq h \leq l$, agents j and g share the same agent expression V_k^h in the hth Pool expression:

$$
\text{l Pool expressions} \left\{ \begin{array}{l} \texttt{Pool\_id}(\ldots, \overset{j}{V_k^1}, \ldots, \overset{g}{V_k^1}, \ldots) \\ \vdots \\ \texttt{Pool\_id}(\ldots, V_k^l, \ldots, V_k^l, \ldots) \end{array} \right.
$$

Moreover, $| \ s \ | = \{ \ (| \ P_i \ |, V_i) \ / \ 1 \leq i \leq m \ \}$.

The P-state of a singleton $\{\texttt{Pool\_id}(E_1, \ldots, E_n)\}$ defined in section 4.3 is denoted $s(\texttt{Pool\_id}(E_1, \ldots, E_n))$. The P-state of the union of two families can be computed from the P-states of these two families, by the operation $\sqcap$:

Property 1.1 *Let s (resp. s') be the P-state of family $\mathcal{F}_1$ (resp. $\mathcal{F}_2$),*
s $\sqcap$ s' is the smallest set obtained by :
If $(P_k, V_k) \in s$ and $(P_h', V_h') \in s'$ and $P_k \cap P_h' \neq \emptyset$ then $(P_k \cap P_h', V_k.V_h') \in s \sqcap s'$
($V_k.V_h'$ is the concatenation of vectors V_k and V_h').
s $\sqcap$ s' is the P-state of $\mathcal{F}_1 \cup \mathcal{F}_2$.

Indication of proof: from the property, if $\mathcal{P}$ and $\mathcal{Q}$ are partition of $\{1, \ldots, n\}$ then so are

$$\mathcal{P} \sqcap \mathcal{Q} = \{P \cap Q / \ P \in \mathcal{P}, \ Q \in \mathcal{Q}, P \cap Q \neq \emptyset\} \square$$

Moreover, the indetermined P-state denoted ω is introduced. It is the P-state associated to an empty set of Pool expressions. It is assumed that: $\omega \sqcap s = s \sqcap \omega = s$ and $| \ \omega \ | = \emptyset$.

1.2 Extension to PCCS expressions

First, an extended P-state S is defined as a mapping such that :
∀Pool_id, $S(\texttt{Pool\_id})$ is a P-state of a Pool expression family of Pool_id.
The operations over P-states are naturally extended :

$$| S |: \texttt{Pool\_id} \mapsto | S(\texttt{Pool\_id}) |$$
$$S \sqcap S' : \texttt{Pool\_id} \mapsto S(\texttt{Pool\_id}) \sqcap S'(\texttt{Pool\_id})$$

The indetermined extended P-state denoted Ω is defined by:
$$\forall \texttt{Pool\_id}, \ \Omega(\texttt{Pool\_id}) = \omega.$$

Now, the extended P-state S(P) associated with each P can be computed by :

$$S(0) = \Omega \qquad S(a.P) = S(P) \qquad S(P[f]) = S(P) \qquad S(P \setminus L) = S(P)$$

$$S(P + Q) = S(P \mid Q) = S(P) \sqcap S(Q)$$

$$S(\texttt{Pool\_id}(E_1, \ldots)) = \Omega \ \sqcap \ s(\texttt{Pool\_id}(E_1, \ldots))$$

Recursion is treated like for Φ-equality, i.e., a new construction is defined :
$\Delta \rightsquigarrow S(P) = S$, where Δ is a set of equalities $S(P_i) = S_i$.
It means that S(P)=S under the assumption that for all i, $S(P_i) = S_i$.
Hence, the axiom and the rule :

$$\Delta \cup \{S(P) = S\} \rightsquigarrow S(P) = S \qquad \qquad \frac{S(P) = S}{\Delta \rightsquigarrow S(P) = S}$$

The Recursion is processed by :

$$\frac{\Delta \cup \{S(A) = \Omega\} \rightsquigarrow S(E) = S}{S(A) = S} (A \stackrel{def}{=} E)$$

For the same reasons that Φ-equality, the computation of S(P) is always finite.
And the Property 4.6 about P-states and Permutability can be extended :

Property 1.2 $P \stackrel{P}{=} Q \Leftrightarrow \mid S(P) \mid = \mid S(Q) \mid$

Sketch of proof: by structural induction over P + Property 4.6 □.

Moreover, since the computation of $\sqcap$ is polynomial with the arity of each pools of agents, the computation of the P-state is polynomial with the length of the system PCCS description, i.e., the sum of the length of the PCCS expressions which represents the whole behaviour and the length of all needed expressions $A \stackrel{def}{=} E$.

Strategy Construction in Infinite Games with Streett and Rabin Chain Winning Conditions

Nils Buhrke*
Helmut Lescow*
Jens Vöge*

ABSTRACT We consider finite-state games as a model of nonterminating reactive computations. A natural type of specification is given by games with Streett winning condition (corresponding to automata accepting by conjunctions of fairness conditions). We present an algorithm which solves the problem of program synthesis for these specifications. We proceed in two steps: First, we give a reduction of Streett automata to automata with the Rabin chain (or parity) acceptance condition. Secondly, we develop an inductive strategy construction over Rabin chain automata which yields finite automata that realize winning strategies. For the step from Rabin chain games to winning strategies examples are discussed, based on an implementation of the algorithm.

1 Introduction

In recent years, methods of automatic verification for finite–state programs have been applied successfully, which have clearly reached the level of practical use. For the existing automata theoretic results on finite–state program synthesis the situation is quite different. Not only explicit formulations of algorithms but also experience in nontrivial examples are missing. The present paper offers an algorithm for finite–state program synthesis from automaton specifications; we also discuss some examples based on an implementation.

The foundations of finite–state program synthesis were laid in the work of Büchi and Landweber [BL69]. Papers exploiting further the approach include Pnueli, Rosner [PR89], Abadi, Lamport, Wolper [ALW89], and Nerode, Yakhnis, Yakhnis [NYY92]. Recently, the paradigm of program synthesis has attracted increasing attention in the context of discrete event

*Institut für Informatik und Praktische Mathematik, Christian-Albrechts-Universität Kiel, D-24098 Kiel, email: {nb, hel, jv}@informatik.uni-kiel.de. Supported by Deutsche Forschungsgemeinschaft, projects Th 352/3-2 and Th 352/5-1.

and discrete control systems ([RW89], [KG95], [AMP95]). Unfortunately, however, these papers do not present directly implementable synthesis algorithms; and also the original Büchi-Landweber paper, while describing an algorithm, is not feasible.

We adopt the following game theoretic framework (see [Tho95] for more detailed background). The interaction between two parties (say, a program and its environment) is modeled by two players, called 0 and 1 here, of an "infinite game" (or "Gale-Stewart game" [GS53]). In a play of the game, both parties perform actions in turn, thus building up an infinite computation. In the state-based description to be assumed in this paper, an action causes a transition in a state graph, and referring to the alternation between the two players, we suppose that this state graph is partitioned into two sets such that the transition relation induces a bipartite graph with respect to these two sets. The two players' actions can then be viewed as movements of a token through this "game graph" along the graph edges. By conditions on the visited (or infinitely often visited) states it can be specified which computations ("plays") cause a win of player 0. As we identify player 0 with the party "program" and player 1 with the "environment", this winning condition for player 0 defines the set of "desired computations" as given by the specification.

The synthesis problem for these games asks for programs that realize winning strategies for player 0, i.e. allow player 0 to choose transitions that ensure his win whatever player 1 does. Büchi and Landweber [BL69] showed that one can effectively compute the set of states from where (as start of a play) player 0 wins, and that such a winning strategy is always realizable by a finite automaton.

In applications (e.g. in problems of discrete control) a natural type of winning condition is the so-called "Streett form" [Str82], i.e. a conjunction of conditions of the form

"if state set U_k is visited infinitely often then state set L_k is visited infinitely often".

Short:
$$(*) \quad \bigwedge_{1 \leq k \leq r} (Inf(\pi) \cap U_k \neq \emptyset \Rightarrow Inf(\pi) \cap L_k \neq \emptyset).$$

Finite game graphs with such winning conditions (for player 0) can be viewed as finite Streett automata (in the sense of ω-automata theory [Tho90]), known to characterize the regular ω-languages.

The computational difficulties in constructing winning strategies for such games are due to two phenomena: First the size of memory needed in winning strategies, secondly the recursive descent by which the given game graph is reduced when a strategy is constructed.

In this paper we develop an algorithm for strategy synthesis in Streett games which proceeds in two steps (by which the above mentioned phenomena are handled separately). First, we transform Streett games to games with "Rabin chain winning condition" (or "parity winning condition" [Mos91]). The blow–up of the game graphs in this step corresponds to the introduction of sufficient memory for winning strategies. The second step is the construction of memory–less winning strategies for these Rabin chain games; it involves a decomposition of the game graph. Other approaches might merge these two aspects (e.g. following [McN93], [TW94], [YY93]), but for experiments it seems useful to be able to study the two effects separately.

The first step has some resemblance to the reduction of games with the Muller winning condition to the Rabin chain condition (see e.g. Emerson, Jutla [EJ91], Thomas [Tho95]). We use a new version of the "latest appearance record". This data structure is hidden already in Rabin's paper [Rab69, lemma 3.8], and appeared in many forms (Gurevich, Harrington [GH82], Büchi [Büc83], Muchnik [Muc92], Safra [Saf92], Muller, Schupp [MS95]). We use a form, called "index appearance record" here, where in a Streett game with winning condition (∗) the indices of referenced sets L_k in the order of their last visits are kept in a record, together with two pointers. This is similar to Büchi's "order vector with hit position" [Büc83]. As a result we obtain a rather simple transformation with the (previously known) time complexity polynomial in the number of states but exponential in the number of pairs.

The actual synthesis algorithm starting from a game with Rabin chain or parity winning condition involves an induction (over the cardinality of the state space of the game) following the approach of [McN93, section 3] and [Tho95]. The time complexity of this synthesis problem is still open; our algorithm has an exponential upper bound but seems to allow practical use.

The paper is structured as follows: Section 2 introduces the terminology, section 3 the transition from Streett games to Rabin chain games, and section 4 presents the synthesis algorithm. In the final section we discuss the synthesis algorithm in a small example. The algorithm is implemented: more experiments with examples seem necessary to find appropriate heuristics for choosing pivot states which help to minimize backtracking in the synthesis algorithm.

We thank Wolfgang Thomas for many helpful discussions during the preparation of this paper.

2   Definitions and Notation

In the context of infinite games, it proved to be useful to consider a type of "ω-automaton" introduced by McNaughton [McN93] where we abstract from the labels of transitions, since the acceptance (or winning) condition depends only on visits of states; moreover, each state is associated with just the player whose turn it is to make the next move.

So a *finite-state game* is given by a bipartite finite directed graph G and a "winning condition". The idea is that two players, called player 0 and player 1, are moving a token alternatively from vertex to vertex along edges in the game graph. A game graph is of the form $G = (Q, Q_0, Q_1, E)$ with $Q = Q_0 \cup Q_1$ and $E \subseteq (Q_0 \times Q_1) \cup (Q_1 \times Q_0)$ where Q_i is the set of vertices where it is the turn of player i to move the token. Since we are interested only in infinite computations it is convenient to demand that each vertex of the game graph has at least one outgoing edge.

A *play* π is an infinite sequence of states from Q visited by the token in successive moves, i.e., a sequence $\pi \in Q^\omega$ with $(\pi(t), \pi(t+1)) \in E$ for all t. The winner of a play is declared by a *winning (or accepting) condition* $Win : Q^\omega \to \{0, 1\}$ that maps a play π to i iff the play π is won by player i. So a game Γ is given by a pair $\Gamma = (G, Win)$. In the sequel, we also use the term "state" for "vertex".

In this paper we deal with Rabin games and Streett games (referring to the analogous acceptance conditions for ω-automata). These games are characterized by special winning conditions. A *Rabin condition* is given by a system $\Omega \subseteq 2^Q \times 2^Q$, and the function Win defined by $Win(\pi) = 0$ iff

$$\exists (L, U) \in \Omega \quad \text{s.t.} \quad Inf(\pi) \cap L = \emptyset \wedge Inf(\pi) \cap U \neq \emptyset$$

where $Inf(\pi)$ is the set of vertices visited infinitely often during the play π. A Rabin game is called *Rabin chain game* if the set of accepting pairs Ω consists of pairs (E_k, F_k) that form a chain by set inclusion: $E_1 \subseteq F_1 \subseteq E_2 \subseteq \ldots \subseteq F_r$ (cf. [Mos91]).

The *Streett condition* (following [Str82]) is dual to the Rabin condition in the sense that a play π is won by player 0 in a Rabin game iff π is accepted for player 1 in the corresponding Streett game. So the Streett acceptance condition is given by a system $\Omega \subseteq 2^Q \times 2^Q$ where the function Win is defined by $Win(\pi) = 0$ iff

$$\forall (L, U) \in \Omega : Inf(\pi) \cap U \neq \emptyset \Rightarrow Inf(\pi) \cap L \neq \emptyset.$$

A *strategy for player* i in the game Γ is a function which associates with a partial play ending in Q_i a state in Q_{1-i}. W.l.o.g. a strategy may be defined as a partial function $\sigma : Q^* Q_i \to Q_{1-i}$ with $\sigma(p_1, \ldots, p_k) = p_{k+1}$ such that $(p_k, p_{k+1}) \in E$. The strategy σ is called a *winning strategy* if, for any choice of moves of player $1 - i$, it induces a play won by player i.

Büchi and Landweber showed that finite automata (with fixed finite memory M) are sufficient to realize winning strategies for games on finite graphs (cf. [BL69]). Due to this a strategy for player i can be defined, using a finite (memory) set M, as a function $\sigma : Q_i \times M \to Q_{1-i}$ and using a function $\varphi : Q \times M \to M$ for updating the memory with each move of the token.

For a finite game graph $G = (Q, Q_0, Q_1, E)$ we call $\hat{G} = (\hat{Q}, \hat{Q}_0, \hat{Q}_1, \hat{E})$ a *game–extension by memory* if there is a finite set M and a memory–update function $\varphi : Q \times M \to M$, s.t. $\hat{G}$ is characterized by M and φ as follows

$$
\begin{aligned}
(i) \quad & \hat{Q} &=& \; Q \times M, \\
(ii) \quad & \hat{Q}_i &=& \; Q_i \times M, \text{ for all } i \in \{0, 1\}, \\
(iii) \quad & \hat{E} &=& \; \{((q, m), (q', m')) : (q, q') \in E \text{ and } \varphi(q', m) = m'\}.
\end{aligned}
$$

The game $\Gamma = (G, Win)$ may be simulated by the game $\hat{\Gamma} = (\hat{G}, \widehat{Win})$ when we define $\widehat{Win}(\hat{\pi}) := Win(Pr_1(\hat{\pi}))$ for all $\hat{\pi} \in \hat{Q}^\omega$, where Pr_j is the projection to the j-th components of an ω-sequence of tuples.

Thus, a strategy is describable by an extended game graph where all edges from states in Q_i not of the form $((q, m), (\sigma(q, m), \varphi(q, m)))$ are deleted. We call a strategy for player i *no-memory* if no additional memory is required, i.e. the strategy is a function $Q_i \to Q_{1-i}$. It can be described by the game graph where all but one outgoing edges from states in Q_i are deleted.

3 From Streett games to Rabin chain games

Between the games given in normal form described by Büchi [Büc83, §5] and the games with Rabin chain condition introduced by Mostowski [Mos91] is a close relation. If these games are played on finite graphs the winning strategies may be given as subgraphs on the game graph, which are called no–memory strategies. Büchi [Büc83, §12] showed how to transform Muller games into games in normal form. The same technique is presented (in simpler terminology and in the simpler case of finite–state games) in Thomas [Tho95] for constructing Rabin chain games out of Muller games. In both cases the memory needed for constructing winning strategies in the main part consists of the well known "latest appearance record" or "order vector".

For building Rabin chain games out of Streett games in our case we extend the "index appearance record", introduced by Muller and Schupp [MS95], by two pointers as done by Safra [Saf92]. For this transformation we present here an easily implementable algorithm of time complexity polynomial in the size of states and exponential in the number of Streett conjunctions. The same can be done for Rabin games.

Let us introduce some conventions to talk about the properties of winning plays in a Streett game. Usually, we assume the following situation:

(*) Let $\Gamma = (G, Win)$ be a Streett game defined over a finite game graph $G = (Q, Q_0, Q_1, E)$ and a finite sequence of Streett pairs $\Omega = (L_k, U_k)_{k \in \{1,\dots,r\}}$ with $L_k, U_k \subseteq Q$, for $k \in \{1,\dots,r\}$, and $L_r = U_r = Q$, s.t. for all plays $\pi \in Q^\omega$ we have $Win(\pi) = 0$ iff for all $k \in \{1,\dots,r\}$ the following condition holds: $Inf(\pi) \cap U_k \neq \emptyset$ implies $Inf(\pi) \cap L_k \neq \emptyset$.

For a given play $\pi \in Q^\omega$ we say that player 0 *reaches* an index $k \in \{1,\dots,r\}$ in the play π at position t if $\pi(t) \in L_k$, and player 1 reaches the index k in the play π at t if $\pi(t) \in U_k$. An index $k \in \{1,\dots,r\}$ reached infinitely often in a play $\pi \in Q^\omega$ by player $i \in \{0,1\}$ is called *frequent* for player i on the play π.

It is quite clear that for a play $\pi \in Q^\omega$, player 0 wins iff the indices that are frequent for player 1 are also frequent for player 0 on the play π, formally

$$\{1 \leq k \leq r : Inf(\pi) \cap U_k \neq \emptyset\} \subseteq \{1 \leq k \leq r : Inf(\pi) \cap L_k \neq \emptyset\}.$$

In a play of a Streett game as in (*) we associate to each position an *index appearance record* (iar) consisting of permutations. The record at a position is given by shifting the indices reached for player 0 in the previous record to the right keeping the remainder in its previous ordering. A start record for the first position is defined. As an auxiliary notion we need a so–called shift function.

Definition 1 *Assume* (*). *For each* $q \in Q$ *and a permutation* $iar = (i_1, i_2, \dots, i_r)$ *of* $\{1,\dots,r\}$, *let* $L(iar, q)$ *be the subsequence of iar consisting of those* i_j *where* $q \in L_{i_j}$. *Similarly, let* $\overline{L}(iar, q)$ *be the (complementary) subsequence of iar with the* i_j *such that* $q \notin L_{i_j}$. *The value of the shift function* $sh : Perm(\{1,\dots,r\}) \times Q \to Perm(\{1,\dots,r\})$ *is defined by*

$$sh(iar, q) := \overline{L}(iar, q)L(iar, q).$$

The crucial point in defining the Rabin chain winning condition are the "hit positions" for each player. Hit functions were invented by Büchi [Büc83] to characterize games by a winning condition in normal form. In our case it would be sufficient to use one hit function which denotes the least hit position of both players and an extra function for the owner of the hit position, which is Büchi's original version. For a simpler argumentation, however, we proceed with two hit functions, one for each player.

Definition 2 *Assume* (*). *The hit function* $hit_i : Perm(\{1,\dots,r\}) \times Q \to \{1,\dots,r\}$ *for player* $i \in \{0,1\}$ *over* $t < \omega$ *is defined by*

$$hit_i(iar, q) := \mu p \in \{1,\dots,r\} : q \in \begin{cases} L_{iar(p)} & \text{if } i = 0, \\ U_{iar(p)} & \text{if } i = 1. \end{cases}$$

The hit functions for both players are well–defined, since the Streett condition contains the pair $(L_r, U_r) = (Q, Q)$. The pair may be added to every Streett condition without changing the winning plays of the game.

For the whole play in the Streett game a sequence of extended index appearance records is defined as follows:

Definition 3 *Assume* (∗). *The function* $IAR : Q^\omega \to Perm(\{1, \ldots, r\})^\omega$ *associates with any* $\pi \in Q^\omega$ *an* ω–*sequence* $IAR(\pi)$ *of iar's defined by*

$$IAR(\pi)(0) := (1, 2, \ldots, r),$$
$$IAR(\pi)(t) := sh(IAR(\pi)(t-1), \pi(t)), \text{ for } t > 0.$$

The sequence of hit positions for each player on a play is given by the following definition.

Definition 4 *Assume* (∗). *The hit function* $HIT_i : Q^\omega \to \{1, \ldots, r\}^\omega$ *over* ω–*sequences is defined for player* $i \in \{0, 1\}$ *by*

$$HIT_i(\pi)(0) := r,$$
$$HIT_i(\pi)(t) := hit_i(IAR(\pi)(t-1), \pi(t)), \text{ for } t > 0.$$

Before we can convert Street games to Rabin chain games we need the following lemma, which give us a link between the least infinite–hit positions of each player and the winner of each play.

Lemma 5 *Assume* (∗), *let* $\pi \in Q^\omega$ *be a play in* Γ *and let*

$$p_0 := \mu p : p \in Inf(HIT_0(\pi))$$

be the least infinite–hit position of player 0 *in the play* π. *Then the play* π *is won by player* 0 *iff for all* $p_1 \in Inf(HIT_1(\pi))$ *we have* $p_0 \leq p_1$.

Proof. Let $\pi \in Q^\omega$ be a play in the game Γ and $\alpha := IAR(\pi)$ the infinite sequence of the index appearance records on π and $p_0 := \mu p : p \in Inf(HIT_0(\pi))$.

Let $t_0 < \omega$ be a position in π such that from t_0 onwards all the indices reached for both players are frequent ones, and $p_0 \leq HIT_0(\pi)(t)$ for all $t > t_0$. Then for all $t \geq t_0$ the sets

$$F(t) := \{\alpha(t)(p) \in \{1, \ldots, r\} : p_0 \leq p \leq r\}$$

are equal to the set $F(t_0)$ and consist of the frequent indices for player 0 on π. In the following we will prove that a play $\pi \in Q^\omega$ is a win for player 0 if and only if for all infinite–hit positions $p_1 \in Inf(HIT_1(\pi))$ of player 1 we have $p_0 \leq p_1$. This is done in two steps.

"⇒": Let π be a winning play for player 0 and $p_1 \in Inf(HIT_1(\pi))$. Then there exist infinitely many indices $t_1 < t_2 < \ldots < \omega$ with $t_0 < t_1$ and $HIT_1(\pi)(t_i) = p_1$. Since π is winning for player 0 all indices reached after t_0 are in $F(t)$, so we get $p_0 \leq p_1$.

"⇐": Assume now that there exists a $p_1 \in Inf(HIT_1(\pi))$ with $p_1 < p_0$. For all $p < p_0$ and $t_0 < t$ we have that $\alpha(t_0)(p) = \alpha(t)(p)$, which means that α is not changed for positions less than p_0 after the position t_0. So player 1 reaches infinitely often an index which is not in the set of the frequent indices for player 0 on the play π. So we get $Win(\pi) = 1$.

□

Theorem 6 *Assume* (∗). *Then there is a memory extension* $\hat{\Gamma} = (\hat{G}, \widehat{Win})$ *of the game* Γ *with the finite game graph* $\hat{G} = (\hat{Q}, \hat{Q}_0, \hat{Q}_1, \hat{E})$ *and where* $\widehat{Win}$ *is a Rabin chain winning condition s.t. for all plays* $\hat{\pi} \in \hat{Q}^\omega$ *in the game* $\hat{\Gamma}$ *we have*

$$(+) \qquad Win(Pr_1(\hat{\pi})) = 0 \text{ iff } \widehat{Win}(\hat{\pi}) = 0.$$

Proof. We have to construct in the following a finite memory set M, a memory update function $\varphi : Q \times M \to M$ and the sequence of Rabin chain pairs. Then we have to prove that the two games are equivalent in the sense of $(+)$.

The finite set M of memory is given by

$$M := Perm(\{1, \ldots, r\}) \times \{1, \ldots, r\} \times \{1, \ldots, r\}.$$

The function $\varphi : Q \times M \to M$ is given for $(q, iar, h_0, h_1) \in Q \times M$ by

$$\varphi(q, iar, h_0, h_1) := (sh(iar, q), hit_0(iar, q), hit_1(iar, q)).$$

The Rabin chain acceptance condition $(E_1, F_1, E_2, F_2, \ldots, E_r, F_r)$ is built up inductively for $k \in \{1, \ldots, r\}$ and $F_0 := \emptyset$ by

$$E_k := F_{k-1} \cup \{(q, iar, h_0, h_1) \in Q \times M : h_1 = k-1 \text{ and } k \le h_0 \le r\},$$
$$F_k := E_k \ \cup \{(q, iar, h_0, h_1) \in Q \times M : h_0 = k \qquad \text{and } k \le h_1 \le r\}.$$

Note that E_1 is the empty set. It is easy to see that for all $k \in \{1, \ldots, r\}$ the sets E_k consist exactly of this states for which the hit position for at least one of the players is less than k.

Let $\hat{G} = (\hat{Q}, \hat{Q}_0, \hat{Q}_1, \hat{E})$ be the memory–extended game graph by the finite memory set M and the memory–update function φ. Define $\widehat{Win} : \hat{Q}^\omega \to \{0, 1\}$ over the Rabin chain $(E_1, \ldots, F_r)$. Then $\hat{\Gamma} = (\hat{G}, \widehat{Win})$ is a Rabin chain game. Finally we show that the two games are equivalent, w.r.t. $(+)$.

Therefore let $\hat{\pi} \in \hat{Q}^\omega$. Define $\pi := Pr_1(\hat{\pi})$. Then $\pi \in Q^\omega$, $HIT_0(\pi) = Pr_3(\hat{\pi})$ and $HIT_1(\pi) = Pr_4(\hat{\pi})$. By Lemma 5, $Win(\pi) = 0$ iff for all $p_1 \in Inf(HIT_1(\pi))$ the least infinite–hit position for player 0 is less or equal than p_1 iff there exists an index $k \in \{1, \ldots, r\}$ with $Inf(\hat{\pi}) \cap F_k \ne \emptyset$ and $Inf(\hat{\pi}) \cap E_k = \emptyset$. The last equivalence follows from the construction of the Rabin chain. Therefore $Win(\pi) = 0$ iff $\widehat{Win}(\hat{\pi}) = 0$. □

From Theorem 6 it follows directly that the generation of the states, of the edges and of the winning condition for a Rabin chain game based on a Streett game can be done separately. For the states and the winning condition it suffices to use simple enumeration routines with time complexity $O(n2^{r\log r})$. In the case of the edges the construction is also done by enumeration in time $O(n^2 2^{r\log r})$, whereby we have to use the hit–function and the shift–function as in Theorem 6.

Theorem 7 *The above construction yields, starting from a Streett game with n states and r accepting pairs, an equivalent Rabin chain game in time $O(n^2 2^{r\log r})$.*

Let us add a remark on games with special type of Streett winning condition: Assume a game (∗) has a Streett winning condition such that $L_1 \subseteq L_2 \subseteq \ldots \subseteq L_r$. In this special case we can extract a Rabin chain game immediately by defining the following winning condition assuming that $F_0 := \emptyset$ and $U_0 := \emptyset$:

$$E_k := F_{k-1} \cup U_{k-1} \text{ and } F_k := E_k \cup L_k, \text{ for all } k \in \{1,\ldots,r\}.$$

The proof is similar to the proof of Theorem 6 by defining the hit functions over the states $q \in Q$ for both players by

$$hit_0(q) := \mu k \leq r : q \in L_k \quad \text{and} \quad hit_1(q) := \mu k \leq r : q \in U_k.$$

It follows from the next section that Rabin chain games allow no–memory winning strategies. Hence in the case of Streett games with monotone increasing L–sets both players have a no–memory strategy.

4 Strategy construction for Rabin chain games

In this section we construct a deterministic winning strategy for a Rabin chain game. In the following we always mean by strategy a no–memory strategy.

Strategies will be presented by functions $\sigma : Q \rightarrow Q \cup \{\bot\}$. Such a function contains two strategies (given by the induced maps from Q_0 to $Q_1 \cup \{\bot\}$, resp. from Q_1 to $Q_0 \cup \{\bot\}$). If a player has no winning possibility in a state q this is indicated by $\sigma(q) = \bot$. Otherwise his strategy is to select $\sigma(q) \in Q$.

For each game (G, Win) with $\Omega = (E_1, F_1, \ldots, E_r, F_r)$ there is a dual game $(\overline{G}, \overline{Win})$, where players are changed: $\overline{G} = (Q, Q_1, Q_0, E)$. The acceptance condition can be complemented by shifting the state sets by one:

$$\overline{\Omega} = (\emptyset, E_1, F_1, E_2, \ldots, F_{r-1}, E_r, F_r, Q).$$

We construct a strategy by induction on the size of game graphs. So we need a notion of subgame. A game (G', Win') is called a subgame of

(G, Win) if $Q' \subseteq Q$ and $G' = (Q', Q_0 \cap Q', Q_1 \cap Q', E \cap (Q' \times Q'))$. The acceptance condition must be $\Omega' = \emptyset$ if $F_r \cap Q' = \emptyset$ and otherwise $\Omega' = (E'_l, F'_l, \ldots, E'_r, F'_r)$ with $l = \min\{k \in \{1, \ldots r\} | F_k \cap Q' \neq \emptyset\}$ and for $k \in \{l, \ldots, r\}$: $E'_k = E_k \cap Q'$ and $F'_k = F_k \cap Q'$. Furthermore, in the underlying graph at least one transition must leave each state. This is the only condition for a subset $Q' \subseteq Q$ to induce a subgame.

We define a function $reach()$ which over Q computes the set R of states from which a player i can force a visit in a given "target set" T. More precisely, the function $reach(Q_i, E, T)$ in Figure 1 determines the states $R \subseteq Q \setminus T$ from which player i can force a visit in T; simultaneously a function $\sigma : R \to Q \cup \{\bot\}$ is computed which defines a "strategy" to ensure this. The word "strategy" here only refers to the domain R which is computed by $reach()$.

> **function** $reach(Q_i, E, T)$:
>   **return** $Reach(Q_i, E, T, T)$
>
> **function** $Reach(Q_i, E, T, T')$:
> $R := \emptyset$
> $\rho := \emptyset$
>   **if** $T' = \emptyset$ **then**
>   **return** (R, ρ)
>   **else**
>   **for each** $q \in T'$ **do**
>   **for each** $p \in E^{-1}(q) \setminus T$ **do**
>   **if** $p \in Q_i$ **then**
> $R := R \cup \{p\}$
> $\rho := \rho \cup (p \mapsto q)$
>   **else**
> $t := true$
>   **for each** $q' \in E(p)$ **do**
>   **if** $q' \notin T$ **then**
> $t := false$
>   **if** t **then**
> $R := R \cup \{p\}$
> $\rho := \rho \cup (p \mapsto \bot)$
> $(R', \rho') := Reach(Q_i, E, T \cup R, R)$
>   **return** $(R \cup R', \rho \cup \rho')$

FIGURE 1. Function $reach()$

In the functions $reach()$ and $strategy()$ the notations $E(p) := \{q | (p, q) \in E\}$ and $E^{-1}(q) := \{p | (p, q) \in E\}$ are used for describing the transition relation E.

The computation of function $reach()$ starts with setting $R = \emptyset$. If there is a state $q \in Q_0 \setminus (T \cup R)$ with a transition leading into $T \cup R$ this state is added to R. If there is a state $q \in Q_1 \setminus (T \cup R)$ with all transitions leading into $T \cup R$ this state is also added to R. These steps are repeated until there is no further state to add. This construction ensures that $Q' = Q - R$ induces a subgame.

A strategy for a Rabin chain game (G, Win) with $G = (Q, Q_0, Q_1, E)$ and $\Omega = (E_1, F_1, \ldots, E_r, F_r)$ can be determined by the recursively defined function $strategy()$ of Figure 2: It returns a triple (V_0, V_1, σ), where V_i is the winning set for player i and $\sigma : Q \to Q \cup \{\bot\}$ is a strategy function. We divide the problem in four different cases of which three are quite simple.

(a) The trivial case is $|Q| = 0$. On this graph winning sets are empty and the strategy function is also empty.

(b) If the acceptance condition is empty ($\Omega = \emptyset$), player 0 cannot win. Thus winning sets are $V_0 = \emptyset$ and $V_1 = Q$. For the states of player 0 the value of the strategy function is $\bot$, for the states of player 1 any of the directly reachable states can be chosen.

(c) If the graph has a non–empty acceptance condition with $E_1 = \emptyset$ the case can be reduced to the dual game $(\overline{G}, \overline{Win})$ with $\overline{G} = (Q, Q_1, Q_0, E)$ and

$$\overline{\Omega} = (F_1, E_2, \ldots, F_{r-1}, E_r, F_r, Q) \quad \text{if } F_r \neq Q \text{ or}$$
$$\overline{\Omega} = (F_1, E_2, \ldots, F_{r-1}, E_r) \quad \text{if } F_r = Q.$$

(d) If none of the previous conditions holds the situation is more complicated. We select a pivot state $p \in E_1$. Player 1 wins if he can visit this state infinitely often. By applying $reach(Q, E, \{p\})$ we compute all states $R \subseteq Q \setminus \{p\}$ from which player 1 can force a visit of p. This function also computes a strategy ρ to get there. Then we determine a strategy for the remaining subgame $(G \setminus (R \cup \{p\}), Win')$ with $\Omega' = \Omega \setminus (R \cup \{p\})$ which results from the original game by removing all states of $R \cup \{p\}$. By induction hypotheses we get winning sets V_0, V_1 and a strategy σ for this subgame. Now we have a strategy for all states but p which leads to two possible cases:

1. Player 1 can prevent player 0 from entering V_0. Then player 0 has a winning strategy on V_0 and player 1 on the remaining set $V_1 \cup R \cup \{p\}$. Let's assume that in state p the choice of $q \in Q \cup \{\bot\}$ is a way for player 1 to avoid entering V_0. Then the strategy for the whole game is $\rho \cup \sigma \cup \{p \mapsto q\}$.

2. Player 1 cannot prevent entering V_0 in state p. Then we only know that player 0 has a winning strategy on V_0. We compute all further states from which player 0 can force entering V_0. We name this set R' and the strategy ρ'. Again the remaining

function $strategy(Q, Q_0, Q_1, E, (E_1, F_1, \ldots, E_r, F_r))$:

(a)   **if** $size(Q) = 0$ **then**
     return $(\emptyset, \emptyset, \emptyset)$

(b)   **elseif** $r = 0$ **then**

$$\text{return } (\emptyset, Q, Q \to Q \cup \{\bot\} : \begin{array}{ll} p \mapsto \bot & \text{if } p \in Q_0, \\ p \mapsto q \in E(p) & \text{if } p \in Q_1 \end{array})$$

(c)   **elseif** $E_1 = \emptyset$ **then**
     if $F_r = Q$ **then**
       $(V_1, V_0, \sigma) := strategy(Q, Q_1, Q_0, E, (F_1, E_2, \ldots, F_{r-1}, E_r))$
     else
       $(V_1, V_0, \sigma) := strategy(Q, Q_1, Q_0, E, (F_1, E_2, \ldots, F_{r-1}, E_r, F_r, Q))$
     return (V_0, V_1, σ)

(d)   **else**
     select $p \in E_1$
     $(R, \rho) := reach(Q_1, E, \{p\})$
     $(V_0, V_1, \sigma) := strategy(Q, Q_0, Q_1, E, (E_1, F_1, \ldots, E_r, F_r), R \cup \{p\})$

(d1)   **if** $(p \in Q_0 \land E(p) \cap V_0 = \emptyset) \lor (p \in Q_1 \land E(p) \setminus V_0 \neq \emptyset)$ **then**
     if $p \in Q_0$ **then**
       $q := \bot$
     else
       select $q \in E(p) \cap V_1$
     return $(V_0, \; V_1 \cup \{p\} \cup R, \; \rho \cup \{(p \mapsto q)\} \cup \sigma)$

(d2)   **else**
     $(R', \rho') := reach(Q_0, E, V_0)$
     $(U_0, U_1, \sigma') := strategy(Q, Q_0, Q_1, E, (E_1, F_1, \ldots, E_r, F_r), R' \cup V_0)$
     return $(U_0 \cup R' \cup V_0, \; U_1, \; \sigma|V_0 \cup \rho' \cup \sigma')$

function $strategy(Q, Q_0, Q_1, E, (E_1, F_1, \ldots, E_r, F_r), R)$:
   if $F_1 \setminus R = \emptyset$ **then**
     return $strategy(Q, Q_0, Q_1, E, (E_2, F_2, \ldots, E_r, F_r), R)$
   else
     return $strategy(Q \setminus R, \; Q_0 \setminus R, \; Q_1 \setminus R, \; E \setminus (R \times R),$
       $(E_1 \setminus R, F_1 \setminus R, \ldots, E_r \setminus R, F_r \setminus R))$

FIGURE 2. Function $strategy()$

subgraph induces a subgame $(G \setminus (V_0 \cup R'), Win')$ with $\Omega' = \Omega \setminus (V_0 \cup R')$. By induction hypotheses we get winning sets U_0, U_1 and a strategy σ' for this subgame . Thus the strategy for the whole game is $\sigma|_{V_0} \cup \rho' \cup \sigma'$.

This function terminates because in each recursive call the number of states or the length of the acceptance condition is reduced. The computation time of $strategy()$ excluding its recursive calls is bounded by a polynomial. The function $strategy()$ calls itself at most twice for smaller subgames. Thus the strategy algorithm has an exponential worst case complexity of $O(2^{|Q|})$.

5 Applying the synthesis algorithm

5.1 A simple type of Rabin chain games

Let $G = (Q, Q_0, Q_1, E)$ be a game graph. As usual the edge relation E is a subset of $(Q_0 \times Q_1) \cup (Q_1 \times Q_0)$. For the vertices in Q we add

- an irreflexive partial order $\prec$ and
- a vertex labeling T with $T(p) \in \{t, f\}$ for all $p \in Q$

such that

$$(*) \quad \neg(p \prec q \vee q \prec p) \Rightarrow \\ [(r \prec p \iff r \prec q) \wedge (p \prec r \iff q \prec r) \ \vee \ T(p) = T(q)].$$

Condition $(*)$ requires that two states which are incomparable w.r.t. $\prec$ have either identical labels or are comparable to the same states.

For any set $M \subseteq Q$ of vertices the set $min(M)$ of minimal elements of M w.r.t. $\prec$ is uniquely defined.

In order to gain a Rabin chain game we use the winning condition:

$$\text{Player 0 wins a play } \pi \iff \text{ for all } p \in min(Inf(\pi)) : T(p) = t.$$

Let us verify that this is indeed a Rabin chain game. We construct the sets E_i, F_i as follows:

$$\begin{aligned}
E_1 &= \{p \in Q \mid \neg \exists q \in Q \ T(q) = t \wedge q \prec p\}, \\
F_1 &= \{p \in Q \mid \forall q \in Q \setminus E_1 \ T(q) = f \Rightarrow p \prec q\}, \\
E_{i+1} &= \{p \in Q \mid \neg \exists q \in Q \setminus F_i \ T(q) = t \wedge q \prec p\}, \\
F_{i+1} &= \{p \in Q \mid \forall q \in Q \setminus E_{i+1} \ T(q) = f \Rightarrow p \prec q\}.
\end{aligned}$$

Assume we have a play π such that for all $p \in min(Inf(\pi))$ $T(p) = t$ holds. Then there is an i such that $Inf(\pi) \cap F_i \neq \emptyset$ and $Inf(\pi) \cap E_i = \emptyset$. Otherwise there would be a state p in $Inf(\pi)$ with $T(p) = f$ that is minimal in $Inf(\pi)$ w.r.t $\prec$.

Now assume we have a play π and an i such that $Inf(\pi) \cap F_i \neq \emptyset$ and $Inf(\pi) \cap E_i = \emptyset$. By condition $(*)$ we know that

- for all $p \in E_i$ and for all $q \in F_i$ $p \prec q$,
- for all $p \in F_i$ and for all $q \in E_{i+1}$ $p \prec q$.

Then by definition of F_i the $\prec$-minimal vertices p of $Inf(\pi)$ are in $Inf(\pi) \cap F_i$ and for these vertices $T(p) = t$ holds.

So the above definition leads indeed to a Rabin chain game.

Example 8 Let $Q_0 = \{(n,0) \mid n \in \{0,\ldots,7\}\}$ and $Q_1 = \{(n,1) \mid n \in \{0,\ldots,7\}\}$, and let $(n,i) \prec (m,j) \iff n < m$ for all $i, j \in \{0,1\}$. The edge relation E is given is given in terms of auxiliary functions $f_i : Q_0 \to Q_1$ and $g_i : Q_1 \to Q_0$ by the following definition:

$$(p, p') \in E \iff \exists i \ (f_i(p) = p' \vee g_i(p) = p').$$

In our example we use the functions:

$$f_1((n,0)) = (n,1), \qquad f_2((n,0)) = \begin{cases} (n+5,1) & \text{if } n \in \{2,6\} \\ (n+1,1) & \text{otherwise,} \end{cases}$$

$$g_1((n,1)) = (n,0), \qquad g_2((n,1)) = \begin{cases} (n+5,0) & \text{if } n \in \{0,4\} \\ (n+1,0) & \text{otherwise.} \end{cases}$$

(Here "+" means addition modulo 8.) So player 0 can use a function f_i to reach a new vertex whereas player 1 uses a function g_i.

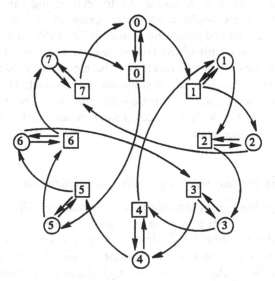

FIGURE 3. Game graph for the Rabin chain game of Example 8

Let T with $T(n,i) = t$ for even n and $T(n,i) = f$ for odd n. By definition player 0 wins iff the minimal number n visited infinitely often is even.

If we represent the states in Q_0 by circles and the ones in Q_1 by squares we get the game graph of Figure 3. Note that by other choices of the functions f_i, g_i many more examples of Rabin chain games can be generated. Beyond the concrete example above, for which an analysis "by hand" is still possible, in the next orders of magnitude we considered various examples from 32 up to 1024 states. We used contrived (however nonrandom) definitions of $\prec$, labeling T, and functions f_i, g_i.

Number of states	"Average time"	"Maximal time"
32	0.1	0.1
48	0.3	0.5
64	0.4	0.6
96	1.3	1.5
128	2.6	4.2
192	5.7	7.7
256	11.0	16.4
384	30.0	49.6
512	74.0	106.9
768	210.0	356.7
1024	469.0	749.5

TABLE 1. CPU time used (in seconds) to compute strategies for example games

The CPU time (on a SUN Sparc 10) for computing the strategies is shown in Table 1. We considered up to ten games of each given size with different edge relations and accepting chains. In the table, the average time as well as the maximal time of the considered cases are noted.

Although the worst case complexity of the algorithm is exponential, it seems applicable to problems of considerable size. Note that the maximal (and average) times we found by our experiments grow moderately even in our preliminary version with an uncontrolled choice of pivots (just using the first in a given enumeration).

5.2 Remarks on the strategy synthesis algorithm

The strategy synthesis algorithm splits a given game graph into two parts, containing the states from which player 0 resp. 1, wins.

The solution for Example 8 is depicted in Figure 4. From the states in the left-hand side, player 0 has a winning strategy as indicated by the chosen displayed edges, from the states in the right-hand part player 1 wins by traversing through the displayed edges.

In general, the critical point in applying the algorithm is the choice of the pivot states (in the "select" line of d) in Figure 2). We see two approaches to handle this problem. A possible heuristic is to select states p where $Reach(p)$ is of maximal size; this reduces the size of the subgame to which the induction hypothesis is applied. However in general this greedy method may fail to find the best descent in reducing the game graph: Note that in case d2, a second use of the inductive hypothesis is necessary which may spoil the optimality of reduction. Another approach would be to introduce a preprocessing of the game graph, yielding an order of pivot elements (similar to preprocessing a linear equation system when applying Gauss elimination). The structure theory of game graphs necessary for this is still missing.

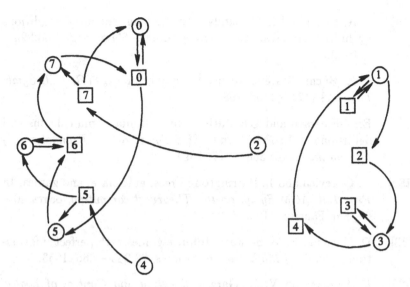

FIGURE 4. Winning strategies for Rabin chain game of example 8

6 Conclusion

We have presented and implemented (for the first time, to our knowledge) an algorithm which synthesizes finite-state winning strategies from automaton specifications of infinite games. In our implementation the necessary pivot choice is still done by the user.

Ongoing work deals with the implementation of algorithms to transform games with other winning conditions into Rabin chain form and of strategy synthesis algorithms in which memory construction and game graph decomposition are combined (as in [McN93], [TW94], and [YY93]).

7 REFERENCES

[ALW89] M. Abadi, L. Lamport, and P. Wolper. Realizable and unrealizable specifications of reactive systems. In G. Ausiello et al., editor, *Automata, Languages, and Programming*, volume 372 of *LNCS*, pages 1 – 17, Berlin, Heidelberg, New York, 1989. Springer-Verlag.

[AMP95] E. Asarin, O. Maler, and A. Pnueli. Symbolic controller synthesis for discrete and timed systems. In P. Antsaklis et al., editor, *Hybrid Systems II*, volume 999 of *LNCS*, pages 1 – 20, Berlin, Heidelberg, New-York, 1995. Springer-Verlag.

[BL69]   J. R. Büchi and L. H. Landweber. Solving sequential conditions by finite-state strategies. *Trans. Amer. Math. Soc.*, 138:295 – 311, 1969.

[Büc83] J. R. Büchi. State strategies for games in $F_{\sigma\delta} \cap G_{\delta\sigma}$. *J. Symb. Logic*, 48:1171 – 1198, 1983.

[EJ91]   E.A. Emerson and C.S. Jutla. Tree automata, mu-calculus and determinacy. In *Proc. 32nd IEEE Symp. on the Foundations of Computing*, pages 368 – 377, 1991.

[GH82]   Y. Gurevich and L. Harrington. Trees, automata, and games. In *Proc 14th ACM Symp. on the Theory of computing*, pages 60 – 65, San Fancisco, 1982.

[GS53]   D. Gale and F. M. Stewart. Infinite games with perfect information. *Annals of Mathematical Studies*, 28:245 – 266, 1953.

[KG95]   R. Kumar and V. K. Garg. *Modeling and Control of Logical Discrete Event Systems*. Kluwer Academic Publishers, Norwell, MA, USA, 1995.

[McN93] R. McNaughton. Infinite games played on finite graphs. *Ann. Pure Appl Logic*, 65:149 – 184, 1993.

[Mos91] A.W. Mostowski. Games with forbidden positions. Technical Report Preprint No. 78, Uniwersytet Gdański, Instytyt Matematyki, 1991.

[MS95]   D.E. Muller and P.E. Schupp. Simulating alternating tree automata by nondeterministic automata: New results and new proofs of the theorems of Rabin, McNaughton and Safra. *Theoretical Computer Science*, 141:69 – 107, 1995.

[Muc92] A. Muchnik. Games on infinite trees and automata with deadends: A new proof for the decidability of the monadic second order theory of two successors. *Bulletin of the European Association for Theoretical Computer Science*, 48:220 – 267, 1992.

[NYY92] A. Nerode, A. Yakhnis, and V. Yakhnis. Concurrent programs as strategies in games. In Moschovakis Y., editor, *Logic from Computer Science*. Springer, 1992.

[PR89]   A. Pnueli and R. Rosner. On the systhesis of a reactive module. In *Proc. 16th ACM Sympos. on Principles of Prog. Lang.*, pages 179 – 190, Austin, 1989.

[Rab69] M. O. Rabin. Decidability of second-order theories and automata on infinite trees. *Transactions of the American Mathematical Society*, 141:1 – 35, 1969.

[RW89]   P. J. G. Ramadge and W. M. Wonham. The control of discrete
          event systems. *Proceedings of the IEEE*, 77, 1:81 – 98, 1989.

[Saf92]   S. Safra.   Exponential determinization for ω-automata with
          strong-fairness acceptance condition. In *Proc. 24th ACM Sym-
          posium on Theory of Computing (STOC)*, pages 275–282, 1992.

[Str82]   R.S. Streett. Propositional dynamic logic of looping and con-
          verse. *Information and Control*, 54:121 – 141, 1982.

[Tho90]   W. Thomas. Automata on infinite objects. In J. van Leeuwen,
          editor, *Handbook of Theoretical Computer Science*, volume B,
          chapter 4, pages 131–191. North-Holland, Amsterdam, 1990.

[Tho95]   W. Thomas. On the synthesis of strategies in infinite games. In
          Ernst W. Mayr and Claude Puech, editors, *STACS 95*, volume
          900 of *LNCS*, pages 1 – 13, Berlin, Heidelberg, New-York, 1995.
          Springer-Verlag.

[TW94]   J.G. Thistle and W.M. Wonham. Control of infinite behaviour
          of finite automata. *SIAM J. of Control and Optimization*,
          32(4):1075 – 1097, 1994.

[YY93]   A. Yakhnis and V. Yakhnis. Gurevich - Harrington's games de-
          fined by finite automata. *Ann. Pure Appl Logic*, 62:265 – 294,
          1993.

Timed Condition/Event Systems: A Framework for Modular Discrete Models of Chemical Plants and Verification of Their Real-Time Discrete Control

Stefan Kowalewski* and Jörg Preußig*

ABSTRACT This paper describes the use of timed Condition/Event (C/E) systems, a real-time extension of the C/E system framework introduced by Sreenivas and Krogh, for building models of chemical plants in a modular fashion and as a basis for the model-based analysis of their discrete control. The approach is illustrated by applying it to the safety control logic of a laboratory batch process.

1 Introduction

Most plants in the chemical industry are controlled by discrete controllers, realized by distributed control systems (DCS), programmable logic controllers (PLC), PC's or dedicated hardware. These controllers have to ensure correct startup and shutdown, realize sequence control, and guarantee safe and reliable process operation. Although there are successful research activities in the field of controller verification (see for example [2], [6], and [7]), up to now the correctness of discrete controllers is only tested manually and no model-based analytical verification methods are applied in practice. The main reason is that the development of a formal model of the uncontrolled plant behavior including all disturbances and operator failures is hardly feasible due to the complexity of such systems. To overcome this situation, modeling procedures have to be developed which make it possible to handle complexity by appropriate structuring strategies. One approach in this direction is modular modeling, i. e. the building of complex system descriptions by setting up small, local models independently

---

*Lehrstuhl für Anlagensteuerungstechnik (Process Control Group) Fachbereich Chemietechnik (Chemical Engineering Dept.) Universität Dortmund, D-44221 Dortmund, Germany, email: stefan@ast.chemietechnik.uni-dortmund.de

from each other and representing the interaction by signals connecting the subsystems. A modeling framework which is particularly well suited for modular modeling are the Condition/Event systems (C/E systems) introduced by Sreenivas and Krogh [9]. C/E systems provide the possibility to couple interconnected discrete event systems by real-time signals in a block diagram and signal flow fashion.

In this paper we will describe the use of the C/E system framework to build discrete models of chemical processes and to analyse discrete controllers for such processes. Since the latter task makes it necessary to treat timing functions in the control programs whereas the original C/E model is untimed, we introduce a real-time extension for C/E systems and describe reachability analysis for timed C/E systems.

The paper is organized as follows. In the next section the basic concept of a C/E system is reviewed and illustrated with the help of a small example. Section 3 presents the real-time extension of C/E systems which is realized by introducing C/E timers and the corresponding analysis. The modeling and analysis approach is then applied to a process control example in Sec. 4. Finally, in Sec. 5, we draw some conclusions, look at the relation of our approach to related work and discuss possible directions for future research.

2 Condition/Event Systems: Basic Concepts

Condition/Event systems were introduced by Sreenivas and Krogh in [9]. The authors were motivated by the observation that in existing DES models the interaction between systems is either based on synchronization of events or conditioning of event occurence depending on state information. Sometimes, both options are used for different purposes as for instance in the supervisory control theory of Ramadge and Wonham [8]. To incorporate both concepts into a single, unified representation of interconnected DES, Sreenivas and Krogh define two classes of signals which can both be input and output signals of one system: *condition signals* and *event signals*. A condition signal $c(\bullet)$ is a right continuous function $c : [t_0, \infty) \to C$ with limits from the left, with C being a nonempty, finite, and countable set of conditions. Therefore, condition signals are time-dependent signals which are piecewise constant. An event signal $e(\bullet)$ is a function $e : [t_0, \infty) \to E_0 = E \cup 0$ for which $e(t_0) = 0$ (the *null* or *zero event*) and $t \in [t_1, t_2] | e(t) \neq 0$ is finite for all finite intervals $[t_1, t_2] \in [t_0, \infty)$ and E is a nonempty, finite, and countable set of events. We may say that event signals are only pointwise "nonzero". The set of all condition or all event signals on $[t_0, \infty)$ is written as $\mathbf{C}(C, t_0)$ or $\mathbf{E}(E, t_0)$, respectively.

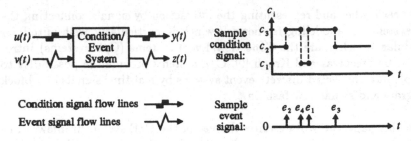

FIGURE 1. Condition/Event signals and systems.

In general, a *C/E system* has a *conditon input signal* $u(t)$, an *event input signal* $v(t)$, a *condition output signal* $y(t)$ and an *event output signal* $z(t)$, as it is illustrated in Fig. 1. The corresponding sets of conditions or events are U, V, Y, and Z, respectively. A C/E system is then defined as a mapping Σ which gives the set of admissable output signal trajectories for each possible input signal trajectory: $\Sigma : \mathbf{C}(U, t_0) \times \mathbf{E}(V, t_0) \rightarrow 2^{\mathbf{C}(Y, t_0) \times \mathbf{E}(Z, t_0)}$, such that for any input $(u(\bullet), v(\bullet)) \in \mathbf{C}(U, t_0) \times \mathbf{E}(V, t_0)$ there exists at least one output $(y(\bullet), z(\bullet)) \in \mathbf{C}(Y, t_0) \times \mathbf{E}(Z, t_0)$ fulfilling $(y(\bullet), z(\bullet)) \in \Sigma(u(\bullet), v(\bullet))$.

In the definition above, a C/E system is characterized by its input/output behaviour. There is no specification or restriction on the model of the internal dynamics of a C/E system. In [9], any formal representation which describes an appropriate input/output relation is called a *C/E model*. One example of a C/E model, based on Petri nets, is presented in [10]. Here, we will consider two different C/E models which realize C/E systems: First, we recall discrete state C/E systems which are used to model untimed DES (Def 1). Then, in Sec. 3, we introduce *C/E timers* (Def. 2) to incorporate quantitative timing information into C/E systems.

Definition 1 (*Discrete State C/E System*): A *discrete state C/E system* is a 9-Tupel $S = (U, V, X, Y, Z, f, g, h, x_0)$, where U, V, X, Y and Z are finite, countable mutually disjoint sets representing the *input conditions*, the *input events* (not including the null event 0, we write V_0 for $V \cup \{0\}$), the *states*, the *output conditions* and the *output events* (again not including the null event, $Z_0 = Z \cup \{0\}$), respectively. f, g and h are functions defined as: $f : X \times U \times V_0 \rightarrow 2^X - \emptyset$, the *state transition function* satisfying $\forall x \in X, u \in U : x \in f(x, u, 0)$, and $g : X \times U \rightarrow Y$, the *condition output function*, and $h : X \times X \times V_0 \rightarrow Z_0$, the *event output function* satisfying $\forall x \in X : 0 = h(x, x, 0)$; and $x_0 \in X$ is the *initial state*. Given a C/E system as defined above and input signals $u(\bullet)$ and $v(\bullet)$, the set of valid state trajectories $x(\bullet)$ and output signals $y(\bullet)$ and $z(\bullet)$ is represented by the following three equations.

$$x(t) \in f(x(t^-), u(t^-), v(t)), \tag{1}$$

$$y(t) = g(x(t), u(t)), \qquad (2)$$
$$z(t) = h(x(t^-), x(t), v(t)), \qquad (3)$$

where $x(t^-)$ is an abbreviation of $\lim_{\Delta \to 0} x(t - \Delta)$ (the same applies to $u(t^-)$). ∎

A C/E system can be regarded as an untimed finite state machine which is embedded in a time-dependent signals space formed by the condition and event input and output signals. The condition input signal constitutes conditions for changes of the state of the system (hence can *disable* or *enable* certain transitions) whereas the event input signal can *force* transitions. Event outputs can be generated if and only if the state of the system changes, condition outputs provide information about the actual state of the system. Transitions can be forced (by event signals) or occur spontaneously, and can be nondeterministic. The two properties $\forall x \in X, u \in U : x \in f(x, u, 0)$ and $\forall x \in X : 0 = h(x, x, 0)$ stated in Def. 1 guarantee that transitions and output events cannot be forced by condition input changes.

To provide a flavour of how technological systems are modeled by means of C/E systems we present a small example. Figure 2 shows a tank which can be filled via an inlet valve and illustrates the corresponding C/E model for the tank level and its influences by its block diagram representation. Condition signal flow lines are characterized by two black rectangles whereas event signal flow lines can be recognized by a lightning symbol. The model is divided into three subsystems, *"valve"*, *"feed pressure"* and *"level"*, which are connected by condition signals and event signals. The dynamic behaviour of each system is represented as a state graph. For a detailed description of the behaviours and interactions between these blocks, the possible successor states and output signal values have to be specified for all combinations of states and input signal values for all three systems. This information is represented for each system by the three functions f, g and h which were introduced in Def. 1. For this example, we will not discuss the complete model but only some aspects of it in order to illustrate the important concepts of forcing and enabling/disabling.

Consider the situation when the tank is empty, the valve is closed and the pressure is sufficient. A transition from *"open"* to *"closed"* in the system *"valve"* will then be indicated to the system *"level"* by the event signal value *"valve opens"* and it will force the transition from *"empty"* to *"medium & rising"*. This is possible because the feed pressure is sufficient which is indicated to the system *"level"* by the condition signal value *"pressure is up"*. So, the transition is enabled by the condition input signal. If the system *"feed pressure"* would be in state *"not sufficient"*, the condition input signal would have the value *"pressure is down"* and therefore disable

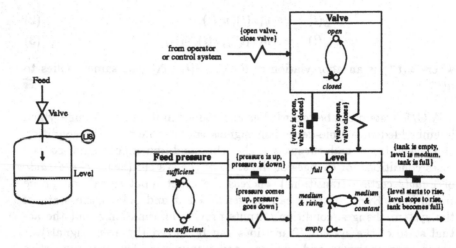

FIGURE 2. Example of a C/E system model.

the transition from *"empty"* to *"medium & rising"*.

An example of a spontaneous event is given by the transition from *"medium & rising"* to *"full"*. It has to be enabled by the condition input *"valve is open"* and *"pressure is sufficient"*, but the actual occurence is spontaneous and cannot be forced by any external input.

The relevant part of the state transition function of the system *"level"* for the behavioural aspects described above is the following (note that $u(t^-)$ and $v(t)$ are pairs of signals because they are determined by the cross product of all input signals coming from different systems):

f(*empty*, (*pressure is up, valve is closed*), (0,*valve opens*))
= {*medium & rising*},

f(*empty*, (*pressure is down, valve is closed*), (0,*valve opens*))
= {*empty*},

f(*medium & rising*, (*pressure is up, valve is open*), (0, 0))
= {*medium & rising, full*}.

3   Timed C/E Systems

3.1   C/E Timers

The C/E system paradigm as described above constitutes an untimed discrete event system model. In technological systems however, transitions usually require a certain amount of time or have to occur within certain time intervals. Consequentially, the qualitative behaviour is strongly influenced by timing constraints. Effective modeling paradigms therefore must allow one to include timing constraints in a natural manner. Since the communication between C/E systems is already defined in terms of continuous time signals, the C/E system paradigm is very well suited to incorporate time without giving up the advantages mentioned above. For this purpose, a special class of C/E models called *C/E timers* are introduced (see Def. 2). The C/E timers are coupled to the untimed logical system part to represent the overall timed behaviour of the system. Thus the timed model remains completely within the original conceptual framework. The advantage is obvious: Describing the timing is part of the modular concept. The untimed dynamics and the timing conditions are seperated and can be modeled independendly. Timing information can be added to an already existing model without changing any block of the C/E block diagram by simply adding the necessary timer blocks and connecting them to the appropriate discrete blocks. We will call such an configuration *timed C/E system*.

Definition 2 *(C/E timer)*: Given an initial time $t_0 \in \Re$ and a *threshold time* $T_\theta \in \Re^+ - \{0\}$, a *C/E timer* θ on $[t_0, \infty)$ is a mapping $\theta : \mathbf{E}(V_\theta, t_0) \to \mathbf{C}(Y_\theta, t_0) \times \mathbf{E}(Z_\theta, t_0)$, with $V_\theta = \{\text{``}t_\theta := 0\text{''}\}$, $Y_\theta = \{\text{``}t_\theta < T_\theta\text{''}, \text{``}t_\theta > T_\theta\text{''}\}$, and $Z_\theta = \{\text{``}t_\theta = T_\theta\text{''}\}$, such that for any event input signal $v_\theta(t) \in \mathbf{E}(V_\theta, t_\theta)$, the output $(y_\theta(t), z_\theta(t))$ is determined by

$$y_\theta(t) = \begin{cases} \text{``}t_\theta < T_\theta\text{''} & if \quad \tau(t) < T_\theta, \\ \text{``}t_\theta > T_\theta\text{''} & if \quad \tau(t) > T_\theta, \end{cases} \tag{4}$$

and

$$z_\theta(t) = \begin{cases} \text{``}t_\theta = T_\theta\text{''} & if \quad \tau(t) = T_\theta, \\ 0 & else \end{cases} \tag{5}$$

in which $\tau : [t_0, \infty) \to [t_0, \infty)$ is the *clock function* given by

$$\tau(t_0) = T_\theta + \epsilon, \epsilon > 0, \tag{6}$$

and for all $t \in [t_0, \infty]$:

$$\dot{\tau}(t) = \begin{cases} 1 & if \quad v_\theta(t) = 0, \\ undefined & else \end{cases} \tag{7}$$

and $\tau(t) = 0$ if $v_\theta(t) \neq 0$. ∎

A C/E timer can be regarded as an alarm clock which is reset and started by the input event "$t_\theta := 0$" and which indicates that it has reached its threshold time T_θ by sending out an event "$t_\theta = T_\theta$". The condition outputs "$t_\theta < T_\theta$" and "$t_\theta > T_\theta$" indicate that the threshold has not yet been reached or has been crossed, respectively.

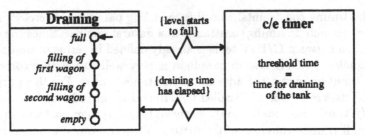

FIGURE 3. Adding time to a C/E system.

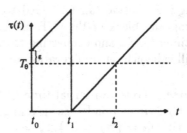

FIGURE 4. Clock function $\tau(t)$.

Figure 3 illustrates this concept for a small example. The left block represents an untimed C/E model for the emptying of a tank filled with liquid, say the tank from the example in Fig. 2. The tank content is drained into two tank wagons which are placed under the outlet valve of the tank one after another, which leads to the four states shown in the state graph. In this model, all transitions are spontaneous. Usually, the time needed to empty the full tank completely can easily be determined. So this information should be incorporated into the model. In Fig. 3, this is done by simply adding a C/E timer to the discrete *"draining"* block which is started by the event *"level starts to fall"* and generates the event *"draining time has elapsed"* after the appropriate time. The transition from *"filling of second wagon"* to *"empty"* is now no longer spontaneous but forced by the event *"draining time has elapsed"*.

Figure 4 shows a sample trajectory of the clock function $\tau(t)$. It is easy to see that T_θ is the only free parameter for the C/E timer behavior, while it is not affected by the value of the initial offset ε. The internal behaviour of a C/E timer is comparable to an integrator with constant input which is reset by an event input (here by *"level starts to fall"* at time t_1) and sends out an event when a threshold is reached (here *"draining time has elapsed"* at time t_2).

3.2   Reachability Analysis

To be useful in the context of controller verification, timed C/E systems must be eligible for reachability analysis. In the following, we propose an algorithm to solve this problem. Since spontaneous transitions are still allowed and time is continuous, the problem arises that the number of possible timed state trajectories becomes infinitely large. However, it is still possible to represent the available information of the past of the system in finite expressions and to determine an upper bound of the possible timed system behaviors. For this purpose, the set of (uncountable many) possible current clock function values of all C/E timers under consideration is represented by a so-called *distance matrix*. A distance matrix M is an n-dimensional matrix which is assigned to an n-tupel $I_M = (\theta_1, \theta_2, \ldots, \theta_{n-1}, now)$ in which each θ_i represents a C/E timer and now stands for the current point of time for which M describes the timing status of the system. For the reachability algorithm, now will be the time when the last state of the currently considered path has been reached. The matrix entries of M have the following meaning:

- For $i < j$, m_{θ_i, θ_j} is interpreted as an upper bound for the distance between the last reset of the i-th and the j-th timer (resp. now) in I_M. If there is no such upper bound m_{θ_i, θ_j} is '∞'. Otherwise, the entries are natural numbers and represent time units.

- For $i > j$, m_{θ_i, θ_j} is interpreted as a lower bound for the distance between the last reset of the i-th and the j-th timer (resp. now) in I_M. These entries are always natural numbers giving a lower bound in time units.

- The entries on the main diagnal are not used and always set to zero.

The reachability analysis is realized by a depth first search algorithm that is given in pseudo code in Figure 5. The algorithm starts in the initial state with no timing information (i.e. the empty distance matrix) and moves along any admissible path of the state graph of a C/E system. In every step of the recursion it determines the possible successor states from logical and time dependent desription of the system, i.e. the state transition function f and the current distance matrix. Depending on the result, it updates the distance matrix and moves to an admissible successor state. The recursion terminates when the current state is visited with the same distance matrix a second time or when it has no more admissible successor states.

For the termination of the algorithm, it is crucial to determine whether a discrete state has been visited already with the same timing information. This is possible because distance matrices provide a canonical representation of this information. A distance matrix M of dimension n is said to be

```
PROCEDURE Main
{
  READ input_system;
  Goto_State(initial_state , empty_distance_matrix);
  WRITE set_of_reachable_states;
}
PROCEDURE Goto_State(state , distance_matrix)
{
  ADD state TO set_of_reachable_states;
  {
    IF distance_matrix NOT_IN set_of_distance_matrices(state)
    {
      ADD distance_matrix TO set_of_distance_matrices(state);
      FIND list_of_admissible_succ_states;
      FOR_ALL succ_states IN list_of_admissible_succ_states;
      {
        FIND succ_distance_matrix;
        Goto_State(succ_state , succ_distance_matrix);
      }
    }
  }
}
```

FIGURE 5. Algorithm in pseudo code.

in *normal form* if two constraints hold for M:

$$\forall i \in \{1, 2, \ldots, n-1\} \quad : \quad m_{\theta_i, now} \leq T_{\theta_i} \vee m_{\theta_i, now} = \text{``}\infty\text{''} \tag{8}$$

$$\forall i \in \{1, 2, \ldots, n-1\} \quad : \quad m_{now, \theta_i} \leq T_{\theta_i} \tag{9}$$

The first constraint postulates that the upper bound $m_{\theta_i, now}$ for the distance between the last reset time of timer θ_i and the current time *now* is always less than or equal the threshold of θ_i or otherwise it is the symbol '∞'. To normalize the distance matrix if this constraint is broken, the symbol '∞' is entered for $m_{\theta_i, now}$. This means that in a normalized distance matrix the irrelevant information for how long a clock might be over its threshold is generalized to the information that this clock simply might be over its threshold.

The second constraint postulates that the lower bound m_{now, θ_i} for the distance between the last reset of a timer θ_i and *now* is always less than or equal the threshold of θ_i. If this constraint is broken, the distance matrix is normalized by deleting the symbol θ_i from I_M and all matrix entries related to clock θ_i from M. Consequentially, a distance matrix in normal form contains no symbols of timers which are definitely over their threshold. Two normalized distance matrices M_1 and M_2 are said to be equal if all entries in the matrices and the tupel I_{M_1} and I_{M_2} are equal. If normalized distance matrices are used to determine whether a state has been visited with the same timing information before, the algorithm in Fig. 5 will terminate

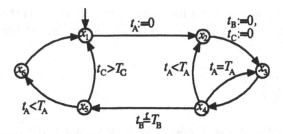

FIGURE 6. Example of a state graph of a C/E system with timers.

because the number of normalized distance matrices for a given timed C/E system is finite.

3.3 Example

We illustrate the basic idea of the reachability algorithm based on distance matrices with the help of a small example. Fig. 6 shows the state graph of a C/E system with three C/E timers, A, B, and C. The threshold times are $T_A = 3$ time units, $T_B = 5$, and $T_C = 6$. The state transitions are labeled according to their temporal conditions. For example, $t_A < T_A$ indicates that this transition may only occur when the clock function value of timer T_A is below its threshold. A transition forced by a timer output is labeled by $t_\theta = T_\theta$. If this case does not include the possibility to stay in the current state, a small "f" is written above the "=". If no condition is assigned to an arc, the transition is not depending on any timer.

Consider the case that the reachability algorithm has followed the path x_1, x_2, x_3, x_4, x_5. The available information about the temporal past at state x_5 is the following: First, timer A was started. Then the system remained in x_2 for an unknown period of time, because the transition to x_3 is purely spontaneous. With this transition, timer B and C were started. The residence times in x_3 and x_4 again are unknown. The transition from x_4 to x_5 is forced by timer B. This means, we know that timer B has just reached its threshold when the system moves to x_5 and that the distance between the instant when the transition from x_2 to x_3 took place and the instant when the transition from x_4 to x_5 occured is exactly 5 time units. So, the last reset of timer A at the transition from x_1 to x_2 is at least 5 time units ago. The corresponding distance matrix is:

$$M(A, C, now) = \begin{pmatrix} 0 & \infty & \infty \\ 0 & 0 & 0 \\ 5 & 5 & 5 \end{pmatrix}$$

Obviously, $M(A, C, now)$ does not fulfill constraint (7) because $m_{A, now} = 5$

and $T_A = 3$. This means that timer A must have reached its threshold, too. For this reason, $M(A, C, now)$ has to be normalized in the following manner.

$$M(C, now) = \begin{pmatrix} 0 & 5 \\ 5 & 0 \end{pmatrix}$$

Based on the information represented by $M(C, now)$, the reachability algorithm will now discover that when the system has moved along the path x_1, x_2, x_3, x_4, x_5, it will not go to x_6 in the next transition because the condition "$t_A < T_A$" is not fulfilled. In fact, x_6 is not reachable.

4 Application

We illustrate the application of the described analysis method to the verification of discrete controllers with the help of a process control example. Consider the flowchart in Fig. 7. It shows a part of a laboratory batch plant at the Chemical Engineering Dept. in Dortmund. In this part of the plant, the following production sequence takes place: Salt solution is filled into tank T1 and then evaporated until a desired concentration is reached. During evaporation, the condenser C1 is in operation and captures the steam coming from T1. When the desired concentration is reached, the material is drained from T1 into T2 as soon as T2 becomes empty. A postprocessing step takes place in T2, before the material can be pumped out of T2 to a subsequent part of the plant. We suppose that in the undisturbed case the operation sequence described above is ensured by the controller and direct our interest to the problem of appropriate control reaction on disturbances. In particular, we look at the consequences of a cooling breakdown in the condenser. This failure can lead to a dangerously high pressure in the condenser tube, if the evaporating is continued. When the heating in T1 is switched off, the pressure in C1 will not rise any more. To make the problem more demanding, we assume that the material in T1 gets solid after a certain time when it cools down and cannot be drained into T2. As a consequence, it is possible that the controller should not switch off the heating immediately after cooling breakdown, because this may lead to solid material in T1. If T2 is still full, it has to wait some time to ensure that T1 can be drained before the material gets solid. However, a meaningful controller will start draining T2 as soon as a cooling breakdown occures, so that no time is lost. The described behavior and more details are represented by the timed C/E system shown in Fig. 8.

The names of the states are based on the following convention: The first character describes the state of T1: $e =$ empty, $p =$ processing (evaporat-

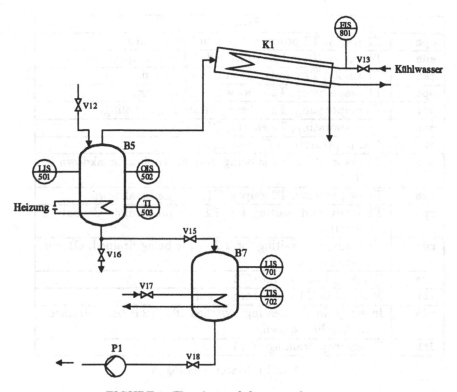

FIGURE 7. Flowchart of the example process.

ing), r = ready (and waiting for T2), d = being drained, i = interrupt (heating switched off before desired concentration was reached), and s = solid; the second character represents T2: e = empty, p = (post-)processing, f = being filled, d = being drained; and the third character symbolizes the state of the condenser: n= not in operation, c = cooling, b = breakdown, and a = pressure alarm (too high). For all devices, an x stands for undetermined. Table 1 and 2 explains the states and timers in more detail.

The verification problem now is to analyze whether a given controller with a waiting time $T_W = 5$ (which means that it waits 5 minutes after cooling breakdown before it will switch off the heating) will prevent the system from reaching the forbidden states **pxa** and **sxx**. Applying reachability analysis shows that for such a controller, the state **sxx** is reachable for the system while it prevents the system from reaching state **pxa**. So, in case of a cooling breakdown, the material in T1 will get solid. Two recursion steps of the algorithm will now be presented in detail.

After 5 steps the algorithm may reaches the state **pdp** if it is currently following a path consisting of the sequence of states: **een, pec, dfn, epn, ppc, pdb**. Starting with the empty distance matrix $M_0(now)$ in the initial

States	
epn	T1 empty, T2 processing, C1 not in operation.
edn	T1 empty, T2 is being drained, C1 not in operation.
een	T1 empty, T2 empty, C1 not in operation.
ppc	T1 evaporating, T2 processing, C1 cooling.
pdc	T1 evaporating, T2 is being drained, C1 cooling.
pec	T1 evaporating, T2 empty, C1 cooling.
pxa	Alarm: pressure in C1 too high.
pdb	T1 evaporating, T2 is being drained, cooling breakdown in C1.
peb	T1 evaporating, T2 empty, C1: cooling breakdown.
rpn	T1 ready and waiting for T2, T2 processing, C1 not in operation.
rdn	T1 ready and waiting for T2, T2 is being drained, C1 not in operation.
dfn	Draining from T1 into T2.
sxx	Material in T1 has become solid.
idb	Interrupt in T1 (heating switched off), T2 is being drained, cooling breakdown.
dfb	Emergency draining of T1.

TABLE 1. States from Fig. 8

Timers		
A	Time between cooling breakdown and pressure alarm if heating is continued.	$T_A = 8$ min
D	Time for draining of T2.	$T_D = 10$ min
E	Minimal time for evaporation in T1.	$T_E = 60$ min
P	Time for processing the material in T2.	$T_P = 40$ min
S	Time between heating switched off and material becoming solid.	$T_S = 4$ min
W	Time which the controller waits after cooling breakdown before it switches off the heating.	$T_W = 5$ min

TABLE 2. Timers from Fig. 8

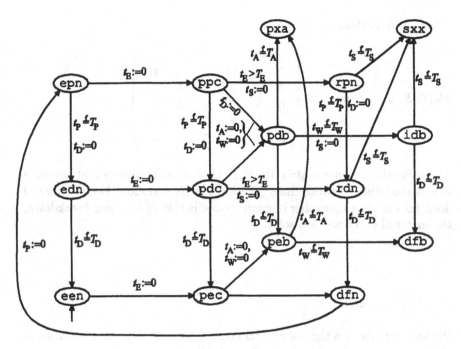

FIGURE 8. State graph for the example.

state **een**, the algorithm then is at state **pdb** with the distance matrix:

$$
M_5(P, E, D, A, W, now) = \begin{pmatrix}
0 & 40 & 40 & 40 & 40 & 40 \\
0 & 0 & 40 & 40 & 40 & 40 \\
0 & 0 & 0 & 0 & 0 & 0 \\
0 & 0 & 0 & 0 & 0 & 0 \\
0 & 0 & 0 & 0 & 0 & 0 \\
0 & 0 & 0 & 0 & 0 & 0
\end{pmatrix}
$$

With this distance matrix the algorithm can only choose the transition to **idb** in its next step, because clock W will reach its threshold before the clocks A and D. Taking the transition from **pdb** to **idb** as the next transition in its 6th step the algorithm calculates the following distance matrix:

$$
M_6(P, E, D, A, S, now) = \begin{pmatrix}
0 & 40 & 40 & 40 & 45 & 45 \\
0 & 0 & 40 & 40 & 45 & 45 \\
0 & 0 & 0 & 0 & 5 & 5 \\
0 & 0 & 0 & 0 & 5 & 5 \\
5 & 5 & 5 & 5 & 0 & 0 \\
5 & 5 & 5 & 5 & 0 & 0
\end{pmatrix}
$$

After normalisation:

$$
M_6(P, E, D, A, S, now) =
\begin{pmatrix}
0 & 40 & 40 & 40 & 45 & \infty \\
0 & 0 & 40 & 40 & 45 & 45 \\
0 & 0 & 0 & 0 & 5 & 5 \\
0 & 0 & 0 & 0 & 5 & 5 \\
5 & 5 & 5 & 5 & 0 & 0 \\
5 & 5 & 5 & 5 & 0 & 0
\end{pmatrix}
$$

Analysing the distance matrix $M_6(P, E, D, A, S, now)$ reveals that the state **sxx** is reachable, because timer S will reach its threshold before timer D does. So, the given controller is incorrect and in case of a cooling breakdown, the material in T1 will get solid.

5 Discussion

We have reported on the use of C/E systems for a model-based verification of discrete controllers for chemical plants. To capture critical timing constraints, the original framework was extended by C/E timers which make it possible to model quantitative time in C/E systems without changing the conceptual framework. A reachabilty algorithm has been sketched. Finally, we described the application of the approach to a laboratory batch plant and parts of its safety control.

The timed C/E system model has many similarities to the timed automata approach by Alur and Dill [1]. In fact, the creation and updating of the distance matrix during the reachability algorithm can be regarded as a method to build the region graph used by Alur and Dill to analyze reachability. We are currently investigating further relations between the two approaches. The reason why timed automata were not applied to model the laboratory plant is twofold. First, they do not provide special support for modular modeling in form of intuitive interaction concepts as C/E systems do. Second, discrete state C/E models were already available for the laboratory batch plant ([4], [3]) and it was necessary to add the timing information without changing the basic framework.

There are several directions of further research. In the described model, transitions can depend at most on the standings of a single timer. We are currently extending the framework to be able to use Boolean connectives on timer queries and compare different timer standings. Since the described analysis method is based on a comprehensive search, we are also interested in symbolic and compositional analysis.

Acknowledgements. Prof. Heiko Krumm and Prof. Sebastian Engell contributed to the presented work by helpful and instructive discussions. We are also grateful to the anonymous referees who helped to improve the presentation.

6 REFERENCES

[1] R. Alur, D. Dill: *The Theory of Timed Automata.* Theoretical Computer Science, 126, 1994: 183-235.

[2] V. D. Dimitriadis, N. Shah und C. C. Pantelides: *Modeling and Safety Verification of Discrete/Continuous Processing Systems Using Discrete Time Domain Models.* Proceedings Workshop Analysis and Design of Event-Driven Operations in Process Systems, Imperial College, London, 10.-11. April 1995.

[3] S. Kowalewski, S. Engell, M. Fritz, R. Gesthuisen, G. Regner, M. Stobbe: *Modular discrete modeling of batch processes by means of condition/event systems.* Workshop Analysis and Design of Event-Driven Operations in Process Systems, Imperial College, London, 10.-11. April 1995.

[4] S. Kowalewski, R. Gesthuisen and V. Romann: *Model-based verification of batch process control software.* Proc. IEEE Conf. on Systems, Man, and Cybernetics, San Antonio, 331-336, 1994.

[5] B. H. Krogh: *Condition/Event Signal Interfaces for Block Diagram Modeling and Analysis of Hybrid Systems.* Proc. 8th Int. Symp. on Intell. Cont. Sys., June 1993.

[6] I. Moon, G. J. Powers, J. R. Burch und E. M. Clarke: *Automatic Verification of Sequential Control Systems Using Temporal Logic.* AIChE Journal 38, 1992.

[7] G. J. Powers und S. T. Probst: *Safety and Operability Analysis of Chemical Process Designs Using Symbolic Model Verification.* AIChE Annual Meeting, San Francisco, USA, 1994.

[8] P. J. Ramadge and W. M. Wonham: *Supervisory control of a class of discrete event processes.* SIAM J. Control Optim. 25(1987): 206-230.

[9] R.S. Sreenivas and B.H. Krogh: *On Condition/Event Systems with Discrete State Realizations.* Discrete Event Dynamic Systems 1(1991): 209-236.

[10] R.S. Sreenivas and B.H. Krogh: *Petri Net Based Models for Condition/Event Systems.* Proc. American Control Conf. 1991, Boston, USA.

Formal Verification of a Partial-Order Reduction Technique for Model Checking

Ching-Tsun Chou*
Doron Peled[†]

ABSTRACT Mechanical theorem proving and model checking are the two main methods of formal verification, each with its own strengths and weaknesses. While mechanical theorem proving is more general, it requires intensive human guidance. model checking is automatic, but is applicable to a more restricted class of problems. It is appealing to combine these two methods in order to take advantage of their different strengths. Prior research in this direction has focused on how to decompose a verification problem into parts each of which is manageable by one of the two methods. In this paper we explore another possibility: we use mechanical theorem proving to formally verify a *meta-theory* of model checking. As a case study, we use the mechanical theorem prover HOL to verify the correctness of a *partial-order reduction* technique for cutting down the amount of state search performed by model checkers. We choose this example for two reasons. First, this reduction technique has been implemented in the protocol analysis tool SPIN to significantly speed up the analysis of many practical protocols; hence its correctness has important practical consequences. Second, the correctness arguments involve nontrivial mathematics, the formalization of which we hope will become the basis of a formal meta-theory of many model checking algorithms and techniques. Our formalization led to a nontrivial generalization of the original informal theory. We also discuss the lessons, both encouraging and discouraging, learned from this exercise.

1 Introduction

Mechanical theorem proving and model checking are the two main methods of formal verification, each with its own strengths and weaknesses. Mechanical theorem proving is more general, but requires intensive human guidance. In practice, only experienced experts can use mechanical theorem

---

*Fujitsu Laboratories of America, 3350 Scott Blvd., Bldg. 34, Santa Clara, CA 95054. **Note:** This work was done when the first author was on leave from UCLA and doing a summer job at AT&T Laboratories.

[†]AT&T Bell Laboratories, 600 Mountain Avenue, Murray Hill, NJ 07974.

provers effectively. Model checking is automatic, but is applicable to only the verification of finite-state systems, and suffer from the state-explosion problem, which inhibits its use in very big systems. Combining the two formal verification methods is appealing, as it has the potential of exploiting the strengths of both methods.

Prior research in this direction, e.g. [9, 11, 17], has focused on how to decompose a verification problem into parts each of which is manageable by one of the two methods. Although some impressive case studies have been conducted, it is still not clear how practical is the combination of theorem proving and model checking in general. The first problem is that some "real-world" systems may not allow any useful decomposition at all. And, secondly, even if a useful decomposition does exist, it may be very hard in practice to find it.

We suggest here another possible approach to combining mechanical theorem proving and model checking: we use mechanical theorem proving to formally verify the *meta-theory* of model checking. By "meta-theory" we mean the mathematical arguments justifying the correctness of model checking algorithms. These arguments can be quite complicated, and are used to justify complex algorithms. Erroneous proofs of algorithms and, more seriously, seemingly correct proofs of incorrect algorithms, are not uncommon in the literature. Using mechanical theorem proving to formally verify the meta-theory, we hope to raise the standard of rigor of, and hence our confidence in, model checking. Furthermore, since the meta-theory of a model checking algorithm needs to be verified only once while the algorithm can be used many times, the high cost of mechanical theorem proving can be amortized. We hope this will make mechanical theorem proving more attractive to practitioners of verification.

As a case study, we use the mechanical theorem prover HOL [5] to verify a *partial-order reduction* technique for cutting down the amount of state search performed by model checkers [16]. We choose this example for two reasons. First, this reduction technique has been implemented in the protocol analysis tool SPIN [7, 8] to significantly speed up the analysis of many practical protocols; hence its correctness has important practical consequences. Second, the correctness arguments involve nontrivial mathematics about sequences, relations, Mazurkiewicz traces [14], deterministic transition systems, and their interactions, whose formal versions we hope will become the basis of a formal meta-theory of many model checking algorithms and techniques.

At this point, a skeptic may ask: how do we know that HOL is free of bugs? And, if HOL turns out to contain bugs, what is the point of this whole exercise? Indeed, we do not know whether HOL is free of bugs. But, as we will explain later, HOL is built in such a way that its correctness depends only on a small kernel of carefully constructed code, which we believe is less error-prone than some model checking programs. To answer the second question, we note that we gained better understanding of the meta-theory from the very act of formalization. Indeed, we were able to obtain a nontrivial generalization of the original informal theory (see Section 2.1 for details). The final formal proof is more elegant and better organized than the original informal proof, and certainly contains less (if any at all!) errors. In general, we believe that formalization is an invaluable tool for gaining better understanding of mathematical arguments.

The rest of this paper is organized as follows. Section 2 describes the partial-order reduction technique to be verified. Section 3 introduces higher-order logic (the logic supported by HOL) and mechanical theorem proving in HOL. Section 4 outlines our proof of the partial-order reduction technique in HOL. Section 5 discusses both encouraging and discouraging lessons learned from this exercise.

2 Partial-Order Reduction

Partial-order reduction is a technique that exploits the commutativity between independent actions of concurrent programs to reduce the space and time requirements of model checking. In the simplest case, consider a program in which two concurrent processes P_1 and P_2 can execute two actions a_1 and a_2 independently, then the two executions $a_1 a_2$ and $a_2 a_1$ can be considered "equivalent" (the precise definition of this equivalence relation will be given shortly). Hence it is sufficient for a model checker to check only one of them. For programs with a high degree of concurrency, the savings thus gained can be considerable.

We shall model programs as *deterministic transition systems* (DTS's). Let A be a set of *actions* and S be a set of *states*. A DTS P is simply a *partial* function from $A \times S$ to S. For any $a \in A$ and $s \in S$, if $P(a, s)$ is defined, then a is *firable* at s and $P(a, s)$ equals the state resulting from *firing* a at s. The set of actions firable at s in P is denoted by $\mathcal{F}(P, s)$. Let A^*, A^ω, and A^∞ denote respectively the sets of finite, infinite, and all sequences over A (i.e., $A^\infty = A^* \cup A^\omega$). We can extend P to a partial function P^* from $A^* \times S$ to S in the obvious way: $P^*(\varepsilon, s) = s$ and $P^*(a^\frown w, s) = P^*(w, P(a, s))$, where ε denotes the empty sequence and $\frown$ denotes sequence concatenation. (Note that $P^*(a^\frown w, s)$ is defined exactly when (a) $P(a, s)$ is defined and equals some state s' *and* (b) $P^*(w, s')$ is also defined.) A finite sequence w is *firable* at a state s iff $P^*(w, s)$ is defined; an infinite sequence is *firable* at s iff all of its finite prefixes are firable at s. A (finite or infinite) sequence that is firable at a state of P is called an *execution* of P. For any $s \in S$, the set of states *reachable* from s in P, denoted $\mathcal{R}(P, s)$, is the set $\{P^*(w, s) \mid w \text{ is finite and firable at } s \text{ in } P\}$.

We say that a DTS Q is a *sub-DTS* of a DTS P iff for any $a \in A$ and $s \in S$:

$$a \in \mathcal{F}(Q, s) \quad \Rightarrow \quad a \in \mathcal{F}(P, s) \wedge (Q(a, s) = P(a, s)) \tag{1}$$

Note that every execution of Q is an execution of P, but not necessarily vice versa.

An *independence relation* for P is an irreflexive and symmetric relation $\perp \subseteq A \times A$ such that for any $a \perp b$ and $s \in S$,

$$a \text{ is firable at } s \;\Rightarrow\; (b \text{ is firable at } s \Leftrightarrow \qquad (2)$$
$$b \text{ is firable at } P(a,s))$$
$$a \text{ and } b \text{ are firable at } s \;\Rightarrow\; (P^*(a^\frown b, s) = P^*(b^\frown a, s)) \qquad (3)$$

The equivalence relation between executions mentioned above is called *trace equivalence*, which was originally proposed for finite sequences by Mazurkiewicz [14] and later extended to infinite sequences by Kwiatkowska [12]. Trace equivalence is defined in five stages:

T1. The *1-step relation* $\doteq \subseteq A^* \times A^*$:
   $v \doteq w$ iff there exist actions a and b and finite sequences x and y such that $a \perp b$, $v = x^\frown a^\frown b^\frown y$, and $w = x^\frown b^\frown a^\frown y$.

T2. The *finite trace equivalence relation* $\equiv^f \subseteq A^* \times A^*$:
   $\equiv^f$ is the reflexive and transitive closure of $\doteq$.

T3. The *finite trace precedence relation* $\sqsubseteq^f \subseteq A^* \times A^*$:
   $v \sqsubseteq^f w$ iff there exists a finite sequence u such that $w \equiv^f v^\frown u$.

T4. The *trace precedence relation* $\sqsubseteq \subseteq A^\infty \times A^\infty$:
   $v \sqsubseteq w$ iff for each finite prefix x of v, there exists a finite prefix y of w such that $x \sqsubseteq^f y$.

T5. The *trace equivalence relation* $\equiv \subseteq A^\infty \times A^\infty$:
   $v \equiv w$ iff $v \sqsubseteq w$ and $w \sqsubseteq v$.

An execution w of P is *fair* [12] iff whenever an action a is firable at some state s in w (i.e., firable after some finite prefix of w is fired), some action b dependent on a (i.e., $a \not\perp b$) must appear later than s in w.

Let Q be the reduced sub-DTS of P, to be constructed by the partial-order reduction algorithm. Let $s_0 \in S$ be an *initial state*. Three conditions will be imposed on Q:

C0. For any $s \in \mathcal{R}(Q, s_0)$, if $\mathcal{F}(P, s) \neq \emptyset$, then $\mathcal{F}(Q, s) \neq \emptyset$.

C1. For any $s \in \mathcal{R}(Q, s_0)$ and finite sequence w firable at s in P, if every action in w belongs to $A \setminus \mathcal{F}(Q, s)$, then every action in w is independent of every action in $\mathcal{F}(Q, s)$.

C2. There exists a *well-founded* relation $\gg \subseteq S \times S$ (i.e., there is *no* infinite descending chain $t_0 \gg t_1 \gg t_2 \gg \cdots$ in S) such that for any $s \in \mathcal{R}(Q, s_0)$, if $\mathcal{F}(Q, s)$ is a *proper* subset of $\mathcal{F}(P, s)$, then $s \gg Q(a, s)$ for every $a \in \mathcal{F}(Q, s)$.

We are now ready to state the main theorems:

Theorem 1 Suppose **C0** and **C1** are true. For any $s \in \mathcal{R}(Q, s_0)$ and $w \in A^\infty \setminus \{\varepsilon\}$ such that w is a *fair* execution of P from s, there exists $a \in \mathcal{F}(Q, s)$ such that $a \sqsubseteq w$.

This theorem essentially says that although Q may not be able to fire w at s, Q can fire some action a at s, resulting in a state s', from which the DTS P can still complete a sequence which is trace equivalent to w (notice that s' is a state of both P and Q). However, this theorem does not guarantee that by repeatedly taking such actions, the sub-DTS Q can generate an execution that is trace equivalent to w. To do so, we need the next theorem, which uses **C2**.

Theorem 2 Suppose **C0**, **C1**, and **C2** are true. For any $s \in \mathcal{R}(Q, s_0)$, $a \in A$, and $w \in A^\infty$ such that $a^\frown w$ is a *fair* execution of P from s, there exists $v \in A^*$ such that $v^\frown a$ is firable at s in Q, a is independent of every action in v, and $v^\frown a \equiv a^\frown v \sqsubseteq a^\frown w$.

Theorem 1 merely guarantees that Q won't be stuck at s. Theorem 2 is stronger: it guarantees that Q eventually can fire what P can fire at s. It is proved by well-founded induction on $\gg$, which exists because of **C2**. Finally, the following theorem justifies partial-order reduction:

Theorem 3 Suppose **C0**, **C1**, and **C2** are true. For any *fair* execution $w \in A^\infty$ of P from s_0, there exists an execution v of Q from s_0 such that $v \equiv w$.

This theorem says that if we partition the (fair) executions of P into equivalence classes of $\equiv$, then the executions of Q must contain at least one representative from each class. A property C is *trace equivalence robust* (or just *robust*) iff:

$$v \equiv w \;\; \Rightarrow \;\; (v \in C \Leftrightarrow w \in C) \tag{4}$$

Therefore, if the property to be checked is trace equivalence robust, then a model checker needs to check only the executions of Q in order to know whether C holds for all executions of P. If P has a high degree of concurrency, Q can be considerably less expensive to check than P.

Because trace equivalent executions differ only in the order of concurrent events, most "natural" properties are robust. For example, both fairness [12] and firability are robust properties. In case the property to be checked is not robust, one can try to refine the trace equivalence relation (by using a smaller independence relation on actions) until the property is robust with respect to it [16]. But, of course, the finer the trace equivalence relation is, the less savings one is likely to get from partial-order reduction.

2.1 Comparison with the original paper

In [16], a modified depth-first search (DFS) algorithm for constructing Q from P (which must be finite) is given. There, a much less abstract version of **C2** in terms of the DFS is used:

C2-DFS. For any s that is about to be closed by the DFS, $\mathcal{F}(Q, s)$ is allowed to be a *proper* subset of $\mathcal{F}(P, s)$ only when $Q(a, s)$ is not on the search stack for each $a \in \mathcal{F}(Q, s)$; otherwise, $\mathcal{F}(Q, s)$ must equal $\mathcal{F}(P, s)$.

To see that **C2-DFS** implies **C2**, let us number the states of Q according to the order in which they are closed by the DFS. Clearly, such a numbering induces a well-founded relation on states. Furthermore, it is a well-known property of the DFS that if a state t is reached from s during the DFS while t is not on the search stack, then t will be closed before s. Hence, t will be numbered with a smaller value than s.

Note that *any* assignment of ordinals to a set of objects induces a well-founded relation on these objects. Conversely, any well-founded relation can be obtained in this manner. Therefore, an equivalent formulation of **C2** is:

C2-Ord. There is an assignment $\mathcal{O}$ of ordinals to states in S such that for any $s \in \mathcal{R}(Q, s_0)$, if $\mathcal{F}(Q, s)$ is a *proper* subset of $\mathcal{F}(P, s)$, then $\mathcal{O}(s) > \mathcal{O}(Q(a, s))$ for every $a \in \mathcal{F}(Q, s)$.

We did not use **C2-Ord** for the technical reason that it is hard to deal with ordinals in HOL.[1]

The more abstract condition **C2** used here shows that DFS is not the only way to construct Q from P. For example, one can use breadth-first search (BFS) as follows: one starts by estimating an upper bound N of the number of states of P. Then the initial state gets the number N and each successive level of the BFS gets a number that is one less than the previous level. A state $s \in \mathcal{R}(Q, s_0)$ will either have $\mathcal{F}(Q, s) = \mathcal{F}(P, s)$, or have all actions in $\mathcal{F}(Q, s)$ leading to states in the next level of the BFS (all of which, incidentally, have the same number).

So our efforts in formalizing (parts of) [16] actually produced a genuine generalization of the theory in [16]: we now know that DFS is not the only algorithm compatible with partial-order reduction. Another (though, from the point of view of model checking, less useful) generalization is that **C2** and hence Theorem 3 are applicable to infinite-state systems as well.

The paper [16] contains actually four partial-order reduction algorithms: P can have or have no fairness assumption, and the construction of Q can be

---

[1] Intuitively, each type in higher-order logic is a set, while the collection of all ordinals is a proper class. So it is impossible to have a "type of ordinals" in higher-order logic (though it is possible to show in higher-order logic that every type can be well-ordered).

carried out before ("off-line") or during ("on-the-fly") the model checking of Q. We have formally verified only the simplest case: fair and off-line. The verification of the other three algorithms needs additional formal theories, such as those about stuttering equivalence [13], Levi Lemma for traces [14], and finite automata on infinite sequences [18]. The work required to develop those formal theories is significant, but not very different from what we have already done.

3   Higher-Order Logic and HOL

Higher-order logic, also known as the *simple theory of types*, was introduced by Alonzo Church [2] as a foundation of mathematics. It is sufficiently expressive to allow the formalization of virtually all of "ordinary mathematics" as *definitional extensions* of a handful of axioms and primitive inference rules. The HOL system, a mechanization of higher-order logic developed by Gordon and others [5], supports this definitional approach to formalizing mathematics by making a clear distinction between *definitions*, which can never introduce any inconsistency, and arbitrary *axioms*, which may introduce inconsistencies and hence should not be used casually. (For an eloquent objection to the casual use of axioms in verification, see the preface of [1].) As is the case in almost all works using HOL, we have not found it necessary to introduce one single axiom in this work: all notions needed are formalized as definitions and all properties desired are proved as theorems of those definitions.

Higher-order logic generalizes first-order logic by allowing quantification over functions. For example, the induction principle for natural numbers can be expressed in higher-order logic by a single formula:

$$\forall P .\ P(0) \wedge (\forall n .\ P(n) \Rightarrow P(n{+}1)) \Rightarrow (\forall n .\ P(n)) \tag{5}$$

Every term t in higher-order logic has a type τ, written $t : \tau$. Intuitively, t denotes a value belonging to the set of values denoted by τ. For example, in (5), we have:

$$n : num \qquad\qquad + : num \rightarrow num \rightarrow num$$
$$P : num \rightarrow bool \qquad \wedge : bool \rightarrow bool \rightarrow bool$$

where *num* is the type of natural numbers 0, 1, 2, ..., *bool* is the type of truth values T and F, and $\alpha \rightarrow \beta$ is the type of functions from α to β, for any types α and β. Note that a formula is just a term of type *bool*. A function $f : \alpha \rightarrow \beta$ can be applied to an argument $a : \alpha'$ only when α and α' are identical; the result $f(a)$ is of type β. For any variable $v : \alpha$ and any term $t : \beta$, the *lambda abstraction* $(\lambda v .\ t)$ denotes a function of type $\alpha \rightarrow \beta$ which, when applied to an argument $a : \alpha$, returns $t[a/v]$, the result of substituting a for v in t. (Note that v need not actually occur in t.)

Primitive terms of higher-order logic are of two kinds: *constants* and *variables*. A constant denotes a fixed value of the appropriate type, while a variable denotes an arbitrary value and hence can be bound by a quantifier. For example, in (5), 0, +, ⇒ are constants, and n and P are (bound) variables. (There is no free variable in (5).) New constants can be introduced using *constant definitions*. For example, the definition:

$$\mathbf{sos}(x)(y) \triangleq x * x + y * y$$

defines a constant $\mathbf{sos} : num \rightarrow num \rightarrow num$ that computes the sum of squares of its arguments.

New types of *literals* can be defined using Melham's *recursive type definition* package [15] (though all literal types used in this paper are in fact non-recursive). For example, Melham's package can take a "BNF" of the form:

$$(\alpha, \beta)ttt \quad ::= \quad \mathbf{aaa} \mid \mathbf{bbb}(\alpha) \mid \mathbf{ccc}(\beta)$$

and define a new *parameterized* type $(\alpha, \beta)ttt$ with three constructors:

$$\mathbf{aaa} : (\alpha, \beta)ttt \qquad \mathbf{bbb} : \alpha \rightarrow (\alpha, \beta)ttt \qquad \mathbf{ccc} : \beta \rightarrow (\alpha, \beta)ttt$$

such that every value of type $(\alpha, \beta)ttt$ equals exactly one of $\mathbf{aaa}$, $\mathbf{bbb}(x)$, and $\mathbf{ccc}(y)$, for some unique x or y. The ability to have parameterized types such as $(\alpha, \beta)ttt$, which can be instantiated by substituting specific types for the *type variables* α and β, is called *type polymorphism* and is an enhancement made by HOL to the original formulation of Church.

There are other definitional mechanisms in HOL in addition to constant definition and recursive type definition, but they will not be needed in this paper.

HOL is implemented using a strongly typed functional programming language ML (for "Meta Language").[2] In HOL, the terms and theorems of higher-order logic are represented by two distinct ML types **term** and **thm**. The only constructors of **thm** are the mechanizations of the primitive inference rules of higher-order logic. (Note that axioms can be viewed as degenerate primitive inference rules.) For example, the primitive inference rule *Modus Ponens*:

$$\frac{\vdash a \Rightarrow b \quad \vdash a}{\vdash b}$$

is implemented in HOL as an ML function **MP:thm->thm->thm** that, if supplied with an implicational theorem **th1** and another theorem **th2** that is α-convertible to the antecedent of **th1**, returns the consequent of **th1** as a theorem (otherwise, **MP** raises an exception). Since ML is strongly typed,

---

[2]In fact, ML was invented for the very purpose of implementing LCF [6], a very influential mechanical theorem prover of which HOL is a descendant.

the only way one can generate an object of type **thm** is by repeated application of these primitive inference rules. (In particular, one cannot "cast" an arbitrary **term** into a **thm**.[3]) This is how HOL ensures the soundness of deductions it makes, and why the correctness of HOL depends only on the small kernel of ML codes implementing the primitive inference rules.

Although every **thm** generated by HOL is ultimately constructed using primitive inference rules, one seldom works directly at such a low level of abstraction when proving theorems in HOL. Since ML is a general-purpose programming language, sophisticated proof strategies, such as forward chaining, backward chaining, rewriting, and decision procedures for decidable theories, can be, and indeed many have been, programmed in HOL by combining primitive inference rules to form *derived proof procedures*. One can perform thousands of primitive inferences with a single invocation of a derived proof procedure. So HOL is an extremely malleable system whose capability is limited only by the user's imagination and programming ability and by the hardware resources of the machine on which HOL is run.

The typographic convention used to write higher-order logic types and terms in this section will be followed in the sequel: type variables are denoted by lowercase Greek letters, type constants by *slanted* identifiers, variables by *italic* identifiers, constants by sans serif identifiers or non-alphabetic symbols, and literals by **typewriter** identifiers. Free variables in a definition or theorem are implicitly universally quantified.

4   Verification of Partial-Order Reduction in HOL

Our verification of partial-order reduction in HOL is organized as a collection of *theories*, each of which consists of a set of definitions and a set of theorems together with their proofs. The dependency relation between the theories is depicted in Figure 1, where $S \rightarrow T$ means that theory T depends upon theory S. The contents of these theories are outlined below.

MISC: This theory proves miscellaneous theorems about natural numbers, lists, conditionals, and so on, that are needed in other theories. It contains no definition.

NUM: This is a theory about a new type *Num* of natural numbers augmented with an infinity element:

$$Num \quad ::= \quad \mathsf{Fin}(num) \mid \mathsf{Inf}$$

where *num* is the (built-in) type of natural numbers. Values of type *Num* are used to denote the "lengths" of sequences (see the theory

---

[3] Some implementations of HOL do contain a function **mk_thm** for doing just that. Clearly, no proof that uses **mk_thm** should be trusted. Our proof does not use **mk_thm**.

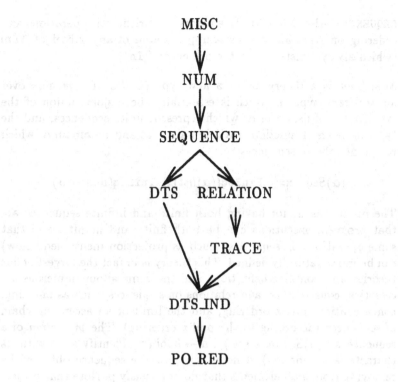

FIGURE 1. Dependencies between our theories

SEQUENCE). Also defined in this theory are arithmetic operations and ordering on *Num* and the least upper bound of any subset of *Num* (which always exists due to the presence of **Inf**).

SEQUENCE: This is a theory about a new type $(\alpha)Seq$ of *sequences* over an arbitrary type α, which is essentially the disjoint union of the type $(\alpha)list$ of lists over α, which represent finite sequences, and the type $num \rightarrow \alpha$ of functions with domain *num* and codomain α, which represent infinite sequences:

$$(\alpha)Seq \quad ::= \quad \texttt{FinSeq}((\alpha)list) \mid \texttt{InfSeq}(num \rightarrow \alpha)$$

The main reasons for having both finite and infinite sequences are that program executions can be both finite and infinite, and that some operations on sequences (such as projection mentioned below) can be more naturally defined. This theory is in fact the largest of our theories and contains definitions and theorems about numerous accessories, constructors, and relations on sequences, such as indexing, concatenation, prefix ordering, and the limit of an ascending chain of sequences (according to the prefix ordering). The *projection* of a sequence $s : (\alpha)Seq$ on a set $p : \alpha \rightarrow bool$ (we identify a set with its characteristic function), denoted $s \downarrow p$, is the sequence obtained by removing from s all elements that do not satisfy p. Note that projection can produce both finite and infinite sequences from an infinite sequence. Projection is defined using limits of projections of finite sequences, which are in turn defined using recursion on lists.

RELATION: This is a theory of *relations*, i.e., objects whose types are of the form $\alpha \rightarrow \alpha \rightarrow bool$. Various properties of relations (e.g., reflexivity, symmetry, transitivity) and operations on relations (e.g., reflexive and transitive closure) are defined. The following is a representative theorem of this theory, which is used several times in the theory **TRACE**:

$$\forall f : \alpha \rightarrow \beta . \forall R\, S .$$
$$\mathsf{Homomorphism}(f)(R)(S) \;\Rightarrow\; \mathsf{Homomorphism}(f)(R^*)(S^*)$$

where R^* and S^* are the reflexive and transitive closures of relations R and S, and **Homomorphism** is defined by:

$$\mathsf{Homomorphism}(f)(R)(S) \;\overset{\triangle}{=}\; \forall x\, y .\, R(x)(y) \;\Rightarrow\; S(f(x))(f(y))$$

Also proved in this theory is the principle of well-founded induction.

TRACE: This is a theory of Mazurkiewicz traces. As outlined in Section 2, we define trace equivalence and precedence in five steps **T1–T5**. We then prove a useful alternative characterization of trace precedence and equivalence:

$$s \sqsubseteq t \quad \Leftrightarrow \quad \forall a\, b\, . \, a \not\perp b \Rightarrow (s \downarrow \{a, b\} \preceq t \downarrow \{a, b\})$$
$$s \equiv t \quad \Leftrightarrow \quad \forall a\, b\, . \, a \not\perp b \Rightarrow (s \downarrow \{a, b\} = t \downarrow \{a, b\})$$

where $\perp$ is the underlying independence relation between actions and $\preceq$ is the prefix relation between sequences. Numerous properties about trace equivalence and precedence are proved.

DTS: This is a theory of *deterministic transition systems* (DTS's), which represent programs. A DTS is a function of type $\alpha \rightarrow \sigma \rightarrow (\sigma)Lift$, where α and σ are respectively the types of actions and states, and $(\sigma)Lift$ is σ augmented with a bottom element representing undefinedness:

$$(\sigma)Lift \quad ::= \quad \text{Up}(\sigma) \mid \text{Bottom}$$

For any DTS P, action a, and state s, if $P(a)(s) = \text{Bottom}$ then a is not *firable* at s in P; otherwise, $\text{Down}(P(a)(s))$ is the state resulting from firing a at s in P, where $\text{Down}(\text{Up}(s)) \triangleq s$. The bulk of this theory is concerned with generalizing the notions of firability and firing from single actions to sequences.

DTS_IND: This is a theory of the interaction between deterministic transition systems and Mazurkiewicz traces. The main definitions are the compatibility of a DTS P with an independence relation (i.e., (2) and (3) of Section 2) and the notion of fairness. The main theorems proved are the robustness of firability and fairness with respect to trace equivalence.

PO_RED: This is where **C0–C2** and Theorems 1–3 of Section 2 are formalized and verified.

Table 1 gives some statistics about our theories: the numbers of definitions, main theorems, lines of code, and primitive inferences performed per theory and per line of code. The last number can be seen as a rough measure of the "density" of each theory. The whole verification project was carried out in 10 weeks of intense programming, but the final ML code takes less than five minutes to run on an SGI Challenger machine with 12 processors and more than 1 gigabytes of physical memory.

5 Lessons Learned

In this section, we shall attempt to answer the following questions: How hard is it to do a formal verification of a nontrivial model checking algorithm? Do the benefits justify the costs? Do we gain better understanding

Theory	Defs.	Thms.	Lines	Inferences	Infs./Line
MISC	0	43	524	15,368	29.33
NUM	14	21	477	9,345	19.59
SEQUENCE	30	128	2,520	107,176	42.53
RELATION	19	28	534	11,904	22.29
TRACE	10	103	1,639	36,679	22.39
DTS	10	21	400	8,563	21.41
DTS_IND	2	22	446	16,889	37.87
PO_RED	5	4	889	53,631	60.33
Total	90	370	7,429	259,555	34.94

TABLE 1. Statistics about our theories

of the verified algorithm? Do we learn something new about the verified algorithm? Is the formal proof more readable than the original informal one?

5.1 Encouraging Lessons

Generalizing the verified algorithm. Doing a formal proof requires mathematical abstraction. This process often produces new insights into the proved problem or algorithm. Defined in mathematical terms, the underlying assumptions and mathematical structures behind the algorithms become clear. In some cases, one realizes that it is possible to generalize or improve the original algorithm. This happened during our verification effort. In order to simplify the proof, the use of DFS in generating the state space was abstracted away and an ordinal numbering of the states was introduced in its stead. This numbering corresponds in DFS to the order in which the search backtracks from nodes. Originally, condition **C2** refers specifically to the DFS stack. In the formal proof it was abstracted into a requirement on an ordinal numbering. The more abstract requirement fits not only DFS but also other search mechanisms, e.g., BFS. This is useful, as sometimes one prefers BFS to DFS in model checking. For example, COSPAN [10] uses BFS because it simplifies the search for the shortest counterexample when a program does not satisfy its specification.

Gaining experience in techniques and tools. The verification attempt was also aimed at learning from the process of doing the verification on a "real-life" problem. This includes: experiencing with the formal verification tool HOL, learning its strengths and weaknesses, and studying how difficult it is to give a formalization of the verification problem in a given logic. Doing the proof, we have studied the feasibility of such a process. This includes the time required to complete such a proof, the level of expertise in the verification tool, the mathematical theories needed, the length of the proof, and the kind of hardware that can carry such a verification task. The main lesson is that such a proof is feasible but requires non-trivial human resources in terms of expertise and time. One of the lessons we learned is the relation between the formal and informal proof. Going through the process of formal verification with a tool such as HOL forced us to be honest in our argumentation. Incantations such as "trivial", "obvious", "immediate from the definition", and "left as an exercise for the reader" do not work. The formal verification has helped to clean the proof and to identify points where "trivial" claims were in fact quite nontrivial.

Developing the machinery to verify similar problems. During the verification, mathematical theories that can support reasoning about related algorithms were developed. We have laid the groundwork of a formal infrastructure that will include the mathematical support for proving various automatic verification algorithms. Some of the theories described in Section 4 can be useful in verifying other model checking reduction algorithms, e.g., symmetry reduction [3, 4]. The theories outlined in Section 4 are not sufficient by themselves, as other algorithms may rely on other theories, e.g., permutation groups. We hope that the combined effort of several such proofs can create the infrastructure for verifying many model checking algorithms. Ideally, after collecting some additional theories related to model checking such as theories of ω-regular languages and automata, verifying a new algorithm would take much less time.

Experimenting with verifying a nontrivial algorithm. Software verification has lost some of its appeal over the last decade, as it was applied mainly to toy examples. In this experiment it was applied to a nontrivial algorithm, whose correctness relies on various mathematical theories. Moreover, the verification was made on a high level description of the algorithm, proving a generic method that can be implemented in many ways rather than just one instance of it. The high level description of the algorithm fits well with the HOL ability to reason about general mathematics and higher order objects. We hope to have demonstrated that formal verification is a practical and useful tool.

Gaining more confidence in an algorithm. Since a lot of effort is spent in creating software verification tools, it is all the more important to pay attention to their correctness. While a verification tool which reports nonexistent bugs ("false negatives") merely wastes time, a verification tool that does not report existing bugs is dangerous, as it creates unjustified confidence. A hand written proof attached to an algorithm is not always sufficient. In many scientific publications the proof of theorems is omitted or only sketched. The algorithm we study here is intricate enough not to be trusted on an intuitive basis. For example, there is a subtle point concerning why condition **C2** is needed when checking liveness properties.

5.2 Discouraging Lessons

The question of the correctness of the verifier. A software tool of the size of HOL is likely to contain some bugs. The ones that concern us are those that allow untrue theorems to be proved. In the past, such bugs have been found in HOL. Although the chance of actually encountering such a bug is insignificantly small, it demonstrates that the use of a formal tool does not guarantee the correctness of a proof. However, one can argue that the additional reliability is mainly achieved by the act of formalization. This argument should be taken with a grain of salt in light of the amount of automation in such tools. For example, in HOL and similar tools, the use of powerful rewriting procedures might produce a big deduction step, which might not always be easy to trace by the person who does the verification.

The possibility of making an error in the formalization of the problem. This seems to be the most severe problem. The first step of the verification is formalizing the theorem to be verified. The use of a specific logic such as higher-order logic requires the translation of the verification problem from a natural language into a formal language. This step is prone to errors. Errors in translating the supporting lemmas for the proof may be discovered when they cannot be proved or when they are insufficient to prove the main theorems.

A partial verification. Verifying algorithms can be done at various levels. One can verify the mathematical theorems that justifies an algorithm, an abstract algorithm given in pseudo-code, or a real implementation of the algorithm in a programming language with a formal semantics. The more abstract proof will be useful for more than one implementation, but would allow a higher level of uncertainty about the correctness of any particular implementation. This work was done at a rather abstract level, concentrating on the mathematical issues.

Poor readability of the proof. Although we gained a lot of new mathematical insights during the development of the HOL proof, the end product is no clearer than the proof in the original paper: the HOL proof code is very difficult to read. It is impractical to replace the informal proof in the paper by the formal HOL proof. Even an expert of both HOL *and* the verified problem can find it difficult to understand the intuition behind the proof given as HOL code. HOL does not impose any proof style which would make the proof a readable document.

The formal proof requires a lot of human resources. The verification effort resulted in almost 7,500 lines of dense proof code. Moreover, it required the complete attention of an HOL expert for 10 weeks. As pointed out in Section 2.1, only a portion of [16] was verified. Although we intended initially to verify a bigger portion of [16], we found it impossible to achieve that goal in the given time frame. We hope that combining several such projects would create a more advanced starting point for future verification efforts.

Acknowledgements

We would like to thank Elsa Gunter for her penetrating remarks (especially regarding the formalization of deterministic transition systems), and Rajeev Alur, Gerard Holzmann, Doug Howe, Robert Kurshan, and Mihalis Yannakakis for their helpful comments.

6 REFERENCES

[1] Robert S. Boyer and J Strother Moore, *A Computational Logic*, Academic Press, 1979.

[2] Alonzo Church, "A Formulation of the Simple Theory of Types", in *Journal of Symbolic Logic*, Vol. 5, pp. 56–68, 1940.

[3] E.M. Clarke, T. Filkorn, S. Jha, Exploiting Symmetry in Temporal Logic Model Checking, 5th International Conference on Computer Aided Verification, Elounda, Greece, June 1993, LNCS 697, 450–462.

[4] E.A. Emerson, A.P. Sistla, Symmetry and Model Checking, 5th International Conference on Computer Aided Verification, Elounda, Greece, June 1993, LNCS 697, 463–479.

[5] Michael J.C. Gordon and Thomas F. Melham (Ed.), *Introduction to HOL: A Theorem-Proving Environment for Higher-Order Logic*, Cambridge University Press, 1993.

[6] M.J.C. Gordon, A.J.R.G. Milner, and C.P. Wadsworth, *Edinburgh LCF: A Mechanized Logic of Computation*, Lecture Notes in Computer Science 78, Springer-Verlag, 1979.

[7] G.J. Holzmann, *Design and Validation of Computer Protocols*, Prentice Hall, 1991.

[8] G.J. Holzmann, D. Peled, An Improvement in Formal Verification, *7th* International Conference on Formal Description Techniques, Berne, Switzerland, 1994, 177–194.

[9] H. Hungar, "Combining Model Checking and Theorem Proving to Verify Parallel Processes", 5th International Conference on Computer Aided Verification, Elounda, Greece, June/July 1993, LNCS 697, pp.154–165.

[10] R.P. Kurshan, Computer-Aided Verification of Coordinating Processes, Princeton University Press, 1994.

[11] R.P. Kurshan and L. Lamport, "Verification of a Multiplier: 64 Bits and Beyond", 5th International Conference on Computer Aided Verification, Elounda, Greece, June/July 1993, LNCS 697, pp.166–179.

[12] M. Z. Kwiatkowska, Event Fairness and Non-Interleaving Concurrency, Formal Aspects of Computing 1 (1989), 213–228.

[13] L. Lamport, What good is temporal logic, in R.E.A. Mason (ed.), Proceedings of IFIP Congress, North Holland, 1983, 657–668.

[14] A. Mazurkiewicz, Trace Theory, in: W. Brauer, W. Reisig, G. Rozenberg (eds.) Advances in Petri Nets 1986, Bad Honnef, Germany, Lecture Notes in Computer Science 255, Springer, 1987, 279–324.

[15] Thomas F. Melham, "Automating Recursive Type Definitions in Higher-Order Logic", pp. 341–386 of G. Birtwistle and P.A. Subrahmanyam (Ed.), *Current Trends in Hardware Verification and Automated Theorem Proving*, Springer-Verlag, 1989.

[16] D. Peled, Combining Partial Order Reductions with On-the-fly Model-Checking, 6th International Conference on Computer Aided Verification, Stanford, CA, USA, 1994, LNCS 818, 377–390.

[17] S. Rajan, N. Shankar, M.K. Srivas, An Integration of Model Checking with Automated Proof Checking, 7th International Conference on Computer Aided Verification, Liège, Belgium, July 1995, LNCS 939, 84–97.

[18] Wolfgang Thomas, "Automata on Infinite Objects", pp.133–192 of Jan van Leeuwen (Ed.), *Handbook of Theoretical Computer Science, Vol. B: Formal Models and Semantics*, The MIT Press/Elsevier, 1990.

Fully Automatic Verification and Error Detection for Parameterized Iterative Sequential Circuits

Tiziana Margaria*

ABSTRACT The paper shows how iterative *parametric sequential* circuits, which are most relevant in practice, can be verified *fully automatically*. Key observation is that monadic second-order logic on strings provides an adequate level for hardware specification and implementation. This allows us to apply the corresponding decision procedure and counter-model generator implemented in the Mona verification tool, which, for the first time, yields 'push-button' verification, and error detection and diagnosis for the considered class of circuits. As illustrated by means of various versions of counters, this approach captures hierarchical and mixed mode verification, as well as the treatment of varying connectivity in iterative designs.

1 Motivation

A clear trend towards reuse of existing designs is the emergence of parametric designs in standard libraries [13]. While such "families of circuits" have been already popular in the hardware verification community for years, where they are the best examples for induction-based reasoning in the hardware application domain, industrial practice did not feature parametric designs in standard libraries because of lack of consolidated methods for their *full-automatic* treatment in the design lifecycle. Thus the pressure towards fully automated methods for the analysis, verification, and fault detection of parametric circuits and their specifications grows with the increasing demand for design reuse. Unfortunately, the standard automata theoretic techniques of the hardware community fail here, because the treatment of automata of unbounded size is required. At this stage, Basin and Klarlund discovered that monadic second-order logic on strings, although 'hopeless' from the complexity point of view, is well-behaved in many practical applications, and, in particular, well-suited for the fully automatic verification of

---

*Fakultät für Mathematik und Informatik, Universität Passau, Innstr. 33, 94032 Passau (D), tel: +49 851 509.3096, fax: +49 851 509.3092, tiziana@fmi.uni-passau.de

parametric *combinational* circuits and of the timing properties of a D-type flip-flop [3]. This general observation led to the development of the **Mona** verification tool [18], whose kernel consists of a non-elementary decision procedure for monadic second-order logic on strings.

In this paper we concentrate on *sequential* circuits, the class of circuits with the most practical relevance for CAD design, and in particular on the uniform treatment of whole families of the parametric iterative kind.

- *Sequential* circuits differ from combinational ones for the presence of clocked registers, or, more generally, state holding devices. Their input/output behaviour over time is usually modelled as a Finite State Machine [19], describing the values taken by the state holding elements and by the outputs over time. The standard model of time is discrete, with one observation point for each clock cycle.

- *Parametric* circuits are actually families of circuits ranging over one or more dimensions, like the width of the datapath as in the n-bit synchronous counter of Section 4.

- *Iterative* circuits exibit regularities of their structures along one dimension, e.g. pipelines or one-dimensional systolic arrays.

Parametric circuits are called iterative when the parametrization involves one dimension only. Examples include n-bit counters, which are sequential, the n-bit ALU of [3], which is combinational, but also the class of systolic arrays called "cellular automata", pipelines, etc..[1]. For this class of circuits, we

- show how they can be *fully automatically* verified,

- loosen the standard hypothesis of constant connectivity, which is inherent to most of the known approaches (see next section), showing how to deal with *variations* of the connectivity between adjacent basic cells as long as these are regular in an informal sense, and finally

- illustrate the impact of the diagnostic features offered by the **Mona** system on fault detection and diagnosis for hierarchical parameterized systems.

Fully automatic approaches can be integrated within existing design environments as 'black boxes' that can be used without additional expertise from the user. In particular, this also applies to Mona, which we integrated in METAFrame, a general environment for the analysis, verification and construction of complex systems.

---

[1] Grid structures where parameters interact (needed e.g. to handle parameterized multipliers) exceed this schema and cannot be handled in this approach.

The remainder of the paper is organized as follows. After a summary of related literature in Section 2, Section 3 sketches the background for the proposed verification method. Sections 4 and 5 illustrate respectively the verification and the fault detection and diagnosis for sequential parametric iterative designs, and finally Section 6 presents a first evaluation.

2 Related Work

Traditional approaches to parametric hardware verification with formal techniques resort to general purpose methods based on inductive reasoning within either first or higher-order logic. First order logic based theorem provers such as Boyer's and Moore's NQTHM [28, 17, 29], or the Larch Prover [1] have been used for years to handle parametric designs, as well as several higher order logic systems like HOL [14, 8, 27], VERITAS [16], or NUPRL [10, 4], and there are studies which compare both approaches [2]. In all of them, verification becomes an activity bound to interactive, computer assisted theorem proving. Thus the user must employ tactics (as in the HOL system) or suggest appropriate lemmas. While such approaches are general and quite powerful, their use is mainly restricted to verification experts as opposed to engineers and CAD designers. Also the approaches of [35, 32, 7, 20, 36] for model-checking, language containment, and process verification require interaction.

We know of two approaches to fully automate the verification of parametric circuits. They are based on symbolic methods:

Rho and Somenzi propose methods to automatically derive invariants from the structure of iterative sequential circuits by resorting to automata-based methods and to BDD-based symbolic manipulation of automata [30, 31]. The derivation process proceeds by greatest fixpoint iteration over state-minimal deterministic representations of the corresponding regular languages. It is successful whenever it stabilizes up to isomorphism. As no characteristic criterion for stabilization is given, the precise class of circuits that can be handled is unclear. The authors only consider circuits with constant connectivity.

Gupta and Fisher [15] introduce a canonical representation for inductive boolean functions (IBF) which resembles an inductive extension of BDDs covering certain classes of inductively-defined hardware circuits. Verification is carried out by symbolic tautology checking on the IBF representation of the circuits. Their results are the most similar to ours, as they cover essentially the same class of circuits, which they call *linear* parameterized sequential circuits. However, besides being complicated, the required coding in a special inductive format has the following drawbacks:

- The coding is bound to a very fine-grained analysis of the recursion pattern and does not directly reflect the structure of the original description. Thus diagnostic information would require to re-establish the connection to the original description.[2]

- The treatment of parametric outputs is very tricky and leads to complicated representations of hierarchical structures.

In contrast, our approach allows a quite straightforward structure-preserving representation of the argument circuits and therefore good support for error diagnosis (Section 5). Moreover, as will be illustrated in the examples, no additional effort is required to treat parametric outputs. This is achieved by using Monadic Second-Order logic on Strings (M2L(Str)) for specification, which Alonzo Church proposed already 30 years ago as an appropriate formalism for reasoning about bitvectors [9]. In fact, this logic is decidable, however, only in non-elementary time: the worst-case complexity is a stack of exponentials of height proportional to the size of the formula, a good reason for it having being considered impractical so long. Fortunately, relevant problems are usually far better behaved and can be solved automatically in reasonable time[3]. The examples of this paper required CPU times ranging from fractions of a second to a few minutes.

3 Background

3.1 The Verification Scenario

The architecture of our verification setup (illustrated in Figure 1) is based on the cooperation between Mona [18] and the METAFrame environment [33]. As circuit descriptions given in a Hardware Description Language can be first translated in the target logic, along the lines introduced in [11, 23, 25][4], proofs can be carried out at the *logic* level and entirely automatically by means of Mona. The result, in form of an automaton or of a minimal counterexample, can be visualized as a graph within the METAFrame environment. The user may interact with both systems simultaneously as illustrated by Figure 2. Currently, METAFrame provides the graphic facilities for the display of the results delivered by Mona. It also allows the user to investigate properties of the graphs by means of hypertext inspectors for nodes and edges.

Mona is a verification tool for a second order monadic logic. Predicates are defined as logic formulas and transformed into minimal automata. The

---

[2]Perhaps this is the reason for not being considered in the paper.

[3]The so popular BDD encodings are also in general exponential, but large classes of hardware circuits have manageable polynomial representations.

[4]In these approaches the semantics of Register-Transfer and gate level descriptions was expressed in terms of first-order logic formulas.

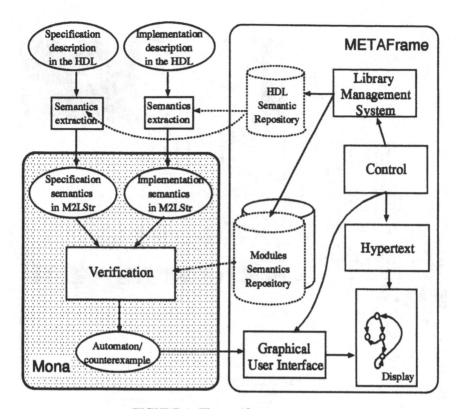

FIGURE 1. The verification scenario

computed automata are persistent objects, that is they are computed only once and stored in a library with their BDD structure. Later references to the predicate cause the precomputed automaton to be loaded and reused. Hence definitions constitute a library of reusable components which remain available for later sessions and the persistency of the precomputed automata supports compositionality with no additional cost: since the automata constitute the semantics of the hardware objects, once the equivalence between two logic objects has been proved they become semantically indistinguishable. In particular, a specification can be then replaced by its implementation (compositional verification) and structural descriptions of a module can be replaced by their behavioral counterpart (mixed-mode verification).

3.2 The Specification Language

The *monadic second-order logic on strings* (M2L(Str)) is one of the most expressive decidable logics known, and it precisley captures regular languages (see [34]). For its syntax we follow [18]. The basic operators are reported in Figure 3, where we distinguish logic terms denoting positions t, string

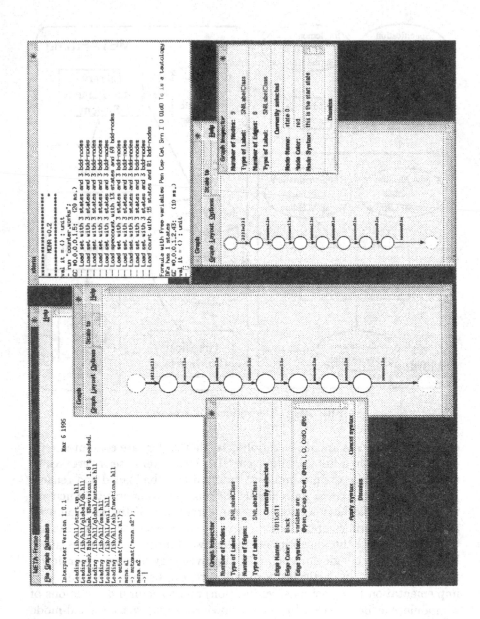

FIGURE 2. Snapshot of a user session

$$t ::= \quad 0 \mid \$ \mid p \mid t + o\, i$$
$$T ::= \quad all \mid P \mid C(T) \mid T_1 \cup T_2$$
$$F ::= \quad tt \mid t_1 = t_2 \mid t_1 < t_2 \mid T_1 = T_2 \mid t \; in \; T \mid \neg F \mid F_1 \,\&\, F_2 \mid$$
$$\quad All \; p\!: F \mid All \; P\!: F$$

FIGURE 3. A basic syntax for M2L(Str)

expressions T, and formulas F:

- First-order expressions t describe string positions (i.e. bitvector addresses) and are built using constants 0 (the starting position), $\$$ (the final position), first-order variables p, and the operator $+o$ which denotes addition modulo the string length. Here i ranges over natural numbers.

- Second-order expressions T describe strings (i.e. bit vectors) in terms of sets of positions whose value is 1 in the string. For instance, all represents strings whose elements are all 1 and union computes the union of the positions of two strings where elements are 1 and $C(T)$ denotes the complement of string T. Here, P ranges over string variables.

- Formulas are interpreted over strings, which correspond to bitvectors of finite, but not necessarily precised length. They have their expected meaning. For example, the conjunction of two formulas is true when both formulas are true. The formula $t \; in \; T$ is true when the position denoted by the interpretation of t is "set" (i.e., 1) in the string interpreting T. Quantification is possible over positions and over strings.

Note that many connectives given here, like e. g. position variables and their connectives, are only included for convenience since they may be encoded within the logic using second-order variables. Internally, Mona uses such an encoding. Similarly, dual connectives like, e.g., ff, the empty string $empty$, string disjunction $\cup$, implication $\Rightarrow$, equivalence $\Leftrightarrow$, existential quantification $\exists$, are available, as well as a short form for Boolean variables, represented as @p, over which quantification is possible too. Predicate definitions are equalities terminated by semicolons, and comments are introduced by the symbol #.

As an example, the following formulas

```
if(@cond, @then, @else) = (@cond => @then) & (~@cond => @else);

inc(Old, New) =
```

```
if(Old = all,
   New = empty,
   Ex j : j notin Old & (All k : k < j => k in Old) &
         All l : (l < j => l notin New) &
                 (l = j => l in New) &
                 (l > j => (l in Old <=> l in New)));
```

define, respectively, a predicate for the usual *if − then − else* construct, and a predicate inc corresponding to the bitvector increment operation by a simple case analysis. If Old, the bitvector we are incrementing, is all ones (i.e., all positions are set) then the result, New, is all zeros (i.e., empty positions are set). Alternatively, there exists a least position j which is zero (i.e. notin Old). In this case the increment operation should clear all the smaller positions in New, set this position, and leave the rest unchanged. This predicate will be used in the specification of the counter in the following section.

Interpretations of formulas are constructed by converting formulas to automata as described in [18]. For any formula ϕ that is not a tautology, a minimal length counterexample can be extracted from the corresponding automaton. This feature is exploited in Sect. 5 for fault detection, diagnosis and testing.

4 Verification of Parametric Iterative Sequential Circuits

We illustrate the flexibility of parameterization allowed in M2L(Str) by giving a behavioral specification, formalizing several architectures of counters based on the well known 74LS163 4-bit counter with enable and synchronous clear, and verifying their correctness.

The same family of counters had been already considered in [24, 26, 25] to study the impact of semantic data abstraction and compositionality in the hierarchical verification of counters of increasing but given word size. There, the semantics had been given in first order logic, and the (fully automatic) verification had been carried out by rewriting and resolution with the OTTER theorem prover. However, this approach was unable to deal with a parametric version of the implementation, a limitation which can be overcome in the fashion described in this paper.

The following four subsections discuss verification problems of increasing difficulty:

1. the parameterized behavioral specification of the counter, which is used to verify the correctness of all the proposed design architectures,

2. the implementation of the 4-bit basic cell, which illustrates how to deal with standard sequential circuits,

3. a parameterized n-bit version of it, which defines a family of iterative sequential circuits. This modelling requires the additional ability to handle variable connectivity, and finally

4. the hierarchical design of a 4×n-parameterized counter constructed as a cascade of n 4-bit modules, where iteration is needed at the hierarchical level, and ranges over the modules.

While induction-based methods are tailored for case 3, but have difficulties with case 2, automata-based methods are tailored for case 2, but fail for case 3. Case 4, being a mixture of 2 and 3, requires a specific and often intricate user interaction in all known approaches. – The handling of faulty designs is delayed to Section 5.

4.1 The Behavioral Specification

The specification defines the behavior of the circuit in terms of its input/output function independently of the word length. Its control part selects one of the four possible operations (*clear, parallel_load, increment, no_op*) according to the values of the control signals, and its data path simply consists of a data register with synchronous clear. Due to the possibility in any state (or data register configuration) of loading any other configuration, transitions are possible between any pair of states.

In [12] the specification is given by the following mode select table and expression for the terminal count TC.

SRn	PEn	CET	CEP	Action (Effect)
L	X	X	X	Reset (Clear)
H	L	X	X	Load ($I \to O$)
H	H	H	H	Count (Increment)
H	H	L	X	No Change (Hold)
H	H	X	L	No Change (Hold)

$$tc = I_o \wedge I_1 \wedge I_2 \wedge I_3 \wedge CET \qquad (*)$$

We may formalize this in M2L(Str) in a fairly direct manner. The functional behavior of the parameterized counter is defined by a direct encoding of this operation select table and of the additional logic equation. To model it, it is sufficient to require the consistency of its behavior over any two consecutive time units: for each operation, the value of the generated output O (which in this simple example coincides with the new state) and of the terminal count tc must be consistent with the previous output/state OldO, the current input I and the current values of the control signals as prescribed by the above table. Note that this modelling turns out to be similar to the one adopted in [18] for the dining philosophers with encyclopedia. Both model essentially an (infinite) family of state transition function. Hardware, however, usually requires an additional function in order express the output values at any clock cycle as a function of the current state for Moore machines, and of the input and the current state for Mealy machines. For the counter, the output function is simply the identity.

The following specification is implicitly parameterized over the length of the datapath (strings I, O, OldO) and uses the predicates if and inc which belong to the basic library and have been already illustrated in the previous section.

```
speccount(@pen,@cep,@cet,@srn,I,O,OldO,@tc) =
  (if(~@srn,(All p: p notin O),
       if(~@pen,(All p: (p in I <=> p in O)),
    if(and(@cet,@cep),inc(OldO,O),
      (All p: (p in OldO <=> p in O)))))
  & (@tc <=> (All j: j in OldO & @cet)));
```

In the following we will concentrate on the relevant phenomena of each implementation style, and limit the Mona syntax to the minimum. The complete descriptions, essentially due to David Basin, are collected in Appendix 1.

4.2 Verification of the Basic Cell

The structure of the gate-level implementation of the 74LS163 4-bit counter, as found in [12], is directly reflected in the structure of the predicate count4bit defined in Appendix 1.1. Its automatic generation from a description in a Hardware Description Language such as, e.g., VHDL [21], ISPS [5] or CASCADE [6] would be straightforward.

Assuming that the input strings are all of length 4 (so their last position, $, is 3), the equivalence of the parameterized specification, restricted to 4-bit strings, with the 4-bit implementation is stated as

```
($ = 0+3 =>
    (count4bit(@pen,@cep,@cet,@srn,@tc,0 in I,0+1 in I,0+2 in I,
            0+3 in I,0 in O,0+1 in O,0+2 in O,0+3 in O,0 in OldO,
            0+1 in OldO,0+2 in OldO,0+3 in OldO) <=>
    speccount2(@pen,@cep,@cet,@srn,I,O,OldO,@tc)))
```

Mona proves this equivalence in 15 s CPU on a SparcStation 20.

4.3 The Iterative Counter: Describing Variable Connectivity

The structure of the n-bit generalization of the counter as shown in in Figure 4 individuates a parametric iterative family of modulo 2^n counters. Its formalization of in a top-down fashion is reported in Appendix 1.2.

Already looking at the description of the 4-bit implementation, we may have noticed that the bit slices do not have all the same inputs/outputs, as

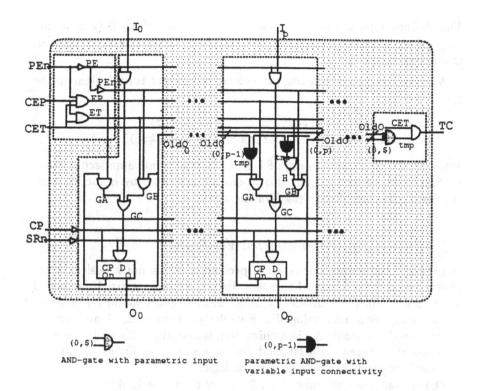

FIGURE 4. Implementation of the n-bit counter

it would be usual e.g. in systolic arrays. In the formalization of the parametric generalization, the ability to describe purely repetitive structures as e.g. in [31] would not suffice. However, since successive slices differ only in a regular manner, we are still capable to formalize this change of pattern within the logic in a natural way.[5]

According to Figure 4, each slice receives inputs from *all the previous* ones, i.e., the pth slice has one data input and one data output more than the $p - 1$th. In particular, the two internal gates indicated in black have a variable number of input lines, which increases by one unit along the n dimension. This is captured by introducing the relation n_and(p,I,@o) which defines an *and* gate with a variable number of input lines controlled by the parameter p:

n_and(p,I,@o) = ((@o) <=> (All j : (j <= p => j in I)));

---

[5]In fact, this circuit belongs to the *linear parametric* class of [15]. It may be modelled by means of their LIBF structures, providing an adequate inductive definition scheme is at hand.

This defines a *parameterized family* of AND gates, which is used in the body of the `computebit` relation and thus it occurs in the description of this family of counters.

We may now prove that this parameterized counter is equivalent to the specification.

```
(speccount(@pen,@cep,@cet,@srn,I,0,@ld0,@tc)
   <=>  count(@pen,@cep,@cet,@srn,I,0,@ld0,@tc))
```

Mona verifies this equivalence in 8 s CPU. In traditional approaches based on first or higher-order logic, this would require proof by induction over the (explicitly formalized) length of the string.

4.4 Hierarchical Parameterized Verification

In practice, the parametric scheme specified above is not a desirable implementation for a family of counters. Having a parameterized number of wires, the fan-in and fan-out[6] of some internal gates would become too large already for a small value of n. Real designs require fan-in and fan-out to be a small constant. A hierarchical implementation of a $4n$-bit counter in terms of a cascade of 4-bit modules (as reported in Figure 5) satisfies this need, and is easily expressed in the logic.

The formalization in Appendix 1.3 is now parameterized in the number of 4-bit units and reuses the `count4bit` predicate to implement the basic cells. Rather than using recursion, the iteration which allocates the modules in the `ripplecount` description is expressed by a predicate `fourth(p)` that is true when the position variable p takes values $3, 7, 11, \ldots$. Internal bit vector variables (`Cep`, `Cet` and `Tc`) represent the vectors of intermediate control values to be propagated between neighbouring 4-bit modules. The rippling of the terminal count `@tc` to the enabling control lines `@cep` and `@cet` of the next module follows the solution indicated in Figure 5.

The equivalence between this implementation and the behavioral specification `speccount` (or, equivalently, the parameterized implementation `count`) can be proven for all counters whose datapath is a multiple of 4-bit:

```
(fourth($) =>
    (ripplecount(@pen,@cep,@cet,@srn,I,0,@ld0,@tc) <=>
        speccount(@pen,@cep,@cet,@srn,I,0,@ld0,@tc)))
```

Mona verifies that this is a tautology in 100 s CPU.

Note that the design of the outer unit is truly hierarchical: we do not need

---

[6]Fan-in is the number of input lines to a gate, fan-out is the number of gates driven by its output.

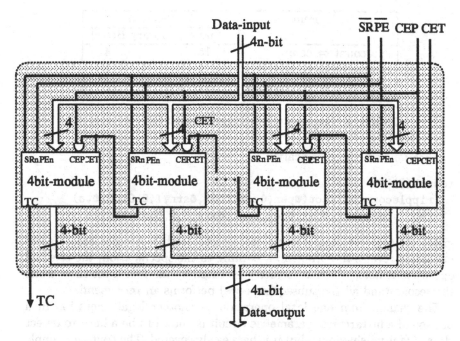

FIGURE 5. Hierarchical implementation of the $4n$ bit counter

to know any interna of the 4-bit cells. The verification at this stage ensures the correct connection of the global control and data inputs and outputs to and from each 4-bit module, independently e.g. also of parameter names. A change to an implementation in terms of 8-bit cells would only require a definition of an *eigth(p)* function and of the corresponding distribution of data inputs and outputs in bunches of 8. This could be generated as well from a HDL description.

5 Fault Detection for Parametric Hierarchical Designs

Mona supports a natural fault detection and diagnosis also for parametric hierarchical hardware designs. This is known to be a difficult problem: the hierarchical structure, intended to yield clarity and transparency, complicates error detection, as the evidence of the faulty behaviour may lie deep inside the modules used in the hierarchical descriptions. This applies in particular to induction-based verification methods.

In order to demonstrate how our approach covers this class of errors, we try to simplify the structure of the parametric hierarchical counter: rather than rippling the control signals between the modules, we connect CEP directly to the TC of the preceding module. The attempt to verify the

Theorem	Verification	
	Flat	Library Based
speccount ⇔ count	15	4
speccount ⇔ count4bit	8	1
speccount ⇔ ripplecount	100	5

TABLE 1. Summary of verification results: CPU times in s

implication wrt. the specification

```
fourth($) =>
  (ripplecount-direct(@pen,@cep,@cet,@srn,I,O,OldO,@tc)
   => speccount(@pen,@cep,@cet,@srn,I,O,OldO,@tc)))
```

yields the counterexample shown in Figure 2 (right). A quick analysis immediately reveals the problem: according to the specification, the selected operation is *hold*, which is correctly executed by the first 4-bit slice, while the second (and all the subsequent ones) performs an *increment!*

The change from one legal operation to another legal operation in a portion of a hierarchical parametric circuit is known to be a hard to detect class of faulty behaviours, but it is here easily covered. The counterexample reports values which distinguish the behaviour of the implementation and of the specification. The problem is here due to the Tc, which is set by the first module and it is erroneously propagated to both Cep and Cet of the second; hence the second module receives the op-code of the increment operation.

Trying to establish *equivalence* rather than implication leads to another counterexample (Figure 2 (left)), which violates the converse implication.

Interestingly, since the verification of a formula works by construction of its full semantics in terms of the corresponding minimal automaton, the cost of the error detection is independent of the fault class. In particular, faults in the data path are not more expensive to detect than faults in the control part. A more detailed discussion of the automatic generation of counterexamples for test and diagnosis purposes can be found in [22].

6 Evaluation and Future Work

The verification results reported in Table 1 clearly show the advantages of a library-based verification approach. The semantics of logic predicates can in fact be computed separately and stored as BDDs in a library (see section 3.1), so that predicates must only be evaluated once, and can be referenced in the course of a verification at virtually no cost. Already in the case of the considered counters the availability of the precompiled predicates accounts for performance improvement factors (flat vs. library based verification) up to 20. This feature suggests the scalability of the proposed approach to quite more complex verification problems.

The logic and the verification method presented here at the gate and register-transfer level allow us to capture in a common framework a wider spectrum of abstraction levels, ranging from switch to gate, register transfer, and architecture or protocol. In fact, by proceeding hierarchically in a library-based way, verification is only necessary relative to the few basic components of each abstraction level, thus avoiding completely the need of handling large circuits at low abstraction levels.

By modelling hardware primitives as relations, rather than functions, we capture both ends of the spectrum, where bidirectionality of the signals plays a central role. Our formalism can not only express the functionality of transistors, buses, and the like, but also diverse kinds of operators, functions, and predicates, useful in specifying their behavior. For example, one may define temporal operators and reason about time dependent specifications [3] or synchronization properties of distributed systems [18] whose modelling is similar to the one adopted for sequential parametric hardware. The possibility of hiding completely to the end user the interna of Mona and of its input language once they are integrated into a CAD design environment is a central feature for the practicability of this verification method in an industrial environment.

Acknowledgements

The author is indebted to Michael Mendler and Claudia Gsottberger for their precious contribution in discussions and in the final realization of the case studies, and to Falk Schreiber, who helped combining Mona and METAFrame. Thanks are also due to David Basin and Nils Klarlund for earlier discussions, help in getting acquainted with Mona, and for their initial implementation of the counter and other examples in Mona.

7 REFERENCES

[1] M. Allemand: "*Formal verification of characteristic properties*: Proc. TPCD'94 (Theorem Provers in Circuit Design - Theory, Practice, and Experience), Bad Herrenhalb (D), Sept.'94, LNCS N. 901, pp. 292-297.

[2] C. Angelo, L. Claesen, H. De Man: "*A Methodology for Proving Correctness of parameterized hardware Modules in HOL*," Proc. CHDL'91, Marseille (F), April 1991, IFIP Transactions, North-Holland, pp.63-82.

[3] D. Basin, N. Klarlund: "*Hardware verification using monadic second-order logic*," Proc. CAV '95, Liège (B), July 1995, LNCS N. 939, Springer Verlag, pp. 31-41.

[4] D. Basin, P. DelVecchio: *"Verification of combinational logic in Nuprl,"* In "Hardware Specification, Verification and Synthesis: Mathematical Aspects", Ithaca, New York, 1989. Springer-Verlag.

[5] M. Barbacci, G. Barnes, R. Cattell, D. Siewiorek: *"The ISPS Computer Description Language"*, Tech. Rep. CMU-CS-79-137, Carnegie-Mellon University, Computer Science Department, Aug. 1979.

[6] D. Borrione, C. Le Faou: *"Overview of the CASCADE multi-level hardware description language and its mixed-mode simulation mechanisms,"* Proc. 7th Int. Conf. on Computer Hardware Description Languages (CHDL'85), Tokyo (Japan), Aug. 1985.

[7] M. Browne, E. Clarke, O. Grumberg: *"Reasoning about networks with many identical finite state processes,"* Information and Computation, 81(1), Apr. 1989, pp. 13-31.

[8] A. Camilleri, M. Gordon, T. Melham: *"Hardware verification using higher-order logic,"* In D. Borrione (ed.), "From HDL Descriptions to Guaranteed Correct Circuit Designs", pages 43–67. Elsevier Science Publishers B. V. (North-Holland), 1987.

[9] A. Church: *"Logic, arithmetic and automata,"* Proc. Int. Congr. Math., Almqvist and Wiksells, Uppsala 1963, pp. 23-35.

[10] R. L. Constable et al.: "Implementing Mathematics with the Nuprl Proof Development System," Prentice-Hall, Englewood Cliffs, NJ, 1986.

[11] H. Eveking: *"Axiomatizing Hardware Description Languages,"* Int. Journal of VLSI Design, 2(3), pp. 263-280, 1990.

[12] "Databook of Analog and Synchronous Components", Fairchild - 1993.

[13] A. de Geus: "High Level design: A design vision for the '90s," Proc. IEEE Int. Conf. on Computer Design, p.8, 1992.

[14] M. Gordon: *"Why higher-order logic is a good formalism for specifying and verifying hardware,"* In G. J. Milne and P. A. Subrahmanyam, editors, "Formal Aspects of VLSI Design", North-Holland, 1986.

[15] A. Gupta, A. Fisher: "Parametric Circuit Representation Using Inductive Boolean Functions," Proc. CAV'93, Elounda (GR), June 1993, LNCS N. 697, pp.15-28.

[16] F.K. Hanna, N. Daeche: *"Specification and verification using higher-order logic: a case study,"* In G.J. Milne and P.A. Subrahmanyam, editors, "Formal Aspects of VLSI Design", pp. 179–213. Elsevier, 1986.

[17] W. Hunt: *"Microprocessor design verification,"* Journal of Automated Reasoning, 5(4):429–460, 1989.

[18] J. Henriksen, J. Jensen, M. Jørgensen N. Klarlund, R. Paige, T. Rauhe, A. Sandholm: *"Mona: Monadic second-order logic in practice,"* Proc. of TACAS'95, Aarhus (DK), May 1995, LNCS 1019, Springer Verlag, pp. 89-110.

[19] Z. Kohavi: "Switching and finite automata theory", Computer Science Series, McGraw Hill, New York, NY (USA), 1970.

[20] R. Kurshan, K. McMillan: *"A structural induction theorem for processes,"* Proc. 8th ACM PODC Symposium, Edmonton (CAN), Aug. 1989, pp. 239-247.

[21] IEEE: "Standard VHDL Language Reference Manual", 1988, IEEE Std. 1076-1987.

[22] T. Margaria, M. Mendler: "Automatic Treatment of Sequential Circuits in Second-Order Monadic Logic", 4th GI/ITG/GME Worksh. on Methoden des Entwurfs und der Verifikation digitaler Systeme, Kreischa (D), March 1996, Shaker Verlag.

[23] T. Margaria: "First-Order theories for the verification of complex FSMs," Aachener Informatik-Berichte Nr.91-30, RWTH-Aachen, Dec. 1991.

[24] T. Margaria: "Efficient RT-Level Verification by Theorem Proving", IFIP World Congr.'92, Madrid (E), Sept. 1992, North-Holland pp. 696-702.

[25] T. Margaria: *"Verifica formale della correttezza del progetto di sistemi digitali,"* Dissertazione di Dottorato (in Italian), Politecnico di Torino, Turin (I), Feb. 1993.

[26] T. Margaria, B. Steffen: "Distinguishing Formulas for Free", EDAC–EUROASIC'93: IEEE European Design Automation Conference, Paris (France), February 1993.

[27] T. Melham: *"Using recursive types of reasoning about hardware in higher order logic,"* In Int. Working Conf. on The Fusion of Hardware Design and Verification, pp. 26–49, July 1988.

[28] L. Pierre: "The Formal Proof of the "Min-max" sequential benchmark described in CASCADE using the Boyer-Moore theorem prover," Proc. IMEC-IFIP Worksh. on Applied Formal Methods for Correct VLSI Design, Leuven (B), Nov. 1989, pp. 129-149.

[29] L. Pierre: *"An Automatic Generalization Method for the Inductive Proof of Replicated and Parallel Architectures,"* Proc. TPCD'94, Bad Herrenhalb (D), Sept.'94, LNCS N. 901, pp. 72-91.

[30] J.K Rho, F. Somenzi: "Inductive Verification for Iterative circuits", Proc. DAC'92, Anaheim (CA), June 1992, pp. 628-633.

[31] J.K Rho, F. Somenzi: "Automatic Generation of Network Invariants for the verification of Iterative sequential Systems", Proc. CAV'93, Elounda (GR), June 1993, LNCS N. 697, pp.123-137.

[32] A. Sistla, S. German: "*Reasoning with many processes*," Proc. LICS'97, Ithaca, NY, June 1987, pp. 138-152.

[33] B. Steffen, T. Margaria, A. Claßen. "The META-Frame: An Environment for Flexible Tool Management," Proc. TAPSOFT'95, Aarhus (Denmark), May 1995, LNCS N. 915, Springer Verlag.

[34] W. Thomas: "*Automata on infinite objects*," In J. van Leeuwen, editor, *Handbook of Theoretical Computer Science*, vol. B, p. 133–191. MIT Press/Elsevier, 1990.

[35] P. Wolper: "*Expressing interesting properties of programs in propositional temporal logic*," Proc. POPL'86, St. Petersburg, Jan. 1986, pp. 184-192.

[36] P. Wolper, V. Lovinfosse: "*Verifying properties of large sets of processes with network invariants*," Proc. Automatic Verification Methods for Finite Systems, LNCS 407, Springer Verlag, 1989, pp 68-80.

1   Descriptions of the Synchronous Counters

In the following examples gates and modules are encoded as relations over booleans as in this fragment of the basic library:

```
notrel(@a,@b) = (~@a) <=> @b;
andrel(@a,@b,@c) = (@a & @b) <=> @c;
orrel(@a,@b,@c) = (@a | @b) <=> @c;
```

1.1   The 4-bit Basic Cell of the Counter

The structural implementation of the 4-bit basic cell of the synchronous counter is formalized in mona as the following relation over its external ports @pen,@cep,@cet,@srn,@tc,@i0,@i1,@i2,@i3,@o0,@o1,@o2,@o3 and the previous state values @oo0 ... @oo3.

```
count4bit(@pen,@cep,@cet,@srn,@tc,@i0,@i1,@i2,@i3,
          @o0,@o1,@o2,@o3,@oo0,@oo1,@oo2,@oo3) =

  (Ex @pe: Ex @ep: Ex @pen1: Ex @et:              # decode operation
    (notrel(@pen,@pe) & and3rel(@pen,@cep,@cet,@ep) &
```

```
            andrel(@cep,@cet,@et) & notrel(@pe,@pen1)) &
(Ex @ga0: Ex @gb0: Ex @gc0: Ex @gi0: Ex @h0:      # set 1st output
            andrel(@pe,@i0,@gi0) & notrel(@et,@h0) &
            andrel(~@oo0,@ep,@ga0) & and3rel(@h0,@pen1,@oo0,@gb0) &
            or3rel(@ga0,@gi0,@gb0,@gc0) & andrel(@srn,@gc0,@o0)) &
(Ex @ga1: Ex @gb1: Ex @gc1: Ex @gi1: Ex @h1:      # set 2nd output
            andrel(@pe,@i1,@gi1) & nandrel(@oo0,@et,@h1) &
            and3rel(~@oo1,@oo0,@ep,@ga1) & and3rel(@h1,@pen1,@oo1,@gb1) &
            or3rel(@ga1,@gi1,@gb1,@gc1) & andrel(@srn,@gc1,@o1)) &
(Ex @ga2: Ex @gb2: Ex @gc2: Ex @gi2: Ex @h2:      # set 3rd output
            andrel(@pe,@i2,@gi2) & nand3rel(@oo0,@oo1,@et,@h2) &
            and4rel(~@oo2,@oo0,@oo1,@ep,@ga2) &
            and3rel(@h2,@pen1,@oo2,@gb2) &
            or3rel(@ga2,@gi2,@gb2,@gc2) & andrel(@srn,@gc2,@o2)) &
(Ex @ga3: Ex @gb3: Ex @gc3: Ex @gi3: Ex @h3:      # set 4th output
            andrel(@pe,@i3,@gi3) & nand4rel(@oo0,@oo1,@oo2,@et,@h3) &
            and5rel(~@oo3,@oo0,@oo1,@oo2,@ep,@ga3) &
            and3rel(@h3,@pen1,@oo3,@gb3) &
            or3rel(@ga3,@gi3,@gb3,@gc3) & andrel(@srn,@gc3,@o3)) &
(Ex @w0: Ex @w1: Ex @w2: Ex @w3:                  # set tc
            notrel(~@oo0,@w0) & notrel(~@oo1, @w1) & notrel(~@oo2,@w2) &
            notrel(~@oo3,@w3) & and5rel(@w0,@w1,@w2,@w3,@cet,@tc)));
```

This formula directly encodes the structure of the circuit and could be
automatically generated from a description of this module in a gate-level
hardware description language.

1.2   The Family of Parametric Counters

The parametric structure of the family is formulated in a top-down fashion
and organized according to functional units:

```
count(@pen,@cep,@cet,@srn,I,O,Old0,@tc) =
  (Ex @pe: Ex @ep: Ex @pen1: Ex @et:
     notrel(@pen,@pe) & and3rel(@pen,@cep,@cet,@ep)
     & andrel(@cep,@cet,@et) & notrel(@pe,@pen1)
     & computebit(@pe,@ep,@et,@pen1,@cet,@srn,I,O,Old0)
     & Ex @tmp: n_invand($,compl(Old0),@tmp) & andrel(@tmp,@cet,@tc));
```

The 4 parts of the above definition 1) declare the ports as booleans, which
correspond to values on internal wires; 2) compute internal signals which
decode the selected operation (this is identical to the 4-bit version); 3) compute the new value of the output/state by means of the
computebit relation, and 4) compute the terminal count @tc using the
auxiliary relation

```
n_invand(I,@o) = @o <=> All j : (j notin I);
```

which defines an *n-bit inverted and* gate.

Dealing with the first slice as a special case (having no predecessors implies a different internal structure, which could be reduced to the generic one with the introduction of 1-input gates), the computation in a generic slice is defined as follows:

```
computebit(@pe,@ep,@et,@pen1,@cet,@srn,I,O,OldO) =    #compute one bit
   (All p: Ex @h: Ex @ga: Ex @gb: Ex @gc:
      if(p = 0, (notrel(@et,@h)),
                (Ex @tmp: n_and(p -o 1,OldO,@tmp) &
                          nandrel(@tmp,@et,@h)))
     & if(p = 0, (andrel(@ep,notsetp(0,OldO),@ga)),         # set GA
                 (Ex @tmp: n_and(p -o 1,OldO,@tmp) &
                  and3rel(@tmp,notsetp(p,OldO),@ep,@ga))) &
     & and3rel(@h,@pen1,setp(p,OldO),@gb)                   # set GB
     & (Ex @gi: andrel(setp(p,I),@pe,@gi)                   # set GC
              & or3rel(@ga,@gi,@gb,@gc))
     & andrel(@gc,@srn,setp(p,O)));                         # set O
```

1.3 A Hierarchical Family of 4—bit Counters

The partitioning of the datapath in 4-bit portions is described by the predicate fourth(p) that is true when the position variable p takes values $3, 7, 11, \ldots$.

```
fourth(p) = (Ex S : (0 notin S & 0+1 notin S & 0+2 notin S &
               (All p : (p >= 0+3 =>
                          (p in S <=> (p -o 1 notin S & p -o 2 notin S &
                                       p -o 3 notin S)))))
     & p in S);

ripplecount(@pen,@cep,@cet,@srn,I,O,OldO,@tc) =
   (Ex Cep: Ex Cet: Ex Tc:
      (All p: fourth(p) =>
                 count4bit(@pen,p in Cep,p in Cet,@srn,p in Tc,
                           p -o 3 in I, p -o 2 in I, p -o 1 in I, p in I,
                           p -o 3 in O, p -o 2 in O, p -o 1 in O, p in O,
                           p -o 3 in OldO, p -o 2 in OldO,
                           p -o 1 in OldO, p in OldO) &
               (~(p=$) => (andrel(p in Tc,@cep,p+4 in Cep) &
                           (p+4 in Cet <=> p in Tc))) &
               (0+3 in Cep <=> @cep) &
               (0+3 in Cet <=> @cet) &
               (@tc <=> ($ in Tc))));
```

Every time fourth(p) holds, a count4bit cell is instantiated. It is connected to the preceding 4 input and output ports and it computes the counter relation over these values. The rippling of the terminal count @tc to the enabling control lines @cep and @cet of the next module follows the solution indicated in Figure 5. Finally, the internal control signals CEP and CET are connected to the global ones and the global terminal count is defined to be the last position of TC.

Priorities for Modeling and Verifying Distributed Systems

Rance Cleaveland*
Gerald Lüttgen*
V. Natarajan*
Steve Sims*

ABSTRACT This paper illustrates the use of priorities in process algebras by a real-world example dealing with the design of a safety-critical network which is part of a railway signaling system. Priorities in process algebras support an intuitive modeling of distributed systems since undesired interleavings can be suppressed. This fact also leads to a substantial reduction of the sizes of models. We have implemented a CCS-based process algebra with priorities as a new front-end for the NCSU Concurrency Workbench, and we use model checking for verifying properties of the signaling system.

1 Introduction

Process algebras, e.g. CCS [13], provide a formal framework for modeling and verifying distributed systems. In the past decade, a number of automatic verification tools for finite state systems expressed in process algebras have been developed [10], and their utility has been demonstrated by several case studies [1, 7]. Most of these case studies are based on process algebras that provide simple mechanisms for modeling nondeterminism and concurrency. Many extensions to these *plain* languages have been proposed, including priorities [2, 6, 8, 14]. Priorities in particular are needed to model the often used concept of *interrupts*, especially in hardware and communication protocols.

This paper presents a case study of a real-world system which shows the benefits of priorities for modeling and verifying distributed systems. Our example is based on a case study by Glenn Bruns [5] dealing with

*Department of Computer Science, North Carolina State University, Raleigh NC 27695-8206 USA, e-mail: {rance, luettgen, nvaidhy, stsims}@eos.ncsu.edu.
Research supported by NSF/DARPA grant CCR-9014775, NSF grant CCR-9120995, ONR Young Investigator Award N00014-92-J-1582, NSF Young Investigator Award CCR-9257963, NSF grant CCR-9402807, and AFOSR grant F49620-95-1-0508.
Research support for the second author provided by the German Academic Exchange Service under grant D/95/09026 (Doktorandenstipendium HSP II / AUFE).

the design of a safety-critical part of a network used in British Rail's Solid State Interlocking (SSI) [11], a system which controls railway signals and points. Bruns modeled and verified a high-level design of the system that abstracted from low-level implementation details. He used plain CCS for modeling the system, a temporal logic for specifying properties of the system, and the Edinburgh Concurrency Workbench [10] for verifying that these properties hold for the model.

We investigate an elaboration of Bruns' case study using a process algebra with priorities [8]. We augment his model in two ways based on key concepts of the SSI system described in the original design document [11]. First we add an error-recovery scheme that is invoked when a communication link fails, and second we add a backup line in order to make the system fault-tolerant. In both cases the use of priorities enables the development of elegant and intuitive models. We also show that, by eliminating invalid interleavings, priorities can dramatically cut the number of states and transitions in our systems. This is particularly significant since the large complexity of practical problems often prevents their automatic verification. We verify our models by showing that several safety properties hold using the NCSU Concurrency Workbench. This verification tool is a re-implementation of the Edinburgh Concurrency Workbench that offers similar functionality, but is faster, able to handle larger systems, and gives diagnostic information when a verification routine returns false.

The remainder of the paper is structured as follows. In Section 2 we present the process algebra with priorities that we use in this paper. Section 3 gives an introduction to the railway signaling system and presents our models. Section 4 discusses our verification results. Finally, we give our conclusions and directions for future work in Section 5.

2 A Process Algebra with Priorities

The process algebra with priorities we consider in this paper is based on the language proposed in [8]. We extend this language with a multilevel priority scheme but disallow the prioritization and deprioritization operator. Therefore, our process algebra is basically CCS [13] where priorities, modeled by natural numbers, are assigned to actions. We use the convention that smaller numbers mean higher priorities; so 0 is the highest priority. Intuitively, visible actions represent potential synchronizations that a process may be willing to engage in with its environment. Given a choice between a synchronization on a high priority and one on a low priority, a process should choose the former.

Formally, let $\{ \Lambda_k \mid k \in \mathbb{N} \}$ denote a family of pairwise-disjoint, countably infinite sets of *labels*. Intuitively, Λ_k contains the "ports" with priority k that processes may synchronize over. Then the set of *actions* A_k with priority k may be defined by $\mathcal{A}_k =_{df} \Lambda_k \cup \overline{\Lambda}_k \cup \{\tau_k\}$, where $\overline{\Lambda}_k =_{df} \{\overline{\lambda} \mid \lambda \in \Lambda_k\}$ and $\tau_k \notin \Lambda_k$. The set of all ports Λ and the set of all actions $\mathcal{A}$ are defined by $\bigcup\{\Lambda_k \mid k \in \mathbb{N}\}$ and $\bigcup\{\mathcal{A}_k \mid k \in \mathbb{N}\}$, respectively. For better readability we write $a{:}k$ if $a \in \Lambda_k$ and $\tau{:}k$ for τ_k. An action $\lambda{:}k \in \Lambda_k$ may be thought of as representing the receipt of an input on port λ which has priority k, while $\overline{\lambda}{:}k \in \overline{\Lambda}_k$ constitutes the deposit of an output on λ. The invisible actions $\tau{:}k$ represent internal computation steps with priority k. In what follows, we use $\alpha{:}k, \beta{:}k, \ldots$ to range over $\mathcal{A}$ and $a{:}k, b{:}k, \ldots$ to range over Λ. We also use $\lambda{:}k$ to represent elements in $\mathcal{A}_k \setminus \{\tau{:}k\}$ and extend $^-$ to all visible actions $\lambda{:}k$ by $\overline{\overline{\lambda}{:}k} =_{df} \lambda{:}k$. Finally, if $L \subseteq \mathcal{A} \setminus \{\tau{:}k \mid k \in \mathbb{N}\}$ then $\overline{L} = \{\overline{\lambda}{:}k \mid \lambda{:}k \in L\}$. For the sake of simplicity, we also write $\tau \in M$ where $M \subseteq \mathcal{A}$ if $\tau{:}k \in M$ for some $k \in \mathbb{N}$.

The *syntax* of our language is defined by the following BNF.

$$P \quad ::= \quad nil \quad \mid \quad \alpha{:}k.P \quad \mid \quad P + P \quad \mid \quad P|P$$
$$P[f] \quad \mid \quad P\backslash L \quad \mid \quad C \stackrel{\text{def}}{=} P \quad \mid \quad P \wr P$$

Here f is a *relabeling*, a mapping on $\mathcal{A}$ which satisfies $f(\tau{:}k) = \tau{:}k$ for all $k \in \mathbb{N}$ and $\overline{f(\overline{a}{:}k)} = f(a{:}k)$ for all $a{:}k \in \mathcal{A} \setminus \{\tau{:}k \mid k \in \mathbb{N}\}$. Moreover, a relabeling preserves priority values, i.e. for all $a{:}k \in \mathcal{A} \setminus \{\tau{:}k \mid k \in \mathbb{N}\}$ we have $f(a{:}k) = b{:}k$ for some $b{:}k \in \Lambda_k$. Further, $L \subseteq \mathcal{A} \setminus \{\tau{:}k \mid k \in \mathbb{N}\}$, and C is a constant whose meaning is given by a defining equation. Additionally, we include the *disabling* operator $\wr$ which is closely related to the corresponding operator in LOTOS [4].

We adopt the usual definitions for *closed* terms and *guarded recursion*. We call the closed guarded terms *processes*. $\mathcal{P}$ represents the set of all processes and is ranged over by $P, Q, \ldots$. Note that our framework allows an infinite number of priority levels although there is a maximum priority.

The *semantics* of our language is given by a labeled transition system $\langle \mathcal{P}, \mathcal{A}, \longrightarrow \rangle$ where $\mathcal{P}$ is the set of processes, and $\longrightarrow \subseteq \mathcal{P} \times \mathcal{A} \times \mathcal{P}$ defined in Table 1 is the transition relation. We will write $P \stackrel{\alpha{:}k}{\longrightarrow} P'$ instead of $\langle P, \alpha{:}k, P' \rangle \in \longrightarrow$, and we say that P *may engage in action* α *with priority k and thereafter behaves like process P'*.

The presentation of the operational rules requires *initial action sets* which are inductively defined on the syntax of processes, as usual. Intuitively, $I_k(P)$ denotes the set of all initial actions of P with priority k, $I_{<k}(P)$ the set of all initial actions of P with a higher priority than k, and $I(P)$ the set of all initial actions of P. Moreover, we define $I_{<0}(P) =_{df} \emptyset$. Note that the initial action sets are independently defined from the transition relation $\longrightarrow$; so the transition relation is well-defined.

Intuitively, $\alpha{:}k.P$ may engage in action α with priority k. The *summation operator* $+$ denotes *nondeterministic choice*. The process $P + Q$ may behave like process P (Q) if Q (P) does not preempt it by performing a higher prioritized τ-action. The *restriction operator* $\backslash L$ prohibits the execution of actions in $L \cup \overline{L}$ and may be seen as permitting the *scoping* of actions. $P[f]$

TABLE 1. Operational semantics

$$\alpha{:}k.P \xrightarrow{\alpha:k} P$$

$P \xrightarrow{\alpha:k} P'$,	$\tau \notin I_{<k}(Q)$	implies	$P + Q \xrightarrow{\alpha:k} P'$
$Q \xrightarrow{\alpha:k} Q'$,	$\tau \notin I_{<k}(P)$	implies	$P + Q \xrightarrow{\alpha:k} Q'$
$P \xrightarrow{\alpha:k} P'$,	$\tau \notin I_{<k}(P|Q)$	implies	$P|Q \xrightarrow{\alpha:k} P'|Q$
$Q \xrightarrow{\alpha:k} Q'$,	$\tau \notin I_{<k}(P|Q)$	implies	$P|Q \xrightarrow{\alpha:k} P|Q'$
$P \xrightarrow{\alpha:k} P', Q \xrightarrow{\bar{\alpha}:k} Q'$,	$\tau \notin I_{<k}(P|Q)$	implies	$P|Q \xrightarrow{\tau:k} P'|Q'$
$P \xrightarrow{\alpha:k} P'$,	$f(\alpha{:}k) = \beta{:}k$	implies	$P[f] \xrightarrow{\beta:k} P'[f]$
$P \xrightarrow{\alpha:k} P'$,	$\alpha{:}k \notin (L \cup \overline{L})$	implies	$P\backslash L \xrightarrow{\alpha:k} P'\backslash L$
$P \xrightarrow{\alpha:k} P'$,	$\tau \notin I_{<k}(Q)$	implies	$P \, \rangle \, Q \xrightarrow{\alpha:k} P' \, \rangle \, Q$
$Q \xrightarrow{\alpha:k} Q'$,	$\tau \notin I_{<k}(P)$	implies	$P \, \rangle \, Q \xrightarrow{\alpha:k} Q'$
$P \xrightarrow{\alpha:k} P'$,	$C \stackrel{\text{def}}{=} P$	implies	$C \xrightarrow{\alpha:k} P'$

behaves exactly as process P where the actions are renamed according to f. The process $P|Q$ stands for the *parallel composition* of P and Q according to an *interleaving semantics* with *synchronized communication* on complementary actions on some priority level k resulting in the internal action $\tau{:}k$. However, if Q (P) is capable of engaging in a higher prioritized internal action or in a synchronization, then lower prioritized actions of P (Q) are preempted. The process $P \, \rangle \, Q$ behaves like P and, additionally, it is capable of *disabling* P by engaging in Q. The side conditions ensure that its semantics is consistent with that of the summation operator. In practice, Q is often an *interrupt handler*. Finally, $C \stackrel{\text{def}}{=} P$ denotes a *constant definition*, i.e. C is a recursively defined process that is a distinguished solution to the equation $C = P$. The side conditions of the operational semantic rules guarantee that high-priority τ-actions have preemptive power over low-priority actions. The reason that high-priority visible actions do *not* have priority over low-priority actions is that visible actions only indicate the potential of a synchronization, i.e. the potential of progress, whereas τ-actions describe complete synchronizations, i.e. *real* progress, in our model.

The usual definition of strong bisimulation – as introduced in [13] – is a congruence relation over $\mathcal{P}$ [8]. In the context of our process algebra with priorities we will refer to it as *prioritized strong bisimulation*.

In the following case study, it is sometimes useful to have visible actions that have preemptive power over lower prioritized actions. More precisely, such an action, e.g. $a{:}k$, is signaling that certain events have occurred, i.e. it plays the role of an *atomic proposition*. We give $a{:}k$ preemptive power by inserting a $\tau{:}k$-loop at the origin states of transitions which are labeled by $a{:}k$. For example the process $a{:}0.P$ is rewritten to $C \stackrel{\text{def}}{=} a{:}0.P + \tau{:}0.C$. For the sake of simplicity, we write $\#a{:}0.P$ as a shorthand for C.

3 Modeling a Railway System

In this section we model a network used in a *safety-critical railway signaling system*. The basic design is adapted from [5]. However, instead of CCS we use the process algebra of Section 2 as it allows a more intuitive modeling of the system. Further, we extend the model by an *error-recovery scheme* and a *fault-tolerant network link* in order to reflect the underlying design document [11] more precisely. Since in both cases *interrupt mechanisms* come into play, the use of a process algebra with priorities is needed for reflecting the design correctly.

3.1 Solid State Interlocking

Our example is embedded in *British Rail's Solid State Interlocking* (SSI) system [5, 11], which adjusts and controls *signals* and *points* along rail routes. Its aim is to prevent situations which may lead to a collision or derailment of trains. Therefore, a formal verification of the design of the SSI and its environment is of particular importance.

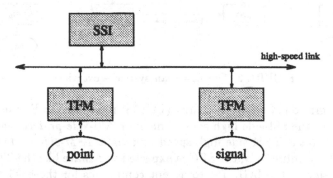

FIGURE 1. The SSI environment – overview

Figure 1 shows the basic design of the interlocking system. It consists of three different components: the SSI, several *trackside functional modules* (TFM), and a *high-speed link* which connects the TFMs with the SSI. The SSI is the main logical unit of the system. It is connected to a control panel to which a signal operator can input her/his commands. The SSI checks the validity of those commands and sends them to the TFMs along the track via the high-speed link. A TFM connects a signal or a point to the network. Its task is to listen to the network in order to receive messages for adjusting its signal or point and to send status information about the signal or point to the SSI.

The pattern of communication between the SSI and the TFMs is as follows. The SSI sends cyclically a message to each TFM. The message includes the TFM's address and the status for the corresponding signal or point (e.g. signal on/off). After sending a message the SSI waits a short time for the addressed TFM to respond with the current state of its signal or point. This *polling* scheme reflects the safety-critical design of the system since it leads to a quick detection of failures. For example, if the addressed TFM does not respond then either the TFM or the connection between the SSI and the TFM is broken. Moreover, if the corresponding signal or point has autonomously changed its state, it is forced to return to its proper state. The disadvantage of the polling scheme is its communication overhead, which necessitates an expensive high-speed network. This expense is even worse if the distance between some TFMs and the SSI is very large. Therefore, the question arises as to whether distant high-speed links can be connected via a low-grade link without violating safety requirements. Our case study will concentrate on this aspect of the SSI system since the use of a high-speed link is known to satisfy the requirements on the error-free delivery of commands and timely detection of failures [5].

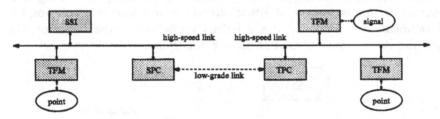

FIGURE 2. The slow-scan system – overview

The integration of a low-grade link (LGL) is illustrated in Figure 2. It is connected to the SSI-side high-speed link via a *SSI-side protocol converter* (SPC) and to the TFM-side high-speed link via a *TFM-side protocol converter* (TPC). Intuitively, the SPC is expected to behave like the TFMs on the other side of the LGL, i.e. to accept commands for those TFMs and to respond to the SSI with their current states, but the SPC occasionally sends these commands along the LGL and receives new status information about those TFMs. On the other side, the TPC should mimic a SSI. We refer to the part of the system which consists of SPC, LGL, and TPC as the *slow-scan system*. In order not to violate safety conditions of the overall system, the slow-scan system is expected to satisfy properties of the following kind. If the low-grade link fails, then the TPC (SPC) will detect the problem and stop sending messages to the TPC-side TFMs (SSI). The TFMs are also expected to change signals to red and to lock points in their current setting if they stop receiving messages.

3.2 The Slow-scan Model

In the following, we formally model the slow-scan system in three steps. First, we present the system as in [5] and discuss the advantages of priorities for modeling. In the second step, we augment our model with an *error-recovery scheme* and remodel the low-grade link in a *full-duplex* fashion. Finally, we show how the required fault-tolerance of the system [11] can be reflected in our design.

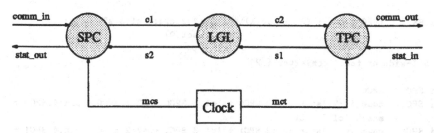

FIGURE 3. The LGL model

Tables 2 and 3 contain the model of the slow-scan system as it is accepted by the NCSU Concurrency Workbench where the symbol * introduces comments. The front end of the workbench for the process algebra with priorities was generated by the process algebra compiler PAC [9] and uses the following syntactical notations for expressions: bi C P for the process algebra term $C \stackrel{\text{def}}{=} P$, and 'a:k for the action $\overline{a}{:}k$.

Figure 3 shows the channels between the three parallel components of the slow-scan system; it also includes an additional clock. Since the correct behavior of our system depends on time constraints, which cannot be modeled in our process algebra directly (cf. [15]), we use the clock in our model to signal the progression of time to the SPC and TPC via the channels mcs and mct, respectively.

The low-grade link is modeled by two parallel unidirectional links. Since we are concerned with the design of a system we choose a poor capacity (or bandwidth) link, capacity one for each direction, and we abstract from message headers and contents. Moreover, the SPC and TPC should be able to deliver a message to and get a message from the medium at any time. If no capacity in a link is left, a new message overwrites a message which is already in the medium, and an overfull error occurs. Therefore, a link behaves for each direction as an input-enabled one-place buffer. Additionally, it offers the action 'outu to its environment if the buffer is empty. With respect to its reliability, we assume that a link can fail because of a broken wire (action 'fail_wire) or if its buffering capacity is exceeded (action 'fail_overfull). If an error has occurred, the medium enters the error state CommF in which it only accepts messages but never delivers any messages.

TABLE 2. The slow-scan model (Part 1)

```
* level 0: fail_overfull, det, mcs, mct
* level 1: -
* level 2: out (c2, s2), fail_wire, comm_in, comm_out, stat_in, stat_out
* level 3: in (c1, s1)
* level 4: outu (c2u, s2u), tick


* Slow-scan system

bi SS      (SPC | LGL | TPC | Clock)\{c1:3,c2:2,c2u:4,s1:3,s2:2,s2u:4,
                                      mcs:0,mct:0}


* SSI-side protocol converter (SPC)

bi SPC     SPC0
bi SPC0    comm_in:2.'stat_out:2.SPC0 + 'c1:3.SPC0 + s2:2.SPC0 + s2u:4.SPC0 +
           mcs:0.'c1:3.SPC1
bi SPC1    comm_in:2.'stat_out:2.SPC1 + 'c1:3.SPC1 + s2:2.SPC0 + s2u:4.SPC1 +
           mcs:0.'c1:3.SPC2
bi SPC2    comm_in:2.'stat_out:2.SPC2 + 'c1:3.SPC2 + s2:2.SPC0 + s2u:4.SPC2 +
           mcs:0.#'det:0.SPCF
bi SPCF    comm_in:2.SPCF + s2:2.SPCF + s2u:4.SPCF + mcs:0.SPCF
```

The states of the SPC are parameterized by a time mark. In each state the SPC is able to accept a message from the SSI (action comm_in) and, subsequently, of responding with the appropriate status information of the requested TFM (action 'stat_out). At least once every clock cycle (action 'mcs) the SPC sends a message over the LGL to the TPC (action 'c1) and increases its internal time-counter by changing its state from SPC0 to SPC1 or from SPC1 to SPC2. If the SPC receives a message (action s2) from the TPC within two time units, it resets its internal time-counter to 0 by changing its state to SPC0. Otherwise, the SPC times out (action 'det) and enters the failure state SPCF. In this state the SPC never sends messages to the SSI or TPC again, but it remains input-enabled.

Up to now, we have not discussed how priorities can be used in modeling the system. However, one has probably already noticed that various parts of the model without priorities would be counterintuitive. For example, if a link has no capacity for an additional message, it should favor outputting a message over accepting a new one, as the latter immediately leads to the failure of the link. Similarly, a link should favor accepting a new message instead of signaling that the buffer is empty. If the clock gives a new time pulse by performing the action 'tick, it should immediately inform the SPC and TPC by performing the (interrupt) actions 'mcs and 'mct. In other words, no action should interfere between the actions 'tick and 'mcs and the actions 'mcs and 'mct. Moreover, the actions 'det and 'fail_overfull

TABLE 3. The slow-scan model (Part 2)

---

* **Track-side protocol converter (TPC)**

```
bi TPC    TPC0
bi TPC0   'comm_out:2.stat_in:2.TPC0 + 's1:3.TPC0 + c2:2.TPC0 + c2u:4.TPC0 +
          mct:0.'s1:3.TPC1
bi TPC1   'comm_out:2.stat_in:2.TPC1 + 's1:3.TPC1 + c2:2.TPC0 + c2u:4.TPC1 +
          mct:0.'s1:3.TPC2
bi TPC2   'comm_out:2.stat_in:2.TPC2 + 's1:3.TPC2 + c2:2.TPC0 + c2u:4.TPC2 +
          mct:0.#'det:0.TPCF
bi TPCF   stat_in:2.TPCF + c2:2.TPCF + c2u:4.TPCF + mct:0.TPCF
```

* **Low grade link (LGL)**

```
bi LGL    Comm[c1:3/in:3,c2:2/out:2,c2u:4/outu:4] |
          Comm[s1:3/in:3,s2:2/out:2,s2u:4/outu:4]

bi Comm   Comm0
bi Comm0  in:3.Comm1 + 'outu:4.Comm0 + 'fail_wire:2.CommF
bi Comm1  in:3.#'fail_overfull:0.CommF + 'out:2.Comm0 + 'fail_wire:2.CommF
bi CommF  in:3.CommF + 'outu:4.CommF
```

* **Clock**

```
bi Clock  'tick:4.'mcs:0.'mct:0.Clock
```

---

are signaling failures which have already occurred, i.e. they should not be delayed. Finally, the failing of the LGL is always possible, i.e. no action of the LGL should be able to preempt the action 'fail_wire.

Based on these observations, we give the actions 'fail_overfull and 'det – which can be viewed as *atomic propositions* – overall preemptive power in our model, i.e. they are translated to #'fail_overfull:0 and to #'det:0, respectively. The actions 'mcs and 'mct are also assigned the highest priority. Thus, they cannot be prevented by any action in the system, and the atomicity of the above mentioned action sequences is guaranteed. Moreover, in the LGL, 'out should have a higher priority than in, and in a higher one than 'outu. The action 'tick is assigned to the lowest priority level, reflecting our design decision to adopt the *maximal progress assumption* of real-time process algebra [15]. This assumption states that time may only proceed if the system cannot engage in a communication. Finally, 'fail_wire is assigned the highest priority-level with respect to the actions of the LGL. These observations lead to the priority scheme of actions for the slow-scan model which is summarized in the beginning of Table 2.

3.3 The Recovery Model

The slow-scan model represents a substantial abstraction from reality since it is not capable of recovering from a failure. Therefore, we augment the slow-scan model by an error-recovery scheme. Moreover, we change the design of the medium to a more realistic *full-duplex* version.

TABLE 4. The recovery model (Part 1)

```
* Low grade link (LGL)

bi LGL      Comm00[c1:3/in:3,s1:3/in':3,c2:2/out:2,s2:2/out':2,
                 c2u:4/outu:4,s2u:4/outu':4,ok:1/online:1]

bi Comm00   in:3.Comm10 + 'outu:4.Comm00 + in':3.Comm01 + 'outu':4.Comm00 +
            'fail_wire:2.CommF + 'online:1.Comm00
bi Comm10   in:3.#'fail_overfull:0.CommF + 'out:2.Comm00 + in':3.Comm11 +
            'outu':4.Comm10 + 'fail_wire:2.CommF + 'online:1.Comm10
bi Comm01   in:3.Comm11 + 'outu:4.Comm01 + in':3.#'fail_overfull:0.CommF +
            'out':2.Comm00 + 'fail_wire:2.CommF + 'online:1.Comm01
bi Comm11   in:3.#'fail_overfull:0.CommF + 'out:2.Comm01 +
            in':3.#'fail_overfull:0.CommF + 'out':2.Comm10 +
            'fail_wire:2.CommF + 'online:1.Comm11
bi CommF    in:3.CommF + 'outu:4.CommF + in':3.CommF + 'outu':4.CommF +
            'repaired:2.Comm00
```

Full-duplex media have the property that if one direction fails then the other should also be considered as unreliable. In the remainder of this section, the action names of both directions of the link will only differ by a trailing prime. As long as the full-duplex medium which is modeled in Table 4 provides service, i.e. it is in one of the states Comm00, Comm10, Comm01, or Comm11, an 'online ('ok) is signaled to the environment. In contrast to the slow-scan model, a broken medium can be repaired in the recovery model. This is modeled by the action 'repaired which is enabled in the failure state CommF and allows the LGL to reset to its initial state Comm00. The recovery of the system as modeled in Table 5 works as follows. If the SPC (TPC) is in its failure state SPCF (TPCF) and detects that the medium has been repaired by receiving the action ok (online), it sends one interrupt (action 'reset) to the clock and another (action 'init) to the TPC (SPC). The invoked interrupt handler of the clock resets the clock. The handler of the TPC (SPC) agrees to that request by sending an acknowledgment (action 'ack_init) back to the SPC (TPC), signaling its reinitialization (action 'recovered), and resetting itself to its initial state. Since we are dealing with abstract models, we leave it open to an implementation how to send interrupt signals between SPC, TPC, and the clock; e.g. one could use the already repaired line.

TABLE 5. The recovery model (Part 2)

```
* level 0: fail_overfull, det, recovered, mcs, mct
* level 1: online (ok), init, ack_init, reset
* level 2: out (c2, s2), fail_wire, repaired,
*          comm_in, comm_out, stat_in, stat_out
* level 3: in (c1, s1)
* level 4: outu (c2u, s2u), tick


* Slow-scan system

bi SS      (SPC | LGL | TPC | Clock)\{c1:3,c2:2,c2u:4,s1:3,s2:2,s2u:4,mcs:0,
                                mct:0,ok:1,init:1,ack_init:1,reset:1}

* SSI-side protocol converter (SPC)

bi SPC     SPC0 [> (init:1.'ack_init:1.#'recovered:0.SPC + ack_init:1.SPC)
...
bi SPCF    comm_in:2.SPCF + s2:2.SPCF + s2u:4.SPCF + mcs:0.SPCF +
           ok:1.'reset:1.'init:1.nil

* Track-side protocol converter (TPC)

bi TPC     TPC0 [> (init:1.'ack_init:1.#'recovered:0.TPC + ack_init:1.TPC)
...
bi TPCF    stat_in:2.TPCF + c2:2.TPCF + c2u:4.TPCF + mct:0.TPCF +
           ok:1.'reset:1.'init:1.nil

* Clock

bi Clock   Clock0 [> reset:1.Clock
bi Clock0  'tick:4.'mcs:0.'mct:0.Clock0
```

If a link has been repaired, the system should reset itself immediately. Therefore, all actions involving the recovery scheme are interrupt actions. However, they should not be able to interfere with the atomicity of the clock signals (actions 'mcs and 'mct). Therefore, the actions ok, online, init and ack_init are assigned to priority level one. The action 'repaired should never be preempted by any communication in which the buffer is involved, so it gets the priority value two. Finally, the action 'recovered is handled as the other 'atomic propositions' 'det and 'fail_overfull.

3.4   The Fault-tolerant Model

We now turn our attention to modeling *fault-tolerance* which is an essential requirement of the SSI [11]. We have already modeled an error-recovery scheme for the medium, which ensures fault-tolerance on a *software-level*. In practice, the *hardware* of the system is also replicated in order to guarantee

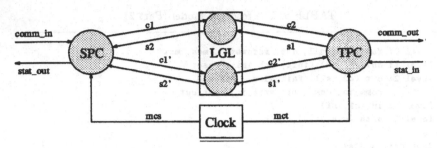

FIGURE 4. The fault-tolerant model

TABLE 6. The fault-tolerant model (Part 1)

```
* level 0: fail_overfull, det, recovered, mcs, mct
* level 1: online (ok, ok'), init, ack_init, switch, ack_switch, reset
* level 2: out (c2, s2), out' (c2', s2'), fail_wire, repaired,
*          comm_in, comm_out, stat_in, stat_out
* level 3: in (c1, s1), in' (c1', s1')
* level 4: outu (c2u, s2u), outu' (c2u', s2u'), tick

* Slow-scan system

bi SS      (SPC | LGL | TPC | Clock)\{c1:3,c2:2,c2u:4,s1:3,s2:2,s2u:4,
                           c1':3,c2':2,c2u':4,s1':3,s2':2,
                           s2u':4,mcs:0,mct:0,ok:1,ok':1,
                           init:1,ack_init:1,reset:1,
                           switch:1,ack_switch:1}
```

better safety-critical behavior [11]. Therefore, we explicitly duplicate the data path in our design. The new situation is depicted in Figure 4, where the LGL consists of the usual link and a spare link whose corresponding actions are annotated by a prime. Our fault-tolerant model, where the 'prime' states of the SPC and TPC indicate that the system works on the second line, behaves as follows. If a failure of the currently used line is detected by the SPC (TPC), i.e. it is in its failure state, and the other line is 'up', then the SPC (TPC) signals its wish to switch the line to the TPC (SPC) by performing the action 'switch. The interrupt handlers react on that request (action 'ack_switch) in the same fashion as in the recovery model. Tables 6 and 7 summarize the necessary changes to our model.

Ideally, we assume the switch to be atomic in the *design* of the slow-scan system, i.e. SPC and TPC switch to the new link at the same time. Using priorities, this can be modeled by giving the actions switch and ack_switch the same priority as the interrupt actions init, ack_init, and ok.

TABLE 7. The fault-tolerant model (Part 2)

```
* SSI-side protocol converter (SPC) ... (changes to TPC analogue)

bi SPC     SPCO [> (init:1.'ack_init:1.#'recovered:0.SPC +
                    ack_init:1.SPC +
                    switch:1.'ack_switch:1.#'recovered:0.SPC' +
                    ack_switch:1.SPC')
...
bi SPCF    comm_in:2.SPCF + s2:2.SPCF + s2u:4.SPCF + mcs:0.SPCF +
           ok:1.'reset:0.'init:1.nil + ok':1.'reset:0.'switch:1.nil

bi SPC'    SPCO' [> (init:1.'ack_init:1.#'recovered:0.SPC' +
                     ack_init:1.SPC' +
                     switch:1.'ack_switch:1.#'recovered:0.SPC +
                     ack_switch:1.SPC)

bi SPCO'   comm_in:2.'stat_out:2.SPCO' + 'c1':3.SPCO + s2':2.SPCO' +
           s2u':4.SPCO' + mcs:0.'c1':3.SPC1'
...
bi SPCF'   comm_in:2.SPCF' + s2':2.SPCF' + s2u':4.SPCF' + mcs:0.SPCF' +
           ok':1.'reset:0.'init:1.nil + ok:1.'reset:0.'switch:1.nil

* Low grade link (LGL)

bi LGL     Comm00[c1:3/in:3,s1:3/in':3,c2:2/out:2,s2:2/out':2,
                  c2u:4/outu:4,s2u:4/outu':4,ok:1/online:1] |
           Comm00[c1':3/in:3,s1':3/in':3,c2':2/out:2,s2':2/out':2,
                  c2u':4/outu:4,s2u':4/outu':4,ok':1/online:1]
```

3.5 State Space of the Models

We have run the NCSU Concurrency Workbench on a SUN SPARC 20 workstation to construct and minimize the state spaces of our models. We refer to the slow-scan model as bruns.pccs, to the recovery model as recovery.pccs, and to the fault-tolerant model as ftolerant.pccs. Moreover, we refer to the slow-scan model where the buffer has been replaced by the full-duplex version as basic.pccs. The CCS models corresponding to bruns.pccs and basic.pccs, which are obtained by leaving out all priority values, are called bruns.ccs and basic.ccs, respectively. Table 8 provides for each model the number of states and transitions of the corresponding transition system and the time (in seconds) needed for constructing it. The table also contains this information for the minimized (with respect to prioritized strong bisimulation) models (cf. "reduced state space").

Table 8 shows that the number of states decreases by over 70% when using the calculus with priorities. Even more impressive is the reduction of transitions by approximately 85%. This results from the fact that we are not able to model the *atomicity of action sequences* and *interrupts* in plain

TABLE 8. Transition system sizes

Model	Global State Space			Reduced State Space		
Name	states	trans.	time	states	trans.	time
bruns.ccs	3527	17122	8	3154	14894	38
bruns.pccs	899	2567	6	766	2094	11
basic.ccs	1114	4721	2	1021	4217	9
basic.pccs	312	801	2	287	713	3
recovery.pccs	1100	2801	20	789	2233	25
ftolerant.pccs	11905	33760	452	7485	26164	552

CCS. That observation demonstrates the utility of priorities for the verification of distributed systems. The large reduction of the fault-tolerant model with respect to prioritized strong bisimulation is due to the symmetry of its design. The minimization of bruns.ccs and basic.ccs with respect to observational equivalence reduces the model to 2057 states / 8280 transitions and 698 states / 2293 transitions, respectively. We are currently implementing an algorithm to compute *prioritized observational* equivalence. The adaption of the corresponding observational equivalence [14] is not suitable for automated verification tools since the weak transition relation is parameterized with (arbitrary) sets of actions. However, we have developed a characterization of the prioritized observational equivalence which uses an alternative weak transition relation that is efficiently computable.

4 Verifying the Railway System

In this section, we specify and verify requirements of the slow-scan, the recovery, and the fault-tolerant model. We use the well-known modal μ-calculus [12] as our specification language and determine the validity of our properties by model checking [3]. For the verification, we use the NCSU Concurrency Workbench on a SUN SPARC 20 workstation with 512 MByte of main memory.

4.1 Requirements of the Slow-Scan System

Since the slow-scan system is embedded in a safety-critical system, we want to verify that our designs satisfy the following required properties.

After a low-grade link fails, either the slow-scan system will eventually detect the error or the link is repaired. Moreover, this property holds after every reinitialization of the system.

The slow-scan system is always capable of continuing to tick. If this property holds, then the system is *deadlock-free*, too.

A failure of the slow-scan system is possible. This property should also be valid after every reinitialization of the system.

A failure is detected only if a failure has actually occurred. Also this property should hold after every reinitialization of the system.

After a low-grade link fails, the slow-scan system will eventually stop responding to the SSI and TFMs if the low-grade link does not recover from the error.

If a failure is detected and the broken line is repaired, then the system will be reinitialized.

All properties – except for the last one – are adapted from [5]. However, since the recovery and the fault-tolerant model are able to recover from an error, the properties of [5] should also hold after every reinitialization of these models.

4.2 Specifying our Requirements in the μ-Calculus

For specifying our requirements we use the modal μ-calculus. Its syntax is defined by the following BNF, which uses a set of variables $\mathcal{V}$ with $X \in \mathcal{V}$.

$$\Phi \quad ::= \quad f\!\!f \quad | \quad X \quad | \quad \neg\Phi \quad | \quad \Phi \wedge \Phi \quad | \quad \langle \alpha{:}k \rangle \Phi \quad | \quad \mu X.\Phi$$

Further, we define the following dual operators: $tt =_{\mathrm{df}} \neg f\!\!f$, $\Phi_1 \vee \Phi_2 =_{\mathrm{df}} \neg(\neg\Phi_1 \wedge \neg\Phi_2)$, $[\alpha{:}k]\Phi =_{\mathrm{df}} \neg\langle \alpha{:}k \rangle(\neg\Phi)$, and $\nu X.\Phi =_{\mathrm{df}} \neg\mu X.(\neg\Phi[\neg X/X])$, where $[\neg X/X]$ denotes the substitution of all free occurrences of X by $\neg X$. Finally, we introduce the following abbreviations where $L \subseteq \mathcal{A}$: $\langle L \rangle \Phi =_{\mathrm{df}} \bigvee \{ \langle \alpha{:}k \rangle \Phi \mid \alpha{:}k \in L \}$, $\langle - \rangle \Phi =_{\mathrm{df}} \langle \mathcal{A} \rangle \Phi$, $\langle -L \rangle \Phi =_{\mathrm{df}} \langle \mathcal{A} \setminus L \rangle \Phi$, $[L]^\infty \Phi =_{\mathrm{df}} \nu X.\Phi \wedge [L]X$, and $\langle L \rangle^* \Phi =_{\mathrm{df}} \mu X.\Phi \vee \langle L \rangle X$.

We use the well-known standard semantics of the modal μ-calculus as e.g. presented in [12]. The model checker integrated in the NCSU Concurrency Workbench is based on [3]. More precisely, it is a *local* model checker for a fragment of the modal μ-calculus. The formulae we intend to verify can be automatically rewritten into semantical equivalent ones which satisfy the syntactic restriction required in [3]. The time and space complexity of the model checker is linear in the size of the formula, in its alternation depth, and in the size of the transition system.

We now formally specify the requirements of the slow-scan system as presented above in the modal μ-calculus. We take particular care in implementing *eventuality* since we want to consider only execution paths in which the clock continues to tick. This *fairness property* is not satisfied by the models themselves since they contain livelocks. As discussed in [5], we are interested in the following notion of *fair eventuality*:

$$even(\Phi) =_{\mathrm{df}} \mu X.(\nu Y.\,\Phi \vee (\overline{[\texttt{tick}]}X \wedge [\overline{-\texttt{tick}}]Y)) \ .$$

Moreover, we need a meta-formula which expresses that the argument formula holds again if the low-grade system has recovered:

$$again(\Phi) =_{\mathrm{df}} [-]^\infty \overline{[\texttt{recovered}]}\Phi \ .$$

Now, we can formalize the desired properties of the slow-scan model and the fault-tolerant model, where Fail $=_{df}$ {fail_wire, fail_overfull}.

After the low-grade link fails (for the first time), the slow-scan system will eventually detect the error or the link is repaired:

$$\text{failures-responded} =_{df}$$
$$[-\text{Fail}]^\infty [\text{Fail}] \, even(\langle \overline{\text{det}} \rangle tt \vee \langle \overline{\text{repaired}} \rangle tt) \ . \tag{1}$$

The formula *failures-responded* holds after every reinitialization of the system again:

$$\text{failures-responded-again} =_{df} again(\text{failures-responded}) \ . \tag{2}$$

Since the formula *failures-responded* is trivially true if the underlying model cannot perform the action 'tick or if it cannot fail, we are also interested in the following two properties. The slow-scan model is always capable of continuing to tick:

$$\text{can-tick} =_{df} [-]^\infty \langle - \rangle^* \langle \overline{\text{tick}} \rangle tt \ . \tag{3}$$

A failure of the slow-scan system is possible:

$$\text{failures-possible} =_{df} \langle - \overline{\text{recovered}} \rangle^* \langle \text{Fail} \rangle tt \ . \tag{4}$$

The formula *failures-possible* holds after every reinitialization of the system again:

$$\text{failures-possible-again} =_{df} again(\text{failures-possible}) \ . \tag{5}$$

A failure is detected only if a failure has actually occurred since the last reinitialization of the system:

$$\text{no-false-alarms} =_{df}$$
$$[-\text{Fail}, \overline{\text{recovered}}]^\infty ([\overline{\text{det}}] ff \vee \langle \overline{\text{fail\_overfull}} \rangle tt) \ . \tag{6}$$

The body of the formula reflects that $\overline{\text{fail\_overfull}}$ signals that a failure has already occurred, i.e. it may be enabled at the same time as $\overline{\text{det}}$. Moreover, the formula *no-false-alarms* should hold after every reinitialization of the system:

$$\text{no-false-alarms-again} =_{df} again(\text{no-false-alarms}) \ . \tag{7}$$

The auxiliary property "the system never responds", which is used below, can be encoded as follows:

$$\text{silent} =_{df} [-]^\infty [\overline{\text{comm\_out}}, \overline{\text{stat\_out}}] ff \ .$$

After a low-grade link fails, the slow-scan system will eventually be silent if the low-grade link does not recover from the error:

$$\text{eventually-silent} =_{df} [-]^\infty [\overline{\text{det}}] \, even(\text{silent} \vee \langle \overline{\text{recovered}} \rangle tt) \ . \tag{8}$$

If a failure is detected and the broken line is repaired, then the system will be reinitialized:

$$react\text{-}on\text{-}repair =_{df} [-]^{\infty} \overline{[\texttt{det}]}([-\overline{\texttt{recovered}}]^{\infty} \overline{[\texttt{repaired}]}$$
$$even(\langle \overline{\texttt{recovered}} \rangle tt)) \ . \tag{9}$$

4.3 Verification Results

We applied the model checker for all models and formulae twice. The first time, we let the model checker construct the state space on the fly as is usual for *local* model checking. The second time, before invoking the model checker, we minimized the models with respect to prioritized strong bisimulation. The verification results are given in Tables 9/10 and 11/12, respectively. The tables show which properties hold for which formulae (columns "ok") and give the CPU time (in seconds) used by the NCSU Concurrency Workbench for checking each formula. The symbol "?" indicates that a computation ran out of memory. The speed-up of the model checker for minimized models is partly due to the fact that the transition systems for our models were constructed in a preprocessing step (minimization) and, thus, are *not* constructed on the fly. Additionally, the times for the verification results with respect to our minimized models do not include the times needed for the minimizations.

TABLE 9. Verification results wrt. the non-minimized models

Non-minimized models	Formula 1 ok	time	Formula 3 ok	time	Formula 4 ok	time	Formula 6 ok	time	Formula 8 ok	time
bruns.ccs	*ff*	1936	*tt*	1811	*tt*	1	*ff*	6	?	?
bruns.pccs	*tt*	1483	*tt*	261	*tt*	1	*tt*	52	*tt*	1164
basic.ccs	*ff*	1460	*tt*	524	*tt*	1	*ff*	19	*tt*	7541
basic.pccs	*tt*	396	*tt*	86	*tt*	1	*tt*	43	*tt*	331
recovery.pccs	*tt*	808	*tt*	495	*tt*	1	*tt*	68	*tt*	1685
ftolerant.pccs	*tt*	1306	?	?	*tt*	1	*tt*	135	?	?

TABLE 10. Verification results wrt. the non-minimized models (continued)

Non-minimized models	Formula 2 ok	time	Formula 5 ok	time	Formula 7 ok	time	Formula 9 ok	time
recovery.pccs	*tt*	1942	*tt*	429	*tt*	492	*tt*	2581
ftolerant.pccs	?	?	?	?	?	?	?	?

In contrast to [5], we could verify most properties automatically and without using any abstractions by hand. However, the formulae *eventually-silent*, *react-on-repair*, and *failures-responded-again* are complicated and

TABLE 11. Verification results wrt. the minimized models

Minimized models	Formula 1		Formula 3		Formula 4		Formula 6		Formula 8	
	ok	time	ok	time	ok	time	ok	time	ok	time
bruns.ccs	*ff*	1570	*tt*	366	*tt*	1	*ff*	18	?	?
bruns.pccs	*tt*	604	*tt*	90	*tt*	1	*tt*	17	*tt*	512
basic.ccs	*ff*	225	*tt*	106	*tt*	1	*ff*	7	*tt*	763
basic.pccs	*tt*	213	*tt*	32	*tt*	1	*tt*	16	*tt*	142
recovery.pccs	*tt*	90	*tt*	86	*tt*	1	*tt*	16	*tt*	423
ftolerant.pccs	*tt*	122	*tt*	864	*tt*	1	*tt*	16	?	?

TABLE 12. Verification results wrt. the minimized models (continued)

Minimized models	Formula 2		Formula 5		Formula 7		Formula 9	
	ok	time	ok	time	ok	time	ok	time
recovery.pccs	*tt*	481	*tt*	96	*tt*	109	*tt*	768
ftolerant.pccs	?	?	*tt*	911	*tt*	1159	?	?

large in size. Therefore, we could not check them automatically for the model **ftolerant.pccs**, which has 7485 states and 26164 transitions after minimization. Although the size of **bruns.ccs** is relatively small, the model checker ran out of memory for the formula *eventually-silent*, which has alternation depth two.

Moreover, our timing results show that using a *local* model checker often gains no advantage. This is because most of the formulae are valid safety properties, and the local model checker has to investigate all states of the models anyway. However, our model checker has quickly detected invalid formulae.

In the prioritized models all properties that could be verified automatically hold as expected. The formula *no-false-alarms* does not hold for the models in plain CCS. This is due to the fact that the atomicity of actions cannot be expressed without priorities. Indeed, there exists an interleaving in the CCS models where one observes a **'det** before a failure has occurred.

Surprisingly, we found the formula *failures-responded* invalid in the model **bruns.ccs** whereas in [5] it is reported to hold. The reason for this is that we left out the actions **c1'** (**s1'**) which occur directly before a **'det** in Bruns' model. Although that reflects our intuition that a **'det** should be signaled as soon as an error is detected, Bruns' modeling does not allow both SPC and TPC to detect the overfull-failure of the medium before the action **'fail_overfull** has occurred.

5 Conclusions and Future Work

We have demonstrated the importance of priorities for modeling and verifying distributed systems by means of a practically relevant case study of the slow-scan part of a railway signaling system. Priorities allow us to favor one communication over another and to make action sequences atomic. While the former helps to model systems more realistically, the latter drastically cuts the number of states and transitions. Our models explicitly reflect safety-critical parts of the slow-scan system, namely an error-recovery scheme and a fault-tolerant medium, which are required in the design document [11]. We have used the NCSU Concurrency Workbench for checking properties of our design. We are currently implementing an algorithm for computing prioritized observational equivalence that will enable us to further reduce the size of our models.

Acknowledgments: We want to thank Girish Bhat for the implementation of his model checker in the NCSU Concurrency Workbench.

6 REFERENCES

[1] J. Baeten, editor. *Applications of Process Algebra*, volume 17 of *Cambridge Tracts in Theoretical Computer Science*. Cambridge University Press, Cambridge, England, 1990.

[2] J. Baeten, J. Bergstra, and J. Klop. Syntax and defining equations for an interrupt mechanism in process algebra. *Fundamenta Informaticae IX*, pages 127–168, 1986.

[3] G. Bhat and R. Cleaveland. Efficient local model-checking for fragments of the modal μ-calculus. To appear in Proceedings of *Second International Workshop on Tools and Algorithms for the Construction and Analysis of Systems* (TACAS '96), 1996.

[4] T. Bolognesi and E. Brinksma. Introduction to the ISO specification language LOTOS. *Computer Networks and ISDN Systems*, 14:25–59, 1987.

[5] G. Bruns. A case study in safety-critical design. In G. Bochmann and D. Probst, editors, *Computer Aided Verification (CAV '92)*, volume 663 of *Lecture Notes in Computer Science*, pages 220–233, Montréal, June/July 1992. Springer-Verlag.

[6] J. Camilleri and G. Winskel. CCS with priority choice. In *Sixth Annual Symposium on Logic in Computer Science (LICS '91)*, pages 246–255, Amsterdam, July 1991. IEEE Computer Society Press.

[7] R. Cleaveland. Analyzing concurrent systems using the Concurrency Workbench. In P. Lauer, editor, *Functional Programming, Concurrency, Simulation and Automated Reasoning*, volume 693 of *Lecture Notes in Computer Science*, pages 129–144. Springer-Verlag, 1993.

[8] R. Cleaveland and M. Hennessy. Priorities in process algebra. *Information and Computation*, 87(1/2):58–77, July/August 1990.

[9] R. Cleaveland, E. Madelaine, and S. Sims. Generating front-ends for verification tools. In E. Brinksma, W. R. Cleaveland, K. G. Larsen, T. Margaria, and B. Steffen, editors, *First International Workshop on Tools and Algorithms for the Construction and Analysis of Systems (TACAS '95)*, volume 1019 of *Lecture Notes in Computer Science*, pages 153–173, Aarhus, Denmark, May 1995. Springer-Verlag.

[10] R. Cleaveland, J. Parrow, and B. Steffen. The Concurrency Workbench: A semantics-based tool for the verification of finite-state systems. *ACM Transactions on Programming Languages and Systems*, 15(1):36–72, January 1993.

[11] A. Cribbens. Solid-state interlocking (SSI): an integrated electronic signalling system for mainline railways. *IEE Proceedings*, 134, Pt. B(3), May 1987.

[12] D. Kozen. Results on the propositional μ-calculus. *Theoretical Computer Science*, 27:333–354, 1983.

[13] R. Milner. *Communication and Concurrency*. Prentice-Hall, London, 1989.

[14] V. Natarajan, L. Christoff, I. Christoff, and R. Cleaveland. Priorities and abstraction in process algebra. In P. Thiagarajan, editor, *Foundations of Software Technology and Theoretical Computer Science*, volume 880 of *Lecture Notes in Computer Science*, pages 217–230, Madras, India, Dec. 1994. Springer-Verlag.

[15] W. Yi. CCS + time = an interleaving model for real time systems. In J. L. Albert, B. Monien, and M. R. Artalejo, editors, *Automata, Languages and Programming (ICALP '91)*, volume 510 of *Lecture Notes in Computer Science*, pages 217–228, Madrid, July 1991. Springer-Verlag.

Games and Modal Mu-Calculus

Colin Stirling*

ABSTRACT We define Ehrenfeucht-Fraïssé games which exactly capture
the expressive power of the extremal fixed point operators of modal mu-
calculus. The resulting games have significance, we believe, within and outside of concurrency theory. On the one hand they naturally extend the iterative bisimulation games associated with Hennessy-Milner logic, and on
the other hand they offer deeper insight into the logical role of fixed points.
For this purpose we also define second-order propositional modal logic to
contrast fixed points and second-order quantifiers.

1 Introduction

This paper further explores the technical contribution that games can make
to understanding concurrency. We define Ehrenfeucht-Fraïssé games which
exactly capture the expressive power of the extremal fixed point operators
of modal mu-calculus. The resulting games have significance, we believe,
within and outside of concurrency theory. On the one hand they naturally
extend the iterative bisimulation games associated with Hennessy-Milner
logic, and on the other hand they offer deeper insight into the logical role
of fixed points. For this purpose we also define second-order propositional
modal logic to contrast fixed points and second-order quantifiers.

There is something very appealing about trying to understand concurrency and interaction in terms of games. They are a very striking metaphor
for the dialogue that a concurrent component can engage in with its environment. One example is [14] where a denotational semantics for concurrent
while programs is presented whose domains are built from strategies. Another is the use of games for understanding linear logic [1]. Within process
calculi, bisimulation equivalence has been pivotal. A number of authors has
noted that it is essentially game theoretic [3, 18, 16] (and [15] extends this
description to bisimulations that are sensitive to causality). In this paper
we build on this game view of bisimulation. In previous work [17] we showed
that local model checking of finite or infinite state processes can be viewed
as a game, without loss of structure. In the finite state case this provides an
alternative perspective from the use of automata, as it also yields fast model

---

*Department of Computer Science, University of Edinburgh, Edinburgh EH9 3JZ,
UK, email: cps@dcs.ed.ac.uk

checking algorithms: furthermore, these games are definable independently of model checking as graph games which can be reduced to other combinatorial games (and in particular to the very important simple stochastic games [6]).

These concerns have practical repercussions. A guiding principle is to find clear theoretical foundations which can, at the same time, enhance tool development. Games can be naturally animated within a tool. They also offer the potential for effective machine user interaction. For instance, in the model checking case not only do they allow a user to know that a process has a property, but also *why* it has it. Games also allow a user to know *why* a process fails to have a property. In both these cases the justification can be given as a winning strategy (which is polynomial in the size of the model checking problem). Therefore, if a user believes incorrectly that a process has a property then she may become convinced otherwise by playing and losing the model checking game against the machine which holds a winning strategy. These techniques are currently being implemented in the Edinburgh Concurrency Workbench. Similar comments apply to the bisimulation game.

Section 2 is a warm up, where we present some well known concepts in a game theoretic fashion. In section 3 we describe modal mu-calculus and the notion of fixed point depth. Section 4 contains the fixed point games and the main theorem whose proof is delayed until section 6. In section 5 we present second-order modal logic and its games, and discuss its relationship with modal mu-calculus. The work reported here for modal logic has benefited from the large literature on games and logic, and in particular from [9, 18] for Ehrenfeucht-Fraïssé games for first-order logic, [4] for their extension to first-order logic with fixed points, and [8] for their extension to (monadic) second-order logic.

2 Bisimulation games

Assume a process calculus such as CCS, with the proviso[1] that all processes are built from a fixed finite set of actions $\mathcal{A}$. Let E_0 and F_0 be two such processes. We define the game $\mathcal{G}_n^0(E_0, F_0)$ as played by two participants, players I and II. Player I wants to show that E_0 and F_0 are distinguishable within n steps whereas player II wishes to demonstrate that they cannot be differentiated. (The superscript 0 will be explained in section 4.) A play of the game $\mathcal{G}_n^0(E_0, F_0)$ is a finite sequence of pairs $(E_0, F_0) \dots (E_m, F_m)$ whose length m is at most n. If part of a play is $(E_0, F_0) \dots (E_i, F_i)$ with $i < n$ then the next move is initiated by player I from the two possibilities in figure 1. Player I always chooses first, and then player II, with full knowledge of

---

[1]This proviso comes into play in Theorem 1 of section 4 (and also in section 5).

$\langle a \rangle$: Player I chooses a transition $E_i \xrightarrow{a} E_{i+1}$, and then
player II chooses a transition with the same label $F_i \xrightarrow{a} F_{i+1}$.

$[a]$: Player I chooses a transition $F_i \xrightarrow{a} F_{i+1}$, and then
player II chooses a transition with the same label $E_i \xrightarrow{a} E_{i+1}$.

FIGURE 1. Game moves

player I's selection, must choose a corresponding transition from the other process.

A player wins a play if her opponent becomes stuck: player I wins the play $(E_0, F_0) \dots (E_i, F_i)$, $i < n$, when she can choose a transition from E_i (or from F_i) and there is no corresponding transition from the other process F_i (or E_i), and player II wins if the processes E_i and F_i are both deadlocked. Player II also wins if the play reaches length n, for then player I has been unable to distinguish the initial processes within n steps.

A strategy for a player is a set of rules which tells her how to move depending on what has happened previously in the play. A player uses the strategy π in a play if all her moves in the play obey the rules in π. The strategy π is a *winning strategy* if the player wins every play in which she uses π. For each game $\mathcal{G}_n^0(E_0, F_0)$ one of the players has a winning strategy, and this strategy is history free in the sense that the rules do not need to appeal to moves that occurred before the current game configuration. If player II has a winning strategy for $\mathcal{G}_n^0(E_0, F_0)$ then we say that E_0 and F_0 are $(0, n)$-game equivalent, which we abbreviate as $E_0 \sim_n^0 F_0$.

Example 1 Consider the two similar vending machines

$$U \overset{\text{def}}{=} \text{1p.(1p.tea.}U + \text{1p.coffee.}U)$$
$$V \overset{\text{def}}{=} \text{1p.1p.tea.}V + \text{1p.1p.coffee.}V$$

Although $U \sim_2^0 V$, player I has a winning strategy for the game $\mathcal{G}_3^0(U, V)$ and so $U \not\sim_3^0 V$. $\square$

Example 2 Let $Cl_{i+1} \overset{\text{def}}{=} \text{tick.}Cl_i$, $i \geq 0$. Therefore Cl_{i+1} is a clock that ticks $i+1$ times before terminating. Let $Cl \overset{\text{def}}{=} \text{tick.}Cl$ be a clock that ticks forever. Assume that $Clock$ is $\sum\{Cl_i : i \geq 1\}$ and $Clock'$ is $Clock + Cl$. Although $Clock'$ can tick forever which $Clock$ cannot do, for every $n \geq 0$, $Clock' \sim_n^0 Clock$. $\square$

Game equivalence and iterated bisimulation equivalence are intimately related. For each $n \geq 0$, let $\sim_n$ be the following relation on processes [13]:

$E \sim_0 F$ for all E and F.

$E \sim_{n+1} F$ iff for each action $a \in \mathcal{A}$,

       if $E \xrightarrow{a} E'$ then $\exists F'. F \xrightarrow{a} F'$ and $E' \sim_n F'$, and

       if $F \xrightarrow{a} F'$ then $\exists E'. E \xrightarrow{a} E'$ and $E' \sim_n F'$.

Fact 1 $E \sim_n^0 F$ *iff* $E \sim_n F$.

Another way of understanding these equivalences uses Hennessy-Milner logic. Let M be the following family of modal formulas where a ranges over $\mathcal{A}$:

$$\Phi ::= \text{tt} \mid \text{ff} \mid \Phi_1 \wedge \Phi_2 \mid \Phi_1 \vee \Phi_2 \mid [a]\Phi \mid \langle a \rangle \Phi$$

The inductive stipulation below states when a process E has a modal property Φ, written $E \models \Phi$. If E fails to satisfy Φ then this is written $E \not\models \Phi$.

$$
\begin{array}{lll}
E \models \text{tt} & & E \not\models \text{ff} \\
E \models \Phi \wedge \Psi & \text{iff} & E \models \Phi \text{ and } E \models \Psi \\
E \models \Phi \vee \Psi & \text{iff} & E \models \Phi \text{ or } E \models \Psi \\
E \models [a]\Phi & \text{iff} & \forall F. \text{if } E \xrightarrow{a} F \text{ then } F \models \Phi \\
E \models \langle a \rangle \Phi & \text{iff} & \exists F. E \xrightarrow{a} F \text{ and } F \models \Phi
\end{array}
$$

The modal depth of a formula Φ, $\text{md}(\Phi)$, is the maximum embedding of modal operators, and is defined as follows:

$$
\begin{array}{lclcl}
\text{md}(\text{tt}) & = & 0 & = & \text{md}(\text{ff}) \\
\text{md}(\Phi \wedge \Psi) & = & \max\{\text{md}(\Phi), \text{md}(\Psi)\} & = & \text{md}(\Phi \vee \Psi) \\
\text{md}([a]\Phi) & = & 1 + \text{md}(\Phi) & = & \text{md}(\langle a \rangle \Phi)
\end{array}
$$

Assume that M_k is the sublogic $\{\Phi : \Phi \in M \text{ and } \text{md}(\Phi) \leq k\}$.

Fact 2 $E \sim_n^0 F$ *iff* $\forall \Phi \in M_n. E \models \Phi$ *iff* $F \models \Phi$.

An easy corollary is that the relations $\sim_n^0$, $n \geq 0$, on processes constitute a genuine hierarchy.

Fact 3 *If* $m < n$ *then* $\sim_n^0 \subset \sim_m^0$.

A binary relation $\mathcal{R}$ between processes is a bisimulation relation provided that whenever $E\mathcal{R}F$, for all $a \in \mathcal{A}$:

       if $E \xrightarrow{a} E'$ then $\exists F'. F \xrightarrow{a} F'$ and $E'\mathcal{R}F'$, and

       if $F \xrightarrow{a} F'$ then $\exists E'. E \xrightarrow{a} E'$ and $E'\mathcal{R}F'$.

Two processes E and F are bisimulation equivalent, written $E \sim F$, if there is a bisimulation $\mathcal{R}$ relating them. To capture $\sim$ (instead of the iterated bismulation relations $\sim_n$) using games the notion of game is extended to encompass plays that may continue forever. Let $\mathcal{G}^0_\infty(E_0, F_0)$ be such a game. If part of a play is $(E_0, F_0)\ldots(E_i, F_i)$ then the next move is initiated by player I from the two moves in figure 1. Again a player wins if her opponent becomes stuck. Also player II wins if the play has infinite length. For each game $\mathcal{G}^0_\infty(E, F)$ one of the players has a (history free) winning strategy, and if it is player II then we write $E \sim^0_\infty F$.

Fact 4 $E \sim^0_\infty F$ *iff* $E \sim F$.

Example 3 Player I has a winning strategy for $\mathcal{G}^0_\infty(Clock', Clock)$. She first chooses the $\langle \text{tick} \rangle$ move, $Clock' \xrightarrow{\text{tick}} Cl$, and so player II has to respond with a transition $Clock \xrightarrow{\text{tick}} Cl_i$, for some $i \geq 0$. So after i further moves the game configuration becomes (Cl, Cl_0), and so player I wins. This example also shows that $\sim \subset \sim^0_n$ for any n. □

3 Modal mu-calculus

Modal mu-calculus, modal logic with extremal fixed points, introduced by Kozen [12], is a very expressive propositional temporal logic with the ability to describe liveness, safety, fairness and cyclic properties of processes. Formulas of the logic, μM, given in positive form are defined as follows

$$\Phi ::= \text{tt} \mid \text{ff} \mid Z \mid \Phi_1 \wedge \Phi_2 \mid \Phi_1 \vee \Phi_2 \mid [a]\Phi \mid \langle a \rangle \Phi \mid \nu Z.\Phi \mid \mu Z.\Phi$$

where Z ranges over a family of propositional variables, and a over $\mathcal{A}$. The binder νZ is the greatest whereas μZ is the least fixed point operator.

When E is a process let $\mathcal{P}(E)$ be the smallest transition closed set containing E: that is, if $F \in \mathcal{P}(E)$ and $F \xrightarrow{a} F'$ then $F' \in \mathcal{P}(E)$. Let $\mathcal{P}$ range over (non-empty) transition closed sets. We extend the semantics of modal logic of the previous section to encompass fixed points. Because of free variables we employ valuations $\mathcal{V}$ which assign to each variable Z a subset $\mathcal{V}(Z)$ of processes in $\mathcal{P}$. Let $\mathcal{V}[\mathcal{E}/Z]$ be the valuation $\mathcal{V}'$ which agrees with $\mathcal{V}$ everywhere except possibly Z when $\mathcal{V}'(Z) = \mathcal{E}$. The inductive definition of satisfaction below stipulates when a process E has the property Φ relative to $\mathcal{V}$, written $E \models_\mathcal{V} \Phi$.

$$
\begin{array}{lll}
E \models_\mathcal{V} \text{tt} & & E \not\models_\mathcal{V} \text{ff} \\
E \models_\mathcal{V} Z & \text{iff} & E \in \mathcal{V}(Z) \\
E \models_\mathcal{V} \Phi \wedge \Psi & \text{iff} & E \models_\mathcal{V} \Phi \text{ and } E \models_\mathcal{V} \Psi \\
E \models_\mathcal{V} \Phi \vee \Psi & \text{iff} & E \models_\mathcal{V} \Phi \text{ or } E \models_\mathcal{V} \Psi \\
E \models_\mathcal{V} [a]\Phi & \text{iff} & \forall F. \text{ if } E \xrightarrow{a} F \text{ then } F \models_\mathcal{V} \Phi \\
E \models_\mathcal{V} \langle a \rangle \Phi & \text{iff} & \exists F. E \xrightarrow{a} F \text{ and } F \models_\mathcal{V} \Phi \\
E \models_\mathcal{V} \nu Z.\Phi & \text{iff} & \exists \mathcal{E} \subseteq \mathcal{P}(E). E \in \mathcal{E} \text{ and } \forall F \in \mathcal{E}. F \models_{\mathcal{V}[\mathcal{E}/Z]} \Phi \\
E \models_\mathcal{V} \mu Z.\Phi & \text{iff} & \forall \mathcal{E} \subseteq \mathcal{P}(E). \text{ if } (\forall F \in \mathcal{P}(E). F \models_{\mathcal{V}[\mathcal{E}/Z]} \Phi \text{ implies } F \in \mathcal{E}) \\
& & \qquad\qquad \text{then } E \in \mathcal{E}
\end{array}
$$

The stipulations for the fixed points follow directly from Tarski-Knaster, as a greatest fixed point is the union of all postfixed points and a least fixed point is the intersection of all prefixed points. The clause for the least fixed point can be slightly simplified as follows: $E \models_V \mu Z. \Phi$ iff

$$\forall \mathcal{E} \subseteq \mathcal{P}(E). \text{ if } E \notin \mathcal{E} \text{ then } \exists F \in \mathcal{P}(E). F \notin \mathcal{E} \text{ and } F \models_{V[\mathcal{E}/Z]} \Phi$$

A formula Φ is closed if it does not contain any free variables: in which case $E \models_V \Phi$ iff $E \models_{V'} \Phi$ for any valuations V and V'. Notice that closed formulas are closed under negation.

There is a large literature on the use of μM for specifying and verifying temporal properties of processes. Here our concern is with trying to understand the role of fixed points in μM. Characterizing the expressive power of particular formulas of μM is no easy matter. We shall show that there is an algebraic characterization which generalizes the well known results of the previous section.

We define the sublogics μM_n^k to be the set of closed formulas whose modal depth is at most n and whose fixed point depth is at most k. In particular, $\mu M_n^0 = M_n$. The modal depth of Φ, $md(\Phi)$, is the maximum embedding of modal operators, and extends the definition from the previous section:

$$
\begin{aligned}
md(tt) &= & 0 &= md(ff) &= md(Z) \\
md(\Phi \wedge \Psi) &= & \max\{md(\Phi), md(\Psi)\} &= md(\Phi \vee \Psi) \\
md([a]\Phi) &= & 1 + md(\Phi) &= md(\langle a \rangle \Phi) \\
md(\nu Z. \Phi) &= & md(\Phi) &= md(\mu Z. \Phi)
\end{aligned}
$$

Similarly, the fixed point depth of Φ, written $fd(\Phi)$, is the maximum embedding of fixed point operators:

$$
\begin{aligned}
fd(tt) &= & 0 &= fd(ff) &= fd(Z) \\
fd(\Phi \wedge \Psi) &= & \max\{fd(\Phi), fd(\Psi)\} &= fd(\Phi \vee \Psi) \\
fd([a]\Phi) &= & fd(\Phi) &= fd(\langle a \rangle \Phi) \\
fd(\nu Z. \Phi) &= & 1 + fd(\Phi) &= fd(\mu Z. \Phi)
\end{aligned}
$$

Let $\mu M_n^k = \{\Phi : \Phi \in \mu M \text{ is closed and } fd(\Phi) \leq k \text{ and } md(\Phi) \leq n\}$.

4 Fixed point games

It is our intention to characterize the families μM_n^k in terms of games which generalize those of section 2. We define the game $\mathcal{G}_n^k(E_0, F_0)$ as played by the two participants, players I and II. For this game we assume k distinct colours $\mathcal{C}_1, \ldots, \mathcal{C}_k$. A play of the game $\mathcal{G}_n^k(E_0, F_0)$ is a finite sequence of pairs $(E_0, F_0) \ldots (E_m, F_m)$ whose length m is at most $k + n$. More precisely, there are two kinds of moves the $\langle a \rangle$ and $[a]$ moves as in figure 1, and the new μ and ν moves: a play contains no more than k fixed point moves, and

⟨a⟩ : If $l < n$ then player I chooses a transition $E_i \xrightarrow{a} E_{i+1}$, and then player II chooses a transition with the same label $F_i \xrightarrow{a} F_{i+1}$.

[a] : If $l < n$ then player I chooses a transition $F_i \xrightarrow{a} F_{i+1}$, and then player II chooses a transition with the same label $E_i \xrightarrow{a} E_{i+1}$.

ν : If $j < k$ then player I obtains the next colour C_{j+1} and paints a subset of $\mathcal{P}(E_i)$ which includes E_i the colour C_{j+1}, and then player II paints a subset of $\mathcal{P}(F_i)$ which includes F_i colour C_{j+1}, and then player I chooses $F_{i+1} \in \mathcal{P}(F_i)$ which is coloured C_{j+1}, and then player II chooses $E_{i+1} \in \mathcal{P}(E_i)$ which is coloured C_{j+1}.

μ : If $j < k$ then player I obtains the next colour C_{j+1} and paints a subset of $\mathcal{P}(F_i)$ which excludes E_i the colour C_{j+1}, and then player II paints a subset of $\mathcal{P}(E_i)$ which excludes F_i colour C_{j+1}, and then player I chooses $E_{i+1} \in \mathcal{P}(E_i)$ not coloured C_{j+1}, and then player II chooses $F_{i+1} \in \mathcal{P}(F_i)$ not coloured C_{j+1}.

FIGURE 2. Fixed point game moves

n modal moves. If part of a play is $(E_0, F_0) \ldots (E_i, F_i)$ with $i < k + n$, and the number of modal moves so far is l and the number of fixed point moves is j, then the next move is initiated by player I from the applicable moves in figure 2. In the case of the fixed point moves, player I first colours a subset of the reachable processes from one of the pair of processes in the current game configuration with the next available colour, and with full knowledge of what player I has done, player II colours a subset of the reachable processes with the same colour from the other process. There is an asymmetry in the colouring between ν and μ, as to whether the current processes are coloured. Next player I, also with full knowledge of what has been coloured so far, picks a reachable process from the set that player II was responsible for colouring: again there is an asymmetry, in the ν case she chooses a coloured process and in the μ case an uncoloured one. Finally player II, with knowledge of all the choices so far, chooses a reachable process that player I was responsible for (in the ν case a coloured process, and in the μ case an uncoloured one). Notice that a process may end up with multiple colours.

A play of $\mathcal{G}_n^k(E, F)$ involves at most k fixed point moves and n modal moves. A game is played until one of the players wins, or until there are no more available moves. The conditions for winning are given in figure 3 where we assume that $(E_0, F_0) \ldots (E_i, F_i)$ is (part of) a play with l modal moves and j fixed point moves. The important new condition is preservation of colours, as given by clause 3 for a win for player I. This means that for

Player I wins

1. If $l < n$ and $E_i \xrightarrow{a} E'$ but $\neg \exists F'.F_i \xrightarrow{a} F'$.
2. If $l < n$ and $F_i \xrightarrow{a} F'$ but $\neg \exists E'.E_i \xrightarrow{a} E'$.
3. If E_i is coloured $C_h, h \leq j$, and F_i is not coloured C_h.

Player II wins

1. If E_i and F_i are both deadlocked and condition 3 above does not hold.
2. If the play has ended, $l = n$ and $j = k$, and 3 above does not hold.

FIGURE 3. Winning conditions

player II to win, she has to make sure that whenever the game configuration reaches (E, F) then the colours of E are included in the colours of F^2.

For each game $\mathcal{G}_n^k(E, F)$ one of the players has a winning strategy (which is no longer history free, as it depends on previous colouring moves). If player II has a winning strategy for $\mathcal{G}_n^k(E, F)$ then we say that E and F are (k, n)-game equivalent, which we write as $E \sim_n^k F$.

Example 1 Player I has a winning strategy for $\mathcal{G}_1^1(Clock', Clock)$. Recall the behaviour of these processes. $Clock \xrightarrow{\text{tick}} Cl_i$ and $Clock' \xrightarrow{\text{tick}} Cl_i$, for any i. However it is also the case that $Clock' \xrightarrow{\text{tick}} Cl$ and $Cl \xrightarrow{\text{tick}} Cl$. Player I's winning strategy consists of making an initial ν move. She paints $Clock'$ and Cl with the colour C_1. Player II must respond by painting $Clock$ and a subset $\mathcal{E} \subseteq \{Cl_i : i \geq 0\}$ the colour C_1. If $\mathcal{E}$ is nonempty then player I chooses the least member of it (with respect to i), and otherwise she chooses $Clock$. Player II must now choose either $Clock'$ or Cl, and either way she will lose at the next step because player I will play a [tick] move, either $Clock' \xrightarrow{\text{tick}} Cl$ or $Cl \xrightarrow{\text{tick}} Cl$, and player II is either stuck or unable to avoid condition 3 for a player I win. $\square$

The main theorem is the following which generalizes Fact 2 of section 2.

Theorem 1 $E \sim_n^k F$ iff $\forall \Phi \in \mu M_n^k. E \models_\nu \Phi$ iff $F \models_\nu \Phi$.

The proof of this result is presented in section 6, where game playing has to be extended to cope with open formulas to provide an inductive mechanism. It shows that there is an exact correspondence between game playing of length (k, n) and having the same properties in μM_n^k. A corollary (using known results [16]) is:

Fact 1 For each k and n, $\sim \subset \sim_n^k$.

---

[2]The asymmetry here between E's and F's colours is because negated variables are not allowed in the logic

We hope that Theorem 1 can be used it to provide a better understanding of how μM formulas express properties. It is possible to define for each formula Φ a signature which represents the sequences of possible moves in a game play. To understand the expressive power of Φ we need only examine those game plays that belong to its signature. This may offer a means for defining filtrations for modal mu-calulus. We hope that these games can be articulated on a machine on small processes and we look forward to examining the feasibility of implementing them. We also hope that Theorem 1 may offer deeper insight into the logical role of fixed points, and the contrast between them and second-order quantifiers. In the next section we define second-order propositional modal logic for this purpose.

An original motivation for this work on games is the issue of fixed point hierarchies. For each k we can define the set $\mu M^k = \bigcup \{\mu M_n^k : n \geq 0\}$. Is there a hierarchy of definability? For each $k \geq 1$ is there a formula $\Phi \in \mu M^k$ such that for all $\Psi \in \mu M^{k-1}$, Φ is not equivalent to Ψ?[3] Using Theorem 1 this reduces to questions about game equivalences (which appear to offer a finer analysis than automata, see [2, 11]). The hierarchy question is more interesting when k in μM^k is alternation depth, instead of fixed point depth[4]. Very recently Bradfield has shown that there is a full alternation depth hierarchy using methods from descriptive set theory [5].

5 Second-order propositional modal logic

We define second-order propositional modal logic, $2M$, as an extension of modal mu-calculus, as follows:

$$\Phi ::= \text{tt} \mid Z \mid \neg\Phi \mid \Phi_1 \wedge \Phi_2 \mid [a]\Phi \mid \Box\Phi \mid \forall Z.\Phi$$

The modality $\Box$ is the reflexive and transitive closure of the family of modalities $[a]$, $a \in \mathcal{A}$, and is included so that fixed points are definable within $2M$: this proposal for $2M$ is due to Howard Barringer. Negation is included explicitly, and we assume the expected derived operators: $\text{ff} \stackrel{\text{def}}{=} \neg\text{tt}$, $\Phi_1 \vee \Phi_2 \stackrel{\text{def}}{=} \neg(\neg\Phi_1 \wedge \neg\Phi_2)$, $\Phi_1 \rightarrow \Phi_2 \stackrel{\text{def}}{=} \neg\Phi_1 \vee \Phi_2$, $\langle a\rangle\Phi \stackrel{\text{def}}{=} \neg[a]\neg\Phi$, $\Diamond\Phi \stackrel{\text{def}}{=} \neg\Box\neg\Phi$, and $\exists Z.\Phi \stackrel{\text{def}}{=} \neg\forall Z.\neg\Phi$.

As with modal mu-calculus we define when a process E has a property Φ relative to $\mathcal{V}$, written $E \models_{\mathcal{V}} \Phi$, where $\mathcal{V}$ is a valuation. The semantic clauses for tt, Z, $\wedge$ and $[a]$ are as in section 3. The new clauses are:

---

[3]For instance, example 1 above shows that μM^1 is more expressive than μM^0.

[4]Preliminary work suggests it is possible to characterize μM_n^k in terms of games when k is alternation depth, but so far these games are very inelegant.

$\langle a \rangle$:   If $l < n$ then player I chooses a transition $E_i \xrightarrow{a} E_{i+1}$, and then player II chooses a transition with the same label $F_i \xrightarrow{a} F_{i+1}$.

$[a]$:   If $l < n$ then player I chooses a transition $F_i \xrightarrow{a} F_{i+1}$, and then player II chooses a transition with the same label $E_i \xrightarrow{a} E_{i+1}$.

$\Diamond$:   If $q < p$ then player I chooses $E_{i+1} \in \mathcal{P}(E_i)$, and then player II chooses $F_{i+1} \in \mathcal{P}(F_i)$.

$\Box$:   If $q < p$ then player I chooses $F_{i+1} \in \mathcal{P}(F_i)$, and then player II chooses $E_{i+1} \in \mathcal{P}(E_i)$.

$\exists$:   If $j < k$ then player I paints a subset of $\mathcal{P}(E_i)$ the colour $\mathcal{C}_{j+1}$, and then player II paints a subset of $\mathcal{P}(F_i)$ the colour $\mathcal{C}_{j+1}$.

$\forall$:   If $j < k$ then player I paints a subset of $\mathcal{P}(F_i)$ the colour $\mathcal{C}_{j+1}$, and then player II paints a subset of $\mathcal{P}(E_i)$ the colour $\mathcal{C}_{j+1}$.

FIGURE 4. Second-order game moves

$$
\begin{aligned}
E &\models_V \neg \Phi & \text{iff} && E &\not\models_V \Phi \\
E &\models_V \Box \Phi & \text{iff} && \forall F &\in \mathcal{P}(E). \ F \models_V \Phi \\
E &\models_V \forall Z.\Phi & \text{iff} && \forall \mathcal{E} &\subseteq \mathcal{P}(E). \ E \models_{V[\mathcal{E}/Z]} \Phi
\end{aligned}
$$

Notice that $\Box$ is definable in μM: assuming Z is not free in Φ, the formula $\Box \Phi$ is $\nu Z. \ \Phi \wedge \bigwedge_{a \in \mathcal{A}} [a] Z$. The operator $\forall Z$ is a set quantifier, ranging over subsets of $\mathcal{P}(E)$.

There is a game theoretic characterization of $2M$, which we briefly describe. Let $2M_{n,p}^k$ be the set of closed formulas whose modal depth with respect to $[a]$ modalities is n, and whose modal depth with respect to $\Box$ is p, and whose quantifier depth is k. A play of the game $\mathcal{G}_{n,p}^k(E_0, F_0)$ is a finite sequence of pairs $(E_0, F_0) \dots (E_m, F_m)$ whose length m is at most $k + n + p$. Again we assume k distinct colours $\mathcal{C}_1, \dots, \mathcal{C}_k$. There are three kinds of moves, the $\langle a \rangle$ and $[a]$ moves as in figure 2, the $\Diamond$ and $\Box$ moves, and the $\exists$ and $\forall$ moves. If part of a play is $(E_0, F_0) \dots (E_i, F_i)$ with $i < k+n+p$, and the number of $\langle a \rangle$, $[a]$ moves so far is l, and the number of quantifier moves is j, and the number of $\Diamond$, $\Box$ moves is q, then player I initiates the next move from those in figure 4. These moves are somewhat simpler than for the fixed point games[5]. A play of $\mathcal{G}_{n,p}^k(E, F)$ involves at most k quanti-

---

[5]Notice that the fixed point moves can almost be built from $2M$ moves: for example, the ν move is almost a $\exists$ move followed by a $\Box$ move.

Player I wins

1. If $l < n$ and $E_i \xrightarrow{a} E'$ but $\neg \exists F'. F_i \xrightarrow{a} F'$.
2. If $l < n$ and $F_i \xrightarrow{a} F'$ but $\neg \exists E'. E_i \xrightarrow{a} E'$.
3. If E_i is coloured $C_h, h \leq j$, and F_i is not coloured C_h.
4. If F_i is coloured $C_h, h \leq j$, and E_i is not coloured C_h.

Player II wins

1. If E_i and F_i are both deadlocked and the conditions 3 and 4 above both fail to hold.
2. If the play has ended, $l = n$, $j = k, q = p$, and conditions 3 and 4 above both fail to hold.

FIGURE 5. Winning conditions

fier moves, and n and p of the respective modal moves. The conditions for winning are given in figure 5 where we assume that $(E_0, F_0) \ldots (E_i, F_i)$ is (part of) a play with $l \langle a \rangle$, $[a]$ moves, $q \diamond$, $\square$ moves, and j quantifier moves. Notice the extra condition for a player I win, because in $2M$ quantification is permitted over negated variables.

E and F are (k, n, p)-game equivalent, written as $E \sim_{n,p}^k F$ if player II has a winning strategy for $\mathcal{G}_{n,p}^k(E, F)$. The following result, as with Theorem 1 of section 4, generalizes Fact 2 of section 2.

Theorem 1 $E \sim_{n,p}^k F$ iff $\forall \Phi \in 2M_{n,p}^k. E \models_V \Phi$ iff $F \models_V \Phi$.

The proof of this result follows closely that of the proof of Theorem 1 of section 4, presented in the next section.

An important question is what the relationship is between closed formulas of μM and $2M$, with respect to particular families of models. Within $2M$ we can define 3-colourability on finite connected undirected graphs. Consider such a graph. If there is an edge between two vertices E and F let $E \xrightarrow{a} F$ and $F \xrightarrow{a} E$. So in this case $\mathcal{A} = \{a\}$, and 3-colourability is given by:

$$\exists X. \exists Y. \exists Z. (\Phi \wedge \square((X \to [a]\neg X) \wedge (Y \to [a]\neg Y) \wedge (Z \to [a]\neg Z)))$$

where Φ, which says that every vertex has a unique colour, is

$$\square((X \wedge \neg Y \wedge \neg Z) \vee (Y \wedge \neg Z \wedge \neg X) \vee (Z \wedge \neg X \wedge \neg Y))$$

In contrast, modal mu-calculus can only express P graph properties (this follows from [10]).

First we have

Proposition 1 μM is a sublogic of $2M$.

Proof: There is a straightforward translation of μM into $2M$. Let Tr be this translation. The important cases are the fixed points: $\mathrm{Tr}(\nu Z.\,\Phi) = \exists Z.(Z \wedge \Box(Z \to \mathrm{Tr}(\Phi)))$ and $\mathrm{Tr}(\mu Z.\,\Phi) = \forall Z.(\Box(\mathrm{Tr}(\Phi) \to Z) \to Z)$. $\quad\Box$

When models are restricted to binary (or n-ary, $n \geq 1$) trees, the closed formulas of $2M$ are translatable into μM. This follows because μM is then equi-expressive to tree automata [7], and $2M$ is easily codable into $S2S$. However this is not the case for processes, as pointed out by Perdita Stevens. $2M$ formulas can distinguish between bisimilar processes which μM formulas are unable to do.

6 Proof of the main theorem

In this section we prove Theorem 1 of section 4, that E and F are (k, n)-game equivalent iff they have the same μM_n^k properties. (The proof of Theorem 1 of the previous section has a similar structure.) To prove this result inductively we need to understand *open* formulas of modal mu-calculus. Therefore we let $\mu M_n^k(X_1, \ldots, X_m)$ be the set of modal mu-calculus formulas with fixed point depth k and modal depth n which also may contain occurrences of any free variable X_i, for $1 \leq i \leq m$. Because $\mathcal{A}$ is finite each $\mu M_n^k(X_1, \ldots, X_m)$ is finite up to logical equivalence.

Proposition 1 *For each k, n and m the set $\mu M_n^k(X_1, \ldots, X_m)$ is finite up to logical equivalence.*

Proof: A straightforward induction on $k + n$. $\quad\Box$

We generalize the game $\mathcal{G}_n^k(E_0, F_0)$ to $\mathcal{G}_n^k(E_0, \overline{U}_i, F_0, \overline{V}_i)$ where $\overline{U}_i$ is a sequence of sets of processes $U_1, \ldots U_m$ and $\overline{V}_i$ is a similar sequence $V_1, \ldots V_m$. The colours for the generalized game are $\mathcal{C}_1, \ldots, \mathcal{C}_m, \ldots, \mathcal{C}_{m+k}$. The colours $\mathcal{C}_1, \ldots, \mathcal{C}_m$ are in use at the start of the game, and vertices U_i and V_i are coloured $\mathcal{C}_i$. The game is played as before (with k fixed point moves and n modal moves) but with $\mathcal{C}_{m+1}$ as the initial available colour. The winning conditions are as before: note however that condition 3 for player I's win extends to the colours in use at the start of play.

Theorem 1 *Player II has a winning strategy for $\mathcal{G}_n^k(E, \overline{U}_i, F, \overline{V}_i)$ iff $\forall \Phi \in \mu M_n^k(X_1, \ldots X_m)$. if $E \models_{\mathcal{V}[\overline{U}_i/\overline{X}_i]} \Phi$ then $F \models_{\mathcal{V}[\overline{V}_i/\overline{X}_i]} \Phi$.*

Proof: Suppose player II has a winning strategy for $\mathcal{G}_n^k(E_0, \overline{U}_i, F_0, \overline{V}_i)$. By induction on $k + n$ we show $\forall \Phi \in \mu M_n^k(X_1, \ldots X_m)$. if $E \models_{\mathcal{V}[\overline{U}_i/\overline{X}_i]} \Phi$ then $F \models_{\mathcal{V}[\overline{V}_i/\overline{X}_i]} \Phi$. The base case is when $k + n = 0$. So Φ is a boolean combination of tt, ff, and the variables X_j, $1 \leq j \leq m$. As player II has a winning strategy, we know that for each such variable X_j, if $E \models_{\mathcal{V}[\overline{U}_i/\overline{X}_i]} X_j$ then $F \models_{\mathcal{V}[\overline{V}_i/\overline{X}_i]} X_j$ (for otherwise player I would win by the winning condition 3). So the result follows. For the general case, assume it holds for

$k + n \leq l$. Assume that $k + n = l + 1$. We proceed by subinduction on Φ. If Φ is tt or ff then it is clear. If it is X_j then the proof is as in the base case. The cases $\Phi_1 \wedge \Phi_2$ and $\Phi_1 \vee \Phi_2$ are routine. Suppose Φ is $[a]\Psi$, and $E \models_{\mathcal{V}[\overline{U}_i/\overline{X}_i]} \Phi$. If E is unable to perform a then, as player II has a winning strategy, F is also unable to do an a and so $F \models_{\mathcal{V}[\overline{V}_i/\overline{X}_i]} \Phi$. Assume that E has an a transition. Consider any transition $F \xrightarrow{a} F'$ (and there is at least one otherwise player I would win the game). Let player I choose this transition as her move which is a $[a]$ move. Player II must respond with $E \xrightarrow{a} E'$ for some E' in such a way that player II has a winning strategy for $\mathcal{G}_{n-1}^k(E', \overline{U}_i, F', \overline{V}_i)$. By the induction hypothesis, as $k + (n - 1) = l$, $\forall \Phi \in \mu M_{n-1}^k(X_1, \ldots X_m)$. if $E \models_{\mathcal{V}[\overline{U}_i/\overline{X}_i]} \Phi$ then $F \models_{\mathcal{V}[\overline{V}_i/\overline{X}_i]} \Phi$. The formula Ψ is in $\mu M_{n-1}^k(X_1, \ldots X_m)$, and $E' \models_{\mathcal{V}[\overline{U}_i/\overline{X}_i]} \Psi$ and so $F' \models_{\mathcal{V}[\overline{V}_i/\overline{X}_i]} \Psi$. Hence for each F' such that $F \xrightarrow{a} F'$, $F' \models_{\mathcal{V}[\overline{V}_i/\overline{X}_i]} \Psi$, and therefore $F \models_{\mathcal{V}[\overline{V}_i/\overline{X}_i]} [a]\Psi$. The case Φ is $\langle a \rangle \Psi$ is similar. Next suppose Φ is $\nu Z. \Psi$. As $E \models_{\mathcal{V}[\overline{U}_i/\overline{X}_i]} \nu Z. \Psi$, therefore $\exists \mathcal{E} \subseteq \mathcal{P}(E). E \in \mathcal{E}$ and $\forall E' \in \mathcal{E}. E' \models_{\mathcal{V}[\overline{U}_i/\overline{X}_i][\mathcal{E}/Z]} \Psi$. Consider the game play where player I makes a ν move and colours $\mathcal{E}$ (containing E) with the next available colour $\mathcal{C}_{m+1}$. As player II has a winning strategy she can respond by colouring a set $\mathcal{F}$ (containing F) with $\mathcal{C}_{m+1}$ in such a way that for any choice $F' \in \mathcal{F}$ there is an $E' \in \mathcal{E}$ such that player II has a winning strategy for the game $\mathcal{G}_n^{k-1}(E', \overline{U}_i\mathcal{E}, F', \overline{V}_i\mathcal{F})$. Via the induction hypothesis, it follows that $\forall F' \in \mathcal{F}. F' \models_{\mathcal{V}[\overline{V}_i/\overline{X}_i][\mathcal{F}/Z]} \Psi$, and as $F \in \mathcal{F}$, it follows by the semantic clause that $F \models_{\mathcal{V}[\overline{V}_i/\overline{X}_i]} \nu Z. \Psi$ as required. The final case Φ is $\mu Z. \Psi$ is similar.

For the other half of the theorem, suppose that $\forall \Phi \in \mu M_n^k(X_1, \ldots X_m)$. if $E \models_{\mathcal{V}[\overline{U}_i/\overline{X}_i]} \Phi$ then $F \models_{\mathcal{V}[\overline{V}_i/\overline{X}_i]} \Phi$. We show that player II has a winning strategy for $\mathcal{G}_n^k(E, \overline{U}_i, F, \overline{V}_i)$. It is in this half of the proof that we appeal to the restriction that $\mathcal{A}$ is a finite set. Again the proof is by induction on $k + n$. The base case is $k + n = 0$. Player I can only win if E is coloured $\mathcal{C}_j$ and F is not. But this contradicts that if $E \models_{\mathcal{V}[\overline{U}_i/\overline{X}_i]} X_j$ then $F \models_{\mathcal{V}[\overline{V}_i/\overline{X}_i]} X_j$. Suppose it holds for $k + n \leq l$. Consider the game where $k + n = l + 1$ and assume that player I has a winning strategy. There are four cases according to the initial move that player I makes under her winning strategy. First, is a $\langle a \rangle$ move, and so $n \geq 1$. Suppose player I chooses $E \xrightarrow{a} E'$. If there are no available transitions from F then there is a contradiction, as $E \models_{\mathcal{V}[\overline{U}_i/\overline{X}_i]} \langle a \rangle tt$ and $F \not\models_{\mathcal{V}[\overline{V}_i/\overline{X}_i]} \langle a \rangle tt$ (and as $n \geq 1$, $\langle a \rangle tt \in \mu M_n^k(X_1, \ldots X_m)$). Otherwise assume that $\{F' : F \xrightarrow{a} F'\} = \{F_1, \ldots\}$. We know that player I can win each game $\mathcal{G}_{n-1}^k(E', \overline{U}_i, F_i, \overline{V}_i)$. By the induction hypothesis there are formulas $\Phi_1, \ldots \in \mu M_{n-1}^k(X_1, \ldots X_m)$ such that $E' \models_{\mathcal{V}[\overline{U}_i/\overline{X}_i]} \Phi_l$ and $F_l \not\models_{\mathcal{V}[\overline{V}_i/\overline{X}_i]} \Phi_l$. However there are only finitely many different $\mu M_{n-1}^k(X_1, \ldots X_m)$ formulas (up to logical equivalence). So $E' \models_{\mathcal{V}[\overline{U}_i/\overline{X}_i]} \bigwedge \Phi_l$ and $F_l \not\models_{\mathcal{V}[\overline{V}_i/\overline{X}_i]} \bigwedge \Phi_l$ and $\bigwedge \Phi_l \in \mu M_{n-1}^k(X_1, \ldots X_m)$.

But then $E \models_{\mathcal{V}[\overline{U}_i/\overline{X}_i]} \langle a \rangle \bigwedge \Phi_l$ and $F \not\models_{\mathcal{V}[\overline{V}_i/\overline{X}_i]} \langle a \rangle \bigwedge \Phi_l$ where $\langle a \rangle \bigwedge \Phi_l$ $\in \mu M_n^k(X_1, \ldots X_m)$ which is a contradiction. So player I cannot have a winning strategy with initial $\langle a \rangle$ move. The second case, an initial $[a]$ move, is similar. The third case is that player I chooses a ν move, so $k \geq 1$, and she colours $\mathcal{E} \subseteq \mathcal{P}(E)$ (containing E) with $\mathcal{C}_{m+1}$ For every colouring choice for player II $\mathcal{F}_1, \ldots$ with $F \in \mathcal{F}_l$ player I can choose $F_l \in \mathcal{F}_l$ such that for every choice by player II of $E_{lj} \in \mathcal{E}$, player I has a winning strategy for $\mathcal{G}_n^{k-1}(E_{lj}, \overline{U}_i \mathcal{E}, F_l, \overline{V}_i \mathcal{F}_l)$. Hence by the induction hypothesis there are formulas $\Phi_{l1}, \Phi_{l2}, \ldots$ for the choice by player I of $F_l \in \mathcal{F}_l$ such that $E_{lj} \models_{\mathcal{V}[\overline{U}_i/\overline{X}_i][\mathcal{E}/Z]} \Phi_{lj}$ and $F_l \not\models_{\mathcal{V}[\overline{V}_i/\overline{X}_i][\mathcal{F}_l/Z]} \Phi_{lj}$. Each $\Phi_{lj} \in \mu M_n^{k-1}(X_1, \ldots X_m, Z)$. There are only finitely many such formulas up to equivalence. Hence, for all $E \in \mathcal{E}$, $E \models_{\mathcal{V}[\overline{U}_i/\overline{X}_i][\mathcal{E}/Z]} \bigwedge_l (\bigvee_j \Phi_{lj})$, and so, as $E \in \mathcal{E}$, $E \models_{\mathcal{V}[\overline{U}_i/\overline{X}_i]} \nu Z. \bigwedge_l (\bigvee_j \Phi_{lj})$, and by definition we know that $F \not\models_{\mathcal{V}[\overline{V}_i/\overline{X}_i]} \nu Z. \bigwedge_l (\bigvee_j \Phi_{lj})$ even though $\nu Z. \bigwedge_l (\bigvee_j \Phi_{lj}) \in \mu M_n^k(X_1, \ldots X_m)$. This contradicts that player I has a winning strategy with an initial ν move. The final case is when player I makes a μ move, and the argument is similar. $\square$

Theorem 1 of section 4 is a corollary of this result, in the case when $m = 0$, and using the observation that closed formulas of μM are closed under negation.

Acknowledgement: Thanks to Faron Moller and Perdita Stevens for comments on an earlier draft.

7 REFERENCES

[1] Abramsky, S., and Jagadeesan, R. (1994). Games and full completeness for multiplicative linear logic. *Journal of Symbolic Logic*, **59**, 543-574.

[2] Arnold, A., and Niwinski, D. (1990). Fixed point characterization of Büchi automata on infinite trees. *J. Inf. Process. Cybern.*, **EIK 26**, 451-459.

[3] Baeten, J. and Weijland, W. (1990). *Process Algebra*. Cambridge Tracts in Theoretical Computer Science, 18.

[4] Bosse, U. (1992). An "Ehrenfeucht-Fraïssé game" for fixpoint and stratified fixpoint logic. *Lecture Notes in Computer Science*, **702**, 100-114.

[5] Bradfield, J. (1995). The modal mu-calculus alternation hierarchy is strict. *Submitted for publication*.

[6] Condon, A. (1992). The complexity of stochastic games. *Information and Computation*, **96**, 203-224.

[7] Emerson, E., and Jutla, C. (1988). The complexity of tree automata and logics of programs. Extended version from FOCS '88.

[8] Fagin, R., Stockmeyer, L., and Vardi, M. (1995). On monadic NP vs monadic co-NP. *Information and Computation*, **120**, 78-92.

[9] Hodges, W. (1993). *Model Theory*. Cambridge University Press.

[10] Immermann, N. (1986). Relational queries computable in polynomial time. *Information and Control*, **68**, 86-104.

[11] Kaivola, R. (1995). On modal mu-calculus and Büchi tree automata. *Information Processing Letters*, **54**, 17-22.

[12] Kozen, D. (1983). Results on the propositional mu-calculus. *Theoretical Computer Science*, **27**, 333-354.

[13] Milner, R. (1989). *Communication and Concurrency*. Prentice Hall.

[14] Moschovakis, Y. (1989). A game theoretic modelling of concurrency. *Procs. 4th IEEE Symposium on Logic in Computer Science*.

[15] Nielsen, M. and Clausen, C. (1994). Bisimulations, games and logic. *Lecture Notes in Computer Science*, **812**, 289-306.

[16] Stirling, C. (1993). Modal and temporal logics for processes. *Notes for Summer School in Logical Methods in Concurrency*. Department of Computer Science, Aarhus University.

[17] Stirling, C. (1995). Local model checking games. *Lecture Notes in Computer Science*, **962**, 1-11.

[18] Thomas, W. (1993). On the Ehrenfeucht-Fraïssé game in theoretical computer science. *Lecture Notes in Computer Science*, **668**.

Generic System Support for Deductive Program Development

Abdelwaheb Ayari*
David A. Basin*

ABSTRACT We report on a case study in using logical frameworks to support the formalization of programming calculi and their application to deduction-based program synthesis. Within a conservative extension of higher-order logic implemented in the Isabelle system, we derived rules for program development that can simulate those of the deductive tableau proposed by Manna and Waldinger. We have used the resulting theory to synthesize a library of verified programs, focusing on sorting algorithms. Our experience suggests that the methodology we propose is well suited both to implement and use programming calculi, extend them, partially automate them, and even formally reason about their correctness.

1 Introduction

Over the last few decades, a variety of methodologies for deductive software synthesis, transformation, and refinement from specification have been suggested, e.g., [4, 5, 8, 9, 12]. Our research investigates general frameworks that support such program development formalisms. That is, how can a framework be used to embed calculi in correctness preserving ways, be applied to the construction of programs hand in hand with their correctness proofs (e.g., synthesis as opposed to verification), simplify and extend previously proposed program development formalisms, and partially or even totally automate program construction. We are currently exploring these questions in the context of calculi for functional program development (reported here), logic programs [1, 3] and circuit synthesis. This work includes support for automated program construction [10, 11].

In this report we focus on the use of a formal metatheory to support the construction of proven correct functional programs. Our work is based on a methodology and calculus, the *deductive tableau system*, of Manna and Waldinger [12], which is a kind of first-order proof system proposed for

---

*Max-Planck-Institut für Informatik, Im Stadtwald, D-66123, Saarbrücken, Germany. Email: {abdu, basin}@mpi-sb.mpg.de

the synthesis of functional programs. Using the Isabelle system, a logical framework developed by Paulson [13], we have recast the deductive tableau as a formal theory that conservatively extends higher-order logic. This is done by formally deriving (as opposed to axiomatizing) proof rules that can simulate deductive tableau derivations. Moreover, deductive tableau proofs construct witnessing functions for proofs of ∀/∃ formulae and, in our work, this is simulated by using higher-order metavariables to stand-in for these witnessing functions; these variables are incrementally instantiated to programs by applying proof rules using higher-order resolution. Resolution, controlled by the interactive or tactic (these are programs which construct proofs) guided application of proof rules, gives us a means not only to verify programs, but also to interactively construct them during proof.

Although our implementation uses a general purpose logical framework that supports a different kind of proof construction (natural deduction) than the deductive tableau, we can use our theory to simulate program derivations possible in the deductive tableau setting. However, because our theory is based on full higher-order logic and Isabelle supports operations on metavariables, we have considerably more flexibility in program development than the original deductive tableau framework offers. For example, we can perform splitting operations on subgoals that are not admitted in Manna and Waldinger's setting (they use nonclausal resolution and simplification to, essentially, operate under positively occurring conjunctions or negatively occurring disjunctions). Another example is that the use of higher-order logic and the Isabelle inductive data-type package allows us to construct recursive programs using well-founded induction where we use resolution to construct well-founded orderings during proofs (this arises in showing the termination of synthesized functions). This leads to a more general approach to induction than is possible in the deductive tableau where inductions are restricted to fixed collections of axiomatized orders. Moreover we gain the flexibility to develop programs first and show their termination later.

Our practical experience with our theory has been positive. Construction of our initial Isabelle theory (definitions, derivation of rules, and supporting tactics) directly utilized the distributed Isabelle HOL theory and standard tactics and, as a result, took only a few days; afterwards, we could immediately apply it to problems of interest. We have reconstructed many of Manna and Waldinger's published examples, and in particular we have synthesized a variety of standard sorting algorithms (e.g., quicksort, merge sort, and insertion sort). All proofs have been formally carried out in Isabelle; full machine checked proofs scripts may be found in [2]. This should be contrasted to the work of Manna and Waldinger; the tableaux in their published papers are generated by hand, since, for many years, they lacked an implementation.

More generally, our work suggests the potential of using frameworks like Isabelle for building prototype implementations and carrying out experiments with such deduction-based development formalisms. The use of a formal metalogic and tactic based prover like Isabelle helps to conceptually clarify the nature of the formalism under consideration (e.g., deductive tableau) since its formalization naturally stratifies into layers: the underlying logic, the derived rules, and the tactics which implement strategies for rule application and program development. Moreover the use of a framework offers certain advantages over a customized implementation; for example, we can formally establish the correctness of proof rules by deriving them. Also, by building our theories on top of standard logics, we can directly benefit from work on decision procedures, rewriting, and other automation for constructing proofs in these logics.

The remainder of this paper is organized as follows. In sections 2 and 3 we briefly review Isabelle and the deductive tableau system. Next, in section 4 we show how the deductive tableau can be interpreted in an Isabelle theory. That is, how each rule of the deductive tableau corresponds to a combination of derived rules and tactics in Isabelle. In section 5 we describe program development by presenting parts of a formal development of quicksort. In section 6 we draw conclusions.

2 Isabelle

Our work requires a theorem prover that implements higher-order logic and supports higher-order unification. We have chosen the Isabelle logical framework [13] although other frameworks such as Pfenning's ELF [14] would also suffice. Isabelle is an interactive theorem prover which serves as a logical framework; this means that its logic is a metalogic in which object logics (e.g., first-order logic, set theory, etc.) are encoded. Isabelle's metalogic is a minimal higher-order logic supporting polymorphic typing. Object logics are encoded by declaring their signature and proof rules. Afterwards, proofs are interactively constructed by applying rules using higher-order resolution. Proof construction may be automated by writing tactics to apply decision procedures, simplifiers, and other kinds of proof construction strategies.

Isabelle's metalogic is based on the universal/implicational fragment of higher-order logic. Universal quantification in the metalogic is represented by !! and implication by ==> . Isabelle manipulates *rules* which are objects of the form

$$[|\phi_1; \ldots; \phi_n|] ==> \phi,$$

where the notation $[|\phi_1; \ldots; \phi_n|] ==> \phi$ is shorthand for the iterated implication $\phi_1 ==> \ldots ==> (\phi_n ==> \phi)$. A rule can also be viewed as a proof-state, for the purposes of top-down proof construction, where ϕ is the goal to be established and the ϕ_i represent the subgoals to be proven. Under this view an initial proof state has the form $\phi ==> \phi$, i.e., it has one subgoal, namely ϕ. The final proof state *is itself* the desired theorem ϕ.

Proof construction in Isabelle is based on higher-order resolution, which is roughly analogous to resolution in Prolog. That is, given a proof state with subgoal ψ and a rule like the one above, then we higher-order unify ϕ with ψ. If this succeeds, then unification yields a substitution σ and the proof state is updated by applying σ to it, replacing ψ with the subgoals $\sigma(\phi_1), \ldots, \sigma(\phi_n)$. Note that since unification is used to apply rules, the proof state itself may contain metavariables. We will show that this supports program transformation and synthesis during proof.

Finally, note that Isabelle supports the hierarchical development of logics and theories and a number of such theories come distributed with the system, along with supporting tactics. For our work we used higher-order logic extended with a theory of inductively defined data-types (in which standard types like lists were defined) and well-founded induction.

3 Deductive Tableau System

Here we give a brief overview of the deductive tableau system. Full details may be found in [12].

A tableau proof starts with a specification of the form $\forall x.\ \exists z.\ Q(x, z)$, where Q is a first-order formula. Such a specification states that for each input x there is an output z satisfying the formula $Q(x, z)$ called the *input-output relation.*[1] A specification is turned into an *initial tableau* by skolemization to $Q(a, f(a))$, where a is an eigenvariable and f is a skolem function which denotes the desired program. Then the term $f(a)$, occurring in the goal $Q(a, f(a))$, is replaced with a new variable, say z, which yields the following initial tableau.

Assertions	Goals	Outputs
		$f(a)$
	$Q(a, z)$	z

This tableau expresses the goal that $Q(a, z)$ is to be proven in some underlying theory, e.g., a first-order theory of lists. Furthermore, the assertion column of the tableau can be augmented with formulae which are known to be valid in the theory. The desired program has, at this stage, the form $f(a) = z$ where the *output variable* z represents the current body of the function f.

---

[1] In general, there may be more than one universally quantified input variable and existentially quantified output variable. However, it will simplify discussion and notation to consider only one of each. Our implementation supports the general case.

A proof is constructed by applying deduction rules which add new rows to the tableau. Each step may incrementally instantiate an output variable. A deduction is successful when the truth value *false* (respectively *true*) appears in the column *assertions* (respectively *goals*). If t is the term appearing in the output column of this final row, then the desired program is $f(a) = t$, where t may depend on a. There are syntactic side conditions (involving so called *primitive expressions*) which guarantee that t is built in an executable way.

Note that, if we ignore the output columns, then the deductive tableau system simply constitutes a calculus for proving the validity of certain first-order sentences in a given theory. Moreover, there is a close relationship between deductive tableau and standard sequent calculi and semantic tableau (c.f. [7]): formulae in the goal column correspond to *goal formulae* on the right-hand side of the sequent, and those in the assertion column correspond to *hypothesis formulae* on the left-hand side of a sequent. So, for example, the conditions above for a successful deduction correspond to a sequent being provable when one of the hypotheses are false or goals are true. We will see though that the rules of the deductive tableau are different from standard sequent/tableau rules because they are based on a non-clausal resolution rule. Further, the deductive tableau system does not allow splitting tableaux; there are no rules that correspond to the sequent calculus rules for conjunction-introduction or disjunction-elimination, which cause branching in proofs.

Nonclausal Resolution

Formulae in different rows of a tableau are combined using nonclausal resolution: this allows simplification and other kinds of logical manipulation. Nonclausal resolution corresponds to a case analysis with simplification and it introduces a conditional term in the output entries. The deductive tableau system contains several such rules depending on whether formulae come from goal or assertion columns.

As an example, consider the following two rows:

$A[P]$		s
	$G[Q]$	t

In the first row $A[P]$ denotes the assertion A with a subformula P. In the second row $G[Q]$ denotes the goal G with a subformula Q. Nonclausal resolution, when applied to these rows, generates the new row

$\neg(A\theta[\mathit{false}]) \wedge G\theta[\mathit{true}]$	*if $P\theta$ then $t\theta$ else $s\theta$*

where θ is the most-general unifier of P and Q. The output entry is a conditional term built using the resolved rows' output entries. There are additional rules for resolution between two assumptions or two goals and other rules derivable from nonclausal resolution.

Induction Rule

Induction is used to develop recursive programs. To prove a goal $Q(a, f(a))$, for an arbitrary element a, we may introduce an *induction hypothesis* that states that the goal holds for all x strictly smaller than a with respect to a well-founded ordering $<_w$. The induction rule introduces an induction hypothesis as an assertion in the tableau.

$$\boxed{if\ (x <_w a)\ then\ Q(x, f(x))}$$

Note that the induction hypothesis contains occurrences of the function symbol f, which denotes the function that we are trying to compute. If the induction hypothesis is used in the proof, terms of the form $f(t)$ can be introduced in the output entries, yielding recursion. To apply induction, a user must choose a well-founded relation $<_w$, which is defined in the current theory, e.g., the *less-than* relation over natural numbers.

4 Interpretation in Isabelle

As discussed above, the deductive tableau is a first-order proof system. Although Isabelle contains a well-developed theory of first-order logic, we have chosen to model the deductive tableau system in an Isabelle formalization of higher-order logic. This gives us more power and flexibility in formalizing and reasoning about well-founded relations. In particular, it allows us to synthesize well-founded relations during proof, in a way analogous to how we synthesize programs.

To simulate deductive tableau it suffices to show how we mimic the initial tableau and application of the proof rules. For the initial tableau, one begins with a specification $\forall a.\ \exists z.\ spec(a, z)$, which specifies some program f. Slipping into Isabelle syntax, we begin our Isabelle proofs by typing

`?H --> ! a.spec(a,?f(a)) .`

We use **typewriter font** for Isabelle syntax. In Isabelle's HOL, the operator ! represents universal quantification, and --> implication.[2] Variables like f and H preceded by ? are metavariables, which can be instantiated by unification during resolution. We will call the metavariable ?H an *output metavariable*; we use it to represent the output column of the tableau where

---

[2]Remember that these are connectives in the declared object logic, and should not be confused with the connectives of Isabelle's metalogic.

the constructed function ?f is "accumulated". This output metavariable allows us not only to record in the proof-state the definition of the function ?f, but it also reflects the logical meaning of proof in a context extended by this definition: the specification follows under the definition of ?f. Our example in section 5 should make this clear. To enforce that output variables are only instantiated with formulae that represent executable programs, we, like in the deductive tableau, incorporate syntactic side conditions on proofs which are enforced by our tactics.

Subgoals play a role in our proofs analogous to subtableaux. Proofs proceed by refining subgoals until no more remain. We have derived rules which can be applied by tactics to simulate deductive tableau steps. Here we briefly discuss our rules corresponding to nonclausal resolution and induction.

Nonclausal Resolution

Nonclausal resolution allows subformulae from two rows to be unified and then replaced by the truth values *true* and *false* respectively; furthermore, its application builds conditional terms. In Isabelle, we define if(C,s,t) to be the term equal to s when C is equivalent to True and t otherwise. We may then derive the following rule which splits on the case C and its negation ~C.

[| ?C ==> ?P(?S); ?~C ==> ?P(?T) |] ==> ?P(if(?C,?S,?T))

This rule says that if we have some predicate ?P(x), then we can prove ?P(if(?C,?S,?T)), when we can prove ?C ==> ?P(?S) and ?~C ==> ?P(?T). Its application can simulate the nonclausal resolution rule of the previous section where ?C corresponds to the unifiable formulae P and Q and ?S and ?T are the output terms for the rows A[P] and G[Q].

Recall that Isabelle is a logical framework and rules are formulae in Isabelle's metalogic; the above case-split rule is not axiomatized, but instead is formally derived. The derivation is simple and consists of expanding the definition of if and propositional reasoning.

This derived rule can be applied for program synthesis and constructs a program containing an if-then statement. In particular, suppose we are synthesizing a program specified by Spec(x,?f(x)). Application of the above proof rule by higher-order resolution will unify ?P to Spec and ?f(x) to the function if(?C(x),?S(x),?T(x)). Instances for ?S(x) and ?T(x) (as well as ?C(x)) will be subsequently synthesized by proving the two subgoals which will correspond to Spec(x,?S(x)) and Spec(x,?T(x)). This use of rules for synthesis will become clearer in section 5.

Induction

The tableau induction rule adds induction hypotheses as assertions in the tableau proofs. We model this with a suitably formulated induction rule.

Isabelle's higher-order logic comes with a theory of relations and inductive definitions. With it, we can directly manipulate relations and reason about their well-foundedness. The well-foundedness of a relation ?r is defined as follows.

```
wf(?r) == !P.(!x.(!y. <y,x>:?r --> P(y)) --> P(x))--> (!x.P(x))
```

The notation `<y,x>:?r` is a proposition that states that the pair `<y,x>` belongs to the relation ?r.

From the definition of well-foundedness, it is a simple matter to formally derive the following well-founded induction rule.

```
[| !x. (!y. <y, x>:?r --> ?P(y)) --> ?P(x); wf(?r) |] ==> !x. ?P(x)
```

This rule formalizes the standard rule of noetherian induction over a well-founded ordering r. It says that to show ?P holds for every x we can show ?P(x) under the assumption of ?P(y) where y is less than x in the ordering ?r. The second assumption insists that ?r is well-founded.

We derive a specialization of this rule for constructing a recursive program ?f by well-founded induction.

```
[| !1. ?f(1) = ?fbody(1);
   !1. (!t. <t, 1>:?r --> ?Spec(t, ?f(t))) --> ?Spec(1,?fbody(1));
   wf(?r)
|] ==> !1. ?Spec(1, ?f(1))
```

We indicated above how the case-split rule is used to synthesize if-then branches. Similarly, the induction rule builds recursive programs. The conclusion ?Spec(1,?f(1)) is suitable for unifying against the translation (into our framework) of deductive tableau specifications. The additional assumption !1. ?f(1) = ?fbody(1) sets up a definition of ?f which can be instantiated during the subsequent proof. Applying the induction hypothesis instantiates ?fbody with a recursive call to ?f and, moreover, this call must be on some smaller argument in the well-founded order defined by ?r; hence this rule builds only terminating programs and ?r represents an ordering upon which recursive calls are smaller. Moreover, when we resolve with this rule, we are not required to give, up front, the ordering ?r; instead, just like with metavariables representing programs, we can incrementally synthesize this relation during subsequent proof steps.

Derived Rules from HOL

The above rules suffice to directly model deductive tableau derivations. Full details of the simulation are provided in [2] and it is proved there (Theorem 6, page 85) that with these rules and with tactics which apply them it is possible to simulate any deductive tableau derivation so that there is a direct correspondence between deductive tableau proof steps and proof steps in Isabelle and moreover the identical program is constructed.

But there is an important difference: in the Isabelle setting we are not constrained to use only the above proof rules and we can construct proofs, which synthesize programs, in ways that have no analog in the deductive tableau system. We can use standard proof rules and tactics for higher-order logic, as well as any derived rules, and this gives us considerable flexibility in constructing proofs. For example, given a goal formula which is a conjunction (or a hypothesis which is a disjunction) in the deductive tableau setting one cannot split the tableau to subtableaux corresponding to each conjunct (or disjunct). Instead one must use nonclausal resolution to perform simplification to true under the conjunctions (or to false under the disjunctions); this isn't very natural and leads to complicated formulae. In our setting, we can directly decompose conjunctions (or disjunctions) by applying the rule for conjunction introduction (or disjunction elimination). Another example of additional flexibility is using metavariables to delay giving well-founded orderings when applying the induction rule.

5 Development of Functional Programs

We have used our theory to develop in Isabelle a number of functional programs including many of Manna and Waldinger's published examples and, in particular, a number of sorting algorithms. Here we consider quicksort. Our entire proof required 23 interactive steps and full details may be found in [2] including: the entire proof script, the supporting theory, and the tactics used in assisting proof construction. In the following we provide some background and a few snapshots from our Isabelle session that illustrate case-splitting, induction, and reasoning about termination.

Sorting may be naturally specified as a relation between an input list and an output list, where the output is an ordered permutation of the input.

```
goal thy ?H --> (! l. perm(l, ?sort(l)) & ordered(?sort(l)))
```

In our formalization, l is of type list over a domain whose elements admit a total order $\leq$.[3] The theory we employ for our development comes with the Isabelle distribution: HOL augmented with a theory of inductive definitions in which lists are defined. It employs standard notation for lists; the empty list is represented by [], the symbol e denotes the append function, hd and tl are the head and tail functions.

Our definitions of the predicates **perm** and **ordered** are taken from Manna

---

[3]This is enforced through the use of type-classes; Isabelle suppresses display of this information.

and Waldinger's development, and formalize the standard permutation and ordered relation on lists.

```
perm([],[])
perm(l1@[u]@l2,t1@[u]@t2) = perm(l1@l2,t1@t2)
perm(l1,l2) --> !a. member(a, l1) = member(a,l2)
ordered([])
ordered([a])
ordered(Cons(a,Cons(b,t))) = (a <= b) & ordered(Cons(b,t))
```

After we enter the above goal, Isabelle responds with the goal to be proven (first line), and subgoals (in this case only 1, the initial goal) which must be proven to establish it:

```
?H --> (! l. perm(l, ?sort(l)) & ordered(?sort(l)))
1. ?H --> ! l. perm(l, ?sort(l)) & ordered(?sort(l))
```

Induction

Our first proof step is induction on l and is invoked by typing

```
by (INDTAC [("f","qsort")] 1);
```

This executes a tactic, INDTAC, which applies the induction schema given in section 4: after some preprocessing, this tactic uses higher-order unification to resolve the goal !1. perm(l, ?sort(l)) & ordered(?sort(l)) with !1. ?Spec(l, ?f(l)), which is the conclusion of the induction rule. Resolution succeeds with ?Spec(l, m) unified with perm(l, m) & ordered(m) and ?f(l) unified with sort(l), and it produces three new subgoals, corresponding to the three assumptions of the induction schema. However, INDTAC immediately discharges the first by unifying it with ?H. Hence, our output metavariable begins accumulating a recursive definition; this is precisely the role that ?H serves.[4] Our tactic also takes an argument which names the function being synthesized qsort. After all this, Isabelle responds with the new proof state:

```
(! l. qsort(l) = ?fbody(l)) & ?H1 -->
(! l. perm(l, qsort(l)) & ordered(qsort(l)))
 1. !!1. [| ?H1;
            ! t. <t, l> : ?r --> perm(t, qsort(t))
                                  & ordered(qsort(t)) |]
        ==> perm(l, ?fbody(l)) & ordered(?fbody(l))
 2. wf(?r)
```

---

[4]To allow the possibility of synthesizing multiple programs (as in quicksort, where we synthesize two additional auxiliary functions) the tactic firsts "duplicates" ?H yielding a new output variable ?H1. This is possible because if we have an hypothesis ?H then we can instantiate it with ?H & ?H1. Instantiation is performed by resolution with &-elimination and results in the new assumptions ?H and ?H1. Hence, we use derived rules to simulate proof under a growing context of definitions.

We are left with two subgoals to prove. The first says we must develop a program **?fbody** (the body of **qsort**) under the assumption that we have a program **qsort** which sorts all lists smaller (under **?r**) than 1. The second insists that **?r** is a well-founded order.

Case Split

Quicksort works by partitioning a non-empty list into those elements greater than and less than some element (usually the head of the list) and sorting the partitions recursively; empty lists are trivially sorted. This analysis requires a case split on whether 1 is empty or not. Hence, we resolve the first subgoal against the case split rule of section 4 and specify that splitting condition is 1 = []. Isabelle returns the proof state:

```
(! l. qsort(l) = if(l = [], ?S(l), ?T(hd(l), tl(l)))) & ?H1 -->
(! l. perm(l, qsort(l)) & ordered(qsort(l)))
  1. !!l. [| ?H1;
             ! t. <t, l> : ?r --> perm(t, qsort(t))
                                  & ordered(qsort(t));
             l = [] |] ==>
         perm(l, ?S(l)) & ordered(?S(l))
  2. !!l. [| ?H1;
             ! t. <t, l> : ?r --> perm(t, qsort(t))
                                  & ordered(qsort(t));
             l ~= [] |] ==>
         perm(l, ?T(hd(l), tl(l))) & ordered(?T(hd(l), tl(l)))
  3. wf(?r)
```

Resolution instantiated **?fbody** with a conditional term and the first subgoal has been replaced by two which construct terms for each case. The remaining subgoal, renumbered to 3, remains unchanged.

Recursive Step and Partitioning

Let us skip ahead 7 steps to see how the use of the induction hypothesis generates recursive programs.

```
(! l. qsort(l) =
        if(l = [], l,
           ?t1(hd(l), tl(l)) @ [hd(l)] @ ?t2(hd(l), tl(l))))
     & ?H1 -->
(! l. perm(l, qsort(l)) & ordered(qsort(l)))
  1. !!l. [| ?H1;
             ! t. <t, l> : ?r --> perm(t, qsort(t))
                                  & ordered(qsort(t));
             l ~= [] |] ==>
         perm(tl(l), ?l1(l) @ ?l2(l)) &
         le(hd(l), ?t2(hd(l), tl(l)))&gr(hd(l), ?t1(hd(l), tl(l)))
```

```
2. !!1. [| ?H1;
         ! t. <t, l> : ?r --> perm(t, qsort(t))
                             & ordered(qsort(t));
         l ~= [] |] ==>
    perm(?l1(1), ?t1(hd(1), tl(1)))&ordered(?t1(hd(1), tl(1)))
3. !!1. [| ?H1;
         ! t. <t, l> : ?r --> perm(t, qsort(t))
                             & ordered(qsort(t));
         l ~= [] |] ==>
    perm(?l2(1), ?t2(hd(1), tl(1)))&ordered(?t2(hd(1), tl(1)))
4. wf(?r)
```

The embryonic form of quicksort has taken shape. We have already solved
the previous subgoal 1 which corresponded to the l = [] case; we have
applied simplification which replaced ?S(1) with the empty list l. We then
simplified the l ~= [] case which resulted in the first 3 subgoals given
above. The first specifies that tl(1) can be decomposed into two lists ?l1(1)
and ?l2(1) and everything in the first list is less than or equal to hd(1)
(this is defined by the predicate le) and the second contains only elements
greater than hd(1) (stated by gr). The second and third subgoal state that
there are lists computed by ?t1 and ?t2, which are permutations of ?l1(1)
and ?l2(1), and are both sorted.

At this point, our generic sorting specification has been specialized into
a specification for quicksort. This is not by chance: In the previous steps
we used our "programmer's intuition" to interactively guide the derivation
towards this specialization by exploiting previously proven properties of
permutation and ordering. The situation in the deductive tableau setting
is analogous: synthesis means guiding the proof in a way that constructs
the desired program in the output column.

Subgoals 2 and 3 are particularly easy to solve; we direct Isabelle to unify
both with their induction hypotheses.

```
(! 1. qsort(1) =
    if(l = [], 1,
        qsort(?t(hd(1), tl(1)))@[hd(1)]@qsort(?ta(hd(1), tl(1)))))
    & ?H1 -->
(! 1. perm(1, qsort(1)) & ordered(qsort(1)))
 1. !!1. [| ?H1;
         ! t. <t, l> : ?r --> perm(t, qsort(t))
                             & ordered(qsort(t));
         l ~= [] |] ==>
    perm(tl(1), ?t(hd(1), tl(1)) @ ?ta(hd(1), tl(1))) &
    le(hd(1), ?ta(hd(1), tl(1))) & gr(hd(1), ?t(hd(1), tl(1)))
 2. !!1. [| ?H1; l ~= [] |] ==> <?t(hd(1), tl(1)), l> : ?r
 3. !!1. [| ?H1; l ~= [] |] ==> <?ta(hd(1), tl(1)), l> : ?r
 4. wf(?r)
```

As a result, **?t1** and **?t2** have been replaced by recursive calls to quicksort. However, subgoals 2 and 3 were not completely solved; there are residual proof obligations. We must later show that the function **?t** (in goal 2) and **?ta** (in goal 3) are applied to arguments "less" then **1** in the ordering **?r**, which must be well-founded if goal 4 is to be provable. In other words, we have used the induction hypothesis twice and in each case we must show that it was on smaller instances under the not yet specified ordering **?r**.

Auxiliary Synthesis and Termination

In the remaining proof we synthesize the functions for **?t** and **?ta** specified in subgoal 1; these are the functions which pick out elements in the tail of **1** which are less than or equal (or, in the case of **?ta**, greater than) the head of **1**. The instantiation of these functions is propagated to the remaining goals; for example, goal 2 becomes

```
!!1. [| 1 ~= [];
       ! x xa. lesseq(x, xa) =
         if(xa = [], xa, if(hd(xa) <= x,
            [hd(xa)] @ lesseq(x, tl(xa)), lesseq(x, tl(xa))))
     |] ==>  <lesseq(hd(1), tl(1)), 1> : ?r
```

and to prove this we must construct a relation **?r** which contains the pair **<lesseq(hd(1), tl(1)), 1>** for all non-empty **1**. Afterwards, we must show that this relation is well-founded (goal 4).

Our termination proofs exploits our use of higher-order logic. Relations are terms in higher-order logic, just like programs, and the explicit use of metavariables allows us to delay commitment to these relations when using the induction hypothesis and synthesize them later by resolution, just like programs. In this example, resolution instantiates **?r** with an ordering true when the first list contains fewer elements than the second, i.e., the relation **{<x, y> | length(x) < length(y)}**. This ordering explains in what sense arguments of recursive calls to quicksort are smaller.

This ordering is shown to be well-founded by construction. We have proven in our theory that certain relations are well-founded and that there are constructors for building new well-founded relations from given well-founded relations. For example, a well-founded relation **s** and a function **f** induce a well-founded relation containing all pairs **<f(x),f(y)>** in the relation **s**. Formally, we have shown that for any well-founded **s**, the relation denoted by **induced_rel(f,s)** is well-founded, where the new relation is defined as follows.

```
induced_rel(f, s) == {q. Ex x y.(q=<x ,y> & <f(x),f(y)>:s)}
```

Given this development, the above ordering is well-founded because we define it as **induced_rel(length, <)**.

Final Proof State

After termination of quicksort and synthesis of all auxiliary programs, the final proof state is the following.

```
[|! 1. qsort(1) =
       if(1 = [], 1,
          qsort(lesseq(hd(1), tl(1))) @ [hd(1)]
          @ qsort(greater(hd(1), tl(1))));
  ! x xa. greater(x, xa) =
       if(xa = [], xa,
          if(hd(xa) <= x, greater(x, tl(xa)),
                          [hd(xa)] @ greater(x, tl(xa))));
  ! x xa. lesseq(x, xa) =
       if(xa = [], xa,
          if(hd(xa) <= x, [hd(xa)] @ lesseq(x, tl(xa)),
                          lesseq(x, tl(xa)))) |]
==> (! 1. perm(1, qsort(1)) & ordered(qsort(1)))
```

The initial output variable has been instantiated to the definition of quicksort and the two auxiliary functions used in this definition. The resulting theorem states that, under these definitions, the quicksort program satisfies the sorting specification. Note that the definitions given can be directly translated into one's favorite functional programming language and correspond to standard presentations of these programs.

Taking Stock

The above proof sketch suggests how algorithms like quicksort can be incrementally developed by interactively applying tactics, which in turn apply proof rules using higher-order resolution. The resulting program is guaranteed to be correct because tactics applied only primitive rules or rules we previously derived. Moreover the derivation separates partial correctness and termination by delaying the choice of the well-founded relations used in showing termination until after all functions have been synthesized. Finally, although perhaps not obvious from the snapshots, our tactics incorporate procedures based on rewriting and propositional reasoning, which make substantial use of standard tactics for HOL to partially automate trivial kinds of reasoning.

6 Related Work and Conclusions

Our case study, highlighting some of the results in [2], is, to our knowledge, the first analysis of how the deductive tableau system can be embedded and extended in a standard theorem prover. It provides evidence that frameworks like Isabelle offer advantages not present in a specialized implementation. First, because Isabelle is a logical framework, we can represent rules of objects logics and prove that they are derivable. Hence, we can formally establish the correctness of rules for deductive tableau style program development. This helps us separate and clarify the underlying logic (HOL), the derived rules, and what tactics and support are necessary to apply the rules. Second, higher-order resolution allows us to directly develop programs along side their correctness proofs either by simulating deductive tableau proofs or taking advantage of the greater flexibility offered by proof in a higher-order metalogic with metavariables. For example we can directly formalize and manipulate well-orderings during proofs. Finally, we can directly utilize standard tactics and libraries that came with the system. This substantially reduces the time needed to create a usable theory with sufficient automation support (e.g., rewriting and propositional reasoning) suitable for carrying out Manna and Waldinger's examples and our own experiments.

The work closest to ours is Coen's [6] who developed his own theory called classical computational logic. He was motivated by the deductive tableau and Constructive Type Theories and his work supports deductive synthesis style proofs in his own classical logic. His goals were rather different than ours: he was not trying to directly model a proposed formalism, but rather create his own specialized theory, with its own advantages and disadvantages. For example, on the system side he had to develop his own tactics for simplification and the like; on the theory side he had to show the correctness of his specialized logic with respect to some appropriate semantics. Also relevant is the work of Regensburger [15] who developed a variant of LCF (Scott's logic of computable functions) as a conservative extension of higher-order logic and applied this to reasoning about programs operating on inductively and co-inductively defined data-types such as streams.

7 References

[1] Penny Anderson and David Basin. Deriving and applying logic program transformers. In *Algorithms, Concurrency and Knowledge (1995 Asian Computing Science Conference)*, pages 301–318, Pathumthani, Thailand, December 1995. Springer-Verlag, LNCS 1023.

[2] Abdelwaheb Ayari. A reinterpretation of the deductive tableaux system in higher-order logic. Master's thesis, University of Saarbrücken, 1995. Available at http://www.mpi-sb.mpg.de/~abdu/dts.ps.Z.

[3] David Basin. Logic frameworks for logic programs. In *4th International Workshop on Logic Program Synthesis and Transformation, (LOPSTR'94)*, pages 1–16, Pisa, Italy, June 1994. Springer-Verlag, LNCS 883.

[4] CIP System Group: F. L. Bauer et al. *The Munich Project CIP, Volume II: The Program Transformation System CIP-S*, volume 292 of *Lecture Notes in Computer Science*. Springer-Verlag, 1987.

[5] Rod M. Burstall and Joseph A. Goguen. Putting theories together to make specifications. In *5th IJCAI*, pages 1045 – 1058, Boston, Mass, 1977.

[6] Martin David Coen. Interactive program derivation. Technical Report 272, Cambridge University Computer Laboratory, Cambridge, November 1992.

[7] Melvin Fitting. *First-Order Logic and Automated Theorem Proving*. Springer-Verlag, New York, 1990.

[8] Berthold Hoffmann and Bernd Krieg-Brückner (Eds.). *Program Development by Specification and Transformation*. Springer LNCS 680, 1993.

[9] Gérard Huet and Bernard Lang. Proving and applying program transformations expressed with second-order patterns. *Acta Informatica*, pages 31–55, 1978.

[10] Ina Kraan, David Basin, and Alan Bundy. Middle-out reasoning for synthesis and induction. To appear in the Journal of Automated Reasoning.

[11] Ina Kraan, David Basin, and Alan Bundy. Middle-out reasoning for logic program synthesis. In *10th International Conference on Logic Programming (ICLP93)*, pages 441–455, Budapest Hungary, 1993.

[12] Zohar Manna and Richard Waldinger. Fundamentals of the deductive program synthesis. *IEEE Transactions on Software Engineering*, January 1992.

[13] Lawrence C. Paulson. *Isabelle : a generic theorem prover; with contributions by Tobias Nipkow*. LNCS-828. Springer, Berlin, 1994.

[14] Frank Pfenning. Logic programming in the LF logical framework. In *Logical Frameworks*, pages 149 – 181. Cambridge University Press, 1991.

[15] Franz Regensburger. *HOLCF: Eine konservative Erweiterung von HOL um LCF*. PhD thesis, Technical University, Munich, 1984.

Extending Promela and Spin for Real Time

Stavros Tripakis*
Costas Courcoubetis*†

ABSTRACT The efficient representation and manipulation of time information is key to any successful implementation of a verification tool. We extend the syntax and semantics of the higher level specification language Promela to include constructs and statements based on the model of timed Büchi automata [2]. We implement these extensions on top of the verification tool Spin.

1 Introduction

Promela [8] is a language for the specification of *interactive concurrent* systems. Such systems consist of a finite number of separate *components*, which act independently one from another, and interact through the exchange of *messages* over message *channels*. A large part of these systems, including communication protocols, asynchronous circuits, traffic or flight controllers, and real–time operating systems can be characterized as *real–time* systems. This characterization comes from the following two observations :

1. the correct functioning of those systems depends on the timely coordination of their interacting components ; and,

2. information is available about the *time delays* encountered during the operation of system processes.

The first observation is crucial when trying to ensure that the system meets its requirements. The second one can be used to develop a more efficient system : knowing with certainty some facts about the delays in a system can lead to concluding that a number of behaviors are impossible, and therefore, can be ignored during system design.

Traditional formalisms for temporal reasoning deal only with the *qualitative* aspect of time, that is, the *order* of certain system events [1]. However,

---

*Department of Computer Science, University of Crete, Heraklion, Greece, and Institute of Computer Science, FORTH

†Partially supported by the BRA ESPRIT project REACT.

[1]An example of a qualitative time property is : "the green light is never switched on after the red one and before the orange one"

real–time systems often demand for a *quantitative* aspect of time, that is, taking into consideration the actual distance in time of certain system events [2]. Hence our motivation to extend Promela for real time. We consider time as *dense*, i.e., an unbounded (although finite) number of events can occur between two successive time moments.

An untimed Promela program consists of a collection of components which interact *asynchronously*. Optionally, a special component can be specified, (called the *never–claim*) which interacts with the rest of the system *synchronously*, and models the complement of the desired system behavior. In the absence of the never–claim, wrong behaviors are coded explicitly into the components in terms of non–progress conditions. In either case, the correctness of the system can be reduced to a language–emptyness problem.

Our verification method consists in considering emptyness of *timed Büchi automata* (TBA) [6, 2] which are Büchi automata extended with a finite number of *clocks*. Based on a timed Promela specification, we construct the equivalent (modulo operational semantics) TBA, and then check if the timed language of the latter is empty.

The work described in this document has been, first of all, to extend the syntax and semantics of untimed Promela for clocks and time information. We call this extended language *Real–Time*–Promela (RT–Promela). Next, we have implemented the TBA verification procedure on top of *Spin* [9], obtaining *RT–Spin*, a tool for the verification of RT–Promela programs. Care has been taken, so that the TBA analysis is absolutely compatible with the existing search algorithms used in untimed Spin. Finally, one of our contributions has been the description of a formal semantics of both untimed and RT–Promela, based on untimed and timed transition systems, respectively.

The rest of this document is organized as follows. Section 2 is a short overview of timed languages and automata. In section 3 we review Promela, give its operational semantics in terms of transition systems, and define the verification problem in the untimed case. RT–Promela is presented in section 5 in the same manner : syntactic extensions, semantics in terms of timed transition systems, verification reduced to language emptyness. In the appendix, we also describe *trace* semantics for individual untimed and RT–Promela processes, and show how one can derive the semantics of the complete specification in a compositional way. Experimental results are presented in section 6.

---

[2] An example of a quantitative time property is : "the orange light will always be switched on at least 5 time units after the red one, followed in at most 0.5 time units by the green one"

2 Timed languages and timed Büchi automata

A Büchi automaton (BA) is a nondeterministic finite-state machine $A = (\Sigma, S, Tr, S_0, F)$. Σ is the input alphabet, S is the set of states, S_0 the set of initial states, and F the set of *accepting states*. $Tr \in S \times \Sigma \times S$ is the transition relation. If $(s, \sigma, s') \in Tr$ then A can move from s to s' upon reading σ.

A *trace* or input word is an infinite sequence $\sigma = \sigma_1 \sigma_2 ..., \sigma_i \in \Sigma$, while a *run* over σ is an infinite sequence $s_0 \overset{\sigma_1}{\mapsto} s_1 \overset{\sigma_2}{\mapsto} ..., s_0 \in S_0, (s_i, \sigma_{i+1}, s_{i+1}) \in Tr, i = 0, 1, ...$ A run r is said to be *accepting* iff there exists a state $f \in F$ such that f appears infinitely often in r. The *language* $\mathcal{L}(A)$ of A is the set of all traces σ such that A has an accepting run over σ.

A *timed* trace or word is a pair (σ, τ), where σ is a trace and τ is a *time sequence*, i.e., an infinite sequence $\tau_1, \tau_2, ..., \tau_i \in R^+$. We only consider strictly increasing, *non–zeno* time sequences, i.e., $\tau_i < \tau_{i+1}$ and $\forall t \in R \exists i, \tau_i > t$. This ensures that time *progresses*, that is, does not converge to a bounded value [3]. A *timed language* is a set of timed traces.

A TBA is a tuple $A = (\Sigma, S, Tr, S_0, F, C)$, where Σ, S, S_0 and F are as in a BA, and C is a finite set of clocks. A transition in Tr has the form (s, σ, s', R, μ), where $R \subseteq C$ are the clocks to be reset to zero, and μ is a *clock constraint* (or *guard*), that is, a boolean conjunction of atoms of the form $y \leq k$, $k \leq y$, $x - y \leq k$ and $k \leq x - y$ for two clocks $x, y \in C$, and an integer constant $k \in N$.

Given a timed word (σ, τ), A starts at a state $s_0 \in S_0$ at time 0. All the clocks of A are active, initialized to zero, and increase at the same rate. At time τ_1 the symbol σ_1 is read and the automaton takes a transition $tr_0 = (s_0, \sigma_1, s_1, R_1, \mu_1)$, only if the values of the clocks satisfy μ_1. The transition is instantaneous, that is, no clocks change, except from the ones belonging in R_1 which are reset to zero. At time τ_2 a new input symbol is read, the next transition is chosen, and so on.

More formally, a run $(\overline{s}, \overline{\nu})$ of a TBA over a timed word (σ, τ) is an infinite sequence $(s_0, \nu_0) \overset{\sigma_1, \tau_1}{\longmapsto} (s_1, \nu_1) \overset{\sigma_2, \tau_2}{\longmapsto} ..., \nu_i \in R^{|C|}$ such that $s_0 \in S_0, \forall x \in C, \nu_0(x) = 0$, and $\forall i = 1, 2, ..., (s_{i-1}, \sigma_i, s_i, R_i, \mu_i) \in Tr, (\nu_{i-1} + \tau_i - \tau_{i-1}) \in \mu_i$, and $\nu_i = \nu_{i-1}[R_i := 0]$ [4]. If such a run exists, then (σ, τ) is *timing consistent*. (σ, τ) is accepting iff it is timing consistent and there exists a state $f \in F$ such that f appears infinitely often in $\overline{s}$. The *timed language* $\mathcal{L}(A)$ of A is the set of all timed traces (σ, τ) such that A has an accepting run over (σ, τ). Languages accepted by TBA are called timed *regular*. It is shown that they are closed under union and intersection, but not under complement [1].

---

[3] An example of a *zeno* time sequence is $0, 1/2, 3/4, 7/8, ...$

[4] The vector ν_i is called a clock *valuation*. $\nu[R := 0]$ is the valuation ν' such that $\forall x \in R, \nu'(x) = 0$ and $\forall x \in C \setminus R, \nu'(x) = \nu(x)$. For $t \in R$, $\nu + t$ is ν' such that $\forall x \in C, \nu'(x) = \nu(x) + t$. Finally, we write $\nu \in \mu$ if ν satisfies μ.

The *synchronous product* of two TBA A_1 and A_2 is a TBA $A = A_1 \otimes_s A_2$ such that $\mathcal{L}(A) = \mathcal{L}(A_1) \cap \mathcal{L}(A_2)$.

3 Untimed Promela

3.1 Language summary

Promela [5] programs consist of *processes*, message *channels*, and *variables*. A specification in Promela consists in two parts : the *system specification part* (system, for short) and the *property specification part* (the never-claim, which is optional). In the first, a number of process *types* are declared which are then instantiated into *real* processes at run time. A process (usually init) can create other processes (of a certain type) by means of the run statement. Processes execute their statements asynchronously, except in the case of atomic statements, or *rendez-vous* handshakes.

The syntax of the never-claim is just like any other process. However, at most one never claim can be present in the specification. Moreover, it should not *participate* in the execution of the system, but rather *monitor* it. By this we mean that every statement inside a claim is interpreted as a condition, and should not have side effects (i.e., send or receive messages, set global variables, execute run statements etc.). Since the system and the claim operate synchronously, the latter can observe the system's behavior step by step, and catch errors.

3.2 The Promela semantics

The operational semantics of an untimed Promela program $\mathcal{P}$ will be specified in terms of a *transition system* (TS), i.e., a (possibly infinite) graph $T = (Q, \rightarrow)$, where Q is the set of nodes, and $\rightarrow \subseteq Q \times Q$ the set of edges. For matters of simplicity, we consider a known number of processes $P_0, P_1, ..., P_m$ which are active right from the start. By convention, P_0 will be the never claim, if specified, otherwise, $P_0 \stackrel{\text{def}}{=} \{ \text{do:: skip od} \}$.

The state of the system is completely described by the contents of channels and memory (global and local variables), as well as the *control location* of each active process P_i. Let gv (resp. lv_i) be the vector representing the current values of global variables (resp. local variables of P_i), and l_i be the location of P_i. The location just after the opening bracket { (resp. just before the closing bracket }) is $start_i$ (resp. end_i). We write $l_i \stackrel{st}{\rightarrow} l'_i$ iff there is a statement st from l_i to l'_i. The variable vectors after executing st are $st[gv]$ and $st[lv_i]$.

---

[5]The reader can refer to [8, 9, 10] for a complete presentation of untimed Promela.

So, states of Q are of the form $q = (l_0, l_1, ..., l_m, lv_0, lv_1, ..., lv_m, gv)$. A statement $l_i' \overset{st_i}{\rightarrow} l_i''$ of P_i is *enabled* at q iff $l_i' = l_i$ and :

1. either st_i is an assignment, skip, or conditional statement satisfied at q ;

2. or st_i is an asynchronous send (resp. receive) to a non-full (resp. from a non-empty) channel ;

3. or st_i is a rendez-vous send and there exists a rendez-vous receive $l_j' \overset{st_j}{\rightarrow} l_j''$ such that $l_j' = l_j$.

Then, $tr = (q, q') \in \rightarrow$ iff there exists a statement $l_0 \overset{st_0}{\rightarrow} l_0'$ of P_0 enabled at q, and :

1. either there exists a statement $l_i \overset{st_i}{\rightarrow} l_i'$ of P_i enabled at q such that $q' = (l_0', ..., l_i', ..., l_m, st_0[lv_0], ..., st_i[lv_i], ..., lv_m, st_i[st_0[gv]])$;

2. or there exists a rendez-vous pair $l_i \overset{st_i}{\rightarrow} l_i'$, $l_j \overset{st_j}{\rightarrow} l_j'$ enabled at q such that $q' = (l_0', ..., l_i', ..., l_j', ..., l_m, st_0[lv_0], ..., st_i[lv_i], ..., st_j[lv_j], ..., lv_m, gv')$, where $gv' = st_i[st_j[st_0[gv]]]$;

3. or no statement of any process $P_i, i > 0$ is enabled at q (such a state is called a *deadlock* one) and $q' = (l_0', ...l_m, st_0[lv_0], ...lv_m, st_0[gv])$ [6].

The initial state of T is $q_0 = (start_0, ..., start_m, lv_0^{init}, ..., lv_m^{init}, gv^{init})$. A *path* of T is a sequence $q_0, q_1, ...$ such that $(q_i, q_{i+1}) \in \rightarrow$.

3.3 Verification in untimed Promela

The *correctness criteria* of $\mathcal{P}$ are implied by the various types of analysis performed using the tool Spin. Locations can be optionally labeled as end, accept, or progress. For a state $q = (l_0, l_1, ..., l_m, ...)$, we define $end(q) = \{l_i \mid l_i = end_i$ or l_i is labeled as end $\}$, and $accept(q) = \{l_i \mid l_i$ is labeled as accept $\}$. A deadlock state q is called *valid* iff $\forall i = 1, .., m, l_i \in end(q)$. We say that $\mathcal{P}$ is :

1. *deadlock free* iff all deadlock states are valid ;

2. ω*-correct* iff for each infinite path p, if $q_1, ...q_k$ is the set of states appearing infinitely many times in p, then $\forall i = 1, ..., k, accept(q_i) = \emptyset$ (i.e., there is no cycle passing by a location labeled as accept).

---

[6] This case corresponds to Promela's *claim-stuttering* semantics.

4 Time extensions

4.1 Syntax

First of all, we add the type clock to the declarations of Promela variables. Clock variables can be scalar or arrays, and are declared globally [7]. Here is an example of the declaration of clocks :

$$\text{clock x, y, z[5];}$$

Next, each statement is expanded with an optional time part, according to the following grammar rules :

$$
\begin{aligned}
\text{stmnt} &::= \quad \text{untimed\_stmnt} \quad | \quad \text{timed\_stmnt} \\
\text{timed\_stmnt} &::= \quad \text{'when' '\{' } \mu \text{ '\}' untimed\_stmnt} \\
&\quad | \quad \text{'reset' '\{' } R \text{ '\}' untimed\_stmnt} \\
&\quad | \quad \text{'when' '\{' } \mu \text{ '\}' 'reset' '\{' } R \text{ '\}' untimed\_stmnt} \\
R &::= \quad \text{clock ',' } R \\
\mu &::= \quad \text{ineq ',' } \mu \\
\text{ineq} &::= \quad \text{clock op int} \quad | \quad \text{clock op clock '+' int} \\
\text{clock} &::= \quad x, y, z \in C \quad | \quad x \text{ '[' expr ']'} \\
\text{op} &::= \quad \text{'<'} \quad | \quad \text{'>'} \quad | \quad \text{'<='} \quad | \quad \text{'>='} \quad | \quad \text{'=='}
\end{aligned}
$$

Here are some examples of timed statements :

$$
\begin{aligned}
&\text{when}\{x < 4, x \geq 2\} \text{ reset}\{x\} \quad &&\text{B!mymesg ;} \\
&\text{when}\{z < 1, y \geq 1\} \text{ reset}\{x, z\} \quad &&\text{a = a*b ;} \\
&\text{when}\{x[i] == 1\} \quad &&\text{goto error ;}
\end{aligned}
$$

The guard μ is interpreted as the *conjunction* of the inequalities it consists of, e.g., "when $\{x < 4, x \geq 2\}$" stands for "when $\{x < 4 \wedge x \geq 2\}$". There is no way to express *disjunctions* using a single statement. Instead, one should use a branching nondeterministic statement, like :

```
if
:: when{x < 4} reset{x} stmnt_part
:: when{x ≥ 2} reset{x} stmnt_part
fi
```

The reason for the above restriction will be clear in section 5, where we discuss our verification methodology.

4.2 The RT–Promela Semantics

The semantics of a RT–Promela program $\mathcal{P}$ is a *timed* TS (TTS) $(Q^\tau, \rightarrow^\tau)$. States of Q^τ are of the form (q, ν) where q is as in section 3.2 and ν is a clock valuation. A timed statement (st, R, μ) is enabled at (q, ν) if st is

---

[7]The reason for this is that the clock–space dimension cannot change at run time.

enabled at q and $\nu \in \mu$. The transition relation $\to^\tau$ contains two types of transitions :

1. Action transitions, $((q,\nu),(q',\nu'))$ (defined as in section 3.2). Each such transition is associated with a pair (resp. triple) of timed statements (st_0, R_0, μ_0), (st_i, R_i, μ_i) (resp. and (st_j, R_j, μ_j)) which are enabled at (q,ν) (this implies $\nu \in \mu_0 \wedge \mu_i \wedge \mu_j$). Let R be $R_0 \cup R_i$ (resp. $R_0 \cup R_i \cup R_j$). Then, $\nu' = \nu[R := 0]$.

2. Time transitions, $((q,\nu),(q,\nu+\delta))$, for $\delta \in \mathbb{R}_+$.

The initial state of T is $(q_0, \mathbf{0})$, $\mathbf{0} = (0, ..., 0) \in \mathbb{R}_+^{|C|}$. The correctness criteria of a RT–Promela program are identical to those defined in section 3.2 except that instead of T we consider $(Q^\tau, \to^\tau)$.

5 Verification using RT–Promela

Our aim is to reduce the verification of the correctness criteria of RT–Promela programs to verification of TBA emptyness, following the approach of [5]. For a RT–Promela program $\mathcal{P}$, we define two TBA $A_\mathcal{P}^\omega$ and $A_\mathcal{P}^{dlock}$, one for each correctness criterion.

5.1 The TBA defined from a RT–Promela program

Then, $A_\mathcal{P}^\omega \stackrel{\text{def}}{=} (Q, Q, Tr, \{q_0\}, F, C)$, where Q, q_0 are as in section 3.2, C is the set of declared clocks, $F = \{q \mid accept(q) \neq \emptyset\}$, and $(q, \sigma, q', R, \mu) \in Tr$ iff $\sigma = s$ and $\mu = \mu_0 \wedge \mu_i$, $R = R_0 \cup R_i$ (or $\mu_0 \wedge \mu_i \wedge \mu_j$, $R_0 \cup R_i \cup R_j$, respectively, in the case of a rendez-vous handshake).

Similarly, $A_\mathcal{P}^{dlock} \stackrel{\text{def}}{=} (\Sigma', Q \cup \{end\}, Tr', \{q_0\}, F', C)$, where $\Sigma' = Q \cup \{\sigma_{end}\}$, $F' = \{end\}$, and $end \notin Q$. Tr' is obtained by adding to Tr a a transition $(q, \sigma_{end}, end, \emptyset, true)$ for each invalid deadlock state q, plus the loop $(end, \sigma_{end}, end, \emptyset, true)$.

The following follows directly from the above definitions.

Theorem 5.1 • $\mathcal{P}$ is deadlock free iff $\mathcal{L}(A_\mathcal{P}^{dlock}) = \emptyset$.

  • $\mathcal{P}$ is ω–correct iff $\mathcal{L}(A_\mathcal{P}^\omega) = \emptyset$.

Let $\mathcal{L}$ be a timed language $\mathcal{L}$. Its *untimed projection* is defined as $unt(\mathcal{L}) = \{\sigma \mid \exists \tau\ s.t.\ (\sigma, \tau) \in \mathcal{L}\}$. Then, $unt(\mathcal{L}) = \emptyset$ iff $\mathcal{L} = \emptyset$ [1]. Thus, it suffices to check the emptyness of $unt(\mathcal{L}(A_\mathcal{P}^{dlock}))$ and $unt(\mathcal{L}(A_\mathcal{P}^\omega))$.

Theorem 5.2 [[1]] For each TBA A there exists a BA U accepting $unt(\mathcal{L}(A))$.

Intuitively, U will also have an extended state space, each state (q, α) containing, apart from the state q of A, the set α of all possible clock valuations.

The latter is generally infinite, due to dense time. To represent such a set, the valuation space $R^{|C|}$ is partitioned into a finite number of *equivalence classes*. Two members ν and ν' of a class α are equivalent in the sense that, if ν belongs to an accepting run $(s_0, \nu_0) \overset{\sigma_1, \tau_1}{\longmapsto} (s_1, \nu_1) \overset{\sigma_2, \tau_2}{\longmapsto} \ldots \overset{\sigma_i, \tau_i}{\longmapsto} (s_i, \nu) \overset{\sigma_{i+1}, \tau_{i+1}}{\longmapsto} (s_{i+1}, \nu_{i+1}) \ldots$, then it can be substituted by ν', which gives another accepting run $(s_0, \nu_0) \overset{\sigma_1, \tau_1}{\longmapsto} (s_1, \nu_1) \overset{\sigma_2, \tau_2}{\longmapsto} \ldots \overset{\sigma_i, \tau_i}{\longmapsto} (s_i, \nu') \overset{\sigma_{i+1}, \tau_{i+1}}{\longmapsto} (s_{i+1}, \nu'_{i+1}) \ldots$, so that the untimed projections of the two runs are the same.

5.2 Checking emptyness efficiently

Checking whether $\mathcal{L}(U) = \emptyset$ is reduced to a reachability analysis (depth-first search) seeking loops which pass by accepting states. The state space of U is constructed *on-the-fly*, i.e., during the dfs. Notice that if Q is finite, then the state space of U is also finite, since the set of equivalence classes C_α is finite. Therefore, termination is ensured.

Each control state q can be visited up to $|C_\alpha|$ times. This number depends on the number of clocks and the constraints, and can be quite large. Thus, we would like to be able to do the analysis in terms of *unions* of equivalence classes. Such a union is called a *clock region*, noted CR. Our goal is to find an efficient way to represent clock regions.

A very popular representation uses *difference bounds matrices* (DBMs) [6]. DBMs are inexpensive as far as storage is concerned. Moreover, they are simple and require low–cost operations. Briefly, a DBM is a square matrix which describes a very simple system of linear inequalities, of the same form as time constraints, that is, x op k, or x op $y + k$, where op $\in \{<, >, \leq, \geq, =\}$, and k is a positive integer constant. Assuming the dimension of a matrix D to be $n \times n$, the set of vectors $\nu \in R^n$ which satisfy the corresponding inequalities will be denoted $\nu(D)$. This set is convex. Then, the idea is to represent a clock region CR by a DBM D, so that $\nu(D) = CR$. At each step during the reachability analysis, a new DBM is computed by transforming the old one. For this, we use a small number of low–cost operations described briefly below. The reader can refer to appendix 1.3 for the precise definitions.

The *intersection* of two DBMs corresponds to the intersection of their regions. The *time–elapse* transformation yields a new DBM which contains all time–successor valuations of the old one, by letting an arbitrary amount of time (possibly zero) elapse. The *clocks–reset* transformation yields a new DBM where some clocks are reset to zero.

In general, more than one DBMs can be used to represent the same set of clock valuations. This is due to the fact that the bounds found in certain inequalities are not "strict" enough. Nevertheless, it is possible to obtain the *canonical* form of a DBM, which is its unique, "minimal" representative. Let $\mathrm{cf}(D)$ denote the canonical form of a DBM D, and D_1, D_2 be two different matrices. Then : $\nu(D_1) = \nu(D_2) \Leftrightarrow \mathrm{cf}(D_1) = \mathrm{cf}(D_2)$.

The use of canonical form reduces the test for equality of two matrices to a test for the equality of their canonical forms. This is in turn reduced, at the implementation level, to a test for pointer equality, since all DBMs are usually stored in a hashing table. The rest of the DBM operations are also simplified by the use of canonical forms.

During the series of transformations, it is possible that the resulting DBM does not "cover" exactly a clock region. Indeed, a clock region is a union of equivalence classes, which is not always convex, while the region represented by a matrix always is. In that case the matrix can be enlarged to include as many points of the region as possible, resulting in a canonical representation [8]. This process is called *maximization*. For a DBM D, and the maximized one, $max(D)$ the following property holds for all other DBM D' :

$$(\forall \alpha \, (\alpha \cap \nu(D) \neq \emptyset \Leftrightarrow \alpha \cap \nu(D') \neq \emptyset)) \Rightarrow \nu(D') \subseteq \nu(max(D)),$$

where α, as usual, denotes an equivalence class.

To prove the correctness of our approach, let us define another automaton, called the *DBM automaton*, denoted A_{DBM}. This plays the same role as U, following exactly the same runs as A does, and keeping track of the possible clock positions at each step.

For a TBA $A = (\Sigma, Q, Tr, Q_0, F, C)$, we define $A_{DBM} \stackrel{\text{def}}{=} (\Sigma, Q', Tr', Q'_0)$ such that :

- the states of A_{DBM} are of the form (q, D), where $q \in Q$ and D is a DBM ;

- the initial states of A_{DBM} are of the form (q_0, D_0), where $q_0 \in Q_0$ and D_0 is the DBM such that $\nu(D_0) = \{0\}$;

- A_{DBM} has a transition $((q, D), \sigma, (q', D'))$ iff $(q, \sigma, q', R, \mu) \in Tr$, and D' is obtained by D by the following sequence of DBM transformations :

$$D \stackrel{\delta}{\longmapsto} D^\delta \stackrel{\mu}{\longmapsto} D^\mu \stackrel{\text{cf}}{\longmapsto} D^{cf} \stackrel{[R:=0]}{\longmapsto} D^0 \stackrel{max}{\longmapsto} D^{max} = D'.$$

In the above sequence, $\stackrel{\delta}{\longmapsto}$ represents the time–elapse transformation, that is, $\forall \nu \in \nu(D), \delta \geq 0, \nu + \delta \in \nu(D^\delta)$. $\stackrel{\mu}{\longmapsto}$ represents the intersection with the constraint μ, that is, $\forall \nu \in \nu(D^\mu)$, ν satisfies μ. $\stackrel{[R:=0]}{\longmapsto}$ represents the clock resets, that is, $\forall \nu \in \nu(D^0), x \in R, \nu(x) = 0$. Finally, $\stackrel{max}{\longmapsto}$ represents the maximization process. Intuitively, the whole series of transformations corresponds to the fact that, being in a state, the system lets the time pass first (this can be zero time) and then executes a statement instantaneously,

---

[8]It is not wrong to add these extra points, since each one of them is equivalent with at least one point in the matrix, thus satisfies exactly the same properties regarding the evolution of the system in time.

moving to another state. In order for the transition to be taken, the time constraints must be satisfied. At the same moment, a number (possibly zero) of clocks are reset to zero.

Not all paths which are discovered during the reachability analysis are valid. Indeed, the presence of time gives meaning only to those infinite executions for which time progresses without bound (recall non–zeno timed traces, defined in section 2). A run of A_{DBM}, $r = (s_0, D_0) \overset{\sigma_1}{\mapsto} (s_1, D_1) \overset{\sigma_2}{\mapsto} \ldots$ over a trace q, is *progressive* iff for each clock $x \in C$:

1. there are infinitely many i's such that D_i satisfies $(x = 0) \vee (x > c_x)$, where c_x is the maximum constant that appears in an inequality of the form x op c_x in the specification ;

2. there are infinitely many j's such that D_j satisfies $x > 0$.

6   Examples

We have implemented the method described above on top of the tool Spin, developed for the validation of concurrent systems [8], by G. J. Holzmann. We have extended Spin to RT–Spin, which performs reachability analysis on the DBM automaton, using as input an RT–Promela program.

We have tested our implementation using a number of examples. We now present three of them. The first one models a simple system of three processes representing a train, a gate, and a controller. The second is a real–time mutual–exclusion protocol, due to Fischer [15]. Both these examples have been taken from [3]. The third has to do with a general–purpose ATM switch [17, 12]. It has been taken from [14], where it has been treated using the selection/resolution model [13] and the tool RT–Cospan [18].

The systems consist of a number of components, modeled as TBA. RT–Promela offers the possibility to use local and global variables, as well as channels. We take advantage of this, and we end up with less components than those described in the original models. For example, we do not need a special automaton to model the global variable in the mutual–exclusion protocol.

The alphabet of each TBA is a set of events. Automata synchronize their actions through shared events. Such an event can occur provided it is enabled in every automaton whose alphabet includes the event. Whenever necessary, synchronization in RT–Promela is done using rendez–vous.

6.1   Modeling the systems using RT–Promela

Train, Gate, Controller (TGC) :

This example deals with an automatic controller that opens and closes a gate at a railway track intersection (see figure 1). Whenever the train

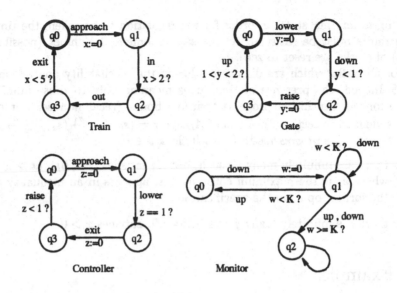

FIGURE 1. Train, Gate, Controller

enters the intersection it sends an **approach** signal at least two minutes in advance to the controller. The controller also detects the train leaving the intersection and this event occurs within five minutes after it started its approach. The gate responds to **lower** and **raise** commands by moving **down** and **up** respectively within certain time bounds. The controller sends a **lower** command to the gate exactly one minute after receiving an **approach** signal from the train. It commands the gate to raise within one minute of the train's exit from the intersection.

The purpose of the verification is to ensure the following safety property [9] : whenever the gate goes down, it is moved back up within a certain upper time bound K. Notice that this implies that the gate *will* eventually come up again. Although this is not immediate from the above property, *liveness* conditions that are associated with each automaton ensure that in every infinite trace, process **Gate** passes infinitely often from state q0, therefore executing infinitely often the transition $q3 \to q0$ which sets the gate up. Returning to the safety property, the automaton **Monitor** models precisely the negation of it, as was explained in section 2. The property is satisfied iff the integer constant K is greater than 6.

---

[9] A *safety* property can be formulated as "never will...". For example "never will processes 1 and 2 be found at their critical sections at the same time"

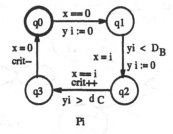

FIGURE 2. Timed mutual exclusion

Timed Mutual Exclusion :

In this protocol, there exist n processes $P_1, ..., P_n$, as shown in figure 2. A process P_i is initially idle, but at any time may begin executing the protocol provided the value of a global variable x is 0. P_i then delays for up to Δ_B time units before assigning the value i to x. It may enter its critical section within δ_c time units provided the value of x is still i. Upon leaving its critical section, it reinitializes x to zero. Global variable crit is used to keep count of the number of processes in the critical section. The auto–increment (auto–decrement) of the variable is done simultaneously with the test (reset of x to zero). This is modeled in RT–Promela using atomic sequences. We need to verify that no two processes are ever in their critical sections at the same time. The property is satisfied iff $\Delta_B > \delta_c$.

A remark needs to be made concerning synchronization between more than two processes. In this case, two or more channels are necessary. The trick is to build a *chain reaction* of receive/send atomic moves in order to propagate the system event to all processes. The method is presented in appendix 1.2 through an example.

Verifying the round–trip delay of an ATM switch :

An ATM switch is a chip used as part of the *Asynchronous Transfer Mode* network protocol for *Broadband Interactive Services Data Networks* (B–ISDN). It consists of four input and four output links, each one of 400 Mbits/sec bandwidth. In ATM, information is transferred in *cells* of fixed length (53 bytes). These cells are routed using *virtual circuits* [10] (VCs), which have different priorities. The *flow–control* mechanism uses a special packet called *token*, which signals to the sender that the receiver is ready to accept a new high–priority cell. Each chip has a flow–control buffer storing the incoming tokens, as well as a cell buffer, used to store the incoming high–priority cells.

---

[10] There exist also *virtual paths*, which are collections of VCs, but will be ignored, since the chip itself cannot distinguish them from VCs

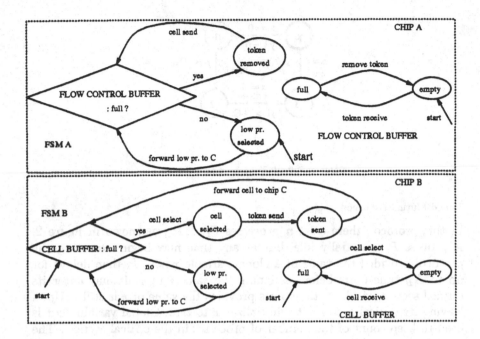

FIGURE 3. Two ATM switches

In our simplified example, we assume two adjacent chips, A and B (figure 3). We are interested in computing the *round-trip* delay. This is defined in [17, 12] as "the delay between the start of two consecutive transmissions of cells of the highest priority", since the chips deal with VCs of different priorities. We make two assumptions :

1. Chip A has always a high priority cell waiting to be transmitted to B.

2. A high priority cell which is sent from B to C is not flow-controlled by C, that is, chip C is always ready to receive it from B.

The first hypothesis allows us to ignore the cell buffer of chip A, while the second allows us to ignore the flow-control buffer of B. The timing assumptions of the system are the following :

1. each chip operates on a cycle of 54 clock *ticks*, that is, between any two packet transmissions, there is a delay of exactly 54 ticks ;

2. the delay between the selection of the next packet to be send and its transmission is between 4 and 10 ticks ;

3. the transmission of a token takes between 11 and 33 ticks ;

4. the transmission of a high priority cell takes exactly 3 ticks ;

K	states	transitions	DBMs	time	memory
5 (erroneous)	26	33	21	0.2	0.8
7 (correct)	32	34	23	0.1	0.9

TABLE 1. Results of train, gate, controller

Based on the above assumptions, we prove that the round–trip delay is never greater than 108 clock ticks, while it cannot be less than 54 ticks. In other words, at most one low priority packet gets transmitted between any two successive transmissions of high priority cells. The specification in RT–Promela can be found in appendix 1.1.

6.2 Proving safety properties

We used three different methods to verify the properties of the systems above. In the case of TGC, the monitor process moves to an error state marked with an **accept** label, where it stays forever. We ran the validator with the "–a" option to search for acceptance cycles. Notice that in this simple case, maximization wasn't necessary. Performance results are presented in table 2.

The specification of fischer's mutual–exclusion protocol includes a never claim monitoring the system and announcing an error if it finds out that more than one processes are in the critical section. We verified the correctness of the protocol when $\Delta_B = 1$, $\delta_c = 2$ for up to 4 processes, while in the case of 5 the validator refused to terminate. On the other hand, the erroneous case ($\Delta_B = 2$, $\delta_c = 1$) is very little affected by the size of the problem, since the error is found and announced early on. We managed to ran the wrong case for more than 23 processes. Performance results are shown in table 2 [11].

Finally, for the ATM switch, we make use of a clock RT which keeps count of the round–trip delay, and test the value of the clock each time a new high–priority cell is sent. If RT is between 54 and 108, it is reset to zero and the system continues normally. If the clock is strictly less than 54 or greater then 108, the error is announced. Performance results are shown in table 2.

Time is measured in seconds, and memory in megabytes.

---

[11]The erroneous version is noted with ⋆. Non-termination is noted with ⊥. The numbers in parentheses are those obtained up to the point where the program has been stopped.

N	version	states	transitions	DBMs	time	mem.
23	⋆	327	352	172	10.1	1.7
5	⋆	93	100	46	0.1	0.9
		⊥ (825,610)	⊥ (1,269,690)	⊥ (32,265)	⊥ (1,724)	⊥ (6)
4	⋆	80	86	39	0.1	0.8
		28,254	43,490	1,869	37.5	2.2
3	⋆	67	72	32	0.1	0.8
		974	1,385	127	0.4	1.2
2	⋆	54	58	17	0.1	0.8
		54	70	13	0.1	0.8

TABLE 2. Results of Fischer's mutual–exclusion protocol

states	transitions	DBMs	time	memory
435	619	510	2.6	1.5

TABLE 3. Results of round–trip delay verification

7 Conclusions

We have presented the theory and practice of the extensions made to Promela to include real–time semantics. The extended language, RT–Promela, allows for a special kind of global variables, which represent the clocks of the system. The statements of the language can contain simple linear constraints which restrict the possible values of a clock, or the relative values of two clocks. This changes the executability semantics of a statement, which can which can be executed only if, in addition to the restrictions imposed by standard Promela, the constraints do not come against the current state of the clocks. The execution of a statement can affect a clock by resetting it to zero.

The semantics of a specification in RT–Promela are given in terms of timed transition systems. The problem of verification is reduced to checking if the set of all possible valid paths (that is, the language of the system) is empty.

This time model permits the specification of a large class of real–time systems. We illustrate its power by three examples, which have been already considered in the bibliography, thus, allow for comparisons.

Putting clocks in an untimed specification usually increases the size of the

model	states	transitions	DBMs	time	memory
untimed	1,298	3,314	—	0.2	1
timed	19,197	47,180	1,225	14	2.3

TABLE 4. Results of leader–election protocol

state space. There are cases where timing constraints restrict the number of possible behaviors of the system, thus creating less states than the untimed model. However, most of the times, the size is significantly increased, up to one or two orders of magnitude, as it is shown in table 2, where we compare the results obtained by an exhaustive dfs performed on an untimed and a timed model of the leader–election protocol [7].

Consequently, future work mainly concerns the research for methods of *reduction*. The size of larger examples makes their analysis prohibitive. The new version of untimed Spin implements the *partial–order* method presented in [16, 11]. It would be interesting to see whether this reduction preserves time properties, and under which conditions. Apart from the above, older methods for on–the–fly *minimization* of the state space exist [4] and should be also tried out.

8 REFERENCES

[1] R. Alur. *Techniques for Automatic Verification of Real-Time Systems*. PhD thesis, Stanford University, 1991.

[2] R. Alur, C. Courcoubetis, and D. Dill. Model-checking for real-time systems. In *Proceedings of the 5th Symposium on Logic in Computer Science*, pages 414–425, Philadelphia, June 1990.

[3] R. Alur, C. Courcoubetis, D. Dill, N. Halbwachs, and H. Wong-Toi. An implementation of three algorithms for timing verification based on automata emptiness. In *RTSS 1992, proceedings*, 1992.

[4] R. Alur, C. Courcoubetis, D. Dill, N. Halbwachs, and H. Wong-Toi. Minimization of timed transition systems. In *CONCUR 1992, proceedings*. Lecture Notes in Computer Science, Springer-Verlag, 1992.

[5] C. Courcoubetis, D. Dill, M. Chatzaki, and P. Tzounakis. Verification with real-time COSPAN. In *Proceedings of the Fourth Workshop on Computer-Aided Verification*, Lecture Notes in Computer Science. Springer-Verlag, 1992.

[6] D. Dill. Timing assumptions and verification of finite-state concurrent systems. In *Proc. Workshop on Computer Aided Verification, CAV89*, Grenoble, June 1989. Lecture Notes in Computer Science, Springer-Verlag.

[7] Dolev, Klawe, and Rodeh. An O(n log n) unidirectional distributed algorithm for extrema finding in a circle. *J. of Algs*, 3:245–260, 1982.

[8] G.J. Holzmann. *Design and Validation of Protocols*. Prentice-Hall, 1990.

[9] G.J. Holzmann. Basic spin manual. Technical report, AT&T, Bell Laboratories, 1994.

[10] G.J. Holzmann. What's new in spin. Technical report, AT&T, Bell Laboratories, 1995.

[11] G.J. Holzmann and Doron A. Peled. An improvement in formal verification. In *Proceedings of the 7th International Conference on Formal Description Techniques, FORTE94*, Berne, Switcherland, october 1994.

[12] M. Katevenis, S. Sidiropoulos, and C. Courcoubetis. Weighted round-robin cell multiplexing in a general purpose ATM switch chip. *IEEE JSAC*, 9(8):1265–1279, 1991.

[13] J. Katzenelson and B. Kurshan. S/r: A language for specifying protocols and other coordinating processes. In *Proc. 5th Ann. Int'l Phoenix Conf. Comput. Commun., IEEE*, 1986.

[14] N. Lambrogeorgos. Verification of real-time systems: a case study of discrete and dense time models, 1993. Available only in greek.

[15] L. Lamport. A fast mutual exclusion algorithm. *ACM Transactions on Computer Systems*, 5(1):1–11, 1987.

[16] Doron A. Peled. Combining partial order reductions with on–the–fly model checking. In *Proceedings of the 6th International Conference on Comptuter Aided Verification, CAV94*, Stanford, California, june 1994.

[17] S. Sidiropoulos. A general purpose ATM switch. architecture and feasibility study, 1991.

[18] P. Tzounakis. Verification of real time systems: The extension of COSPAN in dense time, 1992.

Acknowledgments

We wish to thank Gerard Holzmann for providing numerous answers regarding the implementation, as well as for attentively reading the paper and making useful remarks.

1 Appendix

1.1 Mutual exclusion in RT–Promela

```
#define N 5 /* number of processes */
#define deltaB 1
#define deltaC 2
#define ErRoR assert(0)
clock y[N];
int x, crit;

proctype P ( byte id )
{
    do ::
        reset{y[id]} x==0 ->
        when{y[id]<deltaB} reset{y[id]} x=id+1 ->
        atomic{ when{y[id]>deltaC} x==id+1; crit++; } ->
        atomic{ x=0; crit--; }
    od
}

never{
    skip -> /* to let the processes be activated */
    do
        :: crit>1 -> ErRoR
        :: else
    od
}

init {
    byte proc;
    atomic {
        crit = 0;
        proc = 1;
        do
        :: proc ≤ N ->
                run P ( proc%N );
                proc = proc+1
        :: proc > N -> break
        od
    }
}
```

1.2 Multi-way synchronization in RT-Promela

Assume that four processes wish to synchronize on the signal sync. Then
we have to use three rendez-vous channels and the following specification :
    chan A,B,C = [0] of { byte };
    proctype P1() {   ...   q1: A!sync − >   ... }
    proctype P2() {   ...   q2: atomic { A?sync − > B!sync }   ... }
    proctype P3() {   ...   q3: atomic { B?sync − > C!sync }   ... }
    proctype P4() {   ...   q4: C?sync − >   ... }
In the case of synchronization of timed statements, the constraints and
resets of all of them are grouped together, as if it were a single statement
executed instantaneously.

1.3 DBMs

DBMs

We consider the class $\mathcal{CR}$ of convex polyhedra in $R^{|C|}$ which can be defined
by a set of integer constraints on clocks and clock differences. If we identify
a new fictitious clock x_0 with the constant value 0, the above constraints
can be represented as bounds on the difference between two clock values.
For instance, $x < 5$ can be expressed as $x - x_0 < 5$, and $x > 5$ as $x_0 - x <$
-5. Furthermore, we can introduce ∞ as a bounding value, to represent
inequalities of the form $x < y$ (we write $x - y < \infty$), and $-\infty$ to express
false (we write $x - y < -\infty$). Thus, we can restrict ourselves to upper
bounds without loss of generality. More precisely, each inequality can be
expressed as : $x_i - x_j < k$ or $x_i - x_j \leq k$, for some integer k, or $x_i - x_j < \infty$,
or $x_i - x_j < -\infty$.

A DBM is an $(n+1) \times (n+1)$ matrix D, whose elements (called *bounds*)
are of the form : $d_{ij} = (r, \#)$, $r \in R \cup \{\infty\}$, $\# \in \{<, \leq\}$. D represents
the polyhedron of R^n consisting of all points that satisfy the inequality
$x_i - x_j \# r$, where $d_{ij} = (r, \#)$.

Canonicalization

There are possibly many DBMs defining the same clock region, because
some of the upper bounds need not be tight [12]. For example, $\{x_1 < 2, x_1 \geq$
$1, x_2 \leq 5\}$ can be represented by any matrix D such that $d_{01} = (-1, \leq$
$), d_{02} = (0, \leq), d_{10} = (2, <), d_{20} = (5, \leq)$, and $d_{12} \in \{(2, <), (2, \leq), (3, <$
$), (3, \leq), ...\}, d_{21} \in \{(4, <), (4, \leq), (5, <), (5, \leq), ...\}$.

Then, the idea is to represent D in a *canonical* form, where all upper
bounds are as "tight" as possible. We denote this canonical matrix cf(D).
Dill [6] showed that cf(D) can be computed from D by applying an all-pairs

---

[12] Bounds are ordered lexicographically ($<$ is taken to be strictly less than $\leq$), that
is : $(r, \#) < (r', \#')$ iff $(r < r') \vee (r = r' \wedge \# =< \wedge \#' =\leq)$.

shortest-path algorithm. Moreover, canonicalization leads to easy tests for equality and emptiness of clock regions. A matrix D represents an empty region if a negative-cost cycle (i.e., $(-\infty, <)$) appears during the computation of $cf(D)$.

Elapse of time

As time elapses, clock differences remain the same, since all clocks increase at the same rate. Lower bounds do not change either since there are no decreasing clocks. Upper bounds have to be canceled, since an arbitrary period of time may pass. Let CR be the clock region represented by DBM D, and CR^δ the one represented by D^δ. Then :

$$
\begin{aligned}
d^\delta_{i0} &= (\infty, <) && \text{for all } i = 1, 2, ..., |C| \\
d^\delta_{ij} &= d_{ij} && \text{otherwise}
\end{aligned}
$$

Then it is easy to see that for each equivalence class α such that $\alpha \cap CR \neq \emptyset$, if α' is a time successor of α then $\alpha' \cap CR^\delta \neq \emptyset$.

Intersection and union

Let D and D' be DBMs for CR and CR'. The intersection $CR \cap CR'$ (resp. union $CR \cup CR'$) is represented by the matrix $D^\cap$ (resp. $D^\cup$) such that $\forall i, j, \ d^\cap_{ij} = min\{d_{ij}, d'_{ij}\}$ (resp. $d^\cup_{ij} = max\{d_{ij}, d'_{ij}\}$).

Clock resets

Let CR be the clock region represented by DBM D, and $R \subseteq C$. Then $CR[R := 0]$ is represented by D', defined as follows :

$$
\begin{aligned}
d'_{i0} &= d_{0i} = (0, \leq) && \text{if } i \in R \\
d'_{ij} &= d_{ji} = (\infty, <) && \text{if } i \in R \text{ and } j \in C \setminus R \\
d'_{ij} &= d_{ji} = (0, \leq) && \text{if } i, j \in R \\
d'_{ij} &= d_{ji} && \text{otherwise}
\end{aligned}
$$

Maximization

Let $c^1_{ij}, ..., c^m_{ij}$ be an increasing sequence of bounds, where $c^k_{ij} = (r_k, \#_k)$ corresponds to an atom $x_i - x_j \#_k r_k$ appearing in the program (if no such atom exists, let $m = 1$, $c^1_{ij} = (\infty, <)$). For a DBM D, if $max(D) = D'$, then $d'_{ij} = c^k_{ij}$, such that $d_{ij} < c^k_{ij}, \forall l < k, \ c^l_{ij} < d_{ij}$, and $\forall l' > k, \ d_{ij} < c^{l'}_{ij}$.

Reactive EFSMs – Reactive Promela/RSPIN

Elie NAJM[*]
Frank OLSEN[*†]

ABSTRACT *Reactive Promela*/RSPIN is an extension to the protocol validator *Promela*/SPIN. It enhances the simulation and verification capabilities of SPIN by allowing modular specifications to be analysed while alleviating the state-space explosion problem. *Reactive Promela* is a simple reactive language. The tool RSPIN is a preprocessor for SPIN which translates a *Reactive Promela* specification into a corresponding *Promela* specification. The main function performed by RSPIN is to combine *configurations of Reactive Promela automata* into *Promela proctypes*. The translated specification can then be simulated and verified using SPIN. We present our ideas first in a formal setting then we discuss their implementation in *Reactive Promela* and RSPIN concrete syntax and tool.

1 Introduction

When considering the problem of specification, (de)composition is a central issue. *Promela* provides for two styles of composition of automata: loosely coupled (communication is by FIFO queues) and tightly coupled (communication is by rendezvous). A third style, the synchronous reactive style, has been widely advocated and used in the literature and in industry.

In the synchronous reactive style, a configuration of automata reacts to external events in a synchronous way: a collection of external events is treated thoroughly by the configuration before another collection of events is taken and processed. In other words, the reactive configuration reacts to input events, and it is only at the end of the reaction that new inputs can be considered and processed. This kind of processing is valid when the speed of a reaction is higher than the delay between two consecutive input events.

The reactive style allows for powerful decomposition of specifications, beyond what is possible with merely rendezvous between automata. Fur-

---

[*]Ecole Nationale Supérieure des Télécommunications, 46, rue Barrault, 75013 Paris, France, E-mail: {najm,olsen}@res.enst.fr

[†]This author is now also affiliated with France Telecom–CNET, PAA/TSA/TLR, Issy-les-Moulineaux, Paris, France, E-mail: olsen@ issy.cnet.fr

thermore, it reduces the state space explosion by constraining parallelism between automata.

Whereas Holzmann in [Hol91] proposes ways of reducing the complexity of systems (by incremental composition, minimization, generalization, atomic sequences, layering and structuring techniques, and so on), this is not a feature of the *Promela* language in itself. Instead it is a guideline for how to use the language for large, complex systems.

This paper describes an extension to *Promela*, whereby reactive processes can be defined and instantiated. A reactive process is a configuration of synchronously composed automata. Besides the linguistic extension, this paper also describes a translation mechanism of reactive processes into *Promela* processes. This translation has been implemented in a preprocessor to SPIN, called RSPIN which translates a specification in *Reactive Promela* into an equivalent one in *Promela*.

In order to reason about the extension and about the translation from *Reactive Promela* to *Promela* we use a formalisation of an essential subset of *Promela* (see section 2). In section 3 we formalise the reactive extension model. In section 4 we use these models to formalise the translation algorithms. Section 5 then presents a concrete syntax for *Reactive Promela* with an example. The same section also introduces the RSPIN tool through an example which demonstrates the mapping from *Reactive Promela* to *Promela*.

2 Promela State Machines

The subset of *Promela* that consider can be formally defined using the following settings. We consider first a set L of elementary *Promela* instructions (with typical elements l):

$$L ::= [pred] \mid v = Exp \mid c!Exp \mid c?v$$

These instructions correspond to test, assignment, send, and receive instructions. The send and receive instructions are to bounded channels c. We consider simple channels containing FIFO sequences of simple values.

2.1 PSM processes

We consider PSM processes (with generic element P) as follows: P is a tuple (S, s, T, E) where:

- S is a set of *states*;

- s is either the *initial state* or the *current state*;

- $T \subset S \times L \times S$ is a *transition relation*;

- E is the *environment* of variables in P. It consists of a set of (untyped) variables V (ranging over values in the set VAL) and a mapping of each variable $v \in V$ to a value $val \in VAL$.

We use a dot-notation to access elements of the tuple representing P. $P.T$ is the transition relation T of PSM process P and $P.E$ is the environment of P.

2.2 Semantics of PSM processes

We give the semantics of a PSM process P by a translation function from PSM into a *Labeled Transition System (LTS)* defined by: $(PSM \times \Gamma \times PSM)$[1]. A PSM transition (P, α, P'), also written $P \xrightarrow{\alpha} P'$, means that P can perform action α to become P'.

The following notations are used in the rules:

- $E \vdash Exp \rightarrow val$ denotes that the expression Exp evaluates to val in the environment E.

- $E \oplus (v : val)$ denotes an environment E obtained from E by updating variable v to val.

The translation from PSM to LTS is given by the following set of SOS rules:

TEST

$$\frac{(s, [pred], s') \in T \quad E \vdash pred \rightarrow True}{(S, s, T, E) \xrightarrow{\epsilon} (S, s', T, E)}$$

ASSIGNMENT

$$\frac{(s, v = Exp, s') \in T \quad E \vdash Exp \rightarrow val}{(S, s, T, E) \xrightarrow{\epsilon} (S, s', T, E \oplus (v : val))}$$

SEND

$$\frac{(s, c!Exp, s') \in T \quad E \vdash Exp \rightarrow val}{(S, s, T, E) \xrightarrow{c!val} (S, s', T, E)}$$

---

[1] where $\Gamma ::= \epsilon \mid c!val \mid c?val$, with a typical element α.

RECEIVE

$$\frac{(s, c?v, s') \in T}{(S, s, T, E) \xrightarrow{c?val} (S, s', T, E \oplus (v : val))}$$

2.3 Atomic PSM processes

We now consider a larger subset of *Promela* containing the *atomic{...}* construct. Consequently, our model is extended to reflect this construct. We define atomic PSM processes[2] (with typical element Q is a triple (P, Π, σ) where:

- P is a PSM process.

- Π is a *partitioning* of $P.S$ into a set of disjoint non-empty sets of states, i.e. $\forall p_1, p_2 \in \Pi : p_1 \cap p_2 = \emptyset$ where $p_1 \in P.S, p_2 \in P.S$. Note that there may be some states in $P.S$ that are not in any partition $p \in \Pi$.

- $\sigma = \downarrow \emptyset \mid \downarrow p \mid \uparrow p$ is the current *atomic section* of P. $\downarrow \emptyset$ denotes that P is not in an atomic section, $\downarrow p$ denotes that P has entered atomic section p but is not yet active, and $\uparrow p$ denotes that P is active (executing a sequence of atomic steps) in p.

2.4 Semantics of atomic PSM processes

The semantics of atomic PSM processes is given by two rules. We use the function $\Pi(s)$ defined by $\Pi(s) = p \in \Pi$ (for $s \in p$) and $\Pi(s) = \emptyset$ (for $s \notin \bigcup_{p \in \Pi} p$).

DEACTIVATED–ATOMIC–SEQUENCE

$$\frac{P \xrightarrow{\alpha} P' \quad (\Pi(P'.s) \neq p \ \vee \ \Pi(P'.s) = \emptyset)}{\begin{array}{c} (P, \Pi, \downarrow p) \xrightarrow{\alpha} (P', \Pi, \downarrow \Pi(P'.s)) \\ (P, \Pi, \uparrow p) \xrightarrow{\alpha} (P', \Pi, \downarrow \Pi(P'.s)) \end{array}}$$

---

[2] we do allow for non-atomic PSM processes as a special case where $Q = (P, \emptyset, \downarrow \emptyset)$.

ACTIVATED–ATOMIC–SEQUENCE

$$\frac{P \xrightarrow{\;\alpha\;} P' \quad p \neq \emptyset \quad \Pi(P'.s) = p}{\begin{array}{l} (P, \Pi, \downarrow p) \xrightarrow{\;\alpha\;} (P', \Pi, \uparrow p) \\ (P, \Pi, \uparrow p) \xrightarrow{\;\alpha\;} (P', \Pi, \uparrow p) \end{array}}$$

Figure 1 illustrates the rules and shows the different cases for activation/deactivation of atomic sequences. The transitions numbered (1) to (6) correspond to the first rule (DEACTIVATED–ATOMIC–SEQUENCE), whereas transitions (7) and (8) correspond to the second rule (ACTIVATED–ATOMIC–SEQUENCE).

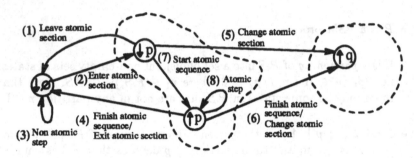

FIGURE 1. Allowable atomic transitions.

2.5 PSM specifications

We now turn to complete PSMs. A PSM specification is a pair $(Procs, Chans)$ where:

- $Procs$ is a set of atomic PSM processes;

- $Chans$ is a set of bounded FIFO channels. If the length of the channel is zero then communication is by rendez–vous, else it is by asynchronous message passing.

2.6 Semantics of PSM specifications

We use the following notations in the rules: $Int(Q)$ means that Q is *interruptible* (i.e. for $Q = (P, \Pi, \sigma)$: $\sigma = \downarrow \emptyset$), $l(c)$ gives the current number of values (messages) in channel c, $\#c$ gives the length of channel c, and $head(c)$ gives the value at the head of the channel c.

SPEC–ASYNCH–SEND

$$\frac{Q_i \xrightarrow{c!v} Q_i' \quad \forall j \neq i : Int(Q_j) \quad l(c) < \#c \quad \#c \neq 0}{(Chans, Procs) \longrightarrow (Chans', Procs')}$$

where
$$Procs' = (Procs - \{Procs'\}) \cup Q_i'$$
$$Chans' = Chans - \{c(v_1, \ldots, v_n)\} \cup \{c(v_1, \ldots, v_n, v)\}$$

SPEC–ASYNCH–RECEIVE

$$\frac{Q_i \xrightarrow{c?v} Q_i' \quad \forall j \neq i : Int(Q_j) \quad l(c) > 0 \quad head(c) = v}{(Chans, Procs) \longrightarrow (Chans', Procs')}$$

where
$$Procs' = (Procs - \{Procs'\}) \cup Q_i'$$
$$Chans' = Chans - \{c(v_1, \ldots, v_n, v)\} \cup \{c(v_1, \ldots, v_n)\}$$

SPEC–RENDEZ–VOUS

$$\frac{Q_i \xrightarrow{c!v} Q_i' \quad Q_j \xrightarrow{c?v} Q_j' \quad \forall k \neq i : Int(Q_k) \quad \#c = 0}{(Chans, Procs) \longrightarrow (Chans, Procs')}$$
$$\text{where } Procs' = (Procs - \{Procs'\}) \cup Q_i' \cup Q_j'$$

The condition that even process Q_j is interruptible is a very strict interpretation of atomic instructions. It prevents rendez–vous communication if the two processes involved are both in an atomic sequence. The rule does permit Q_i to leave, exit or change atomic section while Q_j starts an atomic section.

SPEC–INTERNAL

$$\frac{Q_i \xrightarrow{\epsilon} Q_i' \quad \forall j \neq i : Int(Q_j)}{(Chans, Procs) \longrightarrow (Chans, Procs')}$$
$$\text{where } Procs' = (Procs - \{Procs'\}) \cup Q_i'$$

3   Reactive State Machines

Here we present the *Reactive State Machine (RSM)*, a formalisation of our proposed extension to *Promela*.

Like we did for PSMs, we give the syntax and semantics in an incremental fashion, starting with *RSM automata*, then *RSM processes*, and finally we give the semantics of complete *RSM specifications*. The set of instructions L is the same as the set used in section 2.

3.1   *RSM automata*

In the RSM model a process can be decomposed into a configuration of *RSM automata*. An RSM automaton, A, is a tuple $(S, s, spred, T, E, I)$ where:

- S is a set of states partioned into two disjoint subsets[3]:
  - $SS \subseteq S$ a set of *stable states*
  - $TS \subset S$ a set of *transitory states*

- s is either the *initial state* $\in SS$ or the *current state*.

- $spred : s \rightarrow \{True, False\}$ is a function to determine if a give state is stabel or transitory. $spred(s) = True$ if $s \in SS$ and $spred(s) = False$ if $s \in TS$.

- $T \subset S \times L \times S$ is a *transition relation*

- E is the *environment* of variables in A.

- I is an *interface*[4] consisting of:
  - P_{in} a set of *inports*
  - P_{out} a set of *outports*

A *well-formed* RSM automaton has the following restrictions:

- if $(s, l, s') \in T$ and $s \in SS$ then l is an input action.

- if $(s, l, s') \in T$ and $l = c?x$ then $c \in P_{in}$.

- if $(s, l, s') \in T$ and $l = c!val$ then $c \in P_{out}$.

---

[3]where $S = SS \cup ST$ and $SS \cap ST = \emptyset$
[4]where $P_{in} \cap P_{out} = \emptyset$.

3.2 Semantics of RSM automata

The semantics of an RSM automaton is given by the same rules as for a PSM process.

3.3 RSM processes

An RSM process R is a tuple (A, I, L) where:

- A is a set of RSM automata $\{a_1, \ldots, a_n\}$

- I an *interface*[5] consisting of:

  - C_{in} a set of *input channels*
  - C_{out} a set of *output channels*

- L is a set of *links* taking the following three forms:

  - L_{int} a set of *internal links* represented by the tuple $((a_i, p_i), (a_j, p_j))$, where $p_i \in a_i.P_{out}$ and $p_j \in a_j.P_{in}$.

  - L_{out} a set of *external output links* represented by the tuple $((a_i, p_i), (\bullet, p_j))$, where $p_i \in a_i.P_{out}$ and $p_j \in C_{out}$.

  - L_{in} a set of *external input links* represented by the tuple $((\bullet, p_i), (a_j, p_j))$, where $p_i \in C_{in}$ and $p_j \in \in a_j.P_{in}$.

Some other definitions:

- the *state* of an RSM process R is the tuple $R.s = (a_1.s, \ldots, a_n.s)$, where:

  - the *initial state* is defined as the tuple $(a_1.s_0, \ldots, a_n.s_0)$
  - a state $s = (s_1, \ldots, s_n)$ is a *stable state* iff $\forall s_i : spred_i(s_i) = True$.
  - a state $s = (s_1, \ldots, s_n)$ is a *transitory state* iff $\exists s_i : spred_i(s_i) = False$.

3.4 Semantics of RSM processes

We add the predicate $stable(R) = R.s$ is a stable state. and give the SOS rules for RSM processes:

---

[5]where $C_{in} \cap C_{out} = \emptyset$

RSM–PROC–EXT–SEND

$$\frac{a_i \xrightarrow{\; g!val \;} a'_i \quad ((a_i, g), (\bullet, c)) \in L_{out} \quad c \in C_{out}}{(A, I, L) \xrightarrow{\; c!val \;} (A', I, L)}$$

> where $\begin{aligned} A &= a_1, \ldots, a_i, \ldots, a_n \\ A' &= a_1, \ldots, a'_i, \ldots, a_n \end{aligned}$

RSM–PROC–EXT–RECEIVE

$$\frac{a_i \xrightarrow{\; g?v \;} a'_i \quad ((\bullet, c), (a_i, g)) \in L_{in} \quad c \in C_{in} \quad stable((A, I, L))}{(A, I, L) \xrightarrow{\; c?v \;} (A', I, L)}$$

> where $\begin{aligned} A &= a_1, \ldots, a_i, \ldots, a_n \\ A' &= a_1, \ldots, a'_i, \ldots, a_n \end{aligned}$

RSM–PROC–SYNCH

$$\frac{a_i \xrightarrow{\; g!val \;} a'_i \quad a_j \xrightarrow{\; h?v \;} a'_j \quad ((a_i, h), (a_j, g)) \in L_{int}}{(A, I, L) \xrightarrow{\; \epsilon \;} (A', I, L)}$$

> where $\begin{aligned} A &= a_1, \ldots, a_i, \ldots, a_j, \ldots, a_n \\ A' &= a_1, \ldots, a'_i, \ldots, a'_j, \ldots, a_n \end{aligned}$

A synchronisation between automata a_i and a_j is possible only if a_I can send a message on outport p, a_I can receive a message on inport q, and there is a link between (a_i, p) and (a_j, q).

RSM–PROC–INTERNAL–ACTION

$$\frac{a_i \xrightarrow{\; \epsilon \;} a'_i}{(A, I, L) \xrightarrow{\; \epsilon \;} (A', I, L)}$$

> where $\begin{aligned} A &= a_1, \ldots, a_i, \ldots, a_n \\ A' &= a_1, \ldots, a'_i, \ldots, a_n \end{aligned}$

3.5 RSM specifications

An RSM specification is a triple $(RProcs, Procs, Chans)$ where:

- *RProcs* is a set of RSM processes;

- *Procs* is a set of atomic PSM processes;

- *Chans* is a set of channels.

3.6 Semantics of RSM specifications

The semantics of RSM specifications can simply be given using the rules for PSM specifications where the predicate $Int(R)$ is defined on RSM process R by $Int(R) = stable(R)$.

4 Translating RSMs to PSMs

In the translation of an RSM specification to a PSM specification, each RSM process is translated to a PSM process through a technique of *automata combination*. The next section shows how we use these techniques to extend *Promela* with reactive processes (*rproctypes*), and RSPIN a tool which performs the translation of reactive processes to *Promela* processes (*proctypes*).

The algorithm for automata combination uses standard state space search techniques to create the global state graph representing the combined automaton. The only main difference is that the combined automaton is trimmed from all transitions starting from transitory state vectors and having external inputs.

Once the combined automaton have been obtained we use another algorithm to partion it into disjoint atomic sections. The purpose is to make each possible reaction of the combined automaton atomic. We should note here that the intended behaviour of atomic reactions is only valid when communication is by asynchronous FIFO channels[6].

We can now give the partitioning algorithm, using the notation $s - \bullet \to s'$ to denote the fact that there exists a path from state s to transitory state s', traversing only transitory states. The algorithm is then:

$$\text{For every stable state } s, \Pi(s) =_{def} \{s\} \cup \{s'|s - \bullet \to s'\}$$

We must show that $\Pi(s)$ does not create overlapping partitions. We claim that:

---

[6]In the RSPIN tool there is an option which prevents the partioning from taking place (on a global or a per process basis). This gives the user more flexibility to decide whether to allow rendez-vous communication for reactive processes.

$$\forall s_1, s_2 : \Pi(s_1) \cap \Pi(s_2) = \emptyset$$

The proof is obtained by induction on the length of paths $s_1 - \bullet \rightarrow s$ and $s_2 - \bullet \rightarrow s$ and using the fact that transitions of RSM automata are restricted (syntactically) so that this condition holds:

If $((s_1, l_1, s), (s_2, l_2, s)) \in T \times T$, and if s is a transitory state, then $(s_1, l_1) = (s_2, l_2)$.

5 Reactive Promela and RSPIN

We now present *Reactive Promela*, our proposed extension to *Promela*, and the associated RSPIN tool.

5.1 Syntax of Reactive Promela

The syntax of *Reactive Promela* strongly resembles that of *Promela*, since the aim is to make it as easy as possible to use the extension. The only new keywords added in *Reactive Promela* are the following:

```
automaton   in        inport    link
outport     rproctype  external
```

Below we present the parts of the *Reactive Promela* grammar where it extends the *Promela* grammar. First, a few words on the notation. The new keywords are displayed in capitals (RPROCTYPE), tokens and *Promela* keywords are enclosed within apostrophes (':' and 'goto'), names (references) are displayed in lowercase letters within < ... > (<rproc_name>) and non-terminals in lowercase letters (r_proc). Also, { ... }+ means one or more of the enclosed unit and { ... }* means zero or more units. Units enclosed by [...] are optional.

In *Reactive Promela*, the old process definition: proc ::= PROCTYPE ... is replaced by: proc ::= p_proc | r_proc, where p_proc is the usual *Promela* process, and r_proc is the *Reactive Promela* process defined by:

```
r_proc      ::= RPROCTYPE <rproc_name>
                '(' r_interface ')' r_body
r_interface ::= {r_port_decl}*
r_port_decl ::= INPORT <port_name> | OUTPORT <port_name>
```

```
r_body       ::= {automaton}+ links
automaton    ::= AUTOMATON <autom_name>
                 '(' a_interface ')' a_body
a_interface ::= {a_port_decl}*
a_port_decl ::= EXTERNAL INPORT  <port_name>
             |  EXTERNAL OUTPORT <port_name>
             |  INPORT  <port_name> port_init
             |  OUTPORT <port_name> port_init
port_init    ::= '=' '{' type_list '}'
a_body       ::= '{' {one_decl | a_stmnt}+ '}'
a_stmnt      ::= <port_name> '?' {<var_name>|const}+
             |  <port_name> '!' {a_expr}+
             |  <label_name> ':' a_stmnt
             |  'goto' <label_name>
             |  <var_name> '=' aexpr
             |  'if' options 'fi'
             |  'do' options 'od'
links        ::= LINK '{' {link}+ '}'
link         ::= port '=>' {port}+
port         ::= <port_name> IN <autom_name>
```

The body of an automaton is defined as **a_body**, which is the same as **body** in *Promela* except that **a_body** only allows (for the time being) a subset of the rules of *Promela* (listed in the rule for **a_stmnt**). We have not shown the rule for **a_expr** but it allows most of the usual *Promela* expressions, at least for arithmetic and boolean operations.

To introduce the *Reactive Promela* language and the syntax shown above, we give a simple example of a *Reactive Promela* specification. It consists of a single *rproctype* which encapsulates two *automata*. Figure 2 below shows the specification in a graphical notation for *Reactive Promela*.

The graphical syntax makes it very easy to visualize a *Reactive Promela* specification, and it would certainly be interesting for the user to write or view a specification using a graphical interface. The textual syntax represnting the diagram of figure 2 is:

```
#define NO 0
#define YES 1

chan i1 = [10] of { int, int };
chan o1 = [10] of { bool }; chan o2 = [10] of { int,int };
chan l1 = [10] of { int }; chan l2 = [10] of { int };
chan l3 = [10] of { int }; chan l4 = [10] of { int };

rproctype A
   /* external interface definition */
   (inport  i1, l3; outport o1, l1, l2)
{
   automaton aut1
```

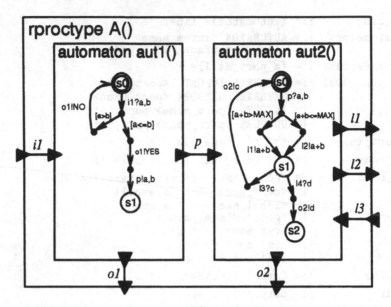

FIGURE 2. A simple rproctype decomposed into two automata.

```
    /* interface definition */
   (external inport i1; external outport o1;
    outport p = { int, int })
{
  int a, b;

 stable0:
  i1?a,b -> if
            :: [a > b]  -> o1!NO; goto stable0
            :: [a <= b] -> o1!YES; p!a,b; goto stable1
            fi;

 stable1: skip
}

automaton aut2
   /* interface definition */
  (external inport  l3, l4; external outport o2, l1, l2;
   inport  p = { int, int })
{
  int a, b, c, d, MAX = 10;

 stable0:
  p?a,b -> if
            :: [a+b > MAX]  -> l1!a+b; goto stable1
            :: [a+b <= MAX] -> l2!a+b; goto stable1
            fi;
```

```
stable1:
 if
 :: 13?c -> o2!c; goto stable0
 :: 14?d -> o2!d; goto stable2
 fi

stable2: skip
}

link { p in aut1 => p in aut2 }
}
```

...other rproctypes() and other Promela proctypes()

5.2   Reactive SPIN

In order to realistically check the correctness of a specification, tool support is essential. Instead of writing a simulator/verifier from scratch we propose to perform a mapping of *Reactive Promela* constructs into corresponding ones in *Promela*. For this purpose we present RSPIN, a preprocessor tool that translates a *Reactive Promela* specification into an equivalent *Promela* specification.

One of the most important aims we hope to achieve through the *Reactive Promela* extension is to provide a way to reduce the state-space explosion problem. There are two ways in which this is done. We have already seen in section 4 that the state space generated by combining RSM automata is not the full crossproduct of reachable states. The other means of reducing the state space is the use of *Promela*'s atomic{...} construct to implement the partitioning function $\Pi(s)$. The effect of this is that the proctypes generated by RSPIN reacts to inputs in an atomic fashion. This means that during simulation or verification, other proctypes are blocked until the reaction is over.

However, it must be noted that the use of atomic reactions is valid only if the channels used are of length greater than zero. In other words, rendez-vous communication is not possible during a reaction. To allow more flexibility we make the encapsulation of reactions as atomic sequences to be optional on a per rproctype basis.

To illustrate how automata are combined we present a part of a *Reactive Promela* specification for the HDLC protocol[7]. To model the protocol in *Reactive Promela* we decompose it into five automata two of which are

---

[7]The example is taken from a course in protocol specification given by Elie Najm at ENST. Modelisation and validation of this example will be presented in more detail elsewhere.

363

shown in figure 3 (the *Transmitter* and the *Window*)[8]. This example shows
the benefit of decomposition: each automaton that make up the rproctype
(i.e. the protocol) have a simple and clearly defined role, but we can still
treat and reason about it as a whole.

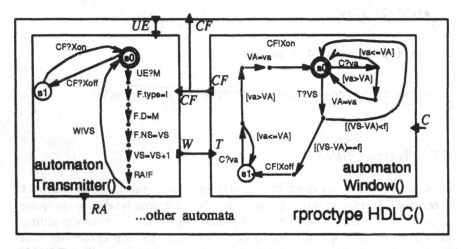

FIGURE 3. The transmitter and the window automata of the HDLC rproctype.

The transmitter can receive a message from the upper protocol (on inport
UE). From this it creates a frame (the structure F) which it sends to the
window (on outport W) as well as to the retransmitter and the acknowledger
(on outport RA). The window's responsibility is to manage the sequence
numbers. When the window is saturated, it notifies the transmitter and
the upper protocol layer (on outport CF) that no more messages can be
sent, until one is acknowledged. From the receiver (not shown) it receives
a message (on inport C) that indicate that the last frame acknowledged.

After combining the two automata in the figure above we get the result
shown in figure 4. In the textual syntax the combined automaton would be
represented as a *Promela* proctype[9]:

```
proctype  combined_Transmitter_Window()
{
  Frame F; /* with fields: type, D, NS */
  int Window_VS, Transmitter_VS, VA, va, f;

  s0:
```

---

[8][8]The three automata not shown are the *Retransmitter*, the *Receiver* and the
Acknowledger.
[9]We ignore the three other automata representing the HDLC protocol.

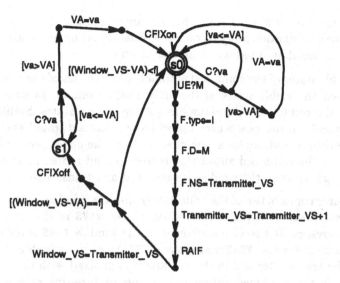

FIGURE 4. The resulting automaton after combining the transmitter and the window.

```
if
:: atomic {
    UE?M -> F.type=I; F.D=M; F.NS=Window_VS;
            Transmitter_VS=Transmitter_VS+1;
            RA!F; Window_VS=Transmitter_VS+1;
            if
            :: [(Window_VS-VA)==f] -> CF!Xoff; goto s1
            :: [(Window_VS-VA)<f] -> goto s0
            fi
    }
:: atomic {
    C?va -> ...
    ...
    }
fi

s1:
  atomic {
    C?va -> ...
    ...
  }
}
```

We can make a few observations about this combined automaton. First we note that the number of states has not increased significantly. This is because the combination process combines transitions and interleaves whole reactions rather than interleaving all transitions.

The stable states of the combined automaton is a subset of the crossproduct between the stable states of the individual automata. In figure 4 we note that the combined automaton has got two stable states. Stable state s0 corresponds to the case where the window is not saturated and where the transmitter is waiting for a new message from the upper protocol layer. In this state the combined automaton is free to send more messages. The other one, s1, is when the window is saturated and transmission blocked.

Communications between the transmitter and the window is reduced to assignment to variables (e.g. the send statement W!VS in the transmitter and the corresponding receive statement in the window T?VS is reduced to the assignment Window_VS=Transmitter_VS). Since the variable VS exists in both the transmitter and in the window it is prefixed with the automaton name in the combined automaton. A more interesting case is where the window notifies both the transmitter and the upper protocol layer that it is saturated. This is an example of a communication with more than one receiver. Between the transmitter and the window this is a pure synchronization which takes the combined automaton to stable state s1 (the saturation state). But we still need to notify the upper layer: therefore the combined automaton keeps the send action CF!Xoff. All other communication actions than those sent between the two automata in figure 4 are kept as they were.

To demonstrate more clearly the benefit provided by *Reactive Promela*'s decomposition technique we would have had to show the combined automaton for all the five automata in the HDLC protocol model have been (unfortunately too big to fit conveniently on one page).

6 Conclusion

In this paper we have presented a formalisation of a subset of *Promela* and of a reactive extension. Then we introduced the *Reactive Promela* language and its associated tool RSPIN. The language belongs to the family of synchronous reactive formalisms and allows a system to be decomposed into a reactive part containing configurations of synchronously communicating automata and a pro-active part containing *Promela* proctypes.

In relation to the other languages in the synchronous reactive family, *Reactive Promela* is an *imperative language*, similar to RC [Bou91], Esterel [BG92], [JLRM], and SL [BdS95]. These languages are distinguished by the notions of *state* and *sequences of statements* that lead from one state to another. In contrast, in the *data-flow languages* like Lustre [CPHP85] and Signal [Gue86], the reaction to input events is evaluated as the solution of a set of equations. There are also some attempts to combine the imperative and data-flow approach, e.g. the language ArgoLus as described in [JLRM].

In *Reactive Promela*, like in the latest version of Esterel and in SL, we disallow hypotheses to be made about the presence or absence of a signal during the reaction. This means that a signal can only be taken into account after it has appeared. In *Reactive Promela* dynamic behavior is represented as extended finite automata, while Esterel and SL are special kinds of process algebras. There are two other major differences between Esterel and SL on one side and *Reactive Promela* on the other: The first is that Esterel and SL use broadcast communication while in *Reactive Promela* communication is via point-to-point channels. The second difference is that in *Reactive Promela*, reactions are triggered by one input event, while in Esterel and SL reactions are triggered by an arbitrary set of input events.

The RSPIN tool translates rproctypes into *Promela* proctypes, so that a *Reactive Promela* specification can be simulated and verified with SPIN. No modifications to the SPIN tool are needed to do this.

We also have some ideas for extensions to *Reactive Promela*/RSPIN. The next probable extensions are handle *Promela* code in RSPIN and to make a graphical interface for X-Windows which would allow the *Reactive Promela* user to write and view automata. A very useful tool for the user of RSPIN would be one which allows traces produced by SPIN to be "mapped to" the initial *Reactive Promela* specification. Other extensions might include an emacs mode for editing *Reactive Promela* specifications. More theoretical issues include the possibility for an rproctype to react to collections of inputs instead of to exactly one input. More work is needed on how properties of *Reactive Promela* specifications can be proven, although it seems that most of the SPIN techniques should be applicable (i.e. special labels, assertions and LTL-formulae). We will also look into how the partial-order reduction methods introduced in recent versions of SPIN can be used with *Reactive Promela* specifications, although we can conjecture that *Reactive Promela* provides this one kind of such reductions "for free": as we have seen in previous sections, RSPIN does not consider all the interleavings of transitions. Instead one interleaving is chosen since the set of outputs generated by the reaction will be the same. For more information on partial order reduction methods see [dSdS95, Pel94, GKPP95, Val90, WG93, God94].

7 REFERENCES

[AF90]   C. André and L. Fancelli. A mixed (asynchronous / synchronous) implementation of a real-time system. In *Euromicro 90, Amsterdam*, 1990.

[BB91]   G. Berry and A. Benveniste. The synchronous approach to reactive and real-time systems. *Another Look at Real Time Programming, Proceedings of the IEEE*, 79:1270–1282, 1991.

[BCGH93] Albert Benveniste, Paul Caspi, Paul Le Guernic, and Nicolas Halbwachs. Data-flow synchronous languages. Rapport de recherche 2089, INRIA, Unité de recherche INRIA Sophia-Antipolis, France., October 1993.

[BdS95]   Frédéric Boussinot and Robert de Simone. The sl synchronous language. Rapport de recherche 2510, INRIA, Unité de recherche INRIA Sophia-Antipolis, France., Mars 1995.

[Ber93a]   G. Berry. Communicating reactive processes. In *Proc. 20th ACM Conf. on Principles of Programming Languages, Charleston, Virginia*, 1993.

[Ber93b]   G. Berry. The semantics of pure esterel. In *Proc Marktoberdorf Intl. Summer School on Program Design Calculi*, LNCS, to appear. Springer-Verlag, 1993.

[BG91]   G. Berry and G. Gonthier. Incremental development of an hdlc entity in Esterel. *Comp. Networks and ISDN Systems*, 22:35–49, 1991.

[BG92]   G. Berry and G. Gonthier. The Esterel synchronous programming language: Design, semantics, implementation. *Science Of Computer Programming*, 19(2):87–152, 1992.

[BN83]   S. Budkowski and E. Najm. Structured finite state automata. a new approach for modelling distributed communication systems. In H. Rudin and C. H. West, editors, *Protocol Specification, Testing and Verification, III*. Elsevier Science Publishers B.V (North-Holland), 1983.

[Bou91]   F. Boussinot. Reactive c: An extension of c to program reactive systems. *Software-Practice and Experience*, 21(4):401–428, 1991.

[CPHP85] P. Caspi, D. Pilaud, N. Halbwachs, and J. Plaice. Lustre, a declarative language for programming synchronous systems. In *Proceedings of ACM Conference on Principles of Programming Languages*. ACM, 1985.

[dSdS95]   Monica Lara de Souza and Robert de Simone. Using po methods for verifying behavioural equivalences. In *Proceedings of FORTE'95*, pages 59–74, October 1995.

[Fer89]   Jean-Claude Fernandez.   Aldebaran: A tool for verification
            of communicating processes. Rapport SPECTRE C14, Lab-
            oratoire de Génie Informatique — Institut IMAG, Grenoble,
            September 1989.

[GKPP95] R. Gerth, R. Kuiper, R. Peled, and W. Penczek. A partial order
            approach to branching time model checking. In *Proceedings of
            ISTCS*, pages 330–339, 1995.

[God94]   Patrice Godefroid. *Partial-Order Methods for the Verification
            of Concurrent Systems: An Approach to the State-Explosion
            Problem*. PhD thesis, UNIVERSITE DE LIEGE, Faculté des
            Sciences Appliquées, 1994.

[Gue86]   P. Le Guernic. Signal, a data-flow oriented language for signal
            processing. *IEEE Trans. ASSP*, 34(2):362–374, 1986.

[Hal93]   N. Halbswachs. *Synchronous Programming of Reactive Sys-
            tems*. Kluwer Academic Press, Netherlands, 1993.

[Hol91]   Gerhard Holzmann. *Design and Validation of Computer Pro-
            tocols*. Prentice-Hall, Englewood Cliffs, N.J., first edition, 1991.

[JLRM]   M. Jourdan, F. Lagnier, P. Raymond, and F. Maraninchi. A
            multiparadigm language for reactive systems.

[Mad92]   E. Madelaine.   Verification tools from the Concur project.
            EATCS Bulletin, 47, 1992.

[MV89]   E. Madelaine and D. Vergamini.   Auto: A verification tool
            for distributed systems using reduction of finite automata net-
            works. In *Proc. FORTE'89 Conference, Vancouver*, 1989.

[Pel94]   D. Peled. Combining partial order reductions with on-the-
            fly model-checking. In *Proceedings of CAV'94*, LNCS 818.
            Springer-Verlag, 1994.

[Plo81]   G. Plotkin. A structural approach to operational semantics.
            Technical report, Comput. Sci. Dept., Aarhus Univ., 1981.

[RdS90]   V. Roy and R. de Simone. Auto and autograph. In R. Kur-
            shan, editor, *proceedings of Workshop on Computer Aided Ver-
            ification*, New-Brunswick, June 1990. AMS-DIMACS.

[Val90]   A. Valmari. A stubborn attack on state explosion. LNCS 531.
            Springer-Verlag, 1990.

[WG93]   P. Wolper and P. Godefroid. Partial order methods for tem-
            poral verification. In *Proceedings of Concur'93*, LNCS 715.
            Springer-Verlag, 1993.

Probabilistic Duration Automata for Analyzing Real-Time Systems

Louise E. Moser[*]

P. M. Melliar-Smith[*]

ABSTRACT [1] We present a novel methodology and tools for analyzing real-time systems that use probability density functions (pdfs) to represent the durations of operations within the system. We introduce the concept of a probabilistic duration automaton in which clocks are defined by pdfs rather than by explicit times. A state of a probabilistic duration automaton is a set of active clocks, and a transition is triggered by the expiration of one or more of these clocks. We present an algorithm for determining the probability that a clock in a state expires, the residual pdfs for the unexpired clocks, the probability of each transition, the probability of each state, and the duration of each state represented as a pdf. The algorithm also calculates the pdfs for durations of intervals between pairs of states within the automaton. These pdfs are used to determine whether a real-time system can meet its probabilistic timing constraints. An example application illustrates the use of this methodology in analyzing the real-time behavior of a four-phase handshaking protocol used in input/output systems.

1 Introduction

Traditionally, real-time systems have been defined by absolute requirements that certain events, typically input or output operations, must occur at or before precisely defined moments in time. To establish that such deadlines are met, existing methodologies and tools use worst-case upper bounds on the durations of operations within the system [8, 13, 14, 15].

Complex real-time systems, however, involve unreliable communication between distributed processors, asynchronous operations, unpredictable heuristic algorithms, and/or recovery from faults; furthermore, modern microprocessors exploit mechanisms such as caching and cycle stealing by

---

[*]Department of Electrical and Computer Engineering, University of California, Santa Barbara, CA 93106.

[1]This work was supported in part by ARPA Grant Nos. N00174-93-K-0097 and N00174-95-K-0083.

high-speed input/output devices. These characteristics introduce significant variations in the time required to produce the results. The worst-case upper bound for the duration of an operation may be substantially worse than the mean duration, but the worst-case upper bound may be realized only very infrequently.

A design based on the worst-case upper bound for the duration of every operation may be unnecessarily conservative, since it must allow for the possibility that each of these rare occurrences coincide. Thus, the performance calculated for the real-time system may be much worse than the performance that the system can actually provide. However, if the real-time system is designed using mean durations, occasionally the system may fail to meet a deadline. Such a failure to meet a deadline may be acceptable, provided that its probability is small enough and can be estimated reasonably accurately.

We describe a novel methodology and tools for analyzing real-time systems that represent the durations of operations by probability density functions (pdfs), rather than by upper and lower bounds. For some real-world applications in which real-time performance is critical, such as the Aegis air defense system, these pdfs are indeed known. The types of questions that our probabilistic analysis methodology can answer are

- What is the duration of the interval between two events, expressed as a probability density function?

- What is the probability of reaching a transient state, and what is the probability of being in a particular state in equilibrium?

- What is the probability that the duration of an operation exceeds the deadline for the operation?

As the basis for this methodology, we introduce the concept of a probabilistic duration automaton in which a clock is a probability density function. In each state of the automaton, several clocks may be active. A transition from one state to another state occurs when one or more active clocks expire; this may result in some of the expired clocks being reset.

We present an algorithm for evaluating such a probabilistic duration automaton. The algorithm determines the probabilities of the transitions out of a state, the rates of flow into a state, and the probability of being in a state. It also determines the probability that an active clock in a state expires, as well as the residual values of the clocks that do not expire, expressed as pdfs. The algorithm calculates the pdfs for the durations of the states and the pdfs for durations of intervals between pairs of states within the automaton. These pdfs are used to estimate the probability that a system can meet its real-time deadlines. Much of the interest of the analysis derives from the care required to ensure that two pdfs are convolved or combined only if they are independent.

As an application of this methodology, we consider the probabilistic timing constraints of a four-phase handshaking protocol used in input/output systems. This example demonstrates that manual analysis of these properties is difficult and that mechanical tools are essential.

2 The Clocks

In our methodology, a clock c is defined by a probability density function $\hat{c}$ that gives the probabilities for the possible durations of an interval between two events. The domain of the pdf, $i.e.$, the set of durations, is a finite set of positive rationals. Multiplication by the least common multiple of the denominators of these rationals yields a set of positive integers. Thus, without loss of generality, we assume that the durations are positive integers. We assume further that all of the pdfs have the same domain $\{1, 2, \ldots, m\}$ for some integer $m \geq 2$. The range of a pdf is a set of non-negative rationals between 0 and 1 such that the sum of these rationals is equal to 1. Thus, a clock c is defined by a pdf

$$\hat{c} : \{1, 2, \ldots, m\} \to [0, 1], \text{ where } \sum_{x=1}^{m} \hat{c}(x) = 1$$

For each duration x, $\hat{c}(x)$ is the probability that the interval from the time at which c was last set until it expires has duration exactly x.

Our methodology exploits the three operations of convolution, residue, and disjunction of pdfs. Convolution gives the pdf for the duration of an interval that is the sequential composition of two intervals, while residue gives the remainder of clock c_1, contingent on clock c_2 expiring before c_1, expressed as a pdf. Some intervals can be formed in several independent ways, each with a probability of occurrence and with its own pdf. Disjunction gives the pdf for the duration of an interval as the sum of these pdfs, weighted by their corresponding probabilities. These three operations are well-known and, thus, we do not define them here. When we employ these operations in our analysis, we must however ensure that the pdfs for the clocks being combined are indeed independent.

3 The Probabilistic Duration Automaton

A state of a probabilistic duration automaton is a set of active clocks. A transition from one state to another state in the automaton corresponds to the expiration of one or more active clocks. More specifically, we have the following definition.

A *probabilistic duration automaton* is defined by

- A finite set $S = \{s_i \,|\, 1 \leq i \leq N\}$ of states, a set $T \subseteq S \times S$ of transitions between states in S, and a set $C = \{c_i \,|\, 1 \leq i \leq M\}$ of clock names

- An initial state in S and a set $\hat{C} = \{\hat{c}_i \,|\, 1 \leq i \leq M\}$ of initial clock values (pdfs), one per clock name

- For each state $s_i \in S$, a set $A_{s_i} \subseteq C$ of clocks that are active in state s_i

- For each transition $(s_i, s_j) \in T$, a set $E_{s_i,s_j} \subseteq A_{s_i}$ of clocks whose expiration in state s_i triggers that transition.

All of the clocks in E_{s_i,s_j} expire at the same moment; none of the clocks in $R_{s_i,s_j} = A_{s_i} - E_{s_i,s_j}$ expires either before or at that moment. The clocks in R_{s_i,s_j} have residual values on the transition (s_i, s_j), and remain active in state s_j, i.e., $R_{s_i,s_j} \subseteq A_{s_j}$. When a clock c is set or reset in any of the states, it is set to the initial clock value $\hat{c} \in \hat{C}$ for that clock. A clock must expire before it can be reset. The clocks that are set or reset on the transition (s_i, s_j) are the clocks in $A_{s_j} - R_{s_i,s_j}$.

Following the standard theory of Markov models, we consider two types of automata: equilibrium automata and transient automata. An *equilibrium automaton* is irreducible (every state can be reached from every other state) and aperiodic (there is no fixed period of returning to any state). The theory of Markov models tells us that, if any initial clock has two or more coprime durations with non-zero probabilities, then the automaton is aperiodic and the equilibrium probabilities of the states are time independent. A *transient automaton* has a single initial state, is reducible, and contains no irreducible subautomata. The probabilities of the states of a transient automaton are time dependent.

4 The Algorithm

A specification of a real-time system determines the set S of states and the set T of transitions of a probabilistic duration automaton, the set A_{s_i} of clocks that are active in state s_i, the set E_{s_i,s_j} of clocks whose expiration cause the transition (s_i, s_j), and the set $\hat{C}$ of pdfs that are the initial values of the clocks when they are set or reset.

Our algorithm determines the duration of each state or, equivalently, the time between the transitions into and out of that state, expressed as a pdf. It also determines the duration of the interval between each pair of states, from the time of the transitions into the first state to the time of the transitions into the second state, expressed as a pdf. To determine these pdfs, the algorithm calculates the probabilities of the transitions out of each state, the rates of flow into each state, the probability of being in a state, and related pdfs. The steps of the algorithm are presented below. Further explanation of the algorithm is given in Section 5.

4.1 Elaboration of the Automaton

The input to the algorithm is a probabilistic duration automaton obtained from the user's specification. If this automaton is reducible but contains an irreducible subautomaton, then the algorithm separates out that subautomaton and analyzes it separately. Such subautomata are replaced by absorbing states in the remaining automaton. Thus, the algorithm partitions the automaton into zero or more equilibrium automata and zero or more transient automata. If the analysis subsequently finds that some of the transition probabilities are zero, then it may be possible to partition the automaton further into simpler equilibrium automata and transient automata.

The algorithm must also eliminate correlations between pdfs before convolving or combining them. We define a state to be *disjunctive* if each of its in-edges has at most one unexpired clock and all of its in-edges have no unexpired clock or the same unexpired clock; otherwise, the state is *non-disjunctive*. A state that is disjunctive has the desirable property that the residual pdfs on its in-edges can be combined. The algorithm splits non-disjunctive states into disjunctive states as outlined below.

1. Until each state with more than one in-edge is a disjunctive state, for each non-disjunctive state with more than one in-edge and for each such in-edge,

    a. Split that state by creating an additional state with

        i. The same set of active clocks as the given non-disjunctive state

        ii. A set of out-edges to the same destinations as the set of out-edges from the state being split, with corresponding in-edges having the same set of expiring clocks

    b. Change the destination of one of the in-edges to be the newly created state.

2. Partition the automaton into zero or more transient automata and zero or more equilibrium automata.

3. Set estimated rates of flow into each state and estimated residual pdfs for each unexpired clock.

Note that, after such elaboration, the automaton may still contain non-disjunctive states having one in-edge and two or more unexpired clocks on that in-edge.

4.2 Calculation for Individual States

For each state of a probabilistic duration automaton, the algorithm determines, the probability of taking a transition out of that state, the conditional pdfs for the duration of the state, the conditional pdfs for the unexpired clocks in the next state, and the rate of flow into the given state (Steps 1-3 below). From these quantities, the algorithm then derives the probability that a clock expires in the state, the pdf for the duration of the state, the pdf for each unexpired clock in the next state, and the probability of being in the given state (Steps 4-7 below).

For each automaton, until convergence is achieved,

1. For each disjunctive state s_i, calculate the residual pdf for the unexpired clock in state s_i from the residual pdfs for that clock on its in-edges, weighted by the rates of flow along those in-edges.

2. For each state s_i (disjunctive or not), trace backwards through the automaton, starting with s_i, until a disjunctive state is found. Denote this sequence of states by $\sigma_1, \ldots, \sigma_n$, where $\sigma_1 = s_h$ is the disjunctive state with the single unexpired clock c_h and $\sigma_n = s_i$. Note that this sequence is unique, that σ_k is non-disjunctive for $1 < k < n$ and that, if s_i is itself disjunctive, then the sequence contains the single state s_i. In the formulas below, we consider each set of possible durations $x_1, \ldots, x_n$ of the states $\sigma_1, \ldots, \sigma_n$ in this sequence.

   For each clock c that is active in some state of this sequence, let l_c be the lowest index in the sequence for which c is active and u_c the highest or upper index. For each clock c that is not active in any state of the sequence, set both l_c and u_c to 0. If a clock is reset at any point in the sequence and is active both before and after that point, regard that clock as two distinct clocks, one before the reset and one after. If c is the unexpired clock in the disjunctive state s_h, let $\hat{c}$ be the residual pdf for c in that state; otherwise, let $\hat{c}$ be the initial pdf corresponding to clock c when it is set or reset. If $l_c = u_c = 0$, extend the domain of $\hat{c}$ to include $x_0 = 0$ and set $\hat{c}(x_0) = 1$. If x is outside the domain of $\hat{c}$, set $\hat{c}(x) = 0$. As usual, interpret an empty sum to be 0 and an empty product to be 1. Set $\delta(p) = 1$ if the predicate p is true and $\delta(p) = 0$ otherwise.

3. For each edge (s_i, s_j) out of state s_i, calculate the following:

a. The probability of taking the edge (s_i, s_j) out of state s_i

$$p_{s_i,s_j} =$$

$$\frac{\displaystyle\sum_{x_1\ldots x_n}\left(\left(\prod_{c\in C-R_{s_i,s_j}}\hat{c}\left(\sum_{l_c\le k\le u_c}x_k\right)\right)\times\left(\prod_{c\in R_{s_i,s_j}}\sum_{x>0}\hat{c}\left(x+\sum_{l_c\le k\le u_c}x_k\right)\right)\right)}{\displaystyle\sum_{\substack{x_1\ldots x_{n-1}\\x_n=0}}\left(\left(\prod_{c\in C-A_{s_i}}\hat{c}\left(\sum_{l_c\le k\le u_c}x_k\right)\right)\times\left(\prod_{c\in A_{s_i}}\sum_{x>0}\hat{c}\left(x+\sum_{l_c\le k\le u_c}x_k\right)\right)\right)}$$

b. The probability of taking the edge (s_i, s_j) out of state s_i, contingent on the duration of the unexpired clock c_h at the start of state s_h being z_h,

$$p_{s_i,s_j|z_h} =$$

$$\frac{\displaystyle\sum_{x_1\ldots x_n}\left(\delta\left(z_h=\sum_{l_{c_h}\le k\le u_{c_h}}x_k\right)\times\left(\prod_{c\in B_R}\hat{c}\left(\sum_{l_c\le k\le u_c}x_k\right)\right)\times\left(\prod_{c\in R_{s_i,s_j}}\sum_{x>0}\hat{c}\left(x+\sum_{l_c\le k\le u_c}x_k\right)\right)\right)}{\displaystyle\sum_{\substack{x_1\ldots x_{n-1}\\x_n=0}}\left(\delta\left(z_h=\sum_{l_{c_h}\le k\le u_{c_h}}x_k\right)\times\left(\prod_{c\in B_A}\hat{c}\left(\sum_{l_c\le k\le u_c}x_k\right)\right)\times\left(\prod_{c\in A_{s_i}}\sum_{x>0}\hat{c}\left(x+\sum_{l_c\le k\le u_c}x_k\right)\right)\right)}$$

Here $B_R = (C - R_{s_i,s_j}) - \{c_h\}$ and $B_A = (C - A_{s_i}) - \{c_h\}$.

c. The pdf for the duration of state $\sigma_n = s_i$, contingent on the edge (s_i, s_j) being taken,

$$\hat{d}_{s_i|s_i,s_j}(z) =$$

$$\frac{\displaystyle\sum_{\substack{x_1\ldots x_{n-1}\\x_n=z}}\left(\left(\prod_{c\in C-R_{s_i,s_j}}\hat{c}\left(\sum_{l_c\le k\le u_c}x_k\right)\right)\times\left(\prod_{c\in R_{s_i,s_j}}\sum_{x>0}\hat{c}\left(x+\sum_{l_c\le k\le u_c}x_k\right)\right)\right)}{\displaystyle\sum_{x_1\ldots x_n}\left(\left(\prod_{c\in C-R_{s_i,s_j}}\hat{c}\left(\sum_{l_c\le k\le u_c}x_k\right)\right)\times\left(\prod_{c\in R_{s_i,s_j}}\sum_{x>0}\hat{c}\left(x+\sum_{l_c\le k\le u_c}x_k\right)\right)\right)}$$

d. The pdf for the unexpired clock $a \in R_{s_i,s_j}$ in state s_j, contingent on the edge (s_i, s_j) being taken,

$$\hat{a}_{s_j|s_i,s_j}(z) =$$

$$\frac{\displaystyle\sum_{x_1\ldots x_n}\left(\hat{a}\left(z+\sum_{l_a\le k\le u_a}x_k\right)\times\left(\prod_{c\in C-R_{s_i,s_j}}\hat{c}\left(\sum_{l_c\le k\le u_c}x_k\right)\right)\times\left(\prod_{c\in R_{s_i,s_j}-\{a\}}\sum_{x>0}\hat{c}\left(x+\sum_{l_c\le k\le u_c}x_k\right)\right)\right)}{\displaystyle\sum_{x_1\ldots x_n}\left(\left(\prod_{c\in C-R_{s_i,s_j}}\hat{c}\left(\sum_{l_c\le k\le u_c}x_k\right)\right)\times\left(\prod_{c\in R_{s_i,s_j}}\sum_{x>0}\hat{c}\left(x+\sum_{l_c\le k\le u_a}x_k\right)\right)\right)}$$

e. From the probabilities p_{s_i,s_j} of the edges (s_i, s_j), calculate the rate f_{s_i} of flow into each state s_i by solving a system of linear flow-balance equations, in the usual manner.

4. From the probabilities p_{s_i,s_j} of the edges (s_i, s_j), calculate the probability that a clock c expires in state s_i by summing the probabilities of the edges on which c expires.

5. From the probabilities p_{s_i,s_j} of the edges (s_i, s_j) and the pdf $\hat{d}_{s_i|s_i,s_j}$ for the duration of state s_i, contingent on the edge (s_i, s_j) being taken, calculate the (unconditional) pdf $\hat{d}_{s_i}$ for the duration of state s_i as a weighted sum.

6. From the probabilities p_{s_i,s_j} of the edges (s_i, s_j) and the pdf $\hat{a}_{s_j|s_i,s_j}$ for the unexpired clock a in state s_j, contingent on the edge (s_i, s_j) being taken, calculate the (unconditional) pdf $\hat{a}_{s_j}$ for the unexpired clock a in state s_j as a weighted sum.

7. From the rate f_{s_i} of flow into each state s_i and the mean duration $\bar{d}_{s_i}$ of state s_i, calculate the probability of being in state s_i by multiplying f_{s_i} by $\bar{d}_{s_i}$ and then normalizing this product over all states.

Note that the equilibrium automata and the transient automata are handled differently in Step 3e, which involves the solution of the system of flow-balance equations, and in Step 7, which as given applies only to the equilibrium automata. For the transient automata, the probability of each non-absorbing state is 0 and the probability of each absorbing state is determined solely by the rate of flow into that state.

4.3 Calculation for Intervals between Pairs of States

The algorithm also determines the residual pdfs for the clocks and the conditional pdfs for the durations of paths and intervals between pairs of states (Steps 1-5 below). From these pdfs, the algorithm then derives the (unconditional) pdfs for the durations of the intervals between pairs of states (Step 6 below).

For each automaton, until convergence is achieved,

1. First consider a single sequence of states $\sigma_1, \ldots, \sigma_n, \sigma_{n+1}$, where $\sigma_1 = s_h$, $\sigma_n = s_i$ and $\sigma_{n+1} = s_j$. Here, the states s_h and s_j are disjunctive and the states σ_k, $1 < k < n + 1$, are non-disjunctive. In Step 3 below, we calculate the pdf for the duration of this path. In Step 5, we calculate the pdf in the more general case, where there are multiple paths between s_h and s_j and the intermediate states of those paths may be either disjunctive or non-disjunctive. This can be generalized further to the case where s_h and s_j are not necessarily disjunctive.

Let the unexpired clocks in states s_h and s_j be c_h and c_j, respectively. We assume here that c_h and c_j are different clocks, i.e., c_h is not the residual clock on the edge (s_i, s_j).

2. For each edge (s_i, s_j) out of state s_i, calculate the rate of flow on the edge (s_i, s_j), contingent on the residual duration of clock c_h at the start of state s_h being z_h and on the residual duration of clock c_j at the start of state s_j being z_j,

$$f_{s_i,s_j|z_h,z_j} = f_{s_h} \times \left(\prod_{1 \leq k \leq n} p_{\sigma_k,\sigma_{k+1}|z_h} \right) \times$$

$$\frac{\displaystyle\sum_{x_1 \ldots x_n} \left(\delta(z_h = \sum_{l_{c_h} \leq k \leq u_{c_h}} x_k) \times \hat{c}_j(z_j + \sum_{l_{c_j} \leq k \leq u_{c_j}} x_k) \times \prod_{c \in C - \{c_h, c_j\}} \hat{c}(\sum_{l_c \leq k \leq u_c} x_k) \right)}{\displaystyle\sum_{x_1 \ldots x_n, x} \left(\delta(z_h = \sum_{l_{c_h} \leq k \leq u_{c_h}} x_k) \times \hat{c}_j(x + \sum_{l_{c_j} \leq k \leq u_{c_j}} x_k) \times \prod_{c \in C - \{c_h, c_j\}} \hat{c}(\sum_{l_c \leq k \leq u_c} x_k) \right)}$$

3. For a single path between states s_h and s_j, calculate the pdf for the duration of that path from the start of s_h to the start of s_j, contingent on the residual duration of clock c_h at the start of s_h being z_h and on the residual duration of clock c_j at the start of s_j being z_j,

$$\hat{d}_{s_h,s_j|z_h,z_j}(y) =$$

$$\frac{\displaystyle\sum_{x_1 \ldots x_n} \left(\delta(y = \sum_{1 \leq k \leq n} x_k) \times \delta(z_h = \sum_{l_{c_h} \leq k \leq u_{c_h}} x_k) \times \hat{c}_j(z_j + \sum_{l_{c_j} \leq k \leq u_{c_j}} x_k) \times \prod_{c \in C - \{c_h, c_j\}} \hat{c}(\sum_{l_c \leq k \leq u_c} x_k) \right)}{\displaystyle\sum_{x_1 \ldots x_n} \left(\delta(z_h = \sum_{l_{c_h} \leq k \leq u_{c_h}} x_k) \times \hat{c}_j(z_j + \sum_{l_{c_j} \leq k \leq u_{c_j}} x_k) \times \prod_{c \in C - \{c_h, c_j\}} \hat{c}(\sum_{l_c \leq k \leq u_c} x_k) \right)}$$

4. Calculate the pdf for the unexpired clock c_j in state s_j, contingent on the edge (s_i, s_j) being taken and on the residual duration of clock c_h at the start of state s_h being z_h,

$$(\hat{c}_j)_{s_i|s_i,s_j,z_h}(z) =$$

$$\frac{\displaystyle\sum_{x_1 \ldots x_n} \left(\delta(z_h = \sum_{l_{c_h} \leq k \leq u_{c_h}} x_k) \times \hat{c}_j(z + \sum_{l_{c_j} \leq k \leq u_{c_j}} x_k) \times \prod_{c \in C - \{c_h, c_j\}} \hat{c}(\sum_{l_c \leq k \leq u_c} x_k) \right)}{\displaystyle\sum_{x_1 \ldots x_n, x} \left(\delta(z_h = \sum_{l_{c_h} \leq k \leq u_{c_h}} x_k) \times \hat{c}_j(x + \sum_{l_{c_j} \leq k \leq u_{c_j}} x_k) \times \prod_{c \in C - \{c_h, c_j\}} \hat{c}(\sum_{l_c \leq k \leq u_c} x_k) \right)}$$

5. For the interval (aggregate of paths) between states s_h and s_j, calculate the pdf for the duration of the interval from the start of s_h to the start of s_j, contingent on the residual duration of clock c_h at the start of s_h being z_h and on the residual duration of clock c_j at the start of s_j being z_j,

$$\hat{d}_{s_h,s_j|z_h,z_j}(y) =$$

$$\frac{\sum_{s_l,y_1,y_2} \delta(y = y_1 + y_2) \times f_{s_l,s_j|z_h,z_j} \times \hat{d}_{s_h,s_l|z_h,z_l}(y_1) \times \hat{d}_{s_l,s_j|z_l,z_j}(y_2)}{\sum_{s_l} f_{s_l,s_j|z_h,z_j}}$$

Here one state s_l is chosen for each path from s_h to s_j.

6. For the interval (aggregate of paths) between states s_h and s_j, calculate the pdf for the duration of the interval from the start of s_h to the start of s_j as the weighted sum

$$\hat{d}_{s_h,s_j}(y) = \sum_{z_h,z_j} \hat{d}_{s_h,s_j|z_h,z_j}(y) \times \hat{c}_h(z_h) \times (\hat{c}_j)_{s_j|s_i,s_j,z_h}(z_j)$$

5 Discussion

We now provide further explanation of the algorithm, with examples to illustrate the problems that can arise if correlated pdfs are not handled properly.

5.1 Eliminating Correlations

The main intricacies of the algorithm arise from the need to eliminate correlations between pdfs that are being combined. For example, consider a state s with two in-edges, where two independent clocks c_1 and c_2 were active in both of the prior states and did not expire, as shown in Fig. 1. Along one edge the residual pdf for c_1 is non-zero for 3 to 5 and the residual pdf for c_2 is non-zero for 7 to 9, while along the other edge the residual pdf for c_1 is non-zero for 10 to 12 and the residual pdf for c_2 is non-zero for 14 to 16. Naively combining the two residual pdfs for c_1 from the two in-edges into a single pdf, and similarly for c_2, would lead to an erroneous conclusion such as that c_2 expires before c_1 or that when c_1 expires the residual pdf for c_2 is non-zero for 2 to 13. This example demonstrates the need to split non-disjunctive states with two or more in-edges, each of which has two or more unexpired clocks, because there is a dependence between the unexpired clocks on those in-edges.

Next consider the example shown in Fig. 2. Here, clocks c_1 and c_2 are active in the initial state s_1. If c_2 expires before c_1, the transition is taken to state s_2 whereas, if c_1 expires before c_2, the transition is taken to state s_3.

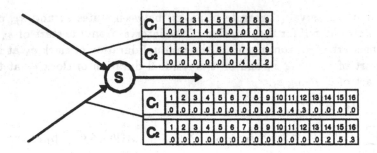

FIGURE 1. An example showing the need to split a non-disjunctive state. In this example, clock c_2 cannot expire before clock c_1 in state s. To ensure this, the state is split, avoiding a disjunction of correlated pdfs.

If c_1 and c_2 expire simultaneously, the transition is taken to state s_6. Clock c_3 becomes active in states s_2 and s_3. If c_1 expires before c_3 in s_2, the transition is taken to s_3 and c_2 becomes active. If c_2 expires before c_3 in s_3, the transition is taken back to s_2 and c_1 becomes active again. If c_3 expires before or simultaneously with c_1 in s_2, the transition is taken to s_4. Similarly, if c_3 expires before or simultaneously with c_2 in s_3, the transition is taken to s_5. Fig. 3 shows the automaton of Fig. 2 after state splitting. It shows the probability of each transition, the probabilities of reaching states s_4, s_5 and s_6, and the pdfs for the durations until those states are reached from s_1.

Now consider the example shown in Fig. 4. Here we have a state s_1 in which three clocks become active: c_1 is non-zero for 2 to 4, c_2 is non-zero for 6 to 10, and c_3 is also non-zero for 6 to 10. When clock c_1 expires, the transition to state s_2 is taken and, when clock c_2 expires, the transition to state s_3 is taken. The residual pdf for c_2 in s_2 is non-zero for 2 to 8, as is the residual pdf in s_2 for c_3. It is incorrect to combine these pdfs and to conclude that the residual pdf for c_3 in s_3 is non-zero for 1 to 6, because they are both obtained from the pdf for c_1 in s_1. This example demonstrates the need to trace backwards through the automaton until a disjunctive state is found, because states with more than one unexpired clock on their in-edges may introduce dependencies between those clocks.

Finally, consider the example in Fig. 5, which illustrates the problem of determining the pdf for the duration of an interval by convolving together the pdfs for the durations of its component states. Here, since c_1 necessarily expires before c_2, the pdf for the duration of state s_1 is non-zero for 1 to 5. Consequently, the pdf for the duration of state s_2, being the residual pdf of c_2 after c_1 has expired, is non-zero for 1 to 9. Simple convolution of the pdfs for the durations of s_1 and s_2 would lead to the incorrect conclusion that the pdf for the duration of the interval consisting of those two states is non-zero for 2 to 14 whereas, in fact, the pdf for that duration is non-zero for 6 to 10.

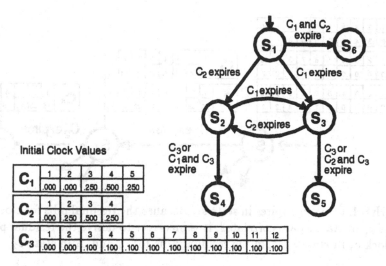

Initial Clock Values

C_1	1	2	3	4	5
	.000	.000	.250	.500	.250

C_2	1	2	3	4
	.000	.250	.500	.250

C_3	1	2	3	4	5	6	7	8	9	10	11	12
	.000	.000	.100	.100	.100	.100	.100	.100	.100	.100	.100	.100

FIGURE 2. A simple probabilistic duration automaton involving six states and three clocks. The initial values of the clocks are also shown.

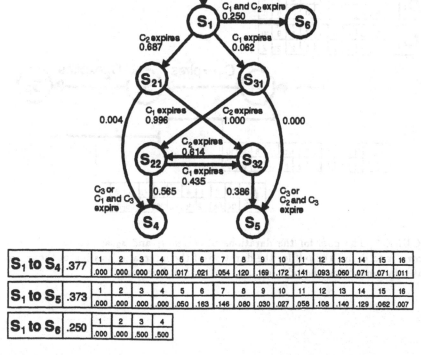

S_1 to S_4 .377	1	2	3	4	5	6	7	8	9	10	11	12	13	14	15	16
	.000	.000	.000	.000	.017	.021	.054	.120	.169	.172	.141	.093	.060	.071	.071	.011

S_1 to S_5 .373	1	2	3	4	5	6	7	8	9	10	11	12	13	14	15	16
	.000	.000	.000	.000	.050	.163	.146	.080	.030	.027	.058	.108	.140	.129	.062	.007

S_1 to S_6 .250	1	2	3	4
	.000	.000	.500	.500

FIGURE 3. The automaton of Fig. 2 after state splitting. For each of the transitions, the probability of that transition is shown. For each of the states s_4, s_5 and s_6, the probability of reaching that state and the pdf for the duration until that state is reached from s_1 are also shown.

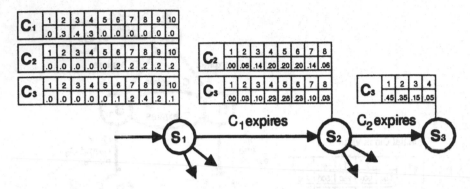

FIGURE 4. Clock c_1 expires in state s_1. Because the residual pdfs for clocks c_2 and c_3 in state s_2 are correlated, it is incorrect to derive the residual pdf for clock c_3 in state s_3 from the residual pdfs for c_2 and c_3 in state s_2.

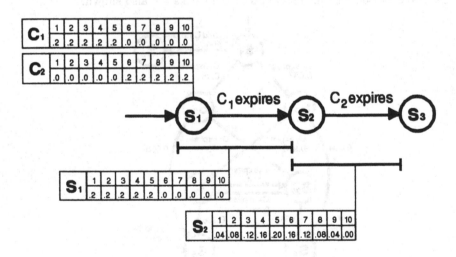

FIGURE 5. The pdfs for the durations of states s_1 and s_2 are correlated. It is incorrect to derive the pdf for the duration of the interval consisting of these two states by convolving the pdfs for their individual durations.

5.2 Disjunctive States

For a disjunctive state, such correlation problems do not arise. We can combine the residual pdfs for the unexpired clock on each of its in-edges into a single pdf, weighting the contribution of the residue on each in-edge by the relative flow of that in-edge.

We are investigating an extension of the algorithm that would allow a disjunctive state to have multiple in-edges and multiple unexpired clocks on those in-edges, provided that all of its in-edges have the same set of unexpired clocks and, for each such clock, the residual pdfs on the in-edges for that clock are equal, with the required or available degree of precision.

Disjunctive states have the advantage over pure state splitting that they substantially reduce the size of the automaton. Unlike the state splitting used in real-time temporal logic decision procedures [14], we can combine states when the pdf for an unexpired clock is a disjunctive composition, whereas such a decision procedure must continue to split states.

5.3 Calculating the Probabilities

As the above examples indicate, we must be careful in calculating the probability p_{s_i,s_j} that the edge (s_i, s_j) is taken when the clocks in E_{s_i,s_j} expire. The analysis must commence with the values determined for those clocks in a disjunctive state or assigned when the clocks were set or reset in a subsequent state, and then consider the effect of the durations of the states since the clocks were determined or set. Fortunately, for each non-disjunctive state, we need only consider a single sequence of prior states since, after state splitting, states with two or more in-edges are disjunctive.

In the numerator for p_{s_i,s_j}, we sum over all of the possible durations $x_1, \ldots, x_n$ of the states in the sequence of prior states, as illustrated by the example in Fig. 6 where $(s_i, s_j) = (s_3, s_4)$, s_1 is the disjunctive state, and c_1 is the unexpired clock on entering that state. Within this summation are two products. The first represents the probability that the expiring clocks (c_1, c_2 and c_3 in Fig. 6) expire at the ends of the states in which they are presumed to expire. Note that a clock c that is set in state σ_{l_c} of the sequence and that expires in state σ_{u_c} has been running for a duration that is the sum of the durations $x_{l_c}, \ldots, x_{u_c}$, as represented by the inner summation. The probability that clock c expires at exactly this moment is determined by the pdf determined for c in the disjunctive state or assigned to c when it was set. The second product provides the probability that the non-expiring clocks (c_4 and c_5 in Fig. 6) do not expire, and is obtained by summing over all larger durations. The denominator for p_{s_i,s_j} represents the probability of reaching state s_i (s_3 in Fig. 6).

The probability density function $\hat{d}_{s_i|s_i,s_j}$ for the duration of state s_i, contingent on the edge (s_i, s_j) being taken, is a variation of the formula for the probability p_{s_i,s_j} of that edge. To determine this pdf, we consider sepa-

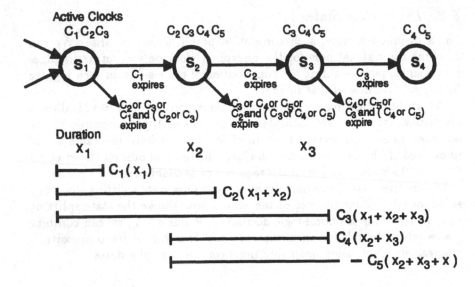

FIGURE 6. An example of a sequence of states preceding the transition (s_3, s_4). State s_1 is a disjunctive state. The figure shows the clocks that are active in each state, the clocks that expire on each transition, and the duration of each state.

rately each possible duration $z = x_n$ for state $s_i = \sigma_n$. Consequently, x_n is excluded from the outer summation in this formula and instead appears as the duration z on the left of the equality. Similarly, the residual pdf $\hat{a}_{s_j|s_i,s_j}$ for clock a in state s_j, contingent on the edge (s_i, s_j) being taken, is obtained by excluding clock a from the last product and instead considering explicitly, as the first factor in the outer product, the probability that clock a survives for an additional duration z.

To calculate the pdfs for the durations of longer intervals, we combine together the durations of shorter intervals, typically the pdfs for the durations from one disjunctive state to the next. Unfortunately, as illustrated in Fig. 5, simple convolution of these pdfs may be incorrect because they may be dependent. Consider the composition of the interval from s_h to s_l and the interval from s_l to s_j, where there is only one unexpired clock c_l on the transition into s_l. We can convolve the pdf for the duration of the interval from s_h to s_l, contingent on c_l having residual duration z_l at the start of s_l, and the pdf for the duration of the interval from s_l to s_j, contingent on c_l having the same residual duration z_l at the start of s_l, since their dependency is fully constrained by that contingency.

Thus, for two disjunctive states s_h and s_j with unexpired clocks c_h and c_j, respectively, we define $\hat{d}_{s_h,s_j|z_h,z_j}$ to be the pdf for the duration of the interval from s_h to s_j, contingent on c_h having residual duration z_h at the start of s_h and on c_j having residual duration z_j at the start of s_j. We make this pdf contingent on the residual durations of the unexpired clocks in both the initial and final states so that we can convolve the pdf for the duration of this interval with the pdf for the duration of either the preceding interval or of the following interval without risk of incorrectness. If more than one path exists from s_h to s_j, the pdfs for the durations of those paths are weighted by the rates of flow along those paths. We then calculate the (uncontingent) pdf $\hat{d}_{s_h,s_j}$ for the duration of the interval from s_h to s_j from the contingent pdfs for that duration and the residual pdfs for the unexpired clocks in the states s_h and s_j.

5.4 Termination

The termination of the state splitting procedure may depend on an approximation, justified by the limited precision of the representation of real numbers in the computer and the uncertainty of the exact values of pdfs in the real world. We are investigating the possibility of not splitting a state if, for each unexpired clock, the differences in the residual pdfs for that clock on the in-edges to that state are sufficiently small. If the analysis shows that we have erred in our estimate of the states that do not need to be split and that for some unexpired clock the pdfs on the in-edges to some state differ significantly, the automaton is enlarged and the analysis is repeated.

6 An Example Application

As an example application, we consider the probabilistic timing constraints of the classical four-phase handshaking protocol used in input/output systems. In its simplest form, the protocol involves two agents, a requester (the processor) and a responder (the device).

The requester sets

- *addr*: a predicate representing the presence of address information on the address bus

- *req*: a boolean control signal indicating to the responder that the requester has placed address information on the address bus.

The responder sets

- *data*: a predicate representing the presence of data on the data bus

- *resp*: a boolean control signal indicating that the responder has received the requester's address information and that the responder has placed information on the data bus for the requester.

Initially, all four of these signals are false.

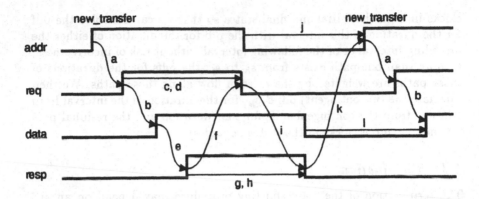

FIGURE 7. The timing diagram for the four-phase handshaking protocol, labeled with clocks. The clocks are pdfs that represent the durations of the indicated intervals.

Duration \ Clocks	1	2	3	4	5	6	7	8	9	10
a,e	.5	.5	.0	.0	.0	.0	.0	.0	.0	.0
c,d,g,h,j,l	.0	.0	.0	.0	.0	.0	.0	.0	.5	.5
b,f,i,k	.0	.2	.4	.2	.1	.05	.02	.01	.01	.01

TABLE .1. The initial values of the clocks, given as pdfs.

The protocol operates in four phases:

1. The requester places information on the address bus and, after a short delay, sets *req* to true.

2. The responder detects that *req* has become true and reads the address information on the address bus. It then places the requested information on the data bus and, after a short delay, sets *resp* to true.

3. The requester detects that *resp* has become true and reads the information on the data bus. At this point, it knows that the responder has detected that *req* has become true and has read the information on the address bus. The requester then sets *addr* and *req* to false.

4. The responder detects that *req* has become false and knows that the requester has read the information on the data bus. The responder then sets *data* and *resp* to false.

Once the requester has detected that *resp* has become false, the requester can restart the cycle by placing further information on the address bus.

The timing diagram is shown in Fig. 7. Each thick time line corresponds to one of the four predicates. The thinner lines with arrowheads are labeled

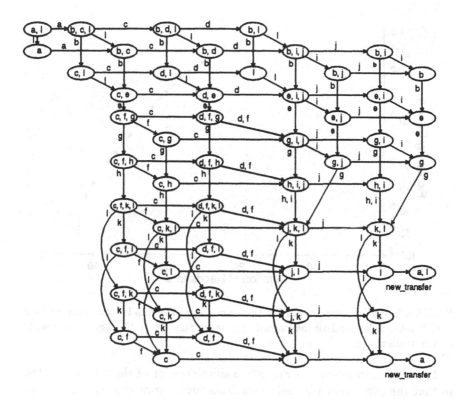

FIGURE 8. The probabilistic duration automaton for the four-phase handshaking protocol. The states are labeled with the active clocks, and the edges with the expiring clocks.

with clocks that define the durations between the indicated transitions. The initial values of the clocks are given in Table 1 as pdfs.

Clock c specifies a lower bound on the duration of the indicated interval; clock d, which is started when clock c expires, imposes an upper bound. When clocks c and f expire, d becomes inactive and, when clocks c and d expire, f becomes inactive. Similarly, when clocks g and h expire, i becomes inactive and, when clocks g and i expire, h becomes inactive.

Clocks j and l specify the lower bounds on the durations for which the signals *addr* and *data* are false, respectively, and impose no upper bounds on these durations. The signal *addr* becomes true when both clocks j and k expire and, in addition, the external predicate *new_transfer* is true. Similarly, the signal *data* becomes true when both clocks b and l expire.

The probabilistic duration automaton for the four-phase handshaking protocol is shown in Fig. 8. The states of the automaton are labeled with the active clocks, and the edges with the expiring clocks. The two states at the bottom right of the diagram are the same as the two states at the top left and, thus, the automaton is an equilibrium automaton.

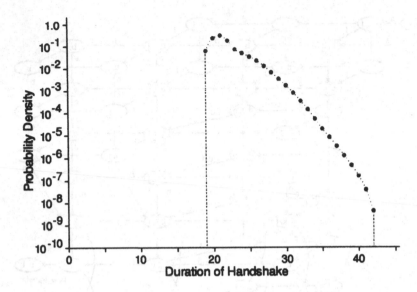

FIGURE 9. The calculated pdf for the duration of the handshake from all four signals being false until all four signals are again false. Note the logarithmic scale on the vertical axis.

The automaton shown in Fig. 8 is a simplification of the full automaton in that the edges that represent simultaneous expiration of clocks are not shown and state splitting has not been performed. After state splitting, the automaton had grown to 262 states and 1162 edges. The calculated pdf for the duration of the handshake is shown in Fig. 9.

Other tools are able to predict the maximum duration of 42, but we are aware of no other tool that can predict the probability of a particular duration for the handshake, a probability that might be of great interest to the designers of real-time systems. The computation (highly unoptimized) required 1 minute 25 seconds on a Sun SPARCstation 20. Only 31 of the states and 81 of the edges had non-zero rates of flow.

7 Related Work

Much work has been done on establishing that real-time systems can meet their deadlines using worst-case analysis with upper and lower bounds, for example [8, 15]. This work diverges from that view, and is more closely related to the work of [1, 3], which develops verification techniques for probabilistic real-time systems. It derives from our work on real-time interval temporal logic [13, 14], and we extend the Büchi automata [2, 16] upon which a decision procedure for such a temporal logic is based. Unlike prior researchers, we introduce the notion of a clock as a pdf, and use pdfs to represent the durations of states, as well as the durations of intervals between pairs of states within the automaton.

Various researchers have developed methodologies for reasoning about probabilistic programs and randomized algorithms. Feldman [4] and Kozen [10] have defined propositional probabilistic dynamic logics, where events occur according to a probability distribution. Courcoubetis and Yannakakis [3] have investigated probabilistic linear-time temporal logics, where probabilistic programs are modeled using Markov chains, and have devised a model-checking algorithm to determine whether a program satisfies its specification in the logic. Hansson and Jonsson [5] have extended the CTL branching-time logic with time and probabilities, and have also provided a model-checking algorithm to determine whether a given Markov chain satisfies a formula of the logic.

Liu, Ravn, Sorensen and Zhou [11] have developed a probabilistic duration calculus for reasoning about, and calculating whether, a given requirement of a real-time system holds with a sufficiently high probability for given failure probabilities of the system. Their calculus is a real-time interval temporal logic in which the user specifies requirements of the system and defines satisfaction probabilities for formulas of the logic. The system model is a finite automaton with fixed transition probabilities; discrete Markov processes are the basis of the calculus.

Jonsson and Larsen [9] have investigated probabilistic transition systems for describing and analyzing reliability aspects of concurrent distributed systems. In [7] Huang, Lee and Hsu have presented a similar extended state transition model, Timed Communicating State Machines, for protocol verification. Ho-Stuart, Zedan and Fang [6] have also described a tool, called the CoS-Workbench, for analyzing and manipulating formal specifications of real-time processes, interpreted as labeled transition systems.

In [12] Lynch, Saias and Segala defined probabilistic timed automata as an extension to I/O automata, which address such questions as whether an algorithm will terminate within time t with probability p. Wu, Smolka and Stark [18] have also introduced probabilistic I/O automata for specifying and reasoning about asynchronous probabilistic systems. However, none of the above approaches uses pdfs to represent clocks, as we do here.

In [1] Alur, Courcoubetis and Dill presented a model-checking algorithm for a probabilistic real-time system modeled as a generalized semi-Markov process, where a specification of the system is given as a deterministic timed automaton. They associate a pdf with each delay and, thus, their approach is similar to ours; however, they assume the existence of a generalized semi-Markov process, whereas we construct it from a given set of pdfs. The completed probabilistic duration automaton constructed by our algorithm can be used as input to their model-checking algorithm. Much closer to our work is the work of Whitt [17], who has investigated the convergence of the construction of generalized semi-Markov processes.

8 Conclusion

We have described a novel methodology and tools for analyzing probabilistic timing properties of real-time systems. In our methodology, clocks are defined as probability density functions, and probabilistic duration automata are defined in terms of the pdfs to which the clocks are set, the clocks that are active in each state, and the clocks that expire on each transition.

The algorithm, which we have implemented, takes as input a probabilistic duration automaton. The probabilistic duration automaton may itself be the user's specification of the real-time system or may be obtained from a temporal logic specification. The algorithm determines the probabilities that clocks in a state expire, the residual pdfs for the other clocks, the probabilities of the transitions, the probabilities of the states, and the pdfs for the durations of the states. The algorithm also determines the pdfs for durations of intervals between pairs of states within the automaton. These pdfs are used to determine whether a real-time system can meet its probabilistic timing constraints.

We plan to integrate this algorithm with a decision procedure for satisfiability checking of interval temporal logic formulas in which the durations of intervals are expressed as pdfs. The decision procedure for this interval temporal logic will construct the automaton from the interval temporal logic formula in the usual manner. Our algorithm will complete this automaton by finding the residual pdfs for the clocks, and the related probabilities and pdfs for the durations. We also plan to extend this methodology to handle continuous pdfs, but different techniques will be required.

9 REFERENCES

[1] R. Alur, C. Courcoubetis and D. Dill, "Verifying automata specifications of probabilistic real-time systems," *Proceedings of the REX Workshop on Real-Time: Theory in Practice*, Mook, The Netherlands (June 1991), Lecture Notes in Computer Science 600, Springer-Verlag, pp. 28-44.

[2] R. Alur and D. Dill, "Automata for modelling real-time systems," *Proceedings of the 17th International Colloquium on Automata, Languages, and Programming*, Warwick, England (July 1990), Lecture Notes in Computer Science 443, Springer-Verlag, pp. 322-335.

[3] C. Courcoubetis and M. Yannakakis, "The complexity of probabilistic verification," *Journal of the Association for Computing Machinery* 42, 4 (July 1995), pp. 857-907.

[4] Y. A. Feldman, "A decidable propositional dynamic logic with explicit probabilities," *Information and Control* 63 (1984), pp. 11-38.

[5] H. Hansson and B. Jonsson, "A logic for reasoning about time and reliability," *Formal Aspects of Computing* 6, 5 (1994), pp. 512-535.

[6] C. Ho-Stuart, H. Zedan and M. Fang, "Automated support for the formal specification and design of real-time systems," *Proceedings of the Nineteenth EUROMICRO Symposium on Microprocessing and Microprogramming*, Barcelona, Spain (September 1993), pp. 79-86.

[7] C. M. Huang, S. W. Lee and J. M. Hsu, "Probabilistic timed protocol verification for the extended state transition model," *Proceedings of the 1994 International Conference on Parallel and Distributed Systems*, Hsinchu, Taiwan (December 1994), pp. 432-437.

[8] S. Jahanian and A. K. Mok, "Modechart: A specification language for real-time systems," *IEEE Transactions on Software Engineering* 20, 11 (November 1994), pp. 933-947.

[9] B. Jonsson and K. G. Larsen, "Specification and refinement of probabilistic processes," *Proceedings of the 6th IEEE Annual Symposium on Logic in Computer Science*, Amsterdam, The Netherlands (July 1991), pp. 266-277.

[10] D. Kozen, "Probabilistic PDL," *Journal of Computer and System Sciences* 30 (1985), pp. 162-178.

[11] Z. Liu, A. P. Ravn, E. V. Sorensen and C. Zhou, "A probabilistic duration calculus," *Proceedings of the Second International Workshop on Responsive Computer Systems*, Saitama, Japan (October 1992), pp. 14-27.

[12] N. Lynch, I. Saias and R. Segala, "Proving time bounds for randomized distributed algorithms," *Proceedings of the Thirteenth Annual ACM Symposium on Principles of Distributed Computing*, Los Angeles, CA (August 1994), pp. 314-323.

[13] L. E. Moser, Y. S. Ramakrishna, G. Kutty, P. M. Melliar-Smith and L. K. Dillon, "A graphical environment for design of concurrent real-time systems," Technical Report 95-18, Department of Electrical and Computer Engineering, University of California, Santa Barbara.

[14] Y. S. Ramakrishna, L. K. Dillon, L. E. Moser, P. M. Melliar-Smith and G. Kutty, "A real-time interval logic and its decision procedure," *Proceedings of the Thirteenth Conference on Foundations of Software Technology and Theoretical Computer Science*, Bombay, India (December 1993), Lecture Notes in Computer Science 761, Springer-Verlag, pp. 173-192.

[15] A. C. Shaw, "Communicating real-time state machines," *IEEE Transactions on Software Engineering* 18, 9 (September 1992), pp. 805-816.

[16] M. Y. Vardi and P. Wolper, "An automata-theoretic approach to automatic program verification," *Proceedings of the Symposium on Logic in Computer Science*," Cambridge, England (June 1986), pp. 322-331.

[17] W. Whitt, "Continuity of generalized semi-Markov processes," *Mathematics of Operations Research* 5, 4 (November 1980), pp. 494-501.

[18] S. H. Wu, S. A. Smolka and E. W. Stark, "Composition and behaviors of probabilistic I/O automata," *Proceedings of the 5th International Conference on Concurrency Theory*, Uppsala, Sweden (August 1994), pp. 513-528.

The Concurrency Factory Software Development Environment

Rance Cleaveland (rance@csc.ncsu.edu)[*]
Philip M. Lewis (pml@cs.sunysb.edu)[†]
Scott A. Smolka (sas@cs.sunysb.edu)[†]
Oleg Sokolsky (oleg@ccc.com)[†]

ABSTRACT

The *Concurrency Factory* is an integrated toolset for specification, simulation, verification, and implementation of real-time concurrent systems such as communication protocols and process control systems. Two themes central to the project are the following: the use of *process algebra*, e.g., CCS, ACP, CSP, as the underlying formal model of computation, and the provision of *practical* support for process algebra. By "practical" we mean that the Factory should be usable by protocol engineers and software developers who are not necessarily familiar with formal verification, and it should be usable on problems of real-life scale, such as those found in the telecommunications industry.

This demo is intended to demonstrate the following features of the Concurrency Factory: the graphical user interface VTView and VTSim, the local model checker for the alternation-free modal mu-calculus, and the graphical compiler that transforms VTView specifications into executable code.

1 Introduction

The *Concurrency Factory* is an integrated toolset for specification, simulation, verification, and implementation of real-time concurrent systems such as communication protocols and process control systems. The project, which is a joint effort between SUNY Stony Brook and North Carolina State

---

[*]Department of Computer Science, N.C. State University, Raleigh, NC 27695-8206, USA. Research supported in part by NSF/DARPA grant CCR–9014775, NSF grant CCR–9120995, ONR Young Investigator Award N00014-92-J-1582, and NSF Young Investigator Award CCR–9257963, and AFOSR grant F49620-95-1-0508.

[†]Department of Computer Science, SUNY at Stony Brook, Stony Brook, NY 11794-4400, USA. Research supported in part by NSF grants CCR–9120995 and CCR–9208585, and AFOSR grants F49620-93-1-0250 and F49620-95-1-0508.

University, officially started in Spring '92, and is currently supported by grants from NSF and AFOSR. Two themes central to the project are the following: the use of *process algebra* (e.g., CCS, CSP, ACP) as the underlying formal model of computation, and the provision of *practical* support for process algebra. By "practical" we mean that the Factory should be usable by protocol engineers and software developers who are not necessarily familiar with formal verification, and it should be usable on problems of real-life scale, such as those found in the telecommunications industry.

The main features of the Concurrency Factory are the following:

- A *graphical user interface*, VTView/VTSim, that allows the non-expert to design and simulate concurrent systems using process algebra. VTView is a graphical editor for hierarchically structured networks of finite-state processes, and VTSim is a sophisticated environment for the simulation and testing of VTView-constructed specifications. We are currently extending the GUI to allow processes to be embedded in states of other processes, thereby permitting compact specifications such as those found in statecharts.

- A *textual user interface* for the language VPL, a simple language for concurrent processes that communicate values from a finite data domain. A VPL compiler translates VPL programs into networks of finite-state processes.

- A *suite of verification routines* that currently includes a linear-time, global model checker for L_{μ_1}, the alternation-free fragment of the modal mu-calculus [CS93], a local model checker for L_{μ_1} [So96], a local model checker for a real-time extension of L_{μ_1} [SS95], and strong and weak bisimulation checkers.

  Care is being taken to ensure that these algorithms are efficient enough to be used on real-life systems. For example, we are investigating how these algorithms can be parallelized [ZS92, ZSS94], and made to perform incrementally [SS94].

- A *graphical compiler* that transforms VTView and VPL specifications into executable code. Our current version produces Facile [GMP89] code, a concurrent language that symmetrically integrates many of the features of Standard ML and CCS. We are also considering adding a concurrent extension of C++ as another target language. The compiler relieves the user of the burden of manually recoding their designs in the target language of their final system.

The Concurrency Factory is written in C++ and executes under X-Windows, using Motif as the graphics engine, so that it is efficient, easily extendible, and highly portable. It is currently running on SUN SPARC-stations under SunOS Release 4.1. The basic organization of the system is depicted in Figure 1.

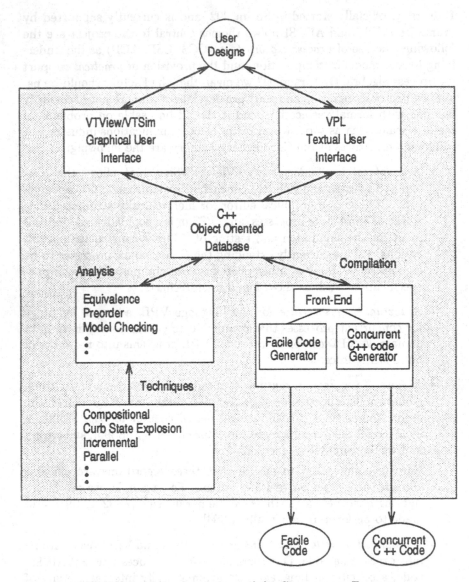

FIGURE 1. Basic organization of the Concurrency Factory.

In what follows, we briefly describe VTView and VTSim, the main components of the demo, and a protocol verification case study.

2 Graphical Editor and Simulator

The graphical user interface of the Concurrency Factory consists of two main components, VTView and VTSim (VT stands for *Verifier's Toolkit*). VTView is a graphical tool supporting the design of hierarchically structured systems of communicating tasks expressed in GCCS, a graphical specification language. GCCS provides system builders with intuitive constructs (buses, ports, links, a subsystem facility, etc.) for designing systems, and it supports both top-down and bottom-up development methodologies. As user designs are entered using VTView, an internal representation is created by invoking the appropriate methods associated with process and network objects.

In contrast with other graphical languages, such as Harel's statecharts and Maraninchi's Argonaute, GCCS is designed to model systems in which processes execute asynchronously (although communication between processes is synchronous). The language is equipped with a formal semantics in the form of a structural operational semantics, à la Plotkin and Milner. The semantics has been "implemented" in the Factory in the form of methods that determine the set of transitions that are possible for a network or a process from a given state. Both the graphical simulator and the method that produces the global automaton from a network of process rely fundamentally on these methods. By encapsulating the semantics of VTView objects, all tools within the Factory are guaranteed to interpret processes and networks consistently.

VTSim permits users to simulate graphically the execution of GCCS systems built using VTView. The tool provides both interactive and automatic modes of operation, and it also includes features such as breakpoints and reverse execution. It also enables users to view the simulated execution of a system at different levels in the structure; one can either choose to observe the simulation at the interprocess level and watch the flow of messages, or one can look at individual processes in order to see why messages are sent when they are.

The demo will illustrate the look-and-feel of VTView and VTSim by considering the well-known Alternating Bit Protocol modeled as a sender and receiver process communicating over an unreliable medium, also modeled as a process.

3 A Case Study: The i-protocol

The Concurrency Factory's local model checker was used to detect and diagnose a non-trivial livelock in the i-protocol, a bidirectional sliding-window protocol employed in the publicly available GNU UUCP file transfer utility. The model checker was dispatched on an instance of the protocol having a window size of 2, and explored about 1.079×10^6 states out of a total estimated global state space of 1.473×10^{12}.

Key to the Factory's success was the use of an abstraction to reduce the message sequence number space from 32 — the constant defined in the protocol's C-code — to $2W$, where W is the window size. This abstraction is shown to preserve the truthhood of all modal mu-calculus formulæ.

4 Conclusions

We have described the Concurrency Factory, a graphical environment that supports the following system development tasks: specification (VTView), simulation (VTSim), verification (model and bisimulation checking), and implementation (Facile graphical compiler). Much work remains to be done on the project, including better state-space management techniques and broader support for real-time systems.

5 REFERENCES

[CS93]   R. Cleaveland and B. U. Steffen. A linear-time model checking algorithm for the alternation-free modal mu-calculus. *Formal Methods in System Design*, 2, 1993.

[GMP89] A. Giacalone, P. Mishra, and S. Prasad. Facile: A symmertric integration of concurrent and functional programming. *International Journal of Parallel Programming*, 18(2), 1989.

[SS94]   O. Sokolsky and S. A. Smolka. "Incremental Model Checking in the Modal Mu-Calculus". In *Proceedings of CAV'94*. LNCS 818, 1994.

[SS95]   O. Sokolsky and S. A. Smolka. Local model checking for real-time systems, In *Proc. 7th CAV* (1995).

[So96]   O. Sokolsky. Efficient graph-based algorithms for model checking in the modal mu-calculus. Ph.D. Thesis, Department of Computer Science, SUNY, Stony Brook (1996), *forthcoming*.

[ZS92]   S. Zhang and S. A. Smolka. Efficient parallelization of equivalence checking algorithms. In M. Diaz and R. Groz, editors, *Proceedings of FORTE '92 – Fifth International Conference on Formal Description Techniques*, pages 133–146, October 1992.

[ZSS94] S. Zhang, O. Sokolsky, and S. A. Smolka. On the parallel complexity of model checking in the modal mu-calculus. In *LICS '94*, July 1994.

The FC2TOOLS Set (Tool Demonstration)

Amar Bouali*
Annie Ressouche†
Valrie Roy*
Robert de Simone†

ABSTRACT

The AUTO/GRAPH toolset developed in our group was a pioneering software for analysis and verification of networks of communicating processes. We describe here the next-generation AUTO/GRAPH, consisting of a modular tool suite interfaced around a common file description format named FC2. The format allows representation of single reactive automata as well as combining networks. This format was developed in the scope of Esprit BRA project 7166:CONCUR2.

In the new implementation, most analysis functions are implemented with redundancy using both *explicit* classical representation of automata, and also *implicit* state space symbolic representation using *B*inary *D*ecision *D*iagrams. The two alternative techniques offer drastically different performances in different cases, and having both at hand in a unified framework is a valuable thing.

Both FC2EXPLICIT and FC2IMPLICIT commands perform synchronised product and reachable state space search. They can minimize results w.r.t. *s*trong, weak, branching bisimulation notions, and produce the result as an FC2 automaton. They can also *a*bstract the system with a notion of "abstract actions", each synthesizing a set of sequences of concrete behaviours (in this sense behavioural abstraction can be seen as reverse from refinement). In addition FC2IMPLICIT has a fast checker for *d*eadlocks, livelock or *d*ivergent states, for which it produces counterexample paths in case of existence, while FC2EXPLICIT allows compositional reduction techniques, mostly in case of "observational" bisimulation minimisations. Several extensions are still underway.

The tool suite is completed by the graphical editor AUTOGRAPH, which allows for graphical depiction of automata and networks as well as recollection of some form of results.

The toolset is available by anonymous ftp. Information can be obtained from the WWW page http://cma.cma.fr/Verification/verif-eng.html, or by e-mailing to fc2team@cma.cma.fr.

---

*CMA/Ecole des Mines de Paris, B.P. 207, F-06904 Sophia-Antipolis cedex
†INRIA , B.P. 93, F-06902 Sophia-Antipolis cedex

– PEP –
More than a Petri Net Tool

Bernd Grahlmann and Eike Best*

ABSTRACT The **PEP** system (Programming Environment based on Petri Nets) supports the most important tasks of a good net tool, including HL and LL net editing and comfortable simulation facilities. In addition, these features are embedded in sophisticated programming and verification components. The programming component allows the user to design concurrent algorithms in an easy-to-use imperative language, and the **PEP** system then generates Petri nets from such programs. The **PEP** tool's comprehensive verification components allow a large range of properties of parallel systems to be checked efficiently on either programs or their corresponding nets. This includes user-defined properties specified by temporal logic formulae as well as specific properties for which dedicated algorithms are available. **PEP** has been implemented on Solaris 2.4, Sun OS 4.1.3 and Linux. Ftp-able versions are available.

KEYWORDS: B(PN)^2, Model checking, Parallel finite automata, **PEP**, Petri nets, Process algebra, Temporal logic, Tool.

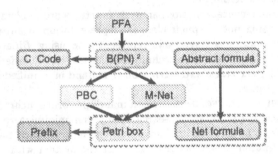

FIGURE 1. Objects used by the **PEP** system.

1 Introduction

In **PEP**[1] [5] two of today's most widely accepted theoretical approaches for the description of parallel systems, viz., Petri nets and process algebras, are combined to model, simulate, analyse and verify parallel systems. The integration of these two approaches, using a common, flexible parallel programming language called B(PN)^2 (**B**asic **P**etri **N**et **P**rogramming Notation), is one of the main characteristics of **PEP**.

---

*Institut für Informatik, Universität Hildesheim, Marienburger Platz 22, D-31141 Hildesheim, {bernd,E.Best}@informatik.uni-hildesheim.de
[1]The PEP project is financed by the DFG (German Research Foundation). The presentation of this paper has also been supported by the HCM Cooperation Network EXPRESS

This paper briefly describes the motivation and rationale behind the **PEP** tool [5]. Its structure and the interdependencies of its different components are explained. The different types of objects used by the **PEP** system are described. The efficiency of the model checking algorithms is demonstrated. An overview over future work and pointers to relevant literature are given.

2 Modelling parallel systems with **PEP**

Users can choose primarily between four types of objects in order to model parallel systems (see figure 1):

1. They can express parallel algorithms in $B(PN)^2$ [6], which is an imperative / predicative programming language whose atomic actions may contain predicates involving the prevalues and the postvalues of variables. Basic command connectives of $B(PN)^2$ are: sequential composition, nondeterministic choice, parallel composition, and iteration. Programs are structured into blocks consisting of a declaration part and an instruction part. Processes can share common memory or use channel communication or both. The implementation of a procedure concept [13] and abstract data types extend $B(PN)^2$ to a complete programming language. $B(PN)^2$ is called **Basic Petri Net Programming Notation** because it has a compositional semantics in terms of low-level (LL) Petri nets called boxes [1].

2. Terms of a process algebra called PBC (**Petri Box Calculus**), which is an extension / modification of CCS [7], can be used. In **PEP**, PBC terms can either be derived automatically from a $B(PN)^2$ program or be designed independently.

3. a) **PEP** allows to design and edit arbitrary labelled P/T-nets. Boxes are a special case which may arise out of a translation from $B(PN)^2$ programs.

   b) Further, **PEP** allows to design and edit high-level (HL) nets, called M-nets [4], on which an alternative net semantics of $B(PN)^2$ programs is based [3].

4. Parallel finite automata (PFA) with $B(PN)^2$ actions as edge annotations can be edited and compiled into $B(PN)^2$ programs [10].

It is up to the user with which kind of object (s)he would like to start the modelling phase. As shown in figure 1, a $B(PN)^2$ program can be compiled into a Petri box in two different ways: using either PBC or a HL net as an intermediate step. The translations produce equivalent LL nets.

Further, the following objects are used in the **PEP** system:

1. In order to allow the user to (model) check a custom designed system property, **PEP** allows the definition of a set of temporal logic formulae in propositional logic on place names, augmented with □ for

'always' and $\Diamond$ for 'possibly at some future point'. Abstract formulae referring to points in the control flow, actions or variable bindings of a $B(PN)^2$ program are handled by an automatic transformation.

2. During verification it may become necessary to calculate the finite prefix of a branching process [8] of an existing LL net. This prefix contains information for model checking [9, 12] a net.

3. A C code generator can produce executable code [14].

In a modelling cycle several different objects are normally created. Typically a $B(PN)^2$ program is written, the corresponding HL net and the LL Petri box are compiled automatically, the prefix is calculated and interesting properties are expressed by formulae. All objects that relate to a single modelling cycle are collected into a machine object called project. A project which is the basic entity handled by the **PEP** system may also contain analysis and verification results or user defined documentation.

3 Structure of the **PEP** prototype

The **PEP** system consists of five different classes of components.

1. Editors for $B(PN)^2$ programs, PBC terms, Petri boxes (LL nets), M-nets (HL nets), formulae, PFA, C code and project documentation.

2. Compilers as follows: $B(PN)^2 \Rightarrow PBC$, $PBC \Rightarrow$ (LL) Petri box, Petri box $\Rightarrow$ prefix, $B(PN)^2 \Rightarrow$ (HL) M-net, (HL) M-net $\Rightarrow$ (LL) Petri box, $B(PN)^2 \Rightarrow$ C code and PFA $\Rightarrow B(PN)^2$.

3. Simulators for HL and LL boxes. The simulation of a $B(PN)^2$ program can be triggered by the simulation of a net, based on references either between actions of the $B(PN)^2$ program and transitions of the corresponding nets or between points in the control flow of the different processes and places of the nets.

4. Some standard algorithms (checking the free choice / T-system properties, liveness, deadlock-freeness, reachability and reversibility) are part of the **PEP** prototype.

5. Three model checking algorithms have been implemented, MC-0 for T-systems [17] and MC-1 and MC-2 [9, 12] for safe Petri nets. They can determine whether a Petri net satisfies a property given in terms of a temporal logic formula. The transparency, and thus the full functionality, of the verification component, is obtained by a formula translator which transforms an abstract formula (such as 'if a program terminates', 'if at some point a variable has a certain value' or 'if a transition is live') into a formula referring to a corresponding Petri net. This offers a comfortable interface to the model checkers.

The components are controlled by a project manager which represents the central part of **PEP** (see Figure 2).

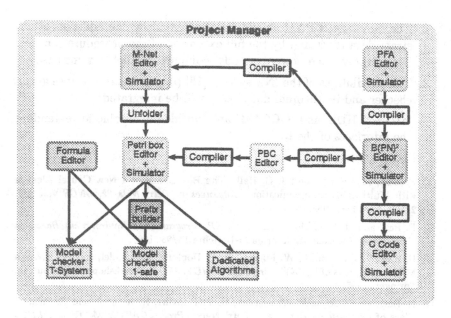

FIGURE 2. Interplay between **PEP** system components. The arrows represent input/output relations between components.

4 Efficiency of the verification component

During the work with the **PEP** system, different case studies have demonstrated that the tool is capable of handling comprehensive examples. As realistic examples a protocol for telephone networks [11] and a pilot behaviour model [15] can be mentioned.

The verification of faulty protocols showed that typical human errors made during the modelling phase can be detected efficiently [11]. Considering a protocol with much more than 1.000.000 states and more than 250.000 states (stubborn set reduced) the calculation of the finite prefix of the branching process was done in less than 1 hour, the verification of 4 interesting properties took 1 minute and the deadlock detection was done in 1 second.

W. Ruckdeschel and R. Onken [15] state '... *the* **PEP** *model checker is used to investigate large fusions of subnets characterized by 'exploding' reachability graphs. Some subsystems which could not be analysed via reachability graph were successfully unfolded by* **PEP** ...'

5 Future work

Our experiences have prompted us to consider the following future aims:

1. A model checker for HL Petri boxes should be developed and implemented, in such a way that the unfolding into LL Petri boxes – often yielding too big nets for realistic problems – can be avoided if desired.

2. The language $B(PN)^2$ should be augmented by the addition of abstract data types and by the full extension of the procedure concept. This improves the power to model complex parallel systems easily.

3. The possibilities of the INA system [16] (in particular, its state graph checker and its theorem data base) will be integrated.

4. 'SDL', 'VHDL' and 'OCCAM' are considered suitable for extending the interfaces of the tool.

6 REFERENCES

[1] E. Best, R. Devillers and J. G. Hall. The Box Calculus: a New Causal Algebra with Multi-Label Communication. *Advances in Petri Nets 92, LNCS* Vol. 609, 21-69. Springer, 1992.

[2] E. Best and H. Fleischhack, editors. *PEP: Programming Environment Based on Petri Nets.* Hildesheimer Informatik-Berichte 14/95. 1995.

[3] E. Best, H. Fleischhack, W. Frączak, R. P. Hopkins, H. Klaudel, and E. Pelz. An M-Net Semantics of $B(PN)^2$. *Proc. of STRICT*, 85-100, Workshops in Computing. Springer, 1995.

[4] E. Best, H. Fleischhack, W. Frączak, R. P. Hopkins, H. Klaudel, and E. Pelz. A Class of Composable High Level Petri Nets. *Proc. of ATPN'95, Torino, LNCS* Vol. 935, 103-118. Springer, 1995.

[5] E. Best and B. Grahlmann. *PEP: Documentation and User Guide.* Universität Hildesheim. ftp.informatik.uni-hildesheim.de /pub/Projekte/PEP/... or http://www.informatik.uni-hildesheim.de/~pep/HomePage.html 1995.

[6] E. Best and R. P. Hopkins. $B(PN)^2$ – a Basic Petri Net Programming Notation. *Proc. of PARLE, LNCS* Vol. 694, 379-390. Springer, 1993.

[7] E. Best and M. Koutny. A Refined View of the Box Calculus. *Proc. of ATPN'95, Torino, LNCS* Vol. 935, 103-118. Springer, 1995.

[8] J. Esparza, S. Römer, and W. Vogler. An Improvement of McMillan's Unfolding Algorithm. *Proc. of TACAS'96*, 1996.

[9] J. Esparza. *Model Checking Using Net Unfoldings*, 151-195. Number 23 in Science of Computer Programming. Elsevier, 1994.

[10] B. Grahlmann, M. Moeller, and U. Anhalt. A New Interface for the PEP Tool – Parallel Finite Automata. *Proc. of 2. Workshop Algorithmen und Werkzeuge für Petrinetze*, AIS 22, 21-26. FB Informatik Universität Oldenburg, 1995.

[11] B. Grahlmann. Verifying Telecommunication Protocols with PEP. *Proc. of RELECTRONIC'95, Budapest*, 251-256, 1995.

[12] B. Graves. *Ein Modelchecker für eine Linear-Time-Logik.* Diplomarbeit, Universität Hildesheim, 1995.

[13] L. Jenner. A Low-Level Net Semantics for $B(PN)^2$ with Procedures. In [2].

[14] S. Melzer. Design and Implementation of a C-Code Generator for $B(PN)^2$. In [2].

[15] W. Ruckdeschel and R. Onken. Petri Net Modelling, Analysis and Realtime-Simulation of Pilot Behaviour. *Proc. of ATPN'95*, 1995.

[16] P. H. Starke. *INA: Integrated Net Analyzer.* Handbuch, 1992.

[17] T. Thielke. Implementierung eines effizienten Modelchecking-Algorithmus. *Petri-Netze im Einsatz für Entwurf und Entwicklung von Informationssystemen*, 127-139. Springer, 1993.

Rapid Prototyping for an Assertional Specification Language

Jorge Cuéllar*†
Dieter Barnard*
Martin Huber*

ABSTRACT

Temporal Language of Transitions (TLT) is a framework for the specification and verification of reactive control systems. *Message Passing Interface* (MPI) is a library for message-passing in a distributed environment. In this paper we present a compiler from TLT to the language C and the library MPI. The development of the compiler raised a number of interesting issues like the implementation of deadlock-free synchronous communication and the scheduling of guarded-commands.

1 Introduction

Today there exists a plethora of formal methods for the specification and verification of distributed and embedded systems. However, in many cases they still lack the recognition as a serious software development technique in industry. One important reason is the perception of a large gap between a correct specification on the one hand and its implementation on the other. This deficiency can be addressed by *rapid prototyping*, which tries to deliver an executable system based on a given specification as early as possible. We present such a tool in the form of a compiler, which inputs (verified) TLT specifications and facilitates their distributed execution on a network of workstations using the MPI library.

2 Temporal Language of Transitions (TLT)

TLT is a compositional framework for the formal treatment of reactive control systems [CH94, BC95, CBH95]. A TLT specification consists of a

---

*Siemens AG, ZFE T SE 1, D-81730 Munich, Germany.
†E-Mail: Jorge.Cuellar@zfe.siemens.de, Tel. (089) 636-47585, Fax. (089) 636-42282.

number of modules. Each module consists of a number of interfaces and a module body. The interfaces and the body each contain a set of declarations of variables and actions, an initially predicate and a set of always-commands. In addition, the body also contains a set of guarded-commands.

Actions are used to express synchronous message-passing. They are typed, and declared as *input* or *output*, depending on whether they are under control of the environment or the given module. A module reacts to input actions using always-commands (thereby making it input-enabled). A module executes output actions using guarded-commands in the usual way.

3 A Compiler for TLT

3.1 The Message-Passing Interface (MPI)

MPI is a library standard for message-passing [MPI94], with support for the language C and SUN/SPARC workstations. We will concentrate here on only a small part of MPI necessary for our compiler: initialization, point-to-point communication, and termination. In MPI the code of all the modules are packed together and then distributed. During initialization, each processor node is assigned an *id* between 0 and $n-1$, from which it determines the appropriate part of the code to execute. A variety of asynchronous and synchronous send/receive primitives is provided (discussed below). A MPI application terminates if all participating nodes decide to do so.

3.2 Synchronous Input and Output

A central issue in the development of the compiler is the realization of synchronous communication. Even though MPI explicitly provides a blocking synchronous send primitive suitable for TLT output actions, it is easy to see that two processes wishing to synchronize simultaneously can deadlock. We therefore make use of the nonblocking synchronous send primitive, which includes the possibility of checking whether a started synchronization has completed. If not, care is taken not to initiate a new synchronization on the same channel (by temporarily disabling the appropriate instructions). TLT input actions are treated dually: the blocking receive primitive is used, but only after checking that there indeed exists a matching output action wishing to synchronize.

3.3 Scheduling

Consider the scheduling algorithm for each module, summarized in Figure 1. Every TLT variable is implemented as a unprimed and a primed C variable. The unprimed versions are assigned initial values where specified. At the the start of the first *execution phase*, their values are copied to the primed versions. This implements the frame axiom for TLT, namely that variables which are not assigned new values retain their current values. Next the scheduler checks for the presence of any input actions; if another module wishes to communicate, the appropriate always command is executed.

After processing the inputs, a nondeterministic selection is made of any enabled instruction (if there exists one). Note that in addition to the explicit guard of an instruction, enabledness is also determined by the ability to perform all of the output actions in the command part (i.e., all previous synchronizations on those particular channels must have been completed). Finally, the primed values are copied back to the unprimed variables before the start of a new execution phase. The execution is repeated ad infinitum. If no inputs are present and no instructions are enabled, the module just stutters.

> *Assign initial values to (unprimed) variables.*
> *Assign unprimed values to primed variables.*
> while (true) do {
> > *Perform always commands triggered by inputs.*
> > *Select and execute an enabled instruction.*
> > *Assign primed values to unprimed variables.*
> }

FIGURE 1. The Scheduler for a TLT Module

This scheduling algorithm renders a true implementation of the TLT semantics for a large class of TLT modules (that respect commutativity conditions similar to [Mis91]). In particular, it is not possible for consistently composed TLT modules to deadlock, since output actions are performed in a nonblocking manner and since all inputs are processed at the start of each phase. This covers the case where two modules wish to synchronize simultaneously, and where one module wants to synchronize twice but the other module has not reacted to the first yet. In this case the second synchronization is disabled temporarily until the first has completed.

3.4 Execution and Logging

Compiled TLT systems can be executed on SUN/SPARC workstations connected by a LAN, with one TLT module executing on each computer. Each module contains a scheduler as explained above. There are two ways in which a user can visualize the execution of a systems. Firstly, provision has been made for ASCII-based input (keyboard) and output (screen). If only one of the modules performs I/O, then the compiler starts this module on the default console. If more than one module wishes to perform I/O, then the compiler adds an I/O manager, i.e. a separate MPI process dedicated handling all I/O requests.

The second possibility is to make use of the MPE (Message Passing Environment) library, which offers extensive logging facilities. If activated, each MPI process creates a local log-file. After (proper) termination, the log-files are collected and integrated, and displayed by the MPE tool upshot. For this purpose, there is a special keyword HALT in TLT, which can be used in instructions to terminate execution for logging puposes. An example is provided in Figure 2, where we compiled and executed a small master/slave system. The top bar represents the master module, the lower two represent the slaves, and the arrows represent MPI communication.

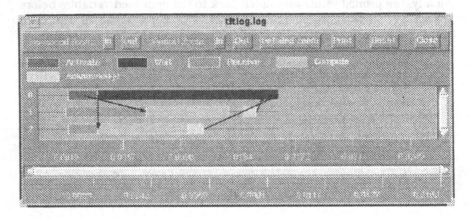

FIGURE 2. MPI/MPE Logging of Master/Slave

4 Conclusion

We have presented a compiler which allows rapid prototyping of TLT specifications. Our goal was to narrow the gap between formal specifications and their implementation. We maintain that the compiler preserves the original (formal) semantics of TLT, even though the synchronous input and output actions of TLT have been replaced by MPI communication. Such prototypes not only serve the role of simulations, but can significantly aid in the understanding of a specification, by visualizing their distributed execution and communication. In addition to numerous small examples, the compiler was used to create a real-time, distributed controller of the FZI production cell simulation [CH94].

Acknowledgements: Christine Roeckl and Dagmar Proell contributed significantly towards the implemenation of the TLT compiler.

5 REFERENCES

[BC95] Dieter Barnard and Simon Crosby. The Specification and Verification of an ATM Signalling Protocol. In *Proc. of 15th IFIP PSTV'95*, Warsaw, June 1995.

[CBH95] Jorge Cuéllar, Dieter Barnard, and Martin Huber. A Solution relying on the Model Checking of Boolean Transition Systems. Submitted as Final Solution to Dagstuhl Seminar of Broy/Lamport, 1994, Siemens Corporate Research and Development, ZFE T SE 1, D-81730 Munich, Germany, 1995.

[CH94] Jorge Cuéllar and Martin Huber. The FZI Production Cell Case Study: A distributed solution using TLT. In *Proc. of the FZI*, volume 891 of *LNCS*. Springer-Verlag, 1994.

[Mis91] Jayadev Misra. Loosely-Coupled Processes. In Springer Verlag, editor, *PARLE'91, Vol. 2*, pages 1–26, 1991. LNCS 506.

[MPI94] MPIF (MPI Forum). MPI: A Message-Passing Interface Standard. Technical report, University of Tennessee, May 1994.

cTc – A Tool Supporting the Construction of cTLA-Specifications

Carsten Heyl*
Arnulf Mester*
Heiko Krumm*

ABSTRACT The design tool cTc has been developed to support the construction and refinement of formal specifications of distributed software systems. It concentrates on the design by stepwise refinement, where refinement steps correspond to the integration of predefined process patterns. cTc processes modules written in the compositional TLA specification style cTLA. It applies the cTLA specification operations and generates the resulting specification modules. We outline the background of cTc and give an overview on its functionality and architecture.

1   Introduction

The compositional TLA specification style cTLA and its application to the design of distributed systems have been discussed in [14] and can be summarized as follows.

cTLA is based on TLA [10] and its understanding of correct refinements [1]. It is a dialect of TLA+ [9] and tailored to the modular description of process systems. Processes perform state transitions on private variables. Process interaction is modelled by joint actions similarly to Lotos [8]. cTLA modules define generic process types. A type may describe elementary processes or subsystems where the subsystems are defined by a set of process instances and their coupling. Due to cTLA style conventions, processes and subsystems inherit their elementary safety and liveness properties to embedding systems. Thus, cTLA can supply specification operations which are based on refinement and process composition, and the application of an operation to a set of argument process types results in a new type which is a correct refinement of the arguments. The utilization of cTLA for the decompositional verification of systems is described in [4, 5].

---

*Universität Dortmund, Fachbereich Informatik, D-44221 Dortmund, Germany, Fax +49 231 755-4730, {heyl|mester|krumm}@ls4.informatik.uni-dortmund.de

According to our experience, the software design for distributed applications mainly deals with the consistent integration and combination of known patterns. This observation also has been made in the broader field of general software engineering leading to the non-formal approach of so-called design patterns (cf. [2]). With respect to this, our approach aims to the formalisation and tool assistance of the design pattern approach. Generic cTLA process types can describe behavioural patterns formally, e.g., distributed algorithms, communication service user scenarios, and application programming interface scenarios can be modelled by re-usable specification modules. The integration of patterns into intermediate system descriptions, the combination of patterns, and the restructuring of system descriptions can be performed by the application of cTLA specification operations.

Several example software developments showed us the suitability of our approach. Furthermore, prototypical tool implementations of the specification operations contributed to the designers' productivity as reported in [14]. Meanwhile, we refined the syntax of cTLA and enriched the set of specification operations. The tool cTc has been developed which supports the enhanced syntax and set of operations.

In the sequel we sketch the notation of the input, output, and commands of cTc by means of the cTLA syntax and specification operations. Furthermore, we address aspects of the implementation of cTc .

2   cTLA syntax and Specification Operations

The following definition of the simple process type *Prepost* gives an impression of the cTLA syntax [7].

```
PROCESS Prepost(tdata : CONST; f(a) : CONST)
BODY
  VARIABLES d : tdata;
            s : {"idle", "pre", "post"} ;
  INIT  ≙   s = "idle";
  ACTIONS   Start(p : tdata) ≙ s = "idle" ∧ d' = p ∧ s'="pre" ;
            Step ≙ s = "pre" ∧ d'=f(d) ∧ s'="post" ;
  WF :      Start,Step;
END
```

The header declares the type name and introduces the generic type parameters. The body starts with the declaration of the private state variables and continues with the definitions of Init-predicate and actions. At last fairness assumptions are expressed.

Seven major specification operations exist: 1. The **compose** operation defines a process system by instantiating process patterns and the coupling of these processes. 2. The **refine** operation supports the refinement of state variables of a pattern. 3. The integrate operation is a composition with a following refinement. 4. The split operation transforms a process into a process system. 5. The array operation introduces an array of process pattern instances. 6. The split actions operation introduces a case decision into an action. 7. The combine operation computes a proposal for a composition. The coupling is implicitly defined by the identity of action names.

As a small example we show an integrate operation application. Process *IAppl1* describes an application of integrate. The imported module *aoi* and the instantiated process type *Auxvar* are shown, *Prepost* has been described above.

```
PROCESS IAppl1
IMPORT aoi;
BODY
  VARIABLES
   id,od : aoi;
   s : {"idle", "pre", "post"} ;
  INTEGRATE
   A : Auxvar(aoi) SUBSTITUTE A.v BY id;
   P : Prepost(aoi, DoubleItems)
       SUBSTITUTE
        P.s BY s,
        P.d BY (IF s="post" THEN od
                         ELSE id);
  ACTIONS
   Start(p : aoi) ≜
     A.Write(p) ∧ P.Start(p);
   Step ≜ A.Stutter ∧ P.Step;
  END
```

```
CONSTANT MODULE aoi
CONSTANTS
 aoi ≜ SET [Nat→Integer];

 double all array elements
 DoubleItems(array : aoi) ≜
  [ FCN n ∈ DOMAIN(array)
      ↦ 2*array[n] ];
END aoi

PROCESS Auxvar(tdata : CONST)
BODY
 VARIABLES
  v : tdata;
 INIT ≜ true;
 ACTIONS
  Write(p : tdata) ≜ v'=p;
 WF : Write;
END
```

The result is:

```
PROCESS IAppl1
IMPORT aoi;
BODY
  VARIABLES id,od : aoi;
            s : {"idle", "pre", "post"} ;
  INIT ≜    true ∧ s = "idle";
  ACTIONS   Start(p : aoi) ≜ id'=p ∧ s="idle"
            ∧ (IF s="post" THEN od ELSE id)'=p ∧ s'="pre";
       Step ≜ id'=id ∧ s="pre" ∧ s'="post"
            ∧ (IF s="post" THEN od ELSE id)' =
              DoubleItems((IF s="post" THEN od ELSE id));
  WF : Start,Step;
END
```

3 cTc Implementation

The main features of cTc [1] are: syntax check of cTLA specification elements and specification operations, type check of specification elements and specification operation application[2], computation of the specification operation results, transformation of cTLA specifications into tTLA+[3] specifications to facilitate the use of existing tools [13] for tTLA+ specifications (e.g. interpreter/animator, browser, model checker, otter theorem prover frontend/lemma generator), and inclusion of tTLA+ CONST modules. cTc has been designed as batch-oriented tool, which detects its desired actions from its input and command line arguments.

It has been implemented [6] in C using the GMD *cocktail* compiler toolset [3]. This toolset consists of scanner, parser, attribute evaluator and transformation generators and provides not only lex/yacc style parsing support but also supplies all routines needed to construct, check, evaluate and transform an attributed syntax tree and all routines needed to use related data structures like symbol tables. Furthermore, extensive test support is available. The scanner and parser has been realized with the *cocktail* *pars/rpp/lalr/rex* tools. The analysis of the static semantic relies on an attribute evaluator generated from an attributed grammar specification by the *ast* tool. Of major importance has been the tree transformation generator *puma*, which was utilized to implement the specification operations, the cTLA to tTLA+ transformation and all unparsing.

From 24K lines problem and language description *cocktail* generated 84K lines C-code. On a Sun ELC workstation (25 MHz SPARC processor) the tools analyses approx. 1000 lines of specification text per second.

4 Concluding Remarks

The modular *cocktail* descriptions for data structures, transformation rules and attribute grammars allowed for easy extension and language evolution.

Despite some small examples, an early tool prototype has been used to support a Message Transfer Agent development [11], resulting in a interoperable SMTP-conformant [16] implementation. The experiences drawn from these first case studies are encouraging. Beside other advantages, the quality of the resulting implementation is very high such that the debugging of the system has been reduced drastically.

Further work includes a tool for automated simplifications and a C-code generator for implementation-near specifications.

---

[1] Acronym for compositional TLA construction.
[2] Based on an extension of the type checking used in a tTLA+ browser [15].
[3] tTLA+ [12] is a tool oriented notation of TLA+ [9].

5 REFERENCES

[1] M. Abadi, L. Lamport: The existence of refinement mappings. *Theoretical Computer Science*, 82(2):253–284, May 1991.

[2] E. Gamma, R. Helm, R. Johnson, J. Vlissides: Design Patterns. Elements of Reusable Object-Oriented Software. 1994

[3] J. Grosch, H. Emmelmann: A Tool Box for Compiler Construction. Compiler Generation Report No. 20, GMD Karlsruhe, Jan 1990.

[4] P. Herrmann, H. Krumm: Compositional Specification and Verification of High-Speed Transfer Protocols. In: S.T. Vuong and S.T. Chanson (Eds.) *Protocol Specification, Testing, and Verification XIV*. 1994.

[5] P. Herrmann, H. Krumm: Re-Usable Verification Elements for High-Speed Transfer Protocol Configurations. In: P. Dembinski and M. Sredniawa (Eds.) *Protocol Specification, Testing, and Verification XV*, 1995.

[6] C. Heyl: Tool Support for the Compositional Design of Distributed Systems in TLA. Diploma Thesis (in German), Univ. Dortmund, Informatik IV, 1995.

[7] C. Heyl, A. Mester: cTLA syntax definition. Univ. Dortmund, Informatik IV. Technical Report RvS-TLA-95/49, Oct 1995.

[8] ISO: *LOTOS: Language for the temporal ordering specification of observational behaviour*. International Standard ISO/IS 8807, 1987.

[9] L. Lamport: TLA$^+$: syntax and semantics. Digital Equipment Corporation, Systems Research Center, Preliminary Version, Feb 1992.

[10] L. Lamport: The Temporal Logic of Actions. *ACM Transactions on Programming Languages and Systems*, 16(3):872–923, May 1994.

[11] K. Luttmann: Formal Design and Implementation of an Internet Mail System. Diploma Thesis (in German), Univ. Dortmund, Informatik IV, 1996.

[12] A. Mester: tTLA+ 1 syntax description. Univ. Dortmund, Informatik IV, Technical Report RvS-TLA-92/4, Jan 1993.

[13] A. Mester, P. Herrmann: Tools for TLA-based Specifications. Univ. Dortmund, Informatik IV, Technical Report RvS-TLA-94/35, 1994.

[14] A. Mester, H. Krumm: Composition and Refinement Mapping based Construction of Distributed Applications. In: Uffe H. Engberg, Kim G. Larsen, Arne Skou (Eds.): *Tools and Algorithms for the Construction and Analysis of Systems*, BRICS NS-95-2, 290–303, Aarhus, Denmark, May 1995

[15] O. Meier: Tool Support for getting into TLA Specifications of Distributed Systems. Diploma Thesis (in German), Univ. Dortmund, Informatik IV, 1994.

[16] J.B. Postel: Simple Mail Transfer Protocol. Request for Comments 821, August 1982

A Tool for Proving Invariance Properties of Concurrent Systems Automatically

Hassen Saïdi*

1 Introduction

We describe a tool for the verification of invariance properties of concurrent systems. Our tool combines model-checking and theorem-proving in the following sense: in order to prove that a predicate P is an invariant of a system S ($S \models Init \Rightarrow \Box P$) it is necessary and sufficient to find a predicate P' weaker than $Init$ and stronger than P, such that P' is preserved by all transitions τ of S, i.e $P' \Rightarrow \widetilde{Pre}[\tau](P')$[1] is valid for each transition τ.

Model-checking consists in computing iteratively the greatest solution of the equation $P \Rightarrow \widetilde{Pre}[\tau](P)$ starting with $P_0 = P$ and taking $P_{i+1} = P_i \wedge \widetilde{Pre}[\tau](P_i)$. This method can be completely automatized under the condition that the above predicates are decidable. However it suffers from the drawback that in the case of infinite state systems convergence is not guaranteed or too slow. Convergence can be accelerated by using *local invariants* extracted from the program obtained by constant propagation, variable domain information, etc ([2], [1]). Convergence can also be forced by using finite abstraction techniques consisting in replacing $\widetilde{Pre}[\tau](P_i)$ by a lower approximation, but in this case, false negative results are possible.

In our tool theorem proving is used for establishing $P_{i+1} \equiv P_i$ that is for testing if the fixed point has been reached. For this purpose we use the PVS theorem prover [7] which implements several decision procedures for decidable sub-classes of formulas. Systems are described in a syntax using PVS declaration and formula syntax. Verification conditions (VC) are extracted automatically by means a "verification condition generator". This generator avoids to generate "trivially true" VCs. For example, if an action τ does not affect the variables on which predicate P depends, the VC $P \Rightarrow \widetilde{Pre}[\tau](P)$ is not generated. Three kinds of verification conditions are generated automatically. The first ones are the PVS type correctness con-

---

*Verimag, Miniparc-Zirst, Rue Lavoisier, 38330 Montbonnot St-Martin, France. Phone: (+33) 76-90-96-43, Fax: (+33) 76-41-36-20. e-mail: saidi@imag.fr.

[1]The predicate $\widetilde{Pre}[\tau](P)$ defines the smallest set of states that have via transition τ only successors satisfying P.

ditions (TCCs) which are generated once. The others, which are updated at each iteration step are the lemmas expressing the fact that P is the invariant we are looking for, that is $P \Rightarrow \widetilde{Pre}[\tau](P)$ and $Init \Rightarrow P$. Tools based on a similar approach are actually designed [4] [3]. However, they are restricted to simple data types as natural numbers, booleans and arrays. Our aim is to use the power of the specification language used in PVS and the proof techniques available to discharge verification conditions. Thus, we allow complex data-types such as buffers and we use powerful proof mechanisms. Our efforts were concentrated on a maximal automatization of the proof process by defining powerful proof strategies. However, it is clear that complete automatization is only possible in the decidable cases, otherwise, the techniques we use are "just heuristics" improving "sometimes" an intrinsically incomplete proof technique. In this case, interactivity with the PVS prover is used when these proof strategies fails.

PVS

PVS is an environment for writing specifications and developing mechanized proofs. It consists of a specification language integrated with a powerful and highly interactive theorem prover. PVS uses higher order logic as a specification language, the type system of PVS includes uninterpreted type, sub-typing and recursively defined data-types. Four sorts characterize this language: **Theory**, **Type**, **Expression** (*term*), **Formula** (*proposition*). Any PVS specification is structured into parameterized theories. A **theory** is a set of declarations consisting of **type**, variable, constant, function and **formula** declarations. The PVS theorem prover implements a set of powerful primitive inference rules with a mechanism for composing them into proof strategies. PVS has emacs as user interface.

2 General Architecture

The organization of the tool (see Figure 1) is inspired by the architecture of PVS. The main entry is a description of a system and a property we want to be invariant, respecting the syntax[2] defined in figure 2. The user controls the verification process by a set of commands.

Writing specifications

A specification is a parallel composition of programs. For the description of a program we use a simple programming language close to Dijkstra's guarded command language (see Figure 2). A program is a tuple $\langle \mathcal{V}, \mathcal{T}, \mathcal{I} \rangle$

---

[2] The grammar is presented using the conventions of [7].

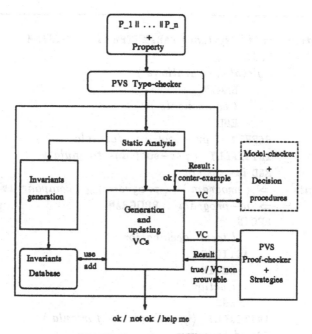

FIGURE 1. Tool architecture

where $\mathcal{V}$ is a set of local program variables, $\mathcal{T}$ is a set of transitions corresponding to the different actions of the program, and $\mathcal{I}$ an initial condition. *global−declaration* and *local−declaration* are sequences of PVS declarations. This shows clearly the power of the language, since we allow program variables of any type definable in PVS (that is natural, rational and real numbers, booleans, enumerated or abstract data-types and functions[3]). Programs may use as basic functions any function definable in PVS by importing predefined or user-defined theories.

Static analysis

Static analysis provides "structural" invariants. They provide informations about values of variables at particular control points. In [2] and [5] several techniques are used to generate automatically this kind of invariants. In our tool we implemented the more powerful ones presented in [1]. Given such a structural invariant I, it is sufficient to prove for each transition τ and predicate P, $I \wedge P \Rightarrow \widetilde{Pre}[\tau](P)$ instead of proving $P \Rightarrow \widetilde{Pre}[\tau](P)$. Since the predicate I is generally a huge formula of the form $\bigwedge_{i=1}^{n} pc = i \Rightarrow Q_i$ where pc is a control variable, it is necessary to eliminate as far as possible the non-relevant conjuncts. For example, when we prove $P \Rightarrow \widetilde{Pre}[\tau](P)$, where action τ moves from control point i to j, we only use the conjuncts of the form $pc = i \Rightarrow Q_i$.

---

[3]This is the way we define arrays and other multi-dimensional data structures.

```
specification  ⇒  id−system [ PARAMETER id ]  :  SYSTEM
               BEGIN
               ⟨ global−declarations ⟩
                     BEGIN
                     ⟨ components ⟩
                     END
               SAFETY : ⟨ pvs−boolean−formula ⟩
               INITIALLY : ⟨ pvs−boolean−formula ⟩
               END id−system
components     ⇒  ⟨ program ⟩ | ⟨ program ⟩ || ⟨ components ⟩
program        ⇒  id−program  :  PROGRAM
               BEGIN
                     ⟨ local−declarations ⟩
               ACTIONS :
                     BEGIN
                     ⟨ action ⟩+
                     END
               INITIALLY : ⟨ pvs−boolean−formula ⟩
               END id−program
action         ⇒  ⟨ pvs−boolean−formula ⟩ --> ⟨ assignement ⟩+
assignement    ⇒  id := ⟨ pvs−expression ⟩
```

FIGURE 2. Specification syntax

Proving verification conditions

A proof session starts by typing the command **M-x prove-invariant (M-x pi)**. A PVS theory containing the lemmas to prove is automatically generated, and the following proof strategy is applied to each of them. First an efficient but incomplete proof strategy for first order predicates is used. It combines rewriting, boolean simplification using BDDs[4], and an arithmetic decision procedure: after rewriting all definitions, the BDD procedure breaks formulas into elementary ones, where other decision procedures such as arithmetic ones can be applied. If the proof fails, another strategy combining automatic induction and decision procedures is applied. If some of them cannot be proved, the user can either try to prove the unproved lemmas using the PVS interactive prover, or start a new proof session with new verification conditions corresponding to the iteration step defined above. In the case that the user knows that the generated VC are decidable predicates – that is a VC that cannot be proved is not true –, he can use the

---

[4]A BDD simplifier is available in PVS as a proof strategy.

command M-x prove-invariant-and-loop (M-x pl) which tries to compute the greatest solution of $P \Rightarrow \widetilde{Pre}[\tau](P)$ implying the property to be proven an invariant, with the risk of non convergence but with the benefits of complete automatization.

3 Future work

We verified with our tool some mutual exclusion examples with finite and infinite state variables, studied in [5]. We also verified some examples involving abstract data types such as buffers. Many features are planned to deal with effective and large systems. We plan to enforce modularity of the descriptions, allowing to verify properties of subsystems of a given complex system. Using compositional rules, we can deduce global properties of systems using some previously proved properties of their components.

Acknowledgments: The author wants to thank Susanne Graf for her helpful comments.

4 REFERENCES

[1] S. Bensalem, Y. Lakhnech, H. Saïdi. *Powerful Techniques for the Automatic Generation of Invariants*. Submitted to CAV'96.

[2] N. Bjørner, A. Browne and Z. Manna. *Automatic Generation of Invariants and Intermediate Assertions*. In U. Montanari, editor, First International Conference on Principles and Practice of Constraint Programming, LNCS, Cassis, France, September 1995.

[3] A. Blinchevsky, B. Liberman, I. Usvyatsky, A. Pnueli. *TPVS: Documentation and Progress Report*. Weizmann Institute Of Science, 1994.

[4] Z. Manna and al. *STeP: The Stanford Temporal Prover*. Department of Computer Science, Stanford University, 1994.

[5] Z. Manna and A. Pnueli. *Temporal Verification of Reactive Systems: Safety*. Springer-Verlag, New York, 1995.

[6] S. Owre, N. Shankar, and J. M. Rushby. *A Tutorial on Specification and Verification Using PVS*. Computer Science Laboratory, SRI International, Menlo Park, CA, February 1993.

[7] S. Owre, N. Shankar, and J. M. Rushby. *The PVS Specification Language*. Computer Science Laboratory, SRI International, Menlo Park, CA, February 1993.

Using the Constraint Language Toupie for "Software Cost Reduction" Specification Analysis

Antoine Rauzy*

ABSTRACT Constraint programming has attracted a considerable interest over recent years. It has been successfully applied to combinatorial optimization problems that were up to now considered as difficult. In this presentation, the constraint language Toupie is used to analyze the specification of a reactive system formulated in terms of the "Software Cost Reduction" method. Our aim is to show that the constraint programming paradigm is relevant for modelization and verification of embedded systems as well.

---

*LaBRI - CNRS URA 1304 - Université Bordeaux 51, cours de la Libération, F-33405 Talence (France), email: rauzy@labri.u-bordeaux.fr .

A Constraint-Oriented Service Creation Environment

Bernhard Steffen*, Tiziana Margaria*,
Andreas Claßen*, Volker Braun*,
Rita Nisius†, Manfred Reitenspieß†

Intelligent Network (IN) services are customized telephone services, like e.g., 1) 'Free-Phone', where the receiver of the call can be billed if some conditions are met, 2) 'Universal Private Telephone', enabling groups of customers to define their own private net within the public net, or 3) 'Partner Lines', where a number of menus leads to the satisfaction of all desires. The realization of these services is quite complex and error prone.

The current trend in advanced IN services clearly evolves towards decoupling Service Processing Systems from the switch network (see e.g. [3]). The reasons for this tendency lie in the growing need for decentralization of the service processing, in the demand for quick customization of the offered services, and in the requirement of rapid availability of the modified or reconfigured services. Service Processing Systems are those elements of the IN architecture which provide *service processing logic and control* but not *connection control and management*, which are provided by the underlying switch system. In particular, they include Service Creation Environments[1], which are interactive environments responsible for the creation, modification, customization and provision of new services.

Service Creation Environments for the creation of IN-services are usually based on classical 'Clipboard-Architecture' environments, where services are graphically constructed, compiled, and successively tested. Two extreme approaches characterize the state of the art: The first approach guarantees consistency, but the creation process is strongly limited in its flexibility to compose Service Independent Building Blocks (SIBs) to new services. The second approach allows flexible compositions of services, but there is little or no feedback on the correctness of the service under creation during the development: the validation is almost entirely located after the design is completed. Thus the resulting test phase is lengthy and costly.

---

*Universität Passau, Innstr. 33, D-94032 Passau (Germany), tel: +49 851 509.3090, fax: +49 851 509.3092, {steffen,tiziana,classen,v.braun}@fmi.uni-passau.de.

†Siemens Nixdorf Informationssysteme AG, Otto-Hahn-Ring 6, D-81739 Munich (Germany), tel: +49 89 636.42393, fax: +49 89 636.48976, rei@rust.mch.sni.de .

[1]The Service Creation Environment Function is a major component of the IN architecture ([1, 4]).

Our environment is used for the reliable, aspect-driven creation of telephone services in a 'divide and conquer' fashion: initial prototypes are successively modified until each component satisfies the current requirements. The entire service creation process is supported by thematic views that focus on particular aspects of the service under consideration. Moreover, the service creation is constantly accompanied by on-line verification of the validity of the required features and the executability conditions for intermediate prototypes: design decisions that conflict with the constraints and consistency conditions of the intended service are immediately detected via model checking. Thus, in addition to the facilities offered by classical 'Clipboard'-Architectures', our approach is characterized by the following four properties:

- during the entire creation process there exists a current executable prototype that can be tested and animated,

- the support through thematic *views*, which provide the required global context and hide unnecessary details, allows the designer to choose a particular aspect of interest, and to develop and investigate the services under that point of view. This supports a much more focussed service development, which concentrates on the design of the aspect currently under investigation,

- a macro facility allows to define whole subservices as primitive entities, which can be used just as SIBs. Macros may be defined on-line and expanded whenever the interna of a macro become important. This supports a truly hierarchical service construction.

- the *global consistency* of each design step with implementation-related or service-dependent frame conditions is *automatically verified*. Thus sources for typical failures can be immediately detected even in the presence of macros.

Figure 1 summarizes the global structure of our approach, which supports an arbitrary decomposition of the design process. This is necessary, since the same Service Creation Environment is shared by teams of users with completely different profiles. According to [2] at least the following user profiles are envisaged:

- The *service programmer* has advanced programming skills and uses the SCE to create new generic functions,

- The *service designer* has logical skills and uses the above functions to create new services,

- The *service provider* is familiar with the specific customer needs and enters customer specific data into the data files.

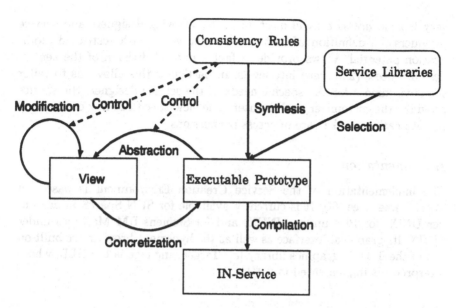

FIGURE 1. The Service Creation Process

We offer the needed design flexibility by means of the second of the following three phases:

1. In a first step, an existing service of similar application profile is loaded from the service library, or a completely new design from scratch is done (under model checking control). Of course this design is supported by the macro facitility. Alternatively, initial executable prototypes could automatically be generated from the set of underlying consistency conditions and constraints, a feature, which is not part of the current version of our service creation environment.

2. The second step consists of aspect-driven modification: the user chooses the aspect of interest, generates the corresponding view abstracting from all irrelevant details, and modifies it where necessary. This is iterated until all relevant aspects have been treated. Due to the on-line verification with the model checker, the executability is preserved and erroneous design steps are immediately detected. It is in this phase, where macros may be required to be expanded in order to resolve 'internal errors'.

3. Current prototypes can at any time be tested, compiled, executed, and, if satisfactory, stored in a data base.

It should be noted that the macro facility covers the standard *stepwise refinement* approaches of the usual tools for service creation. In fact, in combination with our concept of views, macros allow an enormously flexible service development. In addition, views support the realization of a very flexible *access control mechanism*, by allowing designers and service providers the definition of customer specific views with restricted modification potential. Views provide in fact a natural division of the central design process (2nd step) into levels. In particular this allows us to tailor the environment for the specific needs of the service designer, the service provider, the customizer, and the user. The view-specific hiding can be used to automatically take care of access permissions.

Implementation

The implementation of the Service Creation Environment is based on METAFrame (see [6]). It is currently available for SUN SparcStations under UNIX, for PCs under LINUX, and for Siemens RM Machines under SINIX. Its graphical interface as well as the hypertext browser are built on top of the Tcl/Tk graphics library [5]. Target language is the HLL, whose interpreter is implemented in C++.

Acknowledgements

We are grateful to Michael von der Beeck, Achim Dannecker, Philipp Florschütz, Carsten Friedrich, Andreas Holzmann, Marion Klein, Dirk Koschützki, Gerald Lüttgen, Falk Schreiber, Markus Schweighofer, and Matthias Seul for their cooperation in the design and implementation of METAFrame . We also thank the Siemens Nixdorf IN team and the GMRS team for their precious interaction in the definition of the characteristics of the system and for their valuable contributions to the realization of the current product.

1 REFERENCES

[1] J. Aitken: *"Intelligent Networks"*, Seminar, Logica UK Ltd., London, April 26–27, 1995.

[2] P. K. Bohacek, J. N. White: *"Service Creation: The Real Key to Intelligent Network Revenue"*, Proc. Workshop Intelligent Networks '94, Heidelberg, May 24-26, 1994.

[3] E. Crabill, J. Kukla: *"Service Processing Systems for AT&T's Intelligent Network"*, AT&T Techn. Journal, Vol.73(6), 1994, pp.39-47.

[4] ITU CS1 Recommendations, 1993.

[5] J.K. Ousterhout: *"Tcl and the Tk Toolkit,"* Addison–Wesley, April 1994.

[6] B. Steffen, A. Claßen, T. Margaria: *"The METAFrame : An Environment for Flexible Tool Management,"* Proc. TAPSOFT'95, Aarhus (DK), May 1995, LNCS N.915, pp.791-792.

DFA&OPT-MetaFrame: A Tool Kit for Program Analysis and Optimization

Marion Klein*   Jens Knoop†
Dirk Koschützki†   Bernhard Steffen†

ABSTRACT Whereas the construction process of a compiler for the early and late phases like syntactic analysis and code generation is well-supported by powerful tools, the *optimizer*, the key component for achieving highly efficient code is usually still hand-coded. The tool kit presented here supports this essential step in the construction of a compiler. The two key features making it exceptional are (1) that it automatically generates global program analyses for intraprocedural, interprocedural and parallel data flow problems, and (2) that it supports the combination of the results obtained to program optimizations.

1 Overview

Compilers are expected to produce *highly efficient* code. Thus, *optimizers* are integrated in order to detect and remove inefficiencies in application programs. Typically, optimization proceeds in two steps: First, a program analysis, usually a *data flow analysis (DFA)*, which detects the side conditions under which an optimizing program transformation is applicable, and second, the concrete transformation based on the data flow facts computed by the preceding analysis. The algorithms realizing these two steps are usually still hand-coded. As the construction process for essentially every other phase of compilation is well-supported by powerful tools, the construction of the optimizer still belongs to the most expensive, time consuming, and error prone steps in the construction of a compiler.

The DFA&OPT-MetaFrame tool kit supports this essential step of compiler construction. It *automatically* generates efficient DFA-algorithms from concise specifications given in a *modal logic* (cf. [St]). In essence, the DFA-generator of the tool kit works by *partially evaluating* an appropiate *model checker* with respect to the modal formula specifying the data flow property

---

*Lehrstuhl für Informatik II, Rheinisch-Westfälische Technische Hochschule Aachen, Ahornstraße 55, D-52056 Aachen, Germany E-mail: marion@informatik.rwth-aachen.de

†Fakultät für Mathematik und Informatik, Universität Passau, Innstrasse 33, D-94032 Passau, Germany. E-mail: {knoop | koschuetzki | steffen}@fmi.uni-passau.de

of interest (cf. [SCKKM]). The result is a usual iterative DFA-algorithm, which runs on the machine the model checker is implemented on, and which can immediately be integrated into the compiler under construction. A *high level programming language* allows to combine the results of different analyses to optimizing program transformations. It serves as the connecting link for combining program analysis and optimization, such that the tool kit supports the complete process of the optimizer construction.

The benefits of this approach are as follows: The DFA-algorithms required are directly specified in terms of the data flow properties of interest. All the details about the corresponding computation procedures are hidden in the tool kit. This yields concise high-level specifications, simplifies and structures the specification development, and supports the reasoning about features such as correctness and optimality of the DFAs. In fact, the DFA-algorithms required by the program optimizations considered below result from two to five line specifications in a modal logic. They are not only significantly shorter, but also more intuitive than their traditionally specified counterparts. Moreover, our practical experience shows that the generated DFA-algorithms are as efficient as their hand-coded counterparts. Summarizing, we profit from:

- *Concise specifications* directly in terms of the data flow properties

- *Combining* global program analysis (DFA) and optimization

- *Simple reasoning* about DFA and optimization on a very high level

- *Hiding* of all details of the computation procedure

- *No efficiency penalty* in comparison to hand-coded algorithms

- *High flexibility* supporting *rapid prototyping*

2 SCREEN SHOTS FROM A SAMPLE SESSION

We illustrate the usage of the tool kit by means of two screen shots from a sample session. The optimization considered is to remove all *partially redundant computations* in a program (in the example of '$a + b$') by means of the *busy code motion (BCM)* transformation of [KRS1]. This transformation requires the computation of all program points being *down-safe* and *up-safe* for a computation, here '$a + b$'. The results of the corresponding DFA-algorithms, which are automatically generated from the specifications shown in the lower left window, are displayed in the right window of Figure 1, which shows the argument program in an automatically generated and layouted transition system like representation. The states represent program points, and the transitions the control flow and the basic blocks of the underlying procedure. The analysis and optimization process is controlled by means of the high level language, whose commands are executed by an interpreter running in the upper left window.

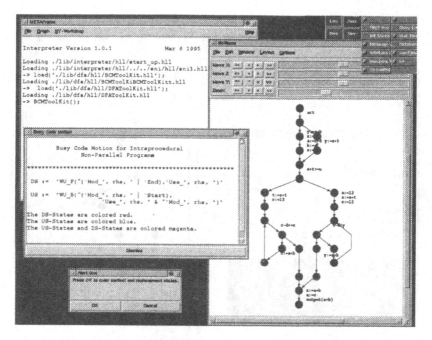

FIGURE 1. First Screen Shot

After computing the set of up-safe and down-safe program points, the
BCM-transformation can be specified within the high level language: (1)
Initializing a new temporary **h** by $a + b$ at all down-safe program points
which have an incoming edge modifying a or b, or an unsafe predecessor.
(2) Replacing all original occurrences of $a + b$ by **h**. The result of the
complete transformation is displayed in the right window of Figure 2.

3 Scope and Current State

The DFA&OPT-METAFrame tool kit supports data flow analysis and optimization of intraprocedural, interprocedural and parallel programs (cf.
[KS, KSV1, KSV2, St]). It is particularly well-suited for optimizations
based on bitvector analyses, which are most relevant in practice due to
their broad scope of powerful and practically relevant optimizations ranging from *code motion* over *assignment motion* and *partial dead code elimination* to *strength reduction* and (via definition-use chains) to *constant
propagation* and *constant folding*. Moreover, all these techniques can be
performed in the parallel and interprocedural program setting as efficiently
as in the sequential intraprocedural one.

The intraprocedural sequential case is fully implemented in the current
prototype of our tool kit, i.e., the program analyses are directly generated
from their modal logic specifications (cf. [SCKKM]). Interprocedural and
parallel DFA-problems are specified in terms of local semantic functionals

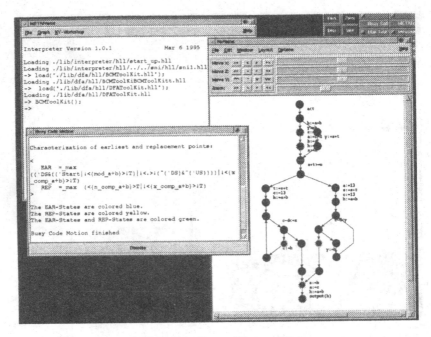

FIGURE 2. Second Screen Shot

giving abstract semantics to statements, the direction of data flow, and
the kind of fixpoint desired as it is common in classical data flow analysis. For the interprocedural setting the current version supports programs
composed of procedures with global variables. An extension to local variables, and value and reference parameters is in progress. The tool kit has
successfully been tested on the program optimizations mentioned above.

4   RELATED WORK

Early approaches to the automatic generation of optimizers concentrated
on peephole optimizations, which do not require global program analyses
(cf. [DF, Ke]). These approaches are contrasted by others which address
the generation of global analyses, but do not support the construction of
program transformations (cf. [AM, YH]). Both steps, i.e., global analyses
and program transformations, are supported by the systems of [VF, WS],
which support intraprocedural optimization. Whereas the system of [VF]
concentrates on 'classical' intraprocedural optimizations, the one of [WS]
is particularly well-suited for local transformations based on data dependency information which are important for the automatic parallelization of
sequential programs. The generality of the DFA&OPT-METAFrame tool kit
that it works for intraprocedural, interprocedural, and parallel programs,
and supports the generation of global program analyses and their combination to optimizations, is in fact exceptional.

5 REFERENCES

[AM]   Alt, M., and Martin, F. Generation of efficient interprocedural analyzers with PAG. In Proc. 2nd Internat. Static Analysis Symposium (SAS'95), Glasgow, UK, Springer-Verlag, LNCS 983 (1995), 33 - 50.

[DF]   Davidson, J. W., and Fraser, C. W. Automatic generation of peephole transformations. In *Proc. ACM SIGPLAN'84 Symp. on Comp. Construct.*, Montreal, Canada, *SIGPLAN Notices 19*, 6 (1984), 111 - 115.

[Ke]   Kessler, R. R. Peep – An architectural description driven peephole transformer. In *Proc. ACM SIGPLAN'84 Symp. on Comp. Construct.*, Montreal, Canada, *SIGPLAN Notices 19*, 6 (1984), 106 - 110.

[KRS1]   Knoop, J., Rüthing, O., and Steffen, B. Optimal code motion: Theory and practice. *Transactions on Programming Languages and Systems 16*, 4 (1994), 1117 - 1155.

[KRS2]   Knoop, J., Rüthing, O., and Steffen, B. The power of assignment motion. In *Proc. ACM SIGPLAN'95 Conf. on Programming Language Design and Implementation (PLDI'95)*, La Jolla, California, *SIGPLAN Notices 30*, 6 (1995), 233 - 245.

[KS]   Knoop, J., and Steffen, B. The interprocedural coincidence theorem. In *Proc. 4th Internat. Conference on Compiler Construction (CC'92)*, Paderborn, Germany, Springer-Verlag, LNCS 641 (1992), 125 - 140.

[KSV1]   Knoop, J., Steffen, B., and Vollmer, J. Parallelism for free: Efficient and optimal bitvector analyses for parallel programs. Accepted for *Transactions on Programming Languages and Systems*.

[KSV2]   Knoop, J., Steffen, B., and Vollmer, J. Parallelism for free: Bitvector analyses $\Rightarrow$ No state explosion! In *Proc. 1st Internat. Workshop on Tools and Algorithms for the Construction and Analysis of Systems (TACAS'95)*, Springer-Verlag, LNCS 1019 (1995), 264 - 289.

[St]   Steffen, B. Generating data flow analysis algorithms from modal specifications. *Science of Computer Programming 21*, (1993), 115 - 139.

[SCKKM] Steffen, B., Claßen, A., Klein, M., Knoop, J., and Margaria, T. The fixpoint-analysis machine. In *Proc. 6th Internat. Conference on Concurrency Theory (CONCUR'95)*, Philadelphia, Pennsylvania, Springer-Verlag, LNCS 962 (1995), 72 - 87.

[VF]   Venkatesh, G. V., and Fischer, C. N. Spare: A development evironment for program analysis algorithms. In *IEEE Transactions on Software Engineering 18*, 4 (1992), 304 - 318.

[WS]   Whitfield, D., and Soffa, M. L. Automatic generation of global optimizers. In *Proc. ACM SIGPLAN'91 Conference on Programming Language Design and Implementation (PLDI'91)*, Toronto, Ontario, Canada, *SIGPLAN Notices 26*, 6 (1991), 120 - 129.

[YH]   Yi, K., and Harrison III, W. L. Automatic generation and management of interprocedural program analyses. In ACM SIGPLAN-SIGACT, (Jan. 1993).

A Construction and Analysis Tool Based on the Stochastic Process Algebra TIPP

Holger Hermanns *
Vassilis Mertsiotakis *
Michael Rettelbach *

ABSTRACT [1] There are many ways to incorporate a notion of time into process algebras in order to integrate functional design and performance analysis. One major research strand, *stochastic* process algebras, concentrates on the annotation of actions with exponentially distributed random variables. This paper presents a tool for the functional analysis and performance evaluation of complex systems based on the stochastic process algebra paradigm. The *TIPP-tool* provides facilities for model specification, reachability analysis, as well as several numerical algorithms for the solution of the underlying Markov chain and the computation of performance measures.

1 Introduction

Stochastic process algebras (SPA) have been introduced as an extension of classical process algebras, like CCS or CSP, with timing information aiming mainly at the integration of functional design and quantitative analysis of computer systems. Time is represented by attaching random variables to every activity in the model, determining their durations [2].

As in classical process algebras, the main characteristic of SPAs is constructivity, i.e. the ability to describe complex systems as a composition of several smaller ones. This concept, together with a powerful abstraction mechanism to hide internal structures, forms the basis of the successful application of SPA for describing and analyzing systems of various domains. The formal foundations of the stochastic process algebra TIPP (*timed processes and performability evaluation*) are presented in [4] and have recently been extended in [5, 7]. They include a formal semantics and an equational theory for congruences that can be seen as stochastic

---

*Universität Erlangen-Nürnberg, IMMD VII, Martensstr. 3, D–91058 Erlangen

[1] This work is supported in part by the Deutsche Forschungsgemeinschaft (*SFB 182*) and by the BRA ESPRIT project 7269 (*QMIPS*).

counterparts of Milner's strong bisimulation and observational congruence.

The TIPP-tool is a prototype modelling tool supporting a LOTOS-oriented input language. Apart from rudimentary facilities to apply functional analysis, it comes up with a set of numerical solution modules for the stationary as well as transient analysis of the *continuous time Markov chain* (CTMC) underlying a TIPP-specification. The tool has been successfully applied to model and analyze various types of parallel and distributed systems, including an Email-system, the alternating bit protocol, a robot control system, and various multiprocessor systems, see [2] for an overview.

2 The language TIPP

The input language of the tool is closely related to LOTOS, but enriched with stochastic timing information. An exponentially distributed random variable is associated with every activity specifying its duration. Hence, every term in our language can be interpreted as a high level description of a CTMC. Exponential distributions can be characterized by a single parameter. Therefore, each activity of the system possesses a specific name and a parameter, called rate, characterizing its duration.

A specification consists of a number of process definitions, each describing a process scheme with generic activity names and activity rates within a behaviour expression. Various constructs are available to describe behaviour expressions, like the prefix operator (;), choice (□), the halt process (**stop**), the hiding operator (**hide**), or the parallel operator |{*action list*}|.

Additionally, process instantiations may occur within behaviour expressions and resemble the invocation of procedures in procedural programming languages such as PASCAL. A process instance is generated by replacing the list of formal action names and action rates by actual action names/rates in the corresponding process definition. A typical specification clearly resembles LOTOS [1]:

```
behaviour System :=
    hide a in P[a](lambda) |{a}| Q[a,b,c](lambda,mu,1)
where
    process P[in](lambda) := (in,lambda);stop
    endproc
    process Q[ready,wait,msg](xi,mu,nu) :=
            (wait,xi);(msg,mu);Q[ready,wait,msg](xi,mu,nu)
            []
            (ready,nu);stop
    endproc
endspec
```

The behaviour of a specification is defined by a structural operational semantics (see [2] for more details) that maps a specification onto its semantic model, a *Markovian labelled transition system* (MLTS) consisting of nodes representing process terms and arcs between them. These arcs are labelled with pairs of actions and rates. Figure 1 shows the semantic model of the above specification.

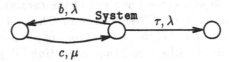

FIGURE 1. Markovian labelled transition system

3   Tool Components

Model descriptions are syntactically and semantically analyzed using a parser written in the functional programming language *Standard ML*. The parser has been generated using the tools *ML-YACC* and *LEXGEN* from the New Jersey ML toolkit. The use of this programming language has shown to be especially useful for implementing the operational semantics. After checking syntactical correctness of a specification the parser applies the operational semantic rules to produce the MLTS. This transition system constitutes the interface between the formal semantics implemented in *ML* and subsequent analysis of the system mostly implemented in *C*. The *C* programming language was chosen in order to allow the efficient solution of very large problems as well as taking advantage of existing libraries for numerical linear algebra [6].

Performance analysis is based on the MLTS where both labels of an arc, denoting the activity name and rate, are regarded as being significant, as are the arc multiplicities. For any SPA model with finite state space the underlying CTMC can be derived directly by associating a state i with each node P of the MLTS. The transitions of the CTMC are the amalgamation of all the arcs joining the nodes, and the transition rate is the sum of the individual activity rates. The activity name information is not incorporated into the CTMC representation but it is often crucial in defining the measures to be extracted from a model.

Characteristic performance and dependability measures based on equilibrium behaviour are extracted via the steady state solution of the CTMC using standard numerical techniques. The resulting values π_i can be interpreted as the probability to observe the behaviour corresponding to each process state i at any time in the steady state. From these values it is straightforward to obtain high-level measures such as throughput, or utilization. The only sufficient condition for a unique equilibrium solution is strong connectivity of the MLTS.

If the latter condition is violated or steady state measures do not give a sufficient insight into the system behaviour, it is possible to carry out transient analysis. Standard algorithms like randomization or calculation of higher moments may be used to find time-related properties of systems. Transient analysis is central to the integration of qualitative and quantitative aspects of model analysis as it allows quantitative implications of qualitative properties of a system to be investigated.

The result of numerical analysis is usually a vector with state probabilities. In order to obtain more sophisticated and expressive results the user can specify measures. This is done via rewards that are assigned to states that match a certain regular expression the user has to specify. This strategy makes use of the fact that the operational semantics associates a distinct process term to every state in the MLTS. Experiment series are also supported by allowing rates to be symbolic variables. The specification of the model as well as the measures and experiments is supported through a graphical user interface. A detailed explanation of the tool and its components can be found in [3].[2]

4 REFERENCES

[1] T. Bolognesi and E. Brinksma. Introduction to the ISO Specification Language LOTOS. In *The Formal Description Technique LOTOS*. North-Holland, 1989.

[2] N. Götz, H. Hermanns, U. Herzog, V. Mertsiotakis, and M. Rettelbach. Constructive Specification Techniques - Integrating Functional, Performance and Dependability Aspects. In *Quantitative Methods in Parallel Systems*. Springer, 1995.

[3] H. Hermanns and V. Mertsiotakis. A Stochastic Process Algebra Based Modelling Tool. In *Proc. of the 11th U.K. Perf. Eng. Workshop for Computer and Telecommunication Systems*. Springer, 1995.

[4] H. Hermanns and M. Rettelbach. Syntax, Semantics, Equivalences, and Axioms for MTIPP. In *Proc. of the 2nd Workshop on Process Algebras and Performance Modelling*. IMMD, Universität Erlangen, 1994.

[5] H. Hermanns, M. Rettelbach, and T. Weiß. Formal Characterisation of Immediate Actions in SPA with Nondeterministic Branching. *The Computer Journal*, 38(7), December 1995. Special issue: Proc. of the 3rd Workshop on Process Algebras and Performance Modelling.

[6] S.K. Kundert and A. Sangiovanni-Vincentelli. A Sparse Linear Equation Solver. Technical report, University of California, Berkeley, 1988.

[7] M. Rettelbach. Probabilistic Branching in Markovian Process Algebras. *The Computer Journal*, 38(7), December 1995. Special issue.

---

[2]More information about the TIPP project are available at the URL http://www7.informatik.uni-erlangen.de/tipp/

UPPAAL in 1995*

Johan Bengtsson[†]   Kim G. Larsen[‡]
Fredrik Larsson[†]   Paul Pettersson[†]   Wang Yi[†]

ABSTRACT UPPAAL[1] is a tool suite for automatic verification of safety and bounded liveness properties of real-time systems modeled as networks of timed automata [12, 9, 4], developed during the past two years. In this paper, we summarize the main features of UPPAAL in particular its various extensions developed in 1995 as well as applications to various case-studies, review and provide pointers to the theoretical foundation.

1 Introduction

UPPAAL is a tool suite for automatic verification of safety and bounded liveness properties of real-time systems modeled as networks of timed automata extended with data variables [12, 9, 4], developed during the past two years. In this paper, we summarize the features of UPPAAL in particular the various extensions developed in 1995 as well as applications to various case-studies, review and provide pointers to the theoretical foundation.

In developing an automatic verification tool, there are two main issues to be considered: a *user interface* which should be easy to use and a *model-checker* which should be efficient. UPPAAL consists of a graphical user interface based on Autograph, that allows system descriptions to be defined graphically and a model-checker that combines *on-the-fly* verification with a *symbolic* technique reducing the verification problem to that of solving simple *constraint systems* [12, 9]. The current version of UPPAAL is able to check for invariant and reachability properties, in particular whether certain combinations of control-nodes of timed automata and constrains on variables are reachable from an initial configuration. Bounded liveness properties can be checked by reasoning about the system in the context of a testing automata. In order to facilitate debugging, the model-checker will report a *diagnostic trace* in case the verification procedure terminates with a negative answer [10].

---

*This work has been supported by the European Communities (under CONCUR2 and RE-ACT), NUTEK (Swedish Board for Technical Development) and TFR (Swedish Technical Research Council)

[†]Department of Computer Systems, Uppsala University, SWEDEN. E-mail: {johanb, fredrikl, paupet, yi}@docs.uu.se

[‡]BRICS (Basic Research in Computer Science, Center of the Danish National Research Foundation), Aalborg University, DENMARK. E-mail: kgl@iesd.auc.dk

[1]The current version of UPPAAL is available on the World Wide Web via the UPPAAL home page http://www.docs.uu.se/docs/rtmv/uppaal.

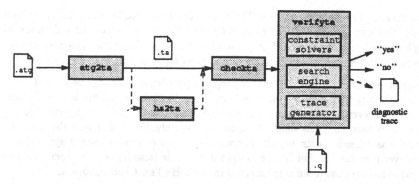

FIGURE 1. Overview of UPPAAL

The current version of UPPAAL is implemented in C++. An overview of UPPAAL is shown in Figure 1.

atg2ta A compiler from the graphical representation (.atg) of a network of timed automata, to the textual representation in UPPAAL (.ta).

hs2ta A filter that automatically transforms linear hybrid automata where the speed of clocks is given by an interval into timed automata [11], thus extending the class of systems that can be analyzed by UPPAAL.

checkta Given a textual representation (in the .ta-format) of a network of timed automata, **checkta** performs a number of simple but in practice useful syntactical checks.

verifyta A model-checker that combines *on-the-fly* verification with constraint solving techniques [12, 9].

2 Extensions in 1995

The UPPAAL model for real-time systems is networks of timed automata with data variables. For detailed descriptions of the model, we refer to [9, 4]. The model-checking algorithms implemented in UPPAAL are developed in [12, 9]. During the past year, we have applied UPPAAL to a number of case-studies reviewed in next section. To meet requirements arising from the case studies, the UPPAAL model and model-checker have been further extended with new features. In the following, we summarize the new features of UPPAAL developed during 1995:

Committed Locations. UPPAAL adopts hand-shaking synchronization between components in a network. The very recent case-study on the verification of Philips Audio Control Protocol with bus-collisions shows that we need to further extend the UPPAAL model with *committed locations* to model behaviors such as atomic broadcasting in real-time systems. The notion of committed locations is introduced in [3]. Our experiences with UPPAAL show that the notion of committed locations implemented in UPPAAL is not only useful in modeling real-time systems but also yields significant reductions in time- and space-usages in verifying such systems.

Urgent Actions. In order to model progress properties UPPAAL uses a notion of *maximal delay* that requires discrete transitions to be taken within a certain time bound. However, in some examples, e.g. the Manufacturing Plant [6], synchronization on certain channels should happen immediately. For this reason the UPPAAL model was extended with *urgent channels*, on which processes should synchronize whenever possible [4]. The notion of urgent channels (also known as *urgent actions* in the literature) has been implemented in both HYTECH and KRONOS.

Diagnostic Traces. Ideally, a model-checker should be able to report diagnostic information whenever the verification of a particular real-time system fails. UPPAAL reports such information by generating a *diagnostic trace* from the initial state to a state violating the property. The usefulness of this kind of information was shown during the debugging of an early version of Philips Audio-Control Protocol [10].

3 Case-Studies

UPPAAL was applied to a number of case-studies and benchmark examples during 1995, including: several versions of Fischers Protocol [1], two version of Philips Audio-Control Protocol [5, 10, 3], a Steam Generator [2], a Train Gate Controller [7], a Manufacturing Plant [6], a Mine-Pump Controller [8] and a Water Tank [11].

In terms of complexity, Philips Audio-Control Protocol with bus-collision is the most serious case-study where UPPAAL is applied so far. The protocol is developed by Philips to exchange information between components (e.g. amplifier, tuner, CD-player, etc.) in one of their high-end audio sets. In [10] Philips Audio-Control Protocol without bus-collision [5] was verified using UPPAAL. In the verification of the protocol, the *diagnostic model-checking* feature of UPPAAL was used for detecting and correcting several errors in an early description of the protocol[2]. Recently a version of Philips Audio-Control Protocol with *two* senders and with *bus-collision handling* was verified using UPPAAL. The result is reported in [3]. This case study is comprehensive compared with previous verification efforts of real-time and hybrid systems described in the literature. During this case-study UPPAAL was extended with *committed locations*, allowing efficient modelling of broadcast communication[3].

---

[2] UPPAAL installed on a Sparc Station 10 running SunOS 4.1.4, with 32 MB of primary memory verifies that the received bit stream is guaranteed to be identical to the sent bit stream in 3.6 seconds.

[3] The verification of Philips Audio-Protocol with Bus Collision was carried out using an extended version of UPPAAL installed on a SGI ONYX machine.

4 Future Extensions

In this paper we have summarized the main features of UPPAAL in particular its recent extensions as well as applications to various case-studies.

Our experience with UPPAAL during the past years shows that in verifying real-time systems, space-consuming is a more serious problem than time-consuming as a verification process must store not only control-nodes searched but also possible clock values associated with the control-nodes. We have introduced the notion of committed locations which is useful in modeling real-time behaviors, and also yields significant reduction in memory-usage. As future work, we shall further develop techniques for minimizing memory-usage. Future work also includes extending the current model-checker of UPPAAL to check bounded liveness properties of [10] and implementing the newly developed compositional model-checking technique of [9].

5 REFERENCES

[1] Martin Abadi and Leslie Lamport. An Old-Fashioned Recipe for Real Time. *Lecture Notes in Computer Science*, 600, 1993.

[2] J.-R. Abrial. Steam-boiler control specification problem. June 1995. International Seminar on Methods for Semantics and Specification.

[3] Johan Bengtsson, David Griffioen, Kåre Kristoffersen, Kim G. Larsen, Fredrik Larsson, Paul Pettersson, and Wang Yi. Verification of an Audio Protocol with Bus Collision Using UPPAAL. Submitted for publication, 1996.

[4] Johan Bengtsson, Kim G. Larsen, Fredrik Larsson, Paul Pettersson, and Wang Yi. UPPAAL— a Tool Suite for Automatic Verification of Real–Time Systems. In *Proc. of the 4th DIMACS Workshop on Verification and Control of Hybrid Systems*, Lecture Notes in Computer Science, October 1995.

[5] D. Bosscher, I. Polak, and F. Vaandrager. Verification of an Audio-Control Protocol. In *Proc. of FTRTFT'94*, volume 863 of *Lecture Notes in Computer Science*, 1994.

[6] C. Daws and S. Yovine. Two examples of verification of multirate timed automata with KRONOS. In *Proc. of the 16th IEEE Real-Time Systems Symposium*, pages 66–75, December 1995.

[7] Thomas A. Henzinger, Pei-Hsin Ho, and Howard Wong-Toi. A Users Guide to HYTECH. Technical report, Department of Computer Science, Cornell University, 1995.

[8] Mathai Joseph, Alan Burns, Andy Welling, Krithi Ramamritham, Jozef Hooman, Steve Schneider, Zhiming Liu, and Henk Schepers. *Real-time Systems Specification, Verification and Analysis*. Prentice Hall, 1996.

[9] Kim G. Larsen, Paul Pettersson, and Wang Yi. Compositional and Symbolic Model-Checking of Real-Time Systems. In *Proc. of the 16th IEEE Real-Time Systems Symposium*, pages 76–87, December 1995.

[10] Kim G. Larsen, Paul Pettersson, and Wang Yi. Diagnostic Model-Checking for Real-Time Systems. In *Proc. of the 4th DIMACS Workshop on Verification and Control of Hybrid Systems*, Lecture Notes in Computer Science, October 1995.

[11] A. Olivero, J. Sifakis, and S. Yovine. Using Abstractions for the Verification of Linear Hybrids Systems. In *Proc. of CAV'94*, volume 818 of *Lecture Notes in Computer Science*, 1994.

[12] Wang Yi, Paul Pettersson, and Mats Daniels. Automatic Verification of Real-Time Communicating Systems By Constraint-Solving. In *Proc. of the 7th International Conference on Formal Description Techniques*, 1994.

Author Index

Springer-Verlag
and the Environment

We at Springer-Verlag firmly believe that an international science publisher has a special obligation to the environment, and our corporate policies consistently reflect this conviction.

We also expect our business partners – paper mills, printers, packaging manufacturers, etc. – to commit themselves to using environmentally friendly materials and production processes.

The paper in this book is made from low- or no-chlorine pulp and is acid free, in conformance with international standards for paper permanency.

Lecture Notes in Computer Science

For information about Vols. 1–977

please contact your bookseller or Springer-Verlag

Vol. 978: N. Revell, A M. Tjoa (Eds.), Database and Expert Systems Applications. Proceedings, 1995. XV, 654 pages. 1995.

Vol. 979: P. Spirakis (Ed.), Algorithms — ESA '95. Proceedings, 1995. XII, 598 pages. 1995.

Vol. 980: A. Ferreira, J. Rolim (Eds.), Parallel Algorithms for Irregularly Structured Problems. Proceedings, 1995. IX, 409 pages. 1995.

Vol. 981: I. Wachsmuth, C.-R. Rollinger, W. Brauer (Eds.), KI-95: Advances in Artificial Intelligence. Proceedings, 1995. XII, 269 pages. (Subseries LNAI).

Vol. 982: S. Doaitse Swierstra, M. Hermenegildo (Eds.), Programming Languages: Implementations, Logics and Programs. Proceedings, 1995. XI, 467 pages. 1995.

Vol. 983: A. Mycroft (Ed.), Static Analysis. Proceedings, 1995. VIII, 423 pages. 1995.

Vol. 984: J.-M. Haton, M. Keane, M. Manago (Eds.), Advances in Case-Based Reasoning. Proceedings, 1994. VIII, 307 pages. 1995.

Vol. 985: T. Sellis (Ed.), Rules in Database Systems. Proceedings, 1995. VIII, 373 pages. 1995.

Vol. 986: Henry G. Baker (Ed.), Memory Management. Proceedings, 1995. XII, 417 pages. 1995.

Vol. 987: P.E. Camurati, H. Eveking (Eds.), Correct Hardware Design and Verification Methods. Proceedings, 1995. VIII, 342 pages. 1995.

Vol. 988: A.U. Frank, W. Kuhn (Eds.), Spatial Information Theory. Proceedings, 1995. XIII, 571 pages. 1995.

Vol. 989: W. Schäfer, P. Botella (Eds.), Software Engineering — ESEC '95. Proceedings, 1995. XII, 519 pages. 1995.

Vol. 990: C. Pinto-Ferreira, N.J. Mamede (Eds.), Progress in Artificial Intelligence. Proceedings, 1995. XIV, 487 pages. 1995. (Subseries LNAI).

Vol. 991: J. Wainer, A. Carvalho (Eds.), Advances in Artificial Intelligence. Proceedings, 1995. XII, 342 pages. 1995. (Subseries LNAI).

Vol. 992: M. Gori, G. Soda (Eds.), Topics in Artificial Intelligence. Proceedings, 1995. XII, 451 pages. 1995. (Subseries LNAI).

Vol. 993: T.C. Fogarty (Ed.), Evolutionary Computing. Proceedings, 1995. VIII, 264 pages. 1995.

Vol. 994: M. Hebert, J. Ponce, T. Boult, A. Gross (Eds.), Object Representation in Computer Vision. Proceedings, 1994. VIII, 359 pages. 1995.

Vol. 995: S.M. Müller, W.J. Paul, The Complexity of Simple Computer Architectures. XII, 270 pages. 1995.

Vol. 996: P. Dybjer, B. Nordström, J. Smith (Eds.), Types for Proofs and Programs. Proceedings, 1994. X, 202 pages. 1995.

Vol. 997: K.P. Jantke, T. Shinohara, T. Zeugmann (Eds.), Algorithmic Learning Theory. Proceedings, 1995. XV, 319 pages. 1995.

Vol. 998: A. Clarke, M. Campolargo, N. Karatzas (Eds.), Bringing Telecommunication Services to the People – IS&N '95. Proceedings, 1995. XII, 510 pages. 1995.

Vol. 999: P. Antsaklis, W. Kohn, A. Nerode, S. Sastry (Eds.), Hybrid Systems II. VIII, 569 pages. 1995.

Vol. 1000: J. van Leeuwen (Ed.), Computer Science Today. XIV, 643 pages. 1995.

Vol. 1001: M. Sudan, Efficient Checking of Polynomials and Proofs and the Hardness of Approximation Problems. XIV, 87 pages. 1995.

Vol. 1002: J.J. Kistler, Disconnected Operation in a Distributed File System. XIX, 249 pages. 1995.

VOL. 1003: P. Pandurang Nayak, Automated Modeling of Physical Systems. XXI, 232 pages. 1995. (Subseries LNAI).

Vol. 1004: J. Staples, P. Eades, N. Katoh, A. Moffat (Eds.), Algorithms and Computation. Proceedings, 1995. XV, 440 pages. 1995.

Vol. 1005: J. Estublier (Ed.), Software Configuration Management. Proceedings, 1995. IX, 311 pages. 1995.

Vol. 1006: S. Bhalla (Ed.), Information Systems and Data Management. Proceedings, 1995. IX, 321 pages. 1995.

Vol. 1007: A. Bosselaers, B. Preneel (Eds.), Integrity Primitives for Secure Information Systems. VII, 239 pages. 1995.

Vol. 1008: B. Preneel (Ed.), Fast Software Encryption. Proceedings, 1994. VIII, 367 pages. 1995.

Vol. 1009: M. Broy, S. Jähnichen (Eds.), KORSO: Methods, Languages, and Tools for the Construction of Correct Software. X, 449 pages. 1995. Vol.

Vol. 1010: M. Veloso, A. Aamodt (Eds.), Case-Based Reasoning Research and Development. Proceedings, 1995. X, 576 pages. 1995. (Subseries LNAI).

Vol. 1011. T. Furuhashi (Ed.), Advances in Fuzzy Logic, Neural Networks and Genetic Algorithms. Proceedings, 1994. (Subseries LNAI).

Vol. 1012: M. Bartošek, J. Staudek, J. Wiedermann (Eds.), SOFSEM '95: Theory and Practice of Informatics. Proceedings, 1995. XI, 499 pages. 1995.

Vol. 1013: T.W. Ling, A.O. Mendelzon, L. Vieille (Eds.), Deductive and Object-Oriented Databases. Proceedings, 1995. XIV, 557 pages. 1995.

Vol. 1014: A.P. del Pobil, M.A. Serna, Spatial Representation and Motion Planning. XII, 242 pages. 1995.

Vol. 1015: B. Blumenthal, J. Gornostaev, C. Unger (Eds.), Human-Computer Interaction. Proceedings, 1995. VIII, 203 pages. 1995.

VOL. 1016: R. Cipolla, Active Visual Inference of Surface Shape. XII, 194 pages. 1995.

Vol. 1017: M. Nagl (Ed.), Graph-Theoretic Concepts in Computer Science. Proceedings, 1995. XI, 406 pages. 1995.

Vol. 1018: T.D.C. Little, R. Gusella (Eds.), Network and Operating Systems Support for Digital Audio and Video. Proceedings, 1995. XI, 357 pages. 1995.

Vol. 1019: E. Brinksma, W.R. Cleaveland, K.G. Larsen, T. Margaria, B. Steffen (Eds.), Tools and Algorithms for the Construction and Analysis of Systems. Selected Papers, 1995. VII, 291 pages. 1995.

Vol. 1020: I.D. Watson (Ed.), Progress in Case-Based Reasoning. Proceedings, 1995. VIII, 209 pages. 1995. (Subseries LNAI).

Vol. 1021: M.P. Papazoglou (Ed.), OOER '95: Object-Oriented and Entity-Relationship Modeling. Proceedings, 1995. XVII, 451 pages. 1995.

Vol. 1022: P.H. Hartel, R. Plasmeijer (Eds.), Functional Programming Languages in Education. Proceedings, 1995. X, 309 pages. 1995.

Vol. 1023: K. Kanchanasut, J.-J. Lévy (Eds.), Algorithms, Concurrency and Knowlwdge. Proceedings, 1995. X, 410 pages. 1995.

Vol. 1024: R.T. Chin, H.H.S. Ip, A.C. Naiman, T.-C. Pong (Eds.), Image Analysis Applications and Computer Graphics. Proceedings, 1995. XVI, 533 pages. 1995.

Vol. 1025: C. Boyd (Ed.), Cryptography and Coding. Proceedings, 1995. IX, 291 pages. 1995.

Vol. 1026: P.S. Thiagarajan (Ed.), Foundations of Software Technology and Theoretical Computer Science. Proceedings, 1995. XII, 515 pages. 1995.

Vol. 1027: F.J. Brandenburg (Ed.), Graph Drawing. Proceedings, 1995. XII, 526 pages. 1996.

Vol. 1028: N.R. Adam, Y. Yesha (Eds.), Electronic Commerce. X, 155 pages. 1996.

Vol. 1029: E. Dawson, J. Golić (Eds.), Cryptography: Policy and Algorithms. Proceedings, 1995. XI, 327 pages. 1996.

Vol. 1030: F. Pichler, R. Moreno-Díaz, R. Albrecht (Eds.), Computer Aided Systems Theory - EUROCAST '95. Proceedings, 1995. XII, 539 pages. 1996.

Vol.1031: M. Toussaint (Ed.), Ada in Europe. Proceedings, 1995. XI, 455 pages. 1996.

Vol. 1032: P. Godefroid, Partial-Order Methods for the Verification of Concurrent Systems. IV, 143 pages. 1996.

Vol. 1033: C.-H. Huang, P. Sadayappan, U. Banerjee, D. Gelernter, A. Nicolau, D. Padua (Eds.), Languages and Compilers for Parallel Computing. Proceedings, 1995. XIII, 597 pages. 1996.

Vol. 1034: G. Kuper, M. Wallace (Eds.), Constraint Databases and Applications. Proceedings, 1995. VII, 185 pages. 1996.

Vol. 1035: S.Z. Li, D.P. Mital, E.K. Teoh, H. Wang (Eds.), Recent Developments in Computer Vision. Proceedings, 1995. XI, 604 pages. 1996.

Vol. 1036: G. Adorni, M. Zock (Eds.), Trends in Natural Language Generation - An Artificial Intelligence Perspective. Proceedings, 1993. IX, 382 pages. 1996. (Subseries LNAI).

Vol. 1037: M. Wooldridge, J.P. Müller, M. Tambe (Eds.), Intelligent Agents II. Proceedings, 1995. XVI, 437 pages. 1996. (Subseries LNAI).

Vol. 1038: W: Van de Velde, J.W. Perram (Eds.), Agents Breaking Away. Proceedings, 1996. XIV, 232 pages. 1996. (Subseries LNAI).

Vol. 1039: D. Gollmann (Ed.), Fast Software Encryption. Proceedings, 1996. X, 219 pages. 1996.

Vol. 1040: S. Wermter, E. Riloff, G. Scheler (Eds.), Connectionist, Statistical, and Symbolic Approaches to Learning for Natural Language Processing. Proceedings, 1995. IX, 468 pages. 1996. (Subseries LNAI).

Vol. 1041: J. Dongarra, K. Madsen, J. Waśniewski (Eds.), Applied Parallel Computing. Proceedings, 1995. XII, 562 pages. 1996.

Vol. 1042: G. Weiß, S. Sen (Eds.), Adaption and Learning in Multi-Agent Systems. Proceedings, 1995. X, 238 pages. 1996. (Subseries LNAI).

Vol. 1043: F. Moller, G. Birtwistle (Eds.), Logics for Concurrency. XI, 266 pages. 1996.

Vol. 1044: B. Plattner (Ed.), Broadband Communications. Proceedings, 1996. XIV, 359 pages. 1996.

Vol. 1045: B. Butscher, E. Moeller, H. Pusch (Eds.), Interactive Distributed Multimedia Systems and Services. Proceedings, 1996. XI, 333 pages. 1996.

Vol. 1046: C. Puech, R. Reischuk (Eds.), STACS 96. Proceedings, 1996. XII, 690 pages. 1996.

Vol. 1047: E. Hajnicz, Time Structures. IX, 244 pages. 1996. (Subseries LNAI).

Vol. 1048: M. Proietti (Ed.), Logic Program Syynthesis and Transformation. Proceedings, 1995. X, 267 pages. 1996.

Vol. 1049: K. Futatsugi, S. Matsuoka (Eds.), Object Technologies for Advanced Software. Proceedings, 1996. X, 309 pages. 1996.

Vol. 1050: R. Dyckhoff, H. Herre, P. Schroeder-Heister (Eds.), Extensions of Logic Programming. Proceedings, 1996. VII, 318 pages. 1996. (Subseries LNAI).

Vol. 1051: M.-C. Gaudel, J. Woodcock (Eds.), FME'96: Industrial Benefit and Advances in Formal Methods. Proceedings, 1996. XII, 704 pages. 1996.

Vol. 1052: D. Hutchison, H. Christiansen, G. Coulson, A. Danthine (Eds.), Teleservices and Multimedia Communications. Proceedings, 1995. XII, 277 pages. 1996.

Vol. 1053: P. Graf, Term Indexing. XVI, 284 pages. 1996. (Subseries LNAI).

Vol. 1055: T. Margaria, B. Steffen (Eds.), Tools and Algorithms for the Construction and Analysis of Systems. Proceedings, 1996. XI, 435 pages. 1996.